Between Culture and Biology

Most of the literature on ont_____ _____ _____ .....ows either a cultural or a biological perspective, defy_____ ___ ... at integration. *Between Culture and Biology* challenges this trend by presenting these divergent perspectives and reflecting their differences and similarities. The chapters emphasize and focus on the degree to which human development is actually embedded within both culture and biology. The book describes the constraints and opportunities for development that derive from both areas, and examines how they can vary according to differing environments and different developmental domains.

The authors themselves come from different scientific sub-disciplines and varying indigenous backgrounds. Their work, mostly based on the presentations and discussions that took place during an organized symposium, provides a unique analysis and comparison of widely differing approaches to the common issue.

HEIDI KELLER is Professor of Psychology at the Department of Psychology of the University of Osnabrück, Germany.

YPE H. POORTINGA is Professor of Cross-Cultural Psychology at Tilburg University in the Netherlands and at the University of Leuven in Belgium.

AXEL SCHÖLMERICH is Professor of Psychology at the Department of Developmental Psychology of the Ruhr-University, Bochum.

Cambridge Studies in Cognitive and Perceptual Development

The aim of this series is to provide a scholarly forum for current theoretical and empirical issues in cognitive and perceptual development. As the twenty-first century begins, the field is no longer dominated by monolithic theories. Contemporary explanations build on the combined influences of biological, cultural, contextual and ecological factors in well-defined research domains. In the field of cognitive development, cultural and situational factors are widely recognized as influencing the emergence and forms of reasoning in children. In perceptual development, the field has moved beyond the opposition of 'innate' and 'acquired' to suggest a continuous role for perception in the acquisition of knowledge. These approaches and issues will all be reflected in the series, which will also address such important research themes as the indissociable link between perception and action in the developing motor system, the relationship between perceptual and cognitive development and modern ideas on the development of the brain, the significance of developmental processes themselves, dynamic systems theory and contemporary work in the psychodynamic tradition, especially as it relates to the foundations of self-knowledge.

Between Culture and Biology

Perspectives on Ontogenetic Development

Edited by

Heidi Keller
University of Osnabrück

Ype H. Poortinga
Tilburg University

Axel Schölmerich
Ruhr-University

CAMBRIDGE UNIVERSITY PRESS

PUBLISHED BY THE PRESS SYNDICATE OF THE UNIVERSITY OF CAMBRIDGE
The Pitt Building, Trumpington Street, Cambridge, United Kingdom

CAMBRIDGE UNIVERSITY PRESS
The Edinburgh Building, Cambridge CB2 2RU, UK
40 West 20th Street, New York, NY 10011-4211, USA
477 Williamstown Road, Port Melbourne, VIC 3207, Australia
Ruiz de Alarcón 13, 28014 Madrid, Spain
Dock House, The Waterfront, Cape Town 8001, South Africa

http://www.cambridge.org

© Cambridge University Press 2002

First published 2002

Printed in the United Kingdom at the University Press, Cambridge

Typeface Times 10/12 pt   *System* LATEX 2$_\varepsilon$ [TB]

A catalogue record for this book is available from the British Library

Library of Congress Cataloguing in Publication data

Between culture and biology : perspectives on ontogenetic development / by
Heidi Keller, Ype H. Poortinga & Axel Schölmerich, eds.
    p.   cm. – (Cambridge studies in cognitive and perceptual development)
Includes bibliographical references and index.
ISBN 0-521-79120-0 – ISBN 0-521-79452-8 (pbk.)
1. Child psychology.   2. Developmental psychology.   3. Child development.
I. Keller, Heidi, 1945–   II. Poortinga, Ype H., 1939–   III. Schölmerich, Axel.
IV. Cambridge studies in cognitive perceptual development.
BF721 .B4138   2002
155 – dc21   2002020173

ISBN 0 521 79120 0 hardback
ISBN 0 521 79452 8 paperback

Contents

Figures

Tables

Notes on contributors

ERNST E. BOESCH studied psychology, philosophy and education in Geneva and served as a school psychologist for the canton of St Gallen from 1943–51. From 1951–82 he was professor of psychology at the University of the Saarland in Saarbrücken, on leave during 1955–8 to direct the International Institute for Child Study (UNESCO) in Bangkok. Until 1987 he was director of the Socio-Psychological Research Centre for Social Development at the University of the Saarland with a main research emphasis on psychological problems of social change in Thailand and Africa. Dr Boesch has over 120 publications to his name, has received honorary doctorates of the universities of Bangkok and Berne and holds honorary membership in several learned societies.

MICHAEL J. CASIMIR is professor of anthropology at Cologne University. After obtaining his Ph.D. in zoology he undertook field research on the ecology, nutrition and behaviour of the eastern lowland gorilla in eastern Zaïre. He went on to do prolonged fieldwork among pastoral nomads – first on ecology, diet and socialization patterns among West Pashtuns in Afghanistan and then on the ecology, diet and economy of nomadic Gujar and Bakkarwal in Kashmir. He has published extensively on various aspects of environmental management, sustainability, nutrition, resource use and risk evaluation. He has taught at the Department of Psychology at the University of Zürich, and at the Departments of Anthropology at the Universities of Göttingen, Hamburg and Münster. He is currently responsible for anthropological research in the framework of the international priority programme on Global Environmental Change: Social and Behavioural Dimensions sponsored by the German Research Council (DFG). He is also responsible for the section on anthropology in the Integrated Management Project for Efficient and Sustainable Use of Fresh Water sponsored by the German Ministry of Education and Research (BMBF) and is a member of the advisory board in anthropology of the DFG.

MICHAEL COLE gained his Ph.D. in psychology at Indiana University in 1962, and was a professor at Rockefeller University from 1969–78. Since 1978 he has been a professor in the Department of Psychology and in the Department of Communication at UC San Diego. At present he is University Professor of Communication and Psychology in the University of California. Dr Cole is best known for several decades of cross-cultural research on learning and development in relation to literacy and schooling. He has spent the past two decades developing effective approaches to improving educational and developmental environments and activities for American children from a variety of ethnic and social class groups. His current research focuses on the creation and sustainability of model cultural systems designed to promote children's development. His most recent books are *Cultural psychology: a once and future discipline* (1966) and *The development of children* (4th edn, with Sheila Cole, 2000).

LUTZ H. ECKENSBERGER gained his diploma degree in psychology in 1964 and, after applied studies on the evaluation of technical schools in Afghanistan, finished his doctorate in 1970. After his habilitation in 1973 he became a professor at the University of the Saarland (Saarbrücken), where he was appointed a full professor in 1976 (Development and Culture). In 1996 he moved to the Johann Wolfgang Goethe University in Frankfurt to become director of the German Institute of International Educational Research and head of the psychology section; he also has a chair of psychology there. In 1985–6 he was fellow of the Center for Advanced Studies in Berlin. Besides his focus on methods and methodology, his interest is in moral development and also in the relation between affects and cognitions, which he studied in environmental and health contexts. He has published two monographs, fifteen collaborations and over ninety journal articles and contributory chapters. He is a member of IACCP and was a member of the Executive Committee from 1984 to 1986, representing western Europe.

HEMA GANAPATHY is a graduate student in the Applied Developmental Psychology doctoral programme at the University of Maryland Baltimore County. Her dissertation research is in cross-cultural parental ethnotheories. She has worked in rural India in the areas of preschool education and women's empowerment and has been a lecturer at The Maharaja Sayajirao University of Baroda there.

PATRICIA M. GREENFIELD received her Ph.D. from Harvard University and is currently professor of psychology at UCLA, where she is a member of the developmental psychology group. Her central theoretical and research interest is in the relationship between culture and human development. She was a resident scholar at the School of American Research in Santa Fe, New Mexico, where she held a fellowship from the National Endowment for the Humanities. She is a past recipient of the American Association for the Advancement of Science Award for Behavioral Science Research, and has received teaching awards from UCLA and the American Psychological Association. Her books include *Mind and media: the effects of television, video games, and computers* (1984), which has been translated into nine languages. In the 1990s she co-edited (with R. R. Cocking) *Interacting with video* (1996) and *Cross-cultural roots of minority child development* (1994). She has done field research on child development and socialization in Chiapas, Mexico, since 1969. A current project in Los Angeles investigates how cultural values influence relationships on multiethnic high-school sports teams. She is also engaged in a cross-cultural teacher-training project called 'Bridging Cultures'.

BARRY S. HEWLETT received his Ph.D. in anthropology from the University of California Santa Barbara in 1987. He has held positions at Southern Oregon University and Tulane University and is currently professor of anthropology at Washington State University in Vancouver. His research has focused on infant development and paternal involvement in hunter-gatherer and horticultural communities, anthropology of infectious disease and evolutionary perspectives of human behaviour. Dr Hewlett is the author of *Intimate fathers: the nature and context of Aka pygmy paternal infant care* (1991), editor of *Father–child relations: cultural and biosocial contexts* (1992) and co-editor of 'Human behavior and cultural context in disease control', a special supplement to *Tropical Medicine and International Health* (1997).

GUSTAV JAHODA is emeritus professor of psychology at the University of Strathclyde in Glasgow. He was one of the pioneers of cross-cultural psychology, carrying out fieldwork on perception, cognition and attitude change, mainly in Africa. Among his other research interests was the development of social and economic concepts in children. After retirement he turned to historical topics, and his latest book is *Images of savages,* which deals with the origins of prejudice in Western culture.

HEIDI KELLER gained her Ph.D. from the University of Mainz and her habilitation from the Technical University of Darmstadt. She is a professor of psychology at the University of Osnabrück and head of its Department of Culture and Development. Her research interests are at the interface between culture and biology. She has begun a major cross-cultural research programme on cultural pathways. She has been a visiting professor at NIH, University of Baroda (Nehru Chair Fellowship) and the University of Costa Rica. She is currently teaching at the Department of Psychology at UCLA. She is invited as a fellow in residence at the Netherlands Institute for the Advanced Study in the Humanities and Social Sciences. Her recent publications include chapters in the *Handbook of psychology* (ed. K. Pawlik and

M. Rosenzweig) and the *International encyclopedia of the social and behavioral sciences* (ed. N. J. Smelser and P. B. Baltes; vol. ed. Nancy Eisenberg). She has edited the *Lehrbuch Entwicklungspsychologie* (Textbook of developmental psychology; 1998) and is currently editing the third edition of the *Handbuch der Kleinkindforschung* (Handbook of infancy research).

MELANIE KILLEN is professor of human development and associate director, Center for Children, Relationships, and Culture at the University of Maryland, College Park. She is the editor of three books including *Morality in everyday life: developmental perspectives* (with D. Hart, 1995). Her research areas include social reasoning about group inclusion and exclusion, social and moral development, cultural influences on development, autonomy, conflict resolution and social interaction.

HANS-JOACHIM KORNADT is professor emeritus of the University of the Saarland, Saarbrücken. Since 1997 he has been adviser to the University of Erfurt. He has been a member (1975–81) of the National Science Advisory Council in Germany as well as chairman of the scientific committee (1980–1). From 1982–4 he was the president of the German Psychological Association. In 1988 he obtained the Japanese-German Research Award. His research interests include pro- and antisocial motivation, socialization, and social change. He has conducted extensive cross-cultural research in east Africa and in east and southeast Asia. Among his publications are *Aggressionsmotiv und Aggressionshemmung* (Motive and repression of aggression) vol. 1 (1982) and, as co-editor, *Japan in transition* (1998).

MICHAEL E. LAMB received his Ph.D. in developmental psychology from Yale University in 1976 and an honorary doctorate in the social sciences from the University of Göteborg in 1995. Between 1980 and 1987 he was professor of psychology, paediatrics and psychiatry at the University of Utah in Salt Lake City and he has been head of the Section on Social and Emotional Development at the National Institute of Child Health and Human Development since 1987. His research is concerned with social and emotional development, especially in infancy and early childhood; the determinants and consequences of adaptive and maladaptive parental behaviour, including child abuse; children's testimony; and the interface of psychology and biology. Dr Lamb is the co-author of *Development in infancy* (1982), *Socialization and personality development* (1982), *Infant–mother attachment* (1985), *Child psychology today* (1982), and *Investigative interviews of children* (1998). He has edited several books on fathers and father–child relationships, including *The role of the father in child development* (1976), founded and co-edited *Advances in developmental psychology*, as well as *Developmental psychology: an advanced textbook* (1984), and has edited other books on various aspects of child development, including day care, infant social cognition, social and personality development, sibling influences, social policy, and parent-child attachment.

JENNIE LEE-KIM is a doctoral student at the University of Maryland, and her research interests include social reasoning about gender roles in Korean families, social and moral development and cultural influences on development.

HEIDI MCGLOTHLIN is a doctoral student at the University of Maryland and her research interests include stereotype and prejudice development and racial attitudes in children and adolescents.

JOAN G. MILLER is a cultural developmental psychologist who received her Ph.D. from the Committee on Human Development at the University of Chicago. Her earliest cross-cultural developmental research examined the development of social attribution among European-American and Hindu Indian populations. More recently she has undertaken programmes of research examining culture and the development of interpersonal morality as well as cultural influences on interpersonal motivation. She is the editor of the newsletter of the International Society for the Study of Behavioural Development as well as the associate editor for theory and method of the *Cross-Cultural Psychology Bulletin*. Having served for several years on the faculty in developmental psychology at Yale University, she presently holds a position as associate research scientist at the Institute for Social Research at the University of Michigan.

YPE H. POORTINGA is part-time professor of cross-cultural psychology at Tilburg University in the Netherlands and at the University of Leuven in Belgium. His most consistent research interest has been in the conditions under which data obtained in different cultural populations can be meaningfully compared. His empirical work has dealt with a variety of topics in culture-comparative research, including information transmission, basic personality variables and emotions, as well as social psychological variables in societies as far apart as southern Africa, India and Indonesia. He has been president of the International Association for Cross-Cultural Psychology (IACCP), the Dutch Psychological Association (NIP) and the European Federation of Psychologists' Associations (EFPA). Currently he is on the executive committees of the International Association of Applied Psychology (IAAP) and the International Union of Psychological Science (IUPsyS).

ANNE E. RUSSON is an associate professor in the Department of Psychology at Glendon College, York University, Toronto. She has been studying intelligence and learning in orang-utans since 1989 in Indonesian Borneo. Her research has been affiliated with the Orang-utan Reintroduction Project since

1994. She has published numerous research and popular articles on orang-utan intelligence, has co-edited an academic book on great-ape intelligence (*Reaching into thought: the minds of the great apes*) and recently published a popular book on orang-utans (*Orang-utans: wizards of the rainforest*).

T. S. SARASWATHI was, until recently, Senior Professor at the Department of Human Development and Family Studies at the Maharaja Sayajirao University of Baroda, India. She is a recipient of numerous professional awards and international fellowships for her contributions to the field of developmental psychology and has published several articles in reputed journals and edited books. She has been (co-)author or (co-)editor of several books and monographs on child development and related fields, including: *Trends and issues in child development, Developmental psychology in India: an annotated bibliography, Human development and family studies: an agenda for research and policy* (with B. Kaur), *Handbook of cross-cultural psychology*, vol. 2 (with John Berry and Pierre Dasen) and an edited volume on *Culture, socialization and human development*. Currently she is a member of the Adolescents in the 21st Century Study Group chaired by Reed Larson and is co-editing *Adolescence in eight regions of the world* with Reed Larson and Bradford Brown.

MICHAEL SCHNEGG studied social anthropology, history, sociology and economics at the University of Cologne. His main research interests include social organization and methods and theories to capture and explain cultural change and variations. He has done extended fieldwork among virtual communities on the Internet and in rural Tlaxcalan villages in Mexico. He is currently a Ph.D. candidate at the University of Cologne.

AXEL SCHÖLMERICH received his Ph.D. from the University of Osnabrück, Germany, in 1990 after studying psychology and educational sciences in Heidelberg, Mainz and Seattle. From 1990–5, he was a Fogarty Fellow at the Section on Social and Emotional Development at the National Institutes for Child Health and Human Development in Bethesda, Maryland. Subsequently, he was professor of psychology at the Department of Psychology in Halle (Saale), and is currently professor of psychology at the Ruhr-University Bochum, Germany. His main research interests include development of emotional regulation, social development, parent–child interactions and culture and migration as contexts for human development.

KAREL SOUDIJN is associate professor of psychology at Tilburg University, having obtained his Ph.D. at the University of Amsterdam. He has published several books and numerous articles on methodology, psychotherapy, interviewing, writing scientific papers and ethics for psychologists.

RODERICK FULATA ZIMBA is a professor of educational psychology at the University of Namibia. He received his Ph.D. from Purdue University, West Lafeyette, Indiana. Formerly he was at the University of Zambia, where he was the founding head of the Department of Educational Psychology, Sociology of Education and Special Education. Recently he has been appointed the director of postgraduate studies at the University of Namibia. He has published and conducted research in early childhood development, moral development, values education, special needs education and on the risk of infection identification and prevention of HIV/AIDS among schoolchildren.

Acknowledgements

For many years the three editors of this book and our colleagues at conferences, in joint research projects and in an international teaching programme have sporadically discussed the issues outlined in this introduction. We made vague plans to pursue the topic more systematically in a workshop or conference. The imminent sixtieth birthday of one of the central contributors to our debates, Lutz Eckensberger, was the catalyst for their realization. The invitational conference at which the foundation was laid for the present volume took place in November 1998 in Wittenberg, Germany. The dates were close enough to Lutz Eckensberger's birthday for us to throw a party, but far enough removed to avoid universal agreement with his views as a birthday present. Not all conference participants were able to contribute a chapter, so in order to cover a broad range of relevant perspectives we solicited a number of additional contributors with important points of view. We are indebted to all who have accepted the challenge to deal with biology, culture and development from their own perspective and research interests.

This book could not have been published without significant help. We acknowledge the financial support of the German Research Foundation, the state of Brandenburg and the Martin-Luther-University of Halle-Wittenberg for granting the initial symposium; we thank Sarah Caro from Cambridge University Press, who has encouraged us during the long editorial procedure; and last but not least, we would like to thank Marita Bojang, who kept track of the contributory manuscripts in her usual competent way and prepared the final draft.

We hope that the readers will enjoy the diversity of views, reflecting some agreement alongside numerous differences, as much as we did during both the congress and the editorial process.

Introduction

Heidi Keller, Ype H. Poortinga and Axel Schölmerich

This book deals with various facets of the long-standing discussion about the relationship between biology and culture, with particular emphasis on how this relationship manifests itself (and maybe changes) during the course of ontogenetic development. The interaction between nature and nurture has fascinated scholars since the beginnings of academic psychology. Developmentalists such as Preyer (1882) in Germany and Carmichael (1925) in the USA, or personologists such as William Stern (1900/1994) have conceptualized these interactions as crucial in their psychological theorizing. Moreover, these views impress by their modernity in stressing the inseparability of the two aspects and their mutual interdependence.

Astonishingly, this early wisdom was hardly built upon in the following decades, during which theorists were devoted either to moulding psychology into a S–R (stimulus–response) framework in which there was no place for more encompassing interactions between organism and environment, or to the promotion of viewpoints of behaviour as almost infinitely pliable, pre-empting the need even to consider such interactions. During this period views on the relationship between culture and biology were primed by both implicit and often explicit views of mutual exclusivity of the physical and the mental or social domain, as if they were separate entities. In this process, much of culture and much of biology disappeared in favour of a trait-oriented understanding of human psychological functioning. Cognitive, emotional and motivational processes tended to be researched in isolation.

Biologically oriented views focused on physiological and neurological mechanisms as the hardware correlates of mental processes. Consequently, the biological embeddedness and the evolutionary history of human behaviour were largely ignored by psychologists; selection pressures and (biological) adaptation processes were seen as regarding other species but not humans. In so far as culture was of concern it was mainly in the form of the proximate environment, with a focus on specific situations rather than on complex contexts comprising ecological, social and psychological processes. With an equally narrow perspective on both biological underpinnings and cultural variation, psychology

1

had truly become to a large extent the science of the laboratory behaviour of the first year psychology students (Keller and Greenfield, 2000). Furthermore, the interest of developmentalists was directed at the formulation of general theories; for example the creative and innovative approach of Jean Piaget did not conceptualize culture or cross-cultural differences for the development of cognitive schemata, although in his theory he saw the environment as crucial.

The isolation of phenomena from their context is a powerful tool in scientific analysis, but only as long as findings are reintegrated into broader frameworks. Are these available and are they valid? On the biological side, the emergence of human ethology and sociobiology have begun to provide such frameworks for the understanding of the biological principles underlying human behaviour, and the advances in understanding neurological structures suggest new organizing principles for behavioural development. On the cultural side, the broader acceptance of culture-informed research in psychology similarly allows a broader perspective on the interactions between nature and nurture. However, there continues to be widespread disagreement on any more precise formulations of such frameworks, especially if one goes beyond the small circle of adherents to a particular school of thinking. Moreover, in broader frameworks of behaviour and culture a developmental perspective as an essential ingredient is lacking. Only when we understand how cross-cultural invariance and variation emerge from the common biological origins in the course of ontogenetic development can we hope to start the journey towards the understanding of human functioning. This is what this book is about.

A complicating factor lies in the various levels of treatises that can be distinguished within both the cultural and the biological perspective. The label 'biology' in psychological theorizing and research comprises processes at the level of genetics, neurobiology and evolutionary biology.

First, a special branch of developmental genetics has begun to receive wider recognition (see Plomin, 1994; Asendorpf, 1998). Genes exert their influences in multiple ways over the entire lifespan. Besides direct influences here and now, there are cumulative effects; genetic activity during early developmental phases can become crystallized neurologically, resulting in a continuation of effects during later phases of the lifespan, e.g. in terms of stability of behavioural consequences. Moreover, genetic influences can be expressed in fixed programmes that translate their effects directly into action, without differential mediation of environmental factors (Mayr, 1974). Such programmes contribute to the universality within the species. Open genetic programmes can be understood as predispositions to learn specific information during specific developmental stages (Keller, ch. 10 this volume), which allows the environment to operate as a switch, contributing to differences between people. Thus, environmental influences are seen as important for both modes of genetic action; yet the role of environment for informing fixed programmes is mainly general whereas the effect of environment informing open genetic programmes is mainly differential (Asendorpf, 1998).

Second, recent advances in neurobiology driven by better techniques and theoretical enhancement also offer challenges and insights for human development. In recent years neurobiology has reached far beyond simply correlating parameters of the brain (e.g. synaptic density) with parameters of behaviour (e.g. memory performance). As the level of resolution of our insight into such structures becomes finer, the complex interplay with environmental stimulation during basic growth periods of the human brain becomes apparent. The prenatal macro-morphological changes in the brain, such as the emergence of the neural tube, outgrowth of neurons, formation of the cortex and production of axons, dendrites and synapses, follow genetic scripts that are relatively independent of experience (although the environment, for example through teratogenetic factors, may exert substantial influence). However, at least during the later period of foetal development, stimulation does play an important role, as sensitivity to language exposure clearly shows (DeCasper and Spence, 1986). The postnatal fine-tuning of the brain is always contingent upon environmental experiences (Nelson, 1999), indicating that processes of physical development can be affected by social conditions (Gottlieb, 1998; Gottlieb, Wahlsten and Lickliter, 1998).

One area of research where genetic and social influences are beginning to converge with developmental evidence is the new field of interpersonal neurobiology. Here evidence is emerging that the brain develops in interaction with social experiences during the first two years of life (Siegel, 1999; Schore, 2000). One consequence of this research is that '. . . it would seem virtually impossible to tease apart that which is innate qua innate from that which is learned qua learned' (Nelson, 1999, p. 425; cf. also Keller, ch. 10 this volume).

Third, evolutionary approaches have added a new dimension to the discussion, when human functioning is analysed with respect to its phylogenetic history. The emergence of sociobiology with Wilson's *Sociobiology: a new synthesis* (1975) initially provoked many negative, even hostile reactions (Lewontin, Rose and Kamin, 1988) from the field of psychology. The idea that in their social behaviour humans also follow an implicit evolutionary logic to optimize their inclusive fitness (Hamilton, 1964) appeared almost blasphemic to many. It has taken a few decades to familiarize psychology – and psychologists – with the idea of the evolutionary descent of behaviour patterns which has eventually made its way into several textbooks on evolutionary psychology (e.g. MacDonald, 1988; Buss, 1999). Some of the authors in this volume argue for more functionalistic and adaptionistic perspectives (see for example, the chapters below by Hewlett and Lamb; Keller; Casimir and Schnegg).

A crucial aspect pertaining to all conceptions of development with a biological flavour is the definition of learning as the acquisition of specific information at specific times during development with specific consequences. Human plasticity does *not* denote the ability to learn everything at any time with predictable results. Probably the most critical question concerns *whether*, and if so *how*, a specific characteristic or behaviour as it is found in a specific cultural context contributes ultimately to individual reproductive fitness (Dunbar, Knight and Power, 1999). In that way the level of proximate functioning is linked to ultimate causes defining the metaperspective and with this the explanatory framework. It is here that psychologists who see behaviour in its typically human aspects as shaped by culture place a different emphasis from their colleagues who argue for more direct linkages between these distinguishable levels of causality.

Likewise the role of culture is conceptualized on several levels. Two major frameworks can be distinguished, designated as psychological universalism and cultural relativism (Berry, Poortinga, Segall and Dasen, 1992). On both levels, context is seen as essential to understanding behaviour, but with quite different emphases on how culture and psychological functioning relate to each other. In psychological universalism (which is not the same as behavioural universalism; cf. Berry et al., 1992) the basic tenet is that all-important psychological functions occur species-wide, as they are rooted in the biological make-up of the human organism, even though this biological make-up is usually not further specified. There are important cross-cultural differences, but these are found in the manifestation of common psychological processes; thus there can be differences in the readiness at which certain cognitive algorithms are available, in the situations which solicit certain emotions, and in the beliefs and norms that control patterns of social interaction (see, for example, the chapters below by Kornadt and by Poortinga and Soudijn).

On the other hand, there are more relativist approaches, especially the school of cultural psychology. Here psychological process is seen as cultural, and thus culture as also residing within the individual. With an emphasis on social construction this perspective sometimes tends to deny any biological functionalism in differentiations between groups (see Miller, 1997). The cultural being 'human' is here regarded as a co-construction of culture and psyche. Although gaining acceptance, this framework also continues to meet with scepticism. Its qualitative character asks for the development of new methodologies and methods, which come with special problems of validity (Greenfield, 1997). A cultural approach is reflected, among others, in the three chapters below by Boesch, Cole and Eckensberger.

A more relativistic orientation also underlies indigenous approaches to the analysis of behaviour and culture. These approaches are rooted in non-Western views on human behaviour and functioning, in a similar fashion as 'mainstream psychology' has been based on Western ideas. The significance of societal culture as context for ontogenetic development is presented in this volume particularly in the chapters by Zimba and by Saraswathi and Ganapathy.

Generally, we would argue that, while taking theories and methods of psychology as a starting point, developmental theories should try to encompass biological principles and cultural variation specifying the relationships between organism and environment during the various phases of the lifespan.

Organization of the book

This volume draws together authors whose previous work is related to the questions and issues mentioned so far. It consists of five parts.

In the first part are three chapters, each of which might be said to survey the area delimited by the three notions of biology, culture and ontogenetic development. Gustav Jahoda does so from a historical perspective. He provides a brief overview of ideas that have been put forward in the past to resolve much the same issues that are the topic of discussion today. He argues that certain major themes have occurred in a variety of guises across historical time. He demonstrates that there is a certain periodic oscillation in the relative weight attached to culture and biology, associated with the prevailing ideologies in society at large.

Anne Russon shows that cultural patterns of transmission are not uniquely human, but occur in other species as well. This establishes the biological basis of culture as a psychological function, and provides important implications about likely properties of this function in humans. She applies a life-history perspective, suggesting that the great-ape culture is coordinated developmentally, in line with interacting biological, psychological and social parameters, with a special emphasis on processes of cultural transmission.

Patricia Greenfield describes several ways in which behaviour within cultural contexts may be linked to evolutionary processes, using examples from her research programme with Zinacantec Indians. She exemplifies different conceptualizations of her thesis that the psychological unity of development arises from maturationally grounded developmental progressions, but that behavioural manifestations of these stage progressions are culture-specific.

Part two contains four chapters by authors who place primary emphasis on cultural context as a major constituent of ontogenetic development. Chapters 4–6 are typical of most studies in psychology addressing culture, in the sense that biological aspects of behaviour, while not entirely ignored in principle, are not explicitly focused upon in the analysis. Cultural practices are reflections of characteristic ways of psychological functioning that are rooted in the sociohistorical past of the society, and thus shape individual development.

T. S. Saraswathi and Hema Ganapathy describe how the Hindu world view influences the way children are brought up. They demonstrate that Hinduism permeates all aspects of daily life including parental ideas, beliefs and practices related to child rearing. Their chapter especially delineates this perspective for parental ethnotheories of child rearing and qualities desired in a 'good child', and in cultural rules governing marriage-partner selection.

Roderick Zimba, writing from a southern African perspective, describes not only how children were traditionally embedded in family and group support structures but also how serious social disruption has challenged such support systems, and has negatively affected socialization patterns. Moreover, in his description of initiation rites Zimba shows how important cultural practices change under the influence of newly arising situational requirements.

Perhaps a culturalist perspective is most clearly represented in the chapter by Ernst Boesch. He deals with existential questions of humankind, taking as a perspective experience of chaos, which occurs in many different themes across the lifespan. In his phenomenologically oriented treatise the ambivalence of chaos as attracting specific facets of humanity as well as threatening others is elucidated.

In the final chapter of part two Joan Miller indicates how biological thinking on development can be incorporated in a culturalist perspective. She argues that individuals always bring along both a common and unique biological apparatus with limitations and facilitations. They also develop always in sociocultural contexts that are historically situated and which impact on their psychological functioning in ways that may be indeterminate.

Part three provides illustrations of culture-comparative studies in which a balance is sought between the universal and the culture-specific in human behaviour and psychological development, with an emphasis on differences in prevailing sociocultural conditions as antecedents of differences in behaviour. In the chapters of this section ontogenetic development is seen as a process that is primarily psychological. Cultural differences are (important) variations on common themes.

Melanie Killen, Heidi McGlothlin and Jennie Lee-Kim deal with one of the most complex aspects of social life: how to balance individual goals with collective concerns of the group. They demonstrate that concerns of the individual and the group coexist in reasoning and that exclusion of individuals occurs in different social and cultural contexts.

Hans-Joachim Kornadt summarizes findings from a longitudinal study about the consequences of differences in early mother–child interaction patterns on the development of aggression in adolescents. Consistent differences are reported between attitudes towards aggression in east-Asian and west-European samples. Kornadt extends his analysis to psychophysiological aspects of aggression and the way these autonomic processes develop.

The fourth part of the book contains three chapters that attempt to explain individual and group differences in terms of sociobiological processes. Here psychological development is conceptualized as the realization of modes of functioning that are potentially available in individuals and are triggered by the requirements of a specific environment.

Heidi Keller's focus is on the human preparedness for acquiring specific information at specific times during ontogeny in order to solve developmental tasks. With a universal repertoire of parenting systems and interactional mechanisms individuals establish specific socialization contexts that prepare their offspring to become competent adults in their respective environments.

Barry Hewlett and Michael Lamb highlight three neo-evolutionary approaches and discuss their implications for developmental psychology with a particular emphasis on the role of culture, introducing the concept of an evolutionary cultural anthropology. They exemplify these approaches with data on parent–infant interactions from Ngandu farmers and Aka foragers living in the same ecology in central Africa, as well as North American middle-class families.

Michael Casimir and Michael Schnegg also use a neo-evolutionary framework – the dual inheritance theory – in order to examine how universal emotional shame is related to physiological processes. With cross-cultural and correspondence analyses they demonstrate an association between emotions and verbal colour labels in a great variety of cultures.

The final part of the volume brings together three chapters that provide metaperspectives. In a sense part five parallels part one, because each of these chapters also attempts to provide an overview of the entire field. However, there is a difference, in that here each chapter tries to provide some kind of closure on how the relationships between biology, culture and ontogenetic development are best conceptualized.

Michael Cole addresses the role of culture in development by considering the question whether any new principles of development appear once a child is born. He exemplifies his view on culture as the species-specific medium of human development. He describes how cultural mediation coordinates individuals with their environment, giving examples from different cultural groups. He argues for different levels in conceptualizing relationships between individuals and environments, stressing the hybrid nature of humans.

Emphasizing that culturally unique manifestations of psychological processes occur at a low level of generality, Ype Poortinga and Karel Soudijn use a distinction between constraints on behaviour and behavioural affordances to demarcate between two realms of research: one where universalist approaches are appropriate and another where relativist approaches are appropriate. They extend their distinction to ontogenetic development and argue that development implies an increase in constraints as well as affordances.

Using important distinctions from philosophy of science as a background, Lutz Eckensberger reviews distinctions between various paradigms (or perspectives) in cross-cultural developmental psychology. Reviewing four such perspectives, namely the physical, biological and cultural perspectives and the perspective of the potentially self-reflective human being, Eckensberger tries to define the relations between them, pointing out that incommensurability can be distinguished from incompatibility and incomparability. It is claimed that, if integration is the goal (instead of assuming demarcation or incommensurability), the first step should be to consider perspectives as complementary to each other, but this step presupposes a mutual respect among scientists who associate themselves with different perspectives.

In the final chapter the editors reflect on the contents of the various parts, trying to bring together certain ideas and noting the wide discrepancies of views in other respects. We hesitantly make some extrapolations to the future, and some suggestions as to how the field of cross-cultural developmental psychology might develop.

This volume both presents a survey of current thinking in psychology on the interfaces between biology, culture and ontogenetic development, and explores the scope for integration of these three notions. We have been more successful in respect of the former than the latter. While working on this project, both before the symposium in Wittenberg that laid its foundations and afterwards, when we were putting this volume together, we were impressed by the book's tremendous range of conceptualizations. Although no single collection of chapters written by authors with disparate views on a common theme can ever hope to provide all relevant information, we hope that the ample collection of ideas reflected here gives a general picture of how the interface between biology, culture and individual development is currently conceptualized, and offers a glimpse of the direction in which it might go in the future.

REFERENCES

Asendorpf, J. B. (1998). Entwicklungsgenetik (Developmental genetics). In H. Keller (ed.), *Lehrbuch Entwicklungspsychologie* (Textbook of developmental psychology). Bern: Huber, pp. 97–118.

Berry, J. W., Poortinga, Y. H., Segall, M. H. and Dasen, P. R. (1992). *Cross-cultural psychology. Research and applications.* Cambridge: Cambridge University Press.

Buss, D. M. (1999). *Evolutionary psychology – the new science of the mind.* Boston: Allyn and Bacon.

Carmichael, L. (ed.) (1925). Heredity and environment. Are they antithetical? *Journal of Abnormal Social Psychology*, 20, 245–60.

DeCasper, A. J. and Spence, M. J. (1986). Prenatal maternal speech influences: newborns' perception of speech sounds. *Infant Behavior and Development*, 9, 133–50.

Dunbar, R., Knight, C. and Power, C. (eds.) (1999). *The evolution of culture.* New Brunswick, NJ: Rutgers University Press.

Gottlieb, G. (1998). Normally occurring environmental and behavioral influences on gene activity: from central dogma to probabilistic epigenesis. *Psychological Review*, 105, 792–802.

Gottlieb, G., Wahlsten, D. and Lickliter, R. (1998). The significance of biology for human development: a developmental psychobiological system view. In W. Damon (chief ed.)/R. R. Lerner (vol. ed.), *Handbook of child psychology*, vol. 1: *Theoretical models of human development*, 5th edn. New York: Wiley, pp. 233–73.

Greenfield, P. M. (1997). Culture as process: empirical methods for cultural psychology. In J. W. Berry, Y. H. Poortinga and J. Pandey (eds.), *Handbook of cross-cultural psychology*, vol. 1: *Theory and method*, 2nd edn. Boston: Allyn and Bacon, pp. 301–46.

Hamilton, W. (1964). The genetical evolution of social behaviour (I and II). *Journal of Theoretical Biology*, 7, 1–52.

Keller, H. and Greenfield, P. M. (2000). History and future of development in cross-cultural psychology. In C. Kagitcibasi and Y. H. Poortinga (eds.), Millennium Special Issue, *Journal of Cross-Cultural Psychology*, 31(1), 52–62.

Lewontin, R. C., Rose, S. and Kamin, L. J. (1988). *Die Gene sind es nicht... Biologie, Ideologie und menschliche Natur.* Munich: Psychologie-Verlags-Union (originally published in 1984 as *Not in our genes. Biology, ideology, and human nature.* New York: Pantheon Books).

MacDonald, K. B. (1988). *Social and personality development. An evolutionary synthesis.* New York: Plenum Press.

Mayr, E. (1974). Behavior programmes and evolutionary strategies. *American Sciences*, 62, 650–9.

Miller, J. G. (1997). Theoretical issues in cultural psychology. In J. W. Berry, Y. H. Poortinga and J. Pandey (eds.), *Handbook of cross-cultural psychology*, vol. 1: *Theory and method*, 2nd edn. Boston: Allyn and Bacon, pp. 85–128.

Nelson, C. A. (1999). Change and continuity in neurobehavioral development: lessons from the study of neurobiology and neural plasticity. *Infant Behavior and Development*, 22(4), 415–29.

Plomin, R. (1994). Nature, nurture, and social development: response. *Social Development*, 3(1), 71–6.

Preyer, W. (1882). *Die Seele des Kindes* (The soul of the child). Leipzig: Grieben.

Schore, A. N. (2000). Attachment and the regulation of the right brain. *Attachment and Human Development*, 2, 23–47.

Siegel, D. J. (1999). *The developing mind. Toward a neurobiology of interpersonal experience.* New York: Guilford Press.

Stern, W. (1994). *Die Differentielle Psychologie in ihren methodischen Grundlagen* (About the psychology of individual differences). Bern: Huber (originally published 1900).

Wilson, E. O. (1975). *Sociobiology: a new synthesis.* Cambridge, MA: Harvard University Press.

Part I

Setting the scene

1   Culture, biology and development across history

Gustav Jahoda

The natural sciences as we know them began some three centuries ago, and their accelerating progress has revolutionized our outlook on the physical world. If one of these predecessors of the time were to be transported into the twenty-first century he would probably be incapable of comprehending the kinds of scientific questions that are being asked today. By contrast, questions about the nature of human nature were being asked from long before the scientific revolution of the seventeenth century, and some of the basic problems of today would not be totally unfamiliar to our distant ancestors. They are, of course, being phrased differently now: the three key terms in the present title were either invented fairly recently ('biology' in 1802), or only began roughly to approximate their current meaning during the latter part of the nineteenth century. It does not follow, however, that before the emergence of this vocabulary there was no awareness of the issues to which it refers.

The aim here is to sketch a range of different approaches dominant in particular periods and to document the recurrence of certain major themes. Given the limitations of space, the coverage will necessarily be highly selective and generally simplified. The selection was governed by a focus on topics mentioned in the title, but it no doubt also reflects my personal bias. The presentation will follow a roughly chronological order, tracing the manner in which key concepts emerged and how their meanings and postulated relationships changed.

One constant thread, concerning the dichotomy of nature versus nurture, has ancient roots in the West; and as usual one can go back to Aristotle. For him all things were potentially what they had the capacity to become; but the external environment might prevent full realization of such potential. For example, an acorn might fail to become an oak because it had fallen on stony ground. As regards humans, the relative weight assigned to nature versus nurture has varied, with the pendulum swinging from one side to the other in different historical eras. It is only very recently that the misleading character of such a dichotomous formulation has come to be recognized.

The preparation of this chapter was supported by a grant from the Nuffield Foundation.

Early background

Differences between human groups have puzzled people since time immemorial, and remarkably similar arguments attributing differences to external influences persisted over more than a millennium. As early as the seventh century Isidorus of Seville (d. 636) commented that, in accordance with diversity of climate, the appearance of men and their colour and bodily size vary, and diversities of mind are also found. The effects of climate, notably of the sun turning the skin black, were debated until the nineteenth century. For most of that period there was of course no strictly 'biological' alternative, since Christian doctrine held that all humans descended from Adam and Eve; only a few unorthodox thinkers such as La Peyère dared to propose multiple creations. None the less, critiques of the climatic hypothesis were voiced, and a typical counter-argument of the kind common in the debate was put forward by Leonardo da Vinci (1452–1519). He denied that the black races of Ethiopia are the product of the sun; 'for if black gets black with child in Scythia [a northern region], the offspring is black; but if a black gets a white woman with child the offspring is grey' (Slotkin, 1965, p. 39).

As well as climate, 'custom' was often used in post-Renaissance Europe to account for human differences; and I have argued in some detail elsewhere (Jahoda, 1993) that its meaning tended to be close to what we know as 'culture'. This comes out clearly in a passage from Descartes (1596–1650), who also was one of the first to put forward a biological approach to psychology:

I...recognised in the course of my travels that all those whose sentiments are very contrary to ours are yet not necessarily barbarians or savages, but may be possessed of reason in as great or even greater degree than ourselves. I also considered how very different the self-same man...may become according as he is brought up from childhood amongst the French or Germans, or has passed his whole life amongst Chinese or cannibals...I thus concluded that it is much more custom and example that persuade us than any certain knowledge. ([1637] n.d., p. 60)

Later John Locke said much the same thing. The arguments were sometimes highly sophisticated. Thus Blaise Pascal (1632–62) wrote: 'Custom is a second nature...But what is nature? For is custom not natural? I am much afraid that nature is itself only a first custom, as custom is a second nature' (Slotkin, 1965, p. 120). This may be compared with Boesch (1991, p. 21): '"Nature" is no antipode to "culture"; nature, as we experience it, is already culture.'

Among these early writings I have not come across anything about child development as we would understand it, but the prolonged helplessness of the offspring of humans as compared with those of animals was repeatedly noted. Also, the child was often seen as a *tabula rasa*. As Pierre Charron (1541–1603), a follower of Montaigne, put it: 'While...the Soul is fresh and clear, a fair and perfect blank ... there can be no difficulty in making it what you please; for this Condition disposes it to receive any manner of impression, and to be moulded into any manner of form' (cf. Slotkin, 1965, p. 115). As shown later in more detail that was essentially what Margaret Mead believed at one stage in her career.

Imitation, later elevated by Gabriel Tarde into a cardinal principle, was said to characterize the child. For instance Bernard Mandeville (1670–1733) suggested that the child adopts customs through its 'fondness of imitation', by aping others. He also anticipated Piaget on animism: 'All young children seem to imagine, that everything feels and thinks in the same Manner as they do themselves: And ... they generally have this wrong opinion of Things inanimate ...' (Slotkin, 1965, p. 267). While such parallels are intriguing, they refer only to scattered observations rather than any systematic approach.

Generally, children were seen as lacking in 'sense' or reason, a deficiency also usually attributed to 'savages'. Hence these were sometimes compared to children, a practice that became extremely widespread during the nineteenth century. But between the seventeenth and nineteenth centuries a radical though only temporary change occurred, at least among a group of leading intellectual figures.

The Enlightenment

The change was made possible by the fading of theological authority, while that of science was rising. A spirit of inquiry prevailed, and the success of the physical sciences led to the belief that similar methods might be applied to the study of human nature regarded as part of, and not, as previously, apart from, nature at large. There would seem to be certain intriguing parallels between Enlightenment ideas and those prevalent during the major part of the twentieth century. I refer here to underlying values and kinds of questions asked, rather than to results obtained, of which there were few.

Eighteenth-century biology was essentially taxonomic, culminating in the classical systematization by Linnaeus. Yet as regards the species *Homo*, he was far from certain where its boundaries should be drawn. There was also a wider discussion about humans' puzzling similarity to apes; but exotic others were not initially seen as specially ape-like, as they were later. Humanity was usually perceived as unitary and, in the words of William Robertson ([1777] 1808, p. 221): 'A human being, as he comes originally from the hand of nature, is everywhere the same.' Differences between human groups were interpreted as a function of stages of progress among societies, perceived as analogous to child development. The stages were seen as related to modes of subsistence, and these in turn were linked to what we would call 'ecologies'. The stages envisaged, which have remained more or less constant to our day, were as follows: hunting, fishing and collecting; pastoralism; agriculture; and, finally, commerce. The whole scheme was reminiscent of Berry's eco-cultural model (Berry, 1976; for details see Jahoda, 1995a). The mental equipment of all humans in all ages was viewed as being closely similar, savages suffering merely from relative ignorance rather than stupidity. Some even considered that this ignorance was often exaggerated, arguing in a manner reminiscent of our 'everyday cognition':

Travellers have exaggerated the mental varieties far beyond truth, who have denied good qualities to the inhabitants of other countries, because their modes of life, manners, and customs have been excessively different from their own. For they have never considered, that when the Tartar tames his horse, and the Indian erects his wig-wam, he exhibits the same ingenuity which an European general does in manoeuvring his army, or Inigo Jones in building a palace. (John Hunter, 1728–93, cited in Slotkin, 1965, p. 212)

Philosophers of the Enlightenment were well aware of what Tomasello et al. (1993, p. 495) called the 'ratchet effect', as indicated by the following passage from Turgot ([1750] 1973, p. 41):

The arbitrary signs of speech and writing, by providing men with the means of securing the possession of their ideas and communicating them to others, have made all of the individual stores of knowledge a common treasure-house which one generation transmits to another, an inheritance which is always being enlarged by the discoveries of each age.

As far as individual development is concerned, the assumption was that of a Lockean *tabula rasa*, expressed in a rather extreme form by Claude-Adrien Helvétius (1715–71). He went so far as to deny the existence of any innate differences, holding that the mind could be completely shaped by what he called 'education'. For him this included not merely teachers, but family, friends, mistresses and so on, as well as chance factors; thus he understood by this term more or less what we would call the sociocultural environment. This approximates the position later adopted by J. B. Watson, though Helvétius did not propose any mechanism whereby the influences were exerted.

Most of these ideas remained purely speculative, though later the need for empirical investigations was appreciated. When the *Société des Observateurs de l'Homme* was founded in 1799, its aims included plans for detailed observations of children's development from the cradle onwards, in evident ignorance that this had already been pioneered by Tiedemann (1787). Another more ambitious project was also mooted, and described as 'an experiment on natural man'. It was proposed to isolate from birth onwards four or six children, half of each sex, so that they would not be in contact with any social institution. These children would be carefully observed for a period of twelve or fifteen years in order to study the development of ideas and of language as governed purely by 'natural instinct' (Jauffret, [1801] 1978).

One study was carried out, namely that of Victor, the well-known 'wild boy' of Aveyron. He was regarded as having been in a pure state of nature when found, and thereby providing an opportunity for a kind of natural experiment. Itard ([1801] 1932) believed that tracking the trajectory of Victor to normal maturity would be a means of throwing light on the general process of becoming civilized or, as we would put it, the acquisition of culture. Unfortunately, as shown by Pinel (a well-known alienist of the time), Victor was profoundly handicapped and made only slight progress.

Even this slight sketch should indicate that the Enlightenment in some important respects adumbrated today's ideas. By the time Napoleon's armies marched over Europe, reaction had already set in, intending to restore after the turmoil of revolution a supposedly traditional order. This included a change in attitudes towards the 'savages', increasingly regarded as irredeemable. Paradoxically, it was the new science that lent its authority to such negative views.

Biology, race and development

The eighteenth century had seen the emergence of biology in its modern sense, pioneered by Linnaeus. Towards the latter part of that century the rise of the anti-slavery movement produced a backlash in which the defenders of slavery postulated the innate inferiority of non-European races, comparing them to apes. Subsequently Cuvier began to transform biology from an essentially taxonomic enterprise into a functional one. The concept of the organization of the nervous system became the key for understanding biological processes in humans as well as animals. Cuvier devised an index of 'animality' depending on the relative size of the facial area. According to this, 'savages' were closer to animals than Europeans. Thereby the path was open to the race-thinking that dominated the nineteenth century, and what had previously been mere opinions about the inferiority of the 'Others' gained the stamp of scientific support. Human differences came to be largely attributed to biological causes, and those like Theodor Waitz (1863) who opposed this trend, adducing culture-historical factors, remained in a minority.

Throughout the nineteenth century differences between 'savages' and civilized peoples, as well as individual differences, were mainly attributed to biological endowment, and strenuous efforts were made to find evidence for this in brain structures. The lengths to which some savants were prepared to go may be illustrated by the bizarre case of the *Société d'autopsie mutuelle*, founded in Paris in 1876 by a group of physical anthropologists. They believed that the link between features of the brain and psychological characteristics had hitherto not been demonstrated for a simple reason: namely, that insufficient information had been available about the people whose bodies had been taken from hospitals and whose brains had been dissected. Hence all members were required to provide an autobiography, from childhood onwards, and later an extensive questionnaire was devised. The agreement was that the surviving members would dissect the brains of the dead ones, and it was hoped that, armed with the requisite detailed knowledge, the relationship of brain structure to personal features could then be firmly established. Alas, they hoped in vain (Dias, 1991).

Going back to the issue of civilized versus 'primitive' societies, the backwardness of the latter came to be explained in terms of differences in child development. During the first half of the nineteenth century reports multiplied that children of 'primitive' races were at least equal in brightness to European children, and were sometimes even believed to surpass them. James Hunt (1865, p. 27), a notorious race propagandist, put it as follows:

With the Negro, as with some other races of man, it has been found that children are precocious; but that no advance in education can be made after they arrive at the age of maturity; they still continue, mentally, children . . .

This alleged phenomenon was labelled 'arrested development', and efforts were made to find a biological explanation for it. The solution arrived at was a supposed early closure of the sutures, i.e. the junctions of the skull bones. One ingenious writer went further and put forward a quaint reason why this should be so: Europeans think more, and the throbbing of the brain produced thereby slows down the process of closure!

The empirically minded Francis Galton was exceptional in seeking some concrete evidence. A questionnaire prepared by him for travellers, missionaries and administrators (reproduced in Pearson, 1924, pp. 352–3) contains the following item:

Children of many races are fully as quick, and even more precocious than European children, but they mostly cease to make progress after the season of manhood. Their moral character changes for the worse at the same time. State if this has been observed in the present instance.

Unfortunately, no answers have been preserved. 'Arrested development' later became somewhat confounded with a more famous theory, the so-called 'biogenetic law', which was applied increasingly to the interpretation of cultural phenomena. In its original version the law referred to embryological development, stating that characteristics held in common by large animal groups usually develop earlier in the embryo than unique features. As such, it was adopted by Darwin and still stands. However, it came to be extrapolated to *postnatal* development and later became known in psychology as the *recapitulation* theory. It was postulated that the cultural stages of the progress of humanity were functionally related to the biologically fixed phases of the psychological maturation of individuals. These phases recapitulate, in miniature as it were, the mental capacities corresponding to the hierarchy of cultural stages; and the progress of individuals in the lower races is arrested when they reach their biological limit. With recapitulation, as with 'arrested development', the question arose as to what caused the cessation of development. The most common answer was that young people of the lower races abandon themselves to unrestrained sex immediately after puberty. It is often not clear whether this was thought of as a biological disposition, or socially determined.

These biological theories coloured nineteenth and early twentieth century ideas about savages and their children. In particular, the equation of adult savages with European children led to absurdities when it came to savage children. It was generally thought that savages do not train their children and let them run wild. In a typical passage Schultze (1900) commented that there cannot be a question of education among *Naturvölker*, since they have little if anything to transmit. Most of the writings were entirely speculative. William Preyer, a pioneer of child psychology, was exceptional in suggesting that explorers should carry out comparisons of small children among uncivilized nations with child behaviour in Germany (Preyer, 1882). The interest was focused less on what 'savage' children are like, and more on the relationship between European children and adult savages. Such comparisons, including even animals, were central to George Romanes' (1880) *Mental evolution in man* as will be documented in more detail later. Letourneau (1881) recommended the study of the dreams of European children as a means of gaining insight into the mentality of savages. The earliest textbooks of child psychology reflected the notion of 'childlikeness'; thus Sully (1895) drew parallels in his classical text between dolls and 'fetishes', or the language of children and that of savages.

From biology to culture

At the turn of the twentieth century the importance of child development for understanding adult society was not yet widely appreciated. Wundt's *Völkerpsychologie* (folk psychology) was intended to throw light on ' . . . those processes, which, owing to their conditions of origin and development, are tied to mental collectivities' (Wundt, 1908, p. 226). This corresponds roughly to what is now meant by 'culture', and in fact in one of his last writings Wundt (1920) conceded that *Völkerpsychologie* and *Kulturpsychologie* (culture psychology) were equivalent concepts. Yet Wundt (1907, p. 336), maintained that ' . . . it is an error to hold . . . that the mental life of adults can never be fully understood except through the analysis of the child's mind. The exact opposite is the case.' Later (1917, p. 195) he referred to the 'exaggeration of the value of child psychology'. It would seem that Wundt, like most of his predecessors over the centuries, regarded child development as something obvious and unproblematic.

It was a misjudgement, made at a time when the new field was emerging. Preyer in Germany, Binet in France and Stanley Hall in America were among those promoting it. Freud, an adherent of the 'biogenetic law', which led him to compare neurotics with children and savages, proclaimed the first five years of life as crucial for later development. Stanley Hall sought to provide evidence of 'recapitulation', mainly by questionnaire methods. He also carried out a cross-national study, replicating an earlier German one of children's knowledge of concepts at the beginning of schooling (Schwabe and Bartolomai, 1870). Others subsequently produced a flood of questionnaire studies of children's moral ideas, one of which is of special interest: Hoyland (1926) carried out a study in India indicating that Indian children were less materialistic and more ethical and religious in their outlook than Western ones.

One of Hall's students, Appleton ([1910] 1976) attempted an empirical test of what she called the 'culture-epoch' theory, based on recapitulation, by comparing the games and play of adults in 'the lowest of savage tribes' with those of American children. It was a valiant effort, but although Appleton claimed that the outcome broadly supported the theory, in hindsight the study suffered from some fatal flaws.

By the first decade of the twentieth century the concept of 'culture' had already come to be more widely used. Its original definition, put forward by Edward Tylor (1871), had listed knowledge, belief, arts, morals and so on 'acquired by man as a member of society'. This notion of culture as something *acquired* or learned was to set the tone for about another century. Tylor never used the term 'culture' in the plural, and it was Franz Boas who began to do so at the end of the nineteenth century. In opposition to the doctrine that race governed the fate of peoples, he argued that culture and history were the essential determinants. He even sought to show that the cephalic index, one of the chief measures of racial identity long used by physical anthropologists, underwent changes in successive generations of immigrants (cf. Stocking, 1982).

While Boas' contribution is well known, that of a German armchair theorist writing at about the same time is not. After a comprehensive survey of ethnographic reports about the development of Negro children, Erich Franke concluded that while race may have some part, the primary factor was the cultural context that influences and constrains the course of their development (cf. Jahoda, 1995b).

Another theorist of that period was James Mark Baldwin, whose *Mental development in the child and the race* (1895), and subsequent works, were based on his own version of recapitulationism. He tried to demonstrate how the history of humankind (which is what he meant by 'the race') is reflected in the growth of the child. But, as has been noted, he was unconcerned with the development of the child within the family context.

While Baldwin was at Johns Hopkins, John Watson had also been recruited to the department there. They were very different characters and the main thing they had in common, it may be noted parenthetically, was that both were expelled from the university: Baldwin for being found in a black brothel and Watson for an extramarital affair. Unlike Baldwin, who had been largely forgotten until Piaget resurrected him, Watson imposed his stamp on a new era of behaviourism. Apparently influenced by Freud, he carried out studies of the emotional conditioning of infants, immortalizing 'Little Albert'. His commonly cited boast of being able to make anyone into anything, irrespective of background and race, concealed his uncertainty about the effects of race. In his autobiography he imagined an 'infant farm' where sets of thirty pure-blooded Negroes, Anglo-Saxons and Chinese would be reared under identical conditions in order to resolve the issue. What is not in doubt is his belief that humans could be extensively moulded into any desired shape.

Watson's extreme environmentalism was in sharp contrast with the biologically oriented 'instinct' theories, inspired by Darwinism, which had led to speculative lists of literally hundreds of supposed instincts. Environmentalism was, however, in harmony with Boas' emphasis on human variability as a function of culture. This was the atmosphere which two prominent students of Boas, Ruth Benedict and Margaret Mead, imbibed. Mead had studied psychology as well as anthropology, and went into the field with test materials. Her position at that time – the 1930s – is clearly set out in the following passage:

... many, if not all, of the personality traits which we have called masculine or feminine are as lightly linked to sex as are the clothing, the manners, and the form of head-dress that a society at a given time assigns to either sex ... the differences between individuals within a culture are almost entirely to be laid to differences in conditioning, especially during early childhood, and the form of this conditioning is culturally determined. (Mead, [1935] 1950, pp. 190–1)

In other words, rather like Helvétius before her, she viewed human nature as more or less infinitely malleable by culture.

In 1930 Freud published his *Civilization and its discontents*, in which the term 'civilization' was more or less equivalent to 'culture-in-general', in the sense of Edward Tylor's original formulation of the concept. Freud postulated an opposition between biology and culture, whereby the latter rested upon the sublimation or suppression of biological urges. As far as development is concerned, the Oedipus complex was viewed by him as being of phylogenetic origin, and thus had to be overcome before an individual could function as a normal member of a culture.

Accordingly, it is not surprising that the most prominent psychoanalytic anthropologist of the period, Geza Roheim, defined culture in a manner that sees it as derivative from biology:

By culture we shall understand the sum of all sublimations, all substitutes, or reaction formations, in short, everything in society that inhibits impulses or permits their distorted satisfaction. (Roheim, 1934, p. 216)

Although as an anthropologist he did discuss cultural differences, he tended to play them down by saying that they are usually exaggerated – a point not without some justification (Roheim, 1950). At any rate, his main stress was on biological universals: all culture, he maintained, is a function of prolonged infancy and the vicissitudes of the libido. Roheim dispensed what he himself called the 'undiluted Freudian wine' (Roheim, 1947, p. 29), viewing development entirely in these terms.

The reason for his strong defence of orthodoxy was that by that time neo-Freudians, notably Kardiner and his group, had considerably watered down the biological aspects and focused on modes of child rearing, themselves viewed as a function of modes of subsistence. But this was done at the cost of pathologizing culture, as exemplified in the following passage: 'The basic personality in Alor is anxious, suspicious, mistrustful, lacking in confidence, with no interest in the outer world' (Kardiner, 1945, p. 170). It should be added that contemporary anthropologists of a Freudian bent usually avoid such pitfalls and often make highly insightful contributions (e.g. Obeyesekere, 1990).

In the Soviet Union Vygotsky, while interested in psychoanalysis, was also critical of it; and it did not enter significantly into his own sociohistorical theory of development, which owed much to Darwinian evolutionism and, to a lesser extent, to Lévy-Bruhl (apart, of course, from numerous other influences analysed by van der Veer and Valsiner, 1991). Put very crudely, one might say that for Vygotsky the young child is a pre-cultural biological organism, which becomes transformed by a series of cultural devices such as language, tools and artefacts into a cultural being and thereby acquires the higher mental processes. At the same time there is of course no clear dividing line between 'natural' and 'cultural':

The growth of the normal child into civilization usually involves a fusion with the processes of organic maturation. Both planes of development – the natural and the cultural – coincide and mingle with one another. The two lines of change interpenetrate one another and essentially form a single line of sociobiological formation of the child's personality. (Vygotsky, cited in Wertsch, 1985, p. 41)

It is also worth noting that Vygotsky did not regard 'primitives' as *biologically* inferior, though agreeing with the then widespread view that they were more restricted to the lower psychological processes. This was because they had not yet been exposed to the historical changes that gradually enabled Europeans to function at a higher level (van der Veer and Valsiner, 1991, p. 212). The Vygotskian approach has been highly influential, but the followers have not been concerned with the biological aspects and have explicitly disclaimed any interest in 'central processes'. This position has been slightly modified by one of the foremost American exponents of sociohistorical theory, who in a recent book (Cole, 1996) has admitted a weak version of modularity – more about this later.

Unlike Vygotsky, who had a literary background, the other great figure in child psychology, namely Piaget, was a biologist. But Piaget was also influenced by Lévy-Bruhl, adopting the notions of a pre-logical mentality and of 'mystic participation'. This became manifest first in his *Language and thought of the child*, where he bracketed together 'defective persons, primitive races and young children'. Such an equation of 'primitives' and European children, which Lévy-Bruhl himself had explicitly denied, harks back to nineteenth-century conventional wisdom. Piaget expounded his position at length in an early paper (Piaget, 1928, 1995). Only a few major features can be singled out.

Piaget referred to the 'astonishing functional similarities between the beliefs of primitives and children's ideas' (1928, p. 193), and went on to list a series of parallels which indicate his acceptance of hoary stereotypes; they include affirmation without proof, absence of logical coherence, 'participation', mystical causality, confusion of sign and the thing signified, and so on. He then went on to ask what could account for these similarities. The answer suggested by Piaget was that, paradoxically, social constraints and egocentrism operate in basically similar ways to produce the same effects. In both cases one has to deal with a mind lacking in education and not effectively socialized, being open to influence by the mere fact of age or power rather than intrinsic truth. Piaget's image of primitive culture is graphically conveyed in the following passage:

In a society where the generations weigh heavily upon one another, none of the conditions required for the elimination of childish mentality can come to light. There is neither discussion nor exchanges of points of view. There is a totality of individuals whose autistic vision will remain ever uncommunicated, and whose communion is assured by the wholly external link of tradition. In such a situation nothing is invented by individuals, and nothing rises above the level of infantile thought. (1928, p. 201)

What is interesting here is that although Piaget was operating with a notion of 'primitive culture' derived from the era of crude biologism, his analysis stressed social factors, notably social interaction, as instrumental in development. Lévy-Bruhl himself retracted much of his original thesis toward the end of his life. But Piaget (1966), in an article where he acknowledged the need for cross-cultural tests of his theory, commented that the recantation had been excessive. Thus although he attempted a cultural explanation of the allegedly inferior cognitive functioning of 'primitives', he continued to hold stereotypical views derived from nineteenth-century biological determinism.

Until well after the Second World War Vygotsky and Piaget were outside the mainstream of psychology, whose centre of gravity had shifted to the USA and was dominated by behaviourism and the environmentalism that corresponded to it. This also largely applied to anthropology and is evident from the definitions of culture in Kroeber and Kluckhohn's (1952) famous monograph. It is usually cited only for its 159 definitions, but contains valuable discussions and analyses.

One can learn from it that only seven of these definitions contained any mention of biology, none of which made any direct link between culture and biology. On the contrary, some of the older definitions referred to culture as a 'superorganic' entity. Explicitly or implicitly, culture was treated as something acquired by individuals during the process of socialization by teaching and learning. This was and remained the dominant stance, and is still reflected by current authors, for instance in the recent edition of the *Handbook of cross-cultural psychology* (Camilleri and Malewska-Peyre, 1997). It is only fairly recently that radical questioning began (for an overview see, e.g. Brightman, 1995).

Before going on to this it is worth considering briefly the ideas of Skinner, the last of the behaviourist luminaries, whose first pronouncements on culture appeared shortly after the publication of the Kroeber and Kluckhohn monograph. He wrote: '...the culture into which an individual is born is composed of all the variables affecting him which are arranged by other people' (Skinner, 1953, p. 419). Culture was for him essentially a matter of *control*, a term that recurs in the discussion. But interestingly, he also made biological comparisons:

The evolution of cultures appears to follow the pattern of the evolution of species. The many different forms of culture, which arise, correspond to the 'mutations' of genetic theory. Some forms prove to be effective under prevailing circumstances and others not, and the perpetuation of the culture is determined accordingly. (p. 434)

He returned to this theme some two decades later in a book that also touched upon child development (Skinner, 1972). Predictably, this consisted for him of the acquisition of a repertoire of behaviour under the contingencies of reinforcement set up by people in the social environment. It would seem that he hardly distinguished between culture and development, since he later (Skinner, 1987, p. 74) defined culture simply as 'the contingencies of social reinforcement maintained by a group'.

Skinner's references to the biological nature of humans are minimal, though he was of course bound to acknowledge the existence of an innate capacity to be reinforced. On the other hand he did elaborate, again in some detail, the parallels between biological and cultural evolution. A culture, according to him, is selected for adaptation to the environment, though he recognized that not all cultural practices are adaptive. But the parallel breaks down when it comes to transmission, since cultural evolution is Lamarckian. This is an aspect of Skinner's thinking that is seldom remembered at a time when similar ideas have come very much to the fore.

Fading of the boundaries

During the heyday of behaviourism the distinction between biology and culture seemed clear-cut, but thereafter this slowly began to change. From the

1960s onwards, behaviourism gradually gave way to the 'cognitive revolution'. The cognitive approach, with its connectionist models taken to characterize the human mind everywhere, constituted a decisive shift away from environmentalism and a concentration on putative central processes. As such it had initially little interest in culture and there were, and still are, those who saw cognitive science as a purely biological approach. Thus Jackendoff (1987, xi) wrote: 'the mind can be thought of as a biological information-processing device'. When it came to issues of development, such a stance was less easy to maintain since the question of how individuals become socialized into a given culture obtrudes itself. Hence there were attempts of various kinds to find answers. A recent example is that of Frawley (1997), who sought to reconcile Vygotsky's culture-historical theory with cognitivism. At the same time, the ancient notion that humans are almost infinitely malleable was decisively abandoned.

Chomsky had long adopted a nativist stance on language, and Fodor (1983) published his highly influential book on 'modularity', that inspired a plethora of research. Much of it addresses the issue of what aspects of cognitive functioning are predetermined by our neural architecture as distinct from those that result from experience. Until recently this would have been expressed in terms of whether not a particular function was innate. But the concept of 'innateness' itself has been subjected to critical scrutiny (Elman et al., 1996), and shown to be much more difficult and complex than had hitherto been realized.

The discussion regarding the number and kinds of modules is somewhat reminiscent of the 'instinct' debate in the early twentieth century. It is worth noting in this connection that the idea of cognition being of two distinct kinds is not a new one. Immanuel Kant, in his *Critique of pure reason* (1781), maintained that the categories of space, time, quantity and relations are not learned from experience, but constitute an intuitive apparatus for making sense of experience and the world. He attributed the cognition of these categories to a soul or self beyond experience. But Jakob Fries (1773–1843), a follower of his, rejected Kant's transcendental principle and suggested that human modes of perception and thinking are a function of our organic constitution, which, as it were, predetermines the categories available to us. Seventy years later William James (1890), in the final chapter of his *Principles of psychology*, came even closer to a concept of modularity since his approach was essentially Darwinian. He argued that there are two quite different kinds of cognition. One consists of the accumulation of facts we learn by experience during our lifetime; the other, which he called 'necessary truths', is the product of evolution.

This brings us to the rise of current evolutionary psychology, which has been comprehensively surveyed by Keller (1997). Hence only a few complementary comments pertinent to the present theme need to be offered.

As far as development is concerned, there is again a historical precedent. George Romanes (1880) was a follower and protégé of Darwin's who treated human psychology as a purely biological product created by evolutionary processes. As far as cognitive development in childhood was concerned, this led him to a bizarre comparative scale: at birth a baby's mental capacity is that of a jellyfish, at three weeks of worms, at fourteen weeks of spiders and crabs, at five months horses, pigs, or cats, and so on. All this was based on the so-called 'biogenetic law', later adopted in psychology under the heading 'recapitulationism' (Haeckel, 1866).

Modern evolutionary psychologists, while necessarily giving priority to biology, all recognize the need to come to grips with culture, though they do so in rather different ways. Tooby and Cosmides (1992) treat culture as a subordinate category, whereby external circumstances trigger domain-specific biological mechanisms, and it is such mechanisms that determine the spread of cultural representations in populations.

They state quite explicitly that 'Human minds, human behaviour, human artefacts, and human culture are all biological phenomena' (pp. 20–1). A rather different approach originated with the biologist Richard Dawkins (1976), who suggested a parallel between genes and units of culture – which he left ill-defined – as 'memes'. According to him memes are subject to the same replication and selection processes as genes, the difference being that memes are much more recent. Hence this new replicator 'is still drifting about in its primeval soup' (p. 192), that soup being culture at an early stage of evolution. This idea was recently taken even further by Blackmore (1999), who regards memes as actively competing for space in human brains and seeking to propagate themselves. The study of such phenomena, which embrace all spheres of human activity, would become the science of 'memetics', a kind of quasi-biology. These are rather extreme positions, not shared by all evolutionary psychologists, some of whom view culture as a so far largely unsolved problem.

Plotkin (1997) describes it as 'one of the last great frontiers of science'. While all these writers are concerned with the relationship between biology and culture, few are particularly concerned with development. This is perhaps rather surprising, since the notion of modularity constitutes a crucial bridge between biology and culture.

Concluding comments

As stated at the outset, the brief sketch offered here is necessarily selective and greatly simplified. None the less, it should be sufficient to indicate that some of the issues that occupy us today are by no means entirely new. The influence of culture, as expressed by the term 'custom', has long been recognized, while the importance of innate biological factors came to the fore during the nineteenth century, predominantly focused on 'race'. On the other hand 'development' was, until the latter part of the nineteenth century, regarded as unproblematic and only gradually attained increasing salience thereafter.

One can also discern a certain periodic oscillation in the relative weight attached to culture and biology. The Enlightenment stressed environmental factors, followed by a shift to biology, which lasted until the first decades of the twentieth century. This gave way in the social sciences to a radical environmentalism that is by no means dead as yet. There is little doubt that these broad movements of thought have been influenced by prevailing ideologies in society at large. It is clear, for instance, that nineteenth-century biological racism was linked to colonialism and imperialism. But as one comes closer to the present the links become less easy to discern for want of the necessary perspective, and their detailed study remains a task for the future.

At any rate, after the prevailing environmentalism of most of the twentieth century there has been a return to biology, not only in psychology but also in anthropology (cf. Sperber, 1996). However, in contrast to the previous century, connectionism is universalistic in orientation and as such initially concerned primarily with the effects of neural architecture, to the exclusion of culture. It is only rather recently, under the influence of neo-Darwinism, that a further change has taken place with a quest to integrate culture and its variations into an evolutionary scheme.

As a result, the former sharp distinction between biology and culture is giving way to the recognition of their interrelationship, though its exact nature as well as its significance for development remains as yet controversial; and so does the question as to the extent to which aspects of development are pre-programmed. So far cross-cultural and cultural psychology have only been marginally affected by the new thinking. If they continue largely to ignore it, they risk being left behind.

REFERENCES

Appleton, L. E. ([1910] 1976). *A comparative study of the play activities of adult savages and civilized children*. Chicago: University of Chicago Press. Reprinted by Arno Press.
Baldwin, J. M. (1895). *Mental development in the child and the race*. New York: Macmillan.
Berry, J. W. (1976). *Human ecology and cognitive style*. New York: Sage.
Blackmore, S. (1999). *The meme machine*. Oxford: Oxford University Press.
Boesch, E. E. (1991). *Symbolic action theory and cultural psychology*. Berlin: Springer.
Brightman, R. (1995). Forget culture: replacement, transcendence, relexification. *Cultural Anthropology*, 10, 509–46.
Camilleri, C. and Malewska-Peyre, H. (1997). Socialization and identity strategies. In J. W. Berry, P. R. Dasen and T. S. Saraswathi (eds.), *Handbook of cross-cultural Psychology*, vol. 2. Boston: Allyn and Bacon, pp. 41–67.

Cole, M. (1996). *Cultural psychology*. Cambridge, MA: Harvard University Press.

Dawkins, R. (1976). *The selfish gene*. Oxford: Oxford University Press.

Descartes, R. ([1637] n.d.). *Discourse de la méthode*. London: Routledge.

Dias, N. (1991). La société d'autopsie mutuelle ou le dévouement absolu au progrès de l'anthropologie. *Gradhiva*, 10, 26–36.

Elman, J. L., Bates, E. A., Johnson, M. H., Karmiloff-Smith, A., Parisi, D. and Plunkett, K. (1996). *Rethinking innateness*. Cambridge, MA: MIT Press.

Fodor, J. A. (1983). *The modularity of mind*. Cambridge, MA: MIT Press.

Frawley, W. (1997). *Vygotsky and cognitive science*. Cambridge, MA: Harvard University Press.

Haeckel, E. (1866). *Generelle Morphologie der Organismen* (General morphology of the organisms). Berlin: Reimer.

Hoyland, J. S. (1926). An enquiry into the comparative psychology of Indian and Western childhood. *Indian Journal of Psychology*, 1, 45–7.

Hunt, J. (1865). On the Negro's place in nature. *Memoirs read before the Anthropological Society of London, 1863/4*. London: Truebner.

Itard, J.-M. ([1801] 1932). *The wild boy of Aveyron*. New York: Century.

Jackendoff, R. (1987). *Consciousness and the computational mind*. Cambridge, MA: MIT Press.

Jahoda, G. (1993). *Crossroads between culture and mind*. Cambridge, MA: Harvard University Press.

(1995a). The ancestry of a model. *Culture and Psychology*, 1, 5–10.

(1995b). Erich Franke on culture and cognitive development. *Psychologie und Geschichte*, 7, 319–38.

James, W. (1890). *Principles of psychology*, 2 vols. New York: Macmillan.

Jauffret, L.-F. ([1801] 1978). Introduction aux memoires. In J. Copans and J. Jamin (eds.), *Aux origines de l'anthropologie française*. Paris: Le Sycomore, pp. 71–85.

Kardiner, A. (1945). *The psychological frontiers of society*. New York: Columbia University Press.

Keller, H. (1997). Evolutionary approaches. In J. W. Berry, Y. H. Poortinga and J. Pandey (eds.), *Handbook of cross-cultural psychology*, vol. 1: *Theory and method*, 2nd edn. Boston: Allyn and Bacon, pp. 215–55.

Kroeber, A. L. and Kluckhohn, C. (1952). *Culture: a critical review of concepts and definitions*. Cambridge, MA: Peabody Museum.

Letourneau, C. (1881). *Sociology based upon ethnography*. London: Chapman and Hall.

Mead, M. ([1935] 1950). *Sex and temperament in three primitive societies*. New York: Mentor.

Obeyesekere, G. (1990). *The work of culture*. Chicago: University of Chicago Press.

Pearson, K. (1924). *The life, letters and labour of Francis Galton*, vol. 2. Cambridge: Cambridge University Press.

Piaget, J. (1928). Logique génétique et sociologie. *Revue Philosophique*, 53, 167–205.

(1966). Nécessité et signification des recherches comparatives en psychologie génétique. *International Journal of Psychology*, 1, 3–13.

(1995). *Sociological Studies*, ed. L Smith. London: Routledge.

Plotkin, H. (1997). *Evolution in mind*. London: Allen Lane.

Preyer, W. (1882). Die Seele des Kindes (The mind of the child). Leipzig: Grieben.

Robertson, W. ([1777] 1808). *The history of America*, vol. 1. London: n.p.

Roheim, G. (1934). *The riddle of the Sphinx*. London: Institute of Psychoanalysis.

(1947). Introduction: Psychoanalysis and anthropology. In G. Roheim (ed.), *Psychoanalysis and the Social Sciences*, vol. 1. New York: International Universities Press, pp. 9–33.

(1950). *Psychoanalysis and anthropology*. New York: International Universities Press.

Romanes, G. J. (1880). *Mental evolution in man*. London: Kegan Paul, Trench.

Schultze, H. (1900). *Urgeschichte der Kultur* (The early history of culture). Leipzig: Biographisches Institut.

Schwabe, H. and Bartholomai, F. (1870). Der Vorstellungskreis der Berliner Kinder beim Eintritt in die Schule (The range of ideas of Berlin children on entering school). In *Berlin und seine Entwicklung: Statisches Jahrbuch fuer Volkswirtschaft und Statistik; Vierter Jahrgang*. Berlin: Guttentag.

Skinner, B. F. (1953). *Science and human behavior*. New York: Macmillan.

(1972). *Beyond freedom and dignity*. New York: Bantam/Vintage.

(1987). *Upon further reflection*. New Jersey: Prentice-Hall.

Slotkin, J. S. (1965). *Readings in early anthropology*. Chicago: Aldine.

Sperber, D. (1996). *Explaining culture*. Oxford: Blackwell.

Stocking, G. W. (1982). *Race, culture, and evolution*. Chicago: University of Chicago Press.

Sully, J. (1895). *Studies of childhood*. London: Longmans, Green.

Tiedemann, D. (1787). Beobachtungen über die Entwicklung der Seelenfähigkeiten bei Kindern (Observations on the development of children's mental capacities). *Hessische Beiträge zur Gelehrsamkeit und Kunst*, 2, 313–33 and 3, 486–502.

Tomasello, M., Kruger, A. C. and Ratner, H. H. (1993). Cultural learning. *Behavioral and Brain Sciences*, 16, 495–552.

Tooby, J. and Cosmides, L. (1992). The psychological foundations of culture. In J. H. Barkow, L. Cosmides and J. Tooby (eds.), *The adapted mind*. New York: Oxford University Press, pp. 19–136.

Turgot, A. R. ([1750] 1973) A philosophical review of the successive advances of the human mind. In R. L. Meek (ed.), *Turgot*. Cambridge: Cambridge University Press.

Tylor, E. B. (1871). *Primitive culture; researches into the development of mythology, philosophy, religion, art, and custom*, 2 vol. London: J. Murray.

van der Veer, R. and Valsiner, J. (1991). *Understanding Vygotsky: a quest for synthesis*. Oxford: Blackwell.

Waitz, T. (1863). *Introduction to anthropology*. London: Anthropological Society.

Wertsch, J. V. (1985). *Vygotsky and the social formation of the mind*. Cambridge, MA: Harvard University Press.

Wundt, W. (1907) *Outlines of psychology*. New York: Stechert.

(1908). *Logik*, vol. 3, 3rd edn. Stuttgart: Enke.

(1917) Völkerpsychologie und Entwicklungspsychologie (Folk psychology and developmental psychology). *Psychologische Studien*, 10, 189–238.

(1920). *Völkerpsychologie*, vol. 10: *Kultur und Geschichte* (Culture and history). Leipzig: Kroener.

2   Comparative developmental perspectives
on culture: the great apes

Anne E. Russon

Interest in nonhuman primate culture owes primarily to the promise of insights into human culture, given the likelihood that evolutionary continuities link human and nonhuman primate processes. Concepts of human culture cannot be applied directly to nonhuman primates, however, because nonhuman primates do not share all the capacities counted as intrinsic to human culture. To enable comparative study, primatologists have focused on what is considered to be the basic defining feature of culture: social transfer of expertise operating across generations, at the group level (e.g. Kummer, 1971; McGrew, 1998; Nishida, 1987). Features considered beyond the reach of nonhuman primates are necessarily treated as secondary.

Defined this way, culture should feature in primate lives because primates characteristically rely on intricate forms of sociality for survival (e.g. Humphrey, 1976; Jolly, 1966; Smuts et al., 1987) and on lifelong learning for much of their expertise (e.g. Fobes and King, 1982; King, 1994; Parker and Gibson, 1990). Within nonhuman primates, the great apes have special importance as humans' sister species. Together, great apes and humans form a clade that diverged from other primates as recently as 16–19 million years ago (Groves, 1989; Pilbeam, 1996). That makes the great apes the closest living genealogical relatives to humans and, on that basis, the species most likely to resemble humans culturally. In that role, great apes are the focus of this chapter.

Because accepted wisdom had placed culture on the human side of the human–nonhuman divide, study has been fixated on establishing incontrovertible evidence for, or against, the existence of culture in great apes. Best evidence has been defined as behaviours or artefacts attributable to social *as opposed to* ecological or individual processes, so criteria have centred on stable social traditions or on special mechanisms for socially transferring expertise such as imitation, teaching or symbolic communication (e.g. Boesch, 1996; McGrew, 1998; Whiten et al., 1999). While this approach has produced convincing evidence that cultures exist in great apes, critics have argued that it promotes flattened and static images of the cultural processes involved (McGrew, 1998; van Schaik, Deaner, and Merrill, 1999; Whiten et al., 1999). Best cases are rarely typical ones, for instance focusing on single, stable traditions precludes the possibility that broader, more flexible cultural systems may operate, and focusing on a narrow set of social mechanisms constricts the view of social information transfer.

Prominent among these lacunae is development. In great apes, acquiring expertise is a protracted affair concentrated in immaturity that can entail years of dedicated study (e.g. Matsuzawa, 1996; McGrew, 1992). Learners' needs and their abilities to understand and absorb new information change with development, as do their preferences for what expertise to acquire socially versus independently and from whom to learn (e.g. King, 1994; Parker and Gibson, 1990; Parker and McKinney, 1999; Russon and Galdikas, 1995). Therefore, individual and social processes that themselves change over time likely intertwine in the process of acquisition – as they do in humans (Boesch and Tomasello, 1998). This chapter discusses approaches to great ape culture that take development into consideration. The aim is to better understand great ape cultures and, through them, to better appreciate human culture.

Missing links: culture and cognition, cognition and development

Many scholars see culture and cognition as intrinsically intertwined in primates, so much so that cognition may be the most important dimension along which cultures vary (e.g. Donald, 1991; Fox, 1972). Differences between primate species in the complexity of their cultures – the behaviours and artefacts produced, the knowledge acquired, and the means of mastering the expertise – may be tied to differences in their cognitive abilities, especially the social learning abilities that govern cultural transmission (e.g. Parker and Russon, 1996; Whiten, 2000).

If primate culture is bound up with cognition, it is equally bound up with development because primate cognition is a product of development. Comparative evidence suggests that human and nonhuman primates share the same developmental sequence of cognitive achievements, in part because their cognition is constructed (Parker and McKinney, 1999). 'Constructed', here, means that each individual's cognitive abilities are emergent products that develop on the basis of experience and that higher abilities are built upon lower-level abilities so they cannot be achieved until prerequisite abilities are in place. Species differ with respect to the highest levels typically attained and the age at which comparable abilities are typically achieved in the life cycle. Evidence suggests four grades of increasingly complex mature cognition – prosimian, haplorhine (except great apes), great ape and human – constructed on the basis of increasingly extended developmental periods in conjunction with accelerated progress through early stages. To the extent that culture and cognition interlock, primate cultural processes should show developmental variation similar to that shown for cognition.

Researchers in the mid 1990s began considering how culture and development are related in great ape cognition, working from Vygotskian views of human development as deeply sociocultural (Rogoff, 1992; Vygotsky, 1962; Whiten, 2000). Two hypotheses resulted, *apprenticeship* (Parker, 1996) and *enculturation* (Call and Tomasello, 1996; Tomasello and Call, 1997; Tomasello, Savage-Rumbaugh and Kruger, 1993).

Apprenticeship

The apprenticeship hypothesis proposes that great ape cognition evolved to depend on specific social inputs during development. Here, apprenticeship means guided participation in shared activities of a routine nature (Rogoff, 1992) and refers to the integrated complex of ecological and social cognitive abilities specific to great apes and hominids.

The hypothesis is that a suite of complex cognitive abilities – imitation, self-awareness, demonstration teaching, and intelligent tool use – co-evolved with the great ape-human clade to enable immatures to acquire a specific form of survival expertise. Ancestral great apes may have faced critical selection pressures from their feeding niche, which is characterized by seasonal reliance on embedded foods like hard-shelled fruits and nest-building invertebrates. Obtaining these embedded foods required special expertise, extractive foraging assisted by intelligent tool use, which required more complex cognitive abilities. (Intelligent tool use means use of a detached object to physically alter another object with an understanding of the causal dynamics involved; Parker and Poti', 1990.) The prolonged ontogeny that distinguishes the great-ape lineage from other nonhuman primates may relate to achieving the necessary cognitive abilities. In great apes, cognitive development and parental support extend into the juvenile period. This helps immatures to develop the cognitive abilities needed to master survival expertise by extending the time and the assistance available. Extending parental support increases pressures on parents, however, especially mothers, by interfering with their further reproduction. Orang-utan interbirth intervals exceed seven years (Galdikas and Wood, 1990), about as long as offspring remain dependent. The apprenticeship complex, notably its social cognitive abilities, may have evolved to help relieve maternal pressures by boosting the capacities of offspring to acquire tool-assisted extractive foraging expertise. This hypothesis puts sophisticated cognitive abilities for social transmission at the core of the evolutionary enhancements that characterize great-ape cognition, with the enhancements realized during development.

Enculturation

Enculturation, in its original anthropological sense, means immersing an agent in a system of meaningful human relations, including language, behaviour, beliefs and material culture; it goes beyond teaching a static set of rules or skills (Miles, 1978; Miles, Mitchell and Harper, 1996). In reference to great apes, it has come to mean rearing them in human settings with the aim of transmitting cultural models and symbolic communication, so that they become active agents within a system of relations, which they come to embody in their own actions and understanding (Miles, 1978, 1999). Some suggest that treating great apes as agents whose behaviours are intentional is the key influence (e.g. Call and Tomasello, 1996; Tomasello et al., 1993). For others, enculturation can be seen as a broadened view of apprenticeship wherein a rich web of cultural processes and forces are at play. Many of the processes entailed in enculturation are within nonhuman primates' reach, so here I will use the term 'enculturation' to refer to immersion in species-typical cultural milieu and 'human enculturation' to refer to immersion in human milieu.

Profound effects have been claimed for the human enculturation of great apes, primarily that it generates higher cognitive abilities than those great apes construct independently or even new abilities that otherwise would not exist (Call and Tomasello, 1996; Tomasello et al., 1993; Tomasello and Call, 1997). Human enculturation is claimed to affect great apes so profoundly that cognitively, human-enculturated great apes are discounted as not representative of their own species. This hypothesis portrays great-ape cognitive abilities as very strongly defined or even determined by the sociocultural context of each individual's development.

Evaluation

Both hypotheses see cultural processes as integral to the development of great apes' cognitive abilities, but they differ on how culture and cognition interact, especially on the degree and direction of influence. The apprenticeship hypothesis posits that cultural input supports the development of cognitive abilities in great apes and may boost it, but within species-defined limits (e.g. developmental timetables, cognitive ceilings). Influences between culture and cognitive development are likely bi-directional because cultural processes themselves depend on the cognitive abilities available. The human enculturation hypothesis presents a more extreme position, that human enculturation enhances great apes' cognitive development to higher than normal levels and that influences flow from culture to cognitive development.

That sociocultural processes are essential to great apes' cognitive development is amply supported. Great apes require unusual sociocultural contexts to develop atypical cognitive abilities; they also rely on sophisticated sociocultural input normally, to support advanced physical cognitive abilities, e.g. in mastering complex food processing expertise. Immatures co-opt social cognitive abilities to assist them in mastering this expertise, up to and probably including imitation, and mothers assist by teaching, including demonstrating facets of the techniques that their offspring find difficult (e.g. Boesch, 1991; Fox, Sitompul and van Schaik, 1999; Inoue-Nakamura and Matsuzawa, 1997; Russon, 1997, 1999a; see reviews by Parker and McKinney, 1999; Tomasello and Call, 1997). The apprenticeship hypothesis is founded on this and additional evidence.

Evidence for the extreme position taken by the human enculturation hypothesis is less extensive, primarily that human-enculturated great apes develop cognitive abilities not known to develop spontaneously, to apparently exceptional levels (e.g. rudiments of language and quantification; see Tomasello and Call, 1997; Tomasello et al., 1993). This evidence represents only conditions that favour human-enculturated great apes. To be culture fair, the claim that human-enculturated great apes' abilities surpass those of wild great apes should also be tested with the tables turned – under wild conditions with cognitively complex wild problems. If this test does not support the claim, differences in their abilities must owe to factors beyond human cultural input and the interaction between culture and cognition, developmentally, may differ from that proposed.

The use of tool sets that incorporate metatools, tools used to make other tools, is one of the few forms of wild expertise that afford this test of the human enculturation position. It is a critical form of expertise because it is the most cognitively sophisticated extractive foraging expertise known in wild great apes (Boesch, 1993; Matsuzawa, 1996). Wild chimpanzees at Bossou, Guinea, develop the abilities to master metatool use. They incorporate rock wedges into the hammer-and-anvil tool sets they use for nut cracking, to level their anvils. The wedges qualify as metatools because they modify or improve the anvil tool (Matsuzawa, 1994). Four captive great apes have also mastered using tool sets that include metatools. Two captive chimpanzees used a rock to break open a bone for food inside, then a fragment of the bone to pierce the cover of a desirable drink (Kitahara-Frisch, Norikoshi and Hara, 1987). A human-enculturated language-trained bonobo (Kanzi) and a captive orang-utan mastered making flake tools, with human tutoring, then used them to cut ropes for access to food (Toth et al., 1993; Wright, 1972).

Wild great apes master metatool use independently but human-enculturated great apes have mastered it only under conditions heavily scaffolded by humans (Parker and McKinney, 1999). Tomasello and Call (1997), proponents of profound effects of human enculturation, concur. Human-enculturated great apes have required assistance to use metatools, so they have not demonstrated cognitive abilities equal to those shown by wild great apes, let alone surpassing them. Reviews of recent studies of other cognitive abilities find, similarly, that the abilities attained by human-enculturated great apes are equalled by free-ranging great apes (Parker and McKinney, 1999). The case that human enculturation boosts great apes' cognitive abilities beyond levels achieved in species-typical rearing conditions, then, is less solid than has been claimed.

Parker and McKinney offer a sensible analysis of the processes involved, based on work by Fischer and his co-workers. Fischer et al. (1993) have shown that an individual's cognitive competence with a given type of problem spans a range of levels, not one fixed level, and that unsupportive contexts elicit low levels in the range while socially supportive contexts elicit high levels. The exceptional performances of human-enculturated great apes have occurred in socially supportive contexts, so they may represent the highest levels in these apes' current competence range.

This does not imply that enculturation makes no significant contribution to great-ape cognitive development. Enculturation likely contributes to great apes' cognitive abilities because it is a normal, species-typical contributor to their cognitive development (Parker and McKinney, 1999; Parker and Russon, 1996). Human enculturation probably induces atypical abilities because great-ape cognition is constructed on the basis of experience, as it is in humans. Individual great apes' cognitive abilities *should* develop as a function of their particular rearing conditions and living problems, as they have in great apes reared in a milieu that demands and tutors quantitative or language abilities. By the same token, however, sophisticated cognitive abilities demanded by problems that occur outside human contexts, such as foraging in the wild, may not develop in human-enculturated great apes, although they do in conspecific-enculturated forest-living great apes. Among ex-captive orang-utans newly freed to forest life, human-enculturated ones stand out painfully for their poor cognitive capabilities. Even after experience with forest foods, climbing devices, and other orang-utans during rehabilitation, in the forest they ignore cues to forest skills from other orang-utans and are inept at recognizing common forest foods as well as figuring out how to obtain foods, travel arboreally and navigate the forest (Russon, 1996). What human enculturation likely offers, then, is refinement of problem-specific cognitive abilities relevant to human contexts – as great ape enculturation refines problem-specific abilities relevant to great-ape contexts.

Of the two hypotheses, apprenticeship offers the better substantiated and the better balanced view of the interplay between culture and development with respect to great-ape cognition: Culture enhances cognition during development, by contributing to the experiences from which cognitive structures are constructed, but subject to psychologically and biologically conditioned opportunities and constraints.

Numerous findings are consistent with this view. Development schedules opportunities for cultural input in great apes, as it does in other mammals, by means of simple biologically designed social tendencies like following and scrounging by immatures (Box and Gibson, 1999). Following others introduces immatures to ranging, navigation and resource locations. When and where close following is tolerated, it also affords proximity, the minimum condition for socially learning manipulative skills (Coussi-Korbel and Fragaszy, 1995). Immature great apes are also dedicated food scroungers from early infancy into the juvenile period and at these developmental levels, scrounging likely enhances their social learning (Russon, 1997). Eating pre-selected, semi-processed, or leftover foods, especially difficult foods, fosters identifying foods in the local repertoire, introduces immatures to items they cannot obtain on their own and shows something of how they are processed. Development also constrains great apes' cultural transmission routes. Mothers initially tolerate their immatures' scrounging but their tolerance wanes as offspring develop. The processing stage at which immature scroungers can take food is therefore progressively restricted, which could provide a step-by-step guide to acquiring the expertise (Russon, 1997). The ability for imitation does not develop in great apes until juvenility, so its availability is constrained with respect to timing and the range of expertise to which it can contribute; great apes also imitate selectively, favouring high-level facets of advanced expertise, notably operations on object–object relations, over low-level motor-action details (Byrne and Russon, 1998; Myowa-Yamakoshi and Matsuzawa, 1999; Russon, 1999a; Russon and Galdikas, 1995). Demonstration teaching has been reported only between mothers and their immature offspring (Boesch, 1991) and learners' choices of imitative models have been found to vary with age (Russon and Galdikas, 1995).

'Life history' perspectives on culture in great apes

The comparative study of primate cognitive development has set the stage for a hypothesis with important implications for culture, namely that cognition within the primates evolved primarily by changes to development (Parker and McKinney, 1999). Evidence suggests that the comparative pattern found across primates in cognitive development is paralleled in other spheres of development (e.g. physical, social). If so, the evolution of cognition within primates may entail the evolution of development itself. Evolution often occurs by changing developmental timetables, or heterochrony, especially timing and rate (McKinney and McNamara, 1991). Based on comparative evidence, development evolved within the primates by terminal extension (extending the developmental period) and acceleration (speeding the rate of development).

   The broad implication is that cognitive evolution within the primates may owe to the evolution of life history strategies. In the biological sense, life history strategies concern the overall patterning of the life cycle for individual members of a species, including features such as longevity, ontogenetic changes, reproduction and philopatry (De Rousseau, 1990; Fleagle, 1999). If life history evolution underpins cognitive evolution in the primates, it likely underpins primate cultural evolution as well. Life history parameters have implications for non-cognitive factors that afford and constrain cultural transmission as well as cognitive ones, e.g. needs, physical capabilities and social roles. Some of these non-cognitive factors also change developmentally, in time with biologically framed schedules that operate roughly in concert with those followed by cognition. All these factors interact when influencing the acquisition of expertise and their interactions are affected by developmental timing, so their roles in cultural transmission should be complex. Evolutionary changes to life history parameters, especially ontogenetic parameters, should have complex effects on cultural transmission and therefore on the cultures created by primate species (Parker and Russon, 1996). Factoring in species-specific life history parameters relevant to these features may then clarify how development and culture interrelate.

Physical capabilities

Ontogenetic parameters that schedule physical change (e.g. dental eruption, manual coordination, brain structures, strength, growth spurts, puberty, reproduction) indirectly affect cultural transmission. Extending and accelerating brain development, for instance, alter mature as well as immature brain structures and, correspondingly, alter cognitive capacities across the life cycle. Infants' physical incompetence (e.g. immature dentition, poor motor coordination) renders social support indispensable; even if social support is mainly physical, it opens opportunities for social information transfer (Box and Gibson, 1999). Puberty can sharply alter growth rates and strength, both of which alter needs and capacities for force-based expertise. Adults face physical losses or liabilities from illness, injury or the encumbrances of adult social roles (e.g. offspring), which again alter needs and capacities. These few examples illustrate that physical development alters the challenges each individual faces in acquiring expertise; by implication, it also alters needs and opportunities for cultural input.

Ecological demands

Understanding life in the wild is important to understanding great-ape cultures because its demands define the expertise needed across the lifespan. Of the ecological demands facing primates – foraging, ranging, predation, etc. – foraging is considered to pose the greatest challenges (e.g. Freeland and Janzen, 1974; Milton, 1984). Foraging may pose unique challenges to great apes.

Great apes are frugivorous by preference but their great size precludes a strictly frugivorous diet (Waterman, 1984). Their diets have therefore broadened to include omnivory, high-quality foods, and 'difficult' foods. Difficult foods are foods protected by anti-predator defences, which make them hard to obtain and prepare for ingestion. Some consider difficult foods to be the distinguishing feature of great-ape diets and obtaining them to be great apes' greatest cognitive challenge (Byrne, 1997; Parker and Gibson, 1979; Russon, 1998). Among great apes' most difficult foods may be permanent or fallback foods that sustain them through periods of food scarcity, such as barks and nest-building invertebrates (Parker and Gibson, 1979; Russon, 1998; Yamakoshi, 1998). For difficult permanent foods, avoidance is not an option; they are, at times, essential to survival. Embeddedness has been suggested as the critical cognitive challenge but many defences that may pose equally difficult challenges are also common; among them are spines, inaccessible locations, companion species like ants that protect the food species, irritant hairs, distasteful exudates, digestive inhibitors and toxins (e.g. Byrne and Byrne, 1991; Parker and Gibson, 1977; Russon, 1998; van Schaik and Knott, 1999). To make matters worse, multiple defences often protect a single food, so difficult foods often pose *multifaceted* problems. *Neesia* sp. seeds that orang-utans eat, for example, are doubly embedded – in a woody, spiny husk that can rarely be broken open *and* in a mass of stinging hairs inside the husk (Fox et al., 1999). Finally, foods themselves grow so the challenges posed by any food may vary. Young leaves are differently defended than mature ones (Waterman, 1984), for instance, and palm hearts are found in palms grading in size from slender immature rosettes on the forest floor to massive crowned trees 30 metres tall (Jones, 1995). Some difficult foods therefore present a set of multifaceted problems, rather than a single, unidimensional one.

This indicates why great apes' techniques for obtaining difficult foods can be highly complex, involving flexible, lengthy manipulative sequences and sometimes complex tool use, and why the acquisition of such techniques can take up to ten years (Byrne and Byrne, 1991; Matsuzawa, 1996; McGrew, 1992; Russon, 1998; van Schaik, Fox and Sitompul, 1996). It also suggests why culture may play an important role. The diversity and multiplicity of defences, the risks of ingesting toxins and the low probability of independently discovering hidden, ephemeral or unpredictable food sources all favour social over individual learning for its greater speed, safety (less error-prone) and power to cue novices to cryptic items and inventive techniques.

Obtaining difficult foods looms even more challenging in life history perspective. The extended developmental change that characterizes great apes' lives effectively alters each individual's experience of these problems across their life cycle. For orang-utans, for instance, hard-shelled foods that are located arboreally become easier to open as strength and cognitive abilities develop, but harder to access as weight increases. Coupled with changes in food items, this means that individual great apes effectively face an unending cycle of *re-solving* the 'same' food problems repeatedly as they and their foods move through their life cycles.

Sociality

Some life history parameters can affect cultural transmission by scheduling social change, such as interbirth interval, subgrouping patterns, philopatry, mating systems and social tolerance (Kummer, 1971; Parker and Russon, 1996; van Schaik et al., 1999). Social tolerance in particular varies with learners' age and sex status, so learners' needs and opportunities for social learning about food techniques should change developmentally, as the experts accessible to them change. For infants, parental tolerance is highest; for juveniles, parental tolerance wanes while same-sex peer tolerance increases; and for adolescents, intolerance grows with same-sex adults and peers but tolerance increases with opposite-sex partners. By channelling the set of potential expert–learner pairs, then, stage-related developmental changes also channel what accessible experts likely know and learners' own abilities to extract information from them. Most work on cultural processes in great apes has focused on mother–offspring transmission because this relationship offers the greatest tolerance during the early period of intensive learning (e.g. Parker and Russon, 1996; Boesch, 1991, 1993). If expertise is to attain cultural status, however, it must be transmitted beyond immediate kin into the wider community. Immatures begin moving into the wider community as juveniles so from this point extrafamilial contacts are likely to affect their social learning.

Culture through the life cycle in orang-utans

The cultural transmission processes associated with acquiring food-related expertise should vary with development because the characteristics that influence acquisition change with age. As new facets of food problems and new capabilities arise, new experts become available or inaccessible to learners. This view of culture and development in great apes jibes well with lifespan models of human development that emphasize the complex and changing nature of the resources, adaptive contexts and needs involved in everyday adaptation (Baltes, Staudinger and Lindenberger, 1999).

To explore this life history perspective on great-ape culture more closely, I will focus on orang-utans, the species I study, because life history parameters vary between species within adaptive arrays. Orang-utans seem unlikely candidates for culture, having been typecast as solitary. They show a distinct sociality, however, albeit a dispersed and muted one (van Schaik and van Hooff, 1996). They pursue long-term relationships beyond the mother–infant unit and may be members of loosely defined communities (van Schaik and van Hooff, 1996). They commonly have few companions but may associate with them for weeks on end. While adults tend to solitude, immatures are actively gregarious (Galdikas, 1995). Paradoxically, orang-utans may be excellent subjects for the study of cultural transmission *because* their sociality is so spare. Their limited social contacts may show social transmission routes more clearly than large interacting groups.

Life history parameters likely to affect individual orang-utans' food-related expertise developmentally are sketched in table 2.1. Figure 2.1 shows

Table 2.1 *Changes in orang-utan food problems and problem-solving capacities*

Stage (age)[7]	Individual capacities		Food problem changes	
	cognitive	physical	age-related	sex-related
Infant 0–4/5	first order (sensorimotor)[8]	maternal dependent weak light (2–15 kg)[7] immature dentition, poor motor control[6]	nursing semi-ready foods scrounged remains simple foods	
Juvenile 4/5–7/8	second order (lower)[8]	maternal help[3] weak[2] light (15–20 kg)[2,7] functional dentition good motor control[6]	weaning foods[1] adult foods[2] low volume[2]	**M** disperse early[3]
Adolescent 7/8–10/15	second order (higher)[8]	strong[10] heavy (20–30 kg)[7,10] **F** early sterility[9] **M** mate guarding[4,7]	adult competition dispersal high volume arboreality	**F** range small, disperse near[11] **M** range large, disperse far[11]
Subadult 9/11–??		**M** stronger heavier (30–50 kg)[7] mate searching[11]		**M** growth diet[5] highly active[5]
Adult 11/20–40+	scaffold[8]	**F** caregiving heavier (30–50 kg)[7] **M** strongest heaviest (50–90 kg)[7] mate competition[11]	reproduction higher volume changed quality arboreality competition association[11]	**F** feed offspring rich diet[5] **M** great mass[11] poorer diet[5] range largest[5] poor mobility[5]

Notes:

1. Life stages are: *Infant* – pre-weaned immature too young to survive independently (Pereira, 1993). *Juvenile* – pre-pubertal immature who can survive losing adult caregivers (Pereira, 1993). *Adolescent* – post-pubertal individual not yet fertile (Pereira and Altmann, 1985). *Subadult* (male only) – post-adolescent lacking adult secondary sexual characteristics (SSCs) but otherwise reproductively mature (van Schaik and van Hooff, 1996). *Adult* – reproductively mature, females at first birth and males as of SSCs and adult reproductive roles.
2. Numbers refer to sources: 1 Altmann (1980); 2 Janson and van Schaik (1993); 3 Horr (1977); 4 Galdikas (1995); 5 Galdikas and Teleki (1981), Rijksen (1978), Rodman (1979), Utami (2000); 6 Joffe (1997); 7 Rijksen (1978); 8 Parker and McKinney (1999); 9 Galdikas (1995), Watts (1985); 10 Bogin (1999); 11 van Schaik and van Hooff (1996).

corresponding social tolerance patterns. Overall, this material indicates that as individual cognitive abilities change, physical capacities, ecological demands, and opportunities for social learning also shift, in tandem and in pace with global life stages. This has several implications for cultural transmission in orang-utans, and probably other great apes.

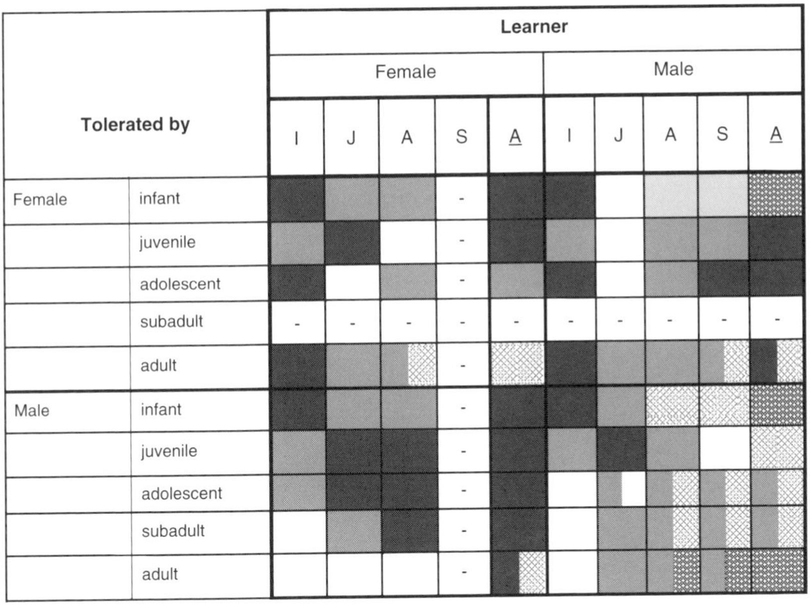

		Learner									
		Female					Male				
Tolerated by		I	J	A	S	A	I	J	A	S	A
Female	infant				-						
	juvenile				-						
	adolescent				-						
	subadult	-	-	-	-	-	-	-	-	-	-
	adult				-						
Male	infant				-						
	juvenile				-						
	adolescent				-						
	subadult				-						
	adult				-						

Figure 2.1 Social tolerance across the lifespan in orang-utans, by age-sex class: predicted tolerance level by group members (rows) for learners (columns).

Notes:
1. Stage-related levels of dyadic social tolerance were established from Galdikas (1995), Mitani (1985), Rijksen (1978), Rodman (1973), van Schaik and van Hooff (1996), Watts and Pusey (1993) and Utami (2000). In dyads for which no information was found, tolerance levels are inferred by interpolating between the tolerance levels for learners in adjacent age/sex-classes.
2. Tolerance levels are approximated in the five grades shown below. Cells shown split, with two tolerance levels, represent ambivalent responses.

Key:

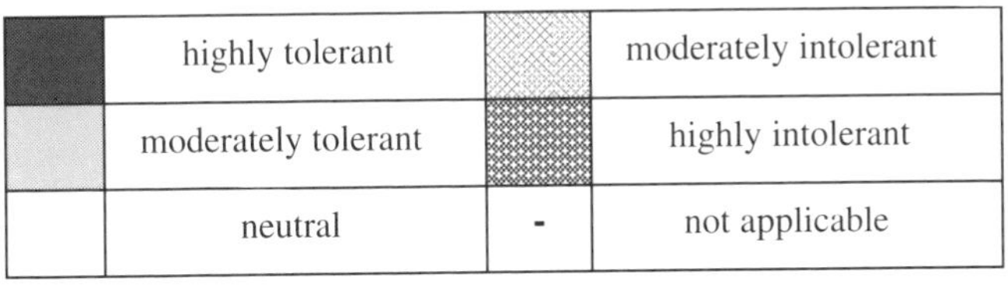

	highly tolerant		moderately intolerant
	moderately tolerant		highly intolerant
	neutral	-	not applicable

First, stage-related tolerance patterns constrain which transmission routes are open to each age/sex class within a community, although other factors may have equal if not greater effects (notably interindividual relationships based on kinship, dominance, mating or affiliation, e.g. Russon and Galdikas, 1995;

Rijksen, 1978; van Schaik and van Hooff, 1996). Adolescent female orang-utans as a class tend to high mutual tolerance, for instance, but are none the less unlikely to share expertise if they are mutual strangers.

Second, stage-related tolerance patterns suggest the types of information likely to be transferred. Infants and young juveniles likely learn mostly from their mothers but they have limited physical and cognitive abilities, so they probably absorb only the simple expertise relevant to these capabilities. They likely focus on identifying foods within their mothers' home range and basic food manipulations, for instance, and are unlikely to acquire expertise from adult males – not only because this association is improbable but also because adult male expertise is likely irrelevant to them and beyond their grasp.

Third, juveniles and adolescents stand out as important in culturally transmitting complex food expertise. Their cognitive and physical capabilities have developed to more powerful levels so they can comprehend and attempt more difficult expertise. They extend their social interests beyond the maternal unit, first as juveniles and mostly to peers, as maternal tolerance wanes (Galdikas, 1995). Adolescents leave their natal range to establish independent home ranges, become highly social and begin associating regularly beyond their natal unit; they sometimes associate with one another for days or weeks, or with adults briefly (Galdikas, 1995; Rijksen, 1978). Learning needs probably intensify for adolescents because their range shift introduces novel foraging problems and physical maturation alters their dietary needs. Conveniently, adolescents' increased sociability enhances opportunities for peer social learning. The importance of these two developmental periods in cultural transmission is further supported by evidence that in imitating, orang-utan learners prefer models performing just beyond their own competence levels (Russon and Galdikas, 1995). At advanced cognitive levels, the cultural system in orang-utans and probably other great apes may be more closely tuned to peer than adult experts, or to horizontal than vertical or oblique transmission.

This makes it likely that the appropriate question about cultural transmission of food processing expertise is not *whether* one route or another predominates – vertical, horizontal, or oblique – but *when* each is prominent. As in humans, the relevance and difficulty of the various components of complex expertise along with changing contexts likely constrain when each is acquired, and so which transmission routes influence learning. Over the lifespan, several routes likely provide input.

Evidence on orang-utan culture

The best evidence from the wild that orang-utans learn socially and use social learning to produce a collective culture concerns tool use at Suaq Balimbing, Sumatra (Fox et al., 1999). Tool use in Suaq orang-utans is habitual and community wide (Fox et al., 1999; van Schaik et al., 1999), including using tools to extract the seeds of *Neesia* sp. fruit from their hard, spiny shells. Suaq is one of two isolated orang-utan communities that consume *Neesia* seeds as a major component of their diet, seasonally. The second community is at Gunung Palung, Western Borneo, but Gunung Palung orang-utans do not use tools to obtain *Neesia* seeds. Circumstances point to cultural transmission as the reason for community-wide tool use in obtaining *Neesia* seeds at Suaq (van Schaik and Knott, 1999; van Schaik et al., 1999). The evidence and the gist of the reasoning are as follows. This tool use is clearly learned. Differential learning capacities or ecological conditions at the community level are *not* plausible accounts for the differential acquisition of this expertise; this tool use is within the capacity of normal orang-utans, opportunities for direct experience with the task and appropriate tool materials are ample at both sites, and the distribution of this expertise at Suaq is bounded by a river, not a change in habitat quality. Despite favourable learning conditions, wild orang-utans almost never invent *Neesia* tool use individually. The only other basis for differential acquisition is cultural, that novices must be introduced to this tool use socially. Opportunities for social transmission are vanishingly rare in non-tool-using communities, given low rates of invention and of social contact. They are exceptionally high in the Suaq community where many orang-utans are tool users, travel and forage in parties and often share food.

Neesia tool-using patterns are consistent with the suggestion that social tolerance affects social transmission. At Gunung Palung, adult males are the main *Neesia* consumers so even if they invented tool use, chances of dissemination are slim because of the intolerance that surrounds them. At Suaq, all age-sex classes eat *Neesia* and use tools to extract ripe *Neesia* seeds. Suaq favours community-level social transmission of tool use not only because there are more tool users but also because tool users' age and sex classes offer broader tolerance. Suaq evidence also indicates that social transmission is affected by developmental changes in social tolerance. During tool sessions at tree holes to obtain invertebrates involving mother–infant dyads and adult female–subadult male consort pairs, infants and non-tool-using consorts closely observed their tool-using partner and manipulated the tool user's tree hole and/or tool (Fox et al., 1999). Both circumstances involved developmentally scheduled intimate dyads.

The mosaic, constructive process involved in acquiring cognitively complex expertise, where social input is one of many contributors, is also evident in Suaq findings on *Neesia*. Fox and colleagues (1999) describe some of a young female's tool use acquisition. At 3–4 years old, Andai often observed her mother, Ani, use tools to probe for invertebrates in tree holes. At 5–6 years, weaned, Andai made her own tools and probed Ani's tree holes after Ani abandoned them, then subsequently initiated a tool session at her own tree hole independently. By 7–8 years, Andai was a frequent and competent tool user.

Additional evidence of a mosaic constructive process involving collective social input derives from my studies of foraging expertise in ex-captive orang-utans reintroduced to free life in Sungai Wain Forest, East Indonesian Borneo (for methodological details, see Russon, 1998, 1999b). Two cases of acquiring complex food-processing expertise are described, for two juveniles initially naive to a difficult food. Observations span five years so they offer a developmental view of part of the acquisition process.

Hearts of palm

Sungai Wain orang-utans regularly eat heart matter (apical meristem) of a local tree palm, *Borassodendron borneensis*, locally called 'bandang'. One strategy underlies all their techniques for obtaining bandang heart, pulling the newest leaf as it emerges at the palm's growing tip then biting heart matter from the leaf's base. This problem changes with palm growth, however. In immature bandang, the heart is in the centre of a small, slender rosette on the forest floor. In mature bandang, it is atop a 10–15 metre trunk, embedded in a massive crown, and encircled by some fifty leaves with razor-edge petioles (the petiole is the stalk attaching the leaf blade to the stem). New leaves also vary in size and desirability. They grow from slender grass-like shoots in rosettes to stout spears in mature trees. Only those grown long enough to grasp and short enough to lack a petiole are chosen. Bandang heart then poses a set of multifaceted problems, naturally graded in difficulty. These orang-utans adjust for this variation by employing two (sub)strategies. The basic strategy, for shoots in small rosettes, is to grab the whole new shoot and pull it out all at once. The mature strategy, for spears in large rosettes or trees, is to subdivide the spear into sections of a few laminae each and pull out sections one by one.

Paul's acquisition of bandang heart expertise illustrates the problem variation, the repeated re-solving and modifying entailed in acquiring effective techniques and probable social input from several members of his community. I began observations in 1995, when Paul was about 5 years old and about six months after his release in Sungai Wain Forest at site K3. Paul was one of three juveniles ranging around K3; others were Enggong and Bento, males about 5 and 6 years old, respectively. In my first month's observations, all three behaved as if naive to bandang heart: they neither ate it nor tried to obtain it, although it was readily available and they ate other items from bandang. It took Paul two years and at least five steps to construct the mature strategy for obtaining bandang heart. One step appeared to involve independent problem solving and other steps implied social learning afforded by stage-related social tolerance.

I first observed Paul eat bandang heart in my second month of observation, during a four-day visit to the K3 area by Sariyem, a 5-year-old female. Sariyem obtained and ate several bandang hearts during her visit. Paul, Enggong and

Bento immediately *scrounged* her discarded leftovers and ate them. They probably learned of this food socially: All three began eating it abruptly after watching Sariyem eat it, never having been seen eating it beforehand, and all first ate her leftovers instead of obtaining the food independently. Social tolerance likely afforded this learning. Two orang-utans proficient in obtaining bandang heart periodically visited K3, Sariyem and an adolescent male named Charlie. The three K3 males tolerated Sariyem but not Charlie (they fled at his sight) so Sariyem's but not Charlie's visits offered social learning opportunities.

Paul alone of the three males tried to obtain bandang heart independently during Sariyem's visit, using the *basic strategy, incorrectly.* He pulled a small shoot, correctly, but ate its tip instead of its base (probably reverting to a food he already knew, the leaf blade). Paul's success over Enggong and Bento probably owed to observing Sariyem closely: she tolerated only Paul in proximity while she obtained bandang hearts. Sariyem used both basic and mature strategies, however, so Paul's partial success and his errors probably owed to his limited understanding, perhaps related to his young age.

Six months later, in 1996, Paul had mastered the *basic strategy* and *enhanced* it with two idiosyncratic tactics, a two-step pull and bracing. In his two-step pull he first pulled the spear down through the side of the crown, which reoriented it sideways and loosened it from the crown, then pulled it outwards, to extract it. He braced by holding a nearby tree, which amplified his pulling force. He successfully accessed mid-sized rosettes using his enhanced basic strategy but often failed on large rosettes and did not even try tall bandang. His tactics did not augment his pulling force enough to handle these larger palms. Given his size, his error was strategic – strengthening himself versus weakening the palm. Probably only adult males have the strength to pull whole large spears (Rodman, pers. comm.). Over the same period, Enggong and Bento mastered basic and mature strategies. Social intolerance plus limited forest experience may explain Paul's slower progress. All three males had similar opportunities to invent techniques: they ranged in the same area, bandang were plentiful, and based on age, Paul's cognitive capacities should have resembled Enggong's. Paul had a year's less experience in Sungai Wain than Enggong or Bento, however. He also suffered Bento's intolerance. Since 1995, Bento regularly foraged, travelled and played with Enggong but drove Paul away. Enggong tolerated Paul but when associating with Bento, Paul was excluded. This left Paul few opportunities to track Enggong's or Bento's advances. This, plus the idiosyncrasy of Paul's tactical enhancements, suggests that Paul invented them. His limited experience and his small size would have constrained them.

By mid 1997, Paul had mastered the *mature* strategy and could regularly obtain heart from tall bandang. He incorporated most tactics used by others (Russon, 1998), e.g. removing debris, making a work seat, bending the section's tip before pulling it to prevent its breaking. Social change probably contributed to his mastery. Bento grew intolerant of Enggong in 1996, probably because Bento was approaching adolescence. This allowed Paul greater access to Enggong; the two became regular companions and Paul often scrounged Enggong's leftovers. In 1996, Paul had not acquired the mature strategy for obtaining heart from large bandang, which is based on subdividing the new leaf spear into sections. Scrounging Enggong's bandang heart leftovers exposed him to spears in sections. It was after months of accompanying Enggong that Paul began to subdivide new leaf spears himself. Individual factors may also have contributed to Paul's progress. The laminae of bandang leaves are separate at the tip, even in new leaf spears, and sometimes a few laminae slipped free accidentally while Paul was pulling the whole spear. Noticing this accidental subdividing then reproducing it deliberately could generate the mature strategy. Finally, the year's development may have brought this within Paul's cognitive reach, however he was exposed to it.

Palm pith

Sungai Wain orang-utans eat pith (parenchyma) from several palm species, bandang included. Their universal strategy is to bite then tear the petiole open lengthwise, pull strips of pith away from the sheath and chew the pith for juice. Growth alters this task in bandang by changing the size, toughness and location of petioles.

I tracked Siti's acquisition of this expertise over 18 months, from her 1996 release at site K5 in Sungai Wain, as a 5-year-old. Immediately post-release Siti associated with Kiki and Ida, two like-aged females who had been her cagemates in 1994. Forest staff, who monitored newly released ex-captives daily, observed none of these three eat bandang pith until Kiki discovered it, independently, after one month in the forest. Kiki chose only tiny rosettes at ground level. Initially she chewed the entire petiole, pith plus sheath, but within 3–4 days began removing and discarding the sheath. Siti and Ida immediately scrounged from Kiki – they chewed her petiole, another petiole on the same plant, or her leftovers. Three weeks after Kiki started removing the sheath, Siti and Ida could obtain pith independently using the same technique. Within another week Siti had enhanced the technique to handle mature bandang trees. She added tactics to contend with their size and arboreal complexities and she made her first bite into mature petioles, U-shaped in cross-section, over one arm of the 'U'. She appeared to have invented these enhancements independently: Kiki took pith only from rosettes at ground level and other orang-utans in the forest made their first bite over the rounded bottom of the 'U'.

A year later, in 1997, Siti associated with three other orang-utans who ranged near K5; both Ida and Kiki had left. Siti's most frequent companion was Judi, a near-adult female about 14 years old. Siti and Judi ate bandang pith frequently in the latter half of 1997, often working the same petiole together, and they shared two idiosyncratic tactics. First, both always chose the second newest petiole for pith, never mature or newest petioles. Orang-utans ranging near K3, located in similar habitat only 4 kilometres from K5, always chose mature petioles for pith. No others near K5 ate bandang pith in the latter half of 1997. No contacts had been reported between orang-utans ranging near K5 and those ranging near other release sites in the forest, bandang are abundant, and each palm has ± 50 mature petioles to one second-newest one, so neither ecological differences nor competition can explain Siti and Judi's choice. Second, both commonly made their first bite into the petiole close to the leaf then tore the petiole open downwards, from the leaf towards the crown. All orang-utans ranging near K3 regularly made their first bite about a third of the way down from the leaf then opened the petiole in both directions. Siti used a third tactic, one not evident in Judi. She chose bandang with a liana or branch running diagonally through the crown. Her first bite into the petiole often cracked the petiole so that it flopped over – almost always, over the liana/branch (figure 2.2). The liana/branch then acted as a hanger that probably helped anchor the petiole while Siti tore it open. I did not notice this pattern until late in my observations so I lack reliable data on its occurrence. Siti used it on at least five occasions, however, so the layout, the place of biting and the hanger were likely deliberate tactics. No others were observed using these three tactics so Siti probably acquired the first two in tandem with Judi and invented the third herself.

These two cases illustrate the multifaceted nature of the problems, the lengthy process of piecing together effective strategies and tactics for solving them, and the 'system' of social input within the community (in the sense of a scheduled set of social inputs) that were involved in acquisition. They also show how developmental changes to cognition, physical capacities, problems and tolerance affect acquisition in concert.

Life history perspectives on culture in other great apes

Some of these developmental patterns may characterize social transmission in the other great apes, who share many life history parameters with orang-utans. Ontogenetic parameters discussed in the apprenticeship hypothesis, and epitomized in chimpanzees' acquisition of stone nut cracking, offer prime examples. Even early stages of acquiring stone nut-cracking expertise are cognitively and socially constrained (Inoue-Nakamura and Matsuzawa, 1997). Wild chimpanzees at Bossou begin manipulating the items used in nut cracking at about six months old, but do not master the basic operations or combine them in appropriate sequences until about $1^1/_2$ and $3^1/_2$ years old, respectively. Infants' social learning opportunities are mainly with their mothers, although with age they increasingly scrounge from and observe other individuals. Scrounging is

Figure 2.2   Siti's hanger. Siti tears open a bandang petiole so that it cracks and flops over the tree from which she is dangling. Farther up the hanger tree are dried remains of three other petioles damaged and hanging in the same way, i.e. she or another orang-utan has used the same hanger technique on this palm in the past.

tolerated in infants but much less so in juveniles; juveniles may even be chased away from nut-cracking sites.

Great ape species differ in their social systems so life history parameters that concern sociality should engender different cultural transmission patterns. Parker and Russon (1996) suggested cultural transmission differences associated with interbirth intervals, subgrouping patterns, philopatry and demography. Further differences may be linked with social tolerance patterns that are developmentally regulated.

In mountain gorillas, for example, infants' only direct social sources of feeding expertise are their mothers, whom they normally accompany when foraging, and the silverback male. Other group members are intolerant of one another's proximity during feeding and dense vegetation obscures visibility beyond a few metres (Byrne and Russon, 1998). One immigrant female in Byrne and Byrne's (1993) study group, Picasso, did *not* use a folding operation to eat stinging nettles (*Laportea alitipes*) when she arrived and had *not* acquired it after five years in the group, although folding is the key operation for minimizing stings and other group members used it. Picasso's offspring, born and raised in the group, had *not* acquired this operation even as a juvenile. All thirty-six other adults and juveniles in the group had. As with *Neesia*, the probable explanation is that novices must be introduced to this operation socially, as infants, and gorilla tolerance patterns denied Picasso's offspring the necessary social opportunities. A similar situation occurred in chimpanzees at Bossou: two adult females did *not* crack nuts with stone tools, but their infants both acquired the expertise normally (Inoue-Nakamura and Matsuzawa, 1997). Non-relatives tolerated infants' observing and even physically contacting them during stone nut cracking, providing opportunities for social learning beyond the mother. The different gorilla and chimpanzee outcomes likely owe to species differences in developmental patterns of social tolerance.

A second example involves differences between chimpanzees and orang-utans in adult male tolerance. Adult male orang-utans show extreme mutual intolerance and avoid one another; any close encounters are invariably agonistic and readily escalate to fights and injuries (van Schaik and van Hooff, 1996). Adult male chimpanzees are mutually tolerant, mutually affiliative and associate in parties (Nishida, 1979; Wrangham, 1979). Based on tolerance, the potential for cultural transmission between adult males should differ between the two species. Vocalizations used by adult males in long-distance communication, orang-utan 'long calls' and chimpanzee 'pant hoots', are consistent with this prediction. Long calls show no evidence of learned similarities between adult males; what stands out is their individuality (Galdikas, 1985). Pant hoots suggest learned similarities between adult males. Adult males mutually alter their pant hoots when chorusing with other males, to converge with one another (Mitani and Gros-Louis, 1998). Adult male pant hoots differ systematically between communities, so convergence may reach collective levels. Socially mediated vocal learning is the favoured explanation (Mitani, Hunley and Murdoch, 1999). Species differences in tolerance linked to age and sex offer a plausible explanation for these behavioural differences.

Discussion

The life history perspective suggests that great-ape culture is coordinated developmentally in line with interacting biological, psychological and social parameters. Affordances and constraints associated with all three sets of parameters alter learners' needs, capabilities and social positions in predictable fashion throughout their lives. Together, these parameters channel what facets of the community's expertise are available to any given learner at any given time. If cultural transmission in great apes is this closely tied to life history parameters, then it operates not as a separate module patched on to an individual learning system nor as a distinct process that intertwines with individual processes in indeterminate fashion. Rather, it appears to be an emergent process in which physical, cognitive and social factors interweave in a developmentally organized fashion, by design. This jibes with views of human culture and development, that see development as a function of co-evolving biological and cultural systems and as an open system with an architecture that is structured, incompletely, by biological, ecological and cultural parameters (e.g. Baltes et al., 1999; Durham, 1991).

One might postulate that human life histories differ so substantially from those of other great apes and human culture is so much more powerful and flexible that biologically and psychologically regulated developmental constraints no longer apply. That this is *not* the case is suggested by studies of at least one human society, Aka pygmies, who are transitional hunter-gatherers (Hewlett and Cavalli-Sforza, 1986). Of common Aka skills, 70 per cent were mastered by late juvenility (10 years old) and 80 per cent by late adolescence (15 years old). Advances continued into adulthood, especially when related to adult sexual division of labour (notably, this echoes findings from lifespan developmental psychology, that biological maturity brings decreases to rates of acquisition but not a halt, e.g. Baltes et al., 1999). The vast majority of skills were transmitted vertically, by same-sex parents who contributed differentially according to their sex-based division of labour. Other transmission routes were also used for particular skills, including oblique routes such as apprenticeship with unrelated masters or group assemblies when experts beyond immediate family were accessible (e.g. dancing), horizontal routes (e.g. skills recently introduced), or multiple routes (e.g. skills with few experts). Similar patterns emerged in fourteen ethnographic studies on transmitting traditional craft skills in a variety of societies; craft skills were chosen as most similar to great apes' complex feeding skills (Shennan and Steele, 1999). Across these societies, transmission routes also vary with the particular skills and the social structures involved.

Developmental approaches promise a rich view of the processes involved in great ape and human cultural transmission, especially how social and individual processes interact. Particularly when development itself is viewed in life history perspective, such approaches offer perspectives on how biological, social and psychological facets of life interact variably across the life cycle.

REFERENCES

Altmann, J. (1980). *Baboon mothers and infants*. Cambridge, MA: Harvard University Press.

Baltes, P. P., Staudinger, U. M. and Lindenberger, U. (1999). Lifespan psychology: theory and application to intellectual functioning. *Annual Review of Psychology*, 50, 471–507.

Boesch, C. (1991). Teaching among wild chimpanzees. *Animal Behavior*, 41, 530–3.

(1993). Aspects of transmission of tool use in wild chimpanzees. In K. R. Gibson and T. Ingold (eds.), *Tools, language and cognition in human evolution*. Cambridge: Cambridge University Press, pp. 171–183.

(1996). Three approaches for assessing chimpanzee culture. In A. E. Russon, K. A. Bard and S. T. Parker (eds.), *Reaching into thought: the minds of the great apes*. Cambridge: Cambridge University Press, pp. 404–29.

Boesch, C. and Tomasello, M. (1998). Chimpanzee and human cultures. *Current Anthropology*, 39(5), 591–614.

Bogin, B. (1999). Evolutionary perspective on human growth. *Annual Review of Anthropology*, 28, 109–53.

Box, H. O. and Gibson, K. R. (eds.) (1999). *Mammalian social learning*. Cambridge: Cambridge University Press.

Byrne, R. W. (1997). The technical intelligence hypothesis: an alternative evolutionary stimulus to intelligence? In A. Whiten and R. W. Byrne (eds.), *Machiavellian intelligence II: evaluations and extensions*. Cambridge: Cambridge University Press, pp. 289–311.

Byrne, R. W. and Byrne, J. M. E. (1991). Hand preferences in the skilled gathering tasks of mountain gorillas (*Gorilla gorilla berengei*). *Cortex*, 27, 521–46.

(1993). Complex leaf-gathering skills of mountain gorillas (*Gorilla g. beringei*): variability and standardization. *American Journal of Primatology*, 31, 241–61.

Byrne, R. W. and Russon, A. E. (1998). Learning by imitation: a hierarchical approach. *Behavioral and Brain Sciences*, 21, 667–721.

Call, J. and Tomasello, M. (1996). The effect of humans on the cognitive development of apes. In A. E. Russon, K. A. Bard and S. T. Parker (eds.), *Reaching into thought: the minds of the great apes*. Cambridge: Cambridge University Press.

Coussi-Korbel, S. and Fragaszy, D. M. (1995). On the relation between social dynamics and social learning. *Animal Behavior*, 50, 1441–53.

De Rousseau, C. J. (ed.) (1990). *Primate life history and evolution*, Monographs in Primatology, 14, New York: Wiley.

Donald, M. (1991). *Origins of the modern mind: three stages in the evolution of culture and cognition.* Cambridge, MA: Harvard University Press.

Durham, W. H. (1991). *Coevolution: genes, culture and human diversity.* Stanford, CA: Stanford University Press.

Fischer, K. W., Bullock, D. H., Rotenberg, E. J. and Raya, P. (1993). The dynamics of competence: how context contributes directly to skill. In R. Wozniak and K. W. Fischer (eds.), *Development in context.* Hillsdale, NJ: Erlbaum, pp. 93–117.

Fleagle, J. G. (1999). *Primate adaptation and evolution,* 2nd edn. San Diego: Academic Press.

Fobes, J. L. and King, J. E. (1982). *Primate behavior.* New York: Academic Press.

Fox, E. A., Sitompul, A. F. and van Schaik, C. P. (1999). Intelligent tool use in wild Sumatran orang-utans. In S. T. Parker, R. W. Mitchell and H. L. Miles (eds.), *The mentalities of gorillas and orang-utans: comparative perspectives.* Cambridge: Cambridge University Press, pp. 99–116.

Fox, R. (1972). The cultural animal. In J. Eisenberg and W. S. Dillon (eds.), *Man and beast.* Washington, DC: Smithsonian Press, pp. 15–28.

Freeland, W. J. and Janzen, D. H. (1974). Strategies in herbivory by mammals: the role of plant secondary compounds. *American Naturalist,* 108, 269–89.

Galdikas, B. M. F. (1985). Adult male sociality and reproductive tactics among orang-utans at Tanjung Puting. *Folia Primatologica,* 45, 9–24.

(1995). Social and reproductive behavior of wild adolescent female orang-utans. In R. D. Nadler, B. F. M. Galdikas, L. K. Sheeran and N. Rosen (eds.), *The neglected ape.* New York: Plenum Press, pp. 163–82.

Galdikas, B. M. F. and Teleki, G. (1981). Variations in subsistence activities of male and female pongids: new perspectives on the origins of hominid labor division. *Current Anthropology,* 22, 241–56.

Galdikas, B. M. F. and Wood, J. W. (1990). Birth spacing in humans and apes. *Primates,* 83, 185–91.

Groves, C. P. (1989). *A theory of human and primate evolution.* Oxford: Oxford University Press.

Hewlett, B. S. and Cavalli-Sforza, L. L. (1986). Cultural transmission among Aka pygmies. *American Anthropologist,* 88, 922–34.

Horr, D. A. (1977). Orang-utan maturation: growing up in a female world. In S. Chevalier-Skolnikoff and F. E. Poirier (eds.), *Primate bio-social development: biological, social, and ecological determinants.* New York: Garland, pp. 289–321.

Humphrey, N. K. (1976). The social function of intellect. In P. P. G. Bateson and R. A. Hinde (eds.), *Growing points in ethology.* Cambridge: Cambridge University Press, pp. 303–17.

Inoue-Nakamura, N. and Matsuzawa, T. (1997). Development of stone tool use by wild chimpanzees (*Pan troglodytes*). *Journal of Comparative Psychology,* 111, 159–73.

Janson, C. H. and van Schaik, C. P. (1993). Ecological risk aversion in juvenile primates: slow and steady wins the race. In M. E. Pereira and L. A. Fairbanks (eds.), *Juvenile primates: life history, development, and behavior.* New York: Oxford University Press, pp. 57–76.

Joffe, T. H. (1997). Social pressures have selected for an extended juvenile period in primates. *Journal of Human Evolution,* 32, 593–605.

Jolly, A. (1966). Lemur social behavior and primate intelligence. *Science,* 153, 501–6.

Jones, D. L. (1995). *Palms throughout the world.* Washington, DC: Smithsonian Institute Press.

King, B. J. (1994). *The information continuum*. Santa Fe, NM: School of American Research.

Kitahara-Frisch, J., Norikoshi, K. and Hara, K. (1987). Use of a bone fragment as a step towards secondary tool use in captive chimpanzee. *Primate Report*, 18, 33–7.

Kummer, H. (1971). *Primate societies: group techniques of ecological adaptation.* Chicago: Aldine.

Matsuzawa, T. (1994). Field experiments on use of tools by chimpanzees in the wild. In R. Wrangham, W. McGrew, F. de Waal and P. Heltne (eds.), *Chimpanzee cultures.* Cambridge: Cambridge University Press, pp. 351–70.

(1996). Chimpanzee intelligence in nature and in captivity: isomorphism of symbol use and tool use. In W. C. McGrew, L. F. Marchant and T. Nishida (eds.), *Great ape societies.* Cambridge: Cambridge University Press, pp. 196–209.

McGrew, W. C. (1992). *Chimpanzee material culture: implications for human evolution.* Cambridge: Cambridge University Press.

(1998). Culture in nonhuman primates? *Annual Review of Anthropology*, 27, 301–28.

McKinney, M. and McNamara, K. (1991). *Heterochrony: the evolution of ontogeny.* New York: Plenum.

Miles, H. L. (1978). Conversations with apes: the use of sign language with two chimpanzees. Unpublished Ph.D. dissertation, Yale University.

(1999). Symbolic communication with and by great apes. In S. T. Parker, R. W. Mitchell and H. L. Miles (eds.), *The mentalities of gorillas and orang-utans.* Cambridge: Cambridge University Press, pp. 197–210.

Miles, H. L., Mitchell, R. W. and Harper, S. (1996). Simon says: the development of imitation in an enculturated orang-utan. In A. E. Russon, K. A. Bard and S. T. Parker (eds.), *Reaching into thought: the minds of the great apes.* Cambridge: Cambridge University Press, pp. 278–99.

Milton, K. (1984). The role of food processing factors in primate food choice. In P. S. Rodman and J. G. H. Cant (eds.), *Adaptations for foraging in nonhuman primates: contributions to an organismal biology of prosimians, monkeys and apes.* New York: Columbia University Press, pp. 249–79.

Mitani, J. C. (1985). Mating behavior of male orangutans in the Kutai Game Reserve, Indonesia. *Animal Behavior*, 33, 391–402.

Mitani, J. C. and Gros-Louis, J. (1998). Chorusing and call convergence in chimpanzees: test of three hypotheses. *Behavior*, 135, 1041–64.

Mitani, J. C., Hunley, K. L. and Murdoch, M. E. (1999). Geographic variation in the calls of wild chimpanzees: a reassessment. *American Journal of Physical Anthropology*, 47, 133–51.

Myowa-Yamakoshi, M. and Matsuzawa, T. (1999). Factors influencing imitation of manipulatory actions in chimpanzees (*Pan troglodytes*). *Journal of Comparative Psychology*, 113(2), 128–36.

Nishida, T. (1979). The social structure of chimpanzees of the Mahale Mountains. In D. A. Hamburg and E. R. McCown (eds.), *The great apes.* Menlo Park, CA: Benjamin-Cummings, pp. 73–121.

(1987). Local traditions and cultural transmission. In B. B. Smuts, D. L. Cheney, R. M. Seyfarth, R. W. Wrangham and T. T. Struhsaker (eds.), *Primate societies.* Chicago: University of Chicago Press, pp. 462–74.

Parker, S. T. (1996). Apprenticeship in tool-mediated extractive foraging: the origins of imitation, teaching and self-awareness in great apes. In A. E. Russon, K. A. Bard and

S. T. Parker (eds.), *Reaching into thought: the minds of the great apes*. Cambridge: Cambridge University Press, pp. 348–70.

Parker, S. T. and Gibson, K. R. (1977). Object manipulation, tool use and sensorimotor intelligence as feeding adaptations in cebus monkeys and great apes. *Journal of Human Evolution*, 6, 623–41.

(1979). A model of the evolution of language and intelligence in early hominids. *Behavioral and Brain Sciences*, 2, 367–407.

Parker, S. T. and Gibson, K. R. (eds.) (1990). *'Language' and intelligence in monkeys and apes: comparative developmental perspectives*. New York: Cambridge University Press.

Parker, S. T. and McKinney, M. L. (1999). *Origins of intelligence: the evolution of cognitive development in monkeys, apes, and humans*. Baltimore: Johns Hopkins University Press.

Parker, S. T. and Poti', P. (1990). The role of innate motor patterns in ontogenetic and experiential development of intelligent use of sticks in cebus monkeys. In S. T. Parker and K. R. Gibson (eds.), *'Language' and intelligence in monkeys and apes*. New York: Cambridge University Press, pp. 219–45.

Parker, S. T. and Russon, A. E. (1996). On the wild side of culture and cognition in the great apes. In A. E. Russon, K. A. Bard and S. T. Parker (eds.), *Reaching into thought: the minds of the great apes*. Cambridge: Cambridge University Press, pp. 430–50.

Pereira, M. E. (1993). Juvenility in animals. In M. E. Pereira and L. A. Fairbanks (eds.), *Juvenile primates: life history, development, and behavior*. New York: Oxford University Press, pp. 7–27.

Pereira, M. E. and Altmann, J. (1985). Development of social behavior in free-living nonhuman primates. In E. S. Watts (ed.), *Nonhuman primate models for human growth and development*. New York: Liss, pp. 217–309.

Pilbeam, D. (1996). Genetic and morphological records of the Hominoidea and hominid origins: a synthesis. *Molecular Phylogenetics and Evolution*, 5(1), 155–68.

Rijksen, H. D. (1978). *A field study on Sumatran orang-utans (Pongo pygmaeus Abelii lesson 1827): ecology, behavior, and conservation*. Wageningen: H. Veenman and Zonen BV.

Rodman, P. S. (1973). Population composition and adaptive organization among orang-utans of the Kutai Reserve. In J. H. Crook and R. P. Michael (eds.), *Comparative ecology and behavior of primates*. London: Academic Press, pp. 171–209.

(1979). Individual activity patterns and the solitary nature of orang-utans. In D. A. Hamburg and E. R. McCown (eds.), *The great apes*. Menlo Park, CA: Benjamin-Cummings, pp. 235–55.

Rogoff, B. (1992). *Apprenticeship in thinking*. New York: Oxford University Press.

Russon, A. E. (1996). Report on Release Group VI. Report to the Wanariset Orang-utan Reintroduction Project, Wanariset-Samboja, E. Kalimantan, Indonesia.

(1997). Exploiting the expertise of others. In A. Whiten and R. W. Byrne (eds.), *Machiavellian intelligence II: evaluations and extensions*. Cambridge: Cambridge University Press, pp. 174–206.

(1998). The nature and evolution of orang-utan intelligence. *Primates*, 9, 485–503.

(1999a). Orang-utans' imitation of tool use: a cognitive analysis. In S. T. Parker, R. W. Mitchell and H. L. Miles (eds.), *Mentalities of gorillas and orang-utans*. Cambridge: Cambridge University Press, pp. 117–46.

(1999b). Naturalistic approaches to orang-utan intelligence and the question of enculturation. *International Journal of Comparative Psychology*, 12(4), 181–02.

Russon, A. E. and Galdikas, B. M. F. (1995). Constraints on great apes' imitation: model and action selectivity in rehabilitant orang-utan imitation (*Pongo pygmaeus*). *Journal of Comparative Psychology*, 109(1), 5–17.

Shennan, S. J. and Steele, J. (1999). Cultural learning in hominids: a behavioral ecological approach. In H. O. Box and K. R. Gibson (eds.), *Mammalian social learning: comparative and ecological perspectives*. Cambridge: Cambridge University Press, pp. 367–88.

Smuts, B. B., Cheney, D. L., Seyfarth, R. M., Wrangham, R. W. and Struhsaker, T. T. (eds.) (1987). *Primate societies*. Chicago: University of Chicago Press.

Tomasello, M. and Call, J. (1997). *Primate cognition*. New York: Oxford University Press.

Tomasello, M., Savage-Rumbaugh, E. S. and Kruger, A. (1993). Imitative learning of actions on objects by children, chimpanzees, and enculturated chimpanzees. *Child Development*, 64, 1688–705.

Toth, N., Schick, K. D., Savage-Rumbaugh, E. S., Sevcik, R. A. and Rumbaugh, D. M. (1993). Pan the tool maker: investigations into the stone tool-making and tool-using capabilities of a bonobo (*Pan paniscus*). *Journal of Archaeological Science*, 20, 81–91.

Utami, S. S. (2000). *Bimaturism in orang-utan males: reproductive and ecological strategies*. Utrecht: Central Reproductive FSB Universiteit Utrecht.

van Schaik, C. P., Deaner, R. O. and Merrill, M. Y. (1999). The conditions for tool use in primates: implications for the evolution of material culture. *Journal of Human Evolution*, 36, 719–41.

van Schaik, C. P., Fox, E. A. and Sitompul, A. F. (1996). Manufacture and use of tools in wild Sumatran orang-utans. *Naturwissenschaften*, 83, 186–8.

van Schaik, C. P. and Knott, C. (1999). Orang-utan cultures? *American Association of Physical Anthropology*, abstracts, p. 223.

van Schaik, C. P. and van Hooff, J. A. R. A. M. (1996). Toward an understanding of the orang-utan's social system. In W. C. McGrew, L. F. Marchant and T. Nishida (eds.), *Great ape societies*. Cambridge: Cambridge University Press, pp. 3–15.

Vygotsky, L. (1962). *Thought and language*, Cambridge, MA: MIT Press.

Waterman, P. G. (1984). Food acquisition and processing as a function of plant chemistry. In D. J. Chivers, B. A. Wood and A. Bilsborough (eds.), *Food acquisition and processing in primates*. New York: Plenum, pp. 177–211.

Watts, D. P. and Pusey, A. E. (1993). Behavior of juvenile and adolescent great apes. In M. E. Pereira and L. A. Fairbanks (eds.), *Juvenile primates: life history, development, and behavior*. New York: Oxford University Press, pp. 148–71.

Watts, E. (1985). Adolescent growth and development in monkeys, apes, and humans. In E. Watts (ed.), *Nonhuman primate models for human growth and development*. New York: Alan R. Liss, pp. 41–65.

Whiten, A. (2000). Primate culture and social learning. *Cognitive Science*, 24(3), 477–508.

Whiten, A., Goodall, J., McGrew, W. C., Nishida, T., Reynolds, V., Sugiyama, Y., Tutin, C. E. G., Wrangham, R. W. and Boesch, C. (1999). Culture in chimpanzees. *Nature*, 399, 682–5.

Wrangham, R. (1979). On the evolution of ape social systems. *Social Science Information*, 18, 334–68.

Wright, R. V. S. (1972). Imitative learning of a flaked tool technology – the case of an orang-utan. *Mankind*, 8, 296–306.

Yamakoshi, G. (1998). Dietary responses to fruit scarcity of wild chimpanzees at Bossou, Guinea: possible implications for ecological importance of tool use. *American Journal of Physical Anthropology*, 106, 283–95.

3   The mutual definition of culture and biology in development

Patricia M. Greenfield

The classical debate concerning nature and nurture implies a single relationship between biology and environment, even when the issue is resolved as an interaction between both forces. However, contrary to this perspective, my thesis is that there are not one but many relations between cultural environment and biological nature in human development. These relations constitute ways in which culture and biology mutually define and influence each other in development. I am going to illustrate this thesis with six relationships, taken one at a time. These relationships are tentative, meant to stimulate further research and thinking.

The relationships are not alternative perspectives, but complementary principles. By illustrating many principles with examples from the same community, I can present a clear case for complementarity. My research site is the Zinacantec Maya hamlet of Nabenchauk in Chiapas, Mexico. Examples from there and elsewhere show that all six principles are required to understand the roles of culture and biology in the developing human being. They will also illustrate the value of the theoretical principles for understanding real-world phenomena.

While complementarity is highlighted by utilizing material from a single community, at the same time generality is compromised. In addition, the examples are by-products of research designed for other purposes. The principles require not only further investigation in other settings, but also research that is designed to test these particular relationships. In this way, the principles can transcend the research of a few investigators. Finally, it is important to note that the examples presented involve proximal processes and explanations. However, I have also included more speculative interpretations concerning distal processes of adaptation and mutual constituted processes of cultural and biological evolution.

Culture reinforces biology

Zinacantec infants are born with long visual attention spans and restrained motor behaviour, relative to Euro-American newborns in the United States (Brazelton, Robey and Collier, 1969). Beginning with attention, Zinacantec newborns were notable for being more alert than Caucasian babies in the United States. They attentively observed their surroundings for much longer periods than Caucasian babies in the United States, laying the foundation for later observational learning (Brazelton et al., 1969). They did not cry intensely or flail about, demanding that someone react to them.

Given the Asian roots of indigenous groups throughout the Americas, there would be a closer genetic link of Maya peoples with Asian groups such as the Chinese than with Euro-Americans. Indeed, Zinacantec newborns shared this behavioural quality with genetically related but environmentally unrelated groups (Freedman, 1979; Freedman and Freedman, 1969). For example, pre-natal nutrition and the general pregnancy experience of Chinese-American and Euro-American mothers (both groups born in the United States) had to be much more similar to each other than to that of pregnant Zinacantec mothers, who (a) relied on a staple diet of corn and beans, supplemented by small quantities of vegetables and fruit, with extra meat, eggs and beans during pregnancy (Anschuetz, 1966) and (b) continued their subsistence work during pregnancy. Yet the Chinese-American newborns differed in their attentional qualities from the Euro-American newborns, with whom they shared important features of the prenatal environment; instead they resembled the Zinacantec newborns, with whom they shared an Asian ancestry.

Without forgetting the crucial role of the environment in epigenesis, we are led to the conclusion that there is a genetic component to this newborn behaviour of attentiveness. This conclusion is buttressed by the results of behaviour genetics studies that, in finding greater correlations for attention in monozygotic than in dizygotic infant twin pairs, conclude that attention has a significant component of heritability (Freedman, 1965; Freedman and Keller, 1963; Goldsmith and Gottesman, 1981).

Newborn visual attention becomes intense observation and imitation as infancy progresses. Indeed, in the infant tests carried out by Brazelton, Robey and Collier (1969), infants showed interest in imitating object manipulations, but little interest in initiating object play. Later, when we studied how Zinacantec girls learn how to weave, we found that learners showed a remarkable ability to observe an adult teacher attentively for long periods of time (Greenfield, Brazelton and Childs, 1989). The culturally defined way in which weaving apprenticeship progressed provided practice and further reinforcement for the newborn attention span.

Zinacantec newborns also showed a lower level of physical activity, which was in turn reinforced by the cultural environment. Their distinctive level of motor activity seemed to be at least partly a function of genetic factors. This conclusion stems from prior empirical evidence concerning the behaviour of newborns from other ethnic groups. Chinese-American, Navajo and Japanese (Goto Island) babies differed from Euro-American babies in many of the same ways that Zinacantec babies did – for example in their relatively low rate of motor activity (Brazelton et al., 1969; Brazelton, personal communication, 1988; Freedman, 1979; Freedman and Freedman, 1969). Although the Chinese-American sample studied by the Freedmans *shared* critical elements affecting the prenatal environment with the Euro-American sample (e.g. prenatal care, middle-class means to obtain good nutrition), the behaviour of the newborns *differed* in the two groups. On the other hand, Zinacantecs, Navajos, Chinese-Americans, and Goto Islanders, sharing almost nothing relevant to the prenatal environment (e.g. nutrition, prenatal care) did share a common pattern of newborn behaviour. Given the absence of a distinctive aspect of prenatal environment in common, the distinctive shared behaviour must, logically have some genetic basis. Indeed, these groups may have common genetic roots. It is now thought that Navajos have been part of a migration from Asia (Freedman, 1979); Maya Indians also have Asian roots. This conclusion concerning a genetic basis for the shared neonatal motor style is in accord with data from well-controlled behaviour genetics studies in the United States that show infant activity level to have a significant heritable component (Goldsmith and Campos, 1982; Goldsmith and Gottesman, 1981).

I am not arguing against the important role of prenatal environment in development. For example, Zinacantec women themselves used controlled motor movements; thus, pregnant mothers provided their unborn babies with a restrained style of prenatal movement environment that itself was culturally mandated (Haviland, 1978); this environment, according to my first principle, should have *reinforced* an epigenetic pathway toward quiet motor patterns.

Outside the womb, the newborn's relatively low motor activity was immediately reinforced by the Zinacantec culture. The cultural practice of swaddling, itself an adaptive protection against the cold of unheated Zinacantec houses in highland Chiapas, restricted the infants' movements (Brazelton et al., 1969; Greenfield, 1972). Nursing at the slightest sign of movement further lessened motor activity (Brazelton et al., 1969).

These cultural norms for infant care thus *reinforced* newborn motor behaviour, enhancing differences between the activity level of Zinacantec newborns and newborns in the United States. Reinforced by different infant-care practices in the two cultures, this group difference in level of physical activity increased during the first week (when a Euro-American baby at that period would have typically been unrestricted in a crib, free to flail about at will).

Lesser Zinacantec motor activity manifested itself in other ways as development proceeded. Children tested in the first year of life, when compared with United States norms, showed a slower rate in the development of motor milestones. This group difference was greater in the area of motor than mental skills (Brazelton et al., 1969). There was evidence of low motoric activity in older children who sat observing for long periods of time when learning to weave (Childs and Greenfield, 1980; Greenfield, 1984). Less use of an active motoric strategy was also noticed in adults instructing babies in a nesting cup task:

Mothers used the more physically aggressive teaching strategy of 'shoving' the baby's hand less frequently than mothers in the United States in a parallel situation (Greenfield et al., 1989; Kaye, 1977).

A low level of physical activity continued into adulthood. Restricted motion was adaptively reinforced for the Zinacantec mother, who nearly always had a baby on her back and, during her childbearing years, had to perform work under this condition (Haviland, 1978). 'Never a people given to wild gesticulation even at their most excited, Zinacanteco physical restraint is most marked in the behaviour of women' (Haviland, 1978, p. 243). Quite astonishingly, Leslie Haviland's description of female body movement is remarkably reminiscent of Brazelton, Robey and Collier's (1969) observations of Zinacantec newborns:

Feminine body movement is highly controlled and carried out in a narrow circumference. 'Women keep their upper arms tight to their bodies and rarely raise their hands or arms over their heads . . . In short, Zinacanteco women never engage in sweeping, expansive gestures, nor do they allow their limbs to stray outward from their bodies, whether in work or in fun' (Haviland, 1978, p. 243).

Culture appropriates biology

Haviland's description is not merely the way Zinacantec women *actually* moved; this is also the way they *were supposed* to move. The 'is' of biology had become the 'ought' of culture. Although less extreme than for women, the aesthetic value for Zinacantec men involved movement patterns that were equally constrained, in comparison with typical movement patterns in the United States (Devereaux (formerly L. Haviland), personal communication, July, 1989). An innate newborn behaviour ultimately becomes a valued adult behaviour.

The adult woman's restrained style of motor movements, itself a product of epigenetic development, created a prenatal motor environment for her own unborn child. The restrained style of movement of Zinacantec females continued to provide a postnatal motor environment during the baby's first two years of life, when he or she was carried most of the time. In this way, the epigenesis of movement patterns in one generation has the potential to influence the epigenesis of movement patterns in the next. In sum, restrained motor activity was a part of the developing Zinacantec from birth to adulthood, at which point, in pregnant females, it provided a restrained movement environment for the unborn Zinacantec baby, most likely helping to preserve this stylistic feature of body culture into the next generation.

Culture and biology are mutually adapted for survival

The area of motor development is also a good arena for illustrating the mutual adaptation of culture and biology for survival, as well as cultural context as interpretive framework. Sophie, the daughter of American social scientists living in Nabenchauk, walked at nine months of age, about five months earlier than the Zinacantec norms. According to her mother, sociologist/anthropologist Leslie Devereaux, in Zinacantec eyes, her precocious walking made her a 'monster' because, in their particular environment, it was dangerous for a child to walk before understanding language (Devereaux, personal communication, July, 1989). For example, Zinacantec houses always have an open fire in the centre. Because Sophie could propel herself motorically, yet lacked the understanding to stay away from the fire, there was a constant danger that she would fall in. Walking before the development of rational sense and understanding also was considered disruptive to others, as when Sophie would stagger into somebody's weaving.

Zinacantecs were horrified at the problems that resulted from Sophie's early walking. They were amused that her parents, unlike the typical Zinacantec family, had to be on guard all the time to keep her from hurting herself or inadvertently causing some kind of damage (Devereaux, pers. comm., July, 1989).

Breaking cultural norms often reveals most dramatically what the norms are. The cultural context goes unnoticed until it is disrupted. In the case of motor development, Zinacantec reactions to Sophie's deviation from the normal walking age make it clear that Zinacantecs do not merely *tolerate*, but actually *value* late walking. In their cultural context, unlike that of the West, relatively late motor development had a positive social value. Even more important from a theoretical perspective is the fact that this norm was much more adaptive for survival in the Zinacantec environment than the Western norm of *accelerating* motor development would be. If we consider late walking to be related to the typically restrained motor activity that is innate from birth in Zinacantec babies, then we see how this characteristic is well adapted to features of Zinacantec cultural norms such as having a fire on the ground in the centre of the house. At the same time, note that early walking can also be adaptive to environmental conditions, as in the USA, with its technology of cribs, playpens, etc.

Culture selects from biology

The operation of this relationship can, in principle, be distinguished from the operation of the first relationship, 'Culture reinforces biology', in which the biology provides the substrate for one particular behavioural outcome, which can either be reinforced by the environment or not. When 'Culture selects from biology', the relationship under discussion here, the biological substrate provides the foundation for more than one capacity and the environment can reinforce one capacity more than another. My example, drawn from the work of Heidi Keller, comes from the newborn period.

From a biological perspective, neonates all over the world are equipped with special propensities for relating to primary caregivers (Keller and Greenfield, 2000). In order to receive the physical and psychological care required by such immature and helpless creatures, infants are able to attract their caregivers' attention and elicit caregiving motivation reliably with a special repertoire of inborn characteristics such as their facial configuration ('Kindchenschema' or 'babyness'; Lorenz, 1969) and attachment behaviours, signalling distress like crying or fussing, as well as communicative cues like looking, smiling and vocalizing (Bowlby, 1969). They are equipped with a perceptual system that prefers the human face over other visual displays (Fantz, 1963) to facilitate the familiarizing of significant others. Their social orientation is expressed in their preference for company over being alone; they behave differently towards persons as compared with objects (Trevarthen, 1980). They are able to detect contingencies and expect social responsiveness from their interactional partners (Brazelton, Koslowski and Main, 1974). They want to be held and carried and are consoled by body contact (Keller and Greenfield, 2000). Parents are equipped with complementary behavioural propensities to meet the special characteristics of infant behaviours in terms of intuitive parenting programmes: they nurse and carry infants in response to distress, they look and smile at them and approach when they cry.

Infant capacities, as well as the basic components of parenting behaviour, have been identified across a remarkable range of cultures; thus they would appear to have their origin in the evolutionary history that is universal across the human species (Keller et al., 1999). Basically, four systems of parenting can be differentiated which address different infant needs and prompt relevant socialization experiences at the same time. The primary care system (especially nursing) provides infants with a reliable response to distress, thus promoting the infant's trust in his or her social partners. The body contact system (especially carrying) relates the infants to the caregiving environment. The body stimulation system promotes an early motor self, and the face-to-face system induces a sense of agency (Keller, 2000). Caregiving usually consists of contextually shaped mixtures of these parenting systems which reflect cultural variability.

Individualism/independence and collectivism/interdependence: two idealized pathways through universal developmental stages

However, some combinations can be found more reliably than others. The prevalence of the face-to-face system, for example, has been described as a typically Western (Keller and Eckensberger, 1998) or pedagogical (LeVine, 1994) parenting style. The body contact system is described as a non-Western (Keller and Eckensberger, 1998) or paediatric style (LeVine, 1974, 1994), prevalent in farming or pastoral communities. These early experiences lay the ground for developmental trajectories, which, as cultural ideals, require corresponding socialization scripts across developmental stages.

Keller and Eckensberger (1998), as well as Greenfield and Suzuki (1998), have identified idealized pathways that can be termed individualism and collectivism, independence and interdependence, or autonomy and relatedness (Greenfield, 1994; Kagitcibasi, 1996; Markus and Kitayama, 1991). Each path involves selective cultural interpretations of the same maturationally grounded stages. These paths are not binary opposites, but relative emphases and systems of prioritization. They represent life strategies that have proved adaptive in addressing specific environmental problems. Each pathway is a mode around which variation can occur.

First we turn to the developmental path of *individualism* or *independence.* This scenario, most common in European-derived and industrial or commercial societies, consists of an impact of exclusive dyadic attention between caregiver, mainly mother, and infant, plus a special emphasis on face-to-face exchange, especially promoting face-to-face contingency experiences in the infant. In other words, it selectively emphasizes the universal face-to-face system. The mother orients the child from early on to the material world, often mediating the interaction with toys. This pathway also selectively elaborates the infants' innate reactions to objects, providing socialization for the development of technological intelligence – knowledge of how to manipulate the world of objects.

These experiences allow the baby to develop expectancies, predictability and control and thus foster the development of the self as a causal agent. The cultural value of early independence is also supported, for example, with independent sleeping arrangements (cf. Morelli et al., 1992) and the use of baby technology, such as infant seats, to provide precocious physical independence for young babies.

The early conceptions of self and relationships, both to people and to things, that are acquired during these early socialization situations may set the stage for specific ways of developing competence in childhood, e.g. with active exploration, asking questions and formal instructions. The development of an independent or individualistic adult, as described by Markus and Kitayama (1991) or Triandis (1989) might represent the 'better adult' in these environments.

Next we turn to the pathway of *collectivism* or *interdependence*, a developmental trajectory that is more common in rural environments in Africa, Asia, and Latin America. This pathway mainly relies on the prevalence of the body contact system in multiple caretaking environments with childcare as a co-occurring activity. The main socialization context is established through bodily proximity, thus promoting warmth and interrelatedness.

The resulting conception of self as 'co-agent' is based on feelings of interrelatedness. This developmental pathway continues in socializing skills through observation and participation, finally leading to an interdependent (Markus and

Kitayama, 1991) or collectivistic (Triandis, 1989) adult. Thus, a developmental approach identifies mechanisms across lifespan trajectories leading up to the culturally diverse adult forms of development.

Each path involves different cultural interpretations and selective emphases of the same maturationally grounded stage. The cultural environment selects components of the universal inborn repertoire – e.g. the differentiation between object behaviour and person behaviour identified by Trevarthen (1980) for newborns – and shapes the behavioural expressions accordingly. Either object behaviour or person-oriented behaviour can be emphasized by those around the infant. The infant who is given toys to play with on his or her own learns experientially the cultural value of independence and technological intelligence, as described by Mundy-Castle (1974, 1991). Innate reactions to objects are enhanced by the individualistic socializing environment more than the collectivistic one.

In contrast, the infant who has other people to play with and is in constant contact with others learns through experience the cultural value of interdependence and social intelligence, also described by Mundy-Castle (1974, 1991).

Caregiving arrangements carry cultural meanings, and these meanings are reconstructed by infants through implicit messages that may become explicit at maturity, or may rest implicit. Thus, the early biologically predisposed development results in basic cultural learning; the foundation for a selective emphasis on independence or interdependence is laid. These early conceptions of relationship and self are the basis for divergent pathways through childhood and adolescence (Greenfield, 1994; Greenfield and Suzuki, 1998; Keller and Eckensberger, 1998). For example, in middle childhood the collectivistic model can be expressed in unconditional in-group helpfulness, while the individualistic model leads to conditional or negotiated helpfulness – as in the research of Mundy-Castle and Bundy (1988). The collectivistic model can be expressed in an emphasis on socially shared knowledge, while the individualistic model leads to an emphasis on individually possessed knowledge (Greenfield, 1997a, 1997b; Keller and Eckensberger, 1998). The collectivistic model leads to an emphasis on fitting into a group, while the individualistic model leads to an emphasis on individuality and uniqueness (Greenfield et al., 2002; Keller, 1998; Markus and Kitayama, 1991). Adolescence is contingent upon these preceding experiences as a short transition in the collectivistic model, from childhood to adulthood, with early marriage and childbearing and responsibilities for the economic support of the family. In the individualistic model, adolescence is a period of moratorium reserved for education and other forms of self-development.

In adulthood, these early experiences also lay the ground for one's own parenting style, so that intergenerational continuity and transformation are established. Thus, each cultural environment selects different components of the universal infant repertoire and the basis for differentiated cultural socialization is laid.

Culture respects biology

Developmentally gradated tools

My theme here is that *cultures have sets of artefacts and practices that respect and stimulate sensitive periods for cognitive and neural development.* I would like to make the argument that the *developmental timing* and *order* in which Zinacantec girls are exposed to various weaving tools show implicit knowledge of and respect for cognitive development. Specifically, these tools show implicit knowledge of the progression from the preoperational to the concrete operational stage and the timing of this progression. Vygotsky noted how much cognitive history is contained in cultural artefacts and that these artefacts function, in turn, as tools for the stimulation of current cognitive development (Scribner, 1985). I would like to take this line of thinking a step further: not only cognitive history but also cognitive development can be contained in cultural artefacts. To provide evidence for this point, I analyse the cognitive requirements of a developmentally gradated set of Zinacantec weaving artefacts: the toy loom, the warping frame, and the real loom.

Play weaving on the toy loom, illustrated in figure 3.1, is widespread in Nabenchauk. It begins at age 3 or 4, in Piaget's preoperational period. The toy loom is used several years earlier than the real loom and warping frame, which are not used before age 6 or 7, the beginning of the concrete operational period. Preparing the real loom to weave is a concrete operational task, as I shall demonstrate in a moment. Because the toy loom is just slightly different from the real loom, it does not require concrete operational thinking to set up. The difference lies in the ropes between the two sticks, on each side (figure 3.2).

By holding together the two endsticks (top and bottom of the loom in figures 3.1 and 3.2), these ropes permit the warp or frame threads (the white threads in figure 3.2) to be wound directly on the loom. Figure 3.1 shows how the sticks that constitute the loom are connected by a loop of ribbon that goes around the weaver's back (hence the name backstrap) to the post; the tension necessary to keep the loom from collapsing is provided by the weaver, who leans back against the strap. Note that, unlike the real loom (figure 3.3), the top and bottom weaving sticks are connected by the ribbon looped around them.

The real loom (shown in figure 3.3) does not have the side ropes (figure 3.2) or ribbons (figure 3.1) holding the loom frame (top and bottom sticks) together. Note that only the warp threads (multicoloured in figure 3.3) hold the two sticks

Figure 3.1   Play weaving on the toy loom.

Figure 3.2   The difference between a toy loom, shown here, and a real loom (figure 3.3) lies in the ropes between the two sticks.

Figure 3.3   The real loom, without the side ropes.

Figure 3.4   The *komen* or warping frame has a warp already wound on it.

together. However, these threads cannot be wound directly on to the loom (the two end sticks) because if the threads were not there, the loom would collapse; the loom has nothing to hold the two sticks together before the winding of the warp threads begins.

Therefore, a real loom must have the warp prewound on a separate apparatus, the *komen* or warping frame shown (with a warp already wound on it) in figure 3.4.

My thesis is that winding the warp on a *komen* intrinsically involves concrete operational thinking. This is the case because winding on the *komen* requires mental transformation, the essence of concrete operations (e.g. Piaget, [1963]1977). The form of the warp threads wound on the *komen* (figure 3.4) is quite different from the form of the threads on the final loom (figure 3.3). Complex topological transformation is required to understand the connection between how you wind the warp and how the warp looks and functions on the loom. Let me illustrate this point with the sequence in figure 3.5.

Figure 3.5a shows a *komen* or warping frame, ready to begin winding. In figure 3.5b, a girl has begun to wind the threads on the warping frame; in figure 3.5c she has gotten a bit further. Compare this image with figure 3.3. Figure 3.3 shows how the warp turns out (after more of the same with additional

Figure 3.5a   The *komen* or warping frame is ready to begin winding.

Figure 3.5b   A girl has begun to wind the threads on the warping frame.

Figure 3.5c   The girl has further succeeded in winding the threads.

colours) after being transferred to the loom. Note the difference between the U-shaped configuration of threads in figure 3.5c, where the warp threads are still on the warping frame, and figure 3.3, where the warp threads have been straightened out and transferred to the loom. Threads on the left side of the stick

Figure 3.6a   A girl has started winding the warp directly on to the toy loom.

in 3.5c go to one end of the loom (e.g. the top in figure 3.3), while threads on the right side go to the other end (e.g. the bottom in figure 3.3).

This sequence illustrates the important cognitive point: that a complex series of mental transformations is required for a weaver to understand the connection between how the threads are wound on the warping frame and how they end up in the configuration visible on the loom in figure 3.3. Because mental transformations characterize the Piagetian stage of concrete operations, winding a warp on the warping frame in order to set up a backstrap loom is a culture-specific concrete operational task.

I now compare the cognitive level required to set up a 'real' loom with that required to set up a toy loom. Whereas to set up a real loom demands the mental transformations of concrete operations, mental transformations are not required for the toy loom. Because of the extra supporting ropes on the side (figures 3.1 and 3.2), the warp can be wound directly on the loom. The sequence in figure 3.6 illustrates this central point.

In figure 3.6a, a young girl has just started winding the warp directly on to the toy loom, which is already set up. The top and bottom loom sticks (left and right in the photo) are held in place by white string connecting the sticks; one of the two side strings is shown clearly at the top of figures 3.6a and 3.6b.

In figure 3.6b, the young girl continues winding, making repeated figure eights between the end sticks, seen in the photograph. This process of winding figure

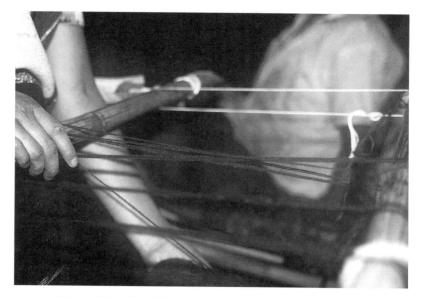

Figure 3.6b   The girl continues winding, making repeated figure eights between the end sticks.

eights makes the cross-configuration we see on the *komen* in figure 3.5b. In this process, there is no mental transformation required to go from the winding process to the set-up loom.

The important conclusion from this analysis is that Piagetian theory is part of the Zinacantecs' implicit ethnotheory of development. Whereas Zinacantec girls start on the toy loom from age 3, they do not set up a real loom before age 6 at the earliest, the normal age range of concrete operations. So, most interestingly, Piagetian theory is implicitly (but not explicitly) built into the developmental progression of Zinacantec weaving tools.

Culture shapes and actualizes biological potential

If we think of Piagetian stages as age-dependent sensitive periods, then learning how to set up a real loom can be seen as an activity that actualizes concrete operations in a culture-specific form.

Cognitive stages as age-dependent sensitive periods for cultural learning

What is the evidence for Piagetian stages as age-dependent sensitive periods and how does play weaving fit into this picture? I should like to draw upon a new theory of primate play by Fairbanks (2000) and propose that it applies both to human play in general and to play weaving in particular. Fairbanks has developed a theory of monkey play that posits its role in stimulating neuromuscular pathways that underlie a particular adult monkey skill. She contrasts her theory with the theory that play functions as direct practice of an adult behavioural skill. She observes that because the peak of each monkey play form occurs years before the adult behaviour, it would not be very useful as practice for the adult behaviour. However, the playful form is most frequent just at the time the relevant neural substrate for that particular activity is developing. For example, play fighting in monkeys reaches its maximum just as the neural circuitry for adult aggression is developing – but years before aggression is required in adult monkey social life.

Could this analysis apply to human play in general and to play weaving in particular? There are several parallels with Fairbanks' theory and data: First, there is the behavioural parallel: just as play fighting occurs in monkeys several years before the real thing, so does play weaving on the toy loom occur several years before weaving utilitarian items on the real loom. Second, Thatcher (1994) presents EEG evidence for spurts in neural development. These spurts are periods of neural instability that serve as developmental transition points in the nervous system. One of these transition points or spurts is at age 4 (Fischer and Rose, 1994), in the age range when play weaving begins.

My theoretical interpretation of these transition points in neural development is that they are sensitive periods – developmental windows – when stimulation, often in the form of culture-specific practices, actualizes maturationally specific neural circuits. It follows from this that play weaving could stimulate neural and neuromuscular pathways that provide a foundation for the later cognitive development required to weave on a real loom.

Fischer and Rose (1994) identify a second spurt in neural development that occurs between ages 6 and 10. This is precisely the period in which weaving on a real loom begins for most Zinacantec girls. It is also Piaget's period of concrete operations, which, as I have tried to illustrate, are indeed required for setting up a real loom. But looking at these matters across cultures, we would not necessarily expect concrete operational children in the United States to be able to set up a loom, beginning with the *komen*. Nor would we necessarily expect Zinacantec children to be able to do Western concrete operational tasks, for example two-way classification. Indeed, we found, through an experiment, that they could not do this task.

In conclusion, the cultural environment *shapes* and *actualizes* the biological potential for concrete operations. Thus my hypothesis is that the concrete operational potential of Zinacantec girls has been actualized by and in the form of weaving-related tasks. In the United States, concrete operations are actualized by different experiences and in different forms; for example, conservation of weight might be actualized by the experience of weighing.

Conclusion

These are the various ways in which I suggest that culture and biology mutually define and influence each other in development. These relationships make it clear that it is much too simple to think of biology on the inside and culture on the outside. The external culture depends on the internal biological capacity for cultural learning. To realize this biological capacity for cultural learning in turn requires an external culture that results from the cultural learning of earlier generations. I hope that this discussion can lead to systematic investigation of these six relationships in a wide variety of cultural settings.

REFERENCES

Anschuetz, M. (1966). To be born in Zinacantan. Ms. on file, Harvard Chiapas Project, Department of Anthropology, Harvard University, Cambridge, MA.

Bowlby, J. (1969), *Attachment and loss*, vol. 1: *Attachment*, New York: Basic Books.

Brazelton, T. B., Koslowski, B. and Main, M. (1974). The origins of reciprocity: The early mother–infant interaction. In M. Lewis and L. A. Rosenblum (eds.), *The effect of the infant on its caregiver*. New York: Wiley, pp. 49–76.

Brazelton, T. B., Robey, J. S. and Collier, G. (1969). Infant development in the Zinacanteco Indians of Southern Mexico. *Pediatrics*, 44, 274–83.

Childs, C. P. and Greenfield, P. M. (1980). Informal modes of learning and teaching: the case of Zinacanteco weaving. In N. Warren (ed.), *Studies in cross-cultural psychology*, vol. 2. London: Academic Press, pp. 269–316.

Fairbanks, L. A. (2000). Behavioral development of nonhuman primates and the evolution of human behavioral ontogeny. In S. Parker, J. Langer and M. Mackinney (eds.), *The evolution of behavioral ontogeny*. Santa Fe, NM: SAR Press, pp. 131–58.

Fantz, R. L. (1963). Pattern vision in newborn infants. *Science*, 140, 296–97.

Fischer, K. W. and Rose, S. P. (1994). Dynamic development of coordination of components in brain and behavior: a framework for theory. In G. Dawson and K. W. Fischer (eds.), *Human behavior and the developing brain*. New York: Guilford Press, pp. 3–66.

Freedman, D. G. (1965). An ethological approach to the genetic study of human behavior. In S. Vandenberg (ed.), *Methods and goals in human behavior genetics*. New York: Academic Press, pp. 141–62.

(1979). Ethnic differences in babies. *Human Nature*, 2, 36–43.

Freedman, D. G. and Freedman, N. (1969). Behavioral differences between Chinese-American and European-American newborns. *Nature*, 224, 1127.

Freedman, D. G. and Keller, B. (1963). Inheritance of behavior in infants. *Science*, 140, 196–8.

Goldsmith, H. H. and Campos, J. J. (1982). Toward a theory of infant temperament. In R. N. Emde and R. J. Harmon (eds.), *The development of attachment and affiliative systems*. New York: Plenum Press, pp. 161–94.

Goldsmith, H. H. and Gottesman, I. I. (1981). Origins of variation in behavioral style: a longitudinal study of temperament in young twins. *Child Development*, 52, 91–103.

Greenfield, P. M. (1972). Studies of mother–infant interaction: toward a structural-functional approach. *Human Development*, 15, 131–8.

(1984). A theory of the teacher in the learning activities of everyday life. In B. Rogoff and J. Lave (eds.), *Everyday cognition: its development in social context.* Cambridge, MA: Harvard University Press, pp. 117–38.

(1994). Independence and interdependence as developmental scripts: implications for theory, research, and practice. In P. M. Greenfield and R. R. Cocking (eds.), *Cross-cultural roots of minority child development.* Hillsdale, NJ: Erlbaum, pp. 1–37.

(1997a). Culture as process: empirical methods for cultural psychology. In J. W. Berry, Y. Poortinga and J. Pandey (eds.), *Handbook of cross-cultural psychology*, vol. 1. *Theory and method.* Boston: Allyn and Bacon, pp. 301–46.

(1997b). You can't take it with you: Why ability assessments don't cross cultures. *American Psychologist*, 52, 1115–24.

Greenfield, P. M., Brazelton, T. B. and Childs, C. (1989). From birth to maturity in Zinacantan: ontogenesis in cultural context. In V. Bricker and G. Gossen (eds.), *Ethnographic encounters in Southern Mesoamerica: celebratory essays in honor of Evon Z. Vogt.* Albany: Institute of Mesoamerican Studies, State University of New York, pp. 177–216.

Greenfield, P. M., Davis, H. M., Suzuki, L. and Boutakidis, I. (2002). Understanding intercultural relations on multiethnic high school sports teams. In S. Ball-Rokeach, M. Gatz and M. A. Messner (eds.), *A sporting chance: the role of sport in urban settings.* Minneapolis: University of Minnesota Press, pp. 141–57.

Greenfield, P. M. and Suzuki, L. (1998). Culture and human development: implications for parenting, education, pediatrics, and mental health. In I. E. Sigel and K. A. Renninger (eds.), *Handbook of child psychology*, vol. 4: *Child psychology in practice*, 5th edn. New York: Wiley, pp. 1059–109.

Haviland, L. K. M. (1978). The social relations of work in a peasant community. Unpublished doctoral dissertation, Harvard University, Cambridge, MA.

Kagitcibasi, C. (1996). *Family and human development across cultures: a view from the other side.* Mahwah, NJ: Lawrence Erlbaum.

Kaye, K. (1977). Infants' effects upon their mothers' teaching strategies. In J. Glidewell (ed.), *The social context of learning and development.* New York: Gardner Press, pp. 173–306.

Keller, H. (1998). Different socialization pathways to adolescence. Paper presented at The 4th Africa Region International Society for the Study of Behavioral Development Conference (ISSBD), Windhoek, Namibia, 20–23 July.

(2000). Human parent–child relationships from an evolutionary perspective. Special Issue of *American Behavioral Scientist* (Evolutionary psychology: potential and limits of a Darwinian framework for the Behavioral Sciences), 43(6), 957–69.

Keller, H. and Eckensberger, L. H. (1998). Kultur und Entwicklung (Culture and development). In H. Keller (ed.), *Lehrbuch Entwicklungspsychologie* (Textbook of developmental psychology). Bern: Huber, pp. 57–96.

Keller, H. and Greenfield, P. M. (2000). History and future of development in cross-cultural psychology. In C. Kagitcibasi and Y. H. Poortinga (eds.). Millennium Special Issue of the *Journal of Cross-Cultural Psychology*, 31(1), 52–62.

Keller, H., Lohaus, A., Völker, S., Cappenberg, M. and Chasiotis, A. (1999), Temporal contingency as an independent component of parenting behavior. *Child Development*, 70, 474–85.

LeVine, R. A. (1974). Parental goals: a cross-cultural view. *Teachers College Record*, 76, 226–39.

(1994). *Child care and culture: lessons from Africa*. Cambridge: Cambridge University Press.

Lorenz, K. (1969). Innate bases of learning. In K. H. Pribram (ed.), *On the biology of learning*. New York: Harcourt, pp. 13–93.

Markus, H. R. and Kitayama, S. (1991). Culture and the self: implications for cognition, emotion, and motivation. *Psychological Review*, 98, 224–53.

Morelli, G. A., Rogoff, B., Oppenheim, D. and Goldsmith, D. (1992). Cultural variation in infants' sleeping arrangements: questions of independence. *Developmental Psychology*, 28(4), 614–21.

Mundy-Castle, A. (1974). Social and technological intelligence in Western and non-Western cultures. *Universitas*, 4, 46–52.

(1991). Commentary and discussion. In P. M. Greenfield and R. R. Cocking (Chairs), *Continuities and discontinuities in the cognitive socialization of minority children*. Proceedings of a workshop, Department of Health and Human Services, Public Health Service, Alcohol, Drug Abuse and Mental Health Administration, Washington, DC, June/July, pp. 573–98.

Mundy-Castle, A. and Bundy, R. (1988). Moral values in Nigeria. *Journal of African Psychology*, 6, 25–40.

Piaget, J. ([1963] 1977). Intellectual operations and their development. In H. E. Gruber and J. J. Vonèche (eds.), *The essential Piaget: an interpretive reference and guide*. New York: Basic Books, pp. 342–58.

Scribner, S. (1985). Vygotsky's uses of history. In J. V. Wertsch (ed.),*Culture, communication, and cognition: Vygotskian perspectives*.Cambridge: Cambridge University Press, pp. 119–45.

Thatcher, R. W. (1994). Cyclical cortical reorganization: origins of human cognitive development. In G. Dawson and K. W. Fischer (eds.), *Human behavior and the developing brain*. New York: Guilford Press, pp. 232–66.

Trevarthen, C. (1980). The foundation of intersubjectivity: development of interpersonal and cooperative understanding in infants. In D. Olson (ed.), *The social foundations of language and thought*. New York: W. W. Norton, pp. 316–42.

Triandis, H. C. (1989). Cross-cultural studies of individualism and collectivism. *Nebraska Symposium on Motivation*, 37, 41–133.

Part II

Perspectives on development informed by culture

4   Indian parents' ethnotheories as reflections of the Hindu scheme of child and human development

T. S. Saraswathi and Hema Ganapathy

Traditional cultural beliefs regarding the value of children and goals of child rearing provide the images and set the standards for developmental theorizing in predominantly Hindu India. Hinduism, often defined as a way of life rather than as a religion in the narrow sense of the word, permeates all aspects of daily life including parental ideas, beliefs and practices related to child rearing.

The present chapter delineates the Hindu world view of human development and examines its pervasive influence on parental ethnotheories of child rearing as evinced in empirical evidence, related beliefs regarding value of children, qualities desired in a 'good child' and in cultural rules governing marriage partner selection. The acknowledgement of the interaction of culture and biology, the central theme of this book, emerges at two levels: (1) Marriage is viewed as a sacrament, that 'sows the seeds of a thousand years' (i.e. determines genetic inheritance) and hence a union between families and not individuals, to be carefully arranged by the experienced elders rather than left to inexperienced young people; (2) The centrality of *karma* associated with the belief in an endless cycle of birth and death (until salvation is attained through *moksha* or *mukti*). Within each lifetime the individual can influence his or her *karma* by balancing 'right' and 'wrong' actions. Each individual starts the next life with the balance of *gunas* (roughly a highly personal and individual unconscious). The constitution of the *guna* is more a metaphysical than a biological inheritance. However, its recognition points to the dominant role attributed to innate predispositions that cannot be altered in a major way by child training and socialization. In sum, culture is seen as providing the context for development and a platform for refining one's predispositions.

The argument may seem metaphysical only, but it permeates daily life practices and acts as the guiding philosophy for both acceptance of the inevitable and the striving for self-actualization. Kakar (1981) comments on this pervasive influence: 'The world image of traditional Hindu culture, ... provides its members with a sanctioned pattern, a template which can be superimposed on the outer world, ... thus helping individuals to make sense of their own lives' (p. 15). Belief in this basic philosophy may also be viewed as the core Indianness that cuts across the regional, caste and linguistic differences that characterize the country. From Kashmir in the extreme north to Kanyakumari at the southern tip, from the illiterate farmer to the scientist working in a hi-tech laboratory, differences only scratch the surface, and the all-pervasive belief regarding the cycle of rebirth and the purpose of life and goodness comes through with surprising transparency.

In the following section we shall detail some of the core concepts regarding the Hindu perspective on human development. This will provide the background for culturally contextualizing parental ethnotheories, beliefs and practices. Major ideas and interpretations presented here draw quite heavily on Sudhir Kakar's presentation of the inner world (1981). Kakar provides a rich tapestry of the Hindu world view, drawing from the Hindu scriptures, medical treatises, epics and folklore as well as from his years of clinical experience as a practising psychoanalyst.

The Hindu world view and the scheme of human development

The core concepts of the Hindu world view are *moksha* or *mukti* (self realization, transcendence, salvation, or a release from worldly involvement and unity with the Infinite) and *dharma* (variously translated as 'law', 'moral duty', 'right action', or 'conformity' with the truth of things (Kakar, 1981)). Be it in an individual's social relations, or during the course of the life cycle, *dharma* is the means to the ultimate goal of *moksha*. The Hindu image of the life cycle or *asramadharma*, drawn from the above, provides the ground plan of an ideal life cycle, and defines the tasks of different life stages. Kakar outlines the stages of the life cycle according to the theory of *asramadharma* and compares it with the eight stages of man. Erikson (1979) has commented on the similarities in the developmental tasks that are said to characterize the later stages of development past that of childhood. However, '(c)ontrasting with Erikson's model, which is clinical and developmental, the Hindu view proposes "ideal" images in the platonic sense' (p. 42; see table 4.1).

The relational value of the stages is summarized succinctly by Ramanujan (1990a) as follows: 'If *brahmacarya* (celibate studentship) is preparation for a full relational life, *grhasthasrama* (householder stage) is a full realization of it... *Vanaprastha* (the retiring forest-dweller stage) loosens the bonds, and *Sanyasa* (renunciation) cremates all one's past and present relations' (p. 54).

The stages from conception to late childhood are detailed separately, as codified through the rites that mark each substage until entry into the stage of apprenticeship, as noted in the fourth stage of school age in the overall life cycle (see table 4.2).

Infancy and early childhood in the Indian tradition are characterized by indulgence. The adult–child interaction is conceptualized as *'palna posna'* – protecting, nurturing; children are not 'reared' or 'brought up'. In other words children are considered as divine and near perfect and adult–child interaction

Table 4.1 *Stages of the life cycle*

	Erikson's scheme		Hindu scheme	
Stage	Specific task and 'virtue'	Stage	Specific task and 'virtue'	
Infancy	Basic trust vs mistrust Hope	Individual's 'prehistory' not explicitly considered	Preparation of the capacity to comprehend *dharma*	
Early childhood	Autonomy vs shame Doubt: willpower			
Play age	Initiative vs guilt Purpose			
School age	Industry vs inferiority	Apprenticeship (*brahmacharya*)	Knowledge of *dharma*: competence and fidelity	
Adolescence	Identity vs identity Diffusion: fidelity			
Young adulthood	Intimacy vs isolation Love	Householder (*garhasthya*)	Practice of *dharma*: love and care	
Adulthood	Generativity vs stagnation Care	Withdrawal (*vanaprastha*)	Teaching of *dharma*: extended care	
Old age	Integrity vs despair Wisdom	Renunciation (*sannyasa*)	Realization of *dharma*: wisdom	

Source: Reprinted from Kakar (1981), p. 43.

is governed by pleasure and nurturance (at least in the stage of infancy) rather than by socialization and training.

Before concluding this section, it is essential to re-examine briefly the concept of *karma*, the third core idea of Hindu world image that links *dharma* and *moksha* and has implications for child development. '*Karma* is not just a doctrine of "reincarnation", "fatalism" or "pre-destination"; it is a promise of hope. Given the innate tendency of the unconscious (*gunas*) toward light (*sattva*), combined with an individual's personal efforts in this direction (*dharma*), *karma* assures that attainment of the goal of existence (*moksha*) is certain even though there are apt to be many setbacks in the process...' (Kakar, 1981, p. 48).

The deep penetration of this Hindu world image in the psyche of the average Indian, regardless of level of scientific training and Western influences, is illustrated convincingly by A. K. Ramanujan, the world-renowned poet-philosopher, in his description of his father. Ramanujan (1990a) talks of the ease with which his mathematician-astronomer father handled simultaneously his expertise in Sanskrit and astrology perceiving no obvious contradictions. This description could well fit a vast majority of educated men and women in contemporary India whose inner world is governed still by the basic Hindu world view, one

Table 4.2 *Stages of childhood: the Hindu scheme of social development*

Childhood period	Stage	Central mode of relationship	Rite marking transition into following stage
I. *Garba*	1. Foetus	Symbiotic (*dauhridya*)	*Jatakarma* (welcoming the new life and ensuring survival)
II. *Ksheerda*	2. Early infancy (0–1 month)	Dyadic intimacy	*Namakarna* (naming ceremony)
	3. Middle infancy (1–3/4 months)	Dyad in family	*Nishkramana* (introduction into the outer world e.g. seeing the moon)
	4. Late infancy (3/4–6/9 months)	Dyad in world	*Annaprasana* (introduction of solid foods)
III. *Ksheerannada*	5. Early childhood (6/9 months–2/3 years)	Dyadic dissolution (psychological birth)	*Chudakarana* (tonsure or shaving the baby's hair)
IV. *Bala*	6. Middle childhood (2/3–5/7 years)	Familial	*Vidyarambha* (initiation of formal education)
V. *Kumara*	7. Late childhood (5/7–8/12 years)	Familial dissolution (social birth)	*Upanayana* (initiation of social birth)

Source: Reprinted from Kakar (1981), p. 43.

which provides stability in the uncertainties of daily life and from which one draws succour at moments of stress and turmoil, to find meaning when struck by tragedy or ill fortune.

In sum, the Hindu world view is characterized by a prescriptive mode with emphasis on the interdependence between the individual and the larger social setting in which he or she is embedded and the interrelatedness within the stages of the present life cycle and between the present life cycle, the past and the future.

The principal directives for leading a good life and for proper child rearing come from two major sources, namely the ancient texts related to medicine, law and healthy living (such as *Susruta Samhita, Caraka Samhita, Ashtanfa Hrdaya*, cited in Singh, 1998; and *Manu Dharma Shastra*, cited in Motwani, 1958) and the rich oral tradition of folklore. While the former are accessible only to those with knowledge of Sanskrit, folklore becomes 'the symbolic language of the non-literate population' (Ramanujan, (1990b), p. 1). The narration of the Vedas alone may be considered invariant in the oral tradition. All other oral transmissions of knowledge exhibit and even invite flexibility. Epics and folk tales lend themselves to reinterpretation and are highly contextualized. The Hindu world view is kept alive through a rich heritage of mythological tales, proverbs and parables that clarify moral dilemmas and provide a rationale for alternative viewpoints. They also guide attitudes towards children, childhood and parenting (Ganapathy, 1998). In the next section, we will examine how the Hindu belief system influences parental beliefs and practices related to child rearing in the contemporary context.

Parental ethnotheories related to child rearing and their linkages to the Hindu world view

With other colleagues we became interested in studying how parental ethnotheories, anchored in the well-defined traditional conceptualizations of man and society, with prescriptions regarding the ideal way of life, and for rearing of children, adapt to the conflicting demands resulting from the fast pace of social change in the contemporary Indian context. We asked ninety-six middle-class parents and twelve grandparents of children ranging in age from infancy to 18 years, four questions: What is the value of having children? What is your conception of a good child? What is your conception of a good parent? What are the sources of your beliefs? (Saraswathi et al., 1998.) The major findings can be summarized as follows:

- Strengthening of the marital bond, a sense of responsibility for procreation and the need for personal fulfilment and satisfaction were cited as the predominant reasons for having children.
- A good child was viewed as one possessing values, good personal qualities (*sanskaras*). The last phrase, i.e. possessing *sanskar*, was interpreted as being respectful of and obedient to parents and other elders; being truthful, modest, trustworthy, compassionate and tolerant, all emphasizing social values.
- In a similar vein, a good parent was viewed as one who would strive to inculcate the values appropriate for a good child and be child oriented in their approach.
- Older members of the family were considered the main source of ideas and beliefs regarding parenting, with mass media and own experience being other sources. Interestingly, religious texts or experts were rarely cited as sources of information.
- When asked about perceived changes in child rearing today compared with when they were children, parents viewed themselves as more lenient (less strict in discipline) and providing more freedom to children to express themselves.

Value of children and desired qualities in a 'good child'

A more recent study by Pant and Saraswathi (2000), examined parents' conceptualizations of an ideal child through in-depth interviews of thirty middle-class Hindu Gujarati couples. Both fathers and mothers were interviewed. Findings related to both the qualities they desire in their children and single out for commendation in children they admire focus on social embeddedness rather than self-maximization. The qualities emphasized by nearly 60 per cent of the respondents include characteristics such as being well behaved, obedient, polite, disciplined, humble and religious. In other words, the parents showed a distinct preference for what they described as a *sanskari* child, one who is obedient, respectful of elders and socially conforming (58 per cent of the responses). This contrasts with the predominant emphasis on self-maximization observed in the American sample (Harwood, Miller and Irizarry, 1995). Self-maximization was operationalized to include independence or self-reliance, self-confidence and the development of the individual's full potential in terms of intellect, verbal facility, skills, abilities etc. Only 20 per cent of the Indian parents' responses emphasized these qualities.

The recurrent theme of cultural transmission through the inculcation of social and moral values as the prime objectives of child rearing and the predominant role of parenting find expression in the results of another recent study on the cultural construction of middle age (Saraswathi, Kurrien and Desai, 2000). Twenty Gujarati Hindu middle-class couples in Surat city were interviewed to obtain data on priorities and satisfactions in middle age (40–60 years). The dominant theme for both husbands and wives focused on the socialization of children and the satisfaction derived from children's successful performance in their education, career and subsequently marriage. Moving through the stages of infancy (*balpan*) characterized by parental indulgence, then *yuvan* or *brahmacharya*, the period of apprenticeship in acquisition of knowledge and skills during adolescence, through the stage of *grahastha* (householder) in early and middle adulthood, the individual is expected to fulfil his duty or *dharma*, resulting in generativity and then readiness for renunciation in old age (*vanaprastha* and then *sanyas*). The life cycle is seen as repeating itself through the next generation, continuing the biological and cultural heritage.

To summarize, the findings of the three studies cited above highlight the emphasis on social embeddedness, adult–child continuity and interpersonal respect and affection. Having a child, and having a child with desirable qualities, is seen as the product of the parents' own *karma*, moderating the pride when children excel, and buffering the pain when children are disabled or become socially deviant. The *dharma* of the householder is grounded in his duty toward fulfilling his responsibilities towards his wife and children, respect for and care of the elderly and contribution to good deeds that will ultimately lead to *moksha* or salvation.

Capturing social change

The world over, there have been noticeable adaptations in the goals, techniques and products of child rearing, consequent to the forces of social change that exert pressures in the contemporary context. India is no exception. The factors contributing to change include demographic transition with high birth rates and falling death rates; increased social mobility; large-scale rural-to-urban migration; blurred caste boundaries; introduction of the market economy with increased emphasis on formal education and technological skills; increases in women's employment and gender awareness; and the breaking of sociocultural barriers as a consequence of satellite communication networks.

Saraswathi and Pai (1997) discuss the significant characteristics of socialization in the contemporary Indian context as the experience of approach-avoidance conflicts in terms of stability and change. Concern has been expressed by educationists, counsellors, social workers and parents in general regarding the stress associated with practically every aspect of change: parent–child relations; educational and occupational goals; women's empowerment. The impact of social change on parental ethnotheories and on the prescriptive mode of the centuries-old tradition warrants examination. A useful paradigm in this regard is one suggested by Goodnow (1998) in studying shared ideas regarding parenting. Her thesis focuses on the *multiplicity* of views held, *competing* viewpoints, uneven distribution of ideas (ranging from core ideas shared by a majority to outliers who differ) and *change* in ideas brought about by both individual characteristics and change in the social context.

In the section that follows, we will briefly summarize the preliminary findings of an ongoing study as an exemplar of parental ethnotheories instantiated in the beliefs and practices of two generations in the choice of a marriage partner.

Interpretations of cultural rules for marriage-partner selection

Besides child-rearing practices, parental ethnotheories also guide socialization for partner selection and guide the profiles of desirable marriage partners. This is particularly significant in the Indian setting wherein marriages are traditionally arranged between families by family elders and not between individuals by mutual choice.

The cultural normative framework and rule systems for marriage-partner selection provide the frame of reference. An empirical study conceptualized in terms of the symbolic action theory (Eckensberger, 1996) was undertaken to understand the cultural rules of marriage-partner selection in the Indian context (Eckensberger, Kapadia and Wagels, 2000). For a better understanding of the meaning of cultural rules the study also examined 'barriers' in terms of conflicts or problems that are likely to occur during the selection process. The investigators were particularly interested in the nature of conflict resolution. These were conceptualized in terms of sociocognitive domains as a reflection of *interpersonal morality* (respecting other persons' ideas and perceptions, and responsibility and care for others); *personal morality* (responsibility for

Table 4.3 *Distribution of responses in the choice of social-cognitive domain in resolution of conflicts related to partner selection (per cent)*

Domain	Fathers (n = 14)	Mothers (n = 14)	Girls (n = 14)	Boys (n = 14)	Unmarried men (n = 4)	Unmarried women (n = 4)	Total (n = 64)
Interpersonal	27	27	22	18	4	1	99
morality	(27.3)	(27.3)	(22.2)	(18.2)	(4.0)	(1.0)	(52.1)
Personal morality	–	1	13	10	2	5	21
		(4.80)	(61.9)	(47.6)	(2.0)	(23.1)	(11.1)
Convention	6	7	–	3	–	–	16
	(37.5)	(43.8)		(18.8)			(8.4)
Personal concern	4	2	6	1	2	3	18
	(22.2)	(11.1)	(33.3)	(5.5)	(11.1)	(16.6)	(9.5)
Mixed domains	3	4	1	3	3	–	14
	(21.4)	(22.2)	(5.5)	(16.6)	(21.4)		(7.4)
Law (dowry-	3	1	3	2	2	1	12
related conflict)	(25.0)	(8.3)	(25.0)	(16.6)	(16.6)	(8.3)	(6.3)

Notes: Owing to multiple responses, totals may exceed n; percentages are given in parentheses.
Source: Eckensberger et al. (2000).

one's own self/life); *convention* (social rules that regulate social interactions and relationships); and *personal concern* (subjective, personalized choice of an individual).

The sample comprised fourteen upper-middle-class Hindu Gujarati families (sixty-four individuals – fathers, mothers, children) and eight unmarried women and men. Hypothetical scenarios formulated on the basis of the common impediments/problems experienced were probed for individuals' subjective interpretations and regulations they saw as appropriate. An example is: 'a girl or boy wants to marry on the basis of self-selection but the parents do not agree'. The interpretations and resolutions of the conflicts were analysed using the sociocognitive domains of reasoning as categories.

The findings (see table 4.3) reveal that although the dominant view among all the respondents was interpersonal morality (52 per cent), personal morality (11 per cent), personal concern (9 per cent), and conventions (8 per cent), also featured in the solutions. Intergenerational differences in the responses are evident. Mothers and fathers resolved the conflicts predominantly by using interpersonal morality and convention, whereas young girls and boys and unmarried men and women also used the domains of personal morality and personal concern in resolving conflicts. The contrast in the use of personal morality as a justification is a noticeable intergenerational difference.

The dominance of an interpersonal, 'duty-based' morality depicts the responsibility and concern embedded in the concept of *dharma* that parents and children have for one another. Parents feel it is their primary duty/responsibility to arrange children's marriages and ensure their well-being. At the same time, children feel it is their duty to uphold the parents' wishes and not hurt them by disobeying. It is noteworthy that the emergence of a distinct category of 'personal morality' indicates that the younger individuals have started asserting their rights (towards themselves) and are giving importance to individual needs as against familial expectations in a crucial area of decision-making.

Conclusion

To recapitulate, this chapter began with an articulation of the key concepts that guide the Hindu image of the life cycle, situating the clear (be it metaphysical rather than biological) recognition of the individual's predispositions in a prescriptive cultural context. The continued influence of this world image, as reflected in parental beliefs and practices, is tempered by observations regarding the moderating impact of social change in at least one crucial practice, namely the choice of a marriage partner. It would, however, be premature to conclude that fifty years of modern history can overwrite 5,000 years of cultural heritage. As we began with the comparison of the Hindu *asramadharma* with Erikson's psychosocial stages of development (Kakar, 1981), it may be apt to conclude with his eloquent observation regarding the possible residual power of a world view that has percolated down the centuries: 'Faced with a traditional world image of such consistency and pervasiveness as the Hindu world, . . . we, observers and diagnosticians of today, cannot ignore or simply leave behind some fundamental questions . . . one such question is that of the residual power, even under conditions of rapid modernization, of the traditional world images . . . ' (Erikson, 1979, p. 16). We have proposed that parental beliefs and practices that instantiate the cultural beliefs and rules offer fertile ground for the study of both continuity and change.

REFERENCES

Eckensberger, L. (1996). Agency, action and culture. Three basic concepts for psychology in general and for cross-cultural psychology in specific. In J. Pandey, D. Sinha and P. S. Bawak (eds.), *Asian contributions to cross-cultural psychology*. Proceedings of the 3rd Regional Asian Conference of the IACCP, Kathmandu, 2–7 January 1992.

Eckensberger, L., Kapadia, S. and Wagels, K. (2000). Social-cognitive domains of thinking in marriage partners selection: the Indian context. Paper presented at the symposium on The Development of Moral Reasoning and Diversity in the Concepts of Being at the 16th Biennial Congress of the International Society for the Study of Behavioral Development, Beijing, 11–14 July 2000.

Erikson, E. H. (1979). Report to Vikram: further perspectives on the life cycle. In S. Kakar (ed.), *Identity and adulthood*. Delhi: Oxford University Press, pp. 13–34.

Ganapathy, H. (1998). *Parental ethnotheories: a framework for understanding the traditional and the modern.* Paper prepared for presentation at the workshop on Writing for Social Science Journals, 13–18 December 1998, Baroda.

Goodnow, J. J. (1998). Collaborative rules: how are people supposed to work with one another? In P. Baltes and U. Staudinger (eds.), *Interactive minds: life-span perspectives on social foundations of cognition.* Cambridge: Cambridge University Press, pp. 313–44.

Harwood, R. L., Miller, J. G. and Irizarry, N. L. (1995). *Culture and attachment. Perceptions of the child in context.* New York: Guilford Press.

Kakar, S. (1981). *The inner world. A psycho-analytic study of childhood in India,* 2nd edn. New Delhi: Oxford University Press.

Motwani, K. (1958). *Manu Dharma Shastra: a sociological and historical study.* Madras: Ganesh and Co.

Pant, P. and Saraswathi, T. S. (2000). Parental ethnotheories: beliefs of Indian parents regarding the value of children and qualities of a good child. Paper presented at the International Conference on Facing Changes in Early Childhood, 5–7 September 2000, University of Malaysia, Kuala Lumpur.

Ramanujan, A. K. (1990a). Is there an Indian way of thinking? An informal essay. In Mckim Marriott (ed.). *India through Hindu categories.* New Delhi: Sage, pp. 41–58.

(1990b). *Who needs folklore? The relevance of oral traditions to South Asian studies.* Honolulu: Center for South Asian Studies.

Saraswathi, T. S., Ganapathy, H., Mithu, P., Dave, K., Pant, P., Khattar, A. and Dave, B. (1998). Parental ethnotheories: beliefs and practices in Indian child rearing. Unpublished manuscript. M.S. University of Baroda.

Saraswathi, T. S., Kurrien, R. and Desai, N. (2000). The cultural construction of middle age among Gujarati Hindus in India. Paper presented at the symposium on Pathways to Development. Biennial Congress of the International Society for Studies in Behavioral Development, Beijing, 11–14 July 2000.

Saraswathi, T. S. and Pai, S. (1997). Socialization in the Indian context. In D. Sinha and H. S. R. Kao (eds.), *Asian perspectives on psychology.* New Delhi: Sage, pp. 74–92.

Singh, A. (1998). Child care in Indian tradition. *Seminar,* 462, 18–23.

5   Indigenous conceptions of childhood development and social realities in southern Africa

Roderick Fulata Zimba

This chapter is about conceptions of childhood and development from the southern African perspective. Nations of Angola, Botswana, Lesotho, Namibia, Malawi, Mozambique, South Africa, Swaziland, Zambia and Zimbabwe are considered here to constitute the southern African region.

The first section deals with clarifications of key concepts used in the presentation. These are embodied in the phrase *indigenous conceptions of childhood development*. In the second section, links are made between conceptions of childhood and manifestations of the development of children from southern Africa. Based on southern African world views, illustrations of indigenous conceptions of childhood and development are provided in the contexts of childcare and development, children's rights and child and youth development in difficult circumstances. In the third section of the chapter, reflections on the possible contribution of the southern African indigenous and cultural conceptions of childhood to the pan-human arena of developmental science are offered.

Key concepts

According to Archard (1993), the conception of childhood is better understood when it is differentiated from the concept of childhood. To him, the

> ...concept of childhood requires that children be distinguished from adults in respect of some unspecified set of attributes. A *conception* of childhood is a specification of those attributes.... I have the concept of childhood if, in my behaviour towards children and the way I talk about them, I display a clear recognition that they are at a distinct and...different stage from adults. (Archard, 1993, p. 22)

He elaborates on this by pointing out that *all* societies at *all* times have had the concept of childhood. However, different societies have, over the centuries, held different conceptions of childhood. Differences have centred on the *extent*, *nature* and *significance* of childhood. Clarifying this further, he posits that conceptions of childhood can differ with respect to *boundaries*, *dimensions* and *divisions* of childhood. Boundaries of childhood focus on when it starts and when it ends. Dimensions of childhood may be understood from moral, juridical, epistemological, ideological and political perspectives. The sense in which conceptions of childhood may differ owing to divisions rests on stages into which the period from the beginning to the end of childhood can be split and what capacities are deemed by different societies to constitute each developmental stage.

Consistent with the work of Ohuche and Otaala (1981), an attempt is made in this chapter to demonstrate some particular southern African *conceptions* of childhood that are due to boundaries, dimensions and divisions of childhood.

The concept of *culture* forms an essential basis for this chapter. According to Brislin (1990), culture confers group membership on people. This comes about through an internalization of identifiable and particular customs, traditions, values, beliefs, practices and ways of reasoning about human life and ways of being such as those of interdependence, relatedness, separateness, independence, 'communalism' and connectedness (Eckensberger and Zimba, 1997; Kagitcibasi, 1996a, 1996b, 1997; Keller and Greenfield, 2000; Snarey, 1985; Triandis, 1990). This reasoning is related in this chapter to how conceptions of childhood and development in southern Africa are influenced by some of these and other ways of being. Kim, Park and Park (2000) state that in addition to providing meaning, direction and coherence to its members, culture allows people to define who they are, to decide what is meaningful, to communicate with others and to manage and utilize their physical and social environmental resources according to *their* desired ends. It is through culture that people think, feel and behave (Berry et al., 1992; Kim et al., 2000; Segall et al., 1990; Shweder, 1991). Moreover, Berry (1976), Kim (1994), Kim et al. (2000), Nsamenang (1992) and Sinha (1998) communicate the message that variations in and varied adaptations to different ecologies and epistemological frameworks create cultural differences in how people from different cultures think, feel and behave. This chapter provides glimpses of how people in the southern African region define who they are, who they wish to become and why they raise their children the way they do.

According to Myers (1995), as a multidimensional construct, *development* is about improving a child's ability to move, coordinate, think, reason, feel and relate to other people. In addition to encompassing physical, mental, emotional and social dimensions in an integral manner, development is perceived to take place continually from conception up to and beyond the attainment of adulthood. Super and Harkness (1997) have described the interactive network as a developmental niche, which requires that children need to interact with people and things in a cultural context. A germane point to the thrust of this chapter is Myers' (1995) contention that the *rate*, *character* and *quality* of a child's development is patterned and influenced by his or her biophysical and social environments. Echoing this, Dawes and Donald (2000) highlight the definition of development to the effect that it is 'the acquisition and growth of the physical, cognitive, social and emotional competencies required to engage fully in family and society' (Aber et al., 1997). How this is translated into unique conceptions of childhood and development in the southern African region is elucidated in this chapter.

The postulation of a child's goal of development as that of adaptation to, mastery of *and* transformation of his or her surroundings appropriately recognizes that different cultural and ecological surroundings place different demands on the child (Myers, 1995). It is held in this chapter that, when understood in this way, the goal of development becomes one of the bases of varied conceptions of childhood and development.

The term *indigenous* in the title of this chapter is used to denote that the conceptions of childhood and development isolated for illustrative purposes are largely native to, originate from and were developed by particular communities of southern Africa to bring about and sustain specific ways of existence and being. This usage of the term derives from and is in line with discourses on indigenous psychologies (Baumrind, 1998; Davidson, 1994; Gergen et al., 1996; Kim, 1990; Nsamenang and Dawes, 1998; Saraswathi, 1998; Serpell, 1976, 1992; Sinha, 1997; Turtle, 1994).

Conceptions of childhood and development in the context of childcare

Childcare entails promoting children's optimal survival, growth and development by meeting their basic needs. These include needs for protection, security, food, health, affection, interaction, stimulation, exploration and discovery (Myers, 1995), leading to socialization into given cultures. In what unique ways have communities in southern Africa done and continue to do this? Answers to this question are given within the rubric of boundaries, dimensions and divisions of childhood.

Boundaries of childhood

In terms of boundaries, it appears that communities in the region are agreed that childhood begins at conception. The age at which adulthood begins is not clear-cut. According to the 1990 African Charter on the Rights and Welfare of the Child, 'a child means every human being below the age of 18 years' (Naldi, 1992, p. 184). This is in line with the 1989 United Nations Convention on the Rights of the Child which stipulates that a child is 'every human being below the age of 18 years unless under the law applicable to the child, majority is attained earlier' (Goodwin-Gill and Cohn, 1994, p. 6). For many communities in the region, however, puberty (which occurs at roughly 12–16 years of age) heralds adulthood (Gelfand, 1979; LeVine et al., 1994). For these communities, childcare should cover the period from conception up to 16 years of age. This implies that in the view of a number of southern Africans, capacities for adult living are expected to be mastered earlier than is the case in other regions of the world. In an integrated manner, these capacities are not limited to biophysical abilities but also extend to moral, social-relational and epistemological realms (e.g. Gelfand, 1979). The discrepancy between the UN and the Organization of African Unity's (OAU) conception of the boundaries of childhood and adulthood on the one hand and the southern African communities' conception of the boundaries on the other poses particular conflicts and tensions pertaining to who is the agent called a child that requires protection from physical and psychological harm and needs nurturance. Owing to this, for instance, cases of child sexual abuse involving persons aged 15 to 16 years become difficult to disentangle if the juridical perspective is relied upon to the exclusion of the indigenous and cultural psychosocial perspective held by communities. This is also the case when the African Charter on the Rights and Welfare of the Child stipulates in article 21 that the minimum age of marriage should, by legislation, be set at 18 years of age.

Dimensions of childhood

The dimensions of childhood to be considered are those of survival and development. The prenatal, perinatal and postnatal stages of children's lives are particularly critical when it comes to survival in southern Africa. The community resources that families in the region have been harnessing for generations and continue to harness in aid of child survival can be illustrated with the following examples.

To the Nama of southern Namibia and the Ndonga of northern Namibia, the protection of the unborn child was and, to a large extent is, enshrined in customs, beliefs and taboos pertaining to the treatment of pregnant mothers (Zimba and Otaala, 1993, 1995). For instance, among the Nama, male spouses, grandparents and other relatives are happy, joyous, grateful, proud and excited to receive news of a pregnancy in the family. One important justification for this is the consideration that the child to be born is a gift from God, and one who would be welcomed as expanding the family.

To further protect the pregnant mother, the Nama employ behavioural taboos, which the mother and her spouse are required to abide by. The main perceived purpose of the taboos is to ensure the safe delivery of healthy babies. It is clear that as dietary guidelines, the taboos are efficaciously valid because a number of them are consistent with modern hygienic and health practices. For instance, pregnant mothers were forbidden from eating fatty and salty foods, bad meat, drinking alcohol, smoking, overworking and exposing themselves to emotional distress (Zimba and Otaala, 1995). It is clear that these prohibitions are based on community experiential knowledge regarding perceived causes of difficult labour, delayed child delivery, complications during delivery and miscarriage. In the event of a miscarriage, the community is supportive of the mother. No blame is ascribed to her alone as her spouse is equally responsible for observing taboos associated with pregnancy.

This rather resilient indigenous mode of social support for the mother and the child is common in southern Africa (Brazelton, Koslowski and Tronick, 1976; Evans, 1994; Gelfand, 1979; LeVine et al., 1994; Mbiti, 1990). Among the Swazi of Swaziland, for instance, the pregnant mother's support is sought not only from sentient extended family members but also from *emadloti* (ancestral spirits) and *tinyanga* (traditional medicine men) (Kuper, 1947; Malan, 1985; M'Passou, 1998; Nxumalo, 1993).

Among the Ndonga of northern Namibia (Zimba and Otaala, 1993), behavioural taboos that centre on the avoidance of social misconduct, conflicts and depression also communicate solutions to complications during childbirth. These taboos emanate from a world view which proposes a link between social and physical reality and suggests solutions to physical problems by making amends in social relations, avoiding social misconduct and obeying behavioural prohibitions (Zimba, 1987, 1994). The world view also relates to the maintenance of harmonious relationships with ancestors whose well-being is held to be injured by the malicious conduct of their living relatives (Mbiti, 1990; M'Passou, 1998; Zimba et al., 1995). For example, the Tsonga of southern Mozambique believe that when injured or offended through a family's involvement in conflicts, the display of unacceptable behaviour and the non-observance of traditional norms and regulations, ancestors can send sickness, scarcity, bad dreams, infertility and misfortune. When all customs and rituals (e.g. the childbirth rituals) are obeyed, ancestral spirits protect their descendants from harm and misfortune (Cruz e Silva and Loforte, 1998).

Continuing to use the Nama of southern Namibia as an example, a notable attribute of the perinatal stage is that a number of children are born outside health facilities and that they are delivered by traditional birth attendants, grandmothers, mothers-in-law, elder sisters and community health workers. With a general breakdown of health systems in most countries of the region, this practice is likely to be widespread. In some countries (e.g. Malawi, Zambia and Zimbabwe), the practice has been integrated into the modern health system. This has been done by running short health courses for traditional birth attendants as part of the general primary healthcare activities. Thus, despite its potential dangers, local and indigenous expertise is used to avoid injury, damage and death of children at birth.

During the postnatal stage (i.e. the period immediately after the birth of a child), Nama mothers, in addition to having their nutritional and material needs met by their spouses, are required by tradition to be confined in their houses for up to three months in order to recuperate and to give undivided attention to their newborn infants. During this period, male spouses are expected, according to custom, not to have sex with their wives earlier than six months, help and assist their wives and not to 'sleep around'. Grandparents and other relatives are expected by custom to ensure that the mothers in confinement and their newborn children are in good health, have enough to eat and are provided with adequate clothing (Zimba and Otaala, 1995). However, widespread poverty and dire economic hardships in the region in general and among the Nama in particular inhibit the optimal functioning of this indigenous support base (Serpell, 1992). This will be elaborated upon below.

Another illustration of the indigenous network of support given to the mother and her newly born baby is provided by Gelfand (1979). She reports that among the Shona of Zimbabwe, the birth of a child is greeted with a happy atmosphere in the family, gifts of various kinds being presented by relatives and friends of the parents. In addition to this, much interest is taken in the newborn by all the family and 'it is not long before the child learns the importance of the extended family' (Gelfand, 1979, p. 2). To enhance the survival of a Shona baby, Gelfand emphasizes the caring function of the traditional midwife.

It should be noted that the customary support and protection given to the mother and her infant by the Shona of Zimbabwe and the Nama of Namibia is commonly practised amongst many rural *and* urban residents of other southern African countries, where the traditional family structure has not yet broken down (Chiswanda, 1998; LeVine et al., 1994; M'Passou, 1998; Mtonga, 1989; Reynolds, 1989).

Conditions for development

Woodhead (1996, p. 12) states that 'each young child has a unique potential for development of human capacities for communication and cooperation, for skill and feeling, for reason and imagination, for practicality and spirituality, for determination and compassion'. To illustrate how this insight is translated into reality in southern Africa, the material and social context of development, the societal goals of development and the media for development will be considered as follows.

(i) Societal goals of child development in a number of communities of the region remain to be essentially pro-social and group-based. Examples are respect, obedience, cooperation, hard work, helpfulness, hospitality, honesty, peace, responsibility and appropriate social decorum (Nxumalo, 1993; Zimba and Otaala, 1993, 1995). The main end point of child development for many adults in the region is teleological in nature (Frankena, 1973). This implies that the main goal of development is towards human solidarity and oneness, in which persons are other-oriented and feel unfulfilled without others (Chingota, 1998).

Using growing up in Malawi as an example, Chingota points out that this does not destroy people's individuality. People remain individuals, but in relation to others. Based on a seminal and comprehensive treatise of African philosophy, epistemology and cosmology, Mbiti (1990, p. 106) expresses this form of being as that in which people say to themselves: 'I am, because we are; and since we are, therefore I am'. When raising children, caregivers normally facilitate the movement towards this endpoint by providing interactional environments that are characterized by family warmth, love, encouragement, commitment, responsiveness, concern for the welfare of the children, undivided attention and social security (Bernard van Leer Foundation, 1994; Evans and Myers, 1994). Because they do not cost money, these attributes can be and are practised under conditions of adversity. For example, in speaking about a Ju/'hoan (one of the bushmen ethnic groups of Namibia) baby, Heckler (1992, p. 13) states that the baby seemed to be 'enveloped in a cocoon, a halo, of warmth and responsiveness. It would seem that a baby's first lesson is "cry and you shall be heard" – or perhaps even deeper and more basic, "be born and you shall be attended". For her needs seemed known and responded to, often before she voiced them herself.' Elaborating on this, Heckler points out that the child was welcomed into a partnership with a society and caregivers whose presence, attention and care focused on the child's needs.

(ii) Reciprocity plays a significant role as a medium of development. From an early age, children in southern Africa, as is the case in other parts of Africa, make contributions to the sustenance of their families while being cared for, and give their time and energy while being taught (Woodhead, 1996). They acquire functional intellectual capacities by observing adults work, participating in household and family duties, helping and cooperating with others. For these children the tasks of growing up, work and learning are interwoven and not separated. Through this, struggles for sustenance nurture the development of young minds. Widely applied in the region, the child-to-child approach, which focuses on children's participation in and contribution to health promotion, child stimulation and development, basic education and nutrition, takes advantage of this indigenous strategy of raising children (Aarons, Hawes and Gayton, 1979; Hawes, 1988; Otaala, 1998).

(iii) The unique media used to stimulate development in the region include those of traditional games, song and dance, stories, riddles, proverbs and rites of passage. It is important to note that development is promoted through purposeful and active face-to-face interaction among children and between adults and children (Reynolds, 1989; Zimba and Otaala, 1995). As can be noticed, the media demand that the process of development and its goals work in synchrony. This is that they are group-based and situated in local social settings. In this context, it would be absurd to expect a child to tell itself stories and teach itself traditional games. It would be plausible, therefore, to expect the outcomes of the dialogue and interactions among children and adults in the settings to include contextualized meanings of being and existence.

Divisions of childhood

In the mainstream psychology literature, divisions of childhood are usually conceptualized in the form of developmental stages. Popularized by developmental psychologists such as Jean Piaget and Lawrence Kohlberg, each stage is characterized by abilities, skills and capacities children are expected to acquire and exhibit once they reach and pass through it. In the 1950s, 1960s and 1970s many studies were undertaken in Africa to validate the universality of Western stage theories of development (Wober, 1975). Among other things, the main thrust of the studies was to demonstrate the manner in which African children acquired and expressed 'stage' concepts, abilities, skills and ways of understanding the world around them (Mwamwenda, 1995; Ohuche and Otaala, 1981; Reynolds, 1989). Notwithstanding the emic and etic debates that took place during this period, the starting point for the majority of the studies was the Western world view of development and its goals (Cole and Scribner, 1974, 1977; Nsamenang, 2000). The African philosophy of life, epistemology, forms of existence, lived experiences, world views and cultural practices did not essentially provoke the studies. The task for many researchers was to study the development of the African children through the lenses of Western psychological theories of development and methods (Evans, 1970). Currently, this way of studying African children is being reconsidered. The main justification for this is captured by Woodhead (1996, pp. 59–60) in the statement that follows. Citing Burman (1994) and supported by Dawes (1999) and Jenks (1996), Woodhead points out that:

conventional theories of child development are about culture as well as about children. The child depicted in Psychology textbooks is in two respects, a cultural invention. The process of child development being studied and the theorists' conceptual representation of that process are both strongly shaped by their shared context, in terms of family organisation, parental roles, expectations of childhood, economic base, political structures, gender/class differentiation, religious beliefs, life expectancies and the like. It is inappropriate to assume that a concept of development derived from one context can or should be the basis for defining good and poor quality in other contexts.

Recognizing this some theorists, researchers and practitioners in the southern African region now attempt to understand the situation and development of children by employing child-context interaction theories of development. These theories enable academics and workers in the area to 'understand how children's development is shaped by their material, social and cultural contexts' (Dawes and Donald, 2000, p. 3). Bronfenbrenner's (1979) ecological framework, Sameroff's (1991) transactional developmental theory and Aber et al.'s (1997) developmental epochs idea are examples of such theories. Although this shift represents an important step towards the authentic understanding of the context and process of child development in the region, an appreciation of the unique and indigenous explication of the process needs to be voiced. Consistent with the focus of this book, the importance of doing this is aptly expressed by Erny (1973, p. 23) who states that:

the newborn, full of potentialities of human nature, is entirely geared toward the future. In the present he is nothing but expectation, power in search of actualization. The culture he is entering without his choice, which will impose itself upon him as he progressively makes it his own, will make some of these possibilities reality, but it will suffocate others which will never emerge. This passage from nature to culture can be considered in two ways. If human nature has only a *biological foundation, common to men and superior monkeys,* culture appears as an efflorescence, a blossoming, the fruit of which exceeds the facilities of the grain. But if instead of being considered at this minimum, nature is looked at in terms of the specifically human, it will appear as all the potentialities of man whose culture is going to actualize only an insignificant number. Then the passage from power to action represents a kind of limitation, *a necessary narrowing.* (Emphasis added)

The point being made here is that there is diversity in the process of *narrowing.* From the southern African perspective, the peculiar aspects of this diversity in the divisions of childhood development require some elucidation. This will be done by providing a brief narrative of the philosophy of life that southern Africans have employed for centuries and in varying degrees continue to employ when creating out of children fully fledged members of various communities. Based on contextualized principles of human development, this will be followed by an analysis of how the philosophy of life is translated into expressions of divisions of childhood and of being. To guard against the chapter turning into a reified and romanticized synthesis of child development principles and practices that have long been discarded and overtaken by processes of modernity, postmodernity and globalization, illustrations of the resilience of the region's indigenous practices of bringing up children will be presented.

Expressed in summary form, indigenous conceptions of *kinship, the family* and *the individual in society* provide us with some understanding of the African philosophy of life. According to Mbiti (1990), kinship could be described as a network stretching in every direction to embrace everyone in a given group. Constituted through blood relationships and marriage, kinship operates in such a way that 'each individual is a brother or sister, father or mother, grandmother or grandfather, or cousin, or brother-in-law, uncle or aunt, or something else, to everybody else. This means that everybody is related to everybody else' (Mbiti, 1990, p. 102). An important feature of kinship is that it includes the departed and the unborn. In this way kinship acts as a communal bond that is based on genealogical *blood relatedness and connectedness* of both sentient and non-sentient beings. With this understanding, a number of African children are born into corporate envelopes of related and linked persons, ancestral spirits and the unborn. Examples of how this functions in southern Africa are provided by communities residing in Malawi (Chakanza, 1998; Chingota, 1998), Swaziland (M'Passou, 1998), Lesotho (Bernard van Leer Foundation, 1994, p. 20), the Eastern Cape (Reynolds, 1989) and Kwa Zulu-Natal of South Africa (Higson-Smith and Killian, 2000).

The indigenous concept of the African family includes parents, children, grandparents, uncles, aunts, brothers and sisters who might have their own children and other immediate relatives. Such a family may be made up of 10 to 100 members who have obligations to one another. In addition to sentient members, departed relatives and the unborn (Mbiti, 1990, pp. 104–5) are included in the family. Whereas the unborn are held to be buds of hope and expectation, the departed, whom Mbiti calls the 'living-dead', actively get involved in the affairs of the families they were sentient members of by overseeing matters pertaining to family fortune, misfortune, care and well-being.

The Zulu of South Africa succinctly express the indigenous view of the individual by noting that *umuntu umuntu ngabantu*, literally meaning that 'a person is only a person with other people'. In other words, 'it is only within a community that a person can be said to truly become a person. Through a person's contributing to the community, the community in turn adds human qualities to that person' (Higson-Smith and Killian, 2000, p. 206).

Although what has been presented is a mere glimpse of the indigenous African philosophy of life, it sufficiently represents a unique world view. One key concept of being in this world view is what Mbiti (1990, p. 103) has called the 'timeless rhythm of human life'. In this view, existence follows a circular pattern through life stages that include death (Erny, 1973). Death does not signify the end of life, but it is a transition to another level of being.

To reflect the indigenous African philosophy of life, divisions of childhood are built on the understanding that in their development, children are moulded and transformed into viable members of particular communities by passing through periods of the unbroken circle of existence. As they do this, children gradually enter into and assume particular forms of personhood, identity and being. Broadly put, the periods are those of conception (encompassing the idea of the unborn as members of families), birth, babyhood, childhood, puberty, adulthood, marriage and death (as embodied in the concept of the living dead) (Chingota, 1998). Although Gelfand (1979) has mapped a developmental pathway similar to the process being presented here on the Shona children's chronological age, the transition from period to period is, in a number of southern African communities, based on maturation and evolvement. Children's capacities for adequate participation in the life of their communities evolve as they interact with and are directly guided by adult members of these communities.

In the region, rituals, rites of passage and initiation ceremonies have indigenously been and, in a number of communities, still are being used to mark and facilitate transition from period to period (Chakanza, 1998; Chingota, 1998; Cruz e Silva and Loforte, 1998; Mbiti, 1991; M'Passou, 1998; Nxumalo, 1993; Phiri, 1998; Reynolds, 1989). In Swaziland, for instance, there are rituals and rites pertaining to the burial of the umbilical cord, the introduction of the baby to the world, the protection of the child from thunder, the initiation of the child into Swazi nationality, puberty initiation, boys' regiments, girls' age cohorts, marriage, funerals and burials (M'Passou, 1998). In addition to the media for development that were provided earlier in the chapter, communities use rites of passage and other means to facilitate children's development through hands-on participation/activity, formal and informal direct teaching, encouragement, demonstration, observation, exposition, reflection and mentoring (Mbiti, 1991; Ocitti, 1973; Phiri, 1998). An example of how this was and is done is provided through an analysis of the *chinamwali* rites of passage and initiation ceremonies as practised by the Chewa, Nyanja, Yao and Lomwe of Malawi.

The *chinamwali* rites of passage are sex-specific. Girls go through their own rites of passage and so do boys. Among the Nyanja and the Yao, two main rites of passage for girls are undertaken. The first one, *chiputu*, is for pre-puberty girls aged 7 to 11 years. During this occasion, girls go into seclusion for up to two weeks to be instructed on the physiological changes that will take place in their bodies, such as menstruation and how to live with it, proper behaviour and decency in dress (Chakanza, 1998). The second *chinamwali* rite of passage is for girls who have experienced their first menstruation flow and for young women. Phiri (1998), has discussed four initiation ceremonies of this rite. In their traditional form, the ceremonies are organized and run by *anankungwi* (special female teachers who are well versed in the norms, morals, beliefs and customs of their societies) and *aphungu* (special female guardians).

Called *chinamwali cha nkangali* by the Chewa, the first initiation ceremony marks the end of childhood and the beginning of womanhood. A *phungu* and a *nankungwi* in this ceremony first instruct an individual girl about the taboos associated with menstruation and about basic hygiene. The girl is also advised by the guardian and the teacher to accept her entry into the status of womanhood and renounce the status of childhood. After obtaining permission from the chief, a senior *nankungwi* sets aside a time when all girls who have recently reached puberty are separated from their society and taken into seclusion away from the village for up to one month. Instruction during the period of seclusion is on moral, customary and sex education. The curriculum includes respect for elders, good manners, decency, cleanliness, proper sexual behaviour and human fertility. In the past, to mark the end of the puberty initiation ceremony, sexual rites were performed between some men called *fisi* and the initiates. Going through the ceremony was, and in a number of cases still is, very important among the Chewa, because without it a girl would not be able to attain the full status of adult womanhood. To emphasize this, the movement from seclusion and the re-entry into the community is marked by festive celebrations.

The second initiation ceremony is performed when a girl who has gone through the puberty initiation ceremony is betrothed and all marriage arrangements have been made. During this ceremony, the girl is instructed by *anankungwi* about how, according to the Chewa custom, to conduct herself in marriage and about how to perform the role of a wife.

In the third initiation ceremony, the newlyweds, as a couple, receive instruction from *anankungwi* on the obligations, duties, privileges and rights of married people. The manner in which a Chewa husband and a Chewa wife should relate to each other is emphasized during the ceremony.

Chinamwali cha chisamba represents the fourth initiation ceremony. This ceremony follows the occurrence of the first pregnancy. The *anankungwi* at this point instruct their 'students' on taboos to be observed, how they should relate to each other during the pregnancy, and how they should care for the child during and after its birth. The knowledge of particular rituals to be observed during this process are emphasized and imparted.

Similar rites of passage are conducted for boys who attain physiological puberty. They are taken to an initiation camp where they reside for up to three weeks and receive instruction from male *anankungwi* about appropriate interaction among people and proper sexual behaviour. On the first day of their stay at the camp, the boys are circumcised. The transition from childhood to manhood is completed when they take a ritual bath after the circumcision wounds have healed. At the end of the three weeks a coming-out ceremony is celebrated with pomp and dignity (Chakanza, 1998).

As a product of culture, cultural practices are dynamic and open to internal and external pressures for change. The rites of passage have not been spared from this as they have been subjected to religious and health pressures. For instance, Christian missionaries have for more than a century attempted to eradicate the *chinamwali* rites of passage in Malawi (Chakanza, 1998; Chingota, 1998; Phiri, 1998). In their pure traditional form some aspects of these rites have been deemed incompatible with Christian beliefs. Sexual rituals between *fisi* and girls to mark the end of the puberty initiation ceremony, for instance, have been judged sinful. Attempts to completely get rid of the rites of passage on religious grounds have failed. Over the years, churches in Malawi have instead accommodated the rites by transforming them in various ways. For instance, the *chinamwali* initiation ceremonies were transformed into *chilangizo*. In general, this relates to the Christian version of the education and guidance that the youth used to receive from *chinamwali* initiation ceremonies. Instead of the *anankungwi* as teachers, *alangizi* (those that guide and instruct) are now engaged (Phiri, 1998). Chingota (1998) has provided a historical progression of the transformation of the *chinamwali* rites of passage into *chilangizo* and the training of *alangizi*. During the period 1876–1994 the traditional rites seemed to be transformed into *miyambo* (generally meaning moral values), *maleredwe* (implying child rearing practices according to Christian principles) and finally into *chilangizo*. Chingota reports that since the late 1940s, there have been two forms of initiation rites, one Christian and the other non-Christian.

Parental responses to the Christian churches' requirements are insightful. Some parents obey them; others send their children to both the Christian and non-Christian initiation rites. The third group of parents chooses to stop being Christians and send their children to the traditional initiation rites (Chakanza, 1998; Phiri, 1998). The responses of the second and third groups of parents provide an important explanation of the resilience of cultural practices such as initiation rites. Because they confer cultural and ethnic identity on the neo-phytes, total eradication of the rites would be tantamount to subverting a people's beliefs, customs, values, world view and philosophy of life.

The health pressures on the Malawian type of initiation rites pertain to the HIV/AIDS risks of infection that girls may be exposed to if HIV-positive men are allowed to participate in sexual rituals with them at the end of the puberty initiation ceremonies (O'Kane, 2000). This threat is real and needs to be met with vigorous modification of the initiation rites so that female neophytes are protected against infection. This would be met with minimum resistance from communities as teaching HIV/AIDS awareness, prevention and sex education in the absence of sexual rituals between the girls and the *fisi* would not dilute the purpose of the rites of passage.

Social realities and development context

In the previous section we have seen how indigenous conceptions of childhood and development, embedded in a general philosophy of life, set the stage for the development of children in many ways. We have pointed out how political and social circumstances influence and interact with existing ideas and practices. In this section two aspects will be further elaborated. These are children's rights and the difficult circumstances in which many children in the region grow up and develop.

Conceptions of childhood and children's rights

Cognizant of the African philosophy of life and world view that were summarized in the preceding section, the African Charter on the Rights and Welfare of the Child recognizes the role of culture in conceptions of childhood and development in two main ways. Firstly, in articles 1 and 21, the charter urges African nations to discourage and eliminate 'harmful social and cultural practices affecting the welfare, dignity, normal growth and development of the child and in particular... those customs and practices discriminatory to the child on the grounds of sex or other status' (Naldi, 1992, p. 191). Secondly, in upholding the integrity of the African conceptions of being, the charter in articles 5, 11 and 31 mandates African nations to ensure the survival, protection and development of the child, the preservation and strengthening of positive African morals, traditional values and conventions, and to raise every child in such a way that he or she has responsibilities towards his or her family and society.

The southern African indigenous perspective on children's rights can be illustrated by looking at how children's best interests are conceptualized and catered for in child-custody cases and in the functioning of the bridewealth (bride price) practice. According to Armstrong (1994), Banda (1994) and Rwezaura (1994), southern African children's best interests are mainly in the form of basic needs for survival and social needs. The basic needs are those of food, water, shelter, medical care and clothing. The contemporary social needs are embodied in the children's rights to education. Based on the concepts of kinship and family that were presented earlier, Armstrong states that children's best interests are not individualized but group based. In Zimbabwe, for example, the Shona customary law requires that children's best interests be congruent with those of the extended family. This being the case, the obligation to ensure that children's best interests are respected does not rest on biological parents alone. It implicates the entire extended family. As a result, the custody of children in times of peace and in times of dispute is ultimately the responsibility of the extended family. In times of peace, parents who may not have the material resources to cater for their child's basic and educational needs may ask a relative with more adequate resources to look after the child. In return the child is expected to perform chores for his or her custodians. A similar situation occurs when urban parents are unable to afford the high cost of accommodation, school fees and childcare facilities. When this happens, a number of them send their children to their relatives in rural areas where the children's best interests are expected to be met at a lower cost.

When parents are in dispute, customary law in most southern African communities dictates that child-custody cases be settled according to either paternal or maternal cultural rights (Armstrong, 1994; Rwezaura, 1994). Under paternal cultural rights as practised by the Shona of Zimbabwe (Armstrong, 1994), it is in the best interests of the child to be associated with his or her paternal family in which familial rather than individual rights are emphasized. Members of the paternal family view and treat the child as 'our child'. Consequently, custody of the child is not given to a single father but to the paternal family. A Shona mother married under customary law, with all *lobola* (bridewealth) obligations met, would understand this from the perspective that the father of her children has paternal rights over the children and give up custody of them.

According to Armstrong (1994), the world view employed in custody cases of this nature is based on spiritual and ritual dimensions. Akin to the 'living-dead' idea, the Shona *cizwarwa* (family groups) entrust matters pertaining to health, marriage and death in the hands of *tateguru* (father's father) ancestral spirits. The *cizwarwa* performs rituals to ensure that *all* members are assisted by the *tateguru*. For the rituals to be effective, *all* members of the paternal family must be present at the *bira* (ritual gathering). By implication, it is in the best interests of the paternal family and its well-being to have custody of all children in order to effectively fulfil its ritual functions. It is also to the best interests of the children because it is their fathers and not their mothers who act as media between their families and the ancestral spirits.

When people are married under common law and its documented statuses, child-custody cases are handled in such a way that the child's best interests become individualized and spouses are placed on an equal footing. However, people's world views remain important for many in the region who take their child-custody cases to community local courts, where customary law (or the living law) and how children are perceived in this law inform their judgements. These judgements are further informed by the practice of the bridewealth.

The bridewealth validates the marriage and effects the transfer of 'the bride's procreative capacity from her family to that of her husband' (Rwezaura, 1994, p. 86). This entitles the husband and his family to claim custody of all the children the wife bears. At the time of separation, this entitlement is claimed as a right by the husband. The productive rights are, however, not transferred from the wife to the husband when the bridewealth has not been paid or when it has not been paid in full. In this instance, the wife and her family would legally claim custody of the children. The husband can reclaim his paternal rights over the children at a latter date by paying the bridewealth in full. In fact the Ndebele, the Swazi and the Manica only pay the full bridewealth when a marriage produces children.

As can be noticed from the preceding paragraph, the process of meeting the children's best interests is linked to the operation of a cultural practice – the transfer of bridewealth from the father's to the mother's family. Once again, this shows that the meeting of the children's best interests is not handled at the individual level but at a corporate family level. Understanding all this at the level of societal conventions produces the insight that children's best interests are conceptualized and catered for in a local and contextualized manner by a number of communities in the southern African region (Dawes, 1999). Attempts to universalize contexts and the senses in which children's best interests are understood and catered for in the region miss this insight (Burman, 1996; Dawes and Cairns, 1998). The wisdom of paying attention to this insight and the influence it has on conceptions of childhood in the region is further clarified in the next subsection of the chapter.

Childhood and youth development in difficult circumstances

In 1990 it was estimated that about 15 per cent of the world's children were living in particularly difficult circumstances. Of these 100 million were working children, 50 million were street children, more than 100 million were abused children and more than 20 million were refugee or displaced children, a number of whom had been physically or psychologically traumatized by armed conflict and natural disasters (Velis, 1995). Because several instances of these circumstances have prevailed for decades and continue to prevail, a number of the children residing in the region form part of the global statistics which, in all probability, have now escalated (Higson-Smith and Killian, 2000; Mufune, 2000; Reynolds, 1996; Wessells and Monteiro, 2000).

For instance, because of migration from rural to urban areas, the structure of the southern African family has changed. Consequently, a number of young men and women of childbearing age migrate to the cities and have children there, far away from the traditional support of extended families and relatives. In some cases the extended family support base is abused by some young people who migrate to urban areas. A number of them leave their children in rural areas in the care of their ageing parents, grandparents, elder siblings and other relatives. In the context of poverty and exhaustion, the majority of such parents are unable to provide the children with adequate care (Zimba, 2000). Moreover, large numbers of men move to urban areas to seek employment. By so doing, they leave their wives in rural areas as single-parent heads of households who are forced to cope with multiple responsibilities of livelihood and childcare (Colletta, Balachander and Liang, 1996; Zimba and Otaala, 1993). Health and nutritional problems ensue from this state of affairs and as a result a number of children die before their fifth birthday.

In addition, the southern African region's adverse living conditions emanate from effects of natural disasters (e.g. the floods that Mozambique, South Africa, Zimbabwe and Zambia had to contend with recently) and diseases such as the HIV/AIDS pandemic, TB and malaria. These conditions disempower and severely erode communities' and families' capacity to optimally raise children. Moreover, liberation wars in Angola, Mozambique, Namibia, South Africa and Zimbabwe dislocated and displaced entire families and in some cases large sections of populations for decades. A number of these families fled from their countries and sought refuge elsewhere in the world. In the region, this exodus overstretched resources in Botswana, Lesotho, Swaziland and Zambia. Long-running civil wars in Angola and Mozambique exacerbated the situation by putting more strain on the region's human and material resources as displaced families from these countries continued to flee and seek refuge in neighbouring countries. Currently, large numbers of refugees fleeing from the Angolan civil war reside in Namibia and Zambia. Political, domestic and community violence, pandemic crime, hunger and starvation and widespread unemployment further disturb the stability of families and communities in many parts of the region (Bernard van Leer Foundation, 1994; Dawes and Donald, 2000; Higson-Smith and Killian, 2000; Wessells and Monteiro, 2000). As a result of these adversities, large numbers of children in the region are raised in the context of depressed, squalid, inadequate amenities and in some cases non-existent social services.

Poverty, violence, crime and disease do not only undermine and place families, communities and civil institutions under siege, but also change the nature of childhood. For instance, in attempts to support their families and survive, a number of children in the region opt to leave school and work on the street (Mufune, 2000). Velis (1995, p. 46) reports that, owing to poverty and other difficult circumstances, the perception of the African child has changed and so has his situation. 'He was the supreme value of the traditional society. Now, for a large number of families, he has become a stepping-stone to survival. They send him out to work, they "place" him (i.e. place him with other extended family members). They exploit him. Once, he was the "child-king", now he is the "child-servant".' When this is viewed in the context of what was presented earlier in the chapter, these sentiments could be an over-exaggeration. The child in poverty-stricken circumstances could be forced to engage in productive work that may go beyond the indigenous requirements of development and education through work and apprenticeship. However, he would be making his own contribution to his family's sustenance. Notwithstanding this, the element of abusing the indigenous family system by exploiting and using children as pawns should be abhorred. For instance, Rwezaura (1994) has illustrated how maternal families could abuse the bridewealth practice to make money. They may demand from paternal families exorbitant bride-prices and childcare fees, hold children as pawns and require that the fathers only have custody of the children after paying all the charges in full. The children could also be exploited by relatives under whose care they may be placed by their poor parents.

Despite all this, adversity can stimulate development. In southern Africa it does this by motivating children to respond to their circumstances in a resourceful, creative, ingenious and versatile manner. For instance, because the majority of them have no access to manufactured toys, they improvise and make toys to play with out of scrap and other available materials (Reynolds, 1989; Zimba and Otaala, 1993, 1995; Mtonga, 1990).

It should be noted that although it has been placed under severe strain by poverty, violence and disease, the indigenous African family in the region has not completely broken down (Bernard van Leer Foundation, 1994; Velis, 1995). Together with the communities of which it is a part, it requires internal and external material and psychosocial support to heal and sustain its resilience (Higson-Smith and Killian, 2000; Wessells and Monteiro, 2000). This process should promote the development and nurturance of sources of resilience in children and other members of their families (Grotberg, 1995). To illustrate that this is plausible, Higson-Smith and Killian (2000) report positive outcomes of a programme that strengthened community sources of resilience to reduce violence and heal wounds of violence in the Kwa Zulu-Natal Province of South Africa.

Families and communities in the region need healing not only from adversities associated with poverty, violence, crime and disease, but also from the ravages of war. Children as integral members of the families and communities are particularly vulnerable and susceptible to trauma emanating from the wars. The children experientially suffer from war trauma as a result of being either participants, victims or observers. For these children childhood becomes a traumatic phase of their lives. Child combatants, for example, may experience chronic fear of retribution, intense feelings of guilt and anxiety and become suspicious of adults. They may also experience flashbacks in which traumatic events from the past come flooding back at unexpected moments to haunt them (Goodwin-Gill and Cohn, 1994). Consistent with this picture, Wessells and Monteiro (2000, p. 181) report that Angolan child combatants and child victims of war display acute psychological disturbances that include 'problems of flashbacks, nightmares and sleep disturbances, concentration problems, heightened alertness or hypervigilance, and avoidance of people and situations that evoke memories of the traumatic events'.

From the Western psychological point of view, the healing of the children's wounds of war would be approached from 'a cultural system saturated with individualistic, materialistic and mechanistic values and world views. Typically, trauma (in this perspective) is viewed as an individual phenomenon, and discourses and practices of healing are steeped in a medical model' (Wessells and Monteiro, 2000, p. 182). There are exceptions to this when entire nations are accused of being perpetrators of either genocide or holocaust. In such cases, the healing process in the West may assume group rather than individual dimensions. Otherwise, the healing process is characteristically individualistic. In African traditional healing, however, the children's wounds are in the majority of cases communal and spiritual (Friedson, 1996). Because of this, Wessells and Monteiro concluded that in Angola, the healing intervention was understood to be communal and spiritual. Wessells and Monteiro (2000, pp. 182–3) based this conclusion on Angolan cosmology that they articulated in the following way:

Particularly in rural areas in Angola, as in much of sub-Saharan Africa, spirituality and community are at the centre of life. The visible world of the living is regarded as an extension of the invisible world of the ancestors. These two worlds are fused into a continuous community of the spirits and those alive today. When a person dies, he or she continues life in the spirit world, which protects the living community. The visible and the spirit world interact continuously, as if the world were a spider's web and any touch of a single thread reverberates throughout the entire structure. It is the invisible world, however, that is most fundamental, and all major events are attributed to it. If the ancestors are not honoured, through the teaching of traditions and the practice of appropriate rituals, their spirits cause problems manifesting in poor health, misfortune, social disruption and even war.

When viewed from this perspective, the child victims of war in Angola may be stressed more by the belief that they and their communities have, for some reason, offended their ancestors and by their inability to obey appropriate burial rituals that would have facilitated movement of their dead relatives' spirits from the visible to the invisible world. The actual objective experiences of war may produce less stress among these children. Because of this, their psychosocial healing should include the observance of appropriate rituals. This does not mean that the link between psychological trauma and these children's experience of war should be severed during the healing process. It means that their healing should benefit from both the indigenous Angolan cultural belief systems and the use of psychological knowledge whose interpretation and meaning have been reconstructed, adapted and situated in the Angolan cosmology where communal rather than individual healing is emphasized (Dawes and Cairns, 1998; Wessells and Monteiro, 2000).

As is the case in Angola and as was the case in Mozambique, the healing of children wounded in the war of liberation in Zimbabwe was, from the indigenous point of view, communal and spiritual. This was so because the war trauma experienced by children was perceived by many Zimbabweans and their *n'anga* (traditional healers) to have been caused by discord in relations between *ngozi* (the aggrieved spirits of innocent victims of war) and the living (Reynolds, 1996). It was believed that the *ngozi,* seeking compensation for their undeserved deaths, attacked the children and caused the symptoms of psychological trauma that they displayed.

The indigenous healing process for the *ngozi* attack on children involved taking the children to a *n'anga* and having him or her diagnose the specific spiritual cause of their trauma, apportion blame for the trauma, ask the children's parents or other family members to appease the *ngozi* by paying compensation and having the children go through a ritual cleansing. Protective medicines were also given to the children to ensure that the *ngozi* did not continue to haunt them. Moreover, the *n'anga* continued to work with the children until their trauma symptoms were averted (Reynolds, 1996).

Contributions of southern African conceptions of childhood to global developmental science

In my view, this chapter contains insights that should be noted afresh by developmental psychologists. Some of these insights are the following:

(i) Human communities employ cosmological ideas and philosophies of life when constructing and evolving cultural identities of who they are and who they wish to become. This process is mirrored in the manner in which they bring up their young. Because it takes place in different biophysical and social environments, this process does not assume a uniform nature across the globe. In southern Africa, as has been illustrated above, a number of communities base the raising of their children on the endpoint of development that is in the form of human solidarity and oneness. Corporate existence in envelopes of related, interdependent and linked persons and ancestral spirits is emphasized. In the envelopes, people become people with others and not as individual entities. With this in mind, development is conceived as a corporate activity in which children pass through periods of what was termed earlier in the chapter as the unbroken circle of existence. As they do this, they enter into and assume particular forms of personhood, identity and being. Although not impervious to internal and external pressures for change and adaptation, this manner of becoming human has, at the core, been shown to withstand sustained subversive onslaught and to remain resolutely resilient. The main reason for this is that a number of individuals, families and communities in the region have resisted the temptation to be alienated from who they believe they are and who they would like to become. This does not necessarily mean that they wish to be cut off from the rest of the world. It means that they wish to coexist with others knowing who they are and what they could contribute to the world if they were allowed to (Azuma, 2000).

(ii) The chapter contains material that demonstrates the wisdom of taking into account unique perceptions of boundaries of childhood, local and contextualized cultural beliefs and practices regarding children's best interests and how these should be catered for, as well as the indigenous trauma-healing processes that are communal and spiritual in nature. The principle to be underlined here is that conceptions of childhood and child development practices emanate from world views and lived experiences of communities; they do not necessarily come from theories of child development (Dawes, 1999). This chapter has attempted to show how this plays out in practice in a number of communities in southern Africa. An important implication of this to note is that any intervention aimed at understanding and stimulating children's development through research, averting their adversity and enhancing their well-being should take into account the region's cosmological and epistemological realities. A feature of the realities worth noting is the immersion of the developing children into communities of *linked*, *'bonded'*, *related* and *interdependent* persons whose existence is understood and expressed in a corporate way. Tearing children away from this world view in order to understand their development at the individual level is inappropriate.

(iii) Because a large number of children in the region are raised and develop under conditions of adversity, the development and enhancement of community sources of resilience becomes crucial. An important point that has been noted above is that a number of communities already have coping strategies that are embodied in traditional child rearing practices and the operation of the kinship and extended family systems. The only problem is that these systems have been severely weakened by internal and external adversity. Because they are linked to indigenous conceptions of childhood and communities' ways of being, these systems need strengthening. This may require additional external psychological resources. It has been emphasized here that when needed these resources should be modified, reconstructed and couched in a manner and language that draws meaning from local conceptual frameworks and belief systems (Blackburn, 1994; Samson, 2000; Serpell, 1997, 1998).

(iv) Reciprocity as a medium of development was given prominence in the chapter. When applied, the principle entails that children in a number of southern African communities that were earlier used as examples make contributions to the sustenance of their families while they develop and are being cared for. In this practice growing up, work and learning are interwoven in a social network where children are enabled actively to participate in their own development and draw upon the fund of their families' and their communities' knowledge, skills and ways of understanding the social, physical and metaphysical worlds. Through direct teaching, demonstration, observation, exposition, reflection and mentoring, families and communities, in a pastoral and corporate way, stimulate and promote children's development. An important outcome of this process is normally the development, in children, of a sense of community and a spirit of interdependence (Keller and Greenfield, 2000). The insight to note here is that southern Africa may have an important contribution to make in a world where the absence of such a sense of community and interdependence among people produces anomie, loneliness and torturous distress.

Concluding remarks

The purpose of this chapter was, among other things, to illustrate how indigenous and cultural conceptions of childhood inform the process of child development in some communities of southern Africa and to reflect on the possible contribution of the region's conceptions of childhood to global developmental science. The most important messages have been sufficiently captured in the last section. The only point I wish to highlight here is the region's socialcultural idea of envelopes of child development. Indigenously, these envelopes were intended to provide developmental contexts in which children's needs for security, safety, love, warmth, empathy and trust were catered for. Moreover, children in these envelopes were, in line with indigenous African world views, accorded the opportunity to become responsible and accountable. Because most communities in the region have been attended by adversity, these envelopes of development have been weakened. One important task for the future, therefore, would be that of mustering research and other resources to support and strengthen the communities' vanguard for resilient response to adversity.

REFERENCES

Aarons, A., Hawes, H. and Gayton, J. (1979). *Child-to-child.* London: Macmillan Education.

Aber, J. L., Gephart, M. A., Brooks-Gunn, J. and Connell, J. P. (1997). Development in context: implications for studying neighborhood effects. In J. Brooks-Gunn, G. J. Duncan and J. L. Aber (eds.), *Neighborhood Policy*, vol. 1: *Context and consequences for children.* New York: Russell Sage Foundation, pp. 44–61.

Archard, D. (1993). *Children: rights and childhood.* New York: Routledge.

Armstrong, A. (1994). School and Sadza: custody and the best interests of the child in Zimbabwe. In P. Alston (ed.), *The best interests of the child: reconciling culture and human rights.* Oxford: Oxford University Press, pp. 150–90.

Azuma, H. (2000). Commentary: indigenous to what? *International Society for the Study of Behavioral Development Newsletter*, 1, 9–10.

Banda, F. (1994). Custody and the best interests of the child: another view from Zimbabwe. In P. Alston (ed.), *The best interests of the child: reconciling culture and human rights.* Oxford: Oxford University Press, pp. 191–201.

Baumrind, D. (1998). From ought to is: a neo-Marxist perspective on the use and misuse of the culture construct. *Human Development*, 41, 145–65.

Bernard van Leer Foundation (1994). *Building on people's strengths: early childhood in Africa.* The Hague: Bernard van Leer Foundation.

Berry, J. W. (1976). *Human ecology and cognitive style: comparative studies in cultural and psychological adaptation.* New York: Sage/Halsted.

Berry, J. W., Poortinga, Y. H., Segall, M. H. and Dasen, P. R. (1992). *Cross-cultural psychology: research and applications.* Cambridge: Cambridge University Press.

Blackburn, C. A. (1994). Resilient children and families. *Coordinators' Notebook*, 15, 16–21.

Brazelton, T. B., Koslowski, B. and Tronick, E. (1976). Neonatal behavior among urban Zambians and Americans. *Journal of American Academy of Child Psychiatry*, 1, 97–107.

Brislin, R. W. (1990). Applied cross-cultural psychology: an introduction. In R. W. Brislin (ed.), *Applied cross-cultural psychology.* Newbury Park, CA: Sage, pp. 9–33.

Bronfenbrenner, U. (1979). *The ecology of human development: experiments by nature and design.* Cambridge, MA: Harvard University Press.

Burman, E. (1994). *Deconstructing developmental psychology.* London: Routledge and Kegan-Paul.

  (1996). Local, global or globalized? Child development and international child rights legislation. *Childhood*, 3, 45–66.

Chakanza, J. C. (1998). Unfinished agenda: puberty rites and the response of the Roman Catholic Church in southern Malawi, 1901–1994. In J. L. Cox (ed.), *Rites of passage in contemporary Africa: interaction between Christian and African traditional religions.* Cardiff: Cardiff Academic Press, pp. 157–67.

Chingota, F. (1998). A historical account of the attitude of Blantyre Synod of the Church of Central Africa Presbyterian towards initiation rites. In J. L. Cox (ed.), *Rites of passage in contemporary Africa: interaction between Christian and African traditional religions*. Cardiff: Cardiff Academic Press, pp. 146–55.

Chiswanda, M. V. (1998). *Hearing mothers and their deaf children in Zimbabwe: mediated learning experiences*. Paper presented at the International Society for the Study of Behavioral Development conference, Windhoek, Namibia, 20–24 July 1998.

Cole, M. and Scribner, S. (1974). *Culture and thought: a psychological introduction*. New York: John Wiley.

(1977). Developmental theories applied to cross-cultural cognitive research. *Annals of the New York Academy of Sciences*, 285, 366–73.

Colletta, N. J., Balachander, J. and Liang, X. (1996). *The condition of young children in sub-Saharan Africa: the convergence of health, nutrition, and early education*. Washington, DC: World Bank.

Cruz e Silva, T. and Loforte, A. (1998). Christianity, African traditional religions and cultural identity in southern Mozambique. In J. L. Cox (ed.), *Rites of passage in contemporary Africa: interaction between Christian and African traditional religions*. Cardiff: Cardiff Academic Press, pp. 35–45.

Davidson, G. (1994). Applying psychology across cultures: an introduction. In G. Davidson (ed.), *Applying psychology: lessons from Asia-Oceania*. Carlton, Australia: Australian Psychological Society, pp. 1–7.

Dawes, A. (1999). Images of childhood in cultural perspective: challenges to theory and practice. Paper presented at the International Interdisciplinary course on children's rights at the Children's Rights Center, University of Gent, Belgium, December, 1999.

Dawes, A. and Cairns, E. (1998). The Machel Study: dilemmas of cultural sensitivity and universal rights of children. *Peace and Conflict*, 4(4), 335–48.

Dawes, A. and Donald, D. (2000). Improving children's chances: developmental theory and effective interventions in community contexts. In D. Donald, A. Dawes and J. Louw (eds.), *Addressing childhood adversity*. Cape Town: David Philip, pp. 1–25.

Eckensberger, L. H. and Zimba, R. F. (1997). The development of moral judgement. In J. W. Berry, P. R. Dasen and T. S. Saraswathi (eds.), *Handbook of cross-cultural psychology*, vol. 2: *Basic processes and human development*. Needham Heights: Allyn and Bacon, pp. 299–338.

Erny, P. (1973). *Childhood and cosmos: the social psychology of the black African child*. New York: New Perspectives.

Evans, J. L. (1970). *Children in Africa: a review of psychological research*. New York: Teachers College Press.

(1994). *Child rearing practices and beliefs in sub-Saharan Africa*. Report of a workshop held in Windhoek, Namibia.

Evans, J. L. and Myers, R. G. (1994). Child rearing practices: Creating programmes where traditions and modern practices meet. *Coordinators' notebook*, 15, 1–15.

Frankena, W. K. (1973). *Ethics*, 2nd edn. Englewood Cliffs, NJ: Prentice-Hall.

Friedson, S. M. (1996). *Dancing prophets: musical experience in Tumbuka healing*. Chicago: University of Chicago Press.

Gelfand, G. (1979). *Growing up in Shona society: from birth to marriage*. Harare: Mambo Press.

Gergen, K. J., Lock, A., Gulerce, A. and Misra, G. (1996). Psychological science in cultural context. *American Psychologist*, 51, 496–503.

Goodwin-Gill, G. S. and Cohn, I. (1994). *Child soldiers: the role of children in armed conflict.* Oxford: Oxford University Press.

Grotberg, E. (1995). *A guide to promoting resilience in children: strengthening the human spirit.* The Hague: Bernard van Leer Foundation.

Hawes, H. (1988). *Child-to-child: another path to learning.* Hamburg: UNESCO Institute for Education.

Heckler, M. (1992). 'Be born and you shall be attended'. An informal progress report on the education of Ju/'hoan children of Namibia presented to the Nyae Nyae Development Foundation. Cited in Bernard van Leer Foundation (1994), p. 13.

Higson-Smith, C. and Killian, C. (2000). Caring for children in fragmented communities. In D. Donald, A. Dawes and J. Louw (eds.), *Addressing childhood adversity.* Cape Town: David Philip, pp. 202–24.

Jenks, C. (1996). *Childhood.* London: Routledge.

Kagitcibasi, C. (1996a). The autonomous-relational self: a new synthesis. *European Psychologist*, 1, 180–6.

(1996b). *Family and human development across cultures: a view from the other side.* Mahwah, NJ: Lawrence Erlbaum.

(1997). Parent education and child development. In M. E. Young (ed.), *Early childhood development: investing in our children's future.* New York: Elsevier, pp. 243–72.

Keller, H. and Greenfield, P. M. (2000). History and future of development in cross-cultural psychology. *Journal of Cross-cultural Psychology*, 31(1), 52–62.

Kim, U. (1990). Indigenous psychology: science and applications. In R. W. Brislin (ed.), *Applied cross-cultural psychology.* Newbury Park, CA: Sage, pp. 142–60.

(1994). Individualism and collectivism: conceptual clarification and elaboration. In U. Kim, H. C. Triandis, C. Kagitcibasi, S. C. Choi and G. Yoon (eds.), *Individualism and collectivism: theory, method and applications.* Thousand Oaks, CA: Sage, pp. 19–40.

Kim, U., Park, Y. S. and Park, D. (2000). The challenge of cross-cultural psychology: the role of the indigenous psychologies. *Journal of Cross-cultural Psychology*, 31(1), 63–75.

Kuper, H. (1947). *An African aristocracy: rank among the Swazi.* London: Oxford University Press.

LeVine, R. A., Dixon, S., LeVine, S., Richman, A., Leiderman, P. H., Keefer, C. H. and Brazelton, T. B. (1994). *Child care and culture: lessons from Africa.* Cambridge: Cambridge University Press.

Malan, J. S. (1985). *Swazi culture.* Pretoria: Africa Institute of South Africa.

Mbiti, J. S. (1990). *African religions and philosophy*, 2nd edn. Oxford: Heinemann Educational.

(1991). *Introduction to African religion*, 2nd edn. Oxford: Heinemann Educational.

M'Passou, D. (1998). The continuing tension between Christianity and rites of passage in Swaziland. In J. L. Cox (ed.), *Rites of passage in contemporary Africa: interaction between Christian and African traditional religions.* Cardiff: Cardiff Academic Press, pp. 15–33.

Mtonga, M. (1989). In discussions with the author.

(1990). *Children's games and plays in Zambia*. Unpublished Ph.D. thesis, Queen's University, Belfast.

Mufune, P. (2000). Street youth in southern Africa. *International Social Science Journal*, 164, 233–43.

Mwamwenda, T. S. (1995). *Educational psychology: an African perspective*, 2nd edn. Durban: Butterworth.

Myers, R. (1995). *The twelve who survive: strengthening programmes of early childhood development in the Third World*, 2nd edn. Ypsilanti, MI: High/Scope Press.

Naldi, G. J. (1992) (ed.). *Documents of the Organization of African Unity*. London: Mansell.

Nsamenang, A. B. (1992). *Human development in cultural context: a Third World perspective*. Newbury Park, CA: Sage.

(2000). Issues in indigenous approaches to developmental research in sub-Saharan Africa. *International Society for the Study of Behavioral Development Newsletter*, 1, 1–4.

Nsamenang, A. B. and Dawes, A. (1998). Developmental psychology as political psychology in sub-Saharan Africa: the challenge of Africanisation. *Applied Psychology*, 47(1), 73–87.

Nxumalo, A. M. (1993). Indigenous education among the Swazi. *Swaziland Institute for Educational Research*, 13, 101–09.

Ocitti, J. P. (1973). *African indigenous education as practiced by the Acholi of Uganda*. Nairobi, Kampala and Dar es Salaam: East African Literature Bureau.

Ohuche, R. O. and Otaala, B. (1981) (eds.). *The African child and his environment*. Oxford: Pergamon Press.

O'Kane, M. (2000). Malawi: the land of the dying. *Mail and Guardian*, 16(28), 14–20 July 2000, 36.

Otaala, B. (1998). Health through the school, part two: Proceedings of a writers' workshop and consolidated recommendations.

Phiri, I. A. (1998). The initiation of *Chewa* women of Malawi: a Presbyterian woman's perspective. In J. L. Cox (ed.), *Rites of passage in contemporary Africa: interaction between Christian and African traditional religions*. Cardiff: Cardiff Academic Press, pp. 129–56.

Reynolds, P. (1989). *Childhood in crossroads: cognition and society in South Africa*. Grand Rapids, MI: Wm. B. Eerdmans.

(1996). *Traditional healers and childhood in Zimbabwe*. Athens, OH: Ohio University Press.

Rwezaura, B. (1994). The concept of the child's best interests in the changing economic and social context of sub-Saharan Africa. In P. Alston (ed.), *The best interests of the child: reconciling culture and human rights*. Oxford: Oxford University Press, pp. 82–116.

Sameroff, A. J. (1991). The social context of development. In M. Woodhead, P. Light and R. Carr (eds.), *Becoming a person*. London: Routledge/The Open University Press, pp. 167–89.

Samson, A. (2000). Commentary: an Australian perspective on indigenous psychology. *International Society for the Study of Behavioral Development Newsletter*, 1, 12–13.

Saraswathi, T. S. (1998). Many deities, one God: towards convergence in cultural and cross-cultural psychology. *Culture and Psychology*, 4(2), 147–60.

Segall, M. H., Dasen, P. R., Berry, J. W. and Poortinga, Y. H. (1990). *Human behavior in global perspective: an introduction to cross-cultural psychology.* New York: Pergamon.

Serpell, R. (1976). *Culture's influence on behavior.* London: Methuen.

Afrocentrism: what contribution to the science of developmental Psychology? Paper presented at the Yaounde International Workshop on Child Development and National Development in Africa, Yaounde, Cameroon, 6–10 April 1992.

(1997). Social intervention and psychological theory (lessons from some recent studies in Zambia). *African Social Research*, 37/38, 40–60.

(1998). The impact of psychology on Third World development. *African Social Research*, 39/40, 1–18.

Shweder, R. A. (1991). *Thinking through cultures: expeditions in cultural psychology.* Cambridge, MA: Harvard University Press.

Sinha, D. (1997). Indigenizing psychology. In J. W. Berry, Y. H. Poortinga and J. Pandey (eds.), *Handbook of cross-cultural psychology*, vol. 1: *Theory and method*, 2nd edn. Needham Heights, MA: Allyn & Bacon, pp. 129–69.

(1998). Changing perspectives in social psychology in India: a journey towards indigenization. *Asian Journal of Social Psychology*, 1, 17–32.

Snarey, J. (1985). Cross-cultural universality of socio-moral development: a critical review of Kohlbergian research. *Psychological Bulletin*, 97, 202–32.

Super, C. M. and Harkness, S. (1997). The cultural structuring of child development. In J. W. Berry, P. R. Dasen and T. S. Saraswathi (eds.), *Handbook of cross-cultural Psychology*, vol. 2: *Basic Processes and Human Development*, 2nd edn. Needham Heights, MA: Allyn & Bacon, pp. 1–39.

Triandis, H. C. (1990). Theoretical concepts that are applicable to the analysis of ethnocentrism. In R. W. Brislin (ed.), *Applied cross-cultural psychology.* Newbury Park, CA: Sage, pp. 34–55.

Turtle, A. (1994). Implications for Asian psychology of the adoption of a stance of theoretic indigenization. In G. Davidson (ed.), *Applying psychology: lessons from Asia-Oceania.* Carlton, Australia: Australian Psychological Society, pp. 9–13.

Velis, J-P. (1995). *Blossoms in the dust: street children in Africa.* Paris: UNESCO.

Wessells, M. and Monteiro, C. (2000). Healing wounds of war in Angola: a community-based approach. In D. Donald, A. Dawes and J. Louw (eds.), *Addressing childhood adversity.* Cape Town: David Philip, pp. 176–201.

Wober, M. (1975). *Psychology in Africa.* London: International African Institute.

Woodhead, M. (1996). *In search of the rainbow: pathways to quality in large-scale programmes for young disadvantaged children.* The Hague: Bernard van Leer Foundation.

Zimba, R. F. (1987). A study on forms of social knowledge in Zambia. Unpublished doctoral dissertation, Purdue University, West Lafayette, IN.

(1994). The understanding of morality, convention and personal preference in an African setting. *Journal of Cross-cultural Psychology*, 25(3), 369–93.

(2000). Informal observations conducted by the author while collecting data for a research project on inclusive education support given to students with special needs in Basic Education schools of the Ondangwa West Educational Region of Namibia.

Zimba, R. F. and Otaala, B. (1993). Child care and development in Uukwaluudhi, north-
ern Namibia. In K. K. Prah (ed.), *Social science research priorities for Namibia.*
Eppindust: The University of Namibia and the Council for the Development of
Economic and Social Research in Africa, pp. 57–67.

(1995). *The family in transition: a study of child rearing practices and beliefs among
the Nama of the Karas and Hardap regions of Namibia.* Windhoek: UNICEF
Windhoek office and The University of Namibia.

Zimba, R. F., Otaala, B., Lester, L., Solomons, H., Ilonga, M., Abrishamian, N. and
Shipena, H. (1995). *Survey on child care and development in the Erongo region:
the case of Mondesa and Omatjete communities.* Windhoek: UNICEF/Bernard van
Leer Foundation.

6   The myth of lurking chaos

Ernst E. Boesch

Dedication

In a new publication the well-known sociobiologist Edward O. Wilson asserts that the moral commandments are not of transcendental origin, as many philosophers and theologians believe, but a result of the interaction of biology and culture (Wilson, 1998). Even theologians can hardly object to this because, as human genes also have to be God-given, unbelievers too would be subject to a genetically based morality. Unfortunately, however, even disregarding the problem of divine origin, such general formulations are not very enlightening. One should rather ask how culture and biology interact to bring about moral consciousness and action; a question that would need to be discussed by means of concrete examples. The following reflections, no matter how unusual they may appear, may contribute to this end, and it is thus appropriate to dedicate them to Lutz Eckensberger in appreciation of his creative work in matters that are of mutual interest to us.

Genesis and characteristics of myth

As a child I was told stories, fairy tales, in which man-eating wolves and giants appeared, witches caught disobedient children or bewitched them, where princes were changed into frogs, and other gruesome events occurred. Efforts to guard against or to avoid such harm pervaded all these fairy tales, and although usually successful, the anxious feeling remained that they could also have failed.

Later these fairy tales were replaced by histories, events of alleged historic truth, and on closer inspection, these were no more pleasing. There was torture, crucifixion, blinding, death by fire, walling-in and alive burials, and even if in these cases, for the glory of the fatherland, the good usually also won in the end (though less often than in fairy tales), the history of my country did not appear to be a series of triumphs but rather one of dangers – often survived only by a hair's breadth.

An extended version of this chapter appears in Boesch (2000) (in German).

116

Reality soon caught up with the stories, even if in its own way. There were the aggressive boys of the neighbourhood whom one could only outrun in breathless flight, paternal beatings that in contrast could not be avoided, even if one did not understand the reasons for them; then frightening family quarrels were followed by poverty and hardship brought about by the breakdown of the area's industry. And, as if that were not enough, a hubris began to stir in nearby Germany in the figure of a Führer whose brutal screaming speeches on the radio were both repulsive and frightening. Up to the day on which we, in uniform, said goodbye to friends with a 'Till we meet again – God willing'.

All these things and more, from the fairy tale to the Second World War, as different as they are, have one thing in common: the threat of chaos – at times even in reality – that allowed hostility to penetrate the apparently ordered and solid, thus revealing its fragility. It clearly showed that destructive forces were steadily at work, forces of an anti-order one could also all too easily succumb to, if not on one's guard.

This being on one's guard was often not easy. What was order, what anti-order? The beatings by my father, for instance; what were they? Harshly they destroyed a hitherto untroubled order and trust. Simultaneously, however, they imposed another kind of order – enforced not simply by coercion, but also by a feeling of affection, which somehow survived the punishment. Even the Nazis were different from the dragons, witches and demons of fairy tales, the pure spawn of chaos: they promised a new order, capable of convincing more than a few. To distinguish between order and anti-order was definitely not simple, and it was determined less on rational grounds than by secret wishes and anxieties, yes even aesthetic impressions – Hitler's way of speaking was so repulsive that anything he said would have been repulsive too.

A threat to order may be difficult to recognize, and its consequences unforeseeable. But the difficulty may also be due to deeper reasons. Let us return to the fairy tales, for example the story about Adam and Eve. Though the snake may well have represented anti-order, it was not threatening. It did not force Eve to eat the apple, but only persuaded her. Yet why did it succeed? Was it not because Eve was already so inclined? For this reason it was considered a sin. Here began the long story of sin – a dominant theme of Christian history and a concept which for the apostle Paul became a cornerstone of Christian belief.

Sin is inner chaos; it is anti-order emanating from ourselves, an anti-order we are born with, as not only the Bible proclaims. Thus young churchgoers are soon taught that they are 'poor sinners, incapable of good, inclined towards evil', and each forbidden stirring confirms it – stealing an apple, maltreating an animal, telling a lie, feeling sexual desire, jealousy, envy or dark Oedipal stirrings: In all such situations young people experience an inner anti-order, perhaps not very consciously, yet no less real.

That our inside hides forces of anti-order may even become physically manifest: there are pimples, rashes, fevers, diarrhoea and ulcers – not to mention the chaotic urges of sex, and they all divulge that even our bodies contain seeds of chaos, which it is essential to forestall and to prevent germinating. The chaotic lurks everywhere, we gradually notice, and even in ourselves we do not always succeed to separate what is welcome from what is bad. How, for instance, does one distinguish between righteous and unholy anger, between love and lust? Moral conflict becomes an inescapable companion of efforts to avoid chaos.

We all, in our own way, undergo such experiences. Not every childhood is overshadowed by war and crisis, by conflicts, illness or death. Still the threat to order, whether from the inside or the outside, is familiar to everyone. Though different, our actual experiences all have something in common: that things we are familiar with, which we rely on, are potentially threatened. We all experience such feelings from time to time. When, however, such a threat is thought to be ever present, as a fundamentally destructive force and not just as a single danger, then the ever-lurking calamity makes us constantly vigilant and circumspect and leads to the myth of lurking chaos.

A myth is not a theory, not a precise idea, but a kind of 'guiding pattern', a structural pre-formation, as I attempted to define it elsewhere (Boesch, 1991). Myth guides our perception, our interpretation and explanation in a specific direction, and it does so mainly unconsciously, unquestioned – it determines the self-evident, as it were, the 'thus-is-the-world' and 'thus-we-should-be'. One notices the closeness to Lévi-Strauss (e.g. 1973), for whom myth was not a concrete fable, but a fundamental structure of thought. 'Structure of thought', however, may be too restrictive, and so I rather tend to see in myth a kind of as yet unspecified 'mould' of receptivity and evaluation, from which then emerge only those stories which we usually call 'myths'. We may compare it to sympathy and antipathy, which are often purely spontaneous reactions, both emotional and structural, yet hardly substantiated rationally, but which can powerfully determine what we perceive about a person and how we interpret this.

Thus, at first still undetermined in content, this 'myth-mould' is filled in, concretized in different ways depending on the culture, engendering 'myth-stories' from general explanations of the world and of fate to the small things of everyday life. And so the different models and admonitions a child grows up with – to stay clean, not to swear, to do this but not that, to admire this but loathe that – are not only practically based; the accompanying references to the calamity which would otherwise occur often betray the mythical derivation. Thus, they warn a child in Thailand that 'those who insult their parents, will be a *preta* in their next life' (a tree-high spirit, with a mouth the size of a needle's eye, suffering tormenting hunger, not able to speak, but only to wail); Catholic doctrine teaches that 'people who lie will end up in purgatory' – such and similar sayings exemplify myth-derived popular wisdoms. And to protect a child from such dire consequences, serious punishments may be considered justified.

Perhaps this is the point at which to indicate an effect of growing up in the sphere of myth. Let us remember a phenomenon from speech development: in the early phases of life a child is capable of forming more phonemes than are contained in its language community. In time the sounds not used 'fall into disuse' and, when learning a foreign language later on, they have to be laboriously acquired anew – sometimes largely unsuccessfully. It appears justified, then, to assume that originally available but unused 'functional potentials' disappear, while others are strengthened and differentiated through practice, and we might imply that myths act in a similar way: they develop and reinforce certain action orientations and let others wither away.

Ways of handling myth

As has been suggested, concrete experiences contribute to forming the 'myth-moulds', i.e. the basic reaction and evaluation tendencies, which then in turn determine the reception and interpretation of concrete experiences. In other words, myths result from generalizations of concrete experiences; once they exist, they give experiences their deeper meaning and are at the same time reinforced by them. These circular processes, however, are selective; they may emphasize certain types of experience and disregard others, a selectivity which may render myths largely resistant to occurrences contradicting them. The more so because the basic pattern of a myth can be concretized in a variety of ways, obsolete contents can easily be replaced by seemingly more adequate ones. Let us then examine how cultural groups handle the myth of lurking chaos.

The Aztecs of Mexico were a people with a remarkably high culture. Successful and dreaded warriors, they were, within the short time of one century, capable of establishing a strong state with a differentiated hierarchy of nobles and priests under an absolute monarch. They invented their own system of pictographic writing, composed historic documents and literary works, developed an astronomy, a system of numbers and in particular a complex, diversified religion. They believed in a variety of gods and spirits who demanded manifold sacrifices and rituals. Much of this was similar to what was customary everywhere: plants and animals which were offered to the gods, prescriptions for behaviour such as fasting, ritual bathing, sexual abstinence. In contrast other things were more unusual: blood offerings through self-mutilation or human sacrifice.

The cruelty of these sacrifices need not be described in detail here. Suffice it to say that during great religious festivals thousands of humans were ritually killed, to offer their hearts to the sun. Because, so it was believed, the sun needed human blood to shine. But not just anyone's blood, it had to be 'good' blood: that of warriors or nobles, if necessary even from one's own people. Often wars were waged – in mutual agreement – for the single purpose of obtaining prisoners for those sacrifices, so that even one's own warrior, having fled the enemy's imprisonment in order to avoid sacrificial death, would be executed at home. The sacrificed persons were highly respected; as heavenly companions of the sun, it was believed, they would carry on living in heaven (Krickeberg, 1979).

This was in no way a cheerful culture. 'What deep-seated pessimism', wrote Krickeberg, 'resonates in the words with which a newborn child was greeted by older relations: You will see, know and learn to taste suffering, misfortune and revulsion. You have come to the site of enduring sorrow and affliction, where pain occurs, where it is pitiful' (1979, p. 218). Hence the upbringing of children was strict, even cruel; the children were not only expected to learn to avoid unacceptable actions, but also to bear pain. Severe punishments were thus frequent: the children were wounded, exposed to blistering heat or peppered smoke, and the sight of the bloody sacrificial feasts must have shaped them very early in life.

It is not my aim here to present a detailed account of the Aztecs and their beliefs. But what I have portrayed seems to be a paradigmatic example of the 'myth of lurking chaos'. It impressively shows the belief that without suitable protective measures the world would be in danger of sinking into chaos, in the process losing all that made life worth living. And the power of this belief resulted in the creation of defensive rituals of such cruelty that they considerably lowered the group's quality of life – which these measures were supposed to be safeguarding. However, it seems that misery was still considered better than death.

The example is not as extraordinary as it appears. If we differentiate between the belief, i.e. the basic myth, and the actions that it leads to, we will discover a variety of behaviours and convictions that a belief in 'lurking chaos' might engender. It seems that some kind of fear of chaos induces human beings everywhere to invent suitable apotropaic (protective) measures. A kind of fundamental anxiety – the myth mentioned – may concretize itself differently, depending on the time or culture, just as the protective measures themselves might be quite different. Thus Christians, on the one hand, personified this anxiety in God whose anger or moods manifested themselves in the expulsion from Paradise, in the Deluge, the destruction of Sodom and Gomorrah, in Job's suffering or in the threatening apocalypse of the Last Judgement; on the other hand, the anxiety induced the idea of the fallen angel Satan, who constantly attempted to oppose the divine order. To avoid God's anger and Satan's temptations, unremitting vigilance and war against evil was required; a purpose served not only by prayers, pilgrimages and various rituals but also by uglier particulars of our history – denunciation, torture and executions of heretics and witches, the persecution of Jews or religious wars and crusades with their attendant excesses. These examples might appear to be past misconceptions to us, but in a different ideological cloak and in other concretizations we find similar things right up into modern times. In the nineteenth century, based on progress made in the field of biology, the witch-mania of former times was replaced by a new theory of race, which reactivated the anti-Semitism that had gradually been fading – in this case the 'myth of lurking chaos' obviously also played a role. 'So the proportion of Aryan blood, which alone upholds the edifice of our society, is close to disappearing', wrote Jean Finot in 1906, and for Richard Wagner's friend H. St. Chamberlain true culture 'is being obstructed by the influence of bastardisation, steadily weakening and finally consuming originality and vitality' – as cited with relish by M. Dippel in 1934. Thus I wrote about 'a secular repetition, formulated in quasi-scientific terms, of the myth that the fate of the world depends on the result of the battle between ... good and evil, light and darkness, yin and yang, God and the Devil. This old assumption occurs here in the shape of the irreconcilable opposition between the Dolichocephalic and Brachycephalic or more specifically between Aryans and Jews' (Boesch, 1971, p. 86). Hitler did not invent something new, but just added human sacrifices to what was extant – only uglier than those of the Aztecs. However, the threat with chaos did not emanate from Jews alone, but also from the 'yellow danger', the 'red flood of communism' and others, up to asylum-seekers and immigrants who to some even nowadays threaten the purity of German culture.

The Aztecs, as I said, presented us with a paradigmatic example of the 'myth of lurking chaos'. By doing the right thing one is able to avert the danger. This example reveals an ambivalence: people are vulnerable, even threatened by destruction; at the same time, however, they have the power to avert this threat, even to make fate look kindly upon them. The gods, no matter how powerful and destructive they may be, can be influenced by magic, prayers, suitable behaviour and sacrifices to grant our wishes.

In addition the example underlines something else. The chaos one fears is more than disorder. Disorder can be tidied up, its causes can be removed – 'traffic chaos' is disorder, not chaos. The chaos meant here is anti-order, an ultimate threat. When it occurs, its effect is final – perhaps even more final than death, which we can after all survive through our children, our works or at least through a testament. Therefore something apocalyptic is characteristic of chaos, basically similar to that kind of 'free-floating anxiety' (Freud), in which one feels an impending disaster, unspecified, all engulfing, yet is unable to grasp its reasons. More psychologically, the myth of lurking chaos threatens to abolish our action potential. This makes comprehensible the compulsive zeal with which we pursue preventive actions. Accordingly, the order we seek for countering chaos is different from the settled routine of everyday life, which at times we even want to escape. Such escape, though, does not search for chaos, but for diversion, for adventure, something different that not only possesses its own order but implies, additionally, the promise of being able to return to the customary comforts. The 'burdensome order', as Peter Orlik called it, may constrain us, but usually does not abolish our action potential, just as adventure does not really threaten it, but rather allows us to test and confirm it. Basically, the order opposed to chaos is that of paradise, an order that promises safeness without constraint; a myth of harmonious well-being, implying somehow an action potential so complete that it is hardly necessary any longer.

However, between disorder and chaos, just as between order and paradise, there is a symbolic relationship: each specific disorder we experience may intimate the absolute one, and thus it becomes a symbol. The same is true for every appealing order – in art for instance: It symbolizes order *as such*, the permanent harmony between the I and the world. Thus these symbolic qualities of concrete experience in everyday life act as reinforcers of the myth and thereby keep it alive.

Sacrifices, magic and prayers are direct attempts to influence the ominous. Let us look now at a more subtle example of dealing with 'lurking chaos'. In an article on the mask I described carnival as an apotropaic 'staging' of chaos (Boesch, 1998). During carnival the customary rules of behaviour are suspended, what is usually forbidden or disapproved of is allowed, from sexual licence to, in former times, physical aggression; the representative 'guardians' of order in everyday life are derided, laughed at, their weaknesses often irreverently uncovered. In this way order 'turned upside-down' becomes a representation of chaos, and it not only remains unpunished, but also amuses, relaxes, liberates – on condition, however, that the return to everyday life remains foreseeable. In this way carnival symbolizes both chaos and the ability of human beings to curb and to control it.

The carnival thus appears to be a second paradigm of handling lurking chaos. In this case sacrifices are no longer offered to avert the ominous; rather chaos is symbolically evoked and simultaneously presented as malleable and controllable. Something similar is also found elsewhere. Think of the fascination with which many people look at scenes of catastrophe, accident or war; in so doing, what otherwise may be an amorphous menace becomes concrete occurrence, something definable which, if need arose, one might even be capable of dealing with; and one feels reassuringly uninvolved, a mere spectator, able to 'zap' out of the scene should it become too threatening. In this case, too, chaos is depicted, but simultaneously experienced as avoidable or even controllable.

This creation and abolition of chaos expresses itself in many often rather subtle ways. One thinks of crime novels, for instance. While reading a novel by the sinologist Robert van Gulik I suddenly noticed its structure: the peaceful world of a Chinese village was disturbed – as would be expected – by a crime, and in the search for its perpetrator suspicion spread out over the previously ordered world, until it gradually seemed to be full of deception, intrigue, criminal conspiracy – order turned into threatening chaos – until finally, the wisdom of

Judge Dee allowed order to be re-established. What, in such a story, captivates the reader? Could it be that in some way the sequence of events activates the myth of lurking chaos and the apprehension of it, but then demonstrates that human wisdom can control it? Just as the carnival represents chaos as both threatening and controllable?

This is a pattern, frequently used in literature, that time and time again rivets the reader. This is true even for tragedies, although their plot seems to convey the opposite, namely helplessness. Yet after the play, when fate has done its cruel work, we get up, perhaps cathartically purified, to go and have an evening drink – after all we were not the victim but the spectator, the calamity on stage did not touch us directly. This pattern: to abolish order but only for a while, always in the position to re-establish it, allows an important dual experience – even if 'only' symbolically. First it underlines our autonomy: we are not simply subjected to an enforced order, but are free to escape it, to disturb it or even destroy it. This raises our self-esteem. No less is done by the other experience, that chaos does not really threaten us because, just as we ourselves abolished order, we are also in a position to re-establish it; a favourite method of self-assurance, especially in our technically powerful times. In the paradigm of carnival – be it by real enactment or vicarious participation – we thus reinforce our action potential twice (Boesch 1991, 1998).

But what if the apotropaic safeguards, the sacrifices, prayers and incantations, the symbolic stagings, remain fruitless? What if anti-order is about to become real? What if not just philosophers or poets invoke or bewail calamity, but disaster really threatens to penetrate our lives? Then other forms of action take over. One of these is *complicity*. One tries to protect oneself by adopting the destructive. The eager and faithful followers believe themselves to be the least threatened. However, complicity goes beyond this mimicry of the anxious. For it not only gives protection but also active satisfactions: praise, social belonging, material profit or even fulfilment of usually taboo sadistic or sexual wishes. In particular, however, complicity bestows an almost unconscious feeling of not only being able to avoid calamity, but also of being able to regulate chaos at will by the power to threaten or to destroy. A self-profit which is all the more enticing the more helpless one originally felt.

There is a secret fascination by chaos in all its forms. We not only want to protect ourselves against it, to preserve our order, but we also want to get to know it; only knowledge promises sufficient action potential. Yet the fascination is more deeply rooted than in the simple need for a prophylactic competence: it springs from those repressions which our socialization imposed on us, consists of that lustful shudder in which we recognize what was once forbidden – even if we only dreamed about it; a prohibition that basically also meant a restriction of our action potential. Complicity can thus become a self-enhancement – hence probably its frightening frequency. One thinks about the French revolution,

National-Socialism, Pol Pot in Cambodia, the Bosnian war. To be the devil himself makes Satan appear benevolent.

These – and other – examples seem to show that complicity is often more than simple compliance, rather it is an identification that fundamentally changes the perception of reality. Thus for instance in Bosnia peaceful Christian and Muslim neighbours, yes even friends, became deadly enemies virtually overnight; Blumenfeld (1998) reports about German soldiers in the First World War who, munching bread, threw hand grenades on to defenceless prisoners, 'just for fun' (according to *Frankfurter Allgemeine Zeitung*). This is no doubt 'complicity with chaos' – to bring it about oneself, to feel one's power over life and death, awakens a feeling of immunity, no matter how deceptive this might be.

From myth to phantasm

This leads to a fourth paradigmatic way of handling the myth of lurking chaos: *fight or flight*. But *what* are we fighting, *what* are we fleeing from? The answer to this question seems easy, if we relate it to resistance fighters or refugees – although their motives would also deserve closer inspection. However, I will rather focus here on those multiple fights and flights that occur without there even being visible external threats. This takes us from the predominantly collective processes, which occupied us up to now, to the more private ones, or put in a different way, from myth to phantasm.

What takes place in the mind of a child who is told that the sun will stop shining if one does not sacrifice the heart of the adorned man being led through the streets in a solemn procession? What in that of the child who learns that Jews, formerly neighbours and playmates, 'are vermin that, like any other vermin, have to be exterminated', to protect the strength of one's own people (Boesch, 1971)? Or the child who is assured that it was born a sinner and is thus destined for eternal damnation, a fate averted only by the sacrifice of the man Jesus? What happens in a child who is assured that America is the land of Satan and must be fought, if necessary, even with acts of terror against children and women? These questions are perhaps unusual, even though the list can easily be increased. However, one can ask more subtly: how does a child react to the fact that it is allowed to do things during carnival which it would be punished for at other times? Or that cruel things, which delight adults, are allowed to happen in a film, although they are otherwise outlawed? Or that it is not allowed to have sexual desires that adults enjoy openly and with pleasure on the TV screen or even demonstrate themselves?

Naturally, in any specific case we do not know the answers. Generally, however, we may assume that the child experiences itself as being in a confusing, sometimes contradictory world, which not only has to be given inner order, but also has to be attuned to oneself. Basically chaos is already there, more in one society, less in another, even if in practice, in the settled order of everyday life, it is not yet existentially dangerous. The child is thus forced to establish structures, with varying degrees of success, but which at any rate impose an individual, subjective pattern on reality. The child selects and rejects, evaluates and weighs, and during these structuralizations it is indeed guided, but not exclusively determined, by the group's myths. The patterns that it forms in the process are not true depictions of the material or social reality, but rather more or less deforming, omitting or highlighting reflections, and they do not concern just the experiential world, but the anticipated world equally – more precisely, that world which the child expects *for itself*, hopes for or is afraid of. These perceiving, transforming as well as anticipating images, bound up with the 'I', are what I call phantasms (Boesch, 1976, 1983, 1991).

Disorder arouses anxiety. Consequently, anxiety is likely to be involved in this structuring activity of the child. Such anxiety at first would spring less from concrete threats than from the confrontation with contradiction, inconsistency and uncertainty. But in association with the factual experience of danger and of failure, supported by cultural myth, the child becomes likely to form individual *phantasms* of lurking chaos in which it will amalgamate its own and social conceptions in differing proportions.

These phantasms probably have a complex structure. They stem from a diffuse, largely emotional basis of confusion, anxiety and hope, which, though not yet given concrete form and content, still largely colour, and at times determine, what visions of the future the child chooses. Thus anticipations of desirable actions and aspirations will be formed progressively, including alternatives deemed possible, according to circumstances and situations. Phantasms will, of course, not be rigid structures, but will be modified in the course of life, adjusting to concrete experiences, thereby becoming more realistic – although their initial emotional inclinations appear to remain rather constant.

Obviously the myth of lurking chaos is not the only myth of a group, just as individuals also form various phantasms. Thus, for instance, a myth of paradise (see below) will counteract the one of lurking chaos, will at times or permanently override it – depending on circumstances. Myths and phantasms constitute dynamic interaction systems linked to the concrete I-world constellations. I cannot elaborate on this here (see, e.g. Boesch 1991, 1998, 2000), but I want to emphasize that the phantasm of lurking chaos may remain latent in fortunate periods of life, and may be activated – in various individual ways – when circumstances become threatening. So, for instance, some Jews fled from Germany in the period before the Second World War, while others stayed. Their reactions, of course, varied for many reasons, but different phantasms of chaos very likely also influenced their perception of danger.

Yet concrete dangers are by no means necessary to arouse phantasms – imagined dangers often do so, maybe even more effectively. Let us take the example of child rearing. Children, apart from everything that they were or are today, also represent the hopes of an imagined future. This future symbolism of the child often obtains great significance. 'My son has stolen an apple – will he become a thief?' Small signs will be interpreted in a far-reaching way; one tends to foresee great promises in virtues, ominous ones in mistakes of the child. Therefore – thus goes traditional belief – one should bend the twig at the outset to have the tree grow straight, and this, if needed, by harsh punishments; should these fail, one might even resort to disinheriting, disowning, in the extreme even to killing, to 'save the family's honour', as happens occasionally. Which, in other words, means preserving a revered order from the invasion of chaos. Thus, in many cultures, the child did not only represent a blessing, but also a threat to the future: it symbolized both order and its abolition. A Thai essay describes the child as uncivilized by nature, a mere animal, which only education would transform into a cultural, or a 'human' being (Boesch, 1998, chapter 'Die Maske'; Yupo, 1957).

Of course, the adult's attitude towards the child is polyvalent, not only, or even predominantly, determined by phantasms of calamity. Here is not the place to pursue this. However, the attitude that a child needs to be 'bent to fit' by the educator, its 'non-culture' to be driven out, is common in many cultures, as it was in Germany up to the recent past. Gradually, however, following Rousseau, the counter-doctrine prevailed that the 'non-culture' rests with the adults, with 'society', and the child would, if unmolested, become a better cultural being than its repressed educators. The movement became influential after the Second World War – the concrete experience of chaos – which had awakened a deep mistrust towards German culture and its proponents. The results, however, in no way corresponded to the ideology. And so today's educators, especially in Germany, feel insecure. At a loss in view of a youth shaped by an anti-authoritarian upbringing, they dare not see in the child, as formerly, a threat to culture, nor the promise of a better world. Such helplessness threatens to reinforce the myth of lurking chaos without, however, activating resistance – resignation prevails because one feels unable to give the dreaded calamity a concrete form.

But this form-giving is important. A study about witch-trials reports that 'during exorcism the priest in Coury ordered the Devil to name the witches present in church. Among the spectators there was an unknown woman farmer from Foucherans... She had sold cherries on the market and had come to the exorcism out of curiosity. The Devil named her as a witch; she was stoned by the populace a few days later and her corpse was burned' (Ernst, 1972, p. 24). How great the fear in the church must have been, when the priest demanded the Devil to name a witch there – and what a relief, when the lot fell to someone else! Exorcism served the battle against calamity, which, as long as it remained indeterminate, was all the more dangerous, being a threat which could emerge from anywhere – even from one's own inner being. To localize a danger increases the action potential: one sees the enemy, can appraise it, and depending on the circumstances either fight or flee. We do not have to reach back into the seventeenth century for this: today's demonizations of asylum-seekers, coloured people, Muslims or Christians fulfil a similar function.

So there are concrete threats, certainly, yet their chaotic potential often remains under cover. Who would have foreseen the holocaust in Hitler's beginnings, who the African AIDS epidemic in harmless enjoyment of sex, who the eschatological threats in the first discoveries of nuclear physics? Where the beginnings of chaos appear to be harmless, it remains unforeseeable – the conditions that open up or bar its way are too complex. Therefore the battle against chaos, just like fleeing from it, is often imaginary, depending on how much a myth or a phantasm has sharpened or obscured our vision. In addition, we often create the threats in our own minds. Literature and art are full of this. Even in the creation myths God and the Devil fight for domination in the world; then one is told of the punishing and condemning God who, if the apostle Paul is to be believed, at the end of time will deliver up the unjust to damnation – and they are in the majority. The great myths of world literature depict, each in its own way, this battle between good and evil – for instance the Ramayana and the Mahabharata in India, the even older epic of Gilgamesh, the Nibelungenlied – and naturally even children's books and fairy tales conjure it up, where usually the good escape doom only thanks to magic and sorcery. In addition, many tales warn of the calamity from the inside – from disobedience, greed or simple carelessness. There are many other examples of the battle against the threatening anti-order in fiction – that of Doctor Faustus against the Devil, that of Captain Ahab against the murderous white whale, that of William Tell against Gessler, that of Antigone against inhumanity or that of various detectives against wrongdoers. In a nearly archetypal way Gotthelf's *Schwarze Spinne* (Black Spider) describes the chaos, that, beginning on the inside, turns into an external threat – which can only be contained by pious devotion, meaning a fight against the 'inner chaos'.

This inside–outside dichotomy surely is the essence of our topic. Obviously the myth is at first external. It is presented to the child and shapes it's world view to a large extent. However, the manifold experiences of anxiety, threat and failure, which the child evaluates and amalgamates with the myth, are internal. Thus, the group's myths will unavoidably influence an individual's perception and anticipation of threats, while the assimilation of the myth will as surely be affected by a person's experience and inclinations. The 'inside–outside dichotomy' turns out to be the interaction between myth and phantasm. An interaction, by the way, portending its own conflicts owing to antagonistic wishes both to be like others and to be oneself.

The myth of lurking chaos seems, in modern western Europe, to be displaced by a different myth: that of *feasibility*. Dangers can be avoided, problems researched and solved, the harmful can be fought, obstacles removed. Even the catastrophes threatening the climate and the environment that many are warning about, the nuclear threat or the atomic 'time bomb', all these are only temporary indispositions that we will eventually master. But, although usually below the surface, the myth of lurking chaos remains and can be activated. The Hong Kong chicken flu, the Ebola or AIDS virus at first set off scenarios of catastrophe revealing the latent virulence of the myth, even though the belief in the power of science soon concealed it. The 'myth of feasibility', or 'mastery', of course, strongly enhances our action confidence and thus efficiently counteracts fears of calamity. Yet, as long as human beings experience threats and failures, corresponding myths and phantasms remain present.

Chaos and guilt

What now, we have to ask, determines the strength of such a phantasm? And what, more basically, would induce an individual to anticipate a generally threatening calamity? Did we not find that the simple experience of misfortune will not necessarily bring about a phantasm of chaos, and that caution, careful planning, circumspect action would appear sufficient to avoid trouble?

To such a general question the answer can only be tentative, since phantasms are, of course, 'over-determined' (Boesch, 1991). I would, however, see an important condition for forming a chaos-phantasm in a breakdown of the action potential, as experienced, for instance, in situations of catastrophe, illness or depression. Yet even a personal feeling of helplessness need not include an anticipation of chaos, as long as it remains limited to oneself; it would have to be exteriorized and generalized to become a fear of chaos. There appears to exist a 'privileged' experience for fulfilling these requirements: guilt. Guilt, no matter of what origin, arises from failure of self-regulation. It somehow corresponds to the apostle Paul's saying, 'What I want to do, I do not do, but what I do not want to do, I do' – independent of its religious connotation. This is an experience of absolute alienation, a negation of our action potential due not to external obstacles but to our inner impotence – in effect, it would be the elemental experience of chaos.

For this reason, the guilty person leans towards self-punishment, which makes him or her inclined to anticipate external threats. Equally, however, the guilty person tries to exonerate himself, to search for mitigations, and this can easily lead him to accuse those who might incriminate him. Others, he then tends to think, are indeed no better, they no less deserve punishment, and such displacement on others, superficially perhaps alleviating his guilt-feeling, is in fact a generalization which favours the forming of a phantasm of external threat as a common punishment.

Look at an additional peculiarity of the phantasm of lurking chaos: it seems to have a quality of absoluteness, somehow implying, similar to the corresponding myth, a global abolition of lifeworthiness. For the Aztecs, without sacrifices the sun would stop shining, and for the nineteenth-century racists the contamination of Aryan blood by Semites meant an end to their civilization. The lurking chaos appears to possess an apocalyptic quality, which raises the question of the relation of guilt to sin. Sin, however, is not equal to guilt. Sin, of course, is anti-order, but at the start it is not experienced, but learned; it belongs to the myth. In contrast, guilt is subjective; its link to sin is circumstantial: one can sin without feeling guilt, and experience guilt although not having sinned. Sin is defined by external prescriptions; guilt, in contrast, results from a failure to uphold inner values. Only when moral prescriptions are internalized, when they have turned into criteria of self-worth, will their violation elicit guilt feelings. Sin then becomes internal, and moral failure would then, too, signify a basic breakdown of self-regulation; in religious terms, it merits damnation; in subjective terms, self-punishment or, in the extreme, even self-destruction.

This, of course, is a hypothesis, and to prove it much clinical material would be needed – which, unfortunately, I do not possess. Let me then illustrate this only by an example taken from literature which, in fact, suggested this hypothesis to me. A Swiss author, Adolf Muschg, known not only for his novels, but also for his often biting criticisms of Switzerland, partly justified, partly not, has in a recent book written almost apocalyptic images of general doom, which are difficult not to understand as a phantasm of 'lurking chaos'. Read the following quotations:

Our rafts are not built for the crossing. Doom travels with them like on the ones of Medusa . . . We are unable to rest until the raft's enlargement has reached the proportions of the *Titanic*. Only then, through the lens of impatience and tragic violation of our limits, doom too is considered worth seeing. (1998, p. 305)

Thus our gods have favoured a race of heroes and heroines, of whom the world can only be terrified, and definitely with reason. Because when they come to know themselves it is always too late. And if there are any survivors, it only remains for them to grow sufficiently with their misfortune so that they too can come to be a misfortune for others. Our gods love insanity, and in this regard we are their equals. (1998, p. 306)

This is the poetic formulation of an individual phantasm of chaos. Less poetically, but in the same vein, Muschg recently expressed himself on TV: 'Now I know what Switzerland lacks: the German experience of bomb-wrecked cities' (Channel 3-sat, 11 October 1998). It sounded like regret. But where is guilt in this case?

Muschg's writings, and in particular this criticism of Switzerland, surprisingly contain much biographical material. Indeed, what are these personal memories doing in a political book? They can of course underline some of his criticisms, but they also risk limiting their general validity. Why would he want to disclose his hurt feelings?

Practising a bit of 'connotation analysis' (Boesch, 1991), one can discover analogies between Muschg's memories and his Parsifal novel *Der rote Ritter* (1993) which I cannot pursue here. Let me only insist on one theme: mother-related guilt feelings. Parsifal, at the outset, caused his mother's death by abandoning her against her will; in the end, ignoring her fate, he sets out to return to her castle – a futile return, of course. In the quoted book, Muschg twice refers to his visiting his dying mother in the hospital – who loudly cried out his name without recognizing the son standing at her bedside.

Can we not recognize here all the elements that make guilt a favourite condition for a phantasm of chaos? In all likelihood, guilt is present, and so is its projection on the figure of Parsifal – and, I tend to presume, also on Muschg's 'fatherland'. A close connotation analysis would also discover compensation-wishes – Parsifal, the greatest among knights, ultimately King of the Holy Grail, whose previous failings have all been pardoned. Of course, these symbols – be it the grail, be it Switzerland – are polyvalent, yet Muschg's apocalyptic reflections quoted above resemble only too well a phantasm of chaos, no less than the Parsifal story seems to seek atonement for guilt. Atonement in the novel and projective accusations in the quoted political book could well fulfil a similar function: to shift guilt on to symbols. The phantasm of lurking chaos turned into literary fiction or political accusation would objectify a self-punishing anxiety and thereby relieve the self.

I admit to feeling somewhat uneasy about presenting such tenuous evidence for the relationship between chaos phantasms and guilt. Yet hypotheses of this kind can never be proved, but at best be made more plausible by accumulating clinical evidence. Which, as already said, I do not possess. Still, I consider the hypothesis to be plausible, and the example given may at least demonstrate its genesis – a process which would deserve more attention than it usually gets (e.g. Claparède, 1934). However, I do not want to imply that guilt plays the same role in all chaos phantasms. Phantasms, of course, are over-determined, guilt may play a key role in their genesis, but so may other factors. The cultural decline by racial pollution, invoked by political ideologists of the nineteenth and twentieth centuries, might have had less to do with guilt than with a host of other motives – yet this would have to be closely analysed. The chaos-guilt hypothesis might, for the moment, at least be useful as a catalyst.

The counter-myth

What is the opposite of guilt? If guilt, as I said, consists of the breakdown of self-regulation, then its opposite would be optimal action potential. Would this then consist of strength, power, invulnerability? Hardly. Optimal action potential would show itself in harmony, in fitting ourselves to a world which in turn fits itself to us. The peacemaker is mightier than the general – with good reason the gospel promises heaven to the peace-loving and not to the proficient. But this optimal harmony, too, is a myth: that of paradise. And paradise, no less than chaos, is also a subject in art – perhaps more so in visual arts than in literature. Though painters such as Hieronymus Bosch, Goya, van Gogh, Picasso, Bacon or Baselitz were also fascinated by chaos, time and time again the paradisiacal is present, from the religious depictions of the Middle Ages to the sunny landscapes of the impressionists or Chagall's angels. Paradise thus becomes the sphere of pure, harmonious order, opposite to chaos, granting ultimate fulfilment. Paradise is a fiction created by the human mind, our experience of it remains purely symbolic, as in art and music. Yet, being constantly challenged by threats – which, other than paradise, can become painfully concrete – we pursue this image with incessant longing. And so, in search of it, we reach out to distant places – the islands of the Pacific, to regions of unspoilt nature – or hope for it in the closeness of love, and where unattainable, we at least surround ourselves with its symbols. To which, besides certain forms of art, also belong the symbols of enjoyment and fulfilment. In this way, the lurking chaos and the enticing paradise form the two fundamental myths of culture whose dynamics reach from magic to science, from religion to politics.

And finally?

What do we get from all this? 'The myth of lurking chaos' was a concept I stumbled on when writing an article on masks (Boesch, 1998). Subsequently, I found it enlightening for various problems, from individual to political hypochondria, from existential fear to fundamentalist compulsions, individual as well as collective, or even from religion to art. But making such phenomena comprehensible does not yet mean explaining them; that would require uncovering the genesis of such myths and phantasms. I tried to illustrate here the direction this could take, but the actual work still remains to be done.

This would, of course – at the outset or later – involve specifying the concepts. What distinguishes the phantasm of lurking chaos from mere caution and circumspection? I do not believe, in the sphere of human existence, in exact definitions of concepts; they obscure rather than enlighten. Nevertheless, the concepts should at least be circumscribed, meaning to clarify their emphasis in relation to others. In this sense, caution and circumspection are more specific than the phantasm of chaos; the latter, less concrete, is therefore more pervasive, more general. While caution might simply motivate one to sign an insurance policy, the phantasm would lead to over-insurance plus the gnawing doubts about whether its cover is sufficient. But before all, phantasm and myth somehow tend towards an existential dimension – they anticipate threats to orders which are vital, be they climate, health, community, religion, democracy or the plans and hopes we have formed for life. Of course, chaos phantasms and myths need not be explicitly present – they may manifest themselves in anxious restraint, in compulsiveness, in a need for social security, in particular avoidances, and so on.

Yet let us not make too-rigid delimitations. What the example means to emphasize is that our actions are not determined only by situational constraints, cognitive taxonomies and rational values, but are also regulated by deeper-lying orientational patterns: cultural myths and individual phantasms. We usually do not heed them enough, less because we repress them than because they represent the obvious, which makes us neither question nor even perceive them. But they penetrate right into our feelings, wishes, evaluations, speech – they remain unconscious and yet powerful, a bit like the discovery by TV crews that angles of presentation, shades of light and colour can shape unawares the reaction of viewers (Winterhoff-Spurk, 1999). And thus, when the Aztecs spoke about the sun, they meant something different than did their Spanish conquerors, and the word Negro had a different colouring for a slave-trader than for Albert Schweitzer. In politics, myths often had more impact than rational discourses, and many a marriage broke up on account of diverging phantasms rather than concrete problems.

In fact, the problem of 'lurking chaos' troubles many minds. In a recently published article Martin Walser (1998) says that nowadays we are well off, 'what we have now, human beings longed for over centuries. But – and this *but* casts a persistent shadow – we do not believe that it could remain thus for long or even forever... Just where does this readiness come from, yes this addiction, to immediately project each civilizatory indisposition to an apocalyptic dimension? From where the fear of soon being lost?' Walser sees the cause for this readiness in our religious imprinting; yet religion is, in the first place, a reaction to a myth of lurking chaos which, I presume, precedes it – even if it nurses and reinforces it. We need this myth, just like our phantasms – it structures our world view, and thus our actions and our selves. To direct, as Walser demands, our eyes from heaven to earth, from the distant to the near, will not spare us the need to deal with experiences of failure, of fear, catastrophe and, in particular with guilt, this disturbing breakdown of self regulation; to form corresponding structures for our actions is a basic requirement of human existence. Thus, even non-Christian cultures know the myth of lurking chaos.

This leads to the question of morality I raised at the beginning. Besides art, is not morality, regardless of its form and content, also an attempt to check or even to avoid the threatening chaos? Certainly, yet simultaneously and inevitably, it intensifies the threat. Sin, as Paul declares, came into the world through the law of God; a dilemma (God both caused sin and punishes it) the apostle attempted to resolve in vain. Moral rules are demands. They aim at shaping human action in ways often contradicting spontaneous inclinations or situational requirements. To violate rules thus becomes tempting at times, is unavoidable at others, and so conflicts, guilt or both result. And both reinforce the myth as well as the phantasm.

Hence one attempts to avoid chaos by means other than moral compliance: by pleasure and enjoyment that promise fulfilment, maybe even paradise. But as Nietzsche says, all desire wants eternity, but will never reach it. So we resort to fiction and dreaming, tend to delude ourselves with all those images of bliss provided by novels, films, travel brochures or other products of a busy entertainment industry. Yet make-believe pleasures tend to increase desire, and this in turn may endanger moral rules. Even striving for pleasure can thus intensify the anticipation of chaos, and does so all the more when inducing guilt – indeed, the pleasure we strive for may evade or disappoint us, an experience which emphasizes the limitation of our action potential; we react to this with frustration, with increased striving, and by stubbornly pursuing our desires we often violate inner norms. But guilt, conscious or unconscious, will lead back to morality, and so the circle of morality–pleasure–guilt begins anew. The lurking chaos repeatedly forces itself upon us – frightening perhaps or simply cautioning – and it may even be indispensable for the regulation of our actions.

Chaos is abolished at best – and only provisionally – in art and music, in which we may experience an I-world harmony without coercion; in love, too, at least as long as it makes no demands. Both art and love suggest the 'fitting oneself to a world which fits itself to us', as I put it above; they induce a premonition of paradise. However, we experience art and love in exceptional moments only, and, of course, they always come to an end, an end with sorrow, risking in turn reawakening the anticipation of lurking chaos.

And finally, there is still the question of whether the apprehensions of lurking chaos are biology or culture. Think of the child's 'functional potentials', mentioned above, of which those not needed fade away, while others are reinforced and differentiated. At first sight the potentials are, of course, biological, the selecting and reinforcing factors cultural – yet are the pressures all external or cultural, or the reactions of the child 'only' psychological? The question, in fact, seems idle. There is nothing about a human being that is not biology, but also nearly nothing that is not culture. How tall we grow, how we walk, talk, laugh, yes even eat and digest, is determined jointly by nature and culture. To look at a beautiful picture changes the blood pressure and skin resistance – culture thus immediately converts itself into nature. Conversely, a momentary condition of nervousness or relaxation will influence our perception. In a cheerful mood the lurking chaos does not worry us, but even a common cold can change this. Biology and culture are so inextricably enmeshed that long debates about their respective 'variance' will not disentangle them. This is all the more so, as we still hardly know enough about culture's nature and ways of action. Yet, 'lurking chaos' should have taught us this much: culture certainly influences the way we think and evaluate, shapes our action and interaction. However, it acts no less below the surface, in those mythical basic dispositions which we now hardly notice. Culture, then, makes us form phantasmic orientations, of which we recognize the more 'rational' manifestations – as goals and fears, affections and antipathies – but which none the less act from a depth that we will hardly ever be able to reflect on. What binds us to our homeland, our partners, or what pulls us from them to faraway places? We would not know how to explain it – and yet it binds or pulls us powerfully. And the force which binds or pulls us – is it biology or culture?

REFERENCES

Blumenfeld, E. (1998). Einbildungsroman (The illusion novel). *Frankfurter Allgemeine Zeitung*, 14 September 1998, p. 50.
Boesch, E. E. (1971). Psychologische Überlegungen zum Rassenvorurteil (Psychological reflections concerning racism). In E. E. Boesch (ed.), *Zwischen zwei Wirklichkeiten* (Between two realities). Bern: Huber, pp. 77–104.
    (1976). *Psychopathologie des Alltags* (Everyday psychopathology). Bern: Huber.
    (1983). *Das Magische und das Schöne* (The magic and the beautiful). Stuttgart: Frommann-Holzboog.
    (1991). *Symbolic action theory and cultural psychology*. Heidelberg: Springer. (Published in French (1995): *L'Action symbolique*. Paris: L'Harmattan.)
    (1998). *Sehnsucht. Von der Suche nach Glück und Sinn* (Yearning. The search for luck and meaning). Bern: Huber.
    (2000). *Das lauernde Chaos. Mythen und Fiktionen im Alltag* (The lurking chaos. Myths and fictions in everyday life). Bern: Huber.
Claparède, E. (1934). *La genèse de l'hypothèse* (The genesis of the hypothesis). Genf: Librairie Kundig.
Dippel, P. G. (1934). *Nietzsche und Wagner: eine Untersuchung über die Grundlagen und Motive ihrer Trennung* (Nietzsche and Wagner: a study about the bases and motives of their separation). Bern: P. Haupt.
Ernst, C. (1972). *Teufelsaustreibungen und Hexenprozesse* (Exorcism and witch trials). Bern: Huber.
Finot, J. (1906). *Race prejudice*. London: Constable.
Krickeberg, G. (1979). *Altamerikanische Kulturen* (Old American cultures). Berlin: Safari.
Lévi-Strauss, C. (1973). *Anthropologie structurale deux* (Structural anthropology two). Paris: Plon.
Muschg, A. (1993). *Der rote Ritter* (The red knight bachelor). Frankfurt an Main: Suhrkamp.
    (1998). *O mein Heimatland* (O my home country). Frankfurt an Main: Suhrkamp.

Walser, M. (1998). Ich vertraue. Querfeldein. Das Gift der Verachtung gegen das Nächste (I trust. Across country. The poison of contempt against the next). *Neue Zürcher Zeitung*, 235, 10–11 October, p. 49.

Wilson, E. O. (1998). Die Zehn Gebote liegen in den Genen (The ten commandments lie in the genes). *Neue Zürcher Zeitung*, 211, p. 57.

Winterhoff-Spurk, P. (1999). *Medienpsychologie* (Media psychology) Stuttgart: Kohlhammer.

Yupo, T. (1957). *Khon* (in Thai). Bangkok: Department of Fine Arts.

7   Integrating cultural, psychological and biological perspectives in understanding child development

Joan G. Miller

Recent years have seen a renewed interest in understanding biological influences on development. This interest has been stimulated, at least in part, by new theoretical developments in evolutionary theory and neuroscience that are extending attention to higher-order psychological functions, as well as by groundbreaking technological advances that make possible mapping of brain cell activity in ways not previously possible (e.g. Berntson and Cacioppo, 2000; Pinker, 1997). However, to date there has been only limited effort to integrate these recent biologically based initiatives with an attention to culture. This neglect is particularly striking, given the invigoration that has occurred in recent years in cultural perspectives, with the growing body of theoretical and empirical work in cultural psychology (e.g. Cole, 1996; Miller, 1997; Shweder, 1990; Shweder et al., 1998). Such work is highlighting the role of cultural meanings and practices in completing the self and in affecting the form of basic psychological processes.

The present chapter examines the question of how to develop approaches to understanding child development that treat biological and cultural factors as sources of patterning of developmental change. The argument is made that it is critical to avoid the reductionism of assuming that biological perspectives provide a deeper level of explanation that supplants cultural analyses, just as it is critical to give greater attention to biological considerations in cultural accounts.

The chapter is organized in four sections. Sections one and two examine ways in which a cultural perspective challenges the tendency, found in many developmental, social psychological and biological accounts, for attention to be given exclusively to psychological processes and to objective contextual factors and not also to cultural meanings and practices in psychological explanation. In turn, the third section provides a select review of empirical research that illustrates ways in which biological and cultural processes are complementary in understanding child development. Finally, challenges are identified for future research, focused on integrating cultural and biological approaches to explanation.

Culture in psychological explanations: limited attention to culture in psychology

The major approaches to explanation in developmental and social psychology consider context primarily in ecological terms and neglect the necessary role of intersubjective or cultural processes in its patterning. As a consequence, there is a tendency in these perspectives to treat basic psychological processes as culturally invariant.

Development viewpoints

Within cognitive developmental and various contemporary constructivist traditions in developmental psychology, such as distinct domain or theory-theory approaches (e.g. Gopnik and Wellman, 1994; Turiel, 1989), the context is treated within a realist framework. From this type of perspective, experience is seen as giving rise to one most veridical representation that can be known in ways that do not depend on how the experience is culturally defined and structured. A major goal of child development is viewed as that of attaining an increasingly adequate understanding of experience, an understanding that is considered to represent the endpoint of child development in a given sphere and thus as essential in adaptation. For example, in work on theory of mind, it is assumed that universally the endpoint of child development is a trait psychology (Wellman, 1990).

Reflecting these assumptions, cognitive developmental viewpoints focus explanatory force mainly on factors in the person, such as the child's cognitive capacities, as well as on factors in the situation, such as the logical or empirical structure that it presents. Enculturation or socialization is treated merely as a vehicle for knowledge acquisition. It is regarded as non-essential, in that it is assumed that the individual can obtain knowledge of the world through direct cognitive processing without the need for cultural input. As Wells, for example, argues in a statement of this position:

It is difficult for anyone who has raised a child to deny the pervasive influence of socialized processing that surely surfaces as causal schemata originate through secondary sources such as parents ... Even though socialized processing may be an important determinant of knowledge about causal forces at one level, it nevertheless begs the question. How is it that the parents knew an answer? The issue is circular. That is precisely the reason that one must consider a more basic factor – namely original processing. (Wells, 1981, p. 313)

Notably, in Piagetian theory and in related constructivist developmental viewpoints, enculturation is considered to be a passive process that may affect the rate of development or the highest level achieved, but that has no impact in determining the nature of the endpoint obtained (Piaget, 1981). As Piaget argued in the case of language, rather than the child's cognitive operations reflecting the structure of language, the child's cognitive capacities develop independently of language and, in turn, make it possible for the child even to comprehend language: 'operativity leads to the structuration of language (of course through a choice among pre-existing linguistic models), rather than the reverse' (p. 309). It is this conception of culture as superfluous that has led to the enduring treatment of cultural approaches as opposed to constructivist viewpoints and to the enduring assumption that active construction of knowledge proceeds autonomously without cultural mediation (Turiel, 1983).

Social psychological perspectives

The tendency within social psychological viewpoints to downplay the importance of cultural considerations may appear surprising, given the concern of the field with understanding social processes and the emphasis placed on the situation in social psychological explanation. However, as may be seen, within social psychological viewpoints, situationism has typically been formulated in ways that accord no essential role to culture.

As approached within this dominant social psychological perspective, the situation is considered objective, in the sense that a given pattern of experience is assumed to present a determinate structure that is at least potentially knowable by the observer (e.g. Kelley, 1987). Importantly, it is also considered subjective, in that it is assumed that the impact of the situation depends upon how accurately the individual interprets it. Thus, for example, it is recognized that observers with different information processing capacities may differ in the degree to which their attributions adequately take into account the information presented in a given situation (e.g. Nisbett and Ross, 1980). Equally, individuals with contrasting schematic understandings may give divergent weight to aspects of the same situation or interpret the meaning of the same situation in different ways (e.g. Markus, Smith and Moreland, 1985).

This type of social psychological perspective gives rise to dualistic modes of explanation, focused on objective factors in the situation, such as the information available to individuals, and on subjective factors within the person, such as individuals' motivational status, cognitive capacities, attitudes, etc. From this viewpoint, culture is assumed to be already taken into account in either the definition of the situation or of the person. Thus, for example, it is recognized, that individuals in different cultural contexts vary in the everyday situations to which they are exposed. However, this stance is consonant with an explanatory focus on the objective situation, in that it merely suggests that the amount or type of information available to individuals may differ in contrasting cultural environments. Within this type of perspective, little consideration is paid to contrasting culturally shared meanings being given to the same objective information. Equally, evidence that individuals from different cultural backgrounds maintain contrasting systems of belief, value, or meaning is assimilated within the present type of model to an individual difference dimension. It is viewed as implying that individual differences in attitudes or understandings may relate to cultural group membership, but not as implying that there is a need to give independent weight to cultural meanings and practices per se in explanation. From this type of perspective, taking culture into account is considered relevant in explaining diversity in psychological outcomes; however, it is not seen as making a necessary contribution in the formulation of basic psychological theory.

Biological viewpoints

In recent years, many diverse types of biologically based approaches to psychological explanation have been developed. Attention here, however, will focus on behavioural genetic and evolutionary perspectives, as two of the dominant viewpoints that have been applied to explaining child development.

In terms of behavioural genetic viewpoints, a dualistic explanatory scheme is adopted, focused on genetic characteristics of the person and on factors in the environment, considered as an objective adaptive context. It is assumed that genetic propensities impact on development both through various direct effects and through the indirect effect of influencing individuals' selection of environments (Plomin, 1986; Plomin and Bergeman, 1991; Scarr and McCartney, 1983). In turn, in terms of environmental influences, it is maintained that the impact of environments on phenotypic behaviour can be understood in probabilistic terms. This idea is captured in the concept of *reaction range*, which is defined as the distribution of observed phenotypical reactions associated with a given genotype (Turkheimer and Gottesman, 1991). Within this framework, the environment is seen as a factor that is necessary for development and that, in extreme cases, can arrest or interfere with development. However, it is not assumed to impact on the direction or endpoint of developmental change. Rather, the assumption is made that the development of basic psychological processes constitute universal features of human experience that may be understood independently of culturally specific learning. As Scarr (1993, p. 1333), for example, argues: 'Becoming human is one matter. Becoming French, Mongolian or African-American is another. Becoming Georges Sand, Ghengis Khan, or Martin Luther King Jr. is still another.'

From this type of behavioural genetic perspective there is assumed to be little empirical need in psychological explanation for the concept of *reaction norm*, which is defined as the range of potential phenotypic reactions associated with a given genotype. Rather, the reaction norm for most psychological propensities is assumed to show no variation within normal human environments.

As applied to explaining human behaviour, this type of behavioural genetic model has characteristically led to a conclusion of universality. A common strategy adopted from this perspective is to define phenomena in terms of constructs in which only one particular form of a behaviour is considered optimum universally rather than in terms of constructs in which alternative forms of a behaviour are considered to be optimum, depending, in part, on the values and practices of the particular group. In defining only one behavioural form of a psychological phenomenon as optimum universally, any cultural variation observed then falls, by definition, within the relatively narrow range defined by this form. For example, in research on intelligence, a general intelligence quotient ('*g*'), which is indexed by scores on conventional IQ tests, is privileged as the most valid index of intelligence (e.g. Bouchard, 1997). No consideration is given to cultural variation in what constitutes intelligence, such as, for example, whether a given culture considers social competence as integral to intelligence (Greenfield, 1997) or privileges synthetic rather than analytic modes of cognition (Peng and Nisbett, 1999). In identifying intelligence exclusively with conventional IQ scores, a situation is created in which cultural groups may be found empirically to differ in the level of intelligence (i.e. '*g*') that they achieve, but, by definition, they cannot be found empirically to show any qualitative variation in the forms of intelligence that they display. To give another example, in the area of parenting, optimum parenting is assumed to take the form universally of an authoritative style – a style that empirically has been observed to be emphasized particularly by middle-class European-American parents (Baumrind, 1971). As critics have argued, however, this type of normative stance fails to recognize the alternative standards of parenting competence that are valued in different cultural communities, such as the stance of *chiao shun* or training emphasized within Chinese-American families (Chao, 1994).

Embodying a somewhat different focus, evolutionary viewpoints call attention to the adaptive functions of behaviours in the ancestral past, as forming broad constraints in which to understand the limits and forms of human psychological processes (e.g. Barkow, Cosmides and Tooby, 1992). Going beyond the early focus of psychologically oriented biological perspectives on functions like reflexes and a sex drive, modern behavioural neuroscience is concerned with functions such as attention and cognition (Berntson and Cacioppo, 2000; Gazzaniga, 2000). It is recognized that natural selection and evolution progressed beyond the limbic system to affect the cortical substrates that underlie advanced cognitive operations.

To date there has been only limited integration of evolutionary viewpoints with cultural accounts. Although it is recognized, within evolutionary viewpoints, that behaviours may at times be maladaptive or may continue to persist even in the absence of the functional constraint to which they were initially adapted, little consideration is typically given to non-functional aspects of behaviour. To the extent that cultural meanings and practices reflect considerations that are based on considerations other than social utility (Shweder, 1984), such meanings and practices and their impact on behaviour tend to be overlooked within evolutionary frameworks.

Evolutionary frameworks have also frequently downplayed the importance of cultural considerations because of their tendency to focus exclusively on highly abstract aspects of human experience. These are aspects that are essential to human survival and that all viable cultures must address, such as the development of attachment, pair bonding, etc. As theorists have noted, the existence of universals can be assumed at this highly abstract level of analysis:

Only extremely poor environments (or impaired organisms) prevent normal species-typical development by depriving the young of opportunities that environment must afford if development is to occur ... From an evolutionary point of view, the culturally universal availability of developmentally appropriate environments is a tautology; how could it be otherwise, if that culture is to survive? (Scarr, 1993, p. 1339)

A cultural perspective does not challenge the existence of psychological universals of this type but rather would question their explanatory sufficiency in accounting for the particulars of human experience and the specifics of human psychological functioning. For example, as LeVine (1990) notes in criticizing the notion of an 'average expectable environment' in Freudian theory, whereas in all cultures emphasis is placed on the development of both autonomy and self-regulation, the form that these phenomena take differs markedly as a function of cultural setting. As an illustration of this, he notes the extensive cultural variation that exists in the universal human capacity of autonomy. Whereas the mature American young adult is expected to show autonomy in choosing his wife and in establishing a separate household, the mature Gusii youth in Kenya is expected to consult his parents in the choice of a wife and to bring her home to his mother for help in setting up their household. In contrast, whereas the Gusii is expected to become increasingly self-sufficient in terms of subsistence activities, such as building his own house, the American youth is expected to show self-sufficiency only in relatively minor domains, such as cleaning his/her own room.

Implications for psychological explanation of cultural psychology

The present section discusses respects in which some of the premises of these developmental, social psychological and biological approaches are challenged by work in the emerging theoretical perspective of cultural psychology (e.g. Bruner, 1990; Cole, 1990, 1996; Miller, 1997, 1999; Shweder, 1990; Shweder and Sullivan, 1993). As will be seen, work from this perspective calls attention to culture as a symbolic medium for human development and highlights that participation in this medium is necessary for the emergence of all higher-order psychological processes.

Symbolic view of culture

A key conceptual contribution of work in cultural psychology is to underscore the need to go beyond exclusively ecological views of the context. A view of the context as an ecological setting has been highly influential within psychological theory. It informs, for example, such groundbreaking approaches as Gibsonian affordance theory (Gibson, 1979), Bronfenbrenner's model of the spheres of human development (Bronfenbrenner, 1979), and the concept of an ecological niche in the Whitings' landmark six-culture study of culture and personality (Whiting and Whiting, 1975). As discussed, it is also key to behavioural genetic and evolutionary arguments.

The anthropological insight that culture represents a symbolic environment does not challenge the importance of these types of ecological views of context, but rather suggests that they are insufficient in themselves. Within recent anthropological views, cultural meanings are understood to have representational functions, in encompassing collectively held understandings about the nature of experience and about the adaptive constraints that experience presents (Shore, 1996; Shweder and LeVine, 1984; Strauss and Quinn, 1997). They are also assumed to have directive functions, in encompassing rules for conduct or social norms. Perhaps most critically, however, cultures are understood to have constitutive functions, in serving to create objects and events whose existence depends, in part, on cultural definition (D'Andrade, 1984). Importantly, this reality-creating or constitutive function of cultures is recognized to be broad, extending not only to the establishment of social institutions (e.g. schools), roles (e.g. student), and artefacts (e.g. desks), but also to the creation of psychological concepts (e.g. intelligence) and epistemological categories (e.g. fairness). Thus, for example, it is recognized that a behaviour cannot be identified as intelligent merely by direct observation of experience but requires the application of socially defined criteria that determine what is meant by and constitutes intelligence in a given community.

These assumptions of symbolic approaches underscore the need to go beyond functional views of culture as bearing a one-to-one relationship to objective ecological constraints. Just as, in the symbolic system of language, there is an arbitrary or open relationship between sound and meaning, there is a partially open relationship between a functional constraint and the cultural meaning or significance that it is accorded. Thus, in a recent example, to understand the reason why Japanese preschool teachers value a low teacher/student ratio over a high one requires consideration of the cultural emphasis that they place on the child as a member of a larger social group, and not merely attention to functional considerations, such as their having the resources to enable them to reduce class size (Tobin, Wu and Davidson, 1989).

Incompleteness thesis

The incompleteness thesis stipulates that experience in a particular cultural environment is essential to the emergence of higher-order psychological processes (Geertz, 1973; Schwartz, 1992; Wertsch, 1995). Such a premise depends on the insight that meanings reflect cultural input. Equally, it depends on the insight of the cognitive revolution that individuals are agentic, actively interpreting and making sense of experience (Bruner, 1990). It follows that if individuals' interpretations of experience depend, in part, on culturally based meanings and practices, and if higher-level psychological processes are affected by these interpretations, then culture is fundamentally implicated in psychological functioning.

Strikingly the incompleteness thesis is highly compatible with evolutionary claims (Shore, 1996). As theorists have noted, the thesis rests on a consideration of the role of symbolic environments in allowing for the type of flexible genetic control characteristic of human adaptation. As Geertz argues in an early statement of this position:

What happened to us in the Ice Age is that we were obliged to abandon the regularity and precision of detailed genetic control over our conduct for the flexibility and adaptability of a more generalized though, of course, no less real, genetic control over it. To supply the additional information necessary to be able to act, we were forced, in turn, to rely more and more heavily on cultural sources – the accumulated fund of significant symbols. Such symbols are thus not mere expressions, instrumentalities, or correlates of our biological, psychological, and social existence; they are prerequisites of it. (Geertz, 1973, p. 49)

From the present perspective, it is expected that qualitative differences will occur in the psychological functioning of individuals inhabiting cultural settings characterized by markedly different meanings and practices. It is also assumed that learning is integral to development, with enculturation an active yet highly social process that impacts on the course and endpoints of child development.

Culture and biology in psychological explanation

The present discussion will focus on illustrative examples of empirical research that is uncovering cultural influences on the nature of basic psychological processes and on the path of child development. While incomplete, the present highly selective survey is intended to convey some of the types of contributions that cultural research is making to developing process understandings of basic psychological phenomena as well as to suggest ways in which cultural accounts are compatible with and dependent on biological processes.

Conceptions of self and others

Psychological theorists treat the capacity for self-awareness as fundamental to psychological functioning and as a biologically based universal. It is assumed that universally individuals maintain some awareness of their mental activity and of themselves as agents who exist in time and space and who act in the world. This type of view of the self underlies, for example, James' (1890) focus on a conscious selfhood or 'I', Allport's (1937) identification of the self as that aspect of personality that allows individuals to realize that they are the same person when they wake each day, as well as Neisser's (1988) conception of an 'ecological self' that perceives itself as situated within a particular physical environment. Arguments for the existence of a universal capacity for self-awareness rest on a consideration of its adaptive role in human sociocultural functioning. As Hallowell, for example, argues:

> . . . it seems necessary to assume self-awareness as one of the prerequisite psychological conditions for the functioning of any human social order, no matter what linguistic and culture patterns prevail . . . the phenomena [sic] of self-awareness in our species is as integral a part of human sociocultural mode of adaptation as it is of a distinctive human level of psychological structuralization. (Hallowell, 1955, p. 75)

In this view, self-awareness is seen as essential to agency and also to the human capacity for higher-order symbolic processes.

In addition to an innate capacity for self-awareness, arguments for a biological basis for perception of self and others have arisen from work on naive psychological concepts. A growing body of evidence is calling into question claims that children are, in effect, blank slates that have no inborn concepts or propensities to acquire particular understandings. Rather, evidence is suggesting that early in development children have available certain core psychological concepts (Gopnik and Wellman, 1994; Wellman, 1990). Young children tend to understand other people's actions in terms of their having certain beliefs about the world, desires, and wants, as well as feelings about having these desires and wants realized. Such understandings, it is further observed, constrain young children's inferences, with other persons understood in mentalistic terms as meaning-making perceivers, actors and emotors. The ideas of a universal capacity for self awareness and of young children being biologically prepared to construct knowledge in certain ways leads to the expectation that significant cross-cultural commonality will exist in social attribution and that this commonality will be somewhat greater early in development than at later ages.

Interestingly, however, these types of biological contributions to development are also compatible with the existence of marked cross-cultural variability in self/other understandings. For example, self-awareness makes it possible for humans, through symbolic means, to formulate and express culturally variable embodiments of the self. Equally, the existence of core psychological understandings (Wellman, 1998) constrains and enables but does not fully determine the developmental endpoints of self/other understandings emphasized within particular cultural populations.

In terms of empirical findings, research on person perception and social explanation among European-American and Hindu Indian populations reveals a common tendency to emphasize concrete and self-involved attributions (Miller, 1984, 1986, 1987). Thus, for example, in explaining behaviours, 8-year-olds in both cultures tend to construct simple narratives that presume a theory of mind. In contrast, whereas over development Americans' attributions show an increasing emphasis on a trait psychology, Indians' attributions show a developmental increase toward a contextualism, characterized by locating an act in terms of its social/spatial/temporal context.

Strikingly, available research on theory of mind shows a similar transition from early cross-cultural developmental commonality to culturally variable endpoints. Research on predominantly Western cultural populations has documented a shift from a 'desire' psychology, focused on simple intentions, to a 'belief' psychology, based on inferences about others' psychological states. Research among Chinese toddlers reveals a similar developmental pattern, with an early use of desire terms, followed by the acquisition at later ages of other types of mental state references (Tardif and Wellman, 2000). However, among various Chinese populations, toddlers employ desire terms earlier than do their English-speaking counterparts, and adults tend not to make the attributions to 'thinking' that are emphasized among English-speaking adults.

In sum, research on person perception and theory of mind points to both biological and cultural influences on the course of development. Evidence suggests that the biological components reflect adaptive capacities of the organism, inborn propensities that constrain and help to pattern the inferences that children make early in development, as well as common processes of learning in which enculturation occurs only relatively gradually. Importantly, however, the available evidence to date points to cultural differences in the course of developmental change and even its patterning at young ages, such as among toddlers. The cross-cultural findings on the cultural-specificity of developmental change imply that present normative models of theory of mind development which treat a trait psychology as the endpoint of child development are not fully adequate to capture the context-oriented endpoints observed in certain collectivist cultures (e.g. Lillard, 1998).

Development of moral understandings

In terms of moral development, the Kohlbergian model of justice morality (Kohlberg, 1971, 1984) argues for a universalistic morality of justice and individual rights, that is based on the realist assumption that the world presents a logical structure that may be deduced by the perceiver. As originally conceived by Kohlberg, this structure is the decontextualized orientation of an observer from the hypothetical perspective of a veil of ignorance, who is without identifying individual difference characteristics or a known position in a social network (Rawls, 1971). The resultant morality is one which gives primacy to the protection of individual rights and that stresses the avoidance of harm and the maximization of individual liberties.

Another related perspective on justice reasoning is offered by distinct domain theorists (Nucci, 1996; Turiel, 1983, 1998a; Turiel, Smetana and Killen, 1991). This model is also grounded in realist assumptions that the world presents one determinate structure which, if properly inferred, leads to a universalistic morality. In contrast to the Kohlbergian emphasis on logical deduction, however, the distinct domain perspective emphasizes processes of induction through which individuals observe the consequences of actions. It is assumed that behaviours that are perceived to result in harm or injustice are categorized in moral terms, based on individuals observing the consequences of these behaviours. In contrast, behaviours that do not involve harm are considered matters for personal decision-making and behaviours that serve solely to coordinate activities of individuals are treated as matters of social convention.

In contrast to these models of justice, Gilligan's model of a morality of caring argues for universals but grounds them in determinate biologically based gender-linked socialization processes (Gilligan, 1977, 1982). It is assumed that males and females, by virtue at least in part of their gender, experience different problems in adaptation. These, in turn, are seen as leading to contrasting socialization experiences and contrasting sense of self. In particular, as a girl develops she is seen as maintaining both an attachment to and an identification with her mother. This gives rise to an assumed connected sense of self and an associated morality of caring. In contrast, the male is assumed to identify with his father. In seeking to overcome the inequality that he experiences in relation to his father, the boy develops an autonomous sense of self and associated morality of justice. These two orientations are portrayed as universals, based on these fundamental biologically grounded problems in adaptation:

(T)he different dynamics of early childhood inequality and attachment lay the groundwork for two moral visions – one of justice and one of care . . .

Although the nature of the attachment between child and parent varies across individual and cultural settings and although inequality can be heightened or muted by familial and societal arrangements, all people are born into a situation of inequality and no child survives in the absence of adult connection. Since everyone is vulnerable both to oppression and to abandonment, two stories about morality recur in human experience. (Gilligan and Wiggins, 1987, p. 281)

This account focuses on deep universals of experience and dismisses cultural variation as only superficial content effects that have no fundamental impact on the development of self and morality (Miller, 1994).

Studies of moral judgement suggest the importance of both biological and cultural processes in patterning moral judgement. In terms of justice morality, research utilizing Kohlbergian measures reveals that conventional forms of justice reasoning tend to be found universally, with moral development proceeding in an invariant stage sequence in all cultures (for reviews, see Eckensberger and Zimba, 1997; Edwards, 1986; Miller, in press; Snarey, 1985). In turn, research that has employed the cognitively simpler procedures of the distinct domain perspective has provided evidence that at very young ages in all cultures children distinguish between domains of morality, based on considerations of harm, and domains of social convention, based on arbitrary matters of social coordination, and domains of personal choice, that do not involve either harm or social coordination concerns (Turiel, Killen and Helwig, 1987). It can be inferred that this commonality in moral appraisal reflects, at least in part, the adaptive importance to individual and group survival of being able to identify harm and the creation of systems to reduce its incidence through social sanction.

However, even with these common aspects of justice morality, cultural considerations affect the priority that is given to justice considerations in everyday moral judgement. Thus, for example, there is a greater tendency for justice obligations to be subordinated to interpersonal responsibilities in cultures that treat the latter as fundamental moral duties, such as Indian and Chinese cultural groups (Miller and Bersoff, 1992; Keller et al., 1998). Also, individuals from cultures emphasizing relational as compared with individualistic beliefs and practices show a greater tendency to consider behaviour as under the control of situational influences and not to hold agents morally accountable for them. Thus, for example, Hindu Indians have been found more frequently than European-Americans to absolve agents of moral accountability for justice breaches performed under the agent's emotional duress, immaturity or other potentially extenuating situational factors (Bersoff and Miller, 1993; Miller and Luthar, 1989). A greater emphasis also appears to be placed on contextual sensitivity in moral codes grounded in Confucian as compared with Judeo-Christian cultural traditions (Dien, 1982). In other cases, the existence of a shared abstract respect for individual rights and protection from harm has been found to give rise to marked variation in everyday moral judgement to the extent that individuals hold contrasting epistemological assumptions about the nature of persons deserving protection from harm or regarding what constitutes harm. For example, in maintaining a greater cultural emphasis on hierarchy, orthodox Hindu Indian populations consider it as morally justifiable to accord unequal privileges to females relative to males (Shweder, Mahapatra and Miller 1987).

More profound challenges to the universality of the morality of justice come from evidence that morality, in certain cases, is constructed around spiritually based issues that are orthogonal to concerns with justice or welfare. It has been shown, for example, that orthodox cultural populations both in the USA and India ground their judgements to Kohlbergian moral dilemmas in terms of consequences related to suffering and spiritual degradation (Haidt, Koller and Dias, 1993; Jensen, 1997; Shweder and Much, 1987). These types of considerations give rise to moral orientations focused on considerations such as disgust, disrespect, and sacrilege that may entail no considerations at all of harm or injustice. For example, Haidt et al. (1993) observed that American and Brazilian research participants tend to consider a brother and sister kissing each other on the mouth as offensive and immoral behaviour, even while judging the behaviour to be harmless.

In terms of interpersonal morality, evidence suggests that in all cultures morality encompasses concerns that are particularistic and partial, in the sense of applying to specific others with whom there is an in-group bond, such as a friend or family member. It has also been found that the same types of contextual factors tend to be taken into account cross-culturally. Thus, for example, both European-American and Hindu Indian populations regard it as more undesirable to fail to meet the needs of someone in a life-threatening as compared with a minor-need situation, as well as to fail to meet the needs of a friend or relative as compared with a stranger (Miller, Bersoff and Harwood, 1990). Likewise, to the extent that responsibilities to meet the needs of others are affected by considerations of affinity and liking, such effects tend to be in the same direction cross-culturally (Miller and Bersoff, 1998), with failure to meet the other's needs seen as always a greater moral violation in cases in which there is high as compared with low liking for the other (Miller and Bersoff, 1998). These common effects of context highlight common features of interpersonal morality that may have adaptive advantage and link human society to its ancestral past. Thus the sensitivity to in-group relations and to affective bonds as well as to level of need all may reflect, at least in part, calculations related to degrees of biological relatedness and to human survival.

Early developmental commonality in moral judgement also provides some indication of universal biologically based aspects of child development. For example, it has been observed that American and Indian 7-year-olds tend to share a view that parents have a responsibility to meet the needs of their children, with American 7-year-olds making such judgements more frequently than do American adults (Miller et al., 1990). It appears to be the case that this developmental commonality reflects certain shared aspects in the experience of children who, in all cultures, come into the world totally dependent on care-givers for their survival and thus may be biologically prepared to construct the understanding that it is natural for parents to be responsive to their young.

However, even with this evidence of considerable cross-cultural common-ality in the nature of interpersonal morality, research also uncovers marked cultural variability in its scope and form. Thus, for example, with respect to the cultural emphasis placed on individual freedom of choice, European-American populations are more prone to treat interpersonal responsibilities as matters for personal decision-making than are Hindu Indian populations (Miller et al., 1990; Miller and Bersoff, 1992). As compared with Hindu Indians, European-Americans also tend to give much greater weight to personal affinity and liking in gauging interpersonal responsibilities, resulting in a more contingent sense of interpersonal commitment (Miller and Bersoff, 1998). Furthermore, Indians consider it as morally required, rather than as beyond the scope of morality, to give priority to the needs of others in the face of personal hardship or sacrifice, and show a greater tendency than is shown by European-Americans to experi-ence satisfaction in such cases (Miller and Bersoff, 1995). Other cross-cultural research indicates the existence of a range of related yet qualitatively distinct interpersonal moral concerns emphasized in different cultural communities. These include, for example, an outlook found in various Buddhist communities that embodies a view of life as suffering and of negative karma as accumulating through transgressions (Huebner and Garrod, 1991, 1993), as well as an empha-sis on promotion of a state of harmony with others found in various small-scale communities, such as among the Maisin people of Papua New Guinea (Tietjen and Walker, 1985) and among the Black Caribs of British Honduras (Gorsuch and Barnes, 1973).

In sum, the present findings of both cross-cultural commonalities and dif-ferences in moral judgement underscore respects in which morality is simul-taneously biologically and culturally grounded. The salience of moralities of justice and of interpersonal responsibility, the common sensitivity of morali-ties to parameters such as need and relatedness, as well as commonalities in young children's early constructions of morality all speak to possible biologi-cally grounded universals related to fundamental problems in human adaptation and to the care of young. However, cultural meanings and practices also impact on the endpoint of moral reasoning, leading to variation in the forms of moral-ity emphasized in different cultural communities and to marked cross-cultural variation in the application of moral criteria in judgement about concrete situ-ations. Such variation may be considered qualitative to the extent that it cannot be fully accommodated within existing models of moral development and re-quires new theoretical formulations – such as of role-based duties having a post-conventional moral status and of morality entailing considerations that do not involve either issues of harm or welfare.

Challenges in integrating cultural and biological perspectives

It has been seen that both biological and cultural processes contribute in distinctive ways to psychological explanation. However, the conceptual and empirical research undertaken to date has also revealed that at present there is little integration of biological and cultural perspectives. Too often they are presented as mutually exclusive interpretations or as explanations that are each sufficient in themselves. In the present section, brief consideration will be given to some of the challenges that must be addressed in developing perspectives that give weight to both types of considerations in understanding child development.

Beyond biological or cultural determinism

A major challenge for work in this area is to avoid assuming deterministic stances that fail to take into account the multifaceted processes contributing to psychological phenomena. This involves recognizing the insufficiency of either biological or cultural accounts alone and the mutual interdependence of biological and cultural explanations.

In terms of evolutionary and other biological approaches to explanation, it is critical to avoid stances focused exclusively on issues of adaptive advantage. It must be recognized that whereas phenomena may be biologically grounded, biological propensities alone do not fully determine psychological outcomes. To the extent that psychological phenomena reflect culturally based and historically situated meanings and practices, they are, in part, historically contingent rather than fully causally determined. Equally, it is critical to avoid portraying cultural forms in idealistic terms, as unrestrained forms that bear no relationship to biological or other material constraints. It must be recognized that biological affordances, constraints, and propensities represent a positive influence on psychological phenomena and not just an enabler or condition for it.

Process understandings of biological and cultural influences

Challenges also exist in developing a more process-based understanding of biological and cultural influences on psychological development. In terms of neuroscience, this type of stance involves localizing more specifically the physiological determinants of given effects and taking into account the extent to which observed effects are contextually dependent. Thus, for example, in working to identify physiological markers for autism, an assumed theory of mind deficit, there is the challenge of recognizing the multiple ways in which theory of mind itself may be defined and manifest. It is also critical to avoid the post hoc and circular character of certain evolutionary explanations. Thus, for example, functional explanations of behaviour that rely on considerations of adaptive advantage must be formulated in such a way that they can be empirically verified and subject to potential falsification.

In terms of developing more process-oriented cultural approaches, it is important to avoid the stereotypical, if not at times pejorative, generalities associated with such global frameworks as that of individualism/collectivism, the independent/interdependent self dichotomy, or of Eastern/Western viewpoints. This involves recognizing that culture impacts on behaviour in ways that are contextually dependent. It is also critical to give greater weight to the routines and practices through which cultural meanings are embodied. Finally, greater effort needs to be made to develop approaches to culture that attend to individual differences in culturally based psychological orientations and that examine the diverse perspectives of individuals in different positions within power hierarchies (Turiel, 1998b).

More generally, there is a need to develop more sophisticated understandings of the interrelationship of biological and cultural factors. In this regard, for example, it is important to recognize that the interrelationship of biological and cultural factors is bi-directional, with cultural factors patterning at times biological processes and not merely the converse (Shore, 1996). As examples of such effects, theorists are noting the marked differences in health outcomes associated with cultural processes linked to socioeconomic status and ethnicity (Huff and Kline, 1999). In addition, there is a need to go beyond the present tendency to associate biologically based processes solely with the presence of universal effects and culturally based processes solely with effects that are culturally variable. A biological process can lead to variation just as a cultural one can give rise to uniformity.

Conclusion

In conclusion, it must be recognized that individuals are simultaneously biological and cultural beings, with processes at both levels intertwined and mutually influential. It is no more possible to study a human without a biology than it is possible to separate individuals from their culture. Individuals always bring both common and unique biological apparatuses that function as constraints, affordances and propensities and always act in ways that have significance in terms of their adaptive consequences. Equally, individuals always develop in sociocultural contexts that are historically situated and that impact on their psychological functioning in respects that may be open-ended and indeterminate. There is a sense that biological and cultural approaches represent new frontiers and promising future directions for studies of child development. For these frontiers and promises to be realized effectively, however, the perspectives must proceed not in parallel, but in combination.

REFERENCES

Allport, G. W. (1937). *Personality: a psychological interpretation.* New York: Holt.
Barkow, J., Cosmides, L. and Tooby, J. (eds.) (1992). *The adapted mind: evolutionary psychology and the generation of culture.* New York: Oxford University Press.
Baumrind, D. (1971). Current patterns of parental authority. *Developmental Psychology Monographs,* 4(1), part 2.
Berntson, G. G. and Cacioppo, J. T. (2000). Psychobiology and social psychology: past, present, and future. *Personality and Social Psychology Review,* 4(1), 3–15.
Bersoff, D. M. and Miller, J. G. (1993). Culture, context, and the development of moral accountability judgements. *Developmental Psychology,* 29(4), 664–76.
Bouchard, T. J. (1997). IQ similarity in twins reared apart: findings and response to critics. In R. J. Sternberg and E. L. Grigorenko (eds.), *Intelligence, heredity, and environment.* New York: Cambridge University Press, pp. 126–60.
Bronfenbrenner, U. (1979). *The ecology of human development: experiments by nature and design.* Cambridge, MA: Harvard University Press.
Bruner, J. (1990). *Acts of meaning.* Cambridge, MA: Harvard University Press.
Chao, R. K. (1994). Beyond parental control and authoritarian parenting style: understanding Chinese parenting through the cultural notion of training. *Child Development,* 65(4), 1111–19.
Cole, M. (1990). Cultural psychology: A once and future discipline? In J. J. Berman (ed.), *Nebraska Symposium on Motivation,* vol. 38: *Cross-cultural perspectives.* Lincoln: University of Nebraska Press, pp. 279–335.
    (1996). *Cultural psychology: a once and future discipline.* Cambridge, MA: Harvard University Press.
D'Andrade, R. G. (1984). Cultural meaning systems. In R. A. Shweder and R. A. LeVine (eds.), *Culture theory: essays on mind, self, and emotion.* Cambridge: Cambridge University Press, pp. 88–119.
Dien, D. S. F. (1982). A Chinese perspective on Kohlberg's theory of moral development. *Developmental Review,* 2, 331–41.
Eckensberger, L. H. and Zimba, R. F. (1997). The development of moral judgment. In *Handbook of cross-cultural psychology,* vol. 2: *Basic processes and human development,* 2nd edn. Boston: Allyn and Bacon, pp. 299–338.
Edwards, C. (1986). Cross-cultural research on Kohlberg's stages: the basis for consensus. In S. Modgil and C. Modgil (eds.), *Kohlberg: consensus and controversy.* Philadelphia: Falmer Press, pp. 419–30.
Gazzaniga, M. S. (ed.) (2000). *The new cognitive neurosciences.* Cambridge, MA: MIT Press.
Geertz, C. (1973). *The interpretation of cultures.* New York: Basic Books.
Gibson, J. J. (1979). *The ecological approach to visual perception.* Boston: Houghton Mifflin.
Gilligan, C. (1977). In a different voice: women's conceptions of self and of morality. *Harvard Educational Review,* 47(4), 481–517.

(1982). *In a different voice: psychological theory and women's development.* Cambridge, MA: Harvard University Press.

Gilligan, C. and Wiggins, G. (1987). The origins of morality in early childhood relationships. In J. Kagan and S. Lamb (eds.), *The emergence of morality in young children.* Chicago: University of Chicago Press, pp. 277–305.

Gopnik, A. and Wellman, H. M. (1994). The theory theory. In L. A. Hirschfield and S. A. Gelman (eds.), *Mapping the mind: domain specificity in cognition and culture.* New York: Cambridge University Press, pp. 257–93.

Gorsuch, R. L. and Barnes, M. L. (1973). Stages of ethical reasoning and moral norms of Carib youths. *Journal of Cross-Cultural Psychology*, 4, 283–301.

Greenfield, P. M. (1997). You can't take it with you: why ability assessments don't cross cultures. *American Psychologist*, 52(10), 1115–24.

Haidt, J., Koller, S. H. and Dias, M. G. (1993). Affect, culture, and morality, or is it wrong to eat your dog? *Journal of Personality and Social Psychology*, 65(4), 613–28.

Hallowell, A. I. (1955). *Culture and experience.* Philadelphia: University of Pennsylvania Press.

Huebner, A. M. and Garrod, A. C. (1991). Moral reasoning in a Karmic world. *Human Development*, 34, 341–52.

(1993). Moral reasoning among Tibetan monks: a study of Buddhist adolescents and young adults in Nepal. *Journal of Cross-Cultural Psychology*, 24(2), 167–85.

Huff, R. M. and Kline, M. V. (eds.) (1999). *Promoting health in multicultural populations: a handbook for practitioners.* Thousand Oaks, CA: Sage.

James, W. (1890). *Principles of psychology.* New York: Holt.

Jensen, L. A. (1997). Different worldviews, different morals: America's culture war divide. *Human Development*, 40(6), 325–44.

Keller, M., Edelstein, W., Fang, F. and Fang, G. (1998). Reasoning about responsibilities and obligations in close relationships: a comparison across two cultures. *Developmental Psychology*, 34(4), 731–41.

Kelley, H. H. (1987). Causal schemata and the attribution process. In H. H. Kelly, *Attribution: perceiving the causes of behavior.* Hillsdale, NJ: Lawrence Erlbaum, pp. 151–74.

Kohlberg, L. (1971). From is to ought: how to commit the naturalistic fallacy and get away with it in the study of moral development. In T. Mischel (ed.), *Cognitive development and epistemology.* New York: Academic Press, pp. 151–236.

(1984). *The psychology of moral development: the nature and validity of moral stages* (Essays on Moral Development, vol. 2). San Francisco: Harper and Row.

LeVine, R. A. (1990). Infant environments in psychoanalysis: a cross-cultural view. In R. A. Shweder and R. A. LeVine (eds.), *Cultural psychology: essays on comparative human development.* New York: Cambridge University Press, pp. 454–74.

Lillard, A. (1998). Ethnopsychologies: cultural variations in theories of mind. *Psychological Bulletin*, 123, 1–32.

Markus, H., Smith, J. and Moreland, R. L. (1985). Role of the self-concept in the perception of others. *Journal of Personality and Social Psychology*, 49(6), 1494–512.

Miller, J. G. (1984). Culture and the development of everyday social explanation. *Journal of Personality and Social Psychology*, 46(5), 961–78.

(1986). Early cross-cultural commonalities in social explanation. *Developmental Psychology*, 22, 514–20.

(1987). Cultural influences on the development of conceptual differentiation in person description. *British Journal of Developmental Psychology*, 5(4), 309–19.

(1994). Cultural diversity in the morality of caring: individually oriented versus duty-based interpersonal moral codes. *Cross-Cultural Research*, 28(1), 3–39.

(1997). Theoretical issues in cultural psychology. In J. W. Berry, Y. H. Poortinga and J. Pandey (eds.), *Handbook of cross-cultural psychology*, vol. 1: *Theory and method*, 2nd edn. Boston: Allyn and Bacon, pp. 185–28.

(1999). Cultural psychology: implications for basic psychological theory. *Psychological Science*, 10(2), 85–91.

(in press). Culture and moral development. In D. Matsumoto (ed.), *The handbook of culture and psychology*. Oxford: Oxford University Press.

Miller, J. G. and Bersoff, D. M. (1992). Culture and moral judgement: how are conflicts between justice and interpersonal responsibilities resolved? *Journal of Personality and Social Psychology*, 62(4), 541–54.

(1995). Development in the context of everyday family relationships: culture, interpersonal morality, and adaptation. In D. M. Bersoff (ed.), *Morality in everyday life: developmental perspectives*. New York: Cambridge University Press, pp. 259–82.

(1998). The role of liking in perceptions of the moral responsibility to help: a cultural perspective. *Journal of Experimental Social Psychology*, 34(5), 443–69.

Miller, J. G., Bersoff, D. M. and Harwood, R. L. (1990). Perceptions of social responsibilities in India and in the United States: moral imperatives or personal decisions? *Journal of Personality and Social Psychology*, 58(1), 33–47.

Miller, J. G. and Luthar, S. (1989). Issues of interpersonal responsibility and accountability: a comparison of Indians' and Americans' moral judgements. *Social Cognition*, 7(3), 237–61.

Neisser, U. (1988). Five kinds of self-knowledge. *Philosophical Psychology*, 1, 35–59.

Nisbett, R. and Ross, L. (1980). *Human inference: strategies and shortcomings of social judgement*. Englewood Cliffs, NJ: Prentice-Hall.

Nucci, L. P. (1996). Morality and the personal sphere of actions, In E. S. Reed, E. Turiel and T. Brown (eds.), *Values and knowledge* (The Jean Piaget symposium series). Mahwah, NJ: Lawrence Erlbaum pp. 41–60.

Peng, K. and Nisbett, R. E. (1999). Culture, dialectics, and reasoning about contradiction. *American Psychologist*, 54(9), 741–54.

Piaget, J. (1981). *The psychology of intelligence*. Totowa, NJ: Littlefield, Adams and Co.

Pinker, S. (1997). *How the mind works*. New York: Norton.

Plomin, R. (1986). *Development, genetics, and psychology*. Hillsdale, NJ: Lawrence Erlbaum.

Plomin, R. and Bergeman, C. S. (1991). The nature of nurture: genetic influences on 'environmental' measures. *Behavioral and Brain Sciences*, 14, 373–427.

Rawls, J. (1971). *A theory of justice*. Cambridge, MA: Harvard University Press.

Scarr, S. (1993). Biological and cultural diversity: the legacy of Darwin for development. *Child Development*, 64, 1333–53.

Scarr, S. and McCartney, K. (1983). How people make their own environment: a theory of genotype-environment effects. *Child Development*, 54(2), 424–35.

Schwartz, T. (1992). Anthropology and psychology: an unrequited relationship. In T. Schwartz, G. M. White and C. Lutz (eds.), *New directions in psychological anthropology*. New York: Cambridge University Press, pp. 324–49.

Shore, B. (1996). *Culture in mind: cognition, culture and the problem of meaning*. New York: Oxford University Press.

Shweder, R. A. (1984). Anthropology's romantic rebellion against the Enlightenment, or there's more to thinking than reason and evidence. In R. A. Shweder and R. A. LeVine (eds.), *Culture theory: essays on mind, self, and emotion*. Cambridge: Cambridge University Press, pp. 27–66.

(1990). Cultural psychology – what is it? In J. W. Stigler, R. A. Shweder, and G. Herdt (eds.), *Cultural psychology: essays on comparative human development*. New York: Cambridge University Press, pp. 27–66.

Shweder, R. A., Goodnow, J., Hatano, G., LeVine, R. A., Markus, H. and Miller, P. (1998). The cultural psychology of development: one mind, many mentalities. In W. Damon (ed.), *Handbook of child psychology*, vol. I. New York: Wiley, pp. 865–937.

Shweder, R. A. and LeVine, R. A. (1984). *Culture theory: essays on mind, self, and emotion*. Cambridge: Cambridge University Press.

Shweder, R. A., Mahapatra, M. and Miller, J. (1987). Culture and moral development. In J. Kagan and S. Lamb (eds.), *The emergence of morality in young children*. Chicago: University of Chicago Press, pp. 1–90.

Shweder, R. A. and Much, N. C. (1987). Determinants of meaning: discourse and moral socialization. In W. M. Kurtines and J. L. Gewirtz (eds.), *Moral development through social interaction*. New York: Wiley, pp. 197–244.

Shweder, R. A. and Sullivan, M. A. (1993). Cultural psychology: who needs it? *Annual Review of Psychology*, 44, 497–527.

Snarey, J. R. (1985). Cross-cultural universality of social-moral development: a critical review of Kohlbergian research. *Psychological Bulletin*, 97(2), 202–32.

Strauss, C. and Quinn, N. (1997). *A cognitive theory of cultural meaning*. New York: Cambridge University Press.

Tardif, T. and Wellman, H. M. (2000). Acquisition of mental state language in Mandarin- and Cantonese-speaking children. *Developmental Psychology*, 36(1), 25–43.

Tietjen, A. M. and Walker, L. J. (1985). Moral reasoning and leadership among men in a Papua New Guinea society. *Developmental Psychology*, 21(6), 982–92.

Tobin, J. J., Wu, D. Y. H. and Davidson, D. H. (1989). *Preschool in three cultures: Japan, China, and the United States*. New Haven, CT: Yale University Press.

Turiel, E. (1983). *The development of social knowledge: morality and convention*. Cambridge: Cambridge University Press.

(1989). Domain-specific social judgements and domain ambiguities. *Merrill-Palmer Quarterly*, 35(1), 89–114.

(1998a). The development of morality. In N. Eisenberg (ed.), *Handbook of child psychology*, vol. 3: *Social, emotional, and personality development*. New York: Wiley, pp. 863–92.

(1998b). Notes from the underground: culture, conflict, and subversion. In J. Langer and M. Killer (eds.), *Piaget, evolution, and development* (The Jean Piaget symposium series). Mahwah, NJ: Lawrence Erlbaum, pp. 271–96.

Turiel, E., Killen, M. and Helwig, C. C. (1987). Morality: its structure, functions, and vagaries. In J. Kagan and S. Lamb (eds.), *The emergence of morality in young children*. Chicago: University of Chicago Press, pp. 155–243.

Turiel, E., Smetana, J. G. and Killen, M. (1991). Social contexts in social cognitive development. In W. M. Kurtines and J. L. Gewirtz (eds.), *Handbook of moral behavior and development*, vol. 1: *Theory*. Hillsdale, NJ: Lawrence Erlbaum, pp. 307–32.

Turkheimer, E. and Gottesman, I. I. (1991). Individual differences and the canalization of human behavior. *Developmental Psychology*, 27, 18–22.

Wellman, H. (1990). *The child's theory of mind*. Cambridge, MA: MIT Press.

(1998). Culture, variation, and levels of analysis in folk psychologies: comment on Lillard [1998]. *Psychological Bulletin*, 123(1), 33–6.

Wells, G. (1981). Lay analyses of causal forces on behavior. In J. H. Harvey (ed.), *Cognition, social behavior and the environment*. Hillsdale, NJ: Lawrence Erlbaum, pp. 309–24.

Wertsch, J. V. (1995). Sociocultural research in the copyright age. *Culture and Psychology*, 1, 81–102.

Whiting, B. B. and Whiting, J. W. (1975). *Children of six cultures: a psycho-cultural analysis*. Cambridge, MA: Harvard University Press.

Part III

Perspectives on development drawing from the universal and the specific

8   Between individuals and culture: individuals' evaluations of exclusion from social groups

Melanie Killen, Heidi McGlothlin and Jennie Lee-Kim

One of the most complex aspects of social life is how to balance individual goals with collective concerns of the group. This difficult task involves weighing individual values, such as rights and personal goals, with group functioning, such as social expectations, traditions, and group identity. While group memberships are an important source of social identity and group functioning, group memberships also contribute to intergroup conflict. This is because, at times, group identifications conflict with individual goals and liberties. For example, when members of a group hold expectations about who belongs to the group, the result is often exclusion. Depending on the criteria, exclusion may constitute a violation of the rights and liberties of the excluded individuals as well as prejudicial and stereotypical attitudes about others, often resulting in severe moral transgressions (Opotow, 1990). However, there are also times when individual goals are subordinated to group goals in a way that does not result in conflict, and in contexts in which the exclusion of an individual is viewed as legitimate, and not as an insult to another person in the form of a violation of individual rights or psychological harm. As examples, cultural organizations and institutions, such as sports teams, schools, the workplace and family life all involve expectations, and sometimes regulations, that result in the exclusion of individuals from full or partial participation. In some cases, these decisions are viewed as a benefit to all, with a goal of coordinating social interactions among individuals and promoting social group functioning.

Decisions to exclude individuals from groups are an inevitable part of culture, and how members of a given culture evaluate, interpret and resolve intergroup conflicts arising from decisions to exclude requires in-depth analysis and

Thanks are extended to the editors, and to Stacey S. Horn, Judith Smetana, and Elliot Turiel for their feedback and comments on the manuscript, and to the graduate students who have worked on the studies described in this chapter, Alicia Ardila-Rey, Stacey S. Horn, Christina Edmonds, Kerry Pisacane, Christine Theimer Schuette, and Micah Stretch. Some of the research described in this chapter was supported by a grant from the National Science Foundation (SBR9729739) awarded to the first author. In addition, we extend our appreciation to Joseph Hawkins for his support of the work, and to the superintendent, principals, teachers, and students in Montgomery County Public School District (Maryland, USA) for their participation in our research programme.

investigation. For example, when is exclusion, based on group membership, considered to be valid? When is exclusion from the group viewed as wrong from a moral standpoint? When do individuals give priority to the group (the decision to exclude) in contrast to the concerns of the individual (the experience of being excluded)? Many different theories have been proposed to explain the relationship between the individual and the society (see Turiel, 1998), but little research has been conducted to analyse how individuals reason about decisions that involve exclusion. Culture is multifaceted and in our work we have defined culture as a diverse phenomenon with different meanings for individuals depending on the context. In contrast to macro theories of culture, in which culture is defined as a unified set of meaning systems, we define culture at the micro level. Culture is one source of influence on individuals and in order to understand how cultures influence individual social judgements it is necessary to examine how different social categories, such as gender, race, ethnicity, class and nationality, contribute to an individual's evaluations of social events and interactions.

Judgements about inclusion and exclusion

In our research, we have been examining the developmental patterns of intergroup attitudes regarding decisions that involve inclusion and exclusion of individuals from social groups (Horn, in press; Horn, Killen and Stangor, 1999; Killen et al., 2001; Killen and Stangor, 2001; Stangor et al., 2001; Theimer, Killen and Stangor, 2001; Theimer-Schuette, 1999). Our research is guided by a model that draws from moral developmental studies on social reasoning about fairness, justice, and rights (see Killen and Hart, 1995; Turiel, 1998; Turiel, Killen and Helwig, 1987), and social psychological studies on intergroup relationships, including the attitudes, beliefs and judgements that members of one social group have about members of another social group (Macrae, Stangor and Hewstone, 1996; Stangor and Schaller, 1996).

We have focused specifically on judgements about group inclusion and exclusion, that is when is it legitimate to exclude someone from a group and when is it unfair to exclude someone from a group? We have proposed that this type of decision varies depending on the specific context of exclusion as well as other factors such as the reason for exclusion and the developmental level of the respondent. We do not assume that exclusion is strictly a moral transgression. The context of exclusion includes many factors. For example, certain forms of exclusion by cultural groups are considered to be legitimate, such as excluding someone from a sports team who is a poor athlete. However, even in a sports context, in which many forms of exclusion are viewed as legitimate, exclusion based solely on race is viewed as wrong. In some contexts, group functioning (e.g. maintaining a winning team) takes priority over the perspective of the individual (e.g. the rejected person feels bad). In other contexts, individual rights (e.g. the right to be treated equally and to be free from discrimination on the basis of race) take priority over the traditions of the group (e.g. a history of same-race participants). Thus it is necessary to understand the reason for exclusion as well as the context of exclusion, in order to determine when individuals view exclusion as legitimate from a group perspective or wrong from an individual (fairness) perspective.

In our view, the balancing of concerns of the individual and concerns of the group is a universal experience, part of being a member of a culture or social group. In fact, we view these dual aspects of social life as part of our evolutionary heritage (see Killen and de Waal, 2000). Humans as well as nonhuman primates have social goals that involve coordinating individual desires with social group functioning. We postulate that individual and group goals coexist within individuals. Our perspective and our findings lead us to challenge the view that members of 'modern' cultures, such as in the USA, Canada and Europe, are individualistic (giving priority to the individual over the group) and that members of 'traditional' cultures, such as in Japan, China and Latin America, are collectivistic (giving priority to the group over the individual; see Killen and Wainryb, 2000; Turiel, 1998; Turiel et al., 1987). Social life is complex and priorities vary by context, not as a function of national or cultural identity. This view is based on empirical studies, which have shown that individuals give priority to both individualistic and collectivistic concerns in a wide range of cultures (Turiel, 1998; Turiel and Wainryb, 2000). As will be asserted below, our findings on inclusion and exclusion in social group contexts have implications for how cultures are characterized. Characterizing cultures as individualistic (giving priority to the individual) or as collectivistic (giving priority to the group) overlooks complexities in how people evaluate social conflicts and, moreover, perpetuates stereotypes about cultures and members of cultures. First, we will describe our theoretical model, then our research on reasoning about inclusion and exclusion, and finally we will discuss the implications of this work for theories of culture.

Children's domain-specific knowledge

Our theoretical model has been referred to as a social-cognitive domain model, originally proposed by Turiel and his colleagues (for reviews, see Helwig, Tisak and 1990; Killen, 1991; Nucci and Lee, 1993; Smetana, 1995; Tisak, 1995; Turiel, 1998; Turiel et al., 1987). This work has documented that individuals evaluate a wide range of social issues and values using different categories of social reasoning. Individuals from many cultures use reasoning that reflects multiple domains of knowledge, including the moral, societal and psychological. The moral domain refers to principles of how people ought to treat one another with regard to fairness, others' welfare, equality and rights (based on moral philosophical criteria, see Gewirth, 1978; Turiel, 1998). The societal domain (Searle, 1969) refers to behavioural regularities to ensure the smooth functioning of social groups such as conventions, traditions and rituals. The psychological domain refers to individual decision-making such as autonomy, personal goals and personal prerogatives (Nucci, 1996; Nucci and Lee, 1993).

The methodology used to document the existence of these epistemological domains involves assessing how individuals classify, evaluate and justify social issues through the use of individually administered interviews as well as detailed surveys and interactive sorting tasks. A goal of this methodology has been to document whether individuals use the theoretical criteria identified with these domains when evaluating straightforward (prototypic) and complex social events. Without knowing how individuals classify events, incorrect assumptions may be made about the nature of the event (Turiel, 1983). For example, 'refusing to brush one's teeth' may be viewed as wrong but not morally wrong. In order to determine how an individual evaluates an act it is necessary to analyse the way in which the individual classifies the act (e.g. as moral or non-moral). Do individuals believe that the principle or rule underlying a transgression applies to all persons everywhere or just to members of a specific culture? Is the rule or principle under specific authority jurisdiction or contingent on negative consequences? In general, this approach, referred to as the semi-structured interview methodology, originally developed by Piaget (1932), is designed to assess underlying reasoning and judgements.

The findings have shown that children, adolescents and adults use these criteria to distinguish acts as moral, social-conventional, and personal (psychological). As shown in table 8.1, the social judgement assessments used to determine how individuals categorize events include: *generalizability* (does the rule underlying the issue apply to members of other cultures and/or communities?), *authority contingency* (does the act depend upon an authority figure's mandate?), *legitimacy of authority* (how legitimate is it for an authority figure to make rules about the act?), *rule contingency* (does the wrongness of the act depend upon explicit rules or laws?), *rule alterability* (can the rule be changed or totally negated?), *rule utility* and *rule violation* (is the rule good or bad? And is it legitimate to violate the rule?). These criteria provide a means for assessing how individuals classify, evaluate and interpret social issues.

We have listed a sample of the diverse cultural groups that have participated in these studies in table 8.1. Over eighty-five empirical studies have shown that individuals evaluate social issues and events using moral, societal, and psychological reasoning categories (Smetana, 1995; Tisak, 1995). Individuals from Brazil, Canada, Colombia, Germany, India, Indonesia, Israel, Japan, Korea, Nigeria, Spain, Turkey, the UK, the USA, Virgin Islands, Zambia, with varied SES (low, high) statuses, and from different types of communities, rural and

Table 8.1 *Social judgement assessments*

Criterion judgement	Sample question	Culture[a]	Age (yrs)	Citation
Generalizability	Is it all right or not all right to do X in another country/school/religion?	Australia	3–5	Siegal and Storey (1985)
		Korea	5–18	Song, Smetana and Kim (1987)
		St. Croix	6–11	Nucci, Turiel and Encarnacion-Gawrych (1983)
		Af-Am low SES	5–6	Jagers, Bingham and Hans (1996)
		Brazil	9–15	Nucci, Camino and Milnitsky-Sapiro (1996)
		Canada	6–7	Helwig (1997, 1998)
		Religion US	6–11	Nucci and Turiel (1993)
Authority contingency	Would it be OK to do act X if directed to do so by teacher/parent/government?	Australia	3–5	Siegal and Storey (1985)
		Nigeria-rural	8–18	Hollos, Leis and Turiel (1986)
		US	6–10	Davidson, Turiel and Black (1983)
Legitimacy of authority	Is it OK or not OK for parents/teachers/government to make rules about act X?	Canada	6–22	Helwig (1997)
		Korea	7–13	Kim and Turiel (1996)
		US	3–6	Tisak (1993)
Rule contingency	Would act X be OK if there were no rules about it?	St. Croix	3–5	Nucci, Turiel and Encarnacion-Gawrych (1983)
		Australia	3–5	Siegal and Storey (1985)
		Korea	5–18	Song, Smetana and Kim (1987)
		India	8–22	Miller and Bersoff (1992)
		Brazil	9–15	Nucci, Camino and Milnitsky-Sapiro (1996)
		Low/highSES US	15–18	Killen, Leviton and Cahill (1991)
Rule alterability	Is it all right to change this rule?	Nigeria-rural	8–18	Hollos, Leis and Turiel (1986)
		US	6–10	Davidson, Turiel and Black (1983)
Rule utility	Is it a good rule or a bad rule?	Canada	6–22	Helwig (1997)
		US	3–6	Smetana (1985)
Rule violation	Would it be OK or not OK to break rule X?	Canada	6–11; 6–22	Helwig (1997, 1998)
		US	17–20	Turiel, Hildebrandt and Wainryb (1985)
		Af-Am low SES	8,10,12	Astor (1994)

Note: [a]Owing to space limitations, only one US empirical study is listed in each section unless the study involved a non-middle-class sample. There are over 80 studies in the USA using these measures. The US studies have included a range of children from low SES to middle SES as well as from different religious groups such as Amish. Orthodox Jewish. Catholic. We have included a few examples of the variation. However, unless otherwise stated, all of the studies listed include middle-class SES. For additional references, see Turiel (1998).

urban, made judgements that reflect a valuing of group functioning, interpersonal obligations, as well as a valuing of individual rights and matters of fairness (for a sample of studies, see table 8.1). As an example, children from these diverse cultures have evaluated acts of harm (a moral transgression) as wrong in any context, not a matter of authority jurisdiction, and not contingent on rules (see table 8.1). These findings have revealed that individuals classify acts in ways that are consistent with philosophical criteria. Moral acts are those that are classified as generalizable, not alterable, and not contingent upon rules or authority. Societal acts are those that are classified as alterable, contingent upon rules and authority and not generalizable. Personal acts are not defined by generalizability, alterability or contingency (Nucci, 1996; Tisak, 1995), but are decisions that are a matter of personal choice, and up to the individual to decide. These criteria are consistent with definitions from moral philosophy (Gewirth, 1978; Rawls, 1971).

The findings from the social-cognitive domain model are in contrast to traditional developmental theories which characterized development as a series of global stages or levels in which one orientation dominates the child's thinking across all contexts (e.g. heteronymous, preconventional orientations) as proposed by Piaget (1932) and Kohlberg (1984). Rather than postulating that children's thinking forms one coherent whole at a particular point in development, research findings have revealed that children's level of knowledge differs depending on the area of knowledge (see Hart and Killen, 1995; Turiel and Smetana, 1998). As an example, in the area of children's rights, a global view would predict that children's evaluations reflect different levels of reasoning (see Melton, 1980) such that children at Level 1 evaluate rights in terms of authority jurisdiction, children at Level 2 evaluate rights in terms of fairness, and children at Level 3 evaluate rights in terms of abstract principles. However, recent work by Ruck, Abramovitch and Keating (1998), using a domain model, has shown that children evaluate rights about self-determination (e.g. the right to privacy and personal decision-making) differently from rights about nurturance (e.g. the right to be cared for by parents), and use different forms of reasoning depending on the content of the specific circumstances (children use reasons based on parental duty in some situations, and based on rights and fairness in other situations).

Further, a domain-specific view of knowledge is based on the proposition that different types of experiences lead to different constructions of knowledge. For example, peer experiences regarding the sharing of toys has been shown to be important for moral knowledge (e.g. fairness) whereas teacher–child experiences regarding autonomy are related to the development of psychological knowledge (e.g. personal decision-making; see Turiel, 1983, 1998). Parental explanations help children to focus on domain distinctions (Jagers, Bingham and Hans, 1996). To substantiate a domain-specific model of development,

observational findings support the view that there are distinct patterns of social interactions that are domain-related. Children's interactions with parents,
siblings, teachers and peers reflect patterns of discourse and exchange that are
differentiated by the domain of the interaction (Tisak, 1995). Discourse about
events involving harm to another is different from discourse about events involving social conventions and regulations, which is distinct from discourse
about personal autonomy and choice (Killen, 1991; Killen and Smetana, 1999;
Nucci and Weber, 1995; Turiel, 1998). Children's and adults' interactions with
one another involve multiple concerns and orientations.

The research using the domain model has involved the use of prototypic
events (e.g. unprovoked hitting, refusing to share toys) as well as multifaceted
events. The types of multifaceted events have included controversial issues such
as abortion, homosexuality, incest, and pornography (see Turiel, Hildebrandt
and Wainryb, 1985), as well as a range of other issues, such as drug use (Killen,
Leviton and Cahill, 1991; Nucci, Guerra and Lee, 1991) and family duties
(Turiel and Wainryb, 2000). Studies on multifaceted issues have focused on
the ways in which individuals use multiple categories of reasoning (moral,
social-conventional and psychological) in their evaluations of the issues and
the priorities attached to these different forms of reasoning. More recently,
studies have examined the role of culture and the social group on individuals'
evaluations of multifaceted events. That is, how do individuals evaluate issues
that are embedded within complex cultural ideologies and societal expectations?

As an illustration, Wainryb and Turiel (1994) studied how parents and children living in a traditional Arabic culture (the Druze) evaluated family expectations about chores, domestic labour and autonomy from the domain-model
perspective. They interviewed family members and determined when they evaluated family duties using moral, social-conventional and psychological forms
of reasoning. Their findings indicated that males often used psychological reasoning, such as autonomy and self-determination, to justify their independent
roles whereas females used more social-conventional reasoning to explain their
domestic roles in the family context. However, the females also used justifications about fairness and equality when evaluating their views about gender
roles in the family. While men viewed their roles as autonomous, they viewed
women's roles as dependent. Women viewed this discrepancy as unfair, but
condoned it because of the severe negative consequences that would occur if
they objected to it. Women also supported certain aspects of their collective
obligations because of their beliefs about the importance of family. Thus, both
individualistic (self-determination and entitlement) and collectivistic (family,
duties, group) goals were articulated by *both* men and women in this traditional
culture.

The findings from these studies point to the complexities that are inherent
in societal issues. Reasoning about conventions can include many different

types of judgements, ones involving rituals, customs and expectations about social roles. Complex dimensions of the societal domain have been revealed in the studies focusing on multifaceted events more often than in the studies focusing on prototypic events because the items used in the prototypic studies often seemed 'trivial' or 'just a matter of etiquette' (e.g. a social-conventional transgression, such as eating spaghetti with your fingers or not raising your hand in class to talk). However, social-conventional reasoning can be applied to a range of issues from ones that are concrete and seemingly 'trivial' to ones that are abstract and imbued with symbolic and cultural meanings, such as societal expectations about family roles, social expectations about group functioning, group identity and shared beliefs about social norms and customs.

We have been particularly interested in how children and adolescents evaluate events that involve group functioning, group identity and social expectations. This is because little work has been conducted from the domain model to determine how children's and adolescents' attitudes about intergroup relationships, including social expectations, influence their moral decision-making. For example, do children's stereotypes about others influence their judgements about the wrongfulness of harm or unfair distribution? In most of the domain studies, by design, children are asked to evaluate a transgression between two children who are the same gender, ethnicity and age (the social group variables, such as gender, age and ethnicity also match the identity of the interviewee).

Yet, little is known about whether children's stereotypes about ethnicity, race, culture and gender influence their moral evaluations. For example, how do children evaluate a boy's refusal to share with a girl? Or a white child's denial of resources to a black child? Moreover, the context of exclusion involves group activities, which are often stereotypically defined. Excluding a girl from sports involves stereotypic expectations about who plays sports. Our preliminary evidence suggests that stereotypes are influential on children's moral decision-making in some contexts, but not all. Stereotypic judgements take many forms, from expectations about gender roles to beliefs about the role of the individual in society. Before describing our studies on exclusion, we will review the literature on children's judgements about group functioning and social stereotypes.

Children's stereotypic knowledge

A large body of literature on children's stereotyped knowledge indicates that children begin recognizing and thinking about stereotypic expectations as early as the preschool years (Aboud, 1992; Bigler and Liben, 1992; Ruble and Martin, 1998). This includes children in North America (Ruble and Martin, 1998), Europe (see Bennett et al., 1998; Cairns, 1989) and the Mid-East (see Bar-Tal, 1996; Cole et al., in press). Most of this evidence is based on either information-processing models (Martin and Halverson, 1981; Stangor and Ruble, 1989) or cognitive-developmental approaches (Aboud, 1988, 1992; Bigler and Liben, 1992). Stereotypes are defined as overgeneralizations about social groups that take the form of attributions about individuals, and that do not take into account individual variation within the group (see Mackie et al., 1996; Stangor and Schaller, 1996). These beliefs reflect cognitive structures, which contain an individual's perception of knowledge, beliefs, and expectations about social groups (see Macrae et al., 1996). From a social cognitive domain model, thinking about stereotypes shares similarities with thinking about social conventions. Some stereotypes reflect expectations about what makes society function (social group functioning). This is particularly true of gender stereotypes (e.g. gender roles and activities) but it is also true of racial and ethnic stereotypes.

Gender stereotypes are among the first category of stereotypes to emerge in young children. According to Mackie et al. (1996), 'for young children, gender seems to be the most salient category for parsing the social environment...' (p. 46). Gender stereotypes for young children include judgements about sex-appropriate activities (e.g. girls play with dolls), sex-specific characteristics (e.g. daddies are strong), and sex-related future roles (e.g. nurses are women) (Kuhn, Nash and Brucken, 1978). There is less known about racial stereotypes and stereotypes about members of other cultures than about gender stereotypes. What is known suggests that these forms of stereotypes emerge sometime during the preschool or elementary years, depending in part on the type of assessment and measure (see Aboud, 1992; Bar-Tal, 1996; Cole et al., 2001).

Many studies have demonstrated that stereotypes influence children's memory and other social cognitive abilities (e.g. Carter and Patterson, 1982; Kuhn et al., 1978; Liben and Signorella, 1993; Martin and Halverson, 1981). Specifically, these studies have found that children have a better memory for information that is consistent with their stereotypes than for information that is inconsistent with stereotypes. For example, Martin and Halverson (1981) demonstrated the application of this concept to gender stereotypes in a study with kindergarten and first-grade children. Children were read stories about gender consistent and inconsistent activities. After one week, participants recalled with greater accuracy activities that were stereotypically consistent with the gender of the protagonist. Bradbard et al. (1986) found that children demonstrated a better memory for novel objects that were labelled gender-appropriate. Further, Bigler and Liben (1993) demonstrated this phenomenon with racial stereotypes held by preschoolers. Preschoolers with greater racial stereotypes exhibited poorer memory for information that was inconsistent with their stereotypes. Research has also demonstrated that stereotypes affect the way in which children tell stories and learn new information (Hirschfeld, 1995; Jennings, 1975; Koblinsky, Cruse and Sagawara, 1978; Martin, Wood and Little, 1990; Martin and Halverson, 1981; Welch-Ross and Schmidt, 1996). For instance, Koblinsky, Cruse and Sagawara (1978) found that after children were read stories or shown pictures of individuals engaged in gender stereotype-consistent and stereotype-inconsistent activities, they altered stereotypic-inconsistent information so that it became consistent with gender stereotypes.

The findings that children have better memory for information that is stereotype-consistent rather than stereotype-inconsistent sheds light on why stereotypes are hard to change, and what needs to be done in the area of intervention. Stereotyping, like categorization, is one way to process information and to make sense of social phenomena. In many ways, stereotyping stems from societal expectations and shared beliefs. In the area of gender stereotypes, labels attached to males and females often stem from social-role expectations. Because of these role-related expectations, some forms of gender stereotyping are condoned more readily than expectations about racial and ethnic stereotyping, which have complex sociopolitical histories and reflect multifarious societal forces (Minow, 1990; Okin, 1989, 1999).

Social-cognitive domain research on children's gender stereotypes has shown that children evaluate gender-specific expectations as a matter of group norms and cultural consensus (Carter and Patterson, 1982; Stoddart and Turiel, 1985). Children's evaluations of cross-gender behaviour reflect social-conventional reasoning rather than moral justifications. For example, in a study by Stoddart and Turiel (1985) children who stated that a boy wearing a hair barrette was wrong did so for social-conventional, not moral, reasons (e.g. if all boys wore hair barrettes it would be OK, whereas hitting would not be OK even if everyone else did it). While stereotypes in and of themselves may not reflect morally negative behaviour towards others, there is a strong relation between stereotyping and prejudice. Researchers studying adult populations have shown that prejudice (a negative evaluative orientation toward groups) leads to stereotyping, and stereotyping leads to prejudice (Mackie et al., 1996). In general, little is known about when children use stereotypes in social decision-making.

In a review of the research, Aboud (1988) concluded that racial and ethnic attitudes are evident as early as preschool. Aboud's work suggests that cognitive limitations of young children make them more likely than older children to judge different races in a biased way. Like research on gender stereotypes, research on racial stereotypes has found that children associate different characteristics and judgement with certain groups, and that racial attitudes affect children's behaviour (e.g. choice of friends; Aboud, 1992). In general, children's prejudice has been measured by the extent to which children assign negative and positive traits to individuals solely on the basis of their group membership such as gender or race (Aboud, 1992; Bigler and Liben, 1993). For example, the findings on racial attitudes show that, with age, children become capable of assigning positive as well as negative traits to individuals of the 'out-group' (Aboud, 1992). Thus, preschool children display an in-group bias because they assign positive traits to the in-group, and negative traits to the out-group. The ability to assign multiple traits to individuals has been related to changes in cognitive development, such as the acquisition of classification and conservation skills (in which children become capable of simultaneously weighing multiple variables, such as length and width). These findings have led researchers to conclude that children's prejudice, or use of negative stereotypes, declines with age as they become capable of simultaneously weighing multiple variables (Aboud, 1992; Doyle and Aboud, 1995). The assignment of multiple traits is just one aspect of prejudice, however, and more recently researchers have examined other indices of prejudice, ones that focus more specifically on intergroup processes, such as perceptions of within-group variability and between-group variability (Bigler, Jones and Lobliner, 1997). This is necessary because, while the assignment of multiple traits may increase with age, indicating a reduction in prejudice (according to this measure), prejudicial judgements and behaviour are none the less evident in adolescence and adulthood.

In general, researchers have argued that intergroup processes, such as in-group/out-group biases, are important dimensions of prejudice and stereotyping (Bigler et al., 1997; Powlishta, 1995). Social psychologists who have extensively studied in-group/out-group perceptions, attitudes and behaviour in adults have demonstrated that group membership strongly influences individuals' perceptions of social groups (Stangor and Schaller, 1996). One of the predominant findings is that individuals recognize variability of their own group (the in-group) to a much greater extent than that of other groups (the out-group), referred to as the 'out-group homogeneity effect' (Park, Ryan and Judd, 1992). The out-group homogeneity effect potentially leads to stereotyping because the individual assumes that the members of the out-group share the same characteristics; thus labels are attributed to individuals in out-groups without a recognition of the heterogeneity within the out-group. There is a vast literature on judgements about in-group/out-group relationships in the adult social psychology literature (Brewer, 1979; Mackie et al., 1996; Tajfel et al., 1971), but only sparse treatment of the issue by developmental psychologists (for exceptions, see Bennett et al., 1998; Bigler et al., 1997; Yee and Brown, 1992). When children ignore variations within groups and attribute labels based solely on group membership this may be a result of a lack of familiarity with the group.

Depending upon the context, decisions about inclusion and exclusion involve judgements that potentially reflect knowledge and biases about in-group/out-group relationships. Children may exclude others who reflect the out-group because their assumption is that these individuals have characteristics that are undesirable or unfamiliar. As children have more contact with individuals from different social groups, however, they recognize the heterogeneity that exists within groups. This increased recognition of heterogeneity occurs at the same time that there is a decrease in rigidity in stereotypes about gender (Katz and

Ksansnak, 1994) suggesting that these two processes are related. However, very little research has been conducted to understand the connection between the judgements of heterogeneity and moral reasoning.

Social psychological research has shown that adults, who hold stereotypes about others in some situations apply concepts of fairness and equality in other situations (Gaertner and Dovidio, 1986). Gaertner and Dovidio assert that while most adults have strong beliefs about fairness, there are contexts in which exclusion based on race (or gender) is made implicitly, and that individuals are often unaware that they hold these judgements. These contexts are ones in which there is some ambiguity about the features of the context. In straightforward situations involving decisions about others on the basis of race, for example, adults reject race as a reason to act or make a judgement. However, in ambiguous situations, in which the parameters of the situation are unclear, adults' stereotypes about others seem to enter into their decision-making. For example, adults who are offered help from a white or black work partner will respond equally and treat both work partners the same. Yet when an opportunity arises to seek help from a white or black work partner, white adults will seek the help of the white partner more often than they will seek the help of the black work partner (Gaertner and Dovidio, 1986). What is not known is how these adults reason about these types of situations. None the less, Gaertner and Dovidio believe that their findings point to the multiple perspectives held by adults regarding their evaluations of situations involving members of other groups. At times equal treatment is granted and at times differential treatment based on group membership is applied to the situation. The developmental trajectory of these types of judgements is not known. Thus a central aim of our work has been to investigate how children evaluate decisions involving inclusion and exclusion, and particularly in contexts in which stereotypic expectations of groups as well as fairness considerations are made salient.

Reasoning about inclusion and exclusion in multiple contexts

There is a large literature on peer rejection in childhood (Asher and Coie, 1990). Much of it includes analyses of what it is about particular children that leads them to be rejected from peer groups, however, rather than a focus on group dynamics that lead to exclusion. Peer rejection studies have focused on individual children's lack of social skills and social competence as risk factors for peer rejection. The social skills that these particular children lack include perspective-taking, empathy, peer-group entry techniques, and conflict resolution strategies (Putallaz and Wasserman, 1990; Rubin, Bukowski and Parker, 1998). Most of this research, then, has focused on the individual side of peer exclusion; that is: what is it about a particular child that results in his or her rejection or exclusion from a group?

The group side of peer exclusion has received much less attention in the empirical developmental literature (for an exception, see Zarbatany et al., 1996). For example, what are the reasons that groups might exclude a child? Exclusion may be an active decision of a group rather than a result of social deficiencies of the excluded child. One of the aims of our work has been to examine how children evaluate the perceived costs to the social group when an individual is excluded from or rejected from joining the group. The consequences of exclusion for the coherence of the group have to do with a range of judgements, from stereotypic expectations of what makes a group work to considerations about social group identity, group functioning and group expectations. As an illustration, when group membership is used as a reason for exclusion this may stem from stereotypic knowledge (such as when an all-boy baseball team excludes a girl because they think she cannot play baseball) or from knowledge about social group functioning (such as the team will not play as well with someone on it who is not very good at the game).

As mentioned above, over the last several years we have been investigating individuals' evaluations of intergroup relationships, and specifically exclusion from groups involving social stereotypes and social expectations (Horn, in press; Horn et al., 1999; Killen et al., under review; Killen and Stangor, 2001; Killen et al., 2001; Theimer et al., 2001). We have conducted studies in which individuals are asked to evaluate a decision to exclude an individual from a group based on group membership, such as gender, race, ethnicity and adolescent reference groups.

We have found that there are developmental and contextual factors that influence when individuals believe that exclusion is legitimate and when it is wrong. Judgements supporting exclusion are based on group functioning, and judgements rejecting exclusion are typically based on the violations of the rights of the individual (e.g. the right to be treated equally or fairly). These judgements reflect a priority of the group (to maintain group functioning) as well as a priority of the individual (to preserve individual rights). From our model, we theorize that judgements about inclusion and exclusion depend on the context of exclusion and the reason why someone is being excluded. In order to examine these types of issues it is necessary to use methodologies that probe individuals' justifications and interpretations of social events and interactions. While most of our research has been conducted in the USA, we have also conducted a cross-cultural study in Japan (described below; see Killen, Crystal and Watanabe, in press; Watanabe, Crystal and Killen, 2000).

Using the social-cognitive domain model, we predict that when *moral* reasons of fairness, equality and rights are brought to bear on such judgements, the decisions will be non-exclusionary, and consistently so across a variety of contexts. When *social-conventional* reasons, including beliefs about group functioning and social stereotypes, are used as a basis of decision-making, decisions are expected to be exclusionary, group-specific and highly contingent upon the current social context. For instance, child-oriented decisions about inclusion or exclusion from peer groups may be based upon both moral reasons (e.g. 'It's not fair to tell her that she cannot join the club just because she's a girl') and social-conventional reasons ('The group will not work well with a boy because girls know how to do it better'). Social-conventional justifications include group identity ('The boys need their own club'), social expectations ('Boys usually don't like ballet') and social stereotypes ('Girls are too weak to play baseball'). Children and adolescents bring multiple considerations to bear when deciding whether to include or exclude someone from a group context.

Currently we are examining how children and adolescents evaluate exclusion based on race or gender in multiple contexts: friendship, peer groups, and school (Killen et al., in prep.). In this study, we are identifying the criteria that children and adolescents use when making decisions about exclusion. We are probing children's and adolescents' judgements regarding their views on the generalizability, authority jurisdiction of exclusion and social influence (e.g. is social pressure a legitimate reason to exclude someone?). For example, in a friendship context we describe a boy who does not want to be friends with another child because of the child's race (a white child does not want to be friends with a black child) or gender (a boy does not want to be friends with a girl). We then ask the participant for their evaluation of the decision (all right or not all right?). Based on the participant's evaluation we present counter probes. For children who think it's wrong to exclude the child, we ask whether it would be all right: (a) if other friends say it's all right (*social influence*); (b) if it would happen in another country (*generalizability*); or (c) if the parents say it's all right (*authority jurisdiction*). For children who think it's all right to exclude then we ask the same questions in the negative. (What if friends say it's wrong? Or if parents say it's wrong? And what about in another country?) The questions are basically the same for three contexts: friendship, peer club (e.g. a music club excludes a child based on gender or race) and school (e.g. a town does not let black children or girls go to school). Our participants are evenly divided by age (4th, 7th, and 10th grades), gender, and ethnicity (African-American, European-American, Asian-American and Hispanic-American).

Preliminary analyses indicate that children view exclusion from school based on group membership as wrong from a moral viewpoint (e.g. *generalizability*: 'It wouldn't be right to not let girls go to school in other countries'; and *authority jurisdiction*: 'It is not up to the parents to decide; everyone should be able to go to school') and reject social influence in this context. However, exclusion based on group membership in friendship and peer group contexts is multifaceted; children view it as a mixture of moral, social-conventional and personal considerations. One example, from an African-American 10th grade girl, regarding her evaluation of a white boy's decision to not want to be friends with a new neighbour because he is black is the following:

'It's not OK . . . Because he's going to see everybody. He's gonna see black people, he's gonna see white people, he's gonna see Asian people, he's going to see Cambodians, he's gonna see Ethiopians. I mean, yes, people do come from different places, and yes, they do speak different languages. But everybody has a heart, and they also have feelings, and they also know how it is to be put down. And it hurts. So I mean if you're the type of person who says "OK, I don't like you because of a reason like that," it's just wrong.'

This student viewed exclusion in a friendship context as wrong from a moral viewpoint. Exclusion makes someone feel bad. Other children viewed this type of decision as a personal choice, and did not view it as involving moral dimensions.

As an illustration, a 7th-grade boy evaluated the decision of a boy who did not want to be friends with a girl using personal choice reasoning:

'I think it's good because boys and girls don't get that much along. Right now, it's like Tom's a young boy so he should just hang out with boys and not mess with girls. It's his decision who he plays with and who he wants to hang out with.' [Does he have to hang out with her if his parents tell him he should?] 'No, I think he doesn't because his parents don't pick his friends. You pick your friends. Your parents can tell you what kind of people you should hang out with, but you make your own decision.'

Interestingly, the same child had a different reaction to a child who did not want to be friends with someone because of skin colour:

'That's just racism. It's not his decision what colour he is. He should just let him hang out with him. They're not different cause maybe Damon thinks the same things as Jerry. He is the same as Jerry inside but outside they are different.'

Older children often viewed the peer group decision in terms of group identity. One 7th-grade Hispanic boy stated that it was all right to exclude a girl from the music club:

'I think that Mike and his friends are right for not letting her in because it's their club and then like if they don't want girls to join and make it an all boys club it's OK.' [Why?] 'Because they made it up for their own club. If she wanted to make her own group then she can do it and have no boys allowed.'

Some contexts created conflicts for children and this was reflected by their use of a mixture of criteria. For example, for the music club, children often wavered back and forth between viewing exclusion as discrimination and viewing it as necessary for group cohesion and group identity. For example, here is what one European-American, 7th-grade girl said about excluding a girl from an all-boys music club:

'In a way, yes, and in a way no, because it's trying to keep her out just because she's a girl. That's discrimination. But boys, they talk about stuff, that you know, girls just don't like or don't like doing. So I think having their club with those boys is OK. It's up to the boys to decide and it's probably OK to not let her in because she'd just be the only girl and all these boys would be talking about stuff that she wouldn't even know about or like. Boys want to have their own club.' [What if other friends thought the members of the club should let her in?] 'Then I think they should let her in if she really wants to join. She should be able to be in the club if she wants to get in. They don't have a good reason for not letting her in.' [What if the parents said that they should let her in?] 'Then they should listen to the parents. Parents have a voice and the boys are likely to listen to the parents. I still don't think the boys would want her in because she would be the only girl. And that's not OK but they don't have a good reason to not let her in.' [What about in another country?] 'I don't think there would be any difference because with music, everyone likes the same music in all countries. And it's not with culture or anything because everybody usually likes the same music so it wouldn't be OK to not let her in.'

In this example, the participant viewed exclusion as legitimate based on group identity and group functioning. At the same time, she viewed exclusion as unfair and a form of discrimination. This type of vacillation occurred most often for the peer group exclusion and friendship contexts, and rarely for the school context (in which a town denied access to school on the basis of gender or race). In addition, older children, more often than younger children, viewed exclusion as necessary in some contexts to preserve group functioning or group identity and to conform with social expectations and traditions. We are currently analysing children's judgements across the contexts, and as a function of the age, gender and ethnicity of the participant.

The results of this study indicate that children and adolescents weigh both individual concerns (rights of the individual excluded, empathy for the one excluded) and group concerns (group functioning, group identity) when evaluating exclusion. In some contexts, moral criteria were applied (exclusion was viewed as wrong in other places and even when parents condoned it), in other contexts, social-conventional criteria were applied (exclusion was viewed as legitimate if under parental jurisdiction and context-specific), and, at times, children viewed the decision as a matter of personal choice. Exclusion is a multifaceted context, and one in which children weigh many concerns. What is not clear is when judgements about group functioning are actually forms of stereotypic reasoning. For example, the view that a group functions better with 'members who are alike' may be an implicit form of prejudice or stereotyping. Some forms of social-conventional reasoning may reflect stereotypic knowledge and other forms may reflect decisions about group functioning that do not include stereotypic reasoning.

In another illustration of our approach, a recently completed study examined how children and adolescents evaluate acts of peer group inclusion *and* exclusion in contexts that were consistent with gender and racial stereotypes

(Killen and Stangor, 2001). We included contexts in which gender and racial stereotypes were already associated with the activities (e.g. ballet for girls, baseball-card club for boys). Our goal was to determine whether children's stereotypes about others would influence their inclusion decisions. Both inclusion and exclusion decisions were used because we predicted that stereotypes, if invoked, would be more prevalent in inclusion decisions than in exclusion decisions. Inclusion decisions were choices about who would be picked to join a club when there was only space for one more person to join. In addition, we varied the qualifications of those who wanted to join the club.

We interviewed children between 7 and 13 years of age about four types of peer exclusion (girls excluding a boy from ballet, boys excluding a girl from baseball, white children excluding a black child from a math club and black children excluding a white child from basketball team). For each of these exclusion events, three different judgemental contexts were presented to the child – straightforward exclusion as well as two contexts involving inclusion. An 'equal qualifications' context included a decision about who to pick when two children were equally qualified (e.g. Who should the group pick if the boy and girl are equally good at ballet?). An 'unequal qualifications' context included a decision about who to pick when the child who fits the stereotype is better at the activity (e.g. Who should the group pick if the girl is better at ballet?).

We found that children and adolescents made clear distinctions between straightforward exclusion and exclusion in multifaceted contexts. In straightforward exclusion contexts, the vast majority of children (90 per cent) stated that it was wrong to exclude someone, even if they did not conform to the stereotypic expectation, and that it was wrong because it was *unfair* to exclude someone just because of their gender or race. However, in the equal and unequal qualifications context (in which only one of two children could be selected), children made clear distinctions. In the equal qualifications context, the majority of children picked the child who did not fit the stereotype, and gave reasons based on equal treatment ('They should let the boy into the girls' ballet club so he can have a chance to try ballet and then maybe more boys would do it'). In the unequal qualifications context, adolescents picked the child who was better qualified and gave reasons based on *social group processes* ('Pick the girl for ballet so that when they go out to perform for everybody, then they won't mess up'). In the unequal qualifications context, adolescents were more likely than younger children to consider social group processes and social-conventional expectations. In general, children did not overtly use stereotypes to justify their decision (as would be predicted from the adult findings by Gaertner and Dovidio, 1986). However, in complex situations, in which a decision had to be made about who to pick, children picked a child who fitted the stereotype and gave reasons based on group functioning. Overall, children and adolescents displayed multiple orientations; at times, individual rights and fairness were the priority, at times social group processes were the priority.

Gender and race are sensitive issues and students are aware of the social desirability of not revealing stereotypic attitudes. One way to address this concern is to use social group categories, such as cliques, that are not as emotionally charged as gender and race. One study by Horn, Killen and Stangor (1999) focused on adolescents reasoning about social reference groups (cliques). Students were surveyed about their evaluations of the use of retribution for a transgression committed by a group that either did or did not fit the stereotype associated with the activity. Specifically, a student council punishes a group for committing a transgression even though there is not explicit evidence that they did it (e.g. punishment was assigned to either the computer students, often called the 'techies', or the athletes, usually called the 'jocks') for breaking into the e-mail system at school; punishment was assigned to the computer students or athletes for breaking the sound equipment at a school dance in which students got rowdy. Participants were asked for their evaluations of the student council decision to punish the group. We found that, overall, students judged that it would be wrong to punish a group when there was little or no evidence that they committed the transgression. However, students were more likely to condone the punishment when the group fitted the stereotype (e.g. athletes breaking sound equipment) than when the group did not fit the stereotype (e.g. athletes breaking into the email system), indicating that stereotypic knowledge was influential in their moral decision-making.

Horn (in press) followed up on these findings and conducted a direct comparison of adolescents' evaluations of exclusion from social groups (adolescent cliques) with their evaluations of the denial of resources based on social group membership. Horn found that adolescents judged exclusion in terms of social group functioning ('It's OK for the cheerleaders to exclude a girl who is a "gothic" because she won't fit in') *and* others used moral reasons ('It's not OK to exclude her because it's being prejudiced'), but they viewed the denial of resources in moral terms ('It's unfair to deny a scholarship to a jock just because people might think he's not smart'). These findings indicate, again, that exclusion is viewed as multifaceted; group functioning as well as moral considerations are involved in this type of issue.

When do judgements about fairness take priority over knowledge about stereotypes? Based on findings that have shown that preschool-aged children use stereotypic knowledge to justify excluding a child from joining a group, such as excluding boys from doll-play or girls from truck-play (Theimer et al., 2001), a study was conducted to determine whether preschool-aged children ignore fairness or stereotypic expectations when these aspects of the situation are made particularly salient (Killen et al., 2001). The results revealed that young children were more influenced by the fairness issues than by the stereotypic expectations of the situation. Children who judged that it was all right to exclude a boy from doll-playing or a girl from truck-playing changed their judgements when presented with information about the fairness dimension of being excluded. However, children who initially judged it wrong to exclude someone did not change their judgements when presented with information about the stereotypic expectations of the play context. When weighing concerns about fairness and concerns about social group functioning, then, fairness may be a more powerful consideration than social-conventional expectations, such as stereotypes.

Japanese and American children's judgements about exclusion

To what extent does culture have an influence on when children and adolescents focus on the individual concerns or the group concerns (or both)? A study on Japanese and American children's evaluations of peer exclusion (Killen et al., in press) was conducted to examine these issues. Students at 4th, 7th and 10th grades were surveyed regarding their evaluations of six types of reasons given by children for excluding a peer from a group: (1) aggressive behaviour (excluding someone who is aggressive towards others), (2) unconventionality in dress (excluding someone who dyes their hair green), (3) unconventionality in public behaviour (excluding someone who acts like a clown in a restaurant), (4) cross-gender behaviour (excluding a boy who acts like a girl or a girl who acts like a boy), (5) slowness in sports (excluding someone who is a slow runner) and (6) personality traits (excluding someone who acts sad and lonely). These contexts varied in terms of the reasons for exclusion. In addition, we included an in-group condition in which four children rejected a member of their friendship group, and an out-group condition, in which four children rejected a fifth child who wanted to join the group.

We predicted that the context for exclusion would be an important variable for determining students' responses, as well as the gender, age and cultural membership of the participants. For example, we expected that students in both cultures would be more likely to agree with a decision for a group to exclude a child who is aggressive than to agree with a decision for a group to exclude a child who is lonely. We expected that, with age, children would be sensitive to group functioning and would be likely to exclude children from groups in which the inclusion of the child threatened successful group functioning. Cultural theorists predict that Japanese students would be more empathetic towards the lonely child than would the American students (and more likely to disagree with the decision to exclude him/her; see Shweder et al., 1998). Further, American students would be more likely to exclude the child who was a slow runner on the team than would the Japanese students owing to the Americans' competitive orientation. Finally, cultural theorists predict that Japanese students would be less likely to exclude a child in the in-group condition than in the out-group condition (see Markus and Kitayama, 1991).

There were no overall differences between Japanese and American children's responses. American students did not condone or reject exclusion more than did the Japanese students. Importantly, and supporting our expectations, we found that there was a significant effect for the context of exclusion. Children evaluated the types of exclusion differently depending on their age, gender and nationality. We also found that females judged it more wrong to exclude a child from a peer group than did males. In fact, American females were the most likely to judge exclusion as wrong, and the American males were the most likely to judge it as all right (the Japanese females and males fell in the middle). Age-related results revealed that 4th graders were more likely to judge exclusion as wrong than 10th graders for two of the six contexts. These two contexts were the ones that adults would consider it most legitimate to exclude someone (one who is aggressive, and one who does not meet the qualifications for a competitive sport). There were no age differences for the other contexts.

Overall, we found that both American and Japanese students judged it wrong to exclude someone who has a 'sad' personality and less wrong to exclude someone who gets into fights and is aggressive. Supporting cultural theorizing, Americans were less willing to exclude someone who dyed their hair green (unconventional dress is condoned in 'modern' cultures) than were Japanese students (societal expectations of proper dress are emphasized in 'traditional' cultures). However, in contrast to cultural theorizing, American students were less willing to exclude someone who is 'sad and lonely' than were the Japanese students. This is in contrast to cultural theorizing because it is often proposed that members of 'traditional' cultures, such as Japan, are 'interdependent' and emphasize being 'empathetic' towards others whereas members of 'modern' cultures, such as in the USA, would not want to include someone who takes away from the group fun. Yet, students' evaluations were in contrast to this type of interpretation.

We found that Japanese and American students weighed the needs of the individual and the group in similar ways for issues involving aggression and sports but differed on conventions about dress and individual differences. Further, the lack of findings for culture (overall) indicates that these judgements are a result of multiple sources of influence (age, gender and culture), which interact in unique ways. Cultural membership alone does not account for social judgements involving the individual and the group (regarding inclusion and exclusion).

Exclusion in the family context

So far our studies have focused on exclusion in friendship, peer groups and school contexts. Exclusion in the family context involves social expectations that may reflect the strongest form of stereotypic expectations that are related to social group functioning (see Turiel, 1998; Wainryb and Turiel, 1995). Gender role expectations involve beliefs that are used to justify the division of labour in the home and future role identities in society.

Theimer-Schuette (1999) investigated children's judgements about inclusion and exclusion in the home context, and found that, with age, children relied on stereotypic expectations to pick someone to perform a task in the home. Children at 5, 8 and 10 years of age, were asked whether it was all right or not all right for a parent (mother or father) to exclude a son or daughter from an activity that involved gender-stereotypic expectations (e.g. father picks son, not daughter, to help with mowing the lawn or changing the oil in the car; mother picks daughter, not son, to help with cooking or sewing curtains). Children were also given counter probes (emphasizing fairness or stereotypic expectations) to determine how willing children were to change their judgements.

The results revealed that the majority of children chose the child who fit the stereotype, and that they were resistant to probes about fairness. These findings are in contrast to the findings with peer-group scenarios used in other studies (Killen and Stangor, 2001; Killen et al., 2001) in which the majority of children chose non-stereotypic children to be included in peer groups in forced choice situations in which group membership was the only distinguishing feature. Approximately 40 per cent of the children in the family study changed their judgement to pick the non-stereotypic child after hearing a moral probe. This suggests that a significant proportion of children, but not the majority, recognized the issue of fairness in decisions involving the distribution of labour on the basis of gender. The results of this study reveal within-culture variation in judgements about inclusion and exclusion. In this study, expectations about family roles took priority over individual fairness considerations except when fairness issues were made particularly salient (and even then only 40 per cent of the participants give priority to fairness). Scholars in the area of gender and justice have pointed to the family context as one in which fairness and individual rights are often given less priority than societal group expectations, in the USA as well as in other cultures (Minow, 1990; Nussbaum, 1999; Okin, 1989). Currently, we are conducting research on how children and adolescents weigh individual and group considerations when evaluating inclusion and exclusion in Korean family contexts (Lee-Kim et al., in prep.) as well as in other traditional cultures, such as Latin America.

Decisions about inclusion and exclusion bear on the larger set of societal issues involving affirmative action and discrimination (Skrentny, 1996), equality (Nussbaum, 1999; Okin, 1989), rights and civil liberties (Helwig, 1995, 1997; Minow, 1990). As an example, affirmative action involves judgements about how a group should make decisions about including individuals who have historically been excluded from full participation in the culture. Does including one person necessarily involve excluding another person? If so, what is the rationale for making these types of inclusion decisions? Further, women and minority groups have experienced exclusion in a wide range of societal contexts. The justifications for these forms of exclusion most likely involve a range of reasons, invoking moral, social-conventional and psychological explanations. While our research with children and adolescents has not directly examined these societal issues, the findings provide a basis for exploring the developmental origins of judgements about these complex concepts.

Implications of research on inclusion and exclusion for theories of culture

According to cultural theory, it might be expected that persons in 'individualistic' cultures view exclusion based solely on group membership as wrong owing to the violation of individual rights, and that members of 'collectivistic' cultures view exclusion based on group membership as legitimate in order to preserve the functioning of the group and minimize group disruption. While there is little research on the ways in which members of diverse cultures evaluate inclusion and exclusion, there is evidence regarding how members of diverse cultures weigh considerations about the individual (individualism) with considerations about the group (collectivism). Our research on inclusion/exclusion is relevant for general theories of culture because we have shown that 'individual' and 'group' considerations are both integral dimensions of decisions about exclusion. Further, we have shown the importance of context. Exclusion in one context is evaluated quite differently from exclusion in another context. Therefore, assessments of cultural differences in the evaluation of social issues need to be sensitive to the context. At times, however, measures of cultural orientations have been very general, relying on generalized statements about values to demonstrate differences between cultures.

The individual *or* the group?

What is the prevailing view of culture and how has cultural theory characterized psychological orientations in diverse cultures? A common conceptualization of the relation between culture and social development is based on the assumption that cultures can be characterized as *either* individualistic (focused on the individual) or collectivistic (focused on the group) (see Greenfield and Cocking, 1994; Shweder et al., 1998, pp. 898–904; Triandis, 1995). Most of the theorizing and research within this perspective has been on the study of the attributes of individualistic and collectivistic cultures, and of the consequences of individualism/collectivism for the development of individuals and their interpersonal and intergroup relations. Typically, cultures with an individualistic orientation are said to value the person as detached from relationships and from the community, as independent from the social order and as motivated to give priority to the individual. By contrast, collectivistic cultures value individuals according to their interdependent roles within the social system and give priority to the group. Individual social development is presumed to consist of the acquisition of the main cultural orientation. These descriptions of cultural orientations are overly general and do not take into account contextual differences within cultures.

Many researchers have proposed that dichotomies used to characterize cultures are overly simplistic, and that heterogeneity, rather than homogeneity, is more often the case (Killen and Wainryb, 2000; Turiel, 1998; Wainryb and Turiel, 1995). Recently, theorists who have used the individualistic/collectivistic dichotomy to characterize cultures have also asserted that these dimensions coexist in the lives of people in different cultures (Greenfield and Cocking, 1994; Shweder et al., 1998; Triandis, 1995). However, a close examination of many research studies in the field reveals that the assumption that members of traditional cultures are collectivistic and members of non-traditional cultures are individualistic is still quite strong and pervasive (see Killen and Wainryb, 2000, for an analysis of the ways in which coexistence has been defined). In fact, the construct of individualism-collectivism has been used quite frequently as an explanatory model of human thought, emotion and behaviour.

As one illustration, Triandis and his colleagues administered various surveys to adults in a number of countries including England, the USA, France, Germany and Japan (Triandis, 1995) in order to demonstrate that individuals hold these diverse orientations, individualism and collectivism. Survey items involve ratings of very general statements with little context, such as 'It is important to me to maintain harmony with the group' or 'I often do my own thing'. In some cases, these statements contain phrases that are characteristic of cultural ideologies and reflected particular cultural orientations. For example, the survey item 'It is important to me to maintain harmony with the group' reflects a specific Buddhist principle in East Asian cultures. Another survey item, 'I often do my own thing', reflects the language of North American culture. For these types of items, the respondent was asked to rate the statement from 1 (strongly disagree) to 9 (strongly agree). From our perspective, these data are hard to interpret because of the generality of the statements. Maintaining harmony with the group differs depending on the context. Without analyses of the reasoning patterns, interpretations of the items or information about the context, the findings are difficult to assess.

Similarly, other instruments used to assess individualism and collectivism require forced-choice answers to what may be perceived as culturally specific scenarios and open to interpretation (Triandis, 1995). As another illustration, the item, 'The meaning of life can best be understood by: (a) paying attention to the views of parents; (b) through discussion with friends; (c) through individual mediation; (d) through individual exposure to the views of wise people' (p. 211) is ambiguous in terms of what 'the meaning of life' refers to. In this example, the answer to understanding the meaning of life is limited to and framed according to whose advice or interaction you may seek. There is no option for choosing 'all of the above depending on the context'. The nature of the measure inhibits the possibility that individuals have multiple perspectives on deeply held beliefs such as the meaning of life. This can also be seen in another example where respondents are asked 'Happiness is attained by: (a) gaining a lot of status in the community; (b) linking with a lot of friendly people; (c) keeping one's privacy; (d) winning in competition.' The options to choose from provide a narrow definition of how 'happiness' is attained by its description of specific sources (e.g. 'status in community', 'friendly people'); the option of 'all of the above' is also missing. Again, a difficulty with interpreting these responses is that there is no assessment of how individuals reason or justify these items. Further, the items themselves may elicit stereotypic responses, which are then used to label an individual's cultural orientation. The lack of information about the context may contribute to this interpretation.

In our view, the nature of the questions asked and the format of the answers do not allow for understanding the complexities involved in how individuals think or reason about these issues, especially ones that are multifaceted, such as 'the meaning of life'. While the measures used by Triandis (1995) are only one example of work on cultural orientations (for others see Shweder et al., 1998), the constructs that are identified by Triandis, 'individualism' and 'collectivism' have been widely used. We theorize that these constructs are broad templates meant to apply to the psychological orientation of members of cultures across a wide range of cultural contexts, and thus are devoid of contextual meaning.

The individual and the group revisited

From our perspective, interpretations of cultural values are difficult to capture solely through the use of methodologies that are based on ratings of general attitudes or ideological statements such as 'the meaning of life'. Instead, methods need to assess how individuals classify, evaluate and justify everyday social events (see table 8.1). These types of assessments provide multiple ways for revealing the heterogeneity of social judgements, that is judgements that give priority to the individual and judgements that give priority to the group. Being a member of a culture does not determine whether one will give priority to the individual or to the group. Assessments must be conducted to understand these types of social judgements and evaluations.

As one demonstration of the coexistence of multiple orientations within cultures, research on traditional cultures (also referred to as 'collectivistic') has found that children, adolescents and adults give priority to the individual by asserting personal choice and self-reliance, a typically 'individualistic' value. This includes Brazilian (Nucci, Camino and Milnitsky-Sapiro, 1996) and Colombian (Ardila-Rey and Killen, 2001) children in Latin America, Japanese (Killen and Sueyoshi, 1995) and Korean (Kim and Turiel, 1996; Song, Smetana and Kim, 1987) children in Asia, and Jewish and Druze (Wainryb and Turiel, 1994, 1995) children in the Mid-East. Interviews with children in these cultures have shown that children classify certain decisions, such as choice of friends, clothes and activities, as within their personal jurisdiction, and not a matter of authority mandates or regulations. These children view personal goals as a matter of entitlement and rights due to the individual. These findings can be extended to decisions about exclusion such that there may be times when members of traditional cultures would view exclusion as wrong on the basis of rights denied to the individual. At the same time, children in these cultures are concerned about authority, customs and conventions, which reflect group functioning considerations. Similarly, studies have demonstrated the many ways in which persons in 'individualistic' cultures value interpersonal duties and obligations, such as making sacrifices for others and fulfilling familial duties (Killen and Turiel, 1998; Turiel, 1998; Turiel et al., 1987). Thus evidence indicates that children and adults in diverse cultures simultaneously hold multiple concerns with the individual and the group; they are both individualistic and collectivistic in their social orientations.

Conclusions

Exclusion between people based on group membership has contributed to intergroup conflict within and between cultures in many parts of the world. Within cultures, individuals have excluded women and members of minority groups from full participation as citizens. Between cultures, exclusion of individuals has created tensions, antagonisms and, in extreme cases, war and genocide (see Opotow, 1990). Decisions to exclude others involve many different types of considerations; in essence, exclusion is a multifaceted phenomenon. On the one hand, exclusion may involve violations of individual rights, freedoms, and the infliction of psychological harm on another person. On the other hand, exclusion may promote social group functioning, and establish group identities. Cultural ideologies and values play a role in judgements about exclusion, because expectations about groups are often derived from social conventions, traditions and norms. We have discovered that social judgements about exclusion are often multifaceted and involve moral, social-conventional and psychological considerations.

We hypothesize that one way to intervene or to promote change regarding the evaluation of exclusion is to introduce arguments that focus on the fairness and moral dimensions of exclusion, particularly in situations involving stereotypic expectations. Social psychologists studying adult populations have reported that stereotypes (in adults) are very difficult to change (Stangor and Schaller, 1996). Gordon Allport's 'contact hypothesis' predicted that stereotypes will change through direct contact with individuals from other groups when four optimal conditions are met: (1) equal status among members of the group; (2) common goals; (3) no competition between groups; and (4) authority sanction for the contact (for a review, see Pettigrew and Tropp, 2000). The notion is that increased contact diminishes assumptions of homogeneity of the out-group (and increases a recognition of within-group variability). Researchers have found mixed results on the effectiveness of contact (Hewstone and Brown, 1986; Pettigrew and Tropp, 2000). In some cases, increased contact with members of the out-group has had only very small effects on stereotypic thinking in adults; in other cases it had significant influences on the reduction of prejudiced attitudes. We believe that the best chance for changing stereotypic thinking is to initiate interventions prior to adulthood, during early and middle childhood, when these judgements are forming and developing (see also Aboud and Levy, 2000).

In one of our studies with preschool-aged children (Killen et al., 2001), statements about fairness were more compelling and influenced children's judgements about whom to include in a group more than did statements about social-conventional expectations. While this effect was just demonstrated in one context (peer play situations) with one type of exclusion (gender-based) the results suggest that discussions with children about the multiple considerations involved in exclusion decisions may be a vehicle for changing thinking about stereotypic expectations.

In general, children and adolescents in our studies voiced strong concerns about the wrongfulness of exclusion on the basis of gender and race, and particularly so in straightforward exclusion contexts. Despite the pervasiveness of stereotypes about others, children's moral judgements about fairness, equality, and justice, predominated. In complex and ambiguous situations, however, stereotypic thinking and social-conventional expectations play a larger role in children's assessments and evaluations of exclusion. Thus, it is important to understand what makes a situation complex or ambiguous, and how best to understand what considerations are at stake for children and adolescents. Moreover, it is important to understand the underpinnings of social group functioning for individuals. When is social group functioning a legitimate concern and when is it a form of stereotypic expectations?

Our research has implications for individuals and cultures in several ways. First, exclusion decisions necessarily involve considerations of the individual and the group. This means that one's priorities about the individual or about the group are also involved in these types of decisions. We did not find that children in US cultures consistently gave priority to individual considerations, nor did children in our Japanese sample systematically grant priority to the group considerations. Weighing concerns of the individual and the group coexisted in the reasoning demonstrated by our participants. Second, exclusion of individuals occurs in many different social and cultural contexts. We have studied exclusion in friendships, peer groups, adolescent cliques, family contexts, school contexts and cultural contexts. In addition, we have analysed exclusion based on gender, race and ethnicity. Clearly, these decisions are not all the same. Different types of concerns are weighed in each type of exclusion context. What transcends the specific context are principles of fairness, and equality. We have not yet examined whether individuals uphold these principles across a range of social and cultural contexts. This is necessary in order to understand the generalizability of the moral dimensions of exclusion. Third, cultures vary in their stereotypes about others and their expectations about social group functioning. Cross-cultural work reveals the myriad ways in which social group functioning is expressed, conveyed and communicated within a culture (and about members of another culture). Understanding the role that cultural expectations play regarding judgements of exclusion will greatly broaden our understanding of this complex and pervasive social phenomenon.

REFERENCES

Aboud, F. E. (1988). *Children and prejudice*. New York: Basil Blackwell.
  (1992). Conflict and group relations. In C. U. Shantz and W. W. Hartup (eds.), *Conflict in child and adolescent development*. Cambridge: Cambridge University Press, pp. 356–79.
Aboud, F. E. and Levy, S. (2000). Interventions designed to reduce prejudice and discrimination in children and adolescents. In S. Oskamp (ed.), *Reducing prejudice and discrimination*. Mahwah, NJ: Lawrence Erlbaum, pp. 269–93.
Ardila-Rey, A. and Killen, M. (2001). Colombian preschool children's judgements about autonomy and conflict resolution in the classroom setting. *International Journal of Behavioral Development*, 25(3), 246–55.
Asher, S. and Coie, J. (1990). *Peer rejection in childhood*. Cambridge: Cambridge University Press.
Astor, R. A. (1994). Children's moral reasoning about family and peer violence: the role of provocation and retribution. *Child Development*, 65, 1054–67.
Bar-Tal, D. (1996). Development of social categories and stereotypes in early childhood: the case of 'the Arab' concept formation, stereotype and attitudes by Jewish children in Israel. *International Journal of Intercultural Relations*, 20, 341–70.
Bennett, M., Barrett, M., Lyons, E. and Sani, F. (1998) Children's subjective identification with the group and ingroup favouritism. *Developmental Psychology*, 34, 902–9.
Bigler, R., Jones, L. C. and Lobliner, D. (1997). Social categorization and the formation of intergroup attitudes in children. *Child Development*, 68, 530–43.
Bigler, R. and Liben, L. S. (1992). Cognitive mechanisms in children's gender stereotyping: theoretical and educational implications of a cognitive-based intervention. *Child Development*, 63, 1351–63.

(1993). A cognitive-developmental approach to racial stereotyping and reconstructive memory in Euro-American children. *Child Development*, 64, 1507–18.

Bradbard, M. R., Martin, C. L., Endsley, R. C. and Halverson, C. F. (1986). Influence of sex stereotypes on children's exploration and memory: a competence versus performance distinction. *Developmental Psychology*, 22, 481–6.

Brewer, M. B. (1979). In-group bias in the minimal intergroup situation: a cognitive-motivational hypothesis. *Psychological Bulletin*, 86, 307–24.

Cairns, E. (1989). Social identity and intergroup conflicts in Northern Ireland: a developmental perspective. In J. Harbison (ed.), *Growing up in Northern Ireland*. Belfast: Stranmillis College, pp. 115–30.

Carter, D. B. and Patterson, C. J. (1982). Sex roles as social conventions: the development of children's conceptions of sex-role stereotypes. *Developmental Psychology*, 18, 812–24.

Cole, C., Arafat, C., Tidhar, C., Zidan, W. T., Fox, N. A., Killen, M., Leavitt, L., Lesser, G., Richman, B. A., Ardila-Rey, A., and Yung, F. (in press). The educational impact of Rechov Sumsum/Shara'a Simsim, a television series for Israeli and Palestinian children. *International Journal of Behavioral Development*.

Davidson, P., Turiel, E. and Black, A. (1983). The effect of stimulus familiarity on the use of criteria and justification in children's social reasoning. *British Journal of Developmental Psychology*, 1, 49–65.

Doyle, A. B. and Aboud, F. E. (1995). A longitudinal study of white children's racial prejudice as a social-cognitive development. *Merrill-Palmer Quarterly*, 41(2) 209–28.

Gaertner, S. L. and Dovidio, J. F. (1986). The aversive form of racism. In J. F. Dovidio and S. L. Gaertner (eds.), *Prejudice, discrimination, and racism*. Orlando, FL: Academic Press, pp. 61–89.

Gewirth, A. (1978). *Reason and morality*. Chicago: University of Chicago Press.

Greenfield, P. and Cocking, R. (1994). *Cross-cultural roots of minority child development*. Mahwah, NJ: Lawrence Erlbaum.

Hart, D. and Killen, M. (1995). Introduction: Perspectives on morality in everyday life. In M. Killen and D. Hart (eds.), *Morality in everyday life: developmental perspectives*. Cambridge: Cambridge University Press, pp. 1–20.

Helwig, C. C. (1995). Adolescents' and young adults' conceptions of civil liberties: freedom of speech and religion. *Child Development*, 66, 152–66.

(1997). The role of agent and social context in judgements of freedom of speech and religion. *Child Development*, 68, 484–95.

(1998). Children's conceptions of fair government and freedom of speech. *Child Development*, 69, 518–31.

Helwig, C. C., Tisak, M. and Turiel E. (1990). Children's social reasoning in context. *Child Development*, 61, 2068–78.

Hewstone, M. and Brown, R. (1986). Contact is not enough: an intergroup perspective on the 'Contact Hypothesis'. In M. Hewstone and R. J. Brown (eds.), *Contact and conflict in intergroup encounters*. London: Blackwell, pp. 1–44.

Hirschfeld, L. A. (1995). Do children have a theory of race? *Cognition*, 54, 209–52.

Hollos, M., Leis, P. E. and Turiel, E. (1986). Social reasoning in Ijo children and adolescents in Nigerian communities. *Journal of Cross-Cultural Psychology*, 17, 352–74.

Horn, S. S. (in press). Evaluations of exclusion and denial of resources based on peer group membership. *Developmental Psychology*.

Horn, S., Killen, M. and Stangor, C. (1999). The influence of group stereotypes on adolescents' moral reasoning. *Journal of Early Adolescence*, 19, 98–113.

Jagers, R. J., Bingham, K. and Hans, S. L. (1996). Socialization and social judgements among inner-city African American kindergartners. *Child Development*, 67, 140–50.

Jennings, S. A. (1975). Effects of sex typing in children's stories on preference and recall. *Child Development*, 46, 220–3.

Katz, P. A. and Ksansnak, K. R. (1994). Developmental aspects of gender role flexibility and traditionality in middle childhood and adolescence. *Developmental Psychology*, 30, 272–82.

Killen, M. (1991). Social and moral development in early childhood. In W. M. Kurtines and J. L. Gewirtz (eds.), *Handbook of moral behavior and development*, vol. 2. Hillsdale, NJ: Lawrence Erlbaum, pp. 115–38.

Killen, M., Crystal, D. and Watanabe, H. (in press). Japanese and American children's evaluations of peer exclusion, tolerance of difference, and prescriptions for conformity. *Child Development*.

Killen, M. and de Waal, F. B. M. (2000). The evolution and development of morality. In F. Aureli and F. B. M. de Waal (eds.), *Natural conflict resolution*. Berkeley: University of California Press, pp. 352–72.

Killen, M. and Hart, D. (eds.) (1995). *Morality in everyday life: developmental perspectives*. Cambridge: Cambridge University Press.

Killen, M., Lee-Kim, J., McGlothlin, H. and Stangor, C. (under review). *Judgments about inclusion and exclusion in three contexts: friendship, peer, and school*. University of Maryland, College Park.

Killen, M., Leviton, M. and Cahill, J. (1991). Adolescent reasoning about drug use. *Journal of Adolescent Research*, 6, 336–56.

Killen, M., Pisacane, K., Lee, J. and Ardila-Rey, A. (2001). Fairness or stereotypes? Young children's priorities when evaluating group inclusion and exclusion. *Developmental Psychology*, 37(5), 587–96.

Killen, M. and Smetana, J. G. (1999). Social interactions in preschool classrooms and the development of young children's conceptions of the personal. *Child Development*, 70, 486–501.

Killen, M. and Stangor, C. (2001) Children's social reasoning about inclusion and exclusion in gender and race peer group contexts. *Child Development*, 72, 174–86.

Killen, M. and Sueyoshi, L. (1995). Conflict resolution in Japanese social interactions. *Early Education and Development*, 6, 313–30.

Killen, M. and Turiel, E. (1998). Adolescents' and young adults' evaluations of helping and sacrificing for others. *Journal of Research on Adolescence*, 8, 355–75.

Killen, M. and Wainryb, C. (2000). Independence and interdependence in diverse cultural contexts. In S. Harkness and C. Raeff (eds.), *Individualism and collectivism as cultural contexts for development*, New Directions for Child Development 87. San Francisco: Jossey-Bass.

Kim, J. M. and Turiel, E. (1996). Korean and American children's concepts of adult and peer authority. *Social Development*, 5, 310–29.

Koblinsky, S. G., Cruse, D. F. and Sagawara, A. I. (1978). Sex role stereotypes and children's memory for story content. *Child Development*, 49, 452–8.

Kohlberg, L. (1984). *Essays on moral development: the psychology of moral development.* San Francisco: Harper and Row.

Kuhn, D., Nash, S. C. and Brucken, L. (1978). Sex role concepts of two- and three-year-olds. *Child Development*, 49, 445–51.

Lee-Kim, J., Killen, M., Park, Y. and Shin, Y. (in preparation). Gender roles and judgments about exclusion in Korean families. University of Maryland, College Park.

Liben, L. S. and Signorella, M. L. (1993). Gender-schematic processing in children: the role of initial interpretations of stimuli. *Developmental Psychology*, 29, 141–9.

Mackie, D. M., Hamilton, D. L., Susskind, J. and Rosselli, F. (1996). Social psychological foundations of stereotype formation. In C. Macrae, C. Stangor and M. Hewstone (eds.), *Stereotypes and Stereotyping*. New York: Guilford Press, pp. 41–77.

Macrae, C. N., Stangor, C. and Hewstone, M. (eds.) (1996). *Stereotypes and Stereotyping.* New York: Guilford Press.

Markus, H. and Kitayama, H. (1991). Culture and the self: implications for cognition, emotion, and motivation. *Psychological Review*, 98, 224–53.

Martin, C. L. and Halverson, C. F. (1981). A schematic processing model of sex-typing and stereotyping in children. *Child Development*, 52, 1119–34.

Martin, C. L., Wood, C. H. and Little, J. K. (1990). The development of gender stereotype components. *Child Development*, 61, 1891–904.

Melton, G. B. (1980). Children's concepts of their rights. *Journal of Clinical Child Psychology*, 9, 186–90.

Miller, J. G. and Bersoff, D. M. (1992). Culture and moral judgment: how are conflicts between justice and interpersonal responsibilities resolved? *Journal of Personality and Social Psychology*, 62, 541–54.

Minow, M. (1990). *Making all the difference: inclusion, exclusion, and American law.* Ithaca, NY: Cornell University Press.

Nucci, L. P. (1996). Morality and the personal sphere of actions. In E. S. Reed, E. Turiel and T. Brown (eds.), *Values and knowledge.* Mahwah, NJ: Lawrence Erlbaum, pp. 41–60.

Nucci, L. P., Camino, C. and Milnitsky-Sapiro, C. (1996). Social class effects on northeastern Brazilian children's conceptions of areas of personal choice and social regulation. *Child Development*, 67, 1223–42.

Nucci, L. P., Guerra, N. and Lee, J. (1991). Adolescent judgements of the personal, prudential, and normative aspects of drug usage. *Developmental Psychology*, 27, 841–8.

Nucci, L. P. and Lee, J. Y. (1993). Morality and autonomy. In G. G. Noam and T. E. Wren (eds.), *The moral self.* Cambridge, MA: MIT Press, pp. 123–48.

Nucci, L. P. and Turiel, E. (1993). God's word, religious rules, and their relation to Christian and Jewish children's concepts of morality. *Child Development*, 64, 1475–91.

Nucci, L. P., Turiel, E. and Encarnacion-Gawrych, G. (1983). Children's social interactions and social concepts: analyses of morality and convention in the Virgin Islands. *Journal of Cross-Cultural Psychology*, 14, 469–87.

Nucci, L. P. and Weber, E. K. (1995). Social interactions in the home and the development of young children's conceptions of the personal. *Child Development*, 66, 1438–52.

Nussbaum, M. (1999). *Sex and social justice*. Oxford: Oxford University Press.

Okin, S. M. (1989). *Justice, gender, and the family*. New York: Basic Books.

(1999). *Is multiculturalism bad for women?* Princeton: Princeton University Press.

Opotow, S. (1990). Moral exclusion and injustice: an introduction. *Journal of Social Issues*, 46, 1–20.

Park, B., Ryan, C. S. and Judd, C. M. (1992). Role of meaningful subgroups in explaining differences in perceived variability for in-groups and out-groups. *Journal of Personality and Social Psychology*, 63, 553–67.

Pettigrew, T. and Tropp, L. (2000). Does intergroup contact reduce prejudice? Recent meta-analytic findings. In S. Oskamp (ed.), *Reducing prejudice and discrimination*. Mahwah, NJ: Lawrence Erlbaum, pp. 93–114.

Piaget, J. (1932). *The moral judgment of the child*. New York: Free Press.

Powlishta, K. K. (1995). Gender bias in children's perceptions of personality traits. *Sex Roles*, 32, 17–28.

Putallaz, M. and Wasserman, A. (1990). Children's entry behavior. In S. Asher and J. Coie (eds.), *Peer rejection in childhood*. Cambridge: Cambridge University Press, pp. 60–89.

Rawls, J. (1971). *A theory of justice*. Cambridge, MA: Harvard University Press.

Rubin, K. H., Bukowski, W. and Parker, J. (1998). Peer interactions, relationships and groups. In W. Damon, series ed., N. Eisenberg (vol. ed.), *Handbook of child psychology*, vol. 3: *Socialization*. New York: Wiley, pp. 619–700.

Ruble, D. and Martin, C. (1998). Gender development. In W. Damon (series ed.), N. Eisenberg (vol. ed.), *Handbook of child psychology*, vol. 3: *Socialization*. New York: Wiley, pp. 933–1016.

Ruck, M., Abramovitch, R. and Keating, D. (1998). Children's and adolescents' understanding of rights: balancing nurturance and self-determination. *Child Development*, 64, 404–17.

Searle, J. (1969). *Speech acts*. Cambridge: Cambridge University Press.

Shweder, R., Goodnow, J., Hatano, G., LeVine, R., Markus, H. and Miller, P. (1998). The cultural psychology of development: one mind, many mentalities. In W. Damon (ed.), *Handbook of child psychology*. New York: John Wiley, pp. 865–937.

Siegal, M. and Storey, R. M. (1985). Day care and children's conceptions of moral and social rules. *Child Development*, 56, 1001–8.

Skrentny, D. (1996). *The ironies of affirmative action: politics, culture, and justice in America*. Chicago: University of Chicago Press.

Smetana, J. G. (1985). Preschool children's conceptions of transgressions: the effects of varying moral and conventional domain-related attributes. *Developmental Psychology*, 21, 18–29.

(1995). Morality in context: abstractions, ambiguities, and applications. In R. Vasta (ed.), *Annals of child development*, vol. 10. London: Jessica Kinglsey, pp. 83–130.

Song, M. J., Smetana, J. G. and Kim, S. Y. (1987). Korean children's conceptions of moral and social-conventional transgressions. *Developmental Psychology*, 23, 577–82.

Stangor, C., Killen, M., Price, B. F. and Horn, S. (under review). Racial exclusion and intimacy. University of Maryland.

Stangor, C. and Ruble, D. N. (1989). Differential influences of gender schemata and gender constancy on children's information processing behavior. *Social Cognition*, 7, 353–72.

Stangor, C. and Schaller, M. (1996). Stereotypes as individual and collective representations. In C. N. Macrae, C. Stangor and M. Hewstone (eds.), *Stereotypes and stereotyping.* New York: Guilford Press, pp. 3–37.

Stoddart, T. and Turiel, E. (1985). Children's concepts of cross-gender activities. *Child Development,* 56, 1241–52.

Tajfel, H., Billig, M., Bundy, R. P. and Flament, C. (1971). Social categorization and intergroup behavior. *European Journal of Social Psychology,* 1, 149–77.

Theimer, C. E., Killen, M. and Stangor, C. (2001). Preschool children's evaluations of exclusion in gender-stereotypic contexts. *Developmental Psychology,* 37, 1–10.

Theimer-Schuette, C. E. (1999). Children's evaluations of gender roles in a home context. Unpublished doctoral dissertation. University of Maryland, College Park.

Tisak, M. (1993). Preschool children's judgments of moral and personal events involving harm and property damage. *Merrill-Palmer Quarterly,* 39, 375–90.

(1995). Domains of social reasoning and beyond. In R. Vasta (ed.). *Annals of child development,* vol. 11. London: Jessica Kingsley, pp. 95–130.

Triandis, H. (1995). *Individualism and collectivism.* Boulder, CO: Westview Press.

Turiel, E. (1983). *The development of social knowledge: morality and convention.* Cambridge: Cambridge University Press.

(1998). The development of morality. In W. Damon (series ed.), N. Eisenberg (vol. ed.), *Handbook of child psychology,* vol. 3: *Socialization.* New York: Wiley, pp. 863–932.

Turiel, E., Hildebrandt, C. and Wainryb, C. (1985). *Judging social issues: difficulties, inconsistencies, and consistencies.* Monographs of the Society for Research in Child Development, 56 (serial no. 224). Chicago: University of Chicago Press.

Turiel, E., Killen, M. and Helwig, C. C. (1987). Morality: its structure, functions, and vagaries. In J. Kagan and S. Lamb (eds.), *The emergence of morality in young children.* Chicago: University of Chicago Press, pp. 155–244.

Turiel, E. and Smetana, J. G. (1998). Limiting the limits on domains: a commentary on Fowler and heteronomy. *Merrill-Palmer Quarterly,* 44, 293–312.

Turiel, E. and Wainryb, C. (2000). Social life in cultures: judgments, conflict, and subversion. *Child Development,* 71, 250–6.

Wainryb, C. and Turiel, E. (1994). Dominance, subordination, and concepts of personal entitlements in cultural contexts. *Child Development,* 65, 1701–22.

(1995). Diversity in social development: between or within cultures? In M. Killen and D. Hart (eds.), *Morality in everyday life: developmental perspectives.* Cambridge: Cambridge University Press, pp. 283–313.

Watanabe, H., Crystal, D. and Killen, M. (2000). Children's and adolescents' evaluations of peer group inclusion and exclusion in Japan and the United States. Paper presented at the International Society for the Study of Behavioral Development, Beijing, China, July.

Welch-Ross, M. K. and Schmidt, C. R. (1996). Gender-schema development and children's constructive story memory: evidence for a developmental model. *Child Development,* 67, 820–35.

Yee, M. D. and Brown, R. J. (1992). Self evaluations and intergroup attitudes in children aged three to nine. *Child Development,* 63, 619–29.

Zarbatany, L., van Brunschot, M., Meadows, K. and Pepper, S. (1996). Effects of friendship and gender on peer group entry. *Child Development,* 67, 2287–300.

9 Biology, culture and child rearing: the development of social motives

Hans-Joachim Kornadt

Traditionally, culture and biology are two quite distant research areas with different research traditions, different methods, rooted in different theoretical frames of reference. For a long time culture was often seen as too complex to be studied in the nomological way by 'hard' psychological methods. Cross-cultural psychologists accordingly have used culture mainly to enlarge the range of variance in the phenomena they studied. For cultural psychologists, on the other hand (Boesch, 1991; Eckensberger, 1990), the importance of culture consists in the uniqueness of meanings, beliefs and symbols in a particular culture. Therefore hermeneutic and ideographic approaches seem appropriate. However, the awareness concerning cultural influences has increased in psychology over the last decades.

Biology as a natural science is traditionally seen as a strict nomological science, with methods and findings rooted in physics and chemistry. Therefore biology seems to be rather distant from human behaviour and especially culture. Yet, the more we know about genetics and neurophysiological processes, the more psychology tends to become a 'neural' science, while traditional, pure psychological methods and theories seem to become more and more marginal.

In this chapter, the term culture refers mainly to a stored meaning system, effective for socialization and child rearing beliefs. In contrast, biology provides the neurophysiological and endocrinological underpinnings of behaviour. Yet, it is necessary to integrate both conceptions (Plomin and Rutter, 1998; Belsky, Steinberg and Draper, 1991), which will be attempted for the development of social motives in this chapter. A theoretical model will be presented to explain how these different processes interact.

Child rearing and motive development: an empirical study

The importance of early child rearing for motive development will be demonstrated using recent results of a cross-cultural longitudinal study (Kornadt et al., 1992), which deals with the development of aggressiveness and altruism in the framework of a motivational theory (Kornadt, 1982, 1984). The study was stimulated by the finding that in everyday life in Japan almost no aggressive

Table 9.1 *Cross-cultural longitudinal study: number of subjects*

	G	Sw	J	Bi	Bk
Pilot study (1980–1982)					
Adolescents	236	–	691	190	180
Mothers	45	–	52	56	43
Main study (1984–1988)					
Adolescents	137	111	226	235	225
Mother-child pairs	98	30	67	66	63
Follow-up study 9 years later (1994–1997)					
Adolescents	45	–	59	43	25
Mothers	45	–	53	43	25

Notes: G = Germany; Sw = Switzerland; J = Japan; Bi = Bali; Bk = Batak.
The Swiss sample and one Japanese subgroup were not included in the follow-up study since they did not show peculiarities in the main study. For technical reasons not all subjects from the main study could be reached in the follow-up study, the Batak sample could not be completely investigated.

interactions could be observed, between neither adults nor children, and especially not between parents and children. This observation corresponded with particular cultural norms and values, and also with a much lower crime rate in Japan as compared to Western cultures.

From the viewpoint of motivation theory, a relationship between culture-embedded child rearing and the development of motives seemed apparent. In motivation theories, it is a postulate that even qualitative specificities in motives, e.g. different relations of emotions and specific motive-related goals and instrumental patterns, develop according to particular early experiences.

In cooperation with several colleagues[1] a cross-cultural study was carried out with samples from two European cultures (Germany and Switzerland) and three East/South-East Asian cultures (Japan, Batak and Bali (Indonesia)). After a pilot study (1982) in which the procedure was tested and the instruments were validated, the main study was conducted (1986) including eight subsamples. The samples consisted of adolescents about 16 years old and unrelated mothers with children about 5 years old. Nine years later a follow-up study was performed with the same mothers, their children now about 15 years old. The numbers of subjects are shown in table 9.1.

A series of questionnaires, a semi-projective (scenario) technique, and a standardized Aggression-TAT (A-TAT) were administered; for supplementary information interviews and direct observations on playgrounds and in homes were conducted.

[1] Klaus Foppa, Bern; Tamatsu Hayashi, Kyoto; Ma'rat, Bandung; Yoshiharu Tachibana, Gifu; Gisela Trommsdorff, Konstanz, supported by Volkswagen-Foundation, German Research Council (DFG), Japan Foundation, and Japanese Society for the Promotion of Science (JSPS).

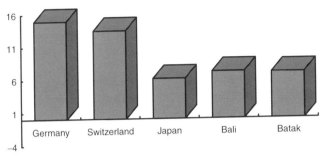

Figure 9.1   Mean aggression scores of 16-year-old adolescents in five cultures, 1986.

Results relevant in the context of this chapter will be summarized under two aspects: universality and culture specificity.

Universal relationships between child rearing and aggression

On all three occasions in 1982, 1986 and 1995 highly significant differences in the aggression motive were found between Western and Asian adolescents. Results of the A-TAT, a theory based method with a reliable scoring technique, are shown in figure 9.1.

As predicted from motivation theory, differences in the child-rearing techniques of mothers were evident, especially in those variables relevant to the development of aggressiveness: for example, the different ways in which mothers dealt with their children in case of conflicts, how mothers interpreted the misbehaviour of their children, and how or whether they approved of aggression. On the aggregate level – taking mothers and non-related adolescents as samples of the same (sub)culture – child rearing correlated in the predicted way with aggressiveness. For instance, across eight subsamples the mean aggression score of the adolescents correlated with evaluation of aggression by mothers ($r = 0.71$), with the mean scores for lack of responsiveness by mothers ($r = 0.82$) and with considerateness of mothers ($r = -0.88$).

The *longitudinal study* underscored the importance of early child-rearing on aggressiveness and altruism at the individual level. Most of the theoretically relevant variables of mothers' behaviour correlated substantially with the motive scores of their children nine years later. For instance, 'positive evaluation/acceptance of aggression' correlated $r = 0.35^{***}$ with aggression, 'benevolent, empathetic interpretation of child's misbehaviour' correlated in contrast $r = -0.41^{***}$, while 'positive evaluation/acceptance of aggression' correlated $r = -0.22^{*}$ with empathy-based (true) altruism and 'friendly setting clear rules' correlated with $r = 0.43^{***}$ (Kornadt et al., 1992).

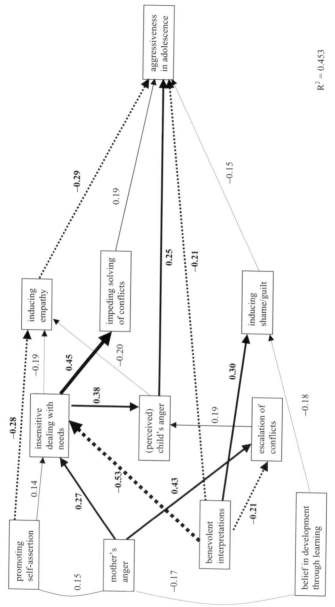

Figure 9.2   Influence of mothers' behaviour in child rearing on aggressiveness of their children nine years later (path analysis, total group without Batak).

Table 9.2 *Significantly frequent reaction sequences following encroachment*

Subjects	Affects	Intention attributed	Subject's intention	Action
Swiss/German	anger/feeling frustrated	malevolent	injure	retaliate
Japanese	anger/feeling	malevolent	complain	deplore
	frustrated/sorrow	benevolent	pro-social	pro-social
		benevolent	pro-social	pro-social
Balinese/Batak	sorrow	benevolent	pro-social	pro-social

Notes: All configurations, p < 0.000.

In Swiss and German subjects the usual aggression motivation is the most frequent sequence, while in Japanese, Balinese and Batak subjects the goal in the activated aggression motive is different (e.g. deplore) or frustration does no aggression motive activate at all.

Since correlations can only test statistical relationships, not causal influences, regression analysis and path analysis were used (see figure 9.2). In this way quantitative data combining very different cultures demonstrated the long-lasting influence of child rearing on social motives.

These results represent the first quantitative evidence of a relationship between early experiences in mother–child interactions and long-term development of social motives across cultures. Similar correlations and paths were also obtained within cultures, demonstrating the validity of these relationships.

Culture-specific relationships

Cultural specificities were found in the motives, and in the mother–child relationship as well as in its long-term effects on social motives of children.

On the basis of an aggression scenario technique subjects described their internal reactions to everyday frustrations. In all cultures the typical frustration–aggression sequence was found as described by the classical frustration–aggression theory of the Yale group and by motivation theory. In the samples from the Western cultures this was the most frequent and almost exclusive reaction. However, in Asian cultures frustration not only led to anger, but also to sorrow, shame or guilt. Moreover, even if the subjects felt angry, aggression was not the only and typical reaction; complaints about the unhappy situation or even pro-social actions were also frequent. Those differences in the sequences were confirmed as statistically significant by the configuration frequency method (see table 9.2).

On the one hand, this finding underscores the notion of a universal aggression motive as reaction toward frustrations expressed in anger feelings, the tendency to interpret the situation as caused by hostile intentions, and a stimulation of aggressive intentions and aggressive actions. However, this sequence is obviously not unavoidable. Besides a genetically based anger reaction including a tendency to aggression, specific 'learning processes' are involved in the development of the complex motive system. In Asian cultures these learning processes can obviously produce a motive system qualitatively quite different from the Western one.

This fits in with the qualitative specifics of the developmental conditions in Asian cultures identified by a similar scenario method. Most impressive was the empathetic way Japanese mothers were able and willing to deal with the needs of their children in case of misbehaviour or in a conflict (see also Trommsdorff and Friedlmeier, 2000). One difference between East and West was the way in which the mother interpreted her child's misbehaviour. When the mother wanted the child to collect the toys before having dinner, and the child did not obey, German mothers quite frequently interpreted their child's behaviour as being caused by bad intentions: 'The child does not obey because he simply wants to make me angry'. She then became angry herself and tended to reject if not to punish her child. Clearly, by this behaviour anger and aversion are likely to escalate.

Interpretations by Japanese mothers included: 'The child does not comply because he is still too immature or too sleepy', or 'He simply enjoys playing too much'. The mother is sympathetic with her child and therefore does not become angry. She tries to maintain their good mutual emotional relationship. In this way a Japanese mother promotes goodwill in her child. Japanese mothers were able to harmonize their own needs with those of their children: In the example of collecting the toys, Japanese mothers suggested a common 'tidy-up-play'; Japanese mothers can give in step by step without permitting any doubt about the rules if the child does not follow instructions. In this way the Japanese mother maintains what Azuma (1984) calls the mother–child 'oneness'. The child in turn again experiences communality and is reluctant to spoil the harmony and to endanger his own security and support.

In the German sample the mother quite often acted from a belief in a natural contrast between her needs and those of her child. She was not willing to compromise her own interests too much. Often she stressed: 'I have my own goal, you might have yours; mine prevails and you have to follow', making the child aware of the contrast between mother and child, being a model of self-centred behaviour directed against the child.

The wider context

In these examples, differences are emphasized. Contrasts between cultures are rarely as sharp and clear-cut. Also, we do not want to postulate an early kind of 'imprinting', which remains an unchangeable or even a unidirectional influence. We rather argue that an interaction circle becomes established within the family, which comprises mutual attitudes, expectations, reactions and effects – stabilizing motives and personality over the years. The correlations between motives in young adolescents and the behaviour, attitudes and values of their mothers are consistent with this argument (for more detail see Kornadt, 1992).

A host of other factors need to be considered: fathers, the extended family, the peer group, customs in school and the broad range of cultural institutions, influencing both mother and child. For instance, the way Japanese mothers are able to harmonize their needs with those of their children, to be responsive, to avoid conflicts without becoming frustrated – all this hinges upon the willingness of the mother to devote her life nearly completely for some years to the well-being of her child, and the acceptance of this devotion can only be understood in the broader context.

Culture and child rearing

In order to achieve a better understanding of these complex social interaction circles, one has to try to understand the broader cultural system. This is what cultural psychologists aim to do. To describe a culture systematically is an ambitious endeavour, impossible in a brief chapter. Therefore I will only mention some key features, accepting the risk of oversimplification.

In the following, Japanese and German cultural norms, beliefs and behaviours will be contrasted. The description of generalized interpretations will occasionally be illustrated by examples from our own data. In spite of these static characterizations, we do believe that cultures are dynamic systems. Both Japan and Germany clearly undergo social and psychological changes, which are well documented in the literature (e.g. Kornadt and Trommsdorff, 1993; Trommsdorff et al., 1998).

Tradition

Usually humans act according to their own experiences and habits. Mothers normally use their own mothers as role models and thereby acquire child-rearing techniques. Intergenerational transmission is therefore one important aspect of culture. If the common rule is to behave patiently with a young child, the mother will tend to do so without question, as certainly until the recent past was the Japanese tradition (Kojima, 1996; Shand, 1985). If the mother wants to devote her life to the well-being of her child, she needs many kinds of social support. Every mother is embedded in her social community where certain *norms* and behavioural *values* are enforced and sanctioned. In Japan it seems (or seemed, see Trommsdorff et al., 1998) to be self-evident that a mother devotes some years of her life to her children. She gives up her job, she spends much of her time together with her child, they even sleep together at the expense of her relationship with her husband. In Germany, the social value is widespread that, even as a mother, a woman should pursue her own aims; if at all possible she should have a job, not only to contribute to the family income but also for her own self-fulfilment. Conflicts of interest between mother and child are perhaps unavoidable. Thus it is understandable that in Germany mothers are inclined to stress their own interests in contrast to those of their children, while in Japan mothers are motivated and know how to reach a compromise. The child becomes motivated to maintain a harmonic relationship by obeying. Thus, in early childhood the Japanese child rarely experiences differences in interests between mother and child.

Naive personality theories and value systems

The broader culturally transmitted *naive theory of human beings* provides the framework for specific attributions of intentions. Japanese mothers in our study believed that development is mostly regulated by internal factors of maturation ('What the child cannot do today will certainly develop later'). In contrast, German mothers believed more in the necessity of actively bringing up and controlling the child ('The child has to learn as soon as possible and I am responsible for it'). This leads to more frequent intervention in the early years, and the child experiencing contrasting goals and conflict.

With respect to the development of aggression, the *evaluation of aggression* itself is relevant in two ways: (1) whether the mother will get angry easily and have aggressive interactions with her child; and (2) the way in which she deals with aggressive behaviour on the part of the child.

The child interacts first with the mother and later with peers and the broader social environment. Here the child experiences how aggression and assistance are in general accepted or rejected, punished or esteemed. In Germany over the last forty years, public attitude has become contradictory in this respect. Aggression was despised in reaction to the Nazi ideology on the one hand, while on the other a critical stance towards powerful authorities became a positive value. Self-assertion and even a certain degree of aggressive opposition was accepted in the service of defending one's view. Accordingly, mothers from the German sample even reported pride in their children when they were disobedient. At the same time, and based on contemporary American influences on cultural goals and educational practices, parents avoided 'to frustrate' a child by imposing strict rules and demands.

However, for the Japanese norms and rules are still taken as justified in themselves and are calmly enforced without hesitation or excitement. Specifically, any sign of aggression has to be avoided. Getting angry or aggressive means losing face. Aggressive adults are seen as immature, children are laughed at good naturedly. Under these conditions it is no surprise that Asian subjects in our study mentioned feelings of pity when aggression occurred at all. Victims were rather ashamed and considered the possibility of their own culpability or guilt. Western subjects in contrast tended to seek revenge.

Self concept

These different evaluations can be seen as concrete instances of the *dichotomy between individualistic and collectivistic cultures* (Hofstede, 1980). Even though this dichotomy is often used in an oversimplistic way, Japan and Indonesia clearly belong to the more collective group of cultures according to many authors like Doi (1973), Azuma (1984), Lebra and Lebra (1974) and Kornadt and Trommsdorff (1993). Germany and Switzerland may be more individualistic. In Japan as well as in Bali (perhaps in Malaysia in general; Geertz, 1981), behaviour has to be polite. Mutual respect and regard for other people, including young children, are emphasized, thus conveying and obeying clear norms. One of the norms is to be a good mother.

Growing up in such a sociocultural environment contributes to the development of a *self concept*, in which the individual sees himself as part of a greater social unit, where it does not make sense to stress independence and individuality ('interdependent self', Markus and Kitayama, 1991). In Western cultures this attitude is maladaptive. Since the Reformation and the Enlightenment the individual has become more and more important. The rejection of traditional rules and individual opposition against social control became especially fashionable during the student revolt in Germany in the late sixties. The ideals of independence, self-realization and assertiveness became prevalent, at least in comparison with common values in Asian cultures.

Religion, seniority and teacher's authority

Moreover, the religious background is important. *Religion* in many aspects underpins the development of a culture, its traditions, social norms and rules and the way individual behaviour is interpreted, supported or negatively sanctioned. The underlying beliefs influence the interpretation of the destiny of a person, the relationship between individuals and society or even the world.

One characteristic aspect for the differentiation between Asian and Western cultures is *the role of authority of parents and teachers*.

In post-war Germany, parents and teachers were reluctant to impose demands which might seem authoritarian. Especially in the family, the idea of equality between parents and children became widespread. What a child should do ought to be negotiated between parents and children. The child is expected to do the

Table 9.3 *Correlations between child rearing and 'true' altruism nine years later*

	'True' altruism				
	overall	G	J	Bi	Bk
setting limits, clear rules	0.43***	0.05ns	0.30*	0.26*	−0.04ns
conflict-solving facilitated	0.31***	−0.03ns	0.28*	0.18ns	0.24ns

right thing out of his own insight. The child's maturity for making a rational decision plays little or no role in this process, leading to frustration of parents and children based on lack of orientation and uncertainty.

In Asian cultures social values and rules are deeply rooted in Hinduism (Bali), Buddhism, Confucianism and Taoism. Traditionally the teacher, in Japan the *sensei*, has high authority. The society is structured in a hierarchical way according to *seniority*. Teaching and learning are of inherent dignity. Therefore the authority of parents and teachers is basically unquestionable. Their main duty is to represent and maintain the highest cultural values, to be a model and to help the growing child to become a good member of society. Even punishment is generally accepted and interpreted as a method (of course, appropriately used) to help the child to grow up. One of the consequences is that demands are carried out without hesitation, thus avoiding uncertainty in the children, giving them a clear orientation and no opportunity to oppose. According to data collected by Trommsdorff (1995), for instance, Japanese adolescents accept demands by their parents as an indicator of their support while young German adolescents see this as hurting their self-esteem and freedom.

Cultural context and developmental outcome

The short discussion in the preceding subsections was to give an impression of the specificities and the complexity of cultures, showing how child rearing is embedded (see Keller and Eckensberger, 1998) in the cultural context with which the child has to interact during the course of development.

Empirical evidence from our research supports the importance of the cultural context in shaping individual developmental trajectories. In table 9.3 the correlations are shown between two contextual child-rearing variables and the ('true') altruism nine years later in the four samples of our longitudinal study.

It should be noted that these two variables are positively related with altruism in Japan, but not in Germany. Trommsdorff and Friedlmeier (2000) have reported similar data.

Biology of social motives

In psychological theories of motive development, biological factors have been mainly discussed on the neurophysiological and endocrinological level (e.g. Brain and Benton, 1981). Today, the role of genetic factors receives increasing interest. For a deeper understanding of the function of biological factors detailed knowledge about functional relationships is needed.

Related hypotheses had already been formulated by Eibl-Eibesfeldt in 1975. He assumes specific inborn behavioural systems and learning dispositions to be universal, for example he provided empirical evidence that children display the same rudimentary aggressive behaviour in all cultures.

Specific functional links between biology and behavioural development were hypothesized in the motivation theory of aggression (Kornadt, 1982, 1984). Biologically rooted emotions were seen as specific starting points for the development of social motives. Kornadt (1982, 1990) assumes that this constitutes the specificity of social motives, allowing a non-arbitrary definition distinguishing the aggression motive from other motives. For aggressiveness, an innate potential to react with anger to insult is postulated. Anger is associated with specific vegetative and motoric reactions as well as facial expressions. These influence in turn the reactions of a social partner or caregiver. Numerous and repeated interactions of this kind constitute the specific emotional experiences of the child which are the basis for the stepwise development of the motive with its internal organization, combining specific emotion-related goals and instrumental patterns (for details see Kornadt, 1990). Similarly, empathy is defined as a biologically rooted reaction to the distress of another person, marking the starting point for the development of 'true' (empathy-based) altruistic motivation (see also Staub, 1986).

First global evidence of heritability

The function of biological factors in motive development can also be illustrated with other findings. Indigenous wisdom about the biological basis of motivation has existed for centuries. Examples are the behavioural differences resulting from the breeding of domesticated dogs, or between geldings and stallions caused by castration, and oxen would never be used for a bullfight. These observations have been supported by experiments on *selective breeding* for aggressiveness by Lagerspetz and Lagerspetz (1971), who found differences from the second generation onwards, increasing up to the nineteenth generation. It may be noted that cross-fostering of the aggressive and non-aggressive selective strains had no effect on aggression. Similar results were found by other investigators using other animals, mostly mammals. Since the basic brain structure, function and biochemical substances are shared among mammals, these results clearly have implications for humans.

Twin studies in humans have resulted in heritability estimates for a variety of motives. The variance explained by heritability for affiliation and achievement motive was 46 per cent respectively 26 per cent in a longitudinal study by Geppert and Halisch (in press), covering a period of fifty years. Christiansen (1974) found a 35 per cent concordance rate for aggressiveness in monozygotic twins and only 13 per cent for dizygotics in a Danish twin study. Rushton and colleagues (1986) found in a study with 573 adult twins that correlation for monozygotic vs. dizygotic pairs were $r = 0.53$ vs. $r = 0.25$ for altruism and $r = 0.40$ vs. $r = 0.04$ for aggressiveness. This resulted in a heritability estimate of 56 per cent for altruism and 72 per cent for aggressiveness.

These heritability estimates provide only basic evidence for the existence of biological underpinnings of social motives. The exact relationship between biological and environmental influences is still unclear, the old nature–nurture controversy will remain unresolved until the function of genes is better understood (Plomin and Rutter, 1998). Therefore studies about brain structure, neural functioning and biochemical processes are essential.

Neuro-anatomical basis of aggression

In the intensively investigated biology of aggression one important aspect refers to the *neuro-anatomical structures* involved. Evidence comes from brain stimulation experiments, and from studies involving lesions of specific areas, covering a wide range of species including human patients. Results show that some areas are involved in activating, others in inhibiting aggressive behaviour (Newman, 1999). The amygdala and hypothalamus play an important role (Trimble and van Elst, 1999). Electrical stimulation in these areas causes the expression of anger in various ways: increased blood pressure and heart rate, and elicited motoric reactions like facial expression and coordinated attack behaviours (biting, hitting and kicking).

However, not one single 'nucleus' is the neuronal basis for the regulation of aggression. A complex neuro-anatomical system is involved including also the frontal lobe, hippocampus, limbic structures and (lower) brain stem, probably in a hierarchical order. The special function of the individual parts and their connectivity is not completely clear. However, this is a difficult issue given the plasticity and individual differences.

Chemical (hormonal) factors

Another kind of evidence comes from studies about the releasing or inhibiting function of *hormones*, *neurotransmitters* or *drugs* for specific motivated behaviour.

Hormonal pathways There are basically two kinds of neuro-chemical functions. One is that hormones and neurotransmitters can activate or inhibit the neuronal system and the actual motivated behaviour. The other is that these substances play an important role during the development of the anatomical structure of the brain and the functions of specific subsystems. Extensively studied hormonal substances, which can promote the display of aggression, are testosterone and its metabolites. Olweus and colleagues (1980) reported a striking covariance between plasma testosterone levels in male adolescents and (self-reported) aggressiveness. Detailed neuro-chemical studies revealed that in the male brain testosterone can activate aggression through three pathways. One is that the relevant structures respond to testosterone itself (i.e. they are androgen sensitive). Another is the oestrogen sensitive pathway where the brain reacts to the oestrogenic metabolite of testosterone. A third pathway is through a synergistic function of both. In adult females also the androgen sensitive pathway exists while the brain is insensitive to the aggression promoting property of oestrogens. There is a clear sexual dimorphism in the sensitivity of neural target tissue. Other relevant systems are the serotonal and dopamine systems. One should also consider the function of various neurotransmitters and their pre- and post-synaptic effects (McGinty, 1999).

Neuro-chemical factors and brain development Individual differences in the sensitivity to these hormones depend on the genotype (Simon et al., 1996), thus the *function of genes* need to be studied in the neuro-chemical processes of gene transmission, in cellular processes and in the process of the development of the brain structure and its function.

The development of the brain can be influenced in certain time 'windows' by hormones or other chemical substances (e.g. drugs) resulting in the anatomical structures or their sensitivity (Kloet et al., 1996). One example is the prenatal influence of testosterone on the neuro-anatomical structures relevant for aggression resulting in masculinization of certain brain structures. This process produces a higher sensitivity to aggression-eliciting stimuli in adults, even in females. In cases of suprarenal gland malfunction, which produces a higher level of testosterone or of androgen medication during the foetal period, more boy-like behaviour in girls has been found (Ferris and Grisso, 1996).

Cortisol and stress feedback The perinatal concentration of several other substances can also influence intracellular processes in the developing brain and thereby influence the sensitivity to hormonal and other stimuli. Important are, for example, nicotine and cortisol. According to King (1996) the hypothalamic–pituitary–adrenal axis (HPA) has a major hormonal function mediating stress responses. During development it undergoes changes, partly dependent on cortisol feedback, which can significantly alter the neuronal structure of the brain. Some of these developmental stages provide a 'window of vulnerability' during which stress of the mother can have long-term behavioural effects on the child.

The studies summarized above illustrate the high relevance of biological processes for motivated behaviour and the formation of enduring dispositions for social motives. Owing to the interaction of numerous factors (RNA and protein synthesis, development and sensitization of steroid receptors etc.) and feedback in the physiological system and its malleability through such environmental events as stress (Francis et al., 1996), genes can never simply determine behaviour.

Integration of cultural and biological factors

The question remains how biology can be integrated in the context of individual child rearing and culture. On the one hand there is our genetic outfit with the innate potential for certain reactions. On the other hand we know that social motives are differentiated systems, formed in a long 'learning' process (Zahn-Waxler et al., 1986; Tremblay, 2000). For example, the aggression motive comprises the disposition to react angrily, the preference to interpret others' intentions as malevolent, their connection with specific individual behaviour patterns and the general acceptance of aggression (Kornadt, 1982).

How can the genetic predisposition and the experience in the social environment interact to form motives? Given the amazing stability of aggressiveness from childhood to adulthood (Zumkley, 1992), we have to study the early processes as one factor contributing to this stability (Staub, 1986).

According to our path-analysis (figure 9.2) and the East–West differences the (harmonious or conflicting) mother–child interaction is the decisive factor. This parental behaviour produces a fundamental experience in the child to feel either content or stressed, to feel secure in a friendly world or insecure in a hostile environment. The effects of accumulated experiences of this kind will certainly exert influence on the child's future development.

Attachment research (e.g. Bowlby, 1982; Cassidy and Shaver, 1999; Grossmann and Grossmann, 1996) has analysed and theoretically formulated the function of early experiences. Attachment is conceptualized as a biologically based motivational system in the infant without specific assumptions about aggression and altruism. It motivates to gain security and to develop a strong affectional bond, to gain proximity or protection from the particular attachment figure. Separation from or loss of that person creates distress and insecurity in the infant. Permanent unresponsive caring or inconsistent availability of the attachment person leads to enduring insecure or ambivalent/avoidant attachment. Insecurely attached children show conflicting and sometimes hostile reactions toward their attachment figure. Attachment theory assumes that these early experiences form fundamental cognitive structures concerning the self–other relationship and related emotions ('working model'), which become one of the basic elements for the personality development.

Building on this, Kornadt's (1992) theoretical model assumes the attachment process to be the decisive starting point for the forming of either pro- or anti-social motives, integrating biological and environmental (including cultural) factors. This is expressed in figure 9.3.

For a brief description in which only the general lines are mentioned, a rough differentiation into two stages may be sufficient.

In the model the process starts with differences in the responsiveness of mothers producing either secure or insecure attachment in the child. Already here genetic factors are relevant for the mother's disposition to be patient or empathetic, which presumably influences the mother's responsiveness. Children also differ in their biological disposition for irritability, anxiety or anger, which in turn may influence their mothers' behaviour. However, culture plays a role in a mother's view about good parenting, and in the tradition she herself experienced during childhood.

In case of insecure attachment a vicious circle becomes established with partly reinforcing positive effects of expressing anger and violent behaviour. Its internal effect is the 'belief' that actions directed against others are necessary in order to satisfy one's own needs. Securely attached children rather strive to restore the harmony by doing what the mother wants in order to avoid further conflicts. A positive circle of mutual affection and harmonizing will be established, reinforcing and stabilizing the secure attachment. Rather than acting in their own interests both parties are solicitous of the other's common well-being.

Thus, the first two to three years of motive development are partly controlled by the quality of attachment. The resulting motive development in middle childhood will be influenced by conditions in the social environment and the products of the earlier processes. Opportunities will be processed by and into the cognitive schemata with the conditioned emotions, related expectations and behaviour patterns developed so far.

Two special aspects in this socialization process worth mentioning are depicted in figure 9.3. The formed characteristics include the receptivity to certain models, seen as affined or opposed to the self. This facilitates the imitation of the relevant behaviour patterns, and the internalization of interpretations and values as provided by the social environment.

Furthermore the child is not passive, provokes certain reactions from the environment (Kuczynski, 2000) and actively seeks niches fitting his or her expectations. In this way adaptive interaction patterns will develop, partly based on characteristics established earlier in the interaction of genetic underpinnings

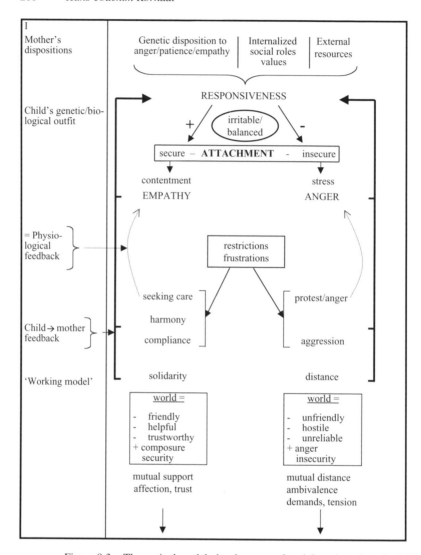

Figure 9.3   Theoretical model: development of social motives. I: early childhood; II: middle childhood.

and environmental conditions. This contributes further to the respective self concept either in terms of being self-assertive and aggressive *against* the interests
of others, or in terms of being well accepted and getting along *with* others.

These central hypotheses about the basic importance of attachment for the
following developmental process is further supported by two different findings.

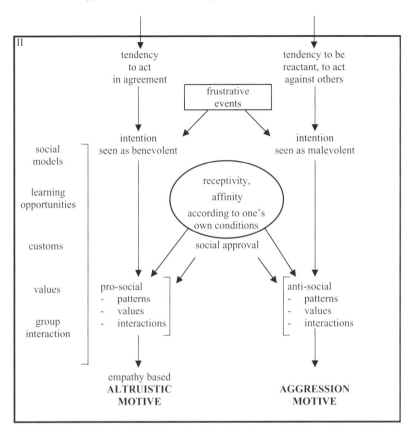

Figure 9.3   (*cont.*)

Over a variety of forty-nine cultures a clear association between 'high infant physical affection', most likely connected with secure attachment, and 'low adult physical violence' was observed in thirty-six of them, as reported by Textor (1967). More important are enduring biological effects of certain experiences. Attachment versus maternal deprivation is especially important: maternal deprivation can alter brain development and physiological responses in adult life. The deprivation operates like stress, activating the HPA axis and causing high cortisol level, which influences the brain function in many ways, as experiments on primates have shown (Kraemer and Clarke, 1996; Kloet et al., 1996).

This theoretical model integrates numerous empirical findings and allows the formulation of more specific hypotheses. Thus further research is suggested.

Conclusion

On the basis of the example of social motives it has been shown here how culture and biology interact in the process of development, and how these interaction processes come about. Undoubtedly there is an inborn capacity to react with specific emotions, such as anger. The first accumulated experiences and their frequency activate and deactivate the emotion and form the biologically based crystallization points for further motive development. But this is not a unilinear process based on one genetic factor. It is the product of internal interaction of many neurochemical processes and feedback loops.

Behaviour of the child is one part of a developing interaction circle which forms the accumulating experience of the child. The caregiver, in turn, acts accordingly to his/her enduring habits and motives, which are based on biology and experiences, and which again are shaped by (culture-bound) understanding of the actual situational context. That means that all experiences of childhood are inevitably culture-related.

It is clear that motives are behavioural systems where biology and culture are deeply intertwined. But so far only the basic principles of interaction are known. Much more research on details is needed. One of the fields is the neuro-chemical formation of the disposition to react with emotions like anger and the connection with the perception of activating conditions. Another field of research is on the first social interactions themselves and the experiences (such as expectations and adaptations) which are at the root of further development.

REFERENCES

Azuma, H. (1984). Secondary control as a heterogeneous category. *American Psychologist*, 39, 970–1.
Belsky, J., Steinberg, L. and Draper, P. (1991). Childhood experience, interpersonal development, and reproductive strategy: an evolutionary theory of socialization. *Child Development*, 62, 647–70.
Bowlby, J. (1982). *Attachment and loss*, vol. 1: *Attachment*. New York: Basic Books.
Boesch, E. E. (1991). *Symbolic action theory and cultural psychology*. Berlin: Springer.
Brain, P. B. and Benton, D. (eds.) (1981). *The biology of aggression*. Alphen van den Rijn, NL: Sijthoff & Noordhoff.
Cassidy, J. and Shaver, P. R. (eds.) (1999). *Handbook of attachment. Theory, research, and clinical applications*. New York: Guilford Press.
Christiansen, K. O. (1974). The genesis of aggressive criminality: implications of a study of crime in a Danish twin study. In J. de Wit and W. W. Hartup (eds.), *Determinants and origins of aggressive behavior*. The Hague: Mouton, pp. 233–53.
Doi, D. (1973). *The anatomy of dependence*. Tokyo/New York: Kodansha International.
Eckensberger, L. H. (1990). On the necessity of the culture concept in psychology: a view from cross-cultural psychology. In F. J. R. van de Vijver and G. J. M. Hutschemakers (eds.), *The investigation of culture. Current issues in cultural psychology*. Tilburg: Tilburg University Press, pp. 153–83.
Eibl-Eibesfeldt, I. (1975). *Krieg und Frieden* (War and peace). Munich: Piper.

Ferris, C. F. and Grisso, T. (eds.) (1996). *Understanding aggressive behavior in children.* New York: New York Academy of Sciences.

Francis, D., DeOrio, J., La Plante, P., Weaver, S., Seckl, J. R. and Meaney, M. J. (1996). The role of early environmental events in regulating neuro-endocrine development. In C. F. Ferris and T. Grisso (eds.), *Understanding aggressive behavior in children.* New York: New York Academy of Sciences, pp. 136–52.

Geertz, C. (1981). *The interpretation of cultures.* New York: Basic Books.

Geppert, U. and Halisch, F. (in press). Genetic vs. environmental determinants of traits, motives, self-referential cognitions, and volitional control in old age: first results from the Munich twin study (GOLD). In A. Efklides, J. Kuhl and E. Sorrentino (eds.), *Trends and perspectives in motivation research.* Dordrecht: Kluwer.

Grossmann, K. and Grossmann, K. E. (1996). Kulturelle Perspektiven der Bindungsentwicklung in Japan und Deutschland (Cultural perspectives on the development of attachment in Japan and Germany). In G. Trommsdorff and H. J. Kornadt (eds.), *Gesellschaftliche und individuelle Entwicklung in Japan und Deutschland* (Societal and individual development in Japan and Germany). Konstanz: Universitätsverlag Konstanz, pp. 215–35.

Hofstede, G. (1980). *Cultures consequences. International differences in work related values.* London: Sage.

Keller, H. and Eckensberger, L. H. (1998). Kultur und Entwicklung (Culture and development). In H. Keller (ed.), *Lehrbuch der Entwicklungspsychologie* (Textbook of developmental psychology). Bern: Huber, pp. 57–96.

King, J. A. (1996). Perinatal stress and impairment of the stress response. In C. F. Ferris and T. Grisso (eds.), *Understanding aggressive behavior in children.* New York: New York Academy of Sciences, pp. 104–12.

Kloet, E. R., Corte, S. M., Rots, N. Y. and Kruk, M. R. (1996). Stress hormones, genotype, and brain organization. In C. F. Ferris and T. Grisso (eds.), *Understanding aggressive behavior in children.* New York: New York Academy of Sciences, pp. 179–91.

Kojima, H. (1996). Japanese child-rearing advice in its cultural social and economic contexts. *International Journal of Behavioral Development,* 19, 373–91.

Kornadt, H. J. (1982). *Aggressionsmotiv und Aggressionshemmung* (Motive and repression of aggression), vol. 1. Bern: Huber.

(1984). Motivation theory of aggression and its relation to social psychological approaches. In A. Mummendey (ed.), *Social psychology of aggression.* Berlin: Springer, pp. 21–31.

(1990). Why motives can be better understood if seen as parts of the personality. In G. L. van Heck, S. E. Hampson, J. Reykowski and J. Zakrzewski (eds.), *Personality psychology in Europe,* vol. 3. Amsterdam: Swets & Zeitlinger, pp. 84–100.

(1992). Common roots and divergent development of altruism and aggression. Working paper no. 62. Saarbrücken: University of Saarland.

Kornadt, H. J., Hayashi, T., Tachibana, Y., Trommsdorff, G. and Yamauchi, H. (1992). Aggressiveness and its developmental conditions in five cultures. In S. Iwawaki, Y. Kashima and K. Leung (eds.), *Innovations in cross-cultural psychology.* Amsterdam: Swets and Zeitlinger, pp. 250–68.

Kornadt, H. J. and Trommsdorff, G. (eds.) (1993). *Deutsch–Japanische Begegnungen in den Sozialwissenschaften* (German–Japanese encounters in social sciences). Konstanz: Universitätsverlag Konstanz.

Kraemer, G. W. and Clark, A. S. (1996). Social attachment, brain function and aggression. In C. F. Ferris and T. Grisso (eds.), *Understanding aggressive behavior in children*. New York: New York Academy of Sciences, pp. 121–35.

Kuczynski, L. (2000). The socialization of parents by children. Paper presented at the 15th IACCP Congress, Pultusk.

Lagerspetz, K. M. J. and Lagerspetz, K. Y. H. (1971). Changes in the aggressiveness of mice resulting from selective breeding, learning, and social isolation. *Scandinavian Journal of Psychology*, 12, 241–8.

Lebra, T. S. and Lebra, W. P. (eds.) (1974). *Japanese culture and behavior*. Honolulu: University Press of Hawaii.

Markus, H. R. and Kitayama, S. (1991). Culture and the self: implication for cognition, emotion, and motivation. *Psychological Review*, 98, 224–53.

McGinty, J. F. (1999). Regulation of neurotransmitter interactions in the ventral striatum. In J. F. McGinty (ed.), *Advancing from the ventral striatum to the extended amygdala*. New York: New York Academy of Sciences, pp. 129–39.

Newman, S. W. (1999). The medial extended amygdala in male reproductive behavior: a node in the mammalian social behavior network. In J. F. McGinty (ed.), *Advancing from the ventral striatum to the extended amygdala*. New York: New York Academy of Sciences, pp. 242–57.

Olweus, D., Mattsson, A., Schalling, D. and Löw, H. (1980). Testosterone, aggression, physical, and personality dimensions in normal adolescent males. *Psychosomatic Medicine*, 42, 253–69.

Plomin, R. and Rutter, M. (1998). Child development, molecular genetics, and what to do with genes once they are found. *Child Development*, 69, 1223–42.

Rushton, J. P., Fulzer, D. W., Neale, M. C., Nias, D. K. B. and Eysenck, H. (1986). Altruism and aggression: the heritability of individual differences. *Journal of Personality and Social Psychology*, 50, 1192–8.

Shand, N. (1985). Culture's influence in Japanese and American maternal role perception and confidence. *Psychiatry*, 48, 52–67.

Simon, N. G., McKenna, S. E., Lew, S.-F. and Cologer-Clifford, A. (1996). Development and expression of hormonal systems regulating aggression. In C. F. Ferris and T. Grisso (eds.), *Understanding aggressive behavior in children*. New York: New York Academy of Sciences, pp. 8–17.

Staub, E. (1986). A conception of the determinants and development of altruism and aggression: motives, the self, and the environment. In C. Zahn-Waxler, E. M. Cummings and R. Iannotti (eds.), *Altruism and aggression*. Cambridge: Cambridge University Press, pp. 135–64.

Textor, R. B. (1967). *A cross-cultural summary*. New Haven, CT: HRAF Press.

Tremblay, R. E. (2000). The development of aggressive behavior during childhood: what have we learnt in the past century? *International Journal of Behavioral Development*, 24, 129–41.

Trimble, M. R. and van Elst, L. T. (1999). On some clinical implications of the ventral striatum and the extended amygdala: investigations of aggression. In J. F. McGinty (ed.), *Advancing from the ventral striatum to the extended amygdala*. New York: New York Academy of Sciences, pp. 638–44.

Trommsdorff, G. (1995). Parent–adolescent relations and changing societies: a cross-cultural study. In P. Noack, M. Hofer and J. Youniss (eds.), *Psychological responses to social change: human development in changing environments*. Berlin: De Gruyter, pp. 189–218.

Trommsdorff, G. and Friedlmeier, W. (2000). Emotion and prosocial behavior – a Japanese–German comparison. Paper presented at the 15th IACCP Congress, Pultusk.

Trommsdorff, G., Friedlmeier, W. and Kornadt, H. J. (eds.) (1998). *Japan in transition*. Lengerich: Pabst.

Zahn-Waxler, C., Cummings, E. M and Iannotti, R. (eds.) (1986). *Altruism and aggression*. Cambridge: Cambridge University Press.

Zumkley, H. (1992). Stability of individual differences in aggression. In A. Fraczek and H. Zumkley (eds.), *Socialization and aggression*. Berlin: Springer, pp. 45–57.

Part IV

Perspectives on development informed
by evolutionary thinking

10 Development as the interface between biology and culture: a conceptualization of early ontogenetic experiences

Heidi Keller

In this chapter it is argued that the analysis of developmental processes allows us to understand the interaction between biological predispositions and environmental information with respect to the initiation of culturally informed developmental pathways. Based on evolutionary theorizing, an organismic metaperspective (Eckensberger and Keller, 1998) is adopted, considering contemporary humans, like any other species, as incorporating evolved behavioural dispositions. The biological heritage and the cultural present are components of the same developmental processes. This view postulates 'transactional relations' between organism and environment, rejecting any simplistic biological determinism. Behavioural development is geared at encompassing developmental tasks, which have specific functions during the life histories of individuals. Thus, development is understood as a teleonomic process instead of pursuing overarching teleological goals. It is argued that the early social experiences of infants with their caregivers set the stage for developmental trajectories that lead to ontogenetic adaptation. A component model of parenting is introduced that captures cross-cultural as well as interindividual differentiations.

Biological underpinnings: the evolutionary heritage

Evolutionary approaches differentiate proximate from ultimate causes when describing behavioural adaptations. The analysis of proximate causes mainly concerns the question how interactive dynamics should be understood (Anastasi, 1958), focusing on somatic, social and psychological processes. The ultimate cause of any proximate adaptation is evaluated in terms of its contribution to optimal genetic reproduction (inclusive fitness, Hamilton, 1964). Therefore, the question *how* has necessarily to be complemented with the question *why* specifying origin and function of developmental patterns (Eckensberger, 1996; Eckensberger and Keller, 1998; Mayr, 1988).

As a result of the ultimate orientation, the evolutionary perspective centres on the gene as the unit of analysis. But, as Mayr (1994, p. 206) has convincingly argued: '... it is not the naked gene, that is exposed to selective forces directly'.

The gene is part of the genotype that is considered as '...a well integrated system analogous to the organ structure of an organism' (Mayr, 1988, p. 129). In fact, it is genotypic information (deoxyribonucleic acid (DNA)) stemming from different gene loci (pleiotropy) as translated into the phenotype that is exposed to selection: 'It is not the genes that live or die, breed or help their relatives, but the realized animal' (Daly and Wilson, 1983, p. 32).

Adaptation as 'selection in progress' (Voland, 1993) centrally depends on variability of the genotypes, which results in humans mainly from sexual recombination.[1] Genetic variability allows the adaptation of the genotype to a multiplicity of environments and environmental changes, although genes are primarily adapted to the environment of the evolutionary past (EEA, *Environment of Evolutionary Adaptedness*), incorporating the 'experiences', i.e. survival enhancing traits, of the ancestors (Delbrück, 1949; Mayr, 1988).

Genes exert their effects in *fixed programmes* which are invariably coded in the DNA of the genotype and in *open programmes* which are environmentally labile and prepared to acquire information through learning (Mayr, 1988). Most macro-morphological changes are tightly controlled by fixed genetic scripts (cf. Nelson, 1999), detailing that the environment is needed but does not exert major differential effects. Open genetic programmes set the stage for differential effects of environmental influences. Proponents of the new field of interpersonal neurobiology (Schore, 1994; Siegel, 1999) argue that the structure and function of the developing brain are determined by how experiences, especially within interpersonal relationships, shape the genetically programmed maturation of the nervous system. The caregiver is providing experiences, which shape genetic potential by acting as a psychobiological regulator of hormones that directly influence gene transcription. Psychoneuroendocrinological changes during critical periods initiate enduring effects at the genomic level which is expressed in the imprinting of evolving brain circuitry (Schore, 2000).

The important message is that social interactions among humans shape neural connections, i.e. the fine-tuning of the brain, as well as the mental representation of experiences and thus the psychological foundation of the individual. The modes in which open programmes influence and direct behaviour are 'legion' (Mayr, 1988, p. 68; MacDonald, 1988), indicating that these interactions occur at a variety of neurophysiological and behavioural levels and are domain specific (Darwinian algorithms, Cosmides and Tooby, 1987).

Therefore, learning based in open genetic programmes cannot be understood as a general mechanism with universal properties: '... the more we have studied learning abilities, the more impressed we have become with their specificity' (Trivers, 1985, p. 102). However, the different modes of learning show biases

---

[1] The estimations for the mutation rate in humans varies between 1.6 (Eyre-Walker and Keightley, 1999) and 3 (Crow, 1999) per 80.000.

that may reflect selective forces. Thus, learning has to be specified with respect to the content that is to be learned and the time at which it is learned. The interplay of content specificity and timing of learning is regarded as specifying 'epigenetic rules' (Wilson, 1975) or 'central tendencies' (MacDonald, 1988) that direct attention to specific (environmental) cues at specific times. Such effects may be weaker or stronger, the classical ethological conception of the sensitive period for imprinting being the strongest case. The acquisition of specific information during specific time windows allows infants 'to learn easily' (Boyd and Richerson, 1985; Draper and Harpending, 1988). The specification of content and timing of learning draws on the implicit notion that the genotype needs specific information from the environment in order to develop its phenotypic appearance (evolved co-designs, Rochat, 1997; inborn environment, Bischof, 1996). Because many aspects of development are activity-dependent, a broad range of individual differences results.

Thus, the foundation of interpersonal differentiation with respect to psychobiological functioning is laid down during the very early years of life and continues to exert influences throughout the life history. Yet we agree with Nelson (1999, p. 425) that '...the first few years of life are (not) a critical period *in general*; rather, it is perhaps wisest to view these years as a critical period for some functions, a sensitive period for others and broadly tuned and receptive to modification for the duration of the lifespan for still others'.

In summary, it can be concluded that human infants are predisposed with open genetic programmes for the acquisition of environmental information, which is of primordial significance for shaping their neurophysiological and psychological development. Yet it can be assumed that the complexity of humans' nervous systems and the multiple facets of the context and environment do not allow the formulation of a single adaptive relation between context and behaviour (cf. Belsky, Steinberg and Draper, 1991; Chisholm, 1992; Greenfield and Suzuki, 1998; Keller, 2000a, 2000b; Keller and Greenfield, 2000; Keller et al., 1999; Lerner and De Stefanis, 1999; Rothbaum et al., 2000).

Learning relationships: the acquisition of a social matrix

The first overarching developmental task that an infant has to master the world over consists of developing relationships with the primary caregiver. Learning relationships can be understood as a developmental process that is guided by epigenetic rules that direct infants' attention to their social partners and allow the easy learning of the parameters that define the relationships within a specific context and, with this, the definition of the contextual foundation of the self.

The constituting interpersonal experiences are embedded in caregiving systems that have evolved as adaptive responses to environmental challenges,

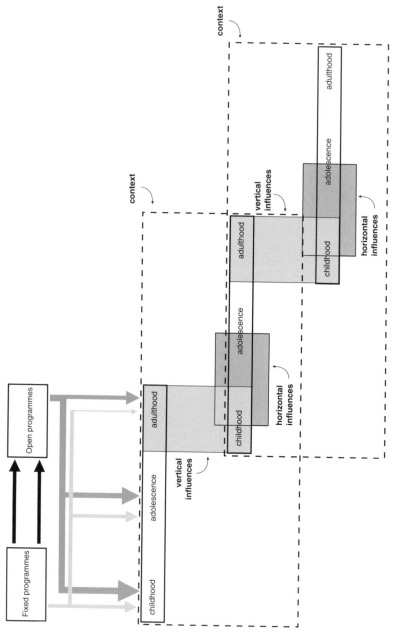

Figure 10.1   Inter- and intragenerational transmission of information.

mainly entailing the regulation of physiological and behavioural functioning (Hofer, 1987), protection from predators (Bowlby, 1969), development of group cohesion (Dunbar, 1996; Keller, 2000b) and the emergence of a sense of self (cf. Keller et al., 1999). It is assumed that caregiving systems consist of a set of genetically prepared behavioural propensities that can be activated due to the challenges of environmental demands. Since contexts only gradually change, contextual continuity over the generations establishes the prevalent socialization framework. This developmental scenario favours vertical social-ization influences where parents prepare their offspring for mastering the same environmental context that they have learned to master. In rapidly changing environments that characterize the (post-) modern world, horizontal influences, e.g. from peers and age mates, increase in importance. Yet the receptivity for those influences is based in the experiences with the early family context. Learn-ing relationships thus consists of decoding information from the significant so-cial partners during the early socialization phase with the consequence of the development of an early conception of an internal working model (Bowlby, 1969) where the emerging self is represented, as well as the relationships with the social partners. Thus, relationship learning is part of an intergenerational transmission process (see figure 10.1).

Figure 10.1 visualizes the individual developmental life history which is roughly differentiated into childhood, adolescence and adulthood (for a more detailed discussion of the lifespan from an evolutionary perspective see Keller, in press), as being informed by fixed and open genetic programmes, thus cov-ering genetic as well as cultural transmission between generations. During the adult phase, individuals create socialization contexts for their offspring, which are contingent upon their own biographical history and their eco-cultural present. Infants actively acquire their social matrix and learn specific modes of relationships within these contexts. Together with horizontal experiences in their eco-cultural environments they proceed through the biographical cycle facing the same developmental tasks.

In our understanding, relationship learning is situated mainly in the earliest developmental period covering the very first months of life. At about three months of age, a developmental transition is postulated in very different cultures. In the Western literature it demarcates the first bio(social) behavioural shift (Cole and Cole, 1989; Emde, 1984), with a first developmental result in the processes of relationship formation (Keller, 1992) when a sense of an emergent self is formed (Stern, 1985). In India, there are ceremonies at about the same time where the infant is exposed for the first time to the sun and the moon (Saraswathi and Pai, 1997, p. 75), thus also opening new developmental contexts. The first three months form the first stage of the reception phase of development (Keller 1998; Keller and Eckensberger, 1998). This phase extends over the first two to three years with the result that the biosocial infant has developed into a cultural child who is recognizable as a member of a distinct culture in terms of appearance and behaviour. The following considerations therefore address specifically the first few months of life.

Infants and caregivers: biological preparedness for relationship formation

Infants are equipped from birth on and even before with specific predispositions (epigenetic rules, central tendencies; cf. Keller, 2000b) to support their own growth and development.

They attract their caregivers' attention, with a repertoire of infant characteristics like the *'Kindchenschema'* ('babyness', Lorenz, 1943) and by retaining juvenile characteristics, which may stimulate surveillance and protection, also from non-family members ('neotony', Mayr, 1982), particularly in cultures where infants are the property of the community, as among the Cameroonian Nso (Yovsi, 2001). Because of their social nature, infants prefer the human face over other perceptual displays (e.g., Fantz, 1963) and behave differently towards people as compared with objects (Brazelton, Koslowski and Main, 1974). They expect responsiveness from their social environment as still-face studies clearly demonstrate (cf. Weinberg and Tronick, 1996). They detect event- as well as person-based contingencies (Keller et al., 1999) and process meaningful language units (phonemes) from their linguistic environment (Keller, 2000c). They are sensitive to stimulation and experience relief from comfort. However, infants are not passive recipients of parental treatment, but participate actively in the acquisition of the relevant information for the construction of the early social matrix (Keller and Eckensberger, 1998; Keller and Greenfield, 2000).

Due to the 'physiological preterm birth' (Prechtl, 1984), which needs not only to be seen as caused by hominid brain growth but constitutes an adaptational pattern in itself, allowing all resources to be invested into growth and development (Keller, in press), newborn infants are highly altricial in many respects. Although they can see, vision is still imperfect, since convergence and acuity are not yet mastered (Kaufmann-Hayoz and van Leeuwen, 1997), vision and movement are not yet coordinated and the memory span covers only about one second. Therefore, they need a special co-designed ('fitting') caregiving environment, which can compensate and complement their behavioural inflexibility and shape the behavioural repertoire that is appropriate for the respective eco-cultural environment. For this purpose also caregivers are endowed with behavioural predispositions to care for and interact with babies.

Humans from about two to three years on display parenting skills which enable them to perceive and process the communicative cues from babies and react in an appropriate manner. We adopt the ethological conception of behavioural systems as relatively independent functional units that comprise behaviours that are coordinated to achieve specific goals, which regulate the interaction intentionally and/or intuitively (Bowlby, 1969; Hinde, 1982). These systems are activated and terminated by endogenous and environmental cues. Our conceptualizing of the parenting systems is more comprehensive than the caregiving system as defined in attachment theory; we see it as the subset of parental behaviours which promote proximity and comfort when the child is in real or potential danger (Cassidy, 1999). It also cuts across descriptive systems like maternal and paternal systems (cf. Harlow, Harlow and Hansen, 1963) or the systems of teaching, feeding and playing (e.g. Cassidy, 1999). We assume that parenting is organized as a pervasive style that is composed from different systems pertaining to the whole of interactional experiences with all caregivers.

These behavioural regulations are mainly performed intuitively and non-intentionally and not based on an understanding of why they are performed (e.g. Heyes and Dickinson, 1993; Keller et al., 1999; Papoušek and Papoušek, 1991). Individuals seem to allocate parental investment differentially into their offspring depending on an intuitive calculation of fertility and mortality rates (Dienes et al., 1995; Hasher and Zacks, 1984; Hill and Hurtado, 1996). Also, biological marker variables such as sex, age and birth order influence caregiving and psychological parenting on an implicit basis (Keller and Zach, in press; Sulloway, 1996; Trivers and Willard, 1973). However, parenting constitutes also a culturally shared activity with explicit scripts about what is considered good or bad for infants. Motor handling in order to increase the speed of development is an example of an explicit parenting strategy in many African societies (Keller, Völker and Yovsi, in prep.; Keller, Yovsi and Völker, in press).

Generally parenting comprises the motivation to care for the infant by nursing, consoling and comforting when distressed, responding to the communicative signals and stimulating growth and development. Mainly family and close kin are involved in early childcare with the mother being the primary caregiver during the early months in virtually all cultures. This holds even if allomothering or multiple caregiving arrangements are prevalent, as in the Central African Efe (Morelli and Tronick, 1991; Tronick, Morelli and Ivey, 1992) or in contexts with extensive paternal care such as the Aka, also in Central Africa (Hewlett, 1991; Munroe and Munroe, 1997). Nevertheless, fathers' absence has detrimental effects, e.g. on child mortality (Hurtado and Hill, 1991). The interplay between the infant, the caregivers and the caregiving environment form individually unique socialization contexts, which represent intuitive regulations and are defined in terms of cultural scripts.

Component model of parenting

So far a general conception of parent–infant interaction has been presented. In the following paragraphs this conception will be differentiated into functional units. We propose to understand caregiving and psychological parenting as occurring within behavioural systems that are considered to have evolved to answer the adaptive problems of our ancestors, which arose during different stages of the evolutionary past. Parenting systems are sets of behaviours that can principally be executed by anybody. We differentiate the parenting systems 'primary care', 'body contact', 'body stimulation', 'object stimulation' and 'face-to-face exchange' as exhaustively describing the experiential array of infants during the first months of life.

The psychological processes and consequences that are initiated within the behavioural framework of the systems are modulated by caregivers' characteristics that fine grain the interactional style. We define these characteristics as constituting interactional mechanisms. They are, basically, the mode of attention (exclusive or shared), sensitivity more towards positive and/or negative infant signals, contingency in terms of prompt reactivity, and emotional warmth. All mechanisms can be effective within all systems of parenting. This does not exclude the possibility that the various systems promote specific mechanisms differently. Systems and mechanisms are considered as universal components of parenting, which are triggered in different compositions according to different environmental demands. The parenting systems constitute mainly explicitly shared cultural conceptions; the interactional mechanisms may operate more on an intuitive basis. The parenting systems together with the interactional mechanisms represent parental investment contexts differing with respect to the energy, time, attention and emotional tone directed at the infant. As such the abundance or scarcity of resources and the 'reproductive value' of the respective child in terms of gender, birth rank and parental age inform intuitive cost–benefit calculations (cf. Keller and Zach, 2002). Thus the flexible organization of parenting allows adaptations to a given situation on a universal scale (cf. Keller, 2000a; Keller et al., 1999; Rothbaum et al., 2000).

Parenting system 1: primary care

Providing primary care for infants in terms of food, shelter and hygiene characterizes any parenting effort and represents certainly the phylogenetically oldest part of the parenting systems. Feeding rates in birds (Borgerhoff Mulder, 1990), caloric consumption with nursing in primates (Paul and Voland, 1997) and other measures of parental energy are assessed as descriptors of parental investment, in both other species and humans. The effort expended on primary care, however, may vary tremendously. In extreme circumstances of poverty and environmental stress nursing may form the main maternal investment that a woman can offer. Hitchcock and Minturn (1963) described the rearing environment of Indian Rajput babies as one in which adults did not pay much attention to them. They were nursed only when they cried, in some cases with remarkable time delays (cf. also De Vries, 1984, for Masai babies).

The psychological function of the parenting effort as expressed in the primary care system would consist of reducing distress (Hitchcock and Minturn, 1963), rather than initiating positive behavioural states or sharing enjoyable moments. The promptness with which an infant receives primary care (and, thus, experiences relief from pain and distress), directly affects the development of security and trust in protection (in the availability and reliability of others) as a primary dimension of the emerging self (Bischof, 1985; Bowlby, 1969; Erikson, 1950). In some cultural environments where health and survival are the main socialization goals, anticipatory responses to infant distress further promote closeness and interpersonal fusion (Keller, Völker, Abels and Yovsi, in prep.; Rothbaum et al., 2000; Yovsi, 2001).

Cultural practices are matched by systems of beliefs and attitudes (Keller, 1996). When, for example, the Rajput mother insists ' . . . that all children are alike' (Hitchcock and Minturn, 1963, p. 317), she is explaining that no special attention has to be paid to infants beyond their physical needs. Equally Ochs and Schieffelin (1984) reported that the Kaluli of Papua New Guinea see their babies as creatures who have 'no understanding', thus explaining why they do not talk to them. Parenting consisting solely of providing primary care for the infant may be characteristic for circumstances that are characterized by extreme mortality, especially high infant mortality. The psychological costs of individual bonding, the disappointment to the mother if the child dies (Cormack, 1974, p. 3) and grief over the loss would hamper the functioning of life.

Parenting system 2: body contact

A second system of parenting can be defined by body contact and extensive carrying. In many different eco-cultural contexts, infants are carried on the bodies of their mothers for a substantial part of the day, mainly tied to the back or across the mother's hip with her arm around them (for example the Aka pygmy mothers carry their infants for about eight hours a day, Hewlett, 1991; cf. also, for the !Kung, Barr et al., 1991; or South American Ache infants spend about 93 per cent of their daylight time in tactile contact with mainly the mother, Hill and Hurtado, 1996; 'back and hip cultures', LeVine, 1990).

Carrying a baby protects him or her against exposure to life-threatening dangers such as fire and/or dangerous animals on the ground. Body contact such as carrying, clinging and grooming in primates supports bonding between mother and infant as well as group coherence (Dunbar, 1996; Harlow and Harlow, 1962). Hofer (1987) describes bodily regulation even in rodents as a phylogenetically old attachment system. The psychological function of body contact mainly consists of the experience of emotional warmth. The permanent close proximity of the mother and other significant caregivers and the resulting bodily stimulation seem to foster an emotional bond that establishes a major transmission mechanism for the development of feelings of relatedness and belonging.

These feelings seem to be associated with the acceptance of norms and values from the previous generation, preparing the individual for a life which is based in harmony and hierarchy among family members or the primary social group (cf. Keller et al., 1999). Yet, parental investment in terms of body contact allows continued participation in subsistence labour, e.g. through farming, fetching water, cooking etc., although carrying a child might compete for a mother's time with other resource-producing activities (Hill and Hurtado, 1996).

Although the primary care system and the body contact system have definite psychological consequences, they are obviously not uniquely human, since they can be observed in many other species as well. The following three systems – two stimulation systems and the face-to-face system – are not found in species other than humans.

Parenting system 3: body stimulation

The third system of parenting is also based in body communication, but as an exclusive dyadic activity. Mothers, but also fathers (like the South American Yanomami (Keller, Schölmerich and Eibl-Eibesfeldt, 1988) stimulate their infants by providing them with motorically challenging experiences through touch and movement, observe the reactions and modulate their own behaviour accordingly. Parental care in terms of body stimulation is an individual response to an individual child.

Body stimulation, which does not usually last for long, can be functionally related to motor development. The motor precocity of the African infant (Geber and Dean, 1959; Super, 1976) has been interpreted as a consequence of early stimulation patterns (Bril, 1989). The specific African body stimulation pattern is based in ethnotheories, like the Nigerian Yoruba concept of mobility and the Nso concept of proper developmental stimulation (Keller, Yovsi and Völker, in press), expressing an appreciation for increasing the speed of development, since children who walk early can start training for household responsibilities like running errands early (Ogunnaike, 1997). Also, Indian baby bathing and massaging have been demonstrated as accelerating developmental progress (Landers, 1989; Walsh Escarce, 1989).

The psychological function of body stimulation might generally consist of intensifying body perception and, thus, the discovery of own-body effectiveness in relation to resources of the environment. The body is experienced as 'agent' situated in the environment (Rochat, 1997, p. 99) and thus the emergence of a body self is promoted. This might be especially adaptive in environments where early motor development like walking helps in controlling environmental hazards, and where body capabilities necessary for subsistence and survival are essential, as in foraging societies. Body stimulation might further enhance somatic development, for example, in order to prepare the body for early reproduction and prepare children for social training.

Parenting system 4: object stimulation

The object stimulation system is aimed at linking the infant to the non-personal world of objects and the physical environment in general. Early object stimulation is pervasive in Western industrialized societies, where the objects may even replace the caregiver (Keller and Greenfield, 2000). Object stimulation is also popular in urban contexts of non-Western societies and is also increasingly recognized in traditional communities with the explicit expectation of fostering cognitive growth (Keller, Yovsi and Völker, in press; Yovsi, 2001). It focuses on shared extradyadic attentional processes and thus initiates and supports metacognitive conceptions. Object stimulation is closely related to exploratory activities (Keller, 1992). However, not all parents over the world value exploration as much as Western parents do during this early part of the lifespan. For example, Rothbaum and colleagues (2000) proposed replacing exploration by accommodation as related to attachment for Japanese developmental trajectories. The psychological function of early object stimulation consists in nurturing the cognitive system and disengaging the infant from the dependency of social relationships at the same time.

Parenting system 5: face-to-face

The fifth parenting system consists of face-to-face exchange, which is especially characterized through mutual eye contact and the frequent use of language (Keller, in press). The evolution of language has accordingly been interpreted as an attachment mechanism which allows group coherence in larger social units. Dunbar (1996) regards the function of language development during human evolutionary history as 'acoustical grooming'. The parental investment into the face-to-face system consists mainly in the exclusive devotion of time and attention into dyadic behavioural exchange. Face-to-face episodes cover only small parts of infants' daily experiences. In a study to assess the social experiences in first- and later-born German infants at three months we found 75 minutes (firstborns) and 66 minutes (laterborns) of situations allowing face-to-face contact with all available caregivers during a 12-hour observation period. The episodes were dispersed over the day and might interrupt other activities, such as bathing or changing (Keller and Zach, in press). Face-to-face exchange follows the rules of pseudo dialogues providing the infant with the experience of contingency perception. Through the prompt answers towards communicative signals, the infant can perceive him- or herself as the cause of the parental action. Thus the infant is informed about his or her uniqueness and self-efficacy (Keller, 1998, 2001). Warmth in face-to-face situations constitutes an independent mechanism (Keller et al., 1999; Lohaus et al., submitted) and is mainly experienced through sharing (positive) emotions, which may prompt feelings of relatedness. The prevalence of the face-to-face parenting system is especially salient in contexts where competition defines the social structure. Western industrialized societies in particular, as well as middle and upper-middle classes in traditional societies, favour parenting practices which are dialogic in nature. In accordance with these practices, cultural beliefs stress the importance of individuality and early independence.

Interactional mechanisms

As has been argued, interactional mechanisms are considered to modulate psychological consequences within the parenting systems. They are conceived of as basically independent of the parenting system and from each other. Yet there are different probabilities of co-occurrence of mechanisms and systems, for example the contingent reactions to negative infant signals can be mainly located in the primary care system, or contingent reactions to positive infant cues can be mainly bound to the face-to-face system. The interactional mechanisms will be outlined in the following paragraphs.

Attention

Cultures differ with respect to the attentional patterns that are prevalent in childcare. In the Western urban middle class where most of the interactional studies reported in the literature were conducted, an exclusive dyadic attentional focus of the caregiver, usually the mother, towards the infant is assumed to represent adequate parenting. Attention towards infants' signals is part of the definition of the conception of sensitivity (Ainsworth et al., 1978), which is one of the major assessment tools of interaction quality in empirical research. Yet exclusive attention is a precious resource that caretakers in most child-rearing contexts cannot afford to allocate extensively. The more popular attentional pattern of caregiving all over the world is constituted by shared attention (Rogoff et al., 1993), conceptualizing caregiving as a co-occurring activity (Saraswathi, 1994). In these cases the caretaker, also usually the mother, attends to extradyadic activities like daily chores as well as to the baby who is usually in close proximity. Co-occurring caretaking is considered as culturally appropriate in many environments where women's economic contribution to the maintenance of the family is needed and mother–infant separation is considered as inadequate. West Cameroonian Nso women watching videotapes of Nso mother–infant interactions emphasized that the infant should be carried on the left side; carrying the infant on the right arm is not good, because it does not enable the mother to carry out other chores effectively (Keller, Völker and Yovsi, in prep.). Co-occurring attention mainly focuses on negative infant signals whereas exclusive dyadic attention is mainly directed at the infant's positive interactional cues.

The pattern of shared attention is perpetuated with older children. In a comparison of attention-seeking efforts and caregivers' responses of African foragers (Efe) and European-American middle-class (Salt Lake City) participants, Verhoef and colleagues (in press) report that Efe children rarely made bids for attention and Efe caregivers rarely interrupted their conversation with the interviewer to attend explicitly to their children. They rather tried to simultaneously attend to the needs of their children who were trying to work a difficult object and to the requirements of the ongoing interview. Salt Lake City toddlers on the contrary repeatedly sought to become the caregivers' primary focus of attention by frequent attention-seeking bids. Mothers were likely to interrupt their conversations to attend to their children. A similar picture emerges from observations with mothers and toddlers for the Indian Dhol-Ki Patti tribe (cf. Mistry, 1993). The women were embarrassed when asked to explore a toy with their 1–2-year-old children, since playing with a child without an ongoing 'useful' occupation was considered as definitely inappropriate (see also Keller and Eckensberger, 1998).

Children experiencing co-occurring attention seldom experience being the centre of attention, but at the same time are never alone since also co-sleeping arrangements support cultural ideals of strong and loyal family bonds where every member accepts the place that is assigned to him or her by cultural customs (Nsamenang and Lamb, 1991, for the Cameroonian Nso; Greenfield, 1994, for Zinacantecan Mayan; Rabinovich, 1998, for Brazilians; Rothbaum et al., 2000, for Japanese). The shared attentional pattern informs the child of being a coagent in a communicative system. The exclusive attention on the other hand that is awarded to a child has consequences for the development of the concept of self as an individually distinct and unique agent.

Sensitivity towards positive and negative signals

As has been outlined with respect to attentional patterns, differential awareness towards positive and negative infant cues is involved in exclusive and co-occurring attention. Sensitivity towards negative infant signals, prevalent in traditional communities, is mostly equivalent with immediate breastfeeding, which can even be anticipatory to infants' demands. 'Whenever an infant opens the mouth the nipple has to be put in', is the expression of a Nso mother's attitude towards infants' fussing and crying (Keller, Yovsi and Völker, in press; cf. Rothbaum et al., 2000, for Japanese mothers; Brazelton, 1977, for Zinacantecan Indians: an infant is never allowed to cry from hunger). This parenting strategy thus can be described as minimizing distress. Western middle-class mothers' responses to infants' distress signals are mainly reactive in the sense that the infant has to demonstrate distress before a reaction is likely to occur. Moreover, mothers' first response is almost never breastfeeding, but changing the body position or trying to distract the infant. Only if these interventions do not work, is (breast)feeding considered. Owing to their exclusive dyadic orientation, Western middle-class parents try to elicit positive interactional cues such as looking, smiling and (positive) vocalizing. This orientation finds its expression in extended face-to-face episodes. This parenting strategy can therefore be described as maximizing positive emotionality.

Besides cultural differences, interindividual differences also have to be taken into consideration, since caregivers within cultures differ with respect to their individual orientation towards positive and negative emotionality. As neurophysiological studies and research on personality functioning have demonstrated, sensitivity for positive and negative emotionality are independent functional systems, which are based in different areas of the brain (Kuhl and Völker, 1998; Völker, 2000).

Warmth

Warmth has been recognized as an important ingredient of parenting across many different cultures (Rohner, 1986) since the early parenting style studies during the 1950s and 1960s (Becker, 1964; Schaefer, 1959), mainly as opposed to parental control (e.g. Kagitcibasi, 1997). Warmth is described as giving and expressing affection and positive affective exchange (MacDonald, 1992), openness and accessibility (Baumrind, 1971), nurturance, understanding, empathy (Hetherington and Frankie, 1967). Behavioural expressions like hugging, kissing or holding are indexed as expressing warmth. MacDonald (1992) conceptualized warmth as an independent parental quality with consequences for the development of early attachment relationships. As contrasted to the conception of security, which is mainly related to negative emotionality, warmth is considered as representing positive emotionality.

Parental warmth during infancy can be expressed in close body proximity. The function of body contact in primates, especially grooming, has been qualified as fostering group coherence. Different primate societies spend up to 30 per cent of their waking hours in reciprocal grooming, which affects the release of endorphins, helping to soothe the groomed partner and hence allowing the development of trust (Dunbar, 1996). Body contact warmth also mediates emotional regulation in the human infant, for example, reducing negative affect (carrying and close proximity are the worldwide most popular responses to distress, cf. Keller and Schölmerich, 1987). Warmth in early parent–infant interactions is also mediated by empathic affect in tonal/vocal parameters of the voice and in the sharing of affective displays in face-to-face exchange.

Warmth generally seems to play an important role for the development of social and emotional competence (Maccoby and Martin, 1983; Mize and Pettit, 1997); it is considered to be an important condition for the development of altruism and sharing (Radke-Yarrow, Zahn-Waxler and Chapman, 1983; Staub, 1979). Besides fostering social coherence, warmth seems to relate to the development of social imitation and role taking. Within the context of social learning theory (Bandura and Huston, 1961), it has been demonstrated that children imitate adult role models more when these display warm and affectionate behaviour (as well as powerful models, Bandura, Ross and Ross, 1963) as compared with cold and distant behavioural models. Maternal nurturance increases imitation from daughters (Mussen and Parker, 1965) and parental warmth predicts identification with parents (Hetherington and Frankie, 1967). Warm and positive affectionate parent–child relationships ' ... are expected to result in the acceptance of adult values by the child, identifying with the parent, and a generally higher level of compliance ... ' (MacDonald, 1992, pp. 761f.).

Contingency

In interactions with babies, parents (as well as caretakers in general) display a propensity for prompt responsiveness to infant cues. Prompt reactivity accordingly is part of different conceptions of parenting, such as Ainsworth's sensitivity rating (Ainsworth et al., 1978) or intuitive parenting (Papoušek and Papoušek, 1991). There are different time spans reported in the literature which are considered as prompt, ranging from two seconds (Millar, 1972) to between five and seven seconds (Perrez et al., 1983), mainly as responses towards distress signals. There is also evidence that parents in fact respond much faster to a substantial part of infants' non-distress signals within a latency window of 200 to 800 milliseconds (Keller et al., 1999; Lohaus et al., 1997; Papoušek and Papoušek, 1991). The necessity of the short time span seems to be related to infants' restricted memory capacity, since habituation studies have demonstrated that infants do not learn that events belong together if the distance between them exceeds one second (Stang, 1989). The parental contingency matches infants' contingency detection mechanisms, which are present from birth on (Gewirtz and Pelàez-Nogueras, 1992). The perception of temporal relationships is seen as constituting a general mechanism of information processing which includes social as well as non-social events (Tarabulsy et al., 1996). With this capacity, infants can relate events to their own actions (cf. Watson, 1967, 1971). Contingency perception does not seem to be dependent upon specific affective displays, although infants enjoy matched affect (Meltzoff, 1990). However, infants' experience of environmental as well as behaviour-based contingencies result in positive affect, whereas the violation of contingency expectations – e.g. during still face situations (Ellsworth, Muir and Hains, 1993) – is accompanied by negative affect and distress. Thus contingency detection seems to be self-rewarding.

The function of the contingency experience based on non-distress face-to-face interaction is considered to promote the acquisition of early perceptually based self-knowledge (cf. Neisser, 1993), by learning that behaviour has consequences (Lewis and Goldberg, 1969) and by seeing their actions reflected in others (Bigelow, 1998). Consequently, contingency experience has been related to the development of beliefs about personal effectiveness (Skinner, 1985) and the predictability of the behaviour of others (Lamb, 1979). The developmental consequence of the contingency experience during early interactions can thus be linked to the development of control beliefs which determine a conception of the self as a causal agent (Keller and Eckensberger, 1998).

Conclusion

We have proposed an understanding of parenting within an evolutionary framework. It is assumed that humans are basically equipped with a set of functionally independent parenting systems and interactional mechanisms which can form contextually and culturally informed alliances. The flexibility of the behavioural organization allows the adaptation of the socialization environment for small infants and the developmental goals of the respective community. The substantial environmental receptivity of the human brain during the early months of life together with learning based in open genetic programmes allow early experiences to be processed in order to form a modal conception of the self which balances the relationships between the psychological dimensions of (1) security (secure self) nourished from the primary care system and contingency towards distress, (2) relatedness (social self), rooted in the body contact system and warmth, (3) body awareness (body self) as mirroring the stimulation context and individuality and (4) distinctness (mind self) based in the object stimulation and the face-to-face system, with contingency towards positive infants' signals and exclusive attention.

The different components (systems and mechanisms) can be regarded as representing a reaction norm, i.e. an ability to respond 'correctly' in various circumstances. 'A clear understanding of phenotypic plasticity, as produced by reaction norms, has important ramifications for all studies of human social behaviour, since much of what we call culture may simply be the result of evolved reaction norms in varying contexts' (Hill and Hurtado, 1996, p. 14). Thus existing phenotypes do not represent infinite, randomly composed patterns.

Environmental challenges promote a single or a few solutions for specific life-history problems. For example, the co-occurrence of the primary care system and the body contact system are conceived of in the literature as an agrarian or paediatric parenting strategy (e.g. LeVine, 1974, 1994), that is differentiated from urban-industrial or pedagogical parenting in which the face-to-face system is emphasized more (cf. Keller, 1998; Keller and Eckensberger, 1998). These different types have been related also to different developmental goals. The agrarian pattern thus represents a more interrelated life style whereas the pedagogical parenting is more related to individualistic developmental goals. However, the variability in the degree of co-occurrence or overlap as well as the variability in the expression of the two modal types is substantial.

We see at least two lines of evidence to support the view of universal propensity and contextual sensitivity of the parenting systems and interactional mechanisms:

1. All systems and mechanisms can be identified in the diverse cultural environments, although differing substantially with respect to the amount and duration of occurrence. In one study Keller, Schölmerich and Eibl-Eibesfeldt (1988) have demonstrated that the face-to-face system exists in populations as spatially distant as Germans, Yanomami Indians and Trobriand Islanders, following the same interactional structure with parents framing the gazes of their infants, even though for different amounts of time. Within this system, a preponderance of contingency towards positive interactional signals can be observed across different cultural contexts (Keller, Chasiotis and Runde, 1992). Also in our recent data base (Keller, Yovsi and Völker, in prep.), we find all systems and all mechanisms in all contexts, although the expressions and the durations seem to differ.

2. A second line of evidence can be derived from research demonstrating that the experience of formal schooling has an impact on specific forms of parenting. Reports from very different cultural environments have demonstrated that the experience of formal Western-style schooling is associated with an increase in face-to-face contact in parenting, the use of language and object stimulation during interactional situations. Greenfield and Childs (1991) have observed this pattern of change in Zinacanteco Indians, Richman and colleagues (1992) in Mexico, and Nsamenang and Lamb (1991) in Cameroonian Nso people (for a summary see Greenfield and Cocking, 1994). The emergence of previously unpopular styles of parenting cannot be attributed to imitation (there are no role models available) or instruction (parenting is not part of the school curriculum). The emergence of the changed patterns of parenting is contingent upon the changing patterns of life as initiated through formal education.

The conception presented here captures intergenerational continuity as well as change in reaction to economic, social and societal demands. From this viewpoint, cross-cultural as well as inter-individual differences are interpreted as psychological adaptations without assuming one single normative pattern of relational development, as is still claimed in attachment theory (e.g. Sroufe and Waters, 1997). Our conception prevents us from accentuating cultural differences as deficit parenting when the Western pattern is not met. Also the Western romantic ideas of perceiving traditional parenting as the natural way seems to be basically a myth. In fact, it is probably impossible to evaluate one parenting style in terms of the cultural standards of another. The proposed component model of parenting allows us to discover cultural conceptions of parenting as well as their qualitative and quantitative variations.

REFERENCES

Ainsworth, M. D. S., Blehar, M. C., Waters, E. and Wall, S. (1978). *Patterns of attachment: a psychological study of the strange situation*. Hillsdale, NJ: Lawrence Erlbaum.

Anastasi, A. (1958). Heredity, environment, and the question 'how'. *Psychological Review*, 65, 197–208.

Bandura, A. and Huston, A. C. (1961). Identification as a process of incidental learning. *Journal of Abnormal and Social Psychology*, 63, 311–18.

Bandura, A., Ross, D. and Ross, S. A. (1963). A comparative test of the status envy, social power and the secondary-reinforcement theories of identification learning. *Journal of Abnormal and Social Psychology*, 67, 527–34.

Barr, R. G., McMullan, S. J., Spiess, H., Leduc, D. J., Yaremko, J., Barfield, R., Francoeur, T. E. and Hunziker, U. A. (1991). Carrying as colic 'therapy': a randomized controlled trial. *Pediatrics*, 87, 623–30.

Baumrind, D. (1971). Current patterns of parental authority. *Developmental Psychology Monograph*, 4(1), Pt 2.

Becker, W. C. (1964). Consequences of different kinds of parental discipline. In M. L. Hoffman and L. W. Hoffman (eds.), *Review of child development research*, vol. 1. New York: Russell Sage Foundation, pp. 169–208.

Belsky, J., Steinberg, L. and Draper, P. (1991). Further reflections on an evolutionary theory of socialization. *Child Development*, 62, 682–5.

Bigelow, A. E. (1998). Infants' sensitivity to familiar imperfect contingencies in social interactions. *Infant Behavior and Development*, 21, 149–62.

Bischof, N. (1985). *Das Rätsel Ödipus: Die biologischen Wurzeln des Urkonfliktes von Intimität und Autonomie* (The Oedipus miracle: the biological roots of the basic conflict between intimacy and autonomy). Munich: Piper.
  Das Kraftfeld der Mythen. Signale aus der Zeit, in der wir die Welt erschaffen haben (The force field of myths. Signals from the time when we created the world). Munich: Piper.

Boesch, C. (1993). Towards a new image of culture in wild chimpanzees? *Behavioral and Brain Sciences*, 16, 514–15.

Borgerhoff Mulder, M. (1990). Kipsigis women's preference for wealthy men: Evidence for female choice in mammals? *Behavioral Ecology and Sociobiology*, 27, 255–64.

Bowlby, J. (1969). *Attachment and Loss*, vol. 1: *Attachment*. New York: Basic Books.

Boyd, R. and Richerson, P. J. (1985). *Culture and evolutionary process*. Chicago: Chicago University Press.

Brazelton, T. B. (1977). Implications of infant development among the Mayan Indians of Mexico. In P. H. Leiderman, S. R. Tulkin and A. Rosenfeld (eds.), *Culture and infancy. Variations in the human experience*. New York: Academic Press, pp. 151–87.

Brazelton, T. B., Koslowski, B. and Main, M. (1974). The origins of reciprocity: the early mother–infant interaction. In M. Lewis and L. A. Rosenblum (eds.), *The effect of the infant on its caregiver*. New York: Wiley, pp. 49–76.

Bril, B. (1989). Die kulturvergleichende Perspektive: Entwicklung und Kultur (The cross-cultural perspective: development and culture). In H. Keller (ed.), *Handbuch der Kleinkindforschung* (Handbook of infancy research). Heidelberg: Springer, pp. 71–88.

Cassidy, J. (1999). The nature of the child's ties. In J. Cassidy and P. R. Shaver (eds.), *Handbook of attachment. Theory, research and clinical applications*. New York: Guilford Press, pp. 3–20.

Chisholm, J. S. (1992). Death, hope and sex: life-history theory and the development of reproductive strategies. *Current Anthropology*, 34(1), 1–24.

Cole, M. and Cole, S. (1989). *The development of children*. New York: Freeman.

Cormack, M. L. (1974). *The Hindu woman*. Westport, CT: Greenwood Press.

Cosmides, L. and Tooby, J. (1987). From evolution to behavior: evolutionary psychology as the missing link. In J. Dupre (ed.), *The latest on the best: essays on evolution and optimality*. Cambridge, MA: MIT Press, pp. 277–306.

Crow, J. F. (1999). The odds of losing at genetic roulette. *Nature*, 397, 292–4.

Daly, M. and Wilson, M. (1983). *Sex, evolution and behavior*, 2nd edn. Boston: PWS Publishers.

De Vries, M. W. (1984). Temperament and infant mortality among the Masai of East Africa. *American Journal of Psychiatry*, 141, 1189–94.

Delbrück, M. (1949). A physicist looks at biology. *Transactions of the Connectical Acadamy of Arts and Science*, 38, 173–90.

Dienes, Z., Altman, G., Kwan, L. and Goode, A. (1995). Unconscious knowledge of artificial grammars is applied strategically. *Journal of Experimental Psychology: Learning Memory and Cognition*, 21, 1322–38.

Draper, P. and Harpending, H. (1988). A sociobiological perspective on human reproductive strategies. In K. B. MacDonald (ed.), *Sociobiological perspectives on human development*. New York: Springer, pp. 340–72.

Dunbar, R. (1996). *Grooming, gossip and the evolution of language*. London: Faber and Faber.

Eckensberger, L. H. (1996). Nature, culture and the question 'why?'. Paper presented at the 14th Biennial Meetings of the ISSBD, Quebec City, 12–16 August.

Eckensberger, L. H. and Keller, H. (1998). Menschenbilder und Entwicklungskonzepte (Models of men and concepts of development). In H. Keller (ed.), *Lehrbuch Entwicklungspsychologie* (Textbook of developmental psychology). Bern: Huber, pp. 11–56.

Ellsworth, C. P., Muir, D. W. and Hains, S. M. J. (1993). Social competence and person–object differentiation: an analysis of the still-face effect. *Developmental Psychology*, 29, 63–73.

Heidi Keller

Emde, R. N. (1984). The affective self: continuities and transformations from infancy. In J. D. Call, E. Galenson and R. L. Tyson (eds.), *Frontiers of infant psychiatry.* New York: Basic Books, pp. 38–54.

Erikson, E. H. (1950). *Childhood and society.* New York: Norton.

Eyre-Walker, A. and Keightley, P. D. (1999). High genomic deleterious mutation rates in hominids. *Nature*, 397, 344–6.

Fantz, R. L. (1963). Pattern vision in newborn infants. *Science*, 140, 296–7.

Geber, M. and Dean, R. (1959). The state of development of newborn African children. *The Lancet*, 1, 1215.

Gewirtz, J. and Pelàez-Nogueras, M. (1992). B. F. Skinner's legacy to human infant behavior and development. *American Psychologist*, 47, 1411–22.

Greenfield, P. M. (1994). Independence and interdependence as developmental scripts: implications for theory, research and practice. In P. M. Greenfield and R. R. Cocking (eds.), *Cross-cultural roots of minority child development.* Hillsdale, NJ: Lawrence Erlbaum, pp. 1–40.

Greenfield, P. M. and Childs, C. P. (1991). Developmental continuity in biocultural context. In R. Cohen and A. W. Siegel (eds.), *Context and development.* Hillsdale, NJ: Lawrence Erlbaum, pp. 135–59.

Greenfield, P. M. and Cocking, R. R. (eds.) (1994). *Cross-cultural roots of minority child development.* Hillsdale, NJ: Lawrence Erlbaum.

Greenfield, P. M. and Suzuki, L. (1998). Culture and human development: implications for parenting, education, pediatrics and mental health. In I. E. Sigel and K. A. Renninger (eds.), *Handbook of child psychology*, vol. 4: *Child psychology in practice*, 5th edn. New York: Wiley, pp. 1059–109.

Hamilton, W. (1964). The genetical evolution of social behavior (I + II). *Journal of Theoretical Biology*, 7, 1–52.

Harlow, H. F. and Harlow, M. K. (1962). Social deprivation in monkeys. *Scientific American*, 207, 136–46.

Harlow, H. F., Harlow, M. K. and Hansen, E. W. (1963). The maternal affectional system of rhesus monkeys. In H. L. Rheingold (ed.), *Maternal behavior in mammals.* New York: Wiley, pp. 254–81.

Hasher, L. and Zacks, R. T. (1984). Automatic processing of fundamental information. *American Psychologist*, 39(12), 1372–88.

Hetherington, M. and Frankie, G. (1967). Effects of parental dominance, warmth and conflict on imitation in children. *Journal of Personality and Social Psychology*, 6(2), 119–25.

Hewlett, B. S. (1991). *Intimate fathers: the nature and context of Aka pygmy paternal infant care.* Ann Arbor: University of Michigan Press.

Heyes, C. and Dickinson, A. (1993). The intentionality of animal action. In M. Davies and G. M. Humphreys (eds.), *Consciousness.* Oxford: Blackwell, pp. 105–20.

Hill, K. and Hurtado, A. M. (1996). *Ache life history. The ecological and demography of a foraging people.* New York: Aldine de Gruyter.

Hinde, R. A. (1982). Attachment: some conceptual and biological issues. In J. Stevenson-Hinde and C. M. Parkes (eds.), *The place of attachment in human behavior.* New York: Basic Books, pp. 60–76.

Hitchcock, J. T. and Minturn, L. (1963). The Rajput of Khalapur, India. In B. B. Whiting (ed.), *Six cultures. Studies of child rearing.* New York: Wiley, pp. 203–362.

Hofer, M. A. (1987). Early social relationships: a psychobiologist's view. *Child Development*, 58, 633–47.

Hurtado, A. M. and Hill, K. (1991). Paternal effect on offspring survivorship among Ache and Hiwi hunter-gatherers: Implications for modeling pair-bond stability. In B. S. Hewlett (ed.), *Father–child relations: cultural and biosocial contexts*. New York: Aldine de Gruyter, pp. 31–55.

Kagitcibasi, C. (1997). Individualism and collectivism. In J. W. Berry, M. H. Segall and C. Kagitcibasi (eds.), *Handbook of Cross-Cultural psychology*, vol. 3: *Social behavior and applications*, 2nd. edn. Boston: Allyn and Bacon, pp. 1–49.

Kaufmann-Hayoz, R. and van Leeuwen, L. (1997). Entwicklung der Wahrnehmung (Perceptual development). In H. Keller (ed.), *Handbuch der Kleinkindforschung* (Handbook of infancy research), 2nd edn. Bern: Huber, pp. 483–507.

Keller, H. (1992). The development of exploratory behavior. *German Journal of Psychology*, 16(2), 120–40.

(1996). Evolutionary approaches. In J. W. Berry, Y. H. Poortinga and J. Pandey (eds.), *Handbook of cross-cultural psychology*, vol. 1: *Theory and method*, 2nd edn. Boston: Allyn and Bacon, pp. 215–55.

(1998). Different socialization pathways to adolescence. Paper presented at the 4th Africa Region International Society for the Study of Behavioral Development Conference (ISSBD), Windhoek, Namibia 20–23 July.

(2000a). Human parent–child relationships from an evolutionary perspective. *American Behavioral Scientist*, special issue: 'Evolutionary psychology: potential and limits of a Darwinian framework for the Behavioral sciences', 43(6), 957–69.

(2000b). Developmental psychology I: prenatal to adolescence. In K. Pawlik and M. R. Rosenzweig (eds.), *International handbook of psychology*. London: Sage, pp. 235–60.

(2000c). Sozial-emotionale Grundlagen des Spracherwerbs (The social-emotional bases of language acquisition). In H. Grimm (ed.), *Enzyklopädie der Psychologie* (Encyclopedia of Psychology) Volume 3: *Sprachentwicklung* (Language acquisition). Göttingen: Hogrefe, pp. 379–402.

(2001). The socialization of competence. Two cultures of infancy. Paper presented at the 7th European Congress of Psychology, London, 1–6 July.

(in press). Evolutionary perspectives on lifespan development. In N. J. Smelser and P. B. Baltes (eds.), *International encyclopedia of the social and behavioral sciences*. Oxford: Elsevier/Pergamon.

Keller, H., Chasiotis, A. and Runde, B. (1992). Intuitive parenting programs in German, American and Greek parents of 3-month-old infants. *Journal of Cross-Cultural Psychology*, 23, 510–20.

Keller, H. and Eckensberger, L. H. (1998). Kultur und Entwicklung (Culture and development). In H. Keller (ed.), *Lehrbuch Entwicklungspsychologie* (Textbook on developmental psychology). Bern: Huber, pp. 57–96.

Keller, H. and Greenfield, P. M. (2000). History and future of development in cross-cultural psychology. In C. Kagitcibasi and Y. H. Poortinga (eds.). Millennium Special Issue of the *Journal of Cross-Cultural Psychology*, 31(1), 52–62.

Keller, H., Lohaus, A., Völker, S., Cappenberg, M. and Chasiotis, A. (1999), Temporal contingency as an independent component of parenting behavior. *Child Development*, 70, 474–85.

Keller, H. and Schölmerich, A. (1987). Infant vocalizations and parental reactions during the first four months of life. *Developmental Psychology*, 23(1), 62–7.

Keller, H., Schölmerich, A. and Eibl-Eibesfeldt, I. (1988). Communication patterns in adult-infant interactions in Western and non-Western cultures. *Journal of Cross-Cultural Psychology*, 19(4), 427–45.

Keller, H., Völker, S., Abels, M. and Yovsi, R. D. (in preparation). Becoming interrelated: early socialization contexts for Cameroonian Nso and Indian Rajput villagers.

Keller, H., Völker, S. and Yovsi, R. D. (in preparation) Conceptions of good parenting in West Africa and Germany.

Keller, H., Yovsi, R. D. and Völker, S. (in press). The role of motor stimulation in parental ethnotheories: the case of Cameroonian Nso and German women. *Journal of Cross Cultural Psychology*.

Keller, H. and Zach, U. (2002). Gender and birth order as determinants of parental behavior. *International Journal of Behavioral Development*.

Kuhl, J. and Völker, S. (1998). Entwicklung und Persönlichkeit (Development and personality). In H. Keller (ed.), *Lehrbuch Entwicklungspsychologie* (Textbook on developmental psychology). Bern: Huber, pp. 207–40.

Lamb, M. E. (1979). The effect of the social context on dyadic social interaction. In M. E. Lamb, S. J. Suomi and G. R. Stephenson (eds.), *Social interaction analysis: methodological issues*. Madison: University of Wisconsin Press, pp. 253–68.

Landers, C. (1989). A psychobiological study of infant development in South India. In J. K. Nugent, B. M. Lester and T. B. Brazelton (eds.), *The cultural context of infancy*. Norwood: Ablex, pp. 169–207.

Lerner, R. M. and De Stefanis, I. (1999). The import of infancy to individual, family, and societal development. *Infant Behavior and Development*, 22(4), 475–82.

LeVine, R. A. (1974). Parental goals: a cross-cultural view. *Teachers College Record*, 76, 226–39.

(1990). Infant environments in psychoanalysis: a cross-cultural view. In J. W. Stigler, R. A. Shweder and G. Herdt (eds.), *Cultural psychology: essays on comparative human development*. Cambridge: Cambridge University Press, pp. 454–74.

(1994). *Child care and culture: lessons from Africa*. Cambridge: Cambridge University Press.

Lewis, M. and Goldberg, S. (1969). Perceptual-cognitive development in infancy: a generalized expectancy model as a function of the mother–infant interaction. *Merrill-Palmer Quarterly*, 15(1), 81–100.

Lohaus, A., Keller, H., Ball, J., Elben, C. and Völker, S. (submitted). The concept of maternal sensitivity. Components and relations to warmth and contingency.

Lohaus, A., Keller, H., Völker, S., Cappenberg, M. and Chasiotis, A. (1997). Intuitive parenting and infant behavior: concepts, implications, and empirical validation. *Journal of Genetic Psychology*, 158(3), 271–86.

Lorenz, K. (1943). Die angeborenen Formen möglicher Erfahrung (The inborn forms of potential experiences). *Zeitschrift für Tierpsychologie*, 5(2), 235–409.

Maccoby, E. E. and Martin, J. A. (1983). Socialization in the context of the family: parent-child interaction. In P. H. Mussen (series ed.), E. M. Hetherington (vol. ed.), *Handbook of Child psychology*, vol. 4. *Socialization, personality, and social development*, 4th edn. New York: Wiley, pp. 1–101.

MacDonald, K. B. (1988). *Social and personality development. An evolutionary synthesis.* New York: Plenum Press.
  (1992). Warmth as a developmental construct: an evolutionary analysis. *Child Development*, 63, 753–73.
Mayr, E. (1982). *The growth of biological thought.* Cambridge, MA: Harvard University Press.
  (1988). *Towards a new philosophy of biology.* Cambridge, MA: Belknap Press.
  (1994). Evolution – Grundfragen und Missverständnisse (Evolution – basic questions and misunderstandings). *Ethik und Sozialwissenschaften*, 5(2), 203–9.
Mead, G. H. (1980). *Gesammelte Aufsätze* (Selected writings), 2 vols, ed. Hans Johas. Frankfurt am Main: Suhrkamp.
Meltzoff, A. N. (1990). Foundations for developing a concept of self: the role of imitation in relating self to other, and the value of social mirroring, social modeling, and self-practice in infancy. In D. Cicchetti and M. Beeghley (eds.), *The self in transition: infancy to childhood.* Chicago: University of Chicago Press, pp. 139–64.
Millar, W. S. (1972). *A study of operant conditioning under delayed reinforcement in early infancy.* Monographs of the Society for Research in Child Development, 37, 1–44. Chicago: University of Chicago Press.
Mistry, J. (1993). Guided participation in Dhol-Ki-Patti. In B. Rogoff, J. Mistry, A. Göncü and C. Mosier (eds.), *Guided participation in cultural activity by toddlers and caregivers.* Monographs of the Society for Research in Child Development, series no. 236, vol. 58(8). Chicago: University of Chicago Press, pp. 102–25.
Mize, J. and Pettit, G. S. (1997). Mothers' social coaching, mother–child relationships style and children's peer competence: is the medium the message? *Child Development*, 68(2), 312–32.
Morelli, G. A. and Tronick, E. Z. (1991). Parenting and child developments in the Efe foragers and Lese farmers of Zaire. In M. H. Bornstein (ed.), *Cultural approaches to parenting.* Hillsdale, NJ: Lawrence Erlbaum, pp. 91–114.
Munroe, R. L. and Munroe, R. H. (1997). A comparative anthropological perspective. In J. W. Berry, Y. H. Poortinga and J. Pandey (eds.), *Handbook of cross-cultural psychology*, vol. 1: *Theory and method*, 2nd edn., Boston: Allyn and Bacon, pp. 171–214.
Mussen, P. H. and Parker, A. L. (1965). Mother nurturance at girls' incidental imitative learning. *Journal of Personality and Social Psychology*, 2, 94–7.
Neisser, U. (1993). The self perceived. In U. Neisser (ed.), *The perceived self: ecological and interpersonal sources of self-knowledge.* New York: Cambridge University Press, pp. 3–21.
Nelson, C. A. (1999). Change and continuity in neurobehavioral development: lessons from the study of neurobiology and neural plasticity. *Infant Behavior and Development*, 22(4), 415–29.
Nsamenang, A. B. and Lamb, M. E. (1991). Attitudes and beliefs regarding childbirth and perinatal care among the Nso of Northwest Cameroon. Unpublished manuscript.
Ochs, E. and Schieffelin, B. (1984). Language acquisition and socialization. Three developmental stories and their implications. In R. Shweder and R. LeVine (eds.), *Culture theory: essays on mind, self and emotion.* Cambridge: Cambridge University Press, pp. 276–322.

Ogunnaike, O. A. (1997). Yoruba toddlers: relating cognitive performance to family sociodemographics and mediating factors in the child's environment. Unpublished doctoral dissertation, Tufts University, Medford.

Papoušek, M. and Papoušek, H. (1991). Early verbalizations as precursors of language development. In M. E. Lamb and H. Keller (eds.), *Infant development. Perspectives from German-speaking countries.* Hillsdale, NJ: Lawrence Erlbaum, pp. 299–328.

Paul, A. and Voland, E. (1997). Die soziobiologische Perspektive. Eltern-Kind-Beziehungen im evolutionären Kontext (The sociobiological perspective: parent–child relationships in an evolutionary context). In H. Keller (ed.), *Handbuch der Kleinkindforschung* (Handbook of infancy research). Bern: Huber, pp. 121–47.

Perrez, M., Achermann, E. and Diethelm, K. (1983). Die Bedeutung der sozialen Kontingenzen für die Entwicklung des Kindes im ersten Lebensjahr (The meaning of social contingencies for the development of the infant during the first year of life). *Verhaltensmodifikation,* 4, 114–29.

Prechtl, H. (1984). *Continuity of neural functions from prenatal to postnatal life.* London: Spastics International Medical Publications.

Rabinovich, E. P. (1998). Comparative study of sleeping arrangements and breastfeeding in Brazilian children. Paper presented at the 14th Congress IACCP, Bellingham, USA, 3–7 August.

Radke-Yarrow, M., Zahn-Waxler, C. and Chapman, M. (1983). Children's prosocial disposition and behavior. In E. M. Hetherington (ed.), *Handbook of child psychology,* vol. 4. New York: Wiley, pp. 469–545.

Richman, A. L., Miller, P. M. and LeVine, R. A. (1992). Cultural and educational variations in maternal responsiveness. *Developmental Psychology,* 28(4), 614–21.

Rochat, P. (1997). Early development of the ecological self. In C. Dent-Read and P. Zukow-Goldring (eds.), *Evolving explanations of development. Ecological approaches to organism-environment systems.* Washington, DC: American Psychological Association, pp. 91–121.

Rogoff, B., Mistry, J., Göncü, A. and Mosier, C. (1993). *Guided participation in cultural activity by toddlers and caregivers.* Monographs of the Society for Research in Child Development, serial no. 236, vol. 58(8). Chicago: University of Chicago Press.

Rohner, R. P. (1986). *The warmth dimension: foundations of psychological acceptance–rejection theory.* Beverly Hills, CA: Sage.

Rothbaum, F., Pott, M., Azuma, H., Miyake, K. and Weisz, J. (2000). The development of close relationships in Japan and the United States: paths of symbiotic harmony and generative tension. *Child Development,* 71(5), 1121–42.

Saraswathi, T. S. (1994). Women in poverty context: balancing economic and child care needs. In R. Borooah, K. Cloud, S. Seshadri, T. S. Saraswathi, J. T. Peterson and A. Verma (eds.), *Capturing complexity. An interdisciplinary look at women, households and development.* New Delhi: Sage, pp. 162–78.

Saraswathi, T. S. and Pai, S. (1997). Socialization in the Indian context. In H. S. R. Kao and D. Sinha (eds.), *Asian perspectives on psychology.* New Delhi: Sage, pp. 74–92.

Schaefer, E. S. (1959). A circumflex model for maternal behavior. *Journal of Abnormal and Social Psychology,* 59, 226–35.

Schore, A. N. (1994). *Affect regulation and the origin of the self. The neurobiology of emotional development*. Hillsdale, NJ: Lawrence Erlbaum.

(2000). Attachment and the regulation of the right brain. *Attachment and Human Development*, 2, 23–47.

Siegel, D. J. (1999). *The developing mind*. New York: Guilford Press.

Skinner, E. A. (1985). Determinants of mother sensitive and contingent responsive behavior. The role of child rearing beliefs and socioeconomic status. In I. E. Sigel (ed.), *Parental belief systems: the psychological consequences for children*. Hillsdale, NJ: Lawrence Erlbaum.

Sroufe, A. and Waters, E. (1997). On the universality of the link between responsive care and secure base behavior. *ISSBD-Newsletter*, 31(1), 3–5.

Stang, W. (1989). Lernen visueller Kontingenzen bei dreimonatigen Säuglingen (Learning of visual contingencies in three month old infants). Unpublished Dissertation. Free University Berlin.

Staub, E. (1979). *Positive behavior and morality: Socialization and development*, vol. 2. New York: Academic Press.

Stern, D. N. (1985). *The interpersonal world of the infant*. New York: Basic Books.

Sulloway, F. (1996). *Born to rebel: birth order, family dynamics, and creative lives*. New York: Pantheon Books.

Super, C. M. (1976). Environmental effects on motor development: a case of African infant precocity. *Developmental Medicine and Child Neurology*, 18, 561–7.

Tarabulsy, G. M., Tessier, R. and Kappas, A. (1996). Contingency detection and the contingent organization of behavior in interactions: implications for socioemotional development in infancy. *Psychological Bulletin*, 120, 25–41.

Trivers, R. L. (1985). *Social evolution*. Menlo Park, CA: Benjamin Cummings.

Trivers, R. L. and Willard, D. E. (1973). Natural selection of parental ability to vary the sex ratio of offspring. *Science*, 179, 90–2.

Tronick, E. Z., Morelli, G. A. and Ivey, P. K. (1992). The Efe forager infant and toddler's pattern of social relationships: Multiple and simultaneous. *Developmental Psychology*, 28(4), 568–77.

Verhoef, H., Morelli, G. A. and Anderson, C. (in prep.). 'Please don't interrupt me, I'm talking.' Cultural variations in toddlers' attention-seeking efforts and caregivers' responses.

Voland, E. (1993). *Grundriß der Soziobiologie* (Outline of sociobiology). Stuttgart/Jena: Fischer.

Völker, S. (2000). Eine Analyse von Interaktionsmustern zwischen Mutter und Kind im dritten Lebensmonat: Die Bedeutung von Wärme und Kontingenz (An analysis of interactional patterns between mother and three-month-old infants). Unpublished Doctoral Dissertation, University of Osnabrueck, Department of Psychology and Health Sciences.

Walsh Escarce, M. E. (1989). A cross-cultural study of Nepalese neonatal behavior. In J. K. Nugent, B. M. Lester and T. B. Brazelton (eds.), *The cultural context of infancy*. Norwood: Ablex, pp. 65–86.

Watson, J. S. (1967). Memory and 'contingency analysis' in infant learning. *Merrill-Palmer Quarterly*, 13, 55–76.

(1971). Cognitive-perceptual development in infancy: setting for the seventies. *Merrill-Palmer Quarterly*, 17, 139–52.

Weinberg, M. K. and Tronick, E. Z. (1996). Infant affective reactions to the resumption of maternal interaction after the still-face. *Child Development*, 67, 905–14.

Wilson, E. O. (1975). *Sociobiology*. Cambridge, MA: Harvard University Press.

Yovsi, R. D. (2001). An investigation of breastfeeding and mother–infant interactions in the face of cultural taboos and belief systems. The case of Nso and Fulani mothers and their infants of 3–5 months of age in Mbvem, sub-division of the Northwest province of Cameroon. Doctoral Dissertation, University of Osnabrück.

11 Integrating evolution, culture and developmental psychology: explaining caregiver–infant proximity and responsiveness in central Africa and the USA

Barry S. Hewlett and Michael E. Lamb

This chapter describes three neo-evolutionary or neo-Darwinian approaches and their implications for developmental psychology. Many developmental psychologists view 'evolutionary' perspectives as 'hard-wired', 'biological' or 'genetic' explanations of human development largely because so much public and scholarly attention has been given to one of these neo-evolutionary approaches – evolutionary psychology. Cover stories about evolutionary psychology have appeared in *Time* and *Newsweek*, and evolutionary psychology courses now exist at several major universities. Although evolutionary psychology is described in this chapter, emphasis is given to two lesser-known approaches to neo-evolutionary thought – evolutionary ecology and evolutionary cultural anthropology. Particular emphasis is placed upon the position and role of culture within neo-Darwinian thought. Few developmentalists are aware that the culture concept (i.e. culture as symbolic, historical, transmitted non-genetically generation to generation) exists within an evolutionary framework. Recent research on caregiver–infant proximity and responsiveness among Aka foragers, Ngandu farmers and urban industrialists from Washington DC are utilized to illustrate the neo-evolutionary approaches.

Evolutionary approaches

There are many brands of evolutionary thought within psychology, ecology and anthropology, but the neo-evolutionary or neo-Darwinian approaches described in this chapter emphasize relatively recent contributions to Darwin's theories of natural and sexual selection. Core neo-evolutionary theories include kin

We are grateful to the Aka, Ngandu and Euro-American families for so graciously allowing impersonal behavioural observations by strange anthropologists and psychologists. We want to thank Donald Shannon, Patricia Evans, Hope Hallock, Nan Hannon, Nancy Kimmerly, Christina Larson, and Laura Scaramella for their assistance in data collection and analysis. We acknowledge and thank the government of the Central African Republic for authorizing the research. The National Institute of Child Health and Human Development supported the research.

selection theory (Hamilton, 1964), parental investment theory (Trivers, 1972), reciprocal altruism theory (Axelrod, 1984) and life history theory (Charnov, 1993) which built upon, clarified and expanded Darwin's ideas of natural and sexual selection. According to Darwin (1859), for instance, the measure of 'fitness' in natural and sexual selection was the number of offspring an individual left behind. Hamilton's (1964) kin selection theory expanded this idea by pointing out that an individual's genes existed beyond self and own offspring. As a result, an individual could enhance his or her reproductive fitness by helping any individual that shared genes with him or her (nieces, nephews, cousins). Several books describe these central neo-evolutionary theories (Daly and Wilson, 1983; Trivers, 1987). From this point on, we drop the 'neo' prefix from 'evolutionary' or 'Darwinian' because our focus is on these recent conceptual frameworks.

Before describing the three evolutionary approaches it is important to mention briefly a few basic concepts that they have in common. First, the unit of natural selection and the focus of evolutionary studies are individuals rather than groups. Humans live in groups and have cultural practices and beliefs because those groups enhance the survival and reproductive fitness of individuals. Second, evolutionists are interested in ultimate rather than proximate explanations. Ultimate explanations focus on the ways in which particular behaviours enhance the reproductive fitness of individuals whereas proximate explanations focus on social, psychological, hormonal or cultural factors. They are different kinds of explanations and they are neither necessarily contradictory nor mutually exclusive. Developmental psychologists may attribute teenage males' risk-taking in sports or sexual relations by reference to identity formation processes or as a result of high levels of male testosterone. An evolutionist would be interested in explaining *why* particular males make these risky choices, *why* testosterone evolved to increase male risk-taking, or *how* the risk-taking relates to an individual's reproductive fitness. Ultimate and proximate explanations are different levels of explanation and are not necessarily contrary to one another. It is also important to remember that evolutionary theories were developed to explain cross-species patterns and are therefore not anthropocentric.

Diversity within evolutionary thought

Table 11.1 summarizes some of the theoretical diversity within evolutionary thought. The core theories of evolutionary thought were developed in the 1960s and 70s and by the early 1980s clear differences had emerged among evolutionary researchers working with humans. One group of scholars, including Nick Blurton Jones, Pat Draper, Melvin Konner and Magdi Hurtado, conducted quantitative behavioural field studies of infants and children in relatively remote small-scale cultures (foragers, pastoralists and

Table 11.1 *Three evolutionary approaches*

	Evolutionary psychology	Evolutionary ecology	Evolutionary cultural anthropology
Tries to explain	Human universals, human nature	Human behavioural diversity, reproductive tradeoffs in different environments	Cultural diversity, culture change, gene–culture interactions
Key constraints	Genetically based cognitive modules	Natural and social/demographic environments	Cultural mechanisms
Time for adaptive change to take place	Long-term (genetic)	Short-term (phenotypic)	Varies by cultural mechanism
View of culture	Culture is the manufactured product of evolved psychological mechanisms	Culture is the product of individuals trying to enhance reproductive fitness; culture as epiphenomena	Culture has its own properties, can take its own course and can drive or co-direct genetic evolution
View of child development	Development influenced by specific genetically based modules of the mind that emerge during development	Children of all ages are trying to maximize their reproductive fitness in their various 'niches'	Cultural mechanisms and histories influence parental ideologies, caregiving practices
Topics of study in child development	Language acquisition, attachment, cooperation, aggression, maternal sensitivity	Parenting strategies, child abuse and neglect, attachment, father involvement	Attachment

Note: Adapted from Smith (2000) and Hewlett (2001).

horticulturalists) in Africa and South America. They hypothesized that many childcare practices (e.g. frequent holding, birth spacing, timing of weaning, parent–child interactions) were 'adaptive' in that they maximized the reproductive fitness of children or adults in particular natural and sociodemographic environments. By comparison, David Buss, Don Symons, Martin Daly and Margo Wilson, John Tooby and Leda Cosmides conducted research in contemporary complex cultures, often studying college undergraduates using pencil and paper questionnaires. They were critical of the first group's 'fitness maximizing' research because it did not contribute to a better understanding of human nature and cognition, and they did not value efforts to demonstrate that specific parenting behaviours increased reproductive success. Instead, they wanted to identify specific universal modules, information-processing programmes, or algorithms of the mind that helped palaeolithic hunter-gatherers solve recurring adaptive problems in the environment of evolutionary adaptation (EEA) originally defined by John Bowlby (1969). These researchers eventually termed their approach evolutionary psychology (EP) while the first group called their approach evolutionary ecology (EE) or human behavioural ecology.

Table 11.1 identifies some of the distinctions between these two approaches. Most importantly, evolutionary psychologists identify several content-specific modules in the mind while evolutionary ecologists view the mind as a general-purpose fitness-maximizing mechanism. Evolutionary psychologists are interested in identifying biologically based (i.e. genetic) universals of the human mind that evolved during the EEA and continue to shape human behaviour. Current research emphasizes identification of the universal behavioural modules while their biological bases (i.e. specific genes or location in brain) are often assumed. For instance, EPs describe a kin recognition module that contributes to the differential care of biological as opposed to step-children (i.e. step-children are more frequently neglected and abused; Daly and Wilson, 1985). The language acquisition device is another module of the mind that enables children quickly to acquire the structure and meaning of language (Chomsky, 1965; Pinker, 1994).

Evolutionary ecologists, on the other hand, tend to view human behaviour as more flexibly and adaptively responsive to diverse natural and sociodemographic environments and thus focus on explaining behavioural diversity in varied environments. Individuals of any age have only so much time and energy and are believed to enhance their reproductive fitness by maximizing their time and energy in a given environment. For instance, Lamb and colleagues (1984), Belsky (1997) and Chisholm (1996) hypothesize that children's attachment styles (i.e. secure, avoidant, resistant) are adaptations to particular rearing environments (e.g. high mortality, family stress). Belsky and Chisholm hypothesize that attachment styles lead to fitness-maximizing reproductive strategies later in life. For EEs, most behaviour (what individuals do) is culture; they make little effort to understand individuals' ideas about what they do. In their view, culture does not have particular or special properties and for some evolutionary ecologists the concept of culture is not necessary (Betzig, 1997). EEs emphasize that there are no specific genes for the behaviours that they describe since the mind is a general-purpose fitness-maximizing mechanism that allows individuals to evaluate the fitness consequences of alternative behaviours in particular environments.

The final approach in table 11.1 is referred to as evolutionary cultural anthropology (ECA) – an evolutionary approach that focuses on the evolutionary nature of culture and social reproduction. Others refer to this research tradition as the dual transmission (genes–culture) or coevolutionary approach (Durham, 1992; Smith, 2000). We prefer to call it evolutionary cultural anthropology because its proponents aim to understand specific properties of culture and cultural diversity (Boyd and Richerson, 1985; Cavalli Sforza and Feldman, 1981) – the domains of cultural anthropology – and because all three approaches are 'dual' to the extent that all consider biology–culture/behaviour interactions. Although most ECA theorists are theoretical biologists or geneticists, they aim at understanding culture, often using analogies and models derived from population genetics and epidemiology. Culture is usually defined by ECAs as information or knowledge that is symbolic, socially transmitted and historic (i.e. modified from prior forms; Durham, 1992). The specific units of cultural communication are referred to as memes (Blackmore, 1999; Dawkins, 1976) or semes (Hewlett et al., 2002). Cultural inheritance is, of course, quite distinct from genetic inheritance (e.g. inheritance of culture from individuals other than parents, cultural inheritance takes place faster or more slowly than genetic inheritance) and ECAs aim to identify and describe the nature of cultural inheritance systems. The approach is evolutionary in that culture has all the elements under which natural selection takes place (e.g. production of variability, heritability, fitness effects) and cultural mechanisms contribute to more efficient learning than trial and error. Efficient mechanisms of transmission enhance reproductive fitness.

Many of these researchers have a background in population genetics and know very well that genetic mechanisms can produce genetic maladaptations. For instance, if parents from West Africa are heterozygous for the sickle-cell trait, they have a 25 per cent chance of producing an offspring who is homozygous for the sickle-cell trait, which leads to death at an early age. If genetic mechanisms produce maladaptation, it seems reasonable to hypothesize that cultural mechanisms could produce maladaptive patterns as well. ECAs point out that the identification of mechanisms underlying genetic transmission revolutionized genetics and that a better understanding of cultural transmission mechanisms could do the same for cultural anthropology. Consequently, ECA

Table 11.2 *Mechanisms of cultural transmission identified by evolutionary cultural anthropology research*

Mechanism	Description	Features	Age most frequent
Vertical transmission	Child adopts semes of parents	Genetic transmission analogy, contributes to conservation of culture, semes slow to change	Infancy and early childhood
Horizontal transmission	Child adopts semes of unrelated individuals	Epidemiological transmission analogy, frequency of interaction with individuals with the semes determines likelihood of transmission (e.g. high frequency of interaction leads to greater likelihood of transmission and rapid change)	Early childhood (between generations); late childhood and adolescence (within generations)
Group effect	Child adopts commonly observed semes	Also called frequency dependent bias, contributes to conservation of culture; semes slow to change	Late childhood and adolescence
One-to-many transmission	Child adopts semes of teacher, leader, mass media	Contributes to rapid culture change, common today but rare in most of human history	Late childhood and adolescence
Indirect bias	Child adopts semes of individuals with status	Children adopt semes of individuals with status (TV and sports stars, etc.) because the individuals believe the seme may lead to reproductive success	Adolescence
Imposition	Child adopts semes imposed upon him/her	Leader imposes laws regulating aspects of culture/semes (e.g. marriage); assumes high stratification; emphasis on lack of free choice	Adolescence
Many-to-one transmission	Child adopts semes from group organized to transmit these semes	Initiation ceremonies, most conservative form of transmission, semes slow to change	Late childhood and adolescence

research has focused on identifying, describing and modelling (often mathematically) mechanisms of cultural transmission. Table 11.2 briefly describes the basic characteristics of some of the key mechanisms identified by evolutionary cultural anthropologists. We have placed them in a developmental context.

The concept of 'niche construction' (Laland, Odling-Smee and Feldman, 1999) is a recent conceptual contribution by ECA theorists. Some species, including humans, modify natural selection pressures within their environments by creating a niche (e.g. burrow, nest) that produces a separate constellation of selective pressures (the constructed niche creates its own set of problems), which may or may not enhance reproductive fitness of the individuals. Over time the niches and the consequences of the selective pressures are inherited. This is a potentially important contribution to ECA because culture increases the abilities of humans to construct new niches. Current work focuses on how innovative artefacts or technologies can lead to dramatic changes in the social and natural environment, which in turn create other selective pressures.

The ECA approach has motivated the smallest number of researchers and few empirical studies have been conducted in this area. Researchers have demonstrated that many aspects of kinship and family organization are a result of demic diffusion, vertical cultural transmission and group effect rather than adaptations to natural or social environments, or cultural diffusion (Burton et al., 1996; Guglielmino et al., 1995; Hewlett et al., 2002). Demic diffusion involves the movement of people with their culture; a new group replaces earlier populations often because of technological or other cultural innovations. The Bantu expansion in central Africa and European colonization of the Americas are classic examples of demic diffusion. The features of vertical transmission and group effect are described in table 11.2. ECA theorists believe that the distribution and diversity in infant caregiving and caregiver–infant sensitivity are the result of demic diffusion and vertical transmission of these semes (i.e. culture history) rather than 'adaptations' to particular natural or social environments.

In summary, proponents of all three of the evolutionary approaches discussed here are interested in understanding interactions between culture and biology, but EPs emphasize universal biology, EEs emphasize the natural and social environment and ECAs emphasize the nature and structure of culture. Each approach asks somewhat different questions and employs its own methodological toolkit to address those questions, so it is not surprising that at times there are conflicts between authors affiliated with each of the approaches. Still these three approaches provide an opportunity to examine developmental psychology from a holistic and integrative perspective.

Infant caregiving in three cultures

In this section we examine caregiver–infant proximity and responsiveness in three cultures with three distinct modes of production. These aspects of infant care were selected because they are hypothetically linked to attachment theory and social-emotional development in infancy. In the next section of the chapter, we discuss the results of our study in the context of the three evolutionary approaches.

Our studies were initiated to describe the 'ecology' of daily life for infants in several cultures. Most studies of infancy are based upon remarkably few hours (usually two or less) of direct naturalistic observation. The brief observations lead to a characterization of infancy that may apply only to particular contexts – e.g. play, feeding, caregiving contexts. In addition, few researchers have studied infancy in small-scale 'traditional' societies. Specific evolutionary hypotheses were not evaluated in our research, but an evolutionary view of the interactions between biology, ecology and culture guided the research design. Behavioural observations dominated the research (we wanted to observe each infant for at least twelve hours), but we also interviewed parents about their ideas about childhood and their explanations for the behaviours we observed. We also participated in the daily lives of families in two of the three cultures (Aka and Ngandu, but not Euro-Americans) so we were able to talk to parents about their children in a variety of informal contexts (e.g. washing clothes, hunting).

The study and the families

The study consisted of, twenty Aka, twenty-one Ngandu and twenty-one Euro-American families with 3–4-month-old infants. Infants were observed for three hours on four different days for a total of twelve hours per infant. Aka and Ngandu were observed between 6 a.m. and 6 p.m. on all days of the week whereas Euro-Americans were observed between 8 a.m. and 8 p.m. on weekdays only. The naturalistic observational procedure and coding system were modified from the scheme originally developed by Belsky and colleagues (1984). The observer watched for twenty seconds and recorded for ten seconds. After forty-five minutes, the observer took a fifteen-minute break and then resumed observation. Observers noted on a checklist the occurrence of eleven caregiver and ten infant behaviours, six dyadic behaviours, as well as the location, position and identity of the caregiver and infant.

All of the Euro-American infants were firstborns. Only about 15 per cent of the Aka and Ngandu infants were firstborns. About 15 per cent of their fathers had more than one wife. None of the Aka had a formal education or were engaged in a cash economy. All Aka and Ngandu men and women engaged in subsistence activities during the observation period. Most of the Ngandu men and several of the Ngandu women had an elementary education. Men and women engaged in subsistence and market activities, but neither were employed outside of the household. All of the observations took place during the dry season.

All Euro-American parents were college educated and half of them had graduate degrees. All but one of these Euro-American mothers were employed full-time before the birth; they took leave during the first few months after delivery, and all returned to work by the time the infants were a year old. Mothers were always in the house during observations and observations took place primarily during the summer months. All the fathers were employed full-time and all infants had their own crib in their own room. The mean family income in 1991 was about $80,000 per year.

Background

The Aka foragers and Ngandu farmers in this study are neighbours in the rural southern region of the Central African Republic (population density less than one person per square km) where they make a living in the same dense humid tropical forest. The Aka and Ngandu have similar relatively high mortality (infant mortality is 10–20 per cent) and fertility (4–6 live births per woman).

The Aka and Ngandu live in very different physical and social settings. The Aka live in camps of 25–35 related (by blood or marriage) individuals who live in 5–8 dome-shaped houses that occupy about 37 square metres. Ngandu villages consist of 50–400 related (including clan affiliation) individuals. Each house is at least ten feet away from the next, but there are no walls or fences between houses. Polygyny is about 40 per cent among the Ngandu and about 15 per cent among the Aka. The EA households were all located in relatively wealthy suburban Washington DC. Each house had several bedrooms and a large backyard. Infant mortality is less than 1 per cent and the total fertility rate is less than 2.0.

Aka and Ngandu have frequent social, economic and religious interactions and see each other caring for infants on a regular basis, yet have distinct modes of production, male–female relations, and patterns of infant care. The Aka are net-hunting foragers (also known as hunter-gatherers), move their villages several times a year, have minimal political hierarchy (i.e. chiefs with little or no power over others) and relatively high gender and intergenerational egalitarianism. The Ngandu are slash-and-burn farmers, relatively sedentary, and have stronger chiefs and marked gender and intergenerational inequality. Upper-middle-class Euro-Americans have the greatest level of political and socioeconomic hierarchy, relatively high gender equality and low intergenerational egalitarianism.

Aka and Ngandu cultures share more and are in many ways more egalitarian than Euro-American cultures, but Aka sharing and egalitarianism are also substantially greater than among the Ngandu. The Ngandu focus on maintaining egalitarianism and sharing between households; households that accumulate more than others and do not share with neighbouring families are prime targets of sorcery, which is believed to cause illness or death. Sharing between households is not as frequent as it is among the Aka (i.e. not daily) and there is marked inequality within Ngandu households, with men and the elderly receiving more than others. The Aka, on the other hand, share with many people in many households on a daily basis and there is greater gender and age egalitarianism. Upper-middle-class neo-local families rarely share with others outside the household, but regularly share food and resources with household members (i.e. between husband and wife). Differences between individuals in food or other resources are evaluated on a near-daily basis.

Aka infants are carried in slings on the left-hand side of the caregiver's body whereas Ngandu infants are tied rather snugly on the caregivers' backs. When the adults are sitting, both Aka and Ngandu care providers place infants on their laps or between their legs, facing outwards. When infants are laid down, they are always placed on their backs. Aka infants sleep with their parents and siblings whereas Ngandu infants often sleep with their mothers (or in separate cots, when husbands come to visit). EA infants sleep alone in their own room in a crib.

Upper-middle-class EA infants are placed in a variety of technological devices – infant seats, swings, etc. – generally facing towards the parent. Caregivers are usually home alone with the infant and there are few adult or juvenile visitors. EA infants have the most caregiving devices (e.g. clothes, diapers, baths, and toys) and the Ngandu have more caregiving devices than the Aka. Some Ngandu parents make small chairs, beds or mats for the infants to lie on. Ngandu infants also have more clothes than Aka, are often dressed more warmly than adults even in the middle of a hot day and are washed once or twice a day. By comparison, Aka infants seldom have more than a protective forest cord around their waists and are infrequently given a complete bath. Both Aka and Ngandu caregivers carefully keep insects and debris off their infants.

Patterns of caregiver–infant proximity and responsiveness

Here we summarize some of our results on the holding, feeding, and fussing/crying experiences of Aka, Ngandu, and Euro-American 3–4-month-olds. The data are described in greater detail elsewhere (Hewlett et al., 1998, 2000) and statistical tests of significance have been omitted for readability. All 'caregivers' in the EA sample were mothers or fathers, whereas the Aka and Ngandu had several other categories of caregivers. The majority of Aka and Ngandu caregivers were adults, so the following descriptions of 'caregiver' proximity and responsiveness refer primarily to adult proximity and responsiveness.

Holding/touching   Figure 11.1 summarizes different proximal behaviours and demonstrates marked differences among groups in the frequencies

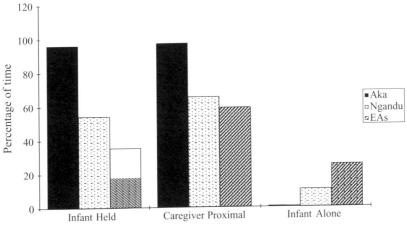

Figure 11.1   Percentage of time Aka, Ngandu and US infants were held, were within proximity (i.e. arm's reach) and were left alone.

with which infants were held, proximal (defined as within an arm's reach of caregiver), or were alone (i.e. caregiver not in room or not in sight). Aka infants were almost always held and never alone, whereas Ngandu infants were held half as frequently as Aka but significantly more than EA infants. There were no significant differences between the Ngandu and EA samples with respect to how often the caregivers were within arm's reach of the infants.

The holding differences between Aka and the other two groups occurred, in part, because caregivers in the other two groups put their infants down when they fell asleep whereas the foragers continued to hold/touch their infants while they slept. Ngandu adults held their infants 44 per cent of the time when they slept and 60 per cent of the time while they were awake, whereas the Aka held their infants 94 per cent of the time while they slept and 98 per cent of the time while they were awake. The Euro-American infants were held 22 per cent of the time while sleeping and 44 per cent of the time while they were awake. The asleep-versus-awake holding differences were highly significant when the Ngandu and Euro-Americans were compared, but not when the Aka and Ngandu were compared.

If we estimate the time infants were held/touched over 24-hour periods, the differences between the groups become even greater. Aka infants sleep with parents, Ngandu infants sleep with their mothers and EA infants sleep in their own beds in their own rooms. With this taken into consideration, Aka infants are held/touched 99 per cent of the time, Ngandu infants are held/touched 79 per cent of the time and EA infants are held/touched 18 per cent of the time.

Table 11.3 *Infant feeding among Aka foragers, Ngandu farmers and Euro-American urban industrialists (age 3 months)*

	Aka	Ngandu	EAs
Number of infants	20	21	21
Percentage of daylight observation intervals with feeding	15.2	12.6	12.5
Mean number of feeding bouts per hour	4.0	2.2	1.6
Mean number of minutes per feeding bout	2.4	3.4	4.7
Percentage of infants that received non-maternal breastfeeding	55.0 (11/20)	9.5 (2/21)	0.0
Mean percentage of time infants received non-maternal breastfeeding	8.4 (0–49)	1.6 (0–27)	0.0

Feeding

Table 11.3 summarizes the frequency and duration of infant feeding. There were no statistically significant differences among the three groups in the percentage of observation intervals in which infant feeding occurred, but there were significant differences between Aka and Ngandu and between Aka and Euro-Americans in the frequency of feeding/nursing. Aka caregivers fed their infants about twice as frequently as did Ngandu or Euro-American caregivers. The Aka were also distinguished by the frequency with which women other than mothers breastfed their infants – more than 50 per cent of the Aka infants were breastfed by someone other than their mothers sometime during the observational period. All EA infants received some bottle-feeding and were sometimes fed by their father or other care providers.

Caregiver–infant responsiveness

There were no differences among the three groups with respect to the frequencies with which caregivers showed affection (hugging, kissing) to their infants, but there were significant differences in the length of time infants fussed or cried and the frequency and nature of responsiveness to fuss/cry events. Table 11.4 summarizes the frequencies of fussing and crying in the three groups. The Aka infants fussed and cried the least, the EAs were intermediate and the Ngandu infants fussed and cried significantly longer than infants in both other ethnic groups.

Figure 11.2 indicates how caregivers responded to instances of fussing or crying. Fifty to sixty per cent of the time caregivers in all groups tried to soothe fussing/crying infants by rocking, singing or verbalizing to the infants. Aka caregivers were more likely to respond by nursing the infants whereas

Table 11.4 *Mean percentage of time and frequency of fussing or crying among Aka foragers, Ngandu farmers and Euro-American urban industrialists*

	Aka	Ngandu	Euro-Americans
Mean percentage of time fussing	3.06	9.45	6.33
Mean frequency of fussing bouts per hour	2.59	4.69	4.38
Mean percentage of time crying	1.66	3.79	1.80
Mean frequency of crying bouts per hour	0.80	1.58	1.02

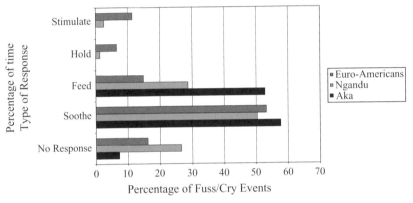

Figure 11.2   Types of caregiver responses to Aka, Ngandu and US infant fussing or crying.

EAs were more likely to respond by holding or stimulating the infant. Aka caregivers did not respond by holding because the infants were almost always already being held when the fussing/crying started. It was interesting to find that Ngandu caregivers were the least likely and the Aka the most likely to respond to fuss/cry events.

In summary, Aka caregivers were the most proximal and responsive to infant feeding and crying, Ngandu caregivers were more proximal to their infants than EA caregivers but less responsive than EAs to infant fussing and crying. Aka infants were the most likely to experience multiple caregiving.

Applying evolutionary approaches

In this final section we examine the caregiver–infant proximity and responsiveness data in light of the three evolutionary approaches described earlier in this chapter. Proponents of each evolutionary approach ask somewhat different questions, but all help to provide an integrated understanding of infant caregiving.

Evolutionary psychology

Evolutionary psychologists have conducted few systematic studies of infant caregiving, so what we present here is based upon our understanding of this approach and how it might be applied to the analyses of infant caregiving.

Evolutionary psychologists would emphasize that, in order to explain caregiver–infant interactions, it is necessary to understand the adaptive problems (i.e. recurring conditions that affected reproductive fitness) of caregivers and infants in the EEA and the modules or design features of their minds that developed under EEA conditions. One way to identify modules is to look for cross-cultural commonalities, possibly paying more attention to hunter-gatherer groups like the Aka since their way of life is closest to the EEA. One adaptive problem faced by humans was the relative helplessness or altriciality of newborns. Owing to the evolution of bipedalism and increased brain capacity, human infants are more immature at birth than newborn chimpanzees and other higher primates. In particular, they are unable to grasp and hold on to their caregivers at birth. In addition, several common patterns of caregiver–infant interactions are evident in this cross-cultural study: (1) infant fussing or crying gets the attention of caregivers and somebody responds most of the time; (2) mothers are most likely to be caregivers and most likely to respond, but several other people also respond, especially among the Aka; (3) mothers and several others know how to soothe crying infants; (4) most caregivers are genetically related to the infants; (5) infants are soothed, among the Aka in particular, by feeding, but they can be soothed by several other means; and (6) infants respond to caregivers besides their mother.

Given the adaptive problem and the cross-cultural commonalities, EPs might suggest that human infants have a fuss/cry or infant vocalization module and an attachment or proximity module. The attachment or proximity module is the classic system described by Bowlby (1969). Infants cannot run, hide or protect themselves from predators or infanticidal males (Hrdy, 1999) so they seek the proximity of particular others by crying for, reaching for, or smiling at these individuals. Infants who did this were more likely to survive in the EEA than infants who did not have these behaviours.

Indeed, fussing or crying might represent a separate module for infant communication, because although fussing and crying are linked to attachment, they also permit communication with others before infants can speak to or crawl to others. Crying can be helpful in communicating hunger, illness, temperature (e.g. too cold), discomfort (e.g. wet) or jealousy (e.g. caregivers spending too much time with other children).

Caregivers are believed to have their own suite of modules: a kin recognition module, an infant communication module and a proximity module. First, caregivers interested in enhancing reproductive fitness must be able to identify their own infants. This module is common to many primates (Silk, 2001) and most caregivers in all three cultures were genetically related to the infant. In the EEA, caregivers who responded to related infants who were fussing or crying would have experienced greater reproductive success than caregivers who responded to any crying infant, related or not.

Second, caregivers also need to know how to interpret and respond to crying and other aspects of infant communication. Experience and learning certainly enhance these abilities, but EPs argue that most individuals in these cultures learn rather quickly how to interpret, respond to and communicate with infants. For instance, many of the mothers and fathers in the EA sample never took care of infants until they had their own, yet learned to respond to crying and other forms of infant communication. The use of 'motherese' by caregivers is another example of the infant communication module in that it appears to be used 'naturally' or with minimal training. Bornstein and colleagues (1992a, 1992b) also describe several cross-cultural and developmental universals in maternal speech and responsiveness. Considerable intracultural and intercultural variability in sensitivity is expected, but most caregivers quickly learn how to communicate and respond to infants.

There is also cross-cultural evidence that kin, mothers in particular, try to maintain proximity to their young infants. Infants among most hunter-gatherer groups like the Aka are held in the caregivers' arms or laps all day and night (Hewlett et al., 2000). Although proximity-seeking behaviours encourage caregiver proximity, hours of behavioural observations indicate that hunter-gatherers maintain proximity with no or very few signals from their infants (e.g. they continue holding infants when they fall asleep). This makes evolutionary sense as mothers and other kin would be better able to protect, feed and transmit culture when their infants were near by.

Recent research indicates that 3–4-month-old infants are able to recognize faces, but unlike older infants they seldom fuss/cry when held by a stranger and can be soothed by several other individuals besides mother (Lamb, Bornstein and Teti, 2002). This suggests either that the brain is not developed enough to establish stranger anxiety or that it was important in the EEA for young infants to compensate for their helplessness by soliciting care from many caregivers.

The infant and caregiver modules described above are speculative, but an EP approach emphasizes the importance of considering evolved design features of the mind that were selected for in the EEA. Humans have a long history and it is likely that the human mind has adapted to deal with recurring problems. Our interpretation and understanding of caregiver–infant interactions is likely

Table 11.5 *Evolutionary ecology characterizations of parent–child sensitivity in three modes of production*

Study	Foragers	Farmers	Urban-industrialists (middle or high SES)
Draper and Harpending, 1982; Belsky et al., 1991	Parents have fewer children due to demands of mobile life so parents are sensitive, supportive, positively affectionate and responsive to infant demands.	Parents want many children and are less responsive, relatively harsh, rejecting, insensitive or inconsistent in their care.	Parents want a few 'quality' children so parents are sensitive, supportive, positively affectionate and responsive to infant demands.
LeVine et al., 1994	not discussed	Parents are concerned about survival so parents maintain physical proximity (hold), are quick to respond to fuss/cry and breastfeed frequently.	Parents are concerned about cognitive development because mortality is low so they hold infants less, and are not as responsive. Frequent face-to-face interaction and stimulating verbal interaction are emphasized.
Blurton Jones, 1993	Parents are concerned about survival so are nurturant and warm, quick to respond to infant requests and hold infants frequently to protect them from danger and exposure.	Parents are 'production enhancers' and consequently unresponsive to infants' demands. Sibling care is utilized to decrease demands on mother.	Parents want to increase the reproductive success of offspring so begin to teach children cognitive skills – frequent face-to-face interaction, stimulation. Responsiveness not important.

to be constrained without some consideration and understanding of evolved templates of the mind.

Evolutionary ecology

The EE perspective emphasizes the ways in which rearing conditions influence infant caregiving. What are the reproductive costs and benefits of different forms of parental investment in this environment? What are the fertility and mortality parameters? How many other caregivers are available? What reproductive tradeoffs are associated with investing now as opposed to later in children? EEs assume that individuals (caregivers as well as infants) try to maximize their reproductive fitness in specific environments.

For instance, kin selection theory predicts that individuals will be more inclined to help those who are biologically related. EEs also use parent–offspring conflict theory to help explain parent–child interactions (Trivers, 1972). Parent–offspring conflict theory emphasizes that parents and their offspring do not have identical reproductive interests – they share half of each other's genes and they are most concerned about their own interests. Given this, the care infants receive may not be optimal from the infants' perspective because parents are concerned about their own health as well as the well-being of other offspring. Infants thus try to extract more time and energy from caregivers than caregivers are willing to provide. Caregivers and infants are interested in their own fitness and in particular social contexts these interests may conflict.

By comparison to EPs, EEs have developed several hypotheses to explain caregiving in the three modes of production represented in the three cultures in this study (i.e. foraging, farming and urban industrialism). This is not unexpected as EEs are interested in explaining behavioural diversity rather than human universals.

Table 11.5 summarizes three models used by EEs to explain caregiving in the three modes of production. Draper and Harpending (1982) were among the first to use evolutionary theory to explain differences in parental sensitivity to their children, suggesting that individuals raised in an 'intimate' husband–wife context, with low marital stress and contributions to subsistence by both parents, develop a reproductive strategy that emphasizes parental effort (proximal caregiving that was very responsive to infant needs). Individuals raised in 'aloof' father-absent households develop reproductive strategies that emphasize mating effort (i.e. keeping and finding mates and less proximal and sensitive caregiving).

This work provided the basis for later work by Belsky (1997) and Chisholm (1996) on the relationships between family rearing environments, attachment, and parental reproductive strategy. They hypothesized that families with stable ('intimate') husband–wife relations and minimal socioeconomic stresses provided sensitive caregiving which in turn promoted 'secure' attachment patterns in infancy as well as parenting effort (i.e. greater investment and responsiveness with fewer children) reproductive strategies in adulthood. By comparison, families with father absence and greater social and economic stress are less proximal and sensitive to their infants. This promotes 'insecure' attachments in infancy and a mating effort reproductive strategy in adulthood. It is important to emphasize that, from this perspective, both parents and infants try to maximize their reproductive fitness in the different environments in which they live.

LeVine and colleagues (1994) also advanced an approach consistent with evolutionary ecology. They indicated that parental goals were adaptations to different levels of infant mortality. Agrarian (like the Ngandu in this study) parental goals focused on the survival, health and physical development of infants because infant mortality levels were high – often only half of the children survived to reproductive age. In order to monitor and respond to health and survival indicators, agrarian parents were expected to keep their infants close (holding or keeping them in proximity), respond quickly to fussing or crying and feed infants on demand. This contrasted with urban industrial parental goals that emphasized active engagement, social exchange, stimulation and proto-conversations with infants. LeVine reasoned that urban parents were concerned with the acquisition of cognitive skills essential for survival when infant mortality is low, children cost more and contribute less and there is a competitive labour market operating through an academically graded occupation hierarchy. He predicted that urban industrial parents would be less proximal and responsive to fussing and crying since infant health was not a priority.

The third model in table 11.5 identifies three basic parental investment strategies characterized, respectively, by 'survivorship', 'production' and 'offspring reproductive success' (ORS) enhancers (Blurton Jones, 1993). The survivorship-enhancing and production-enhancing patterns are similar to the parental and mating effort patterns described by Draper and Harpending (1982) in the first model. Blurton Jones (1993) suggested that forager–farmer differences in caregiving were due to differential environmental hazards (e.g. predators); he proposed that forager parents invest more time and energy in each child to ensure 'survivorship' in an especially hazardous environment whereas farmers emphasize 'production'. Parents who adopted the ORS enhancing pattern, like LeVine's prototypical urban industrial parents, were expected to have very few offspring, invest heavily in their children's cognitive development and minimize the importance of caregiver proximity and responsiveness. Blurton Jones (1993, p. 311) associated the survivorship-enhancing strategy with low-fertility hunting and gathering groups, the production-enhancing strategy with high-fertility agricultural societies and the ORS-enhancing strategy with high-socioeconomic status parents in industrial societies.

There are several similarities and also clear differences among the models' assumptions and predictions. Most important from an evolutionary ecology approach is that local ecologies – rearing environment and health risks – are central to each of the models. LeVine used differences in infant mortality to explain differences between the agrarian and industrial parental infant care-giving, whereas Blurton Jones emphasized threats to infant and child survival (e.g. predators) to explain the proximal and sensitive caregiving practices of survivorship-enhancing hunter-gatherers.

Important differences exist between the three models in their characteriza-tion of group differences in caregiving, however. Most importantly, LeVine described farmers, such as the Ngandu, as proximal (holding or staying close to their infants), responsive, and sensitive to their infants whereas the other two models suggested that farmers provide relatively harsh, rejecting and insensitive parenting. Draper and Harpending proposed similarities between foragers and EAs whereas LeVine and Blurton Jones suggested that these groups differed.

The data presented in the previous section raise serious questions about LeVine's depiction of 'indulgent' (i.e. frequent holding and feeding, rapid re-sponse to fussing/crying) agrarian parents. Infants among the agrarian Ngandu fussed and cried substantially more than the EA infants, they were fed almost as frequently (bouts per hour) as EA infants, and there were no differences be-tween EA and Ngandu infants with respect to the amounts of time that infants were near caregivers during the day. EA infants were not held as often and they were more likely than Ngandu infants to be alone. Such findings support Draper and Harpending's and Blurton Jones' characterizations of agrarian care-givers, with parents emphasizing 'production' and minimal responses to infant demands. Analyses of the distal-verbal measures in previous papers (Hewlett et al., 1998) tended to support LeVine's and Blurton Jones' predictions regarding urban industrial caregivers' emphasis on cognitive development, however.

In another paper, Hewlett et al. (2000) identified several problems with EE explanations of forager infant proximity and responsiveness. Some of them are listed below.

1. Most studies reveal few differences in fertility and mortality between foragers and simple farmers (Bentley et al., 1993; Hewlett, 1991). Specifically, Aka women have more live births than do Ngandu or EA women (6.2, 4.3 and 1.8 respectively), but hold their infants more often and respond to fussing and crying more quickly and consistently.

2. A study of the causes of ninety-nine deaths (fifty-seven male, forty-two female) among Aka infants indicated that infants and young children never died from snakebites or predator attacks (Hewlett et al., 1986).

3. Aka and Ngandu both have high (by Western standards) infant mortality rates (both above 10 per cent). If one caregiving pattern did lead to greater survival and better child health parents should adopt the behaviours that increased

survivorship (i.e. towards Aka frequent holding and sensitivity). Aka and Ngandu see each other's caregiving on a regular basis and are therefore clearly aware of alternative patterns.

4. Aka allow their infants to play with 'dangerous' sharp instruments such as digging sticks, spears, axes, knives and machetes while Ngandu and EA parents do not.

5. Aka caregivers are not as vigilant as Ngandu and EA caregivers in trying to keep older infants and young children away from hot pots and pans. Young Aka are allowed to crawl around hot pots and fires.

6. Interviews with twenty Aka and twenty Ngandu parents revealed that: (a) parents felt there were just as many poisonous snakes in the village as there were in the forest; (b) snakes, insects and predators were not identified by Aka or Ngandu parents as important health risks for infants; (c) both Aka and Ngandu parents felt that Ngandu infants were more fragile but this did not lead Ngandu parents to hold their infants or respond to them more frequently; and (d) both groups of parents felt that crying could lead to illness, but this did not lead the Ngandu to respond as quickly as Aka parents to crying infants.

We thus suggest a few alternative hypotheses. The first is consistent with EE and will be discussed here while a second hypothesis is consistent with ECA and will be mentioned in the following section. Our EE hypothesis suggests that holding and sensitive infant caregiving among foraging groups like the Aka contribute to the development of individuals who are more trusting, autonomous and generous (Hewlett et al., 2000). Hunter-gatherer life is characterized by deep and broad sharing and egalitarianism. Studies among the Aka and other hunter-gatherers indicate that it is not unusual for individuals to share 80 per cent of the food they obtain by hunting or collecting with most of the families in a camp (Gurven et al., in press; Kitanishi, 1996). If children learn to trust themselves and others, they are more likely to give and share extensively with others. Individuals trust that others will be generous with food, caregiving and other resources. A secure sense of self also contributes to autonomy, another common feature of forager life (Gardner, 1991), and egalitarianism. A secure sense of self and trust in others decreases the potential for ranking and evaluation of others by gender, age or features. This hypothesis helps to explain why EA and Ngandu caregivers may be less responsive to infant needs – it is less important to promote trust and sharing in these cultures – but does not help to explain why the Ngandu are least responsive to crying.

In summary, the EE perspective emphasizes the impact of sociodemographic factors (e.g. availability of fathers, predators, and socioeconomic conditions) and the importance of cooperation and sharing between individuals in explaining the three patterns of caregiver proximity and responsiveness in the three cultures.

Evolutionary cultural anthropology

The final evolutionary approach examines the ways in which specific features of culture and social reproduction shape caregiver–infant proximity and responsiveness. The ECA approach suggests that culture exerts its own set of unique forces on infant care. By comparison to juveniles in higher primate species, human children have a remarkable ability to imitate and acquire knowledge, information and behaviours from others – i.e. to acquire culture. ECAs are particularly interested in the processes of cultural transmission and acquisition. They pay close attention to the history and transmission of caregiving ideologies, artefacts of caregiving and cultural practices or 'habits' associated with caregiving. Like the EP approach, specific ECA studies of infant care do not exist so this description should be considered exploratory.

The ECA approach is similar to recent analyses of the relationships between attachment theory and culture (Rothbaum et al., 2000). Their analysis suggests that maternal sensitivity and infant attachment patterns are substantially different in Japan and the USA because of dramatic differences in what cultural anthropologists call 'culture cores' – general schema that pervade and shape developmental trajectories throughout the lifespan. The Japanese schema places priority on collectivism, interdependent conceptions of self, empathy, compliance and propriety towards others (called symbolic harmony). By comparison, middle-class US parents emphasize individualism (independent conceptions of self) and exploration (called generative tension). The preferred patterns of social relations affect parent–infant proximity and responsiveness. According to Rothbaum and colleagues, Japanese parents are more proximal and responsive in order to promote infant dependency and sense of interrelatedness. 'Japanese mothers meet their infants' needs even before they are expressed, thereby blurring the self-other distinction' (p. 1126). Selfless devotion and indulgence (*amae*) is expected of Japanese mothers. US parents, on the other hand, prefer to wait for the infant's cues before responding. Rothbaum and colleagues cite a number of studies showing that Japanese parents are more proximal than US parents: Japanese mothers hold and carry their infants more than US parents, co-sleep more frequently and are more likely to use snugglies to carry infants rather than strollers or walkers. Rothbaum and colleagues suggest that Japanese parents are more responsive to infant needs such as hunger and fussing and crying, but unfortunately no data were presented to support the statement. This is problematic because both Aka and Ngandu caregivers in this study were more proximal to their infants than the US parents were, while US parents were more responsive to their infants' fussing and crying than Ngandu parents were.

Proponents of ECA argue that culture and cultural history have substantial effects on caregiver–infant proximity and responsiveness. However, the ECA approach is distinct from Rothbaum and colleagues' and other 'cultural' approaches to infant care (e.g. Harwood, Miller and Irizarry, 1995; Super and Harkness, 1986) in that it tries to identify specific evolutionary-based processes and mechanisms that lead to the prominence of culture in explaining human behaviour (see table 11.2). The work by Freedman and Gorman (1993) on attachment is probably one of the best examples of an ECA approach to infant care. Freedman and Gorman describe how the attachment process and the associated development of internal working models (IWMs) help to explain the emotional basis of conservative vertical transmission – i.e. IWMs shape how we feel about relations with others and this in turn shapes our responsiveness to infants' needs. This early patterning of social relations (a type of schema) becomes what ECAs call 'marker traits' (Boyd and Richerson, 1985) – patterns of language, dress and social relations that are acquired in infancy and early childhood. ECAs point out that individuals are more likely to acquire culture (or semes) later in childhood and adolescence from people with marker traits similar to their own.

ECAs hypothesize that peoples with a common history are likely to have common patterns of infant care due to particular patterns of transmission – vertical transmission and group effect. Bantu peoples in Africa, Polynesians in Oceania and Indo-Europeans in Europe and the Americas share a common history, in that all expanded their ranges and displaced previous inhabitants. The culture cores of these peoples are conserved by vertical transmission and group-effect mechanisms. Individuals in each of these expansionist groups are expected to have similar patterns of infant proximity and responsiveness, and this implies that infant care may or may not be reproductively adaptive to particular natural or social environments. To better understand the phylogenetic history of caregiver proximity and responsiveness, we need comparable systematic data from many cultures around the world, but unfortunately these data do not exist.

Systematic interviews with Aka and Ngandu children and adults indicated that infant caregiving practices (how to soothe a fussy infant, how to hold and carry an infant) were learned from their parents (Hewlett and Cavalli Sforza, 1988; also Hewlett, unpublished data). Most individuals, especially among the Aka, reported that they learned these skills from both their mothers and fathers, although some mentioned only one parent. Aka and Ngandu respondents usually knew these skills by age ten. Behavioural observations were consistent with interview data; when young children cared for infants, their parents usually supervised them. Vertical transmission and group effect are thus the principal mechanisms by which infant care is transmitted in these two groups. Although comparable systematic data was not obtained from EA parents, many EA parents today rely upon the advice of paediatricians or family doctors, 'how to' books, and close friends who have children. Parents (mothers, in particular) may be consulted, but they seldom live near (especially in upper-middle-class families).

Infant care among EAs appears to be transmitted primarily by way of horizontal and one-to-many mechanisms. These differences in primary transmission mechanisms imply that Aka and Ngandu caregiving is more conservative and is likely to have a deeper phylogenetic history, whereas the transmission of EA caregiving is consistent with rapid change and short histories in a highly variable environment. ECAs point out that horizontal and one-to-many types of transmission are more likely to lead to maladaptation (i.e. to reduce reproductive fitness of individuals) because there may be less time to respond to feedback from the environment.

The mechanisms of transmission for EAs help to explain some of the relatively rapid changes in EA infant care practices. For example, US parents today are encouraged to hold infants more often, feed more on demand rather than on a schedule, and to respond quickly to fussing, crying or other infant needs. This contrasts with recommendations offered by experts in infant care manuals in the mid-twentieth century (e.g. Spock, 1946). The changes in recommended practices are integrated and take meaning within the culture core, which is transmitted more vertically and through group effect (also called frequency dependent bias). This is one limitation of the analysis conducted by Rothbaum and colleagues (2000) – they emphasize the differences between Japanese and US cultural cores, but give the impression that infant care practices in Japan and the US have not changed much since the 1950s.

In the previous section we questioned EE explanations for the high levels of infant proximity and responsiveness among the Aka. The frequent holding and feeding as well as the sensitive responsiveness to fussing and crying cannot be explained entirely by high infant mortality and dangers in the environment. We hypothesized that extensive sharing is another important 'ecological' factor to consider, but it is also important to consider the role of culture. Although our analysis of parental ideologies is not complete, Aka parents clearly do not view their environment as particularly dangerous for their infants. Parents are not preoccupied with infant health and survival – indeed they allow infants and young children to play with all kinds of sharp objects and to wander around and touch hot pots and pans. Aka parents talk about keeping their children physically and emotionally close to them throughout the lifespan. Aka respondents say that Ngandu parents may love and keep their infants and young children close to them, but the Aka are different in that they love and keep their children close at all ages. The Aka and many other foragers have vertically transmitted internal working models that value remarkable responsiveness and sensitivity to infants' needs. Even the most engaged EA parents are unlikely to hold their infants all day and to nurse their infant four times an hour. Ngandu parents, on the other hand, value respect and deference towards others. One may hypothesize that Ngandu caregivers let infants cry relatively long to help develop deference to the needs of older individuals. But deference and respect to the group are the reasons given for the reverse – immediate response to infants' needs – among the Japanese.

Finally, the recent work on niche construction within the ECA approach also suggests that we should pay particular attention to the material culture of caregiving. The Aka have few material artefacts associated with infant care while EAs have several. Our observational data indicate that 3–4-month-old EA infants spend about 55 per cent of their daylight hours in some sort of device (infant seat, car seat, crib, etc.). Niche construction theorists indicate that such artefacts or particular technologies can lead to separate selective forces. For instance, infant seats are constructed niches which affect the infant's temperature, movement, eye contact, etc. Over time, they could lead to changes in either biological or cultural evolution.

In summary, the ECA approach indicates that caregiver–infant proximity and responsiveness are influenced by a variety of cultural transmission mechanisms and that both the phylogenetic history of a culture and ontogenetic enculturation play a role in explaining these behaviours.

Integration

The evolutionary perspective is undergoing an evolution of its own! At first it was thought to be a unified perspective, often called 'sociobiology'. As more researchers from a variety of disciplines and backgrounds applied the evolutionary perspective, they began to distinguish among the three approaches described in this chapter. Although considerable work is still needed within each of these approaches, there is increasing interest in trying to integrate the three approaches.

Figure 11.3 is a heuristic and integrative model for the study of human development. The model has several distinguishing features. First, biology, environment and culture are defined and conceptually separated from the behaviour that one wants to understand (e.g. caregiver proximity and sensitivity in this study). If one wants to consider alternative hypotheses about the impacts of biology, environment and culture on particular behaviours, it is essential to clearly define and distinguish these factors. This is particularly important for 'cultural' approaches as most sociocultural researchers do not distinguish between behaviour and culture. ECAs define culture and describe its unique features. Second, the model and all the approaches are based on a unified body of theory – all are 'evolutionary'. The underlying unity enables those who focus on biology or culture to communicate with each other. Researchers using different evolutionary approaches often disagree, but an underlying commonality exists which enables communication and the potential for synthesis and theoretical development. This does not mean that all other theoretical approaches should be incorporated into an evolutionary approach. Evolutionary approaches

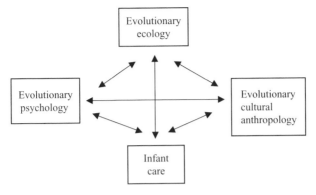

Figure 11.3 Heuristic model for interpreting and analysing behaviour from an evolutionary perspective.

are limited in that they focus on individuals and ultimate kinds of explanations. Finally, the model is integrative in that it assumes that it is unlikely that any behaviour is entirely biological, cultural or environmental.

Biology, culture or environment may explain a certain percentage of the variability, but it is necessary to integrate the three approaches. For instance, evolved modules associated with the attachment process (e.g. proximity) contribute to the emotional basis for conservative vertical cultural transmission. It is also likely that evolved modules exist for cultural transmission mechanisms, such as indirect bias, where individuals adopted semes from people of status (see table 11.2). Individuals in the EEA who adopted semes from reproductively successful collectors, archers or caregivers probably experienced greater reproductive success than individuals who learned only through trial-and-error. Likewise, aspects of culture – artefacts and vertical transmission mechanisms – can lead to changes in genes' frequencies (e.g. the adoption of yam cultivation in West Africa led to changes in gene frequencies of the sickle-cell trait) and the evolution of modules. Also, the modules that the EP researchers describe are 'evoked' under specific conditions, which means it is essential to understand the social (EE) and cultural (ECA) contexts of these behaviours.

The natural and social 'environment' in EE is a large and complex set of factors, but it is likely that culture (semes) and evolved psychological modules shape and influence decisions and behaviour in that environment. For instance, EEs might argue that the nature and frequency of caregiver–infant responsiveness is linked to the number and type of alternative caregivers available. Aka fathers are often around their infants and are highly involved in caregiving, but Ngandu fathers are also often around their infants but seldom participate in infant care, in part due to vertically transmitted gender roles.

Summary and conclusions

In this chapter we have described three emergent approaches within evolutionary theory and have illustrated how they might be applied and integrated to understand issues and problems in developmental psychology. The chapter focused on caregiver–infant proximity and responsiveness because these behaviours have implications for understanding social and emotional development. The EP approach indicated that it was essential to understand underlying biologically based modules of the mind that evolved in the EEA due to recurring adaptive problems. Infant communication and proximity modules in infants, like kin recognition, proximity and infant communication modules in adults, were identified as potentially important modules contributing to caregiver–infant proximity and sensitivity. The EE approach emphasized the importance of infants' rearing environments (e.g. availability of alternative caregivers, social stress, environmental hazards, child and adult mortality rates, frequency of sharing). The EE approach is similar to ecological and systems theories in developmental psychology, but distinct in that reproductive fitness and the strategies of both caregivers and infants are the assumed bases for explaining caregiver–infant behaviours in a particular ecology. Finally, the ECA approach indicated that caregiver proximity and sensitivity are influenced by caregivers' beliefs that specific styles of caregiving (e.g. immediate response to fussing/crying) are natural. Caregivers feel they are natural because they have been culturally transmitted and acquired through relatively conservative mechanisms of transmission – vertical and group effect transmission of internal working models and culture cores. This approach is also similar to existing 'sociocultural' theories in developmental psychology, but it is distinct in that it focuses on specific evolutionary-based mechanisms of culture.

As mentioned several times, the approaches are relatively recent developments and so only a few systematic studies within developmental psychology have been conducted. Developmental psychologists are in an excellent position to make substantial contributions to each approach, however, as all of these approaches seldom take ontogenetic development into consideration. Current evolutionary theory focuses on the minds, environments, and cultures of adults; discussion and consideration of children and their development are few and far between. When, how and why do evolved modules emerge? Table 11.2 is the first attempt to try to place the ECA mechanisms of transmission in a developmental context. Developmental psychologists have the knowledge and methodological tools to make important contributions.

In conclusion, evolutionary theory provides one way in which several approaches can be unified. The integrative approach illustrated in figure 11.3 also makes it clear that biology, environment and culture are mutually constituted. In particular, we have tried to emphasize that the culture concept is alive and well within an evolutionary framework and that many who adopt an evolutionary perspective (EEs and ECAs in particular) do not feel that human behaviour is necessarily hard-wired or biologically based (genetic).

REFERENCES

Axelrod, R. (1984). *The evolution of cooperation*. New York: Basic Books.

Belsky, J. (1997). Attachment, mating, and parenting: an evolutionary interpretation. *Human Nature*, 8, 361–81.

Belsky, J., Rovine, M. and Taylor, D. G. (1984). The Pennsylvania Infant and Family Development Project, Part III. The origins of individual differences in infant–mother attachment: maternal and infant contributions. *Child Development*, 55, 718–28.

Belsky, J., Steinberg, L. and Draper, P. (1991). Childhood experience, interpersonal development, and reproductive strategy: an evolutionary theory of socialization. *Child Development*, 62, 647–70.

Bentley, G. R., Goldberg, T. and Jasienska, G. (1993). The fertility of agricultural and non-agricultural societies. *Population Studies*, 47, 267–81.

Betzig, L. (1997). Introduction: people are animals. In L. Betzig (ed.), *Human nature: a critical reader*. New York: Oxford University Press, pp. 1–29.

Blackmore, S. (1999). *The meme machine*. Oxford: Oxford University Press.

Blurton Jones, N. (1993). The lives of hunter-gatherer children: effects of parental behavior and parental reproductive strategy. In M. E. Pereira and L. A. Fairbanks (eds.), *Juvenile primates*. New York: Oxford University Press, pp. 309–26.

Bornstein, M. H. et al. (1992a). Functional analysis of the contents of maternal speech to infants of 5 and 13 months in four cultures: Argentina, France, Japan, and the United States. *Developmental Psychology*, 28, 593–603.

(1992b). Maternal responsiveness to infants in three societies: the United States, France, and Japan. *Child Development*, 63, 808–21.

Bowlby, J. (1969). *Attachment and Loss*, vol. 1: *Attachment*. New York: Basic Books.

Boyd, R. and Richerson, P. J. (1985). *Culture and evolutionary process*. Chicago: University of Chicago Press.

Burton, M. L., Moore, C. C., Whiting, J. W. M. and Romney, A. K. (1996). Regions based on social structure. *Current Anthropology*, 37, 87–123.

Cavalli-Sforza, L. L. and Feldman, M. W. (1981). *Cultural transmission and evolution: a quantitative approach*. Princeton: Princeton University Press.

Charnov, E. L. (1993). *Life history invariants*. Oxford: Oxford University Press.

Chisholm, J. (1996). The evolutionary ecology of attachment organization. *Human Nature*, 7, 1–38.

Chomsky, N. (1965). *Aspects of the theory of syntax*. Cambridge, MA: MIT Press.

Cole, M. (1995). Socio-cultural-historical psychology: some general remarks and a proposal for a new kind of cultural-genetic methodology. In J. V. Wertsch, P. del Rio and A. Alvarez (eds.), *Sociocultural studies of mind*. Cambridge: Cambridge University Press, pp. 187–214.

Daly, M. and Wilson, M. (1983). *Sex, Evolution and behavior*, 2nd edn. Boston: Willard Grant Press.

(1985). Child abuse and other risks of not living with both parents. *Ethology and Sociobiology*, 6, 155–76.

268   *Barry S. Hewlett and Michael E. Lamb*

Darwin, C. R. (1859). *On the origin of species.* New York: Random House.
Dawkins, R. (1976). *The selfish gene.* Oxford: Oxford University Press.
Draper, P. and Harpending, H. (1982). Father absence and reproductive strategy: an evolutionary perspective. *Journal of Anthropological Research,* 38, 255–73.
Durham, W. H. (1992). *Coevolution: genes, culture and human diversity.* Stanford, CA: Stanford University Press.
Freedman, D. G. and Gorman, J. (1993). Attachment and the transmission of culture: an evolutionary perspective. *Journal of Social and Evolutionary Systems,* 16, 297–329.
Gardner, P. M. (1991). Foragers' pursuit of individual autonomy. *Current Anthropology,* 32, 543–72.
Guglielmino, C. R., Viganotti, C., Hewlett, B. and Cavalli Sforza, L. L. (1995). Cultural variation in Africa: role of mechanisms of transmission and adaptation. *Proceedings of the National Academy of Sciences,* 92, 7585–9.
Gurven, M., Kaplan, H. and Hill, K. (in press). From forest to reservation: transitions in food sharing behavior among the Ache of Paraguay. *Journal of Human Evolution.*
Hamilton, W. D. (1964). The genetical evolution of social behavior. *Journal of Theoretical Behavior,* 7, 1–52.
Harwood, R. L., Miller, J. G. and Irizarry, N. L. (1995). *Culture and attachment: perceptions of the child in context.* New York: Guilford Press.
Hewlett, B. S. (1991). Demography and childcare in preindustrial societies. *Journal of Anthropological Research,* 47, 1–47.
(2000). Parental ideologies among Aka foragers and Ngandu farmers. Paper presented at Annual Meetings of the American Anthropological Association, San Francisco.
(2001). Neoevolutionary approaches to human kinship. In L. Stone (ed.), *New directions in anthropological kinship.* Lanham, MD: Rowman and Littlefield, pp. 93–108.
Hewlett, B. S. and Cavalli Sforza, L. L. (1988). Cultural transmission among Aka pygmies. *American Anthropologist,* 88, 922–34.
Hewlett, B. S., de Silvertri, A. and Guglielmino, C. R. (2000). Semes and genes in Africa. *Current Anthropology,* 43, 313–21.
Hewlett, B. S., Lamb, M. E., Leyendecker, B. and Schölmerich, A. (1998). Culture and early infancy among Central African foragers and farmers. *Developmental Psychology,* 34, 653–61.
(2000). Parental investment strategies among Aka foragers, Ngandu farmers, and Euro-American urban-industrialists. In L. Cronk, N. Chagnon and W. Irons (eds.), *Adaptation and Human Behavior.* New York: Aldine de Gruyter, pp. 155–78.
Hewlett, B. S., van de Koppel, J. M. H. and van de Koppel, M. (1986). Causes of death among Aka pygmies of the Central African Republic. In L. L. Cavalli Sforza (ed.), *African pygmies.* New York. Academic Press, pp. 45–63.
Hrdy, S. (1999). *Mother nature: A history of mothers, infants, and natural selection.* New York: Pantheon.
Kitanishi, K. (1996). Variability in the subsistence activities and distribution of food among different aged males of the Aka hunter-gatherers in northeastern Congo. *African Study Monographs,* 17, 35–57.
Laland, K. N., Odling-Smee, F. J. and Feldman, M. W. (1999). Niche construction, biological evolution, and cultural change. *Behavioral and Brain Sciences,* 23, 131–75.

Lamb, M. E., Bornstein, M. H. and Teti, D. M. (2002). *Development in infancy*, 4th edn. Mahwah, NJ: Lawrence Erlbaum.

Lamb, M. E., Thompson, R. A., Gardner, W. P., Charnov, E. L. and Estes, D. (1984). Security of infantile attachment as assessed in the 'strange situation': its study and biological interpretation. *Behavioral and Brain Sciences*, 7, 127–71.

LeVine, R. A., Dixon, S., LeVine, S., Richman, A., Leiderman, P. H., Keefer, C. H. and Brazelton, T. B. (1994). *Child care and culture: lessons from Africa*. New York: Cambridge University Press.

Pinker, S. (1994). *The language instinct*. New York: Morrow.

Rothbaum, F., Pott, M., Azuma, H., Miyake, K. and Weisz, J. (2000). The development of close relationships in Japan and the United States: paths of symbiotic harmony and generative tension. *Child Development*, 71(5), 1121–42.

Silk, J. (2001). Ties that bond: the role of kinship in primate societies. In L. Stone (ed.), *New directions in anthropological kinship*. Lanham, MD: Rowman and Littlefield, pp. 71–92.

Smith, E. A. (2000). Three styles in the evolutionary study of human behavior. In L. Cronk, N. Chagnon and W. Irons (eds.), *Adaptation and human behavior*. New York: Aldine de Gruyter, pp. 27–48.

Spock, B. (1946). *The common sense book of baby and child care*. New York: Suell, Sloan and Pearce.

Super, C. M. and Harkness, S. (1986). The developmental niche: a conceptualization at the interface of child and culture. *International Journal of Behavioral Development*, 33, 23–30.

Trivers, R. L. (1972). Parental investment and sexual selection. In B. Campbell (ed.), *Sexual selection and the descent of man*. Chicago: Aldine de Gruyter, pp. 136–79.

(1987). *Social evolution*. Menlo Park, CA: Benjamin Cummings.

12 Shame across cultures: the evolution, ontogeny and function of a 'moral emotion'

Michael J. Casimir and Michael Schnegg

Our aim in this chapter is to apply a 'dual inheritance theory' and show how 'emotion universals' – in this case shame – are related to physiological processes and linked to social and behavioural similarities across cultures on the one hand and how culture-specific emotions are connected to the learning and coding of specific social and behavioural patterns and conventions on the other. At least since Paul Ekman's major studies (e.g. 1973, 1980, 1989; Ekman and Oster, 1979) on 'basic emotions' and the rise of the constructivist view in anthropology, there has been a controversy over whether emotions are universal or culturally constructed (Armon-Jones, 1986; Averill, 1980; Harré, 1986; Lutz, 1988). Many recent studies have shown that everywhere humans express emotions through metaphors and/or metonyms, which are related to bodily feelings (Kövecses, 1995, 1998), which in turn are generated by autonomic nervous system activities. These activities seem to have a panhuman hard-wired basis (for an overview see Levenson et al., 1992). These findings challenge the cultural constructivist hypothesis, which postulates that different cultures construct emotions in an entirely different manner. However, a comparison of the events which lead to the feelings expressed by these metaphors and metonyms shows that the antecedents and related appraisals do vary greatly between cultures. This underlines the relevance of the criticism levelled by the constructivists, which stresses the analytic indispensability of cognitive factors (Schachter and Singer, 1962) inculcated in the course of childhood and related to the variety of values, norms and behavioural prescriptions obtaining in different societies.

The problems inherent in the theory of 'basic emotions' and the fruitlessness of either/or, nature/culture, nature/nurture dichotomizations can, we suggest, be overcome by following Lyon (1995, 1998; cf. also Leavitt, 1996, p. 531; Lyon and Barbalet, 1994; Morton, 1995; Williams, 2001) in suggesting

Michael J. Casimir would like to thank all those colleagues, students and friends, who helped collect the language data used in this paper, and who are too numerous to mention individually. Without forgetting the usual disclaimer, Christine Avenarius, Monika Böck, Priya Bondre-Beil, Alexander L. Gerlach, Thomas Helmig, Aparna Rao, Birgitt Röttger-Rössler, Peter Tschohl and the editors of the volume were of immense help with their perceptive and critical comments.

that ideational/interpretative and materialist/positivist/analytic approaches be surmounted by using a more comprehensive perspective.

Drawing on data on language use across 135 cultures (see appendix I), we show that the phenomenon of blushing in shameful situations is a panhuman one. This, we suggest, indicates that the emotional mechanisms and physiology involved serve a specific function, which has a long phylogenetic history. The data available on the ontogeny of emotions in early childhood, and especially on the emergence of the feelings of shame, could shed light on its panhuman function. Simultaneously, however, we must allow for some epigenetic modulation and flexibility in early childhood for a linkage to take place with culture-specific behavioural norms. Culture prescribes and constructs the enacting of shame-feelings – it spells out when and why these feelings can or should be experienced and exhibited and when they should be suppressed.

Here we examine shame and embarrassment – the members of the 'family of negative self-conscious emotions'. These have been chosen because they are most suited to reach a clearer understanding of the interrelationship between bodily feelings and the more or less culture-specific antecedents and appraisals leading to emotions (cf. Mesquita and Frijda, 1992; Scherer, 1993a, 1997; Scherer and Wallbott, 1994). Finally, using the cognition/emotion behaviour complex associated in the West with the terms 'shame' and 'embarrassment' and applying Wierzbicka's (1986, 1988, 1992, 1999; Harkins and Wierzbicka, 1997) theory of 'natural semantic metalanguage' (NSM), we demonstrate the interdependence of metaphorical or metonymical language and panhuman physiological reactions and their relationship to universal antecedents and appraisals.

It has become increasingly clear in recent years that only an epigenetic view can explain the similarities and differences in emotional experiences and expressions. In some instances it is true that, as Athanasiadou and Tabakowska (1998, p. xii) wrote, '... while the physiological background as such may well be universal for all human beings, the actual choice of its elements for conceptualisation, and subsequent expression, need not be'. In other instances, however, even this choice appears to follow some universal pattern, for although 'there are no completely universal concepts for emotions; there can nevertheless be similarities in conceptualisation of emotions across different languages and different cultures. This is due to universal human experience, especially physiological experience' (Mikolajczuk, 1998, p. 158). This is why antecedent events, which may lead to evolutionarily 'primitive' reactions, such as an attack or flight, are always accompanied by similar bodily feelings and often conceptualized across cultures in comparable metonyms and metaphors. The metonymic conceptualization of the physiological reaction is an indirect description of the emotion; thus, for example, the metonymic expression for anger could be 'his face turned red with anger'. Metaphors are also often motivated by physiological effects – here, the central metaphor for anger is 'heat' (Mikolajczuk, 1998, pp. 157–8; for a detailed discussion of the 'standard theories of metaphor' see Johnson, 1990, pp. 67–72).

On the origins of the 'negative self-reflexive emotions' and the blushing/flushing complex

An evolutionary perspective always focuses on the function of a given trait or behaviour and it is in this framework that we now discuss the evolution of shame and related emotions. Emotions – and especially the self-centred, reflexive ones – are linked to the social life of the species and must have had a continued adaptive importance. Emde (1980, p. 3), in his biosocial approach to emotional development, stated that:

> ...emotional states represent complex systems of organized functioning inherent in the human person, states that are generally advantageous to the species as well as to the individual in the course of development. Evolutionary considerations seem to highlight both the complexity of emotions and their centrality in social adaptation.

Again, referring to Hamburg's (1964) study, he pointed out that emotions

> ...evolved because of a selective advantage in facilitating social bonds. In reviewing the course of primate evolution, he speculated that group living operated as a powerful adaptive mechanism and that, because of this, the formation of social bonds has been experienced as pleasurable and their disruption as unpleasurable. (Emde, 1980. p. 3)

All members of the family of unpleasant and negative self-reflexive emotions can then be understood as part of the 'social fearfulness complex', which emerged together with the evolution of more complex social structures in the animal kingdom. Lewis (1995) postulated an early form of embarrassment that is not associated with the self's negative evaluation of its action and a second phase when embarrassment does become associated with self-evaluation. 'This [latter] form of embarrassment is related to other negative self-conscious evaluative emotions, such as shame and guilt' (p. 215). In evolutionary terms the early emotional type of embarrassment may be linked to unpleasant feelings (e.g. fear) deriving from the negative reactions experienced by the individual when his/her behaviour went against the expectations of members of the social group. If the same 'wrong' behaviour occurs again and is once again noticed by other group members, expected 'punishment' may cause these feelings of embarrassment. This type of emotion and the accompanying behaviour in the absence of self-recognition is to be found in most species 'below' the higher primates (Gallup, 1970, 1977); a common example is the behaviour of a dog that has done something 'wrong'. Shying away and submissive postures are the usual signs of punishment expectation and can be interpreted as appeasement strategies with the obvious intention of changing the opponent's behaviour (cf. Keltner and Harker, 1998). Should, however, the opponent's strength and dominance be questionable, aggressive motivation may emerge and lead to an attack. In the process of social integration the young individual learns to appraise the qualities and capacities of others, minimizing the risk of 'wrong' behaviour by calculating his chances and also appraising the advantages of flight or fight. As Öhman (1986, p. 130) observes,

> ... the evolutionary origin of social fear is in systems controlling dominance/submissiveness in group-living animals. Biological factors are clearly involved in the determining stimulus and response factors, such as which gestures define displays of dominance and submissiveness, as well as readiness to respond to them. However, learning describes which particular individuals become associated with submissiveness and fear.

It was only later in evolution – at the latest with the emergence of the hominids with their self-reflexive cognitive capacities – that the function of this mechanism was broadened and Lewis' postulated second form of embarrassment/shame evolved.

The exact mechanisms of the physiological process leading to a flush/blush are not clear. They seem to be part or epiphenomena of a general arousal mechanism, which enables the individual to react quickly by supplying the periphery with blood. If such a mechanism indicates aggression/rage in the 'lower' mammals (e.g. the bloodshot eyes of an attacking bull), it probably also existed in primates and early hominids. When the capacity for self-reflection developed in the higher primates, the second form emerged and was linked to the physiological mechanism already present.

Since, arguably, the early hominids had a dark complexion, it was only when some of them became melanin deficient that the reddening of the face was semanticized and now functioned as a signal indicating the emotions, intentions and possible behaviour of the other. This became a new code which, together with other signals indicating the individual's emotions (facial expressions, body postures and, later, language) enhanced communication between individuals, thus leading to cohesion and consensus between group members. Leary et al. (1992) rightly suggested that '...the blush reaction may have emerged for reasons unrelated to social communication and only later came to serve an interpersonal function among light-skinned peoples'. This would mean that a flush-reaction was already fully developed before self-consciousness, complex sex- and age-specific hierarchically organized social structures – and with them the expectations of role performance – came into being. But now its function broadened. If violation of behavioural expectations of group members leads to probable punishment, arousal is likely in the individual who has transgressed these rules, setting the behavioural options to flight (fear) or fight (anger, rage). Such behavioural patterns are well known among many mammals with complex social structures and a 'social submissive system'. From the phylogenetic point of view, it could then be suggested that shame is a specific form of social fear that may lead to feelings of anger and/or rage, enabling the individual to react quickly and aggressively in order to change the behaviour of others (Gilbert and McGuire, 1998; McGuire and Troisi, 1990).

If, however, the neurophysiological mechanisms leading to a shameful blush are different from those leading to a flush in the context of anger/rage, the question arises about the evolution of this new mechanism which functioned as part of an interpersonal communication system. This can only have developed in concert with the evolution of complex social systems, the capacity for self-consciousness and normative value-bound behaviours. If we assume that in early dark-skinned primate/human populations with complex social structures and individual self-consciousness, shame and related emotions (embarrassment, shyness) had already developed, the function of a blush as an appeasement signal is unlikely. Vasodilation and thus blushing in shameful situations occurs in all humans, regardless of visibility; this suggests an early time-point in evolution. In other words, it could not have developed exclusively among those human populations with decreased levels of melanin in the skin. It is also implausible that a physiological blush mechanism, independent from that of a flush, was coupled in 'shameful situations' with lowering the gaze, shying away and other behavioural expressions of confusion and insecurity, since these are also observable in many other mammals living in social groups (cf. Keltner and Harker, 1998).

On the function of shame

Social consensus and the adjustment of the self

A major role of emotions when functioning as facial, vocal, or physiological cues, or when expressed as gestures or body movements, consists of communicating ego's state of mind as part of a series of individual and culture-specific adjustments to the social environment (Greenwald and Harder, 1998; Keltner and Harker, 1998; Lazarus, 1991; Planalp, 1999). Mayer (1974) differentiated between two kinds of behaviour – non-communicative and communicative. Only the latter, he suggested, elicits responses that can be understood and reacted to, if one is to maximize chances of goal attainment. Consequently, he subdivided the emotion 'fear' into that elicited by other species who endanger the well-being of an organism and that elicited by conspecifics.

But we can conceive of blushing as expression of emotion as well as communication, and to see these as dichotomies would, we suggest, be misleading (see Ekman, 1997). It is interesting to observe how the change of colour, which cannot normally be seen by the blusher, affects the other. The blusher only feels the rise in temperature, and even this seems to occur only after the reddening of the face is visible (Shearn et al., 1990) to his/her interlocutor, who might react even before the blusher realizes that the event has been observed. This gives him/her a very brief temporal advantage in which to decide between different reactive strategies. The reaction will depend largely on the culture-specific code that prescribes the correct behaviour in such a situation. Such a code obviously varies according to class, gender and age and also depends on the specific goals pursued in this interaction. For instance, mocking reactions amplify the feelings of shame, typically expressed in the German children's rhyme '*Pfui, pfui schäm dich, alle Leute seh'n dich*' (Fie, fie shame on you, everyone sees you). This may lead to even greater self-focused attention, blushing propensity and fear of blushing (Bögels, Alberts and de Jong, 1996; Shearn et al., 1990), and eventually too many unpredictable reactions which the interlocutor would have to cope with. But the brief period between the moment of observation and the perceived temperature rise may be enough for an empathetic person, or for one who wants to avoid further complications, to politely pretend not to have noticed the embarrassing event. It is clear then, that not only the specific cultural appraisals of the antecedent event but also the behavioural prescriptions and individual goals, which are partly cultural and situation-bound, play a major role in the performance and outcome of (potentially) embarrassing interactions between individuals. Indeed, the 'blushing complex' is a potent mechanism to help or force individuals to adjust to group-specific behavioural expectations, and is thus of great significance in the development and maintenance of social conformity.

Embarrassment and shame function to rapidly integrate and reintegrate an individual into the normative zeitgeist-specific behavioural mainstream of society (cf. Planalp, 1999). When severe punishment (in this or the next world) can be expected for major normative violations, persistent feelings of guilt occur; these may lead to confession and finally to reintegration into a social group, but as Bastian and Hilgers (1991, p. 102) have noted, 'guilt requires shame as a precondition'.

The development of shame and related members of the 'family of self-reflexive emotions'

The results presented in the bulk of the literature dealing with the development of self-reflexive emotions depend on definitions, as well as on the types of observations and experiments conducted. Wierzbicka (1986, 1992, 1999) pointed to the question of generalizability of such findings. Lewis (1992, 1995) has shown that in Western populations the different members of the 'moral', 'social' or 'self-reflexive' family of emotions, i.e. 'shyness', 'embarrassment', 'shame' and 'guilt', can be differentiated. In many languages, speakers do not differentiate linguistically between, for example, embarrassment and shame, shame and guilt or shame and anger (Fisher, 1985; Heron, 1992; Russell, 1989; Schieffelin, 1983, also Lambek and Solway, 2001); alternatively, a multitude of related terms, all belonging to this 'family', are used. We must therefore ask whether, and how many, such emotions which were found to emerge, for example, among children in the United States, are also distinguished or distinguishable in other societies. It is likely that all methods based on language-performing experiments must fail if a specific differentiation of the 'family of negative self-reflexive emotions' based on 'Western terms' is expected.

Cultural norms and values tend to determine which behaviours are considered shameful, and in many cultural contexts blushing can have both positive and negative connotations. The phrase 'he/she blushes', can mean that he/she has trespassed a convention or rule – but it can also mean that the person is well mannered. Here the event of blushing alone – i.e. the phenomenon without further contextualization – cannot be correctly interpreted. A photograph published by Izard (1992, p. 330, fig. 15.1) illustrating 'shame behaviours along with a smile in a ten-year-old boy of northern India' is a good example of how essential culture-specific contextualization is. Many north Indian languages and most languages of Iran and Afghanistan distinguish between situations and feelings, all of which are conducive to behaviour which could be glossed by the single English term 'shame'. Denoted by local terms such as '*sharm*', '*laaj*' and '*hayaa*', these feelings can lead to blushing, lowering one's gaze, veiling, etc., but their antecedents and connotations are varied and several terms in English – such as embarrassment, modesty, respect, well-mannered, but also pride and honour, manliness and femininity – are required to convey the complex contexts of their usage and meaning (cf. Cohen, Vandello and Rantilla, 1998; Lindisfarne, 1998; Menon and Shweder, 1994; Wierzbicka, 1999). Fajans' (1985) discussion of the complexity of 'shame' in the folk model of emotions among the Baining of New Britain and Hermann's (1995) and Jamieson's (2000) studies among the Ngaing of Papua New Guinea and the Miskitu of Kakabila (Nicaragua), respectively, are yet other examples of such variation.

But even if we consider only Western societies, the answers to the questions when and in which sequence the various emotions, understood as different, develop or mature, depend on the analytic methods used – for example on the choice of behaviour patterns and/or language capacities thought to indicate the presence of a given emotion. Is a given behaviour or facial expression a reliable indicator for a specific emotion? Is a parent's report of the first signs of a child's emotional expression a reliable indicator for the presence of a given feeling/emotion, or is this a matter of interpretation? Buss, Iscoe and Buss (1979), for instance, concluded on the basis of parents' judgements of their children's behaviour (including blushing and facial expressions) that '. . . embarrassment begins for most children at 5 years of age'. Does a child's capacity at a given age to name a given emotion or describe a feeling parallel an adult's understanding of this emotion? After all, '. . . thought-feeling structures are not learned or enacted in a vacuum, but in social life' (Strauss, 1992, p. 15). In some languages, such as Chinese, the emotion we gloss as 'shame' is hypercognitive (Heelas, 1986; Levy, 1973, 1984). Shaver and colleagues in 1992 and Wang in 1994 (both in Russell and Yik, 1996) found more than 100 shame-related words which are all translated in Chinese-English dictionaries as 'shame', or as combinations of shame with other emotions. It can be supposed that when a given emotion, or emotion-cluster, is of outstanding cultural importance, children, in accordance with Piaget's concept of *décalage*, comprehend and use such terms earlier than their counterparts in societies where the term is not hypercognitive or even hypocognitive (Heelas, 1986; Levy, 1973). It is therefore not surprising that about 95 per cent of Chinese children understand 'shame' and some related terms as early as at age 2.5–3 years, in stark contrast to American children, of whom only 10 per cent in that age group understood the term 'ashamed' (Russell and Yik, 1996, pp. 180–1). Using a Western sample Harter and Whitesell (1989) showed that only after the emotions 'happiness', 'sadness', 'anger' (cf. Wellman et al., 1995) and 'fear' matured, did children aged 6–7 years understand the feelings glossed by the terms 'pride' and 'shame', and Griffin (1995, p. 224) reports that only at the age of 7–8 years, in the stage of bi-intentional thought did the majority of children report self-conscious emotion experience. Mascolo and Fischer (1995, p. 65) point out '. . . that shame parallels pride development, whereas a positive appraisal develops pride, a negative one shame'. In their view, distress leads to distress/shame and thus to shame (p. 84), while joy leads to pride (p. 73).

Two postulates attempt to explain the emergence of 'shame' (and some related emotions) in human ontogeny. The first focuses on self-recognition, the second sees the emergence of self-consciousness and shame as mutually independent:

I. According to the first postulate, 'shame' can occur only after the infant has developed self-recognition. Only then can the child relate cultural norms, 'inculcated' by the caregiver(s) to its self, classify behaviour as 'wrong', and recognize this as its own fault. Self-consciousness is a prerequisite for empathy (Bischof-Köhler, 1989, 1995; cf. also Zahn-Waxler and Robinson, 1995). During the process of socialization, caregivers 'inculcate' desired and expected behaviour and 'punish' deviations from convention. Bischof-Köhler (1989) rejects Izard's (1980a) and Izard and colleagues' (1980) suggestion that embarrassment develops as early as 8 months of age, because this feeling implies the conscious reflection of the self, which develops much later. Lewis (1992) states that embarrassment and shame are basically the same emotion, but at different levels of intensity. Embarrassment, he points out, is of two types: the first, is more similar to shyness than to shame, and is not related to negative evaluation. Shyness, he states, can be understood as oscillation between fear and interest, or between avoidance and approach, and is not related to self-evaluation in children in the first month of life. The second type of embarrassment is related to negative self-evaluation, and can be understood as less intense shame.

Self-recognition develops not earlier than at 15 months – it is only at 21–24 months that the majority of children tested showed this capacity (Bischof-Köhler, 1989; cf. also DiBiase and Lewis, 1997; Scherer, 1993b; Smiley and Huttenlocher, 1991). Lewis (1992, 1995) also observed that the secondary or self-conscious emotions are observed only in the middle of the second year. This seems to be paralleled by the emergence of one of the typical shame-related behaviours – shying away, which, according to Mascolo and Fischer (1995), can be observed in children about 2 years old; only at the age of 2.5 to 3 years are clusters of such behaviours enacted in shame-related situations.

These various observations support Darwin's (1872/1965) suggestion that very young children, who had not yet imbibed their culture-specific norms, did not feel ashamed:

> Children at a very early age do not blush; nor do they show those other signs of self-consciousness which generally accompany blushing; and it is one of their chief charms that they think nothing about what others think of them. (p. 326)

II. The second postulate is based on the assumption that shame and related feelings can arise even before the development of self-recognition. Ferguson and Stegge (1995) imply that shame develops early in the infant, caused by the experience that its behaviour does not meet the expectations of the care-giver. Here it is thought that the withdrawal of love and/or other negative reactions towards the child elicit fear or guilt, based on anxiety (cf. also Magai, Distel and Liker, 1995; Rosenberg, 1991). Barrett (1995) also stresses the important function of the caregivers. If they show love as a reaction to the child's behaviour, the child experiences his self as loveable. If the caregiver shows negative reactions '... children [are] more likely to believe that they have failed, and to experience the shame of failure' (p. 54). In a comparable approach, based on Bowlby's (1969) 'Attachment theory' and developmental neurophysiology, Schore (1998) demonstrates the functional interaction be-tween the maturation of the orbifrontal cortex, the infant–caregiver behaviour and the development of emotions of the 'shame family'. Barrett (1995, p. 35) suggests that '... general cognitive acquisitions are not viewed as prerequisites for the emergence of entire emotion "families" such as shame or guilt'. Here the crucial question arises whether 'general cognitive acquisitions' include those necessary for self-recognition and self-reflexive emotions, and whether the self can exist or be conceived of without self-awareness/self-consciousness?

In what can be considered an attempt to combine these two conjectures, Lewis (1995), who differentiates 'embarrassment' from 'shame', postulated that an early form of embarrassment, not associated with the self's negative evaluation of the self's action, can be differentiated from a second type of embarrassment, occurring only between the second and third years of life and associated with self-evaluation. 'This form of embarrassment' he writes (p. 215) 'is related to the negative self-conscious evaluative emotions, such as shame and guilt.' He speaks of primary emotions (joy, fear, anger, sadness, disgust and surprise), which occur shortly after birth, or are seen within the first 6 to 8 months of life. Thereafter, with the growing cognitive capacity for self-awareness (15–24 months), these are followed by the 'exposed emotions' (embarrass-ment, empathy and envy). Only then, with the standards, rules and goals learned, by about the third year of life, do the 'self-conscious evaluative emotions' (embarrassment, pride, shame and guilt) emerge (pp. 207–8 and fig. 7.1).

From the above it appears that 'specific emotions such as pride, shame and guilt do not emerge at a single point in development' (Mascolo and Fischer, 1995, p. 72). The links between the elicitation of specific emotions and individual events are established in early childhood and adolescence, and triggered by role models during the process of socialization; specific emotions, especially shame, themselves influence development (Barrett, 1995; Scheff, 1990). Later in life, many of these emotions are mainly released in circumstances, and following events, which generate meaning in the framework of cultural norms and values, because the emergence of such feelings are based on given cultural contextualizations. However, the debate is far from over, and with a look to the future of research on emotional development, Mascolo and Fischer (1995, p. 72) suggested that development should be considered as 'a variable web', rather than as 'a uniform ladder of stages':

It is not fruitful to debate about the point at which an emotion first 'really' emerges in a child. . . . Treatment of emotions as developing at one point or age will lead to unproductive debates . . . Emotions do not emerge fully formed at one age; instead they develop gradually over extended periods of time, taking increasingly complex forms. One can always identify some form of a given emotion or ability at multiple points in development.[1]

All these observations and postulates show that many questions still need to be asked and many problems remain to be solved before we understand those aspects of the intermeshing of biology and culture that bring about the development of emotions. In search of the similarities and differences of emotional patterns in different societies we should start with the assumption that basic human biology is the same everywhere. The analysis of the impact of diverse cultural patterns on the elicitation of different emotions has, however, only just begun. To develop a panhuman model of emotional development we have first

---

[1] These extremely complex issues have been intensely debated and can not be treated here in detail. As early as 1932, Bridges (in Buechler and Izard, 1983, pp. 297ff.) postulated in his differentiation theory that generalized excitement is the only emotion present at birth and that distress develops during the first month. The first signs of anger, he suggested, evolve from distress between the third and sixth months of life and clear indicators of anger were not considered to exist earlier than in the twelfth month. Scroufe (1976, in Buechler and Izard, 1983) is of the opinion, however, that rage emerges before anger at 3 months, and the latter only in the seventh month; according to him anger develops from rage. Charlsworth (1969, in Buechler and Izard, 1983) suggests that 'surprise' (defined as the emotion arising with the recognition of deviation from expectancy) is present in the seventh month. It has also been suggested (Izard, 1980b; Izard et al., 1980) that at birth, the emotions interest, disgust, discomfort and shock can be released and that it is only after about age 6 months that happiness, anger and surprise, and after 1 year sadness and fright, mature. Emde (1980) gave the following mean ages at which mothers felt that given emotions first occurred in their infants: 2.6 months for interest, 2.9 months for joy, 5.6 months for surprise, for anger 6.3 months, for fear 8.1 months, for shyness and distress 9.1 months and 8.9 months, respectively. However, the capacity for the strategic control of emotional expressions develops much later (Saarni, 1991) and is held to be shaped by culture-specific rules and conventions (cf. Goldschmidt, 1976; Lindholm, 1988).

to determine behavioural and terminological similarities across cultures, which allow comparisons and enable us to develop and conduct new experiments.

Blushing and the panhuman shame complex: the 'natural semantic metalanguage' and a cross-cultural approach

The shame-blushing complex is, we believe, eminently suitable for a cross-cultural analysis. Darwin suggested that blushing[2] occurs in all humans, and that its meaning is always related to the same specific emotion(s). Even when among darker-skinned persons the flush was less clearly visible than among fairer ones, he wrote:

> ...there can always be seen the same expression of modesty or confusion; and even in the dark, a rise of temperature of the skin of the face can be felt... (Darwin, 1872/1965, p. 317)

Our starting point was the insight that in many European languages people tend to describe certain emotional states by remarks such as someone's 'face turned red with shame because he was caught red-handed', or again 'he/she turned red with shame', or simply 'he/she blushed'. In terms of Wierzbicka's (1986) NSM, the general structure here is: 'something happens because of this'. As the basis for this analysis we shall use the structure of Wierzbicka's (1986, p. 592; cf. also, 1999, p. 110) formulation:

X was ashamed = X felt as one does when one thinks that other people see that one has done something one should not do, when one thinks that other people may think something bad of one because of that, and when one wants to cease to be seen by other people because of that.

In our context the change in facial colour took place because of, or coincided with, a given emotion, caused by a specific event. It was now conjectured that when, in a given language, native speakers use phrases (see appendix II) in colloquial speech, the physiological phenomena parallel specific events and indicate specific emotional states. Sometimes this relationship between event and the physiological effect is expressed in metonyms or metaphors. These metaphors and metonyms are often related to both physiological changes and culture-specific ideas about the world and its functioning. As Kövecses' (1995, 1998) as well as Athanasiadou and Tabakowska's (1998) studies demonstrate, many such expressions are related to bodily changes or feelings (in cold blood, his/her blood boiled, etc.), which coincide with or parallel emotional changes.

---

[2] The physiological principles involved here were described by Darwin (1872/1965) and it has recently been shown (Drummond, 1997; Mariauzouls, 1996) that active β-adrenergic vasodilation is a major process leading to a blush. Although several precise mechanisms have been postulated (for an overview see Gerlach, 1998), the neurobiology of blushing is still poorly understood (Stein and Bouwer, 1997; Drummond, 1994). It is also not clear whether the same and/or other mechanisms are involved when a flush is caused by anger or rage (Drummond, 1994).

The data and the analysis

On the basis of usage in several European languages, we designed a matrix-form questionnaire, where the emotions joy/happiness, shame, anger, rage, fear, pain, shock and envy listed in rows could be related to one or more colours listed in the columns. The terms 'beaming/shining' were added to the list of colours, because very early it was found that the emotions 'joy' and/or 'happiness' were often related to the expressions 'beaming', 'shining eyes' or 'a shining or bright face'. The term 'shame' was used by us to designate a prototype for all emotions/feelings belonging to the family of more or less negative self-conscious emotions, since in many if not most languages no terminological differentiation is made between shame and embarrassment (and, as we shall see later, even between some other emotion terms).

Only native speakers were interviewed. The task was explained to the informant in his/her native language/dialect or, to bilingual informants, in a European language in which he/she was clearly fluent. Informants were asked to relate facial colour change to emotions. In addition, they were asked to build colloquial sentences expressing these event-relationships. Remembering that in many languages only some 'basic colour terms' (Berlin and Kay, 1969) are used, descriptive terms such as 'colour of blood', 'colour of the sky' or 'leaf coloured' were taken as equivalents of specific colour terms, irrespective of whether a 'basic colour term' was present in a particular language or whether the informant was using a metaphor. All these sentences were recorded either in the local script or transcribed and then translated literally into English, French, German or Spanish. Whenever possible, more than one informant was questioned in order to counter individual and local variation. In our analysis here we shall focus only on the data concerning the emotions shame, rage and anger.

During data collection, in most cases a semantic structure very similar to Wierzbicka's NSM (1986, 1988, 1992) emerged, consisting of the antecedent situation (implicit the appraisal), the emotion term and the related colour. The semantic structures corresponded mostly to one of the four following:

(a) 'He/she turned colour A.'
(b) 'Colour A (in situation C) because of emotion B.'
(c) 'Colour A [occurred (on the face)] because of emotion B.'
(d) 'Because of situation C colour A [occurred (on the face) (because of emotion B)].'

Figure 12.1 shows how frequently emotions were related to facial colour change in 98 of the 135 different languages/dialects analysed.[3] The numbers

---

[3] In the remaining 37 languages no relationship was found to be expressed between any of these emotions and any colour term. However, in many of these languages such sudden emotional transitions were expressed in metaphors indicating the same physiological changes as those which took place in the speakers of the other 98 languages. Hence, it is plausible that had

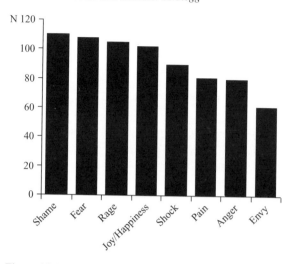

Figure 12.1   Frequency with which emotions were related to colour metaphors in 98 of the 135 languages/dialects recorded.

on the *y*-axis indicate the frequency with which each of the emotions was
associated with *any* colour. Since an emotion can be related to more than one
colour, these values can exceed 98. The figure shows clearly that the differences *between* the emotions are neither high nor significant; nevertheless, some
measure of variation was observed: shame, fear and rage were most frequently
associated with some colour(s), whereas pain, anger and envy were found to
be less so. In a next step we switched perspectives, to examine the frequency
with which specific colours were related to emotions. Figure 12.2 sets out
these results, whereby the frequency with which any given colour was mentioned is represented by the height of the bars. The rank order here is much
more differentiated with red, white and black dominating and red and white
figuring more than four times as often as other colours. Certain colours, such
as red, were related in some languages to multiple emotions, hence the frequency with which these were mentioned well exceeded the language sample
of 135.

Figure 12.3 shows in how many languages each of the emotions shame, anger
and rage is related to a specific colour. Shame, for instance, is associated with
red in 78 of the 98 languages examined. In general red followed by black, and
less frequently white is associated with shame, anger and rage. The frequency

these changes been as visible among the darker complexioned speakers of these 37 languages
as they are among speakers of the remaining 98, they would have also been expressed in similar
metaphors. This logic applies equally to those languages in which no metaphors are used to
indicate the physiological changes. This assumption justifies our not treating these 37 languages
as those with 'negative responses', but rather ignoring them in our calculations.

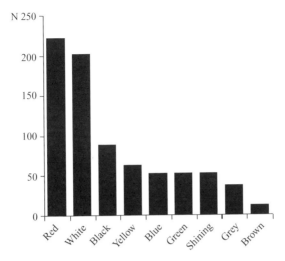

Figure 12.2   Frequency with which colours or colour metaphors were related to emotions in the various sentences recorded. The colours with a high
frequency were often related to multiple emotions.

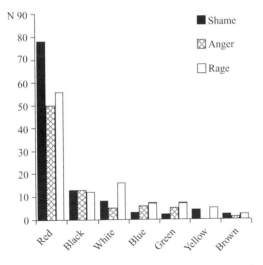

Figure 12.3   Frequency of associations between colours/colour change and
the emotions shame, anger and rage in 98 languages.

of all the other colours is low and roughly equal. Figures 12.4a and 12.4b set
out the geographical distribution of the languages/dialects recorded in which a
connection is made between primarily red and shame, in other words in which
the metaphor 'blushing' is used and others in which it is absent. From these maps

Figure 12.4a   The distribution of 98 languages/dialects in which colour metaphors or metonyms indicating shameful blushing are used.

- ● Official language(s)
- ● Other language(s)

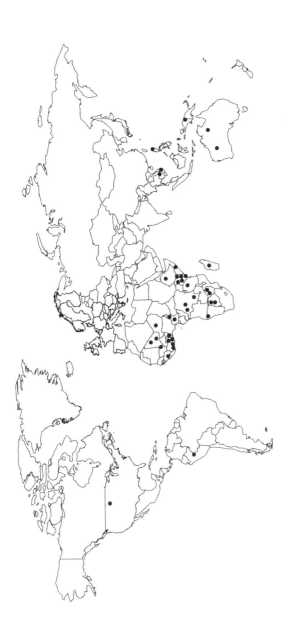

• No colour term/metaphor

Figure 12.4b   The distribution of languages recorded in which no metaphors or metonyms indicating shameful blushing are used.

it can be seen that with only a few exceptions expressions indicating blushing are used by populations with fair complexions.

The few exceptions can, we suggest, be explained as follows. Firstly, when the postulated blushing was hardly visible due to the speaker's relatively dark complexion, red was sometimes substituted by black – a phenomenon that is comprehensible, since a dark complexion becomes darker still when the blood flow into the capillaries intensifies (Darwin, 1872/1965). We can assume that there is a threshold of melanin concentration above which the effect is too small to be noticeable.

Secondly, in many cases, especially when the speakers' complexions were very dark, no colour term was related to shame. Sometimes, however, other metaphors indicating physiological processes were used; many of these point to a rise in temperature – e.g. 'he/she (his/her) (face/neck) became hot because of shame'.

It should also be mentioned that in some languages in Africa shame is often associated with 'red eyes', 'fire', or 'blood'; in Zulu anger is associated with the reddening of the sky or of an inflamed eye and Taylor and Mbense (1998, p. 203) explain that these '. . . expressions testify to the power of the conceptualisation of anger in terms of the body filling up with blood'.

So far we have shown (1) that emotions are related to (facial) colour change in a broad range of languages and (2) which colour(s) is(are) associated with the spectrum of emotions shame, anger, and rage. These findings point to a more generalized pattern in which red (and white, though not analysed here) seem crucial, a result that is strikingly corroborated by correspondence analysis (Greenacre, 1993) of our data. The scatter-plot can be viewed as a 'statistical map' where substantive relations between items are transformed into proximity in the image space. Those colours clustering around a particular emotion are typical for this emotion.[4]

Figure 12.5 shows the plot of the first two dimensions obtained from correspondence analysis. On the horizontal axis that captures 51.9 per cent of the variance in the data, there is a clear split between shame/anger/rage and pain/fear/shock corresponding respectively to red and white. The predominant dimension underlying the relationship between colours and emotions is, however, one that separates white from red and simultaneously pain, fear and shock from shame, anger and rage. On the vertical axis, which explains an additional 30.8 per cent of the variance of the data, a split between envy, mostly associated with green (for which no physiological explanation is available), and all the rest of the emotions and colours is visible.

The results presented from the cross-cultural sample (see appendix I) of 98 out of the 135 languages in which colour metaphors were used to signal

---

[4] Shining/beaming was excluded from this analysis because it occurs only in combination with the emotion joy/happiness. This would introduce a new, partly artificial dimension.

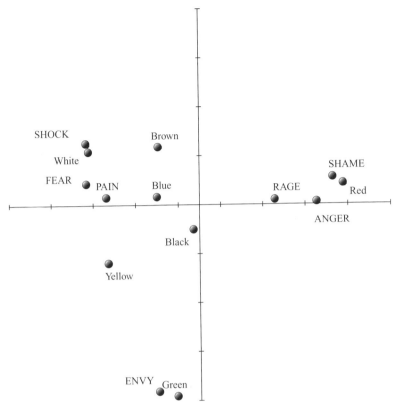

Figure 12.5   Correspondence analysis of the use of colour terms or metaphors and the emotions examined.

emotional change indicate a high degree of universality or *inter*cultural consensus. Yet they leave room for variation, and none of the relationships holds true for *all* individuals, languages or other speech forms. To determine more precisely to what degree these exceptions to the overall pattern are random, or hide substantial differences across languages or cultures, a second sample of informants was interviewed. This *intra*cultural sample consisted of forty-nine German students, socialized in different parts of the country and hence exposed to different German dialects. Though the units of analysis are different (languages in one sample and individuals in the other) this second sample can be used as a control group to determine (1) how similar or different the picture of the emotion-colour relationship can be *within* one language and (2) the degree of difference between the internal variations within this single language sample on the one hand and the languages in the cross-cultural sample taken together on the other. A similar or even lower variation within a single language than that within a cross-cultural sample would strongly support our contention that we are looking at a universal phenomenon. We shall examine both hypotheses separately: first, the similarity of the two colour-emotion spaces and second the relative amount of internal variation in the two samples.

The simplest approach is to compare the relative judgements on each pair of items and to compute from these the absolute differences between the two samples.[5] The index of similarity (S_{ab}) varies between 0 and 1, where 1 indicates total equality between two populations and 0 total difference. Computing this index of similarities for our two samples we retain a similarity value (S_{ab}) of 0.91 between the two.[6] Thus, within one population speaking one language there is roughly the same degree of variation as in a sample composed of members speaking 98 languages.

Still the theoretically more challenging question remains. In spite of sound evidence that forty-nine speakers of one language are as good (if not better) predictors of cross-cultural content as individuals speaking ninety-eight languages/dialects, we do not know the extent of internal variations. Only if the internal variations within the two sample populations are similar can we be certain that there is a universal understanding of the colour-emotion complex.

Variations can be defined as deviation from consensus on a specific judgement. If *all* members of one population agree that there is a relationship between a specific emotion and a specific colour (say shame and red), there is no variation; there exists 100 per cent consensus within this group. The same extent of consensus can also result from an agreed negative judgement: if all members of a group share the notion that there is *no* relationship between any two items (e.g. shame and green) we would also find 100 per cent consensus or zero variation for that pair of items. The amount of variation within one population can be calculated if we sum up all absolute departures from perfect consensus.[7] The index of variation (V) varies between 0 and the number of judgements divided by 2, where 0 indicates no variation and the maximal value total disagreement; this value of maximum variation would be reached if, on each pair of items, 50 per cent of the population agrees with the judgement and 50 per cent

[5] The similarity (S_{ab}) between two sample populations (a and b) can be expressed as $S_{ab} = 1 - \sum |X_{ij}/n - Y_{ij}/m| / k$ where S_{ab} is the index of similarity, X_{ij} is the judgement of the first population about a given pair of items, Y_{ij} the judgement of the second population about a given pair of items, n the size of the first population, m the size of the second population and k the number of pairs. See note 2 for the reasons for taking 98 as the basis of our calculations in the cross-cultural sample.

[6] The validity of the measure is also supported by a Pearson correlation of $r = 0.84$ between the two datasets.

[7] $V_a = \sum X_{ij}/n$ for $X_{ij}/n \leq 0.5 + \sum 1 - X_{ij}/n$ for $X_{ij}/n > 0.5$. All indices are the same as above.

disagrees. The coefficients V_a and V_b for the populations considered here are 5 for the intercultural sample and 6 for the German sample. Given the restriction that the index varies between 0 and 24.5 for the size of the matrices analysed, both values are *very* close to each other. Even more surprising is the fact that the variations within the German sample are greater than those in the sample of ninety-eight languages from all over the world. This points clearly to the existence of a panhuman relationship between experiencing specific physiological effects and the perception of facial colour change. The contexts/situations (antecedents) in which the emotions are felt are, however, culturally constructed, especially in the case of 'shame'.

Shame, fear, anger and rage

The metaphor linked in most languages to the emotions 'fear', 'shock' and 'pain' was either 'white' or terms close to it, such as 'grey', 'ash coloured' or 'pale'. Here, obviously, the principal physiological process is the reverse of blushing or flushing – here blood *withdraws* from the capillaries in frightening situations. In cases of both anger and fear there is a rise in diastolic blood pressure (Ax, 1953; Roberts and Weerts, 1982), but it is significantly higher in cases of intense anger than of extreme fear. Anger and rage (defined as 'anger out of control', Lewis, 1992, p. 153) are accompanied by a higher heart rate, rising blood pressure and higher breathing frequency, and in many cultures/languages the related feelings are expressed with what Kövecses (1995, 1998; see also Lakoff and Kövecses, 1987) termed the 'container under pressure' metaphor. In a shameful situation, however, in the short moment of blushing, neither a rise in blood pressure nor a higher heart rate can be observed (Gerlach, 1998).

An analysis of the subsample of seventy-eight languages in which red was associated with shame reveals that in sixty-two of these (79 per cent) this colour was also associated either with anger or with rage; in fifty-one cases (65 per cent) it was related to anger, and in forty-eight (62 per cent) to rage. In twenty-seven (35 per cent) of these seventy-eight languages red was associated with all the three emotions – shame, anger and rage.

The connotations of the term 'shame' exhibit remarkable fuzziness in many languages and the close relationship between shame, fear and anger (Fisher, 1985; Heron, 1992; Schieffelin, 1983) has often been described. In some societies feelings of anger/rage are feared and should be suppressed; if they arise they lead to the feeling of shame (Dentan, 1978; Levy, 1978; Rosaldo, 1983) in the angry person. In other societies shameful emotions are related to feelings of anger (Fisher, 1985; Heron, 1992; Rosaldo, 1984; Schieffelin, 1983) – a famous example is that of 'running amok' which occurs in Malay society and leads to anger and enraged homicidal attacks (Winzeler, 1990) – which are projected either on the self that has failed socially, or on those who have noticed this failure and thus constitute a danger to the self (cf. also El-Islam, 1994; Okano, 1994; Sachdev, 1990; Sharpe, 1987). This danger may, in turn, lead to anger/rage in the ashamed person. It can be assumed that after the first intense moments of shameful insecurity, confusion, fear, anger or rage may overwhelm one, leading to a secondary flush, and once again to shame. This is in accordance with Lewis' (1992, pp. 149–53) findings that 'the shame–rage connection can lead to a spiral in which the rage itself becomes a new source of shame' (cf. Retzinger, 1987; Scheff and Retzinger, 1991; Schore, 1998).

Conclusion

In the foregoing we saw that the negative self-reflexive emotions belonging to the shame/embarrassment/shyness complex and terminologically differentiated in different languages and societies are often expressed locally by using either the 'shying away' or 'blushing' metonyms, or both. These emotions play an important role in the psychological and behavioural shaping of the individual in childhood and early youth, thus allowing for his/her integration and functioning in a given society. The physiological principle operating on all the occasions glossed by the English term 'shame' also activates the various facial motor patterns. As Ekman (1972, p. 279 in Ekman, 1980, p. 138) noted:

... the elicitors, the particular events which activate the affect program, are in largest part socially learned and culturally variable, and ... many of the consequences of an aroused emotion also are culturally variable ...

The cross-cultural analysis and the related correspondence analysis have shown that the metonyms indicating the reddening, mainly of the face, are used to indicate states of mind – emotions which are part of this shame complex and/or of the anger/rage complex. If the physiology of the shame-blushing complex occurs in all human beings, whether visible or not, it is worthwhile to explore its phylogenetic roots and examine whether it serves similar functions in the social context.

We suggest that there is a panhuman experience deeply rooted in evolution, which first links specific events and appraisals, then leads to the elicitation of these self-reflexive emotions and finally to behaviour which serves the function of enhancing the chances of individual survival. We posit the following: individual emotions in different sets of 'emotion families' are released by events of specific sets of 'event families'. The fuzziness of both sets, between cultures and within 'one' culture over time, is the result of different culture-specific concepts about the world. These emotions are experienced and paralleled by physiological reactions that cause bodily symptoms or syndromes; again, the cultural setting greatly influences which bodily feeling(s) are taken into account when speaking of emotions.

We know that the junction of specific external events with physiological reactions leading to bodily feelings developed in the course of evolution. This development took place in the differential process of optimizing the proximate means of reaching the ultimate goal of maximizing Darwinian fitness. With the evolution of complex social and cultural structures the number of events included in such 'external event families' grew. Feelings of fear and anger were now released, not only by predators, but also by conspecifics and members of the same social group, when hierarchically ordered sex- and age-related norms began to constrain the degrees of freedom. The 'self-conscious emotions' now enabled the individual to react quickly in self-defence. A second function, however, developed in all groups where the flush or blush can be observed: it serves as a signal for the 'other' about ego's state of mind and gives the former the opportunity to react according to his/her own purposes – for the benefit or detriment of the blusher.

The data used in this chapter indicate that whenever a behavioural norm has been violated and this violation has been observed by others, feelings belonging to the family of self-conscious emotions arise in the violator. These are often accompanied by a blush. When a more or less fair complexion renders the blush visible, this reddening of the face expresses and communicates (Ekman, 1997) specific feelings. In these cultures the blushing phenomenon is expressed metonymically or metaphorically in everyday speech, to indicate shame, embarrassment or similar feelings that belong to this 'emotion family'. Such speech is encountered in the hypercognitive and hypocognitive emotion vocabularies of different cultures (Heelas, 1986; Levy, 1973, 1984) with their varied behavioural norms. This points to epigenetic development processes in early childhood and to the flexibility of human 'emotional intelligence'; it enables humans to cope optimally, though differentially, with their specific social environments.

REFERENCES

Armon-Jones, C. (1986). The thesis of constructionism. In R. M. Harré (ed.), *The social construction of emotions*. Oxford: Basil Blackwell, pp. 32–56.

Athanasiadou, A. and Tabakowska, E. (1998). *Speaking of emotions. conceptualization and expression*. Berlin: Mouton de Gruyter.

Averill, J. R. (1980). A constructivist view of emotion. In R. Plutchik and H. Kellermann (eds.), *Emotion: theory, research, and experience*. San Diego: Academic Press, pp. 305–40.

Ax, A. (1953). The physiological differentiation between fear and anger in humans, *Psychosomatic Medicine*, 15, 433–42.

Barrett, K. C. (1995). A functionalist approach to shame and guilt. In J. P. Tangney and K. Fischer (eds.), *Self-conscious emotions. The psychology of shame, guilt, embarrassment, and pride*. New York: Guilford Press, pp. 25–63.

Bastian, T. and Hilgers, M. (1991). Scham als Teil des Minderwertigkeitsgefühls – und die fehlende Theorie der Affekte (Shame as part of feelings of inferiority – and the missing theory of affect). *Zeitschrift für Individualpsychologie*, 16, 102–10.

Berlin, B. and Kay, P. (1969). *Basic color terms: their universality and evolution.* Berkeley: University of California Press.

Bischof-Köhler, D. (1989). *Spiegelbild und Empathie. Die Anfänge der sozialen Kognition* (Mirror image and empathy. The beginnings of social cognition). Stuttgart: Huber.

(1995). The development of empathy in infants. In M. E. Lamb and H. Keller (eds.), *Infant development: perspectives from German-speaking countries.* Hilsdale, NJ: Lawrence Erlbaum, pp. 1–33.

Bögels, S. M., Alberts, M. and De Jong, P. (1996). Self-consciousness, self-focused attention, blushing propensity and fear of blushing. *Personality and Individual Differences*, 21(4), 573–81.

Bowlby, J. (1969). *Attachment and loss*, vol. 1: *Attachment.* New York: Basic Books.

Buechler, S. and Izard, C. E. (1983). On the emergence, functions, and regulation of some emotion expressions. In R. Plutchik and H. Kellermann (eds.), *Emotion: theory, research, and experience*, 2nd edn. San Diego: Academic Press, pp. 305–40.

Buss, A. H., Iscoe, I. and Buss, E. (1979). The development of embarrassment. *Journal of Psychology*, 103, 227–30.

Cohen, D., Vandello, J. and Rantilla, A. K. (1998). The sacred and the social: cultures of honor and violence. In P. Gilbert and B. Andrews (eds.), *Shame: interpersonal behavior, psychopathology, and culture.* New York : Oxford University Press, pp. 261–282.

Darwin, C. (1872/1965). *The expression of emotions in man and animals.* Chicago: University of Chicago Press (Originally published by D. Appleton and Company, London).

(1872/1998). *The expression of the emotions in man and animals.* Definitive edition. Introduction, Afterword and Commentaries by P. Ekman. New York: Oxford University Press.

Dentan, R. K. (1978). Notes on childhood in a nonviolent context: the Semai case. In A. Montagu (ed.), *Learning non-aggression: the experience of non-literate societies*: Oxford: Oxford University Press, pp. 94–143.

DiBiase, R. and Lewis, M. (1997). The relation between temperament and embarrassment. *Cognition and Emotion*, 11(3), 259–71.

Drummond, P. D. (1994). The effect of anger and pleasure on facial blood flow. *Australian Journal of Psychology*, 46(2), 95–9.

(1997). The effect of adrenergic blockade on blushing and facial flushing. *Psychophysiology*, 34, 163–8.

Ekman, P. (ed.) (1973). *Darwin and facial expressions: a century of research in review.* New York: Academic Press.

(1980). *The face of man: expressions of universal emotions in a New Guinea Village.* New York: Garland STPM Press.

(1989). The argument and evidence about universals in facial expressions of emotions. In L. H. Wagner and A. Manstead (eds.), *Handbook of social psychophysiology.* New York: John Wiley, pp. 143–64.

(1997). Should we call it expression or communication? *Innovation*, 10, 333–44.

Ekman, P. and Oster, H. (1979). Facial expressions of emotion. *Annual Review of Psychology*, 30, 527–54.

El-Islam, M. F. (1994). Cultural aspects of morbid fears in Qatari women. *Social Psychiatry and Psychiatric Epidemiology*, 29, 137–40.

Emde, R. N. (1980). Levels of meaning for infant emotions: a biosocial view. In W. A. Collins (ed.), *Development of cognition, affect, and social relations*, *The Minnesota Symposia on Child Psychology*, vol. 13. Hillsdale, NJ: Lawrence Erlbaum, pp. 1–37.

Fajans, J. (1985). The person in social context: the social character of Baining 'Psychology'. In G. M. White and J. Kirkpatrick (eds.), *Person, self, and experience: exploring Pacific ethnopsychologies*. Berkeley: University of California Press, pp. 367–97.

Ferguson, T. J. and Stegge, H. (1995). Emotional states and traits in children: the case of guilt and shame. In J. P. Tangney and K. W. Fischer (eds.), *Self-conscious emotions: the psychology of shame, guilt, embarrassment and pride*. New York: Guilford Press, pp. 174–97.

Fisher, S. F. (1985). Identity of two: the phenomenology of shame in borderline development and treatment. *Psychotherapy*, 22(1), 101–9.

Gallup, G. G. (1970). Chimpanzees: self recognition. *Science*, 157, 86–7.

(1977). Self-recognition in primates. *American Psychologist*, 32, 329–38.

Gerlach, A. L. (1998). *Blushing, embarrassment, and social phobia: physiological, behavioral, and self-report assessment*. Marburg: Tectum Verlag.

Gilbert, P. and McGuire, M. T. (1998). Shame, status, and social roles: psychobiology and evolution. In P. Gilbert and B. Andrews (eds.), *Shame: interpersonal behavior, psychopathology, and culture*. New York : Oxford University Press, pp. 99–125.

Goldschmidt, W. (1976). Absent eyes and idle hands: socialization for low affect among the Sebei'. In T. Schwartz (ed.), *Socialization as cultural communication*. Berkeley: University of California Press, pp. 65–71.

Greenacre, M. J. (1993). *Correspondence analysis in practice*. London: Academic Press.

Greenwald, D. F. and Harder, D. W. (1998). Domains of shame: evolutionary, cultural, and psychotherapeutic aspects. In P. Gilbert and B. Andrews (eds.), *Shame: interpersonal behavior, psychopathology, and culture*. New York: Oxford University Press, pp. 225–45.

Griffin, S. (1995). A cognitive-developmental analysis of pride, shame, and embarrassment in middle childhood. In J. P. Tangney and K. W. Fischer (eds.), *Self-conscious emotions: the psychology of shame, guilt, embarrassment and pride*. New York: Guilford Press, pp. 219–36.

Hamburg, D. A. (1964). Emotions in the perspective of human evolution. In P. H. Knapp (ed.), *Expression of emotions in man*. New York: International University Press, pp. 300–17.

Harkins, J. and Wierzbicka, A. (1997). Language: a key issue in emotion research. *Innovation*, 10(4), 319–31.

Harré, R. M. (ed.) (1986). *The social construction of emotions*. Oxford: Oxford University Press.

Harter, S. and Whitesell, N. R. (1989). Developmental changes in children's understanding of single, multiple, and blended emotion concepts. In C. Saarni and P. L. Harris (eds.), *Children's understanding of emotion*. Cambridge: Cambridge University Press, pp. 81–116.

Heelas, P. (1986). Emotion talk across cultures. In R. M. Harré (ed.), *The social construction of emotions*. Oxford: Oxford University Press, pp. 234–66.

Hermann, E. (1995). *Emotionen und Historizität. Der emotionale Diskurs über die Yali-Bewegung in einer Dorfgemeinschaft der Ngaing, Papua New Guinea* (Emotions and historicity. The emotional discourse on the Yali movement in a village community of Ngaing, Papua, New Guinea). Berlin: D. Reimer Verlag.

Heron, J. (1992). *Feeling and personhood: psychology in another key*. London: Sage.

Izard, C. E. (1980a). Cross-cultural perspectives on emotion and emotion communication. In H. C. Triandis and W. Lonner (eds.), *Handbook of cross-cultural psychology*, vol. 3: *Basic processes*. London: Allyn and Bacon, pp. 185–221.

(1980b). The emergence of emotions and the development of consciousness in infancy. In J. M. Davidson and R. J. Davidson (eds.), *The psychobiology of consciousness*. New York: Plenum Press, pp. 193–216.

(1992). *The psychology of emotions*. New York: Plenum Press.

Izard, C. E. and Buechler, S. (1980). Aspects of consciousness and personality in terms of differential emotions theory. In R. Plutchik and H. Kellerman (eds.), *Emotion: theory and research*, vol. 5: *Emotion, psychopathology and psychotherapy*. London: Academic Press, pp. 165–87.

Izard, C. E., Huebner, R. R., Risser, D., McGuinnes, G. C. and Doughen, L. M. (1980). The young infant's ability to produce discrete emotion expressions. *Developmental Psychology*, 16, 132–40.

Jamieson, M. (2000). It's shame that makes men and women enemies: the politics of intimacy among the Miskitu of Kakabila. *Journal of the Royal Anthropological Institute* (n.s.), 6, 311–24.

Johnson, M. (1990). *The body in the mind: the bodily basis of meaning, imagination, and reason*. Chicago: University of Chicago Press.

Keltner, D. and Harker, L. (1998). The forms and functions of nonverbal signals of shame. In P. Gilbert and B. Andrews (eds.), *Shame: interpersonal behavior, psychopathology, and culture*. New York: Oxford University Press, pp. 78–98.

Kövecses, Z. (1995). Metaphor and folk understanding of anger. In J. A. Russel, J.-M. Fernández-Dols, A. S. R. Manstead and J. C. Wellenkamp (eds.), *Everyday conceptions of emotions: an introduction to the psychology, anthropology and linguistics of emotion*, Series D: Behavioral and social sciences 81. London: Kluwer Academic, pp. 49–71.

(1998). Are there any emotion-specific metaphors? In A. Athanasiadou and E. Tabakowska (eds.), *Speaking of emotions: conceptualization and expression*. Berlin: Mouton de Gruyter, pp. 127–51.

Lakoff, G. and Kövecses, Z. (1987). The cognitive model of anger inherent in American English. In D. Holland and N. Quinn (eds.), *Cultural models in language and thought*. Cambridge: Cambridge University Press, pp. 196–221.

Lambek, M. and Solway, J. S. (2001). Just anger: scenarios of indignation in Botswana and Madagascar. *Ethnos*, 66(1), 49–72.

Lazarus, R. S. (1991). *Emotion and adaptation*. Oxford: Oxford University Press.

Leary, M. R., Britt, T. W., Culip II, W. D. and Tempelton, J. L. (1992). Social blushing. *Psychological Bulletin*, 112(3), 446–60.

Leavitt, J. (1996). Meaning and feeling in the anthropology of emotions. *American Ethnologist*, 23(3), 514–39.

Levenson, R. W., Ekman, P., Heider, K. and Friesen, W. V. (1992). Emotion and autonomic nervous system activity in the Minankabau of West Sumatra. *Journal of Personality and Social Psychology*, 62(6), 972–88.

Levy, R. I. (1973). *Tahitians: mind and experience in the Society Islands*. Chicago: University of Chicago Press.

   (1978). Tahitian gentleness and redundant controls. In A. Montagu (ed.), *Learning non-aggression. the experience of non-literate societies*. Oxford: Oxford University Press, pp. 222–35.

   (1984). Emotion, knowing, and culture. In R. A. Shweder and R. A. LeVine (eds.), *Culture theory: essays on mind, self, and emotion*. Cambridge: Cambridge University Press, pp. 214–37.

Lewis, M. (1992). *Shame: the exposed self*. New York: Maxwell Macmillan Press.

   (1995). Embarrassment: the emotion of self-exposure and evaluation. In J. P. Tangney and K. W. Fischer (eds.), *Self-conscious emotions: the psychology of shame, guilt, embarrassment, and pride*. New York: Guilford Press, pp. 198–218.

Lindholm, C. (1988). The social structure of emotional constraints: the court of Louis XIV and the Pukhtun of North Pakistan. *Ethos*, 16, 227–46.

Lindisfarne, N. (1998). Gender, shame, and culture: an anthropological perspective. In P. Gilbert and B. Andrews (eds.), *Shame: interpersonal behavior, psychopathology, and culture*. New York: Oxford University Press, pp. 246–60.

Lutz, C. (1988). *Unnatural emotions: everyday sentiments on a Micronesian atoll and their challenge to Western theory*. Chicago: University of Chicago Press.

Lyon, M. L. (1995). Missing emotions: the limitations of cultural constructionism in the study of emotions. *Cultural Anthropology*, 10(2), 244–63.

   (1998). The limitations of cultural constructionism in the study of emotions. In G. Bendelow and S. J. Williams (eds.), *Emotions in social life*. London: Routledge, pp. 39–59.

Lyon, M. and Barbalet, J. M. (1994). Society's body: emotion and the 'somatization' of social theory. In T. J. Csordas (ed.), *Embodiment and experience: the existential ground of culture and self*. Cambridge: Cambridge University Press, pp. 48–66.

Magai, C., Distel, N. and Liker, R. (1995). Emotion socialization, attachment, and patterns of adult emotional traits. *Cognition and Emotion*, 9(5), 461–81.

Mariauzouls, C. (1996). Psychophysiologie von Scham und Erröten (The psychology of shame and blushing), Ph.D. thesis, University of Munich.

Mascolo, M. F. and Fischer, K. W. (1995). Developmental transformations in appraisals for pride, shame and guilt. In J. P. Tangney and K. W. Fischer (eds.), *Self-conscious emotions: the psychology of shame, guilt, embarrassment and pride*. New York: Guilford Press, pp. 64–113.

Mayer, E. (1974). Behavior programs and evolutionary strategies. *American Scientist*, 62, 650–9.

McGuire, M. T. and Troisi, A. (1990). Anger: an evolutionary view. In R. Plutchik and H. Kellermann (eds.), *Emotion: theory, research, and experience*. San Diego: Academic Press, pp. 43–57.

Menon, U. and Shweder, R. A. (1994). Kali's tongue: cultural psychology and the power of shame in Orissa, India. In S. Kitayama and H. Markus (eds.), *Emotion and culture*. Washington, DC: American Psychological Association, pp. 241–82.

Mesquita, B. and Frijda, N. H. (1992). Cultural variations in emotions: a review. *Psychological Bulletin*, 112(2), 179–204.

Mikolajczuk, A. (1998). The metonymic and metaphorical conceptualization of *anger* in Polish. A. In Athanasiadou and E. Tabakowska (eds.), *Speaking of emotions: conceptualization and expression*. Berlin: Mouton de Gruyter, pp. 153–90.

Morton, J. (1995). The organic remains: remarks on the construction and development of people. *Social Analysis*, 37, 101–18.

Öhman, A. (1986). Face the beast and fear the face: animal and social fears as prototypes for evolutionary analyses of emotions. *Psychophysiology*, 23(2), 123–45.

Okano, K. (1994). Shame and social phobia: a transcultural viewpoint, *Bulletin of the Manninger Clinic*, 85(3) 323–38.

Planalp, S. (1999). *Communicating emotion: social, moral, and cultural processes*. Cambridge: Cambridge University Press.

Retzinger, S. R. (1987). Resentments of laughter: video studies of the shame-rage spiral. In L. Lewis (ed.), *The role of shame in symptom formation*. Hillsdale, NJ: Lawrence Erlbaum, pp. 151–81.

Roberts, J. R. and Weerts, T. C. (1982). Cardiovascular responding during anger and fear imagery. *Psychological Reports*, 50, 219–30.

Rosaldo, M. Z. (1983). The shame of head hunters and the autonomy of self. *Ethos*, 11(3), 135–51.

(1984). Towards an anthropology of self and feeling. In R. A. Shweder and R. A. LeVine (eds.), *Culture theory: essays on mind, self, and emotion*. Cambridge: Cambridge University Press, pp. 135–57.

Rosenberg, C. (1991). *Understanding shame*. London: Jason Aronson.

Russell, J. (1989). Culture, scripts, and children's understanding of emotions. In C. Saarni and P. L. Harris (eds.), *Children's understanding of emotion*. Cambridge: Cambridge University Press, pp. 293–318.

Russell, J. and Yik, S. M. (1996). Emotion among the Chinese. In M. H. Bond (ed.), *The handbook of Chinese psychology*. Hong Kong: Oxford University Press, pp. 166–88.

Saarni, C. (1991). Children's understanding of strategic control of emotional expression in social transactions. In C. Saarni and P. L. Harris (eds.), *Children's understanding of emotion*. Cambridge: Cambridge University Press, pp. 181–208.

Sachdev, P. S. (1990). *Whakama*: culturally determined behavior in the New Zealand Maori. *Psychological Medicine*, 20, 433–44.

Schachter, S. and Singer, J. E. (1962). Cognitive, social and physiological determinants of emotional state. *Psychological Review*, 69(5), 379–99.

Scheff, T. J. (1990). Socialisation of emotions: pride and shame as causal agents. In T. D. Kemper (ed.), *Research agendas in the sociology of emotions*. Albany: State University of New York Press, pp. 281–304.

Scheff, T. J. and Retzinger, S. M. (1991). *Emotions and violence: shame and rage in destructive conflicts*. Lexington, MA: DC Heath.

Scherer, K. R. (1993a). Studying the emotion-antecedent appraisal process: an expert system approach. *Cognition and Emotion*, 7, 325–55.

(1993b). Les émotions: fonctions et composantes. In B. Rimé and K. Scherer (eds.), *Les émotions*. Neuchâtel: Delachaux et Niestle, pp. 97–133.

(1997). Profiles of emotion-antecedent appraisal: testing theoretical predictions across cultures. *Cognition and Emotion*, 11(2), 113–50.

Scherer, K. R. and Wallbott, H. G. (1994). Evidence for universality and cultural variation of differential emotion response patterning. *Journal of Personality and Social Psychology*, 66, 310–28.

Schieffelin, E. L. (1983). Anger and shame in the tropical forest: on affect as a cultural system in Papua New Guinea. *Ethos*, 11(3), 181–91.

Schore, A. N. (1998). Early shame experiences and infant brain development. In P. Gilbert and B. Andrews (eds.), *Shame: Interpersonal behavior, psychopathology, and culture*. New York: Oxford University Press, pp. 57–77.

Sharpe, J. (1987). 'Shame' in Papua New Guinea. *Group Analysis*, 20, 43–8.

Shearn, D. (1992). Blushing as a function of audience size. *Psychophysiology*, 29(4), 431–6.

Shearn, D., Bergman, E., Hill, K., Abel, A. and Hindis, L. (1990). Facial coloration and temperature responses in blushing. *Psychophysiology*, 27(6), 687–93.

Shweder, R. A. (1996). *Thinking through cultures. expeditions in cultural psychology*. Cambridge, MA: Harvard University Press.

Smiley, P. and Huttenlocher, J. (1991). Young children's acquisition of emotion concepts. In C. Saarni and P. L. Harris (eds.), *Children's understanding of emotion*. Cambridge: Cambridge University Press, pp. 27–49.

Stein, D. J. and Bouwer, C. (1997). Blushing and social phobia: a neuroethological speculation. *Medical Hypotheses*, 49(1), 101–8.

Strauss, C. (1992). Models and motives. In R. D'Andrade and C. Strauss (eds.), *Human motives and cultural models*. Cambridge: Cambridge University Press, pp. 1–20.

Taylor, J. R. and Mbense, T. G. (1998). Red dogs and rotten mealies: how Zulus talk about anger. In A. Athanasiadou and E. Tabakowska (eds.), *Speaking of emotions: conceptualization and expression*. Berlin: Mouton de Gruyter, pp. 191–226.

Wellman, H. M., Harris, P. L., Baberjee, M. and Sinclair, A. (1995). Early understanding of emotions: evidence from language. *Cognition and Emotion*, 9(2), 117–49.

Wierzbicka, A. (1986). Human emotions: universal or culture-specific? *American Anthropologist*, 88(3), 584–94.

(1988). The semantics of emotions: *fear* and its relatives in English. *Australian Journal of Linguistics*, 10(3), 359–75.

(1992). Talking about emotions: semantics, culture, and cognition. *Cognition and Emotion*, 6(3/4), 285–319.

(1999). *Emotions across languages and cultures: diversity and universals*. Cambridge: Cambridge University Press.

Williams, S. (2001). *Emotion and social theory: corporeal reflections on the (ir)rational*. London: Sage.

Winzeler, R. (1990). Amok: historical, psychological and cultural perspectives. In W. J. Karim (ed.), *Emotion of culture: a Malay perspective*. Oxford: Oxford University Press, pp. 97–122.

Zahn-Waxler, C. and Robinson, J. (1995). Empathy and guilt: early origins of feelings of responsibility. In J. P. Tangney and K. Fischer (eds.), *Self-conscious emotions: the psychology of shame, guilt, embarrassment, and pride*. New York: Guilford Press, pp. 143–73.

Appendix I

These follows a list of languages referred to in this paper and the countries in which they are spoken. Bold type indicates the absence of metaphors and metonyms linking facial colours (or colour change) and emotions, while the numbers give the sample of informants for the given language.

Afrikaans	3	Namibia		**Gabry**	**1**	**Chad**	
Akposso	**1**	**Togo**		**Garadjeri**	**1**	**Australia**	
Albanian	2	Albania		German	5	Germany	
Altai	2	S. Russia		**Gourane**	**1**	**Chad**	
Ani	**1**	**Ivory Coast**		Greek	4	Greece	
Arabic / Egyptian	4	Egypt		Greenlandic	3	Greenland	
Arabic / Iraqi	2	Iraq		**Guabibo / Sukuani**	**1**	**Colombia**	
Arabic / Palestinian	5	Palestine		Guajajara	1	Brasilia	
Arabic / Tunisian	3	Tunisia		**Gupapuynu**	**1**	**Australia**	
Armenian	2	Iran		**Gur / Kabre**	**1**	**Togo**	
Ashanti / Twi	**1**	**Ghana**		**Hausa**	**1**	**N. Nigeria**	
Bahasa Indonesian	2	Indonesia		Hebrew	2	Israel	
Baka	**1**	**S.E. Cameroon**		Hindi	6	N. India	
Balinese	1	Indonesia		Hungarian	3	Hungary	
Bambara	**1**	**Mali**		Icelandic	2	Iceland	
Bamilèke	**1**	**Ivory Coast**		Italian	4	Italy	
Bassa	**1**	**Cameroon**		Italian / Venetian	1	Italy / Venice	
Bengali	3	Bangladesh		Japanese	3	Japan	
Bété	**1**	**Ivory Coast**		Javanese	1	Indonesia	
Bhili	4	W. India		Kabyle (Berber)	1	Algeria	
Boran / Galla	**1**	**Kenya**		Kannada	1	S. India	
Bulgarian	3	Bulgaria		Kashmiri	3	N. India	
Catalan	1	Spain		Kazhak	2	Kazakhstan	
Central Bontoc	1	Philippines / Luzon		**Khmer**	**1**	**Cambodia**	
Chagga	**1**	**Tanzania**		**Kikongo**	**1**	**Congo**	
Chanti	3	N.W. Russia		Kirghiz	2	Kyrgyzstan	
Chichewa	**1**	**Zambia**		**Kisuahili**	**2**	**Kenya**	
Chinese	4	China / Peking		Komi	2	Russia	
Chinese / Taiwan	2	China (Taiwan)		Konkani	1	S. India	
Croatian	3	Yugoslavia / Croatia		Korean	2	Korea	
Czech	2	Czech Republic		Kumauni	2	N. India	
Douala	**1**	**Cameroon**		Kurdish	3	Iran	
Dutch	5	Netherlands		Ladakhi	2	N. India	
Eipo / Mek	**1**	**New Guinea**		Lakota	1	USA	
English / British	5	England		**Lamutic / Ewenic**	**1**	**Russia**	
English / American	5	USA		**Laotic**	**2**	**Laos**	
Estonian	1	Estonia		**Lingalla**	**1**	**Congo**	
Ewe	**1**	**Togo**		**Luo**	**1**	**Kenya**	
Finnish	2	Finland		Macedonian	2	Macedonia	
French	4	France		**Malagasy**	**1**	**Madagascar**	
Fulfulde	**1**	**Chad**		Malayalam	1	S. India	

Mansi	2	N.W. Russia
Lamutic / Ewenic	1	Russia
Marathi	1	India
Marwari	4	W. India (Barmer)
Marwari	3	W. India (Jodhpur)
Mongolian	2	Mongolia
Naga / Angami	1	N.E. India
Navajo	1	USA
Neapolitan	1	Italy
Nenets	2	N.W. Siberia
Nepali	2	Nepal
Newari	2	Nepal
Njanumarda	**1**	**Australia**
Norwegian	3	Norway
Oriya	1	E. India
Ossetic	1	S. Russia
Pashtu	2	Afghanistan
Persian / Dari	2	Afghanistan
Persian / Farsi	6	Iran
Peul	**1**	**Tschad**
Polish	2	Poland
Portuguese	1	N. Brazil
Portuguese	4	Portugal
Punjabi	3	N. India
Quechua	1	Peru
Russian	5	Russia
Samoan	1	Samoa

Shoric	1	W. Russia
Sicilian	1	Sicily
Sindhi (Barmer)	2	W. India
Singhalese	2	Sri Lanka
Slovenian	3	Slovenia
Spanish	2	Argentina
Spanish	4	Spain
Spanish	1	Costa Rica
Tamang	1	Nepal
Tamil	1	S. India
Telugu	1	S. India
Temne	**1**	**Sierra Leone**
Thai	1	Thailand
Tibetan	1	Tibet / China
Tigre	**1**	**Ethiopia**
Toba	1	Argentina
Toba Batak	1	Indonesia / Borneo
Tongan	1	Tonga
Tshiluba	**1**	**Congo**
Tulu	1	S. India
Tumbuka	**1**	**Zambia**
Turkish	5	Turkey
U'wa	**1**	**Colombia**
Urdu	4	Pakistan
Vietnamese	1	Vietnam
Yakutic	1	Russia / Yacutia

Appendix II

Examples of metaphors and metonyms indicating shameful feelings in some languages.

Armenian:	amantchouchounits		karmrav			
Literal	from shame		become red			
Translation	he/she became red with shame					

Bahasa Indonesia:	karena	dia	malu	mukanya	menjadi	merah
Literal:		because	he is	ashamed	his face	is	red
Translation:	his face is red because he is ashamed					

Balinese:	gobane	barak	ulian	lek	
Literal:	face	red	because	shame	
Translation:	his face turned red because of shame				

Bengali: notun borer shaathe chokh   miliye   bouer mukh lojjaae laal hoe gaelo
Literal: new groom's   with   eyes having met bride's face shame red became
                                                    shyness with
Translation: the bride blushed when her eyes met those of her new groom

Bulgarian: potscherwenjawam   ot   sram
Literal: becoming red   with   shame
Translation: he/she turned red with shame

Chinese: ta bei shangsi dang zhong piping   jiu   lian   hong se
Literal: he is head/boss in public   criticized therefore face red colour
Translation: because the head/boss was criticized in public his face turned red

Croatian: pocrvenelo mu je lice od   stida
Literal: becomes red him is face with shame
Translation: his face became red with shame

Greenlandic: kanngutsikkami   aapillerpoq
Literal: shame   red
Translation: he/she turned red because of shame

Hungarian: vörös, mint a   paprika
Literal: red   as   the   paprika
Translation: he/she is red as a paprika (from shame or rage)

Kashmiri: washlyok sa vits watse   tember
Literal: shame he with became   copper-coloured
Translation: his face became copper-coloured with shame

Toba: napagaaqtec cha' aye   ncoq
Literal: he/she blushes because he/she is ashamed
Translation: he blushes because he is ashamed

Toba-Batak: marrara   bohina   ala   tarboto   ibana manangko
Literal: becoming red his face because recognized   he   a thief
Translation: he blushed when he was recognized as a thief

Turkish: utanmaktan kipkirmizi   oldu
Literal: shame from very red   has became
Translation: he/she turned red because of shame

Yakutic: kybystan   sireje   kytarda
Literal: having been ashamed face   became red
Translation: his face became red because he has been ashamed

Part V

Metaperspectives

13   Culture and development

Michael Cole

This chapter addresses the role of culture in development by considering a question that I have been thinking about for some time without coming to any fixed conclusion: *Do any new principles of development appear once a child is born?* As a means of motivating this discussion, I begin by asking the reader to consider the following statements by leading developmental theorists. Some of these statements imply strongly that no new principles of development are introduced following birth. Others imply that the change in environmental conditions has a significant impact on the process of development. Still others are ambiguous on the matter:

1. 'Child psychology should be regarded as the embryology of organic as well as mental growth, up to the beginning of...the adult level' (Piaget and Inhelder, 1969, p. vii).
2. 'Neither physical nor cultural environment contains any architectonic arrangements like the mechanisms of growth. Culture accumulates; it does not grow' (Gesell 1945, p. 358).
3. 'The human being is immersed right from birth in a social environment which affects him just as much as his physical environment. Society, even more, in a sense, than the physical environment, changes the very structure of the individual... Every relation between individuals (from two onwards) literally modifies them...' (Piaget, 1973, p. 156).
4. 'A new level of organization is in fact nothing more than a new relevant context' (Waddington, 1947).
5. The levels of generalization in [a child's use of words] correspond strictly to the level of social interaction. Any new level in the child's generalization signifies a new level in the possibility for social interaction (Vygotsky, 1956, p. 423).

How are we to decide the truth of these various statements? Could it really be the case that emergence from the mother into the social group and the acquisition of culture introduce no new principles of human development? And if new principles of development emerge, if the process of development itself changes,

The preparation of this chapter was made possible by a grant from the Spencer Foundation.

in what do these changes consist? I will examine these issues chronologically, beginning with principles of development widely used to account for change between conception and birth.

Embryogenesis

It may seem odd to begin a discussion of culture and development with embryogenesis, a period when it is generally thought that culture plays no role. I choose this starting point because, in my view, individual human development, from before the beginning, is an emergent process resulting from transactions among the so-called factors of development parsed as biological, social and cultural, although the precise nature of these transactions varies throughout ontogeny. Moreover, many developmentalists, as the first quotation from Piaget and Inhelder indicates, believe that embryology provides the model for all that is to follow.

When fertilized, the egg released by the female is the largest human cell, many times the size of a normal body cell, encased within a cell wall called the *zona pellucida*. Almost immediately the zygote undergoes a process of cell division in which the single, relatively gigantic cell divides, and redivides. Each division results in identical-looking cells that are successively smaller. Eventually the zygote becomes packed with such identical cells each the size of an average body cell.

Up to this time, the zygote is a world unto its own, feeding on its own internal matter. But once the zygote has exhausted its internal resources, it must begin to take in nutrients from the outside, from its context. No sooner does this process of interaction of organism and environment begin than the heretofore identical cells of the zygote begin to differentiate. Cells at the periphery of the zygote, through which the nutrients crucial to further growth must pass, begin to look different from the cells near the centre of the zygote. 'A new stage of development' takes place: a blastocyst emerges as a consequence of the fact that cells at its borders make possible new transactions with its environment. Here we see the earliest manifestation of development as differentiation and reintegration. It is an epigenetic process arising from interaction of organism and environment. The mechanism that embryologists have proposed as the stimulus for the specific path of differentiation is called induction. While the mechanisms of induction continue to be the subject of research and theorizing, the overall process illustrates the pattern of change which the embryologist C. H. Waddington (1947) was referring to when he remarked that 'A new level of organization is in fact nothing more than a new relevant context.' A blastocyst is clearly a new level of organization; just as clearly, its development is part and parcel of a new relevant context. In a similar manner, when the blastocyst becomes attached to the wall of the uterus and is transformed into a foetus, a new system of transactions emerges in which a new structure, the umbilical cord, emerges as a 'third part' mediating between organism and uterus.

Another important question of embryonic development is the role of the embryo's activity in the process. Beginning with the first heartbeat early in embryogenesis, the organism becomes and remains active until it dies. However, the functions of this activity are still debated. Viktor Hamburger (1957), an embryologist, asserted

One can make the general statement that organization and structure develop in forward reference to functional activity, but without its participation as a determining agent. Organs are built up first, and thereafter they are taken into use. (p. 54)

Others disagree, arguing that without such activity as, for example, wing movement in embryonic chicks, more complicated neural circuits needed for coordinated movement could not develop adequately. Chickens curarized in early embryology are deprived of the possibility of pruning the profusion of nerve cells that are produced in the brain and spinal cord, rendering them immobile when no longer curarized (Hofer, 1981). Activity may have forward reference, but such anticipation does not appear to be functionless.

Postnatal development

Perhaps nowhere is Waddington's aphorism about the co-development of organism and context more obvious than at birth. Severing the umbilical cord induces a reversal in the direction of the baby's blood flow. Neonates are no longer bound to their environments through a *direct* biological connection. Rather, even essential biological processes occur *indirectly* – they become mediated by the baby's social and cultural environment. The baby's food no longer arrives predigested through the mother's bloodstream. It must now obtain sustenance either through the modification of sucking, grasping and rooting reflexes, in reciprocal interactions with mother, or it must be fed food that has been 'pre-pared'. The process of eating prepared food is neither purely biological nor purely natural. The sociocultural environment of the infant, which was largely muted by the buffering built into prenatal development, becomes an essential aspect of the organism's context, and the interactions that produce development become the special hybrid of natural and sociocultural that is the human way of life.

Following birth, changes in babies' impact on their environments are no less marked than changes in the way the environment acts on them. They make urgent, vocal demands on their caretakers. They become social actors who re-order the social relations among the people around them. At birth, *development becomes a co-constructive process* in which *both* the environment *and* the child are active agents. And after birth, the transactions between baby and context are mediated in a quite obvious way by culture.

Considerations such as these led Hamburger to argue that:

> The ways and mechanisms by which new levels of maturation are achieved are fundamentally different for the embryo and the human person. The most striking contrast is perhaps in the role which the environment plays in the two processes. (1957, p. 53)

Unfortunately, he offers no concrete evidence of how the mechanisms of development change, except to argue that the postnatal environment accentuates individual differences to 'bring them to their full realization' (p. 53). Given the theme of this chapter, I want to focus on that part of the environment referred to as cultural, and its role in mediating the relations between individuals and their social environments.

Culture as the species-specific medium of human development

Over two decades ago Raymond Williams (1976) commented that 'Culture is one of the two or three most complicated words in the English language' (p. 76). Among other resources, he could refer to Alfred Kroeber and Clyde Kluckhohn's classic monograph, *Culture: a critical review of concepts and definitions* (1952/63) that offered more than 250 different definitions. So, the topic needs some discussion here to avoid difficult-to-detect misunderstandings.

In its most general sense, the term 'culture' is used to refer to the socially inherited body of past human accomplishments that serves as the resources for current life of a social group (D'Andrade, 1997). A good starting point for my own view of culture is provided by Kroeber and Kluckhohn's omnibus definition:

> Culture consists of patterns, explicit and implicit, of and for behavior acquired and transmitted by symbols, constituting the distinctive achievements of human groups, including their embodiment in artifacts; the essential core of culture consists of traditional (i.e. historically derived and selected) ideas and especially their attached values; cultural systems may on the one hand be considered as products of action, on the other as conditioning elements of further action. (1952, p. 181)

The major modification I introduce into this classic view is to broaden the definition of artefacts to make them synonymous with what Kroeber and Kluckhohn refer to as culture's essential core. According to this view, which traces its genealogy back to Hegel and Marx, and which is found in many contemporary sources, an artefact is an aspect of the material world that has been modified over the history of its incorporation into goal-directed human action. By virtue of the changes wrought in the process of their creation and use, artefacts are *simultaneously ideal (conceptual) and material.* They are ideal in that their material form has been shaped by their participation in the interactions of which they were previously a part and which they mediate in the present.

This conception of artefacts extends to what Wartofsky (1973) refers to as secondary artefacts, representations of primary artefacts and their modes of use. Secondary artefacts play a central role in preserving and transmitting the kinds of social inheritance referred to as recipes, beliefs, norms, conventions and the like. This extension brings the mental entities psychologists refer to as scripts and schemas into contact with the notion of artefact in a manner akin to Bartlett's (1932) notion of schemas as conventions, which are both material practices and mental structures (this convergence was first pointed out to me by Derek Edwards and David Middleton, see Edwards and Middleton, 1986).

I cannot elaborate here on this conception of culture (see Cole, 1996, for a fuller discussion). What it produces is an understanding of culture as a structured, artefact-saturated medium that is simultaneously ideal and material, inside the head and in the humanly transformed environment, that serves to coordinate newborns with their caretakers within the overall circumstances of the social group. It transforms our notion of the transactional processes involved in development by adding a 'third force' to the ordinary dichotomous view of development as a transactional process.

A very similar view of culture and its role in mediating human activity is summarized by Edwin Hutchins (1995) in the context of his efforts to describe the role of culture in cognition through connectionist modelling, which treats each of the three factors that enter into cognition as representational structures:

Our inventory of representational structure includes *natural structure* in the environment, *internal structure* in the individuals, and *artefactual structure* in the environment. Artefactual structure is a bridge between internal structures. Artefacts may provide the link between internal structures in one individual and those in another individual (as in the case of communication), or between one set of internal structures in an individual and another set of internal structures in that same individual (as is the case in using written records as a memory aid, for example). Internal structures provide bridges both between successive artefactual structures and between natural and artefactual structures. (pp. 161–2)

Cognition, from this point of view, is conceived of as 'the propagation of representational state across representational media that may be internal to or external to individual minds' (p. 160).

Whether starting from the heritage of Hegel and Marx or Hutchins, we arrive at a notion of culture as a medium of coordination and development and as a process of coordinating structures, in a tripartite process.

Examples from early ontogeny

The role of cultural mediation in coordinating individuals with their environments is evident from the first days of postnatal life. The earliest, essential condition for continued development once neonates have been 'precipitated into the group' is that the newcomer must be incorporated into the group's daily life. This incorporation requires that adults are able to accumulate enough resources to accommodate the newcomer while the newcomer gets enough food, care and warmth to continue developing. Super and Harkness (1986) refer to this process as creating a 'developmental niche' for the child. The process of child-group coordination within developmental niches is both universal and culturally variable.

The Ache, a hunter-gatherer people of eastern Paraguay, arrange for their children under 3 years of age to spend 80–100 per cent of their time in direct physical contact with their mothers and are almost never seen more than three feet away (Kaplan and Dove, 1987). A major reason for this form of coordination is that the Ache do not create clearings in the forest when they stop to make camp. Rather, they remove just enough ground cover to sit down upon, leaving roots, trees and bushes more or less where they find them. In consequence, mothers either carry their infants or keep them within arms reach.

Quechua mothers also keep their infants close to them, but in a different way and for different reasons. The Quechua inhabit the 12,000-foot altiplano of Peru, where oxygen is scarce, humidity is extremely low and the temperature reaches freezing an average of 340 days a year (Tronick, Thomas and Daltabuit, 1994). Quechua newborns spend almost all of their time in a specially constructed *manta pouch*, constructed to seal off the child from the outside so that no part of the child's body is exposed except when being changed. Tronick and his colleagues propose that the warmer, more humid, and more stable environment in the pouch helps the infant to conserve energy, reducing the number of calories needed for growth in an environment poor in nutritional resources.

The way in which culturally regulated childcare practices are designed to coordinate infants and caretakers can also be highlighted by contrasting the way parents organize their children's sleeping and eating patterns in the process known as 'getting the baby on a schedule'. This process, an essential part of creating the developmental niche, requires rearrangement of the child's social context as a precondition for its continued development. Bruner (1982) refers to such routines that occur in recurring social events as 'formats', rulebound microcosm(s) in which the adult and child *do* things to and with each other. In its most general sense, it is the instrument of patterned human interaction. Since formats pattern communicative interaction between infant and caretaker before lexico-grammatical speech begins, they are crucial vehicles in the passage from communication to language. Bruner's notion of format is very similar to the way in which Nelson (1981, 1986) talks of generalized event schemas called *scripts*, 'sequentially organized structures of causally and temporally linked acts with the actors and objects specified in the most general way'.

In effect, formats or scripts are event-level cultural artefacts, which are embodied in the vocabulary and habitual actions of adults and which act as structured media within which children can experience co-variation of language and action while remaining generally coordinated with culturally organized forms of behaviour that form the process Hutchins refers to as the 'propagation of structure across representational media'.

Relating past and future: the non-linearity of cultural mediation

With respect to embryogenesis, we have a pretty good idea of the way that the past is related to the future and the present. The genetic code assembled from the past when sperm and egg unite at conception provides the current and future biological constraints within which the biological process of development can take place. It is in this sense that the past enters the future in order that the end can be in the beginning.

There appears to be an analogous set of temporal relationships when the cultural past and present greet the newborn as its cultural future. The name of the cultural mechanism that brings 'the end into the beginning' is *prolepsis*, meaning 'the representation of a future act or development as being presently existing' (*Webster's Dictionary*, 1991). Prolepsis operates throughout ontogeny, but I shall briefly describe only two examples.

Prolepsis: a cultural mechanism of induction?

A basic fact about human nature stemming from the symbolic character of cultural mediation is that when neonates enter the world, they are already the objects of adult, culturally conditioned, interpretation.

In the 1970s paediatrician Aidan Macfarlane recorded conversations between obstetricians and parents at their children's birth. He found that the parents almost immediately start to talk about and to the child. Their comments arise in part from phylogenetically determined anatomical differences between males and females and in part from culturally conditioned experiences they have encountered in their own lives. Typical comments include 'I shall be worried to death when she's eighteen' or 'She can't play rugby'. Putting aside our negative response to the sexism in these remarks, we see that the adults interpret the phylogenetic-biological characteristics of the child in terms of their own past (cultural) experience. In the experience of English men and women living in the 1950s, it could be considered 'common knowledge' that girls do not play rugby and that when they enter adolescence they will be the object of boys' sexual attention, putting them at various kinds of risk. Using this information derived from their cultural past, parents assume that the world will be very much for their daughter as it has been for them and project a probable future for the child, which shapes their current behaviour and thereby their child's experience.

This process is depicted in figure 13.1 by following the arrows from the mother → (remembered) cultural past of the mother → (imagined) cultural *future* of the baby → present adult treatment of the baby.

Two features of this system of transformations are important for understanding the contribution of culture in constituting development. First, and most obviously, we see prolepsis in action: The parents represent the future in the present. Secondly, we see mutual transformations between the ideal and material sides of an artefact (in this case, beliefs about girls, soccer, and society). The parents' (purely *ideal*) recollection of their past and (purely *ideal*) imagination of their child's future becomes a fundamental *materialized* constraint on the child's life experiences in the present. This rather abstract, non-linear process of transformation gives rise to the well-known phenomenon that even adults totally ignorant of the actual gender of a newborn will treat the baby quite differently depending upon its symbolic/cultural 'gender'. For example, they bounce 'boy' infants (those wearing blue diapers) and attribute 'manly' virtues to them while they treat 'girl' infants (those wearing pink diapers) in a gentle manner and attribute beauty and sweet temperaments to them (Rubin et al., 1974).

Macfarlane's example also motivates the special emphasis placed on the *social* origins of higher psychological functions by cultural-historical psychologists (Cole, 1988; Rogoff, 1990; Valsiner, 1988; Vygotsky, 1987; Wertsch, 1985). Humans are social in a sense that is different from the sociability of other species. *Only* a culture-using human being can 'reach into' the cultural past, project it into the future and then 'carry' that conceptual future 'back' into the present to create the sociocultural environment of the newcomer's development.

Space does not permit me to enumerate, let alone analyse, the myriad examples of prolepsis in later development. Bare mention of a few will have to suffice.

Note that in asserting the importance of the social world on the children's development, Piaget sets age 2 as the point at which 'Every relation between individuals literally modifies them'. This is also the time when, according to Vygotsky, children's acquisition of language creates a new level in the generalizations they can make, signifying a new level in the possibility for social interaction. I have already mentioned one of the conditions, in addition to biological integrity of the organism, that appears necessary to the acquisition of language: coordination in the kinds of scripted events Bruner (1982) refers to

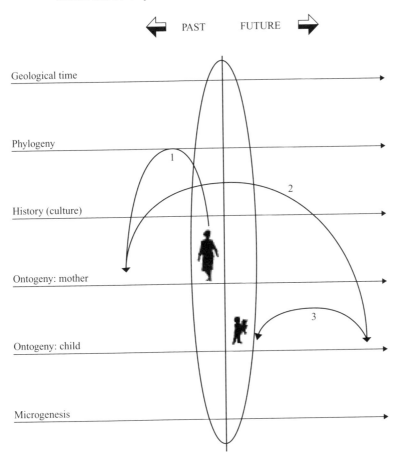

Figure 13.1   Looking backward, looking forward.

Notes: The horizontal lines represent time scales corresponding to the history of the physical universe, the history of life on earth (phylogeny), the history of human beings on earth (cultural-historical time), the life of the individual (ontogeny), and the life of moment-to-moment lived experience (microgenesis). The vertical ellipse represents the event of a child's birth. The distribution of cognition in time is traced sequentially into (1) the mother's memory of her past, (2) the mother's imagination of the future of the child, and (3) the mother's subsequent behavior. In this sequence, the ideal aspect of culture is transformed into its material form as the mother and other adults structure the child's experience to be consistent with what they imagine to be the child's future identity.

as formats, Savage-Rumbaugh et al. (1993) refer to as 'interpersonal routines' and Nelson (1981) refers to as scripts. Rommetveit (1974) has argued that prolepsis is an essential characteristic of intersubjectivity in such scripted activities that makes language possible. Language-mediated interpersonal routines allow conditions in which speakers can presuppose shared knowledge that has not yet been introduced into the interaction, but which is essential to making their utterances interpretable.

Göncü (1993), following Rommetveit (1974) as well as Stone and Wertsch (1984), shows the crucial role of prolepsis in the development of the forms of language-mediated interpersonal routines needed for symbolic play. Tobin, Wu and Davidson (1989) show how prolepsis operates to structure cultural differences in Japanese and American preschool classroom social structures and interactions. Newman, Griffin and Cole (1989) analyse the operation of prolepsis in the organization of classroom science lessons. In all such cases, the structure of social interactions that provide the proximal environment for children's development is constrained by imagined futures, read back into the present as material constraints on development.

Interweaving of phylogenetic and cultural lines of development

For my final example I want to concentrate on a topic which serves to illustrate how the cultural-historical view that I have been seeking to develop can be brought together fruitfully with views that do not ordinarily include cultural mediation as a central mechanism of development.

It is now a standard critique of cultural-psychological approaches to development that, contrary to their own principles, they ignore the crucial contributions of phylogenetic constraints on development (for representative critiques, see Moll, 1994; Smith, 1996; Wertsch, 1985). To make the discussion concrete, I have chosen the development of mathematical thinking as the target domain because there is sufficient evidence about the co-action of phylogeny, ontogeny and cultural organization of thinking in this domain to provide an integrated picture of development and culture's role in it.

Phylogenetic precursors

Research has demonstrated that some birds and non-human primates possess some rudimentary knowledge of number (Klein and Starkey, 1987). For example, Sarah Boysen (1993) has demonstrated that when training in number-related skills is integrated into a way of life that is rich in interpersonal routines, and training grows out of a pre-established relationship based on play, a chimpanzee raised by human beings is capable not only of understanding one-to-one correspondence but can learn to count, to add and even to solve arithmetic problems similar to those achieved by 3-year-old children.

I interpret these data on the phylogeny of arithmetic to indicate that elements of the form of activity we call mathematical thinking can be achieved by nonhuman primates raised in a cultural environment that includes them in a humanlike way. These results fully accord with evidence concerning language in chimpanzees. What then of human ontogeny?

Early ontogeny

Under the influence of Piaget, developmental psychologists spent a great many years assuming that mathematical abilities make their earliest appearance late in infancy as infants become capable of mentally representing an absent object.

Current research leaves no doubt that by the middle of the first year of life, more than a year before they will be able to engage in a simple conversation, babies are able to respond to numerosity and can perform elementary arithmetic operations on a small arrays of objects (Gallistel and Gelman, 1991; Wynn, 1992).

For example, Karen Wynn (1992) showed 4-month-old babies a number of events designed to assess their sensitivity to number and elementary number operations. First a mouse doll was placed on an empty stage while the baby watched. Then a screen was raised to hide the doll from the baby's view. Next a hand carrying an identical doll moved behind the screen and withdrew, without the doll. The screen was then lowered. In half the cases there were two dolls behind the screen (the expected outcome). In the other half of the cases there was only one doll (the unexpected outcome). The babies looked longer at the unexpected outcome. Additional experiments showed that the babies expected $2-1$ to be 1 and $3-2$ to be 1.

In short, it appears that as near to birth as it can be tested for, there is evidence for the presence of what Rochel Gelman (1990) refers to as 'skeletal principles' which provide initial constraints upon which later mathematical understanding can be built. The key argument for the necessity of such constraints is made by Gelman in the following terms:

it is necessary to grant infants and/or young children domain-specific organizing structures that direct attention to the data that bear on the concepts and facts relevant to a particular cognitive domain. The thesis is that the mind brings domain-specific organizing principles to bear on the assimilation and structuring of facts and concepts, that learners can narrow the range of possible interpretations of the environment because they have implicit assumptions that guide their search for relevant data. (p. 4)

The question then becomes, under what conditions will the primitive abilities of the young infant be realized in appropriate behaviours that are a part of its everyday life?

Although there is only spotty evidence of early number-related knowledge in children growing up in societies where mathematical knowledge is not highly elaborated, what little evidence we have indicates that the density of social practices involving the use of mathematical knowledge begins to affect development of mathematical thinking very early. In some cultures, at least, it appears that adult knowledge of mathematical principles does not develop beyond the capacities seen in young infants. Arithmetic operations confined to the 'one, two, many' variety appear to suffice (Lancy, 1983).

Geoffrey Saxe (1991, 1994) studied the development of counting and elementary arithmetic operations (comparison of relative quantity, simple addition) among Oksapmin children of New Guinea who use their body parts as a counting device, and children learn to use this device at an early age. According to Saxe, traditionally the Oksapmin had little need to engage in computations with numbers. When they traded goods within the traditional cultural framework, they ordinarily used various one-for-one or one-for-many exchanges that involved counting, but did not use calculational procedures. Children's ability to use counting to mediate comparisons of number of objects in two arrays or to carry out simple addition is slow to develop. Saxe observed actual arithmetic calculations only among children who began attending school and adults who became involved with the money economy of New Guinea.

These studies fit nicely with the idea that culture builds upon primitive, universal mathematical knowledge based upon skeletal principles specific to this cognitive domain depending upon their centrality to the culturally organized, scripted, formatted activities of everyday life. But they do not tell us much about the dynamics of the process by which children come to acquire the knowledge embodied in the cultural system used by adults for whom new cultural practices have brought the system into more widespread use. Granted the generally accepted view of cultural psychologists that cognitive development occurs within scripted events and that children must actively appropriate the cultural tools of their society in the process of development, how does one make available for analysis the ways in which skeletal principles and cultural practices combine in the process of development?

Research by Saxe, Guberman and Gearhast on the development of arithmetic knowledge among 30–48-month-old American children illustrates how these dynamics work in a manner that links up nicely with the idea of prolepsis introduced earlier and the notion of a zone of proximal development from the Russian cultural-historical tradition (Saxe et al., 1987).

From work on early arithmetic understanding such as that described above, Saxe and his colleagues identified four kinds of numerical tasks (Saxe refers to these tasks as cognitive *functions*) that American children are capable of achieving in early childhood: naming, counting and cardinality (using last count name as the name of the set), comparing and reproducing sets and using arithmetical operations to transform numerical values. They also expected to see various cognitive *forms*, that is strategies for achieving an accurate count of a set or for adding two sets together.

The research began with interviews of mothers about the everyday practices in which issues bearing on number and arithmetic arose. Maternal responses were analysed according to the numerical functions involved, such as identifying and pushing elevator buttons or counting coins, and how these functions were carried out. These data revealed regular age-related changes in the level of arithmetic tasks which children encountered and accomplished.

Next the investigators sought to observe the dynamics of change. They video-taped mothers and children engaging in practices that required either a low-level function such as determining the total number of objects in an array or a higher-level function such as reproducing the total number in one array with a new array. Analyses of the videotapes showed the development of more complex functions and how mothers and children adjusted to each other as subgoals of the task emerged.

For example, in the number reproduction task, mothers were given an array containing three or nine pictures of the Sesame Street Cookie Monster and asked to instruct their child to put as many pennies in a cup as there were Cookie Monsters in the array. Mothers of older or more competent children tried to structure the task in terms of its highest-level goals, while mothers of younger or less-competent children provided instructions focused on simpler goals.

The highest-level instructions simply repeated the overall goal, 'Get just the same number of pennies as there are Cookie Monsters'. If the child had difficulty, the mother might say 'Get nine pennies for the Cookie Monster'. If that failed, the mother might ask 'How many cookie monsters are there?' or 'Count the Cookie Monsters'. When all else failed, 'Get nine pennies' might be the instruction. Saxe (1994) summarizes the pattern of results concerning the way new functions arise in the course of this activity:

Mothers were adjusting their goal-related directives to their children's understandings and task-related accomplishments and...children were adjusting their goal-directed activities to their mother's efforts to organize the task. Further, as children's ability to produce numerical goals of different complexity levels changed with development, they were afforded new opportunities for creating more complex numerical environments. (p. 147)

Research focused on many different activities in different societies supports the conclusion that the principles found in this example operate quite broadly (Saxe, 1994).

Results such as these have produced what appears to be a growing consensus on a model of development that combines the idea of innate skeletal constraints with the idea of cultural mediation in cultural organized, scripted activities.

For example, Lauren Resnick (1994) offers what she calls a 'situated ratio-nalist' synthesis of the cultural historical and skeletal principles points of view. By 'situated' Resnick means a loose collection of theories and perspectives that propose a contextualized (and therefore, particularist) and social view of

316 *Michael Cole*

the nature of thinking and learning. By rationalist she means the theorists who claim a priori biological constraints on the development of domain-specific knowledge (Carey and Gelman, 1991).

Resnick unites the ideas of sociocultural and biological constraints in the concept of a 'prepared structure'.

> Individuals develop their abilities in a domain specific manner, in each situation, on the basis of their prepared structures. These prepared structures are both biological and sociocultural in origin. What changes with development is their relative contributions. (1994, p. 479)

This idea, which appears similar in its essentials to Gelman's, is echoed by several scholars, including Giyoo Hatano (1995) and Howard Gardner (1991).

A tentative summation

The tentative conclusion I would like to draw from this discussion is that it is at least heuristically useful to consider the possibility that all of the statements about development I quoted at the beginning of this chapter are true. Throughout development we see the principles of development present in embryology at work. Development, at least from the time when the zygote begins to interact with the intra-uterine environment, is an epigenetic process of the emergence of more complex structures in which each new level of organization is associated with a new relevant context and a new form of mediation between the individual and at least one other human being.

In the effort to ferret out essential differences in the process after birth my thoughts return repeatedly to the properties of the cultural medium and the forms of interaction which it mediates. During embryogenesis it seems as if phylogenetic/biological processes mediate cultural influences while, following birth, the terms of this mediational process appear to shift. The wing movements of the embryonic chick are certainly anticipatory and the role of the environment as an inducer of differentiation clearly provides the antipode of the epigenetic process. But play, for example, seems anticipatory in a quite different way, and the kinds of moves made by mothers interacting with their children to induce higher levels of mathematical reasoning appear proleptic in a way that the induction of a blastocyst through interaction of the zygote with the intra-uterine environment does not.

In so far as the processes to development are different, it is to the properties of culture and the capacity/requirement of humans to acquire culture that I think we must look to arrive at a more satisfactory answer to my starting question. In so far as it is dominated by phylogenetic influences, development is a Darwinian process of natural selection operating on the random variation of genetic combinations created at conception. But cultural change operates according to a different set of principles: cultural variations are not randomly generated, they are, rather, descended from the successful adaptations of prior generations passed down extrasomatically. While natural selection has the final say, in so far as human behaviour is mediated through culture it is 'distorted' by a Lamarckian principle of evolution. In acquiring culture (and especially, as both Piaget and Vygotsky emphasize, with the acquisition of culture's most flexible form, language), culture becomes a 'second nature' which makes development a goal-directed process in a way in which phylogenetic change is not. As I have argued elsewhere (Cole, 1996), human beings are hybrids. This hybrid nature is central to the process of postnatal development in a way that is not true before birth. Understanding this hybridity is, I suggest, necessary in order to understand if and how the principles of development change once children leave the womb and are precipitated into the social group.

REFERENCES

Bartlett, F. C. (1932). *Remembering*. Cambridge: Cambridge University Press.
Boysen, S. T. (1993). Counting in chimpanzees. In S. T. Boysen and E. J. Capaldi (eds.), *The development of numerical competence: animal and human models*. Hillsdale, NJ: Lawrence Erlbaum. pp. 39–57.
Bruner, J. S. (1982). Formats of language acquisition. *American Journal of Semiotics*, 1, 1–16.
  (1990). *Acts of meaning*. Cambridge, MA: Harvard University Press.
Carey, S. and Gelman, R. (eds.) (1991). *The epigenesis of mind: essays on biology and cognition*. Hillsdale, NJ: Lawrence Erlbaum.
Cole, M. (1988). Cross-cultural research in the sociohistorical tradition. *Human Development*, 31, 137–51.
  (1996). *Cultural psychology: a once and future discipline*. Cambridge, MA: Harvard University Press.
D'Andrade, R. (1997). *Culture. The social science encyclopedia*. London: Routledge.
Edwards, D. and Middleton, D. (1986). Conversation with Bartlett. *Quarterly Newsletter of the Laboratory of Comparative Human Cognition*, 8, 79–89.
Gallistel, R. and Gelman, R. (1991). Preverbal and verbal counting and computation. *Cognition*, 44, 43–74.
Gardner, H. (1991). *The unschooled mind: how children think and how schools should teach*. New York: Basic Books.
Gelman, R. (1990). Structural constraints on cognitive development. Introduction to a special issue of *Cognitive Science*, 14, 79–106.
Gesell, A. (1945). *The embryology of behavior*. New York: Harper and Row.
Göncü, A. (1993). Development of intersubjectivity in social pretend play. *Human Development*, 36, 185–98.
Hamburger, V. (1957). The concept of development in biology. In D. B. Harris (ed.), *The concept of development*. Minneapolis: University of Minnesota Press, pp. 49–58.
Hatano, G. (1995). Cultural psychology of development: the need for numbers and narratives. Annual Meeting of the Society for Research in Child Development, April.

Hofer, M. A. (1981). *The roots of human behavior: an introduction to the psychobiology of early development.* San Francisco: Freeman.

Hutchins, E. (1995). *Cognition in the wild.* Cambridge, MA: MIT Press.

Kaplan, H. and Dove, H. (1987). Infant development among the Ache of eastern Paraguay. *Developmental Psychology, 23,* 190–8.

Klein, A. and Starkey, P. (1987). The origins and development of numerical cognition. In J. A. Sloboda and D. Rogers (eds.), *Cognitive processes in mathematics.* Oxford: Clarendon Press, pp. 39–57.

Kroeber, A. and Kluckhohn, C. (1952/63). *Culture: a critical review or concepts and definitions.* New York: Vintage Books.

Lancy, D. F. (1983). *Cross-cultural studies in cognition and mathematics.* New York: Academic Press.

Moll, I. (1994). Reclaiming the natural line of Vygotsky's theory of cognitive development. *Human Development, 37,* 333–42.

Nelson, K. (1981). Cognition in a script framework. In J. H. Flavell and L. Ross (eds.), *Social cognitive development.* Cambridge: Cambridge University Press, pp. 97–118.

   (1986). *Event knowledge: structure and function in development.* Hillsdale, NJ: Lawrence Erlbaum.

Newman, D., Griffin, P. and Cole, M. (1989). *The construction zone.* New York: Cambridge University Press.

Piaget, J. (1973). *The psychology of intelligence.* Totowa, NJ: Littlefield and Adams.

Piaget, J. and Inhelder, B. (1969). *The psychology of the child.* New York: Basic Books.

Resnick, L. B. (1994). Situated rationalism: biological and social preparation for learning. In L. A. Hirschfeld and S. A. Gelman (eds.), *Mapping the mind: domain specificity in cognition and culture.* New York: Cambridge University Press, pp. 474–93.

Rogoff, B. (1990). *Apprenticeship in thinking: cognitive development in social context.* New York: Oxford University Press.

Rommetveit. R. (1974). *On message structure.* London: Wiley.

Rubin, J. Z., Provezano, F. J. and Luria, Z. (1974). The eye of the beholder: parents' views on sex of newborns. *American Journal of Orthopsychiatry, 44,* 512–19.

Savage-Rumbaugh, E. S., Murphy, J., Sevcik, R. A., Brakke, K. E., Williams, S. L. and Rumbaugh, D. M. (1993). *Language comprehension in ape and child.* Monographs of the Society for Research in Child Development, 58, nos. 3–4, serial no. 233. Chicago: University of Chicago Press.

Saxe, G. B. (1991). *Culture and cognitive development.* Hillsdale, NJ: Lawrence Erlbaum.

   (1994). Studying cognitive development in sociocultural contexts: the development of practice-based approaches. *Mind, Culture, and Activity, 1,* 135–57.

Saxe, G. B., Guberman, S. R. and Gearhart, M. (1987). Social processes in early number development. *Monographs of the Society for Research in Child Development, 52,* serial no. 216.

Smith, L. (1996). With knowledge in mind: novel transformation of the learner or transformation of novel knowledge. *Human Development, 39,* 257–63.

Stone, A. and Wertsch, J. V. (1984). A social interactional analysis of learning disabilities. *Journal of Learning Disabilities, 17,* 194–9.

Super, C. M. and Harkness, S. (1986). The developmental niche: a conceptualization at the interface of society and the individual. *International Journal of Behavioral Development*, 9, 545–70.

Tobin, J. J., Wu, D. Y. H. and Davidson, D. H. (1989). *Preschool in three cultures: Japan, China, and the United States*. New Haven, CT: Yale University Press.

Tronick, E. Z., Thomas, R. B. and Daltabuit, M. (1994). The Quechua manta pouch: a caretaking practice for buffering the Peruvian infant against the multiple stresses of high altitude. *Child Development*, 65, 1005–13.

Valsiner, J. (1988). *Developmental psychology in the Soviet Union*. Bloomington: Indiana University Press.

Vygotsky, L. S. (1956). *Selected psychological investigations*. Moscow: Academy of Pedagogical Sciences Publishers.

(1987). *Thinking and speech*. New York: Plenum Press.

Waddington, C. H. (1947). *Organizers and genes*. Cambridge: Cambridge University Press.

Wartofsky, M. (1973). *Models*. Dordrecht; D. Reidel.

Webster's Ninth New Collegiate Dictionary (1991). Springfield, MA: Mirriam-Webster.

Wertsch, J. V. (1985). *Vygotsky and the social formation of mind*. Cambridge, MA: Harvard University Press.

Williams, R. (1976). *Keywords: a vocabulary of culture and society*. New York: Oxford University Press.

Wynn, K. (1992). Addition and subtraction by human infants. *Nature*, 358, 749–50.

14 Behaviour–culture relationships and ontogenetic development

Ype H. Poortinga and Karel Soudijn

In the literature a large variety of conceptualizations can be found on the how and why of differences in behaviour across cultural populations. In the first part of this chapter, we briefly review various theoretical positions, distinguishing two major dimensions. The first dimension ranges from universalism to relativism and is associated with the contrast between culture-comparative and culturalist research methods, reflected in various chapters of this book. Universalists argue predominantly from the perspective that human behaviour and understanding should be interpreted in terms of shared species-wide psychological processes. Relativists maintain that human psychological functioning, based on constructions of meaning, differs essentially across cultures. The second dimension has to do with the generality of cross-cultural differences. This dimension varies from positions in which such differences are believed to be organized in a systemlike fashion to positions in which such differences are seen as an array of loose and sporadically interconnected, historically developed cultural rules and practices.

Despite the variety of conceptualizations most authors appear to agree that psychological functioning and culture are closely and systematically linked to each other. However, valid interpretations about behaviour–culture relationships are difficult to distinguish from stereotypical convictions that reside mainly in the observer. In this chapter we argue that the field as a whole attributes larger and more systematic effects to cultural context than is merited by the available data.

We suggest that many cultural rules and practices tend to have an aspect of arbitrariness (they might just as easily have turned out to be different) and that valid explanation of cross-cultural differences due to such rules and practices is impossible. Already in this introduction we want to emphasize that the need for having *some* cultural rule has to be distinguished sharply from the question whether there is a psychological reason why a *particular* rule should be as it actually is found to be; in other words, whether there is a reason for having *this* rule over and above having *a* rule.

In order to develop an alternative to approaches presuming systematic and close relationships between culture and behaviour, we introduce the notion of discontinuities, as found in chaos theory and catastrophe theory. The essence of such discontinuities does not lie in the unpredictable and unexplainable with which they are often associated. Chaotic variations exist within certain boundaries; there are constraints that limit the extent of variation. Such boundary conditions lend themselves to analysis in terms of regularities (laws) of psychological functioning. In the space demarcated by such boundaries there are alternatives for choice, which we shall refer to as affordances. Which alternative within an available range is realized in a given instance by an actor (or a population of actors) escapes causal explanation or prediction and lends itself only to analysis by interpretive methods. Thus, the reasons why the Europeans developed a broader technology than the Chinese (Boorstin, 1985), why one group migrates and the other stays, or why one particular researcher makes an important discovery, are unclear.

Discontinuity implies a dimension of time that in psychological analysis requires an ontogenetic perspective. In this connection we address two issues. First, we refer to the classical theme of continuity versus discontinuity in ontogenetic development. In developmental research, unlike in the cross-cultural area, there is experimental evidence for discontinuities of the above-mentioned kind, at least for motor development in infancy. The second point we address is a question which follows from the perspective outlined above. This question is whether development should be seen as an increase in behaviour potential (as it usually is), or whether the empirical record perhaps fits better with a view of increasing constraints that accumulatively limit the range of affordances.

The (non-)identity of psychological functioning across cultures

In this section we describe the first of the two dimensions mentioned in the introduction, ranging from strictly universalist to strictly relativist positions. Relativists tend to see cultural practices as exemplars of underlying differences in psychological functioning, thus emphasizing cultural context as an essential and major constituent of behaviour. In such a position psychological functioning is supposed to differ qualitatively from culture to culture. For example, according to Lutz (1988) the Ifaluk in the Pacific have emotions not found in the USA; according to Wierzbicka (1999) there are in German, and only in German, essential distinctions between *Angst* (anxiety) and *Furcht* (fear), and according to Doi (1973) *amae* (passive love or dependence) is important among the Japanese, but not readily found in Westerners.

On the other hand, variations in cultural practices can also be seen as different manifestations of essentially identical underlying psychological processes. This implies that there are apparently species-wide modes of functioning, often captured with the notion of a 'psychic unity of humankind'. In such a position of universalism both cross-cultural variations in behaviour and invariance of psychological functions are explicitly allowed (Berry et al., 1992). Although recognized in writings on methodology as an essential requirement (van de Vijver and Leung, 1997b), most contributions to the cross-cultural literature do not allow an estimate of the proportion of variance on the dependent variables that can be ascribed to culture; they simply report statistically significant differences. In studies that do provide such estimates interindividual differences tend to be considerably larger than those between cultures (e.g. Poortinga and van Hemert, 2001), providing substance to the universalist perspective.

Most culture-comparative researchers do not exclude qualitative differences pointing to non-universal aspects of behaviour, and most culturalists will not deny species-wide psychological characteristics. At the same time, there are a host of concomitant differences attached to various positions on the universalism-relativism dimension, both in (meta)theoretical outlook and in methodology (for extensive reviews see Lonner and Adamopoulos, 1997, and Miller, 1997, on theory and by Greenfield, 1997, and van de Vijver and Leung, 1997a, on methodology). For example, in more relativist orientations intentionality and historicity of behaviour will be emphasized, while universalists emphasize antecedent-consequent, and often causal, relationships between culture and behaviour. With respect to methods the use of common (mainly Western) instruments across cultural groups is not acceptable for relativists, because of the presumably inescapable imposition of Western ideas (in theory and operationalization) with these methods. On the other hand, universalists tend to question the validity of research methods in qualitative research where plausibility of detailed single-case analyses rather than statistical evidence based on experimental and psychometric analyses of numerous, presumably replicable, events forms the basis for interpretation (e.g. Poortinga, 1998).

With respect to this dimension we take the position that both relativists and universalists have legitimate concerns, although they may not be easy to integrate (Poortinga, 1997). Nevertheless, there is an inherent imbalance between the universalist and the relativist pole. Manifest differences (or culture-specifics) can be explained in terms of similarities in psychological functioning (or universals). However, it is not clear how similarities in overt behaviour can be explained in terms of different psychological functions (Berry et al., 1992). In our opinion cross-cultural research should be designed to allow explicitly for the emergence of qualitative differences as well as invariance, allowing outcomes compatible with a relativist as well as a universalist perspective.

An example of such a strategy is a study of the cognitive structure of emotions in Indonesia and the Netherlands (Fontaine et al., in press). Emotion terms were collected independently in the two countries (to avoid cultural imposition) and analysed separately for the two sets of terms. In both countries a three-dimensional cognitive map was found that accounted for 90 per cent and 88 per cent of the variance, respectively. The two independent datasets were subsequently linked, using as anchor points pairs of terms that met strict criteria of translation equivalence and cognitive equivalence. It was shown that this common solution explained 87 per cent of the variance in the combined dataset. However, a few pairs of terms that met criteria for translation equivalence were found not to be cognitively equivalent (i.e. the two terms of such a pair were located at some distance from each other in the common space). With two such pairs, representing the social emotions of shame and guilt, another study was conducted in which both these emotions were found to be located somewhat further away from anger and closer to fear in Indonesia than in the Netherlands. If we contrast the findings by Fontaine and colleagues with the relativist findings mentioned before, they illustrate the contention, made among others by Mesquita and Frijda (1992), that more detailed studies focusing on a specific (kind of) event, word or practice reveal substantial cross-cultural differences, while studies that encompass a larger domain of behaviour tend to show much smaller differences.

In summary, in analyses that focus more on detail, larger effects for culture tend to be found. However, even if psychological functioning is universal to an important extent, this does not by itself invalidate relativist claims about cultural specificities; it only shifts the balance. Thus, the question whether psychological functions are identical or not identical remains dependent, at least to some extent, on the perspective that a researcher wishes to take.

The (in)coherence of culture

The second dimension outlined in the introduction concerns the question how and to what extent aspects of the behaviour repertoire that are considered characteristic of a cultural population hang together in a psychological sense. For example, Triandis (1996) has used the notion of cultural 'syndromes', referring to shared attitudes, beliefs, norms, role- and self-definitions and values of members of each culture that are organized around a theme. Cultural anthropologists, and also psychologists, tend to talk about 'cultures as systems' (e.g. Geertz, 1973; Rohner, 1984). Such systems may be rather loose, they may even be defined as open systems, but nevertheless the notion of a system cannot be applied unless the constituent elements somehow are interconnected in major ways.

The psychological coherence of cultures in cultural anthropology has not been demonstrated unambiguously. Replication studies in ethnography look so different from each other that respective ethnographers never appear to have observed approximately the same system of values, meanings or drives (cf. Freeman, 1983; Kloos, 1988). In cross-cultural psychology the presumption of coherence in cultures is reflected in postulates of broad ranging differences. In earlier days 'great-divide' theories (Segall et al., 1999) were mainly concerned with cognitive functioning. For example, Lévy-Bruhl (1926) distinguished between two types of thinking, named prelogical and logical. Luria (1971, 1976) concluded from his studies among illiterates in central Asia that they lacked the capability for abstract thinking, a mental faculty that would only develop in an appropriate social context, like the Western school environment. Subsequently this conclusion has been redressed by Cole and Scribner (Cole, 1996; Scribner, 1979; Scribner and Cole, 1981) who demonstrated that the cognitive skills found in a society meet particular features of a particular context.

More recently, major dimensions of differences in respect of social functioning and personality have gained increasing popularity (Hofstede, 1980; Smith and Bond, 1998). Best known is the dimension of individualism-collectivism, originally a value dimension, that has become associated with the most diverse phenomena, including population density and social distribution principles such as equality and equity. Collectivists resolve their conflicts in a more harmonious manner (Leung, 1988), they are more restrained when they meet someone for the first time (Gudykunst, 1983), they attach greater importance to virginity in their marriage partner (Buss, 1989), and they ascribe negative social behaviour relatively more to the situation than to the person of the actor (Miller, 1984). Triandis (1989) refers even to differences in the structure of constitutions and preference for classical music or jazz as related to individualism-collectivism. Other conceptualizations that divide the world along somewhat parallel lines are a dimension of independence versus interdependence and a distinction between more interdependent and more independent notions of the self (Greenfield, 1994; Kagitcibasi, 1990, 1996; Markus and Kitayama, 1991).

We agree that there exist important cross-cultural differences in behaviour repertoire that are associated with the gross national product (GNP) and education. However, the question arises whether these differences are best seen as reflecting internalized psychological characteristics, acquired in early socialization and organized in broad dimensions of social functioning, or as reflecting direct consequences of prevailing external circumstances (cf. Lonner and Adamopoulos, 1997). For example, hunter-gatherers appear to socialize their children towards independence (associated with individualism rather than collectivism), although they live in socially tight-knit bands with large-scale sharing of goods that is considered typical for a collectivist society (e.g. Berry et al., 1992; Hewlett and Lamb, this volume).

Moreover, there is research in which not only preparedness to share was included (as is the case in most questionnaire studies on individualism-collectivism) but also expectations about receiving from others. Hypotheses postulating differences between individualist (or independent) and collectivist (or interdependent) countries could not be confirmed. In fact, largely parallel patterns of scores emerged for collectivist and individualist samples across social categories varying from close relatives, such as children and parents, to remote categories, such as an unknown person and the state. Perceived emotional closeness explained by far the largest proportion of the differences between social categories in all the countries that were included (Fijneman et al., 1996; van den Heuvel and Poortinga, 1999). In these studies (small) cultural deviations from general patterns of scores were found mainly for categories of non-nuclear family members, such as aunts and uncles. These differences happen to coincide with actual differences in family life; in more wealthy countries interactions with and dependencies on members of one's extended family tend to be far less than in most traditional societies. Also research by Georgas and colleagues (e.g. Georgas et al., 1997) has shown that on such variables as frequency of visits and contacts by telephone with nuclear family members, more individualist and more collectivist countries did not show any substantial differences.

The 'success' of the earlier great-divide theories in cognition, as well as the recent ones on social behaviour, in our view has to do with the most common research strategy used in cross-cultural psychology. This strategy amounts to a search for convergent evidence, ignoring the need to establish discriminant validity as well (Campbell and Fiske, 1959). Some difference is observed and then tends to be interpreted in terms of an 'important' dimension that has the danger of acquiring stereotypical character. With a couple of countries and a few dependent variables the probability of finding some cross-cultural difference is much higher than the 0.05 a priori probability presumed in most statistical testing procedures. Even with one variable the probability of finding a difference is larger than this a priori value, if the measurement is affected even in a minor way by (virtually inescapable) cultural bias factors (Malpass and Poortinga, 1986).

In a classification of inferences about culture-behaviour relationships Girndt (2000) has proposed a dimension of generalization that varies from situation-specific to situation-general. Needless to say, notions of culture as a system or syndrome, and of major social dimensions, have a high generality. In contrast, cultural conventions or cultural rules are situation specific; they are also more or less directly observable and imply only limited inferences or generalizations. Rules or conventions are not limited to overt actions; they include, according to Girndt, beliefs, ways to handle problems (e.g. building stone and not wooden houses) and explanations of other rules (looking at someone while talking shows honesty and openness, versus not looking someone in the eye is a matter of respect).

This implies that in a psychological sense a culture can be seen comprising a behaviour repertoire consisting of a large set of conventions (cf. Poortinga et al., 1987). Conventions are perhaps best equated with the words in a dictionary, because of their large number. This analogy is relevant in another way: when translating terms on the basis of a dictionary one is likely to err on shades of meaning, and it can be said that in a similar fashion mismatches occur from one cultural repertoire to another, for example in intercultural communication or in the translation of questionnaires. Even if we have basic knowledge about certain rules of a society, we are likely to err in their proper application. Just as we feel most confident and at ease with our mother tongue, we are also most at ease with our own cultural repertoire and least likely to commit errors.

In summary, broad dimensions of cross-cultural differences in psychological functioning have gained credibility from convergent research strategies, which tend to leave open alternative interpretations. There are few efforts designed to examine discriminant validity, which is aimed at ruling out alternative explanations. The degree of psychological coherence of cultures ultimately is an empirical issue. However, this issue can only be resolved if the alternative is taken seriously that a culture is best seen as a large array of conventions. From our point of view there is in the current literature a tendency of overgeneralization towards broad social and personality dimensions.

Loosening culture–behaviour relationships

There is an aspect of arbitrariness to conventions, evident in many instances, including traffic rules, greeting procedures and religious beliefs. However, the content of a convention should be distinguished from the desirability to have a convention at all on how to act in a certain situation. Traffic rules provide a neat illustration. They are not needed in a world in which people move on foot with limited speed. Traffic complicated by fast mechanical devices is unthinkable without such rules. Only left- or right-hand drive is a parameter of choice, even though difficult to change once a decision has been made. Of course, conventions do not always stand on their own; one way of doing things sometimes excludes other ways; and certain beliefs are incompatible with other beliefs. Also, conventions can have implications and side effects. Certain conventions may even provide a better solution to the category of situations to which they pertain than other conventions. For example, in two-dimensional depictions of three-dimensional objects the convention of drawing in linear perspective, developed during the Renaissance, leads to a more realistic representation than other conventions (Hagen and Jones, 1978). Similarly, the introduction by Arab scientists of the number zero with a meaning dependent on position opened the way to significant advancements in mathematics that are hard to imagine with other conventions. However, this is insufficient justification for ascribing system characteristics to the functioning of individuals in one culture as distinct from those in some other culture without precise specification of the domain to which the notion of system is applied.

Inasmuch as conventions are crystallizations of more or less arbitrary (rather than predestined or predictable) choices made somewhere in history, they are incompatible with the assumption of close culture–behaviour relationships, as discussed in the previous sections. Most theories, both culture-comparative and culturalist, are based on the axiom that culture and behaviour are tightly

Table 14.1 *Levels of constraints and affordances varying from distal to proximal*

	Constraints		Affordances
	Internal	External	
Distal	*genetic transmission (species)* • adaptations	• ecological niche	• pleiotropies and 'spandrels'
	cultural transmission (group) • epigenetic rules	• ecological context • sociohistorical context	• technology • enabling conditions (conventions)
	genetic transmission (individual) • aptitudes	• poor fit in cultural niche	• capacities
	cultural transmission (individual) • enculturation (skills, beliefs, etc) • situation 'meaning'	• socialization to prevailing conditions • actual situation	• enabling conventions (skills, beliefs, etc) • perceived choices
Proximal			

interconnected. The notion that conventions have a certain degree of arbitrariness loosens up such close connections.

Redefining culture–behaviour relationships

The position argued for in this chapter is one in which reference is made to universal psychological processes as well as to culture-specific conventions of a low level of generality. In this section we shall indicate how in our opinion such a position can be conceptualized.

A key observation is that the range of imaginary actions of a person is much larger than the observed range. One way to look at this is from a conception of *constraints* that limit the range of alternative actions actually available to a person. At the same time, in most situations there remain various alternative courses of action open to a person. These can be seen as *affordances* or *opportunities*. For reasons that will become clear later, we place emphasis on constraints rather than on affordances. Constraints can be defined at various levels from distal to proximal; and they can be internal within the person as well as external, imposed by the environment. Affordances can be defined as the space of alternatives left by constraints at each level; affordances in this sense are complementary to constraints. An overview is provided in table 14.1 (cf. also Poortinga, 1992).

At the most general level the scope of human behaviour is determined by the phylogenetic history of our species with selective transmission of genetic materials over many generations as a consequence of natural selection. The results are adaptations that optimize organism-environment fit (e.g. Tooby and Cosmides, 1992). Thus, the environment, or ecological niche in which humans function imposes constraints on adaptation outcomes. Recently it has been argued, notably by Gould (1991), that features of adaptedness may not always be the direct outcome of selection-driven genetic transmission processes. For example, a gene can have various effects on the development of an organism, a phenomenon called *pleiotropy*. In an environment-driven genetic change not only a pertinent effect of a gene will be affected, but all of the effects of that gene on the phenotype (e.g. Lewontin, 1978). Gould speaks about *exaptations* (i.e. features that now enhance fitness, but originally came about for another function) and *spandrels* (i.e. features that have come about as added consequences of other features). Gould sees the complex brain as a feature of the human organism that has opened up many affordances, such as religion, art and technology, for which it hardly can have been developed originally. In the scheme of table 14.1 exaptations and spandrels qualify as affordances.

Cultural transmission at the group level can be distinguished from genetic transmission with the help of a notion like *culturegen* (Lumsden and Wilson, 1981) that forms the basic unit of culture, and refers to a more or less homogeneous set of artefacts and mentifacts. According to these authors transmission takes place via *epigenetic rules*, referring to processes of interaction between genes and environment. Which cultural patterns will develop depends to a major extent on the resources that are available in a given natural environment. There are also patterns that are unlikely to develop, given adverse eco-cultural or sociocultural conditions. In this sense the environment acts as a set of constraints. At the same time, the natural environment provides affordances that have been differentially developed by various cultural populations, and thus have resulted in different enabling conditions, in the form of technologies and conventions on how to manage the environment, including one's social environment.

The next row in the table implies a shift from transmission at the population level to transmission as an individual-level phenomenon. Genetically the individual can be seen as representing a specific subset of the gene pool of a breeding population that tends to show great overlap with his/her cultural population. One's genetic make-up imposes severe restrictions on what can be achieved, in terms of physical as well as mental dimensions. One's environment equally does not provide optimum opportunities for development – think of less than optimal nutrition – thus providing external constraints adding to those inherent in an individual's genetic make-up. Individual capacities need not be seen only in terms of their limiting effects. Specific capabilities also form the basis for the development of individual competencies or skills, which a person can employ to realize desired achievements; in this sense capabilities can also be viewed as affordances.

The final form of transmission distinguished in table 14.1 is cultural transmission at the individual level in the form of enculturation and socialization to prevailing economic conditions and sociocultural context. Enculturation usually refers to all forms of cultural learning, including imitation (cf. Segall et al., 1999). It is a limiting condition in so far as the individual manages only incompletely to learn from experience. External constraints are added by the limited range of experiences available in a given context, as well as by prevalent socialization practices. Child (1954) already saw socialization as the process through which individuals are led to develop a much narrower range of behavioural repertoire than the potentialities they are born with.

The last row of the table refers to concrete situations or stimuli, which we actually face, and which are only a very small part of all possible situations. In so far as a situation demands certain actions and makes other actions inappropriate (e.g. evasive action in the case of physical danger) there are external constraints. Internal constraints are present in so far as a person attributes certain meanings to a situation. At the same time, in most situations the actor can think of alternative possible courses of action that can be conceptualized as affordances.

In psychology, the emphasis is on individual-level explanation. In cross-cultural psychology the focus is also on the interaction of individual and cultural context. Constraints can be seen as the defining characteristic of a culture, i.e. '[c]ulture becomes manifest in shared constraints that limit the behaviour repertoire available to members of a certain group in a way different from individuals belonging to some other group' (Poortinga, 1992, p. 10).

For at least two reasons the distinctions made in this section are not as clear-cut as they are presented in table 14.1. First, constraints and affordances are often two sides of the same medal; for example, growing up in a society enables one to learn a language, but severely limits the learning of other languages. Thus, distinctions are to some extent a matter of perspective. Second, there are interactions between the various levels represented by the rows in the table, as we shall see in a later section. Third, to allow a precise mapping of the boundaries of constraints, and by implication those of affordances, typically requires a large number of observations, often more than are feasible in practice. Therefore, boundaries are not sharply defined; they are fuzzy. As we shall see just now, this limits the empirical utility of the distinctions.

Inasmuch as there are constraints limiting the range of behaviour alternatives these should become manifest in regularities that are open to analysis by experimental and psychometric methods. If we know what the constraints are, we can predict events that will occur (and, perhaps more important, events that will not occur). For example, in psychology learning curves and curves of forgetting have been found to follow such precise trajectories that we even speak about 'psychological laws' (like the law of effect). At the level of a cultural group constraints can pre-empt the development of certain technologies; in concrete terms, it is difficult to imagine that some kind of agriculture could have developed in the Arctic area.

Inasmuch as there is freedom from constraints future events are not predictable beyond their a priori level of probability; only in retrospect can we observe which choice actually has been made in a certain instance. Of course, the realization of one affordance may rule out others and may well have consequences even across rows in table 14.1. Thus individual skills are highly dependent on the technologies that happen to be available in a culture, and so is the range of behaviour alternatives available to a person in many concrete situations. However, this does not detract from the principle of unpredictability of choice within a range of alternatives. This uncertainty is easy to understand for simple events; we appreciate that the probability of throwing a six with a die cannot exceed one-sixth. It is more difficult to understand for complex events. For example, if we know that 80 per cent of the adolescents in a given population get married, we can make the prediction that any specific youngster will marry with a probability of 0.8, but this in itself does not add anything. We can gain further knowledge from other sources of information, which reduces the range of uncertainty (differential percentages of marriage in various subpopulations, signs of interest in the other sex, etc.). In the present terminology this amounts to a more precise specification of constraints, but it does not improve the predictability of the behaviour of a single individual beyond that of the category he or she belongs to.

The essence of the distinction between constraints and affordances for the present chapter is that it creates a complementarity between the two perspectives of universalism and relativism. Culture defined as a set of antecedent conditions is most appropriately analysed by (quasi-)experimental methods. Inasmuch as there are no constraining antecedent conditions, the rules and conventions that have emerged in a certain group lend themselves to description and interpretative analysis (often referred to as qualitative methods), but not to lawful explanation.

Non-linear dynamics as models of choice

In the nineteenth century the botanist Robert Brown observed through a microscope the seemingly random movements of colloid particles in a solution. This Brownian movement, caused by molecules that collide with the particles, more or less follows the laws of Newtonian mechanics. However, the number of collisions and variety of the direction of impact makes the prediction of the pattern of movement of any colloid particle over any length of time utterly impossible. In the twentieth century there have been other developments that show the limits of prediction of concrete events even in highly lawful systems. Well known is the discovery by the meteorologist Lorenz that very slight variations in the initial value of a parameter can lead to rapidly diverging outcomes in computer simulations of atmospheric disturbances. His famous metaphor is that the fluttering of the wings of a butterfly in the rain forest of Brazil could result in a hurricane in North America several days later. This was one of the beginnings of chaos theory about which there are now also writings pertinent to psychology (e.g. Barton, 1994). Another formulation to model sudden changes is the catastrophe theory developed by Thom (1975), the psychological relevance of which has been demonstrated, for example, by Zeeman (1976).

Such models of non-linear dynamics have in common that they make understandable how there can be changes that are essentially unpredictable, even if they take place in a deterministic, lawbound context. However, the most important point to note is that chaos and catastrophes are constrained within boundaries; the weather in a week's time may be beyond prediction, but if it is winter there will not be a hurricane. There is essential unpredictability, but with more or less strict, lawful limitations on the range of variations.

In many models of non-linear changes transitions appear sudden and cannot be mapped; we only can observe the outcomes; i.e. that a change has occurred. At the same time, the fact that behaviour may be difficult to predict does not by itself justify the conclusion that we are dealing with chaotic events. Validation of discontinuities requires the formulation of functions (based on theories and hypotheses) on the basis of which boundary conditions can be specified. If no theory is available any ill-understood change can be labelled as a chaotic change, making the concept of chaos merely an empty metaphor. This tendency already seems to take place in psychology (e.g. Masterpasqua and Perna, 1997).

Constraints and discontinuities in ontogenetic development

Shifting to a developmental perspective we have to consider one further aspect, namely changes that occur in the individual over time. It has been stated repeatedly that cross-cultural psychology has to be developmental, since differences in behaviour can only be understood properly if one knows their ontogenetic history (e.g. Heron and Kroeger, 1981; Keller and Greenfield, 2000). We would like to refer to two theoretical themes, namely the question of continuity and discontinuities in ontogenetic development, and whether it makes sense to see development as a process of increasing constraints on potential rather than as a process of increasing affordances. Beforehand we wish to note that we introduce a simplification by not making any differentiation in cross-cultural differences of developmental outcomes between psychological domains like perception, cognition, social behaviour etc. (Poortinga, Kop and van de Vijver, 1990). We believe that this simplification does not affect the argument of this section in any essential way.

Probably the most impressive theory that postulates clear developmental discontinuities remains that of Piaget (1972). The various stages in cognitive development in his theory are the outcome of continuous processes of accommodation and assimilation that result in stages that are qualitatively different from each other. Stages form cohesive entities (*'structures d'ensemble'*). Piaget expected only small cross-cultural differences even in the age at which each stage would appear. Neo-Piagetian research (e.g. Demetriou and Efklides, 1994) and cross-cultural studies (Dasen, 1972) have shown that the initial unitary conception of each of the various cognitive stages could not be maintained. Apparently, qualitative changes are less comprehensive than Piaget thought. Nevertheless, in respect of the spontaneous emergence of skills that for Piaget were central evidence of the presence of a stage, large differences in time of onset across cultures have been demonstrated for the later stages of cognitive development. A distinction between performance and competence has made sense of these findings. Dasen (1975) found that a limited amount of training led to concrete operational solutions in school-age children who spontaneously manifested only preoperational thinking on tasks of conservation. In the meantime cross-cultural research has demonstrated that abstract thinking, as emerging, for example, in syllogistic thinking, is probably better seen as a set of algorithms (tricks learned at school) than as a separate stage of cognition. Along these lines some convergence between work in the tradition of Piaget and that of Cole and colleagues has been reached, even though there is no complete agreement (Segall et al., 1999; Cole, 1996).

Moreover, recent research has made clear that cognitive processes, which Piaget saw as emerging only with a certain stage, have important precursors. Baillargeon (1995, 1998) has been able to show that infants of a few months already distinguish physically possible from impossible events. Significant progress has also been made in the development of non-linear models to describe developmental trajectories for certain skills (Thelen, 1995; van Geert, 1994). Empirical studies have been conducted in which criteria for discontinuities have been formulated and investigated experimentally. In the area of early motor development observations have been shown to meet such criteria. For example, Wimmers and colleagues (Wimmers, Savelsbergh, Beek and Hopkins, 1998; Wimmers, Savelsbergh, van der Kamp and Hartelman, 1998) could demonstrate that the change from reaching without grasping to reaching with grasping satisfied conditions for a discontinuous change. The rather abrupt change appeared to be a function of arm weight and arm circumference of the babies; a small change in the amount of muscle relative to arm mass occurs which probably reduces the effort of grasping and then allows unflexing of the fingers.

Cross-cultural research has shown age differences in motor development, for example for the onset of walking (e.g. Bril and Lehalle, 1988). Research like that of Wimmers and colleagues should make it possible to identify and even predict natural limits in cross-cultural variation on the range of values over which relevant parameters can extend. However, to the best of our knowledge such an analysis has never been carried out. Moreover, the example of grasping pertains to a well-defined developmental task, in the sense that the parameters can be specified and measured with precision. It is not (yet) clear how models of non-linear change can be tested empirically for developmental changes in more complex domains of behaviour (i.e. domains which are more fuzzy in terms of the definition of parameters) as they occur after infancy. However, we would expect that cross-cultural differences in parameter values will be small.

To avoid any misunderstanding, it is evident also to us that at a concrete level the repertoire of behaviour as the outcome of developmental processes differs markedly across cultures, even at a fairly young age. Barker and Wright (1951) have described in detail the life of a 7-year-old child in the Midwest of the USA. When reading this account one is impressed with the large arsenal of skills and factual knowledge that the child displays in going through daily routines, in and outside school. Although no similar account is available for other societies, it is clear that a description of a day in the life of an Aka pygmy child would look very different (e.g. Hewlett and Lamb, this volume; van de Koppel, 1983). The question is whether such differences are a large accumulation of incidents, or whether there are broader psychological patterns in which these differences become organized.

For example, from an evolutionary perspective Belsky, Steinberg and Draper (1991) have proposed that the interaction of early socialization patterns and available dispositions can lead to different developmental outcomes in terms of reproduction strategies. A harmonious family environment, sensitive to the child and allowing secure attachment, will lead to a late onset of sexual maturation, closer pair bonding and a better environment for the next generation. In contrast, marital discord and an insensitive environment lead to insecure attachment and later to early sexual activity and unstable partner relationships. Support for similar relationships between childhood experiences and the onset of puberty has been reported by Keller and colleagues (cf. Keller, this volume). Keller (1997; Keller and Greenfield, 2000) also suggested links between eco-cultural conditions and parental ethnotheories, which should make sense in terms of the evolutionary criterion of reproductive success.

We do not doubt that extremely negative social conditions can have effects on social development, in a similar sense that nutritional deficits can affect physical (and mental) development. Such conditions of adversity may even occur frequently in some societies at some period of their history (cf. Aptekar and Stöcklin, 1997; Zimba, this volume), but as a rule the young are well cared for in any culture and highly adverse conditions are certainly not 'typical' of childhood in any culture. In this sense, findings like those of Belsky et al. (1991), which pertain to (difficult to define) subgroups of a society, have limited relevance for this chapter. However, there is another issue, pertinent also to developmental research from an evolutionary perspective. Eco-cultural features tend to have a large degree of continuity, at the level of families as well as at the level of cultures. To demonstrate convincingly that effects in adolescence and adulthood are due to conditions of early infancy rather than to an accumulation of experiences during all of childhood would seem to require a discontinuation of the same environment for at least part of the sample in a study, in a similar way that behaviour geneticists have studied identical twins reared together and reared apart. Until researchers succeed in somehow unconfounding effects of the early and of the later environment, explanations assuming such relationships in our opinion remain rather speculative.

The distinctions that we made in the previous sections imply one further issue on which cross-cultural data can throw light. Ontogenetic development, at least until adulthood, tends to be portrayed as a growth in behaviour potential. In a sense this is obvious. An adult person knows more words, has a larger array of cognitive algorithms at his/her disposal and can apply social rules (social etiquette) better than a young child. At the same time, development as realized potential goes together with a simultaneous increase in unrealized potential. For example, neurological development implies that the number of neurons and connections between them is lower in adults than in infant vertebrates (e.g. Rakic, 1995; cf. also Gottlieb, 1998). As far as psychological aspects of development are concerned, a cross-cultural perspective makes the notion of unrealized potential more evident. Children lose the ability early in life to distinguish spontaneously between various phonemes that do not belong to their mother tongue (cf. Harley, 1995). We have already mentioned the opinion of Child (1954) that the socialization of individuals leads to the development of a behavioural repertoire that is more limited than their potential allows.

Which of the two emphases, affordances or constraints, should be considered to be more appropriate depends on their respective validity. In so far as societies not only profess but also realize differences in the socialization of their young, notions of choice and affordance form the preferred mode of explanation. In so far as there are universal patterns of development, and in so far as cross-cultural differences in patterns can be explained in terms of antecedent ecological conditions, developmental patterns are apparently constrained. From the arguments and evidence presented it may be clear that we are more impressed by the cross-cultural similarities in developmental outcomes than by the differences.

In summary, it seems to us that affordances at the level of culture are best explained as due to the accumulation of large numbers of specific experiences each with limited generalization. Genetic constraints which apply species-wide apparently hardly allow for the development of different modes of functioning cross-culturally; the 'valleys of cultural construction' (cf. Harris and Heelas, 1979) are small. The range of affordances that individuals have at their disposal (and that a culture can emphasize) can be seen as limited to specific skills and algorithms, largely developed through contextual experiences and demands. Furthermore, there is at least some evidence, be it so far not beyond early childhood, that supports development as a discontinuous process, but again for specific tasks. We would argue that as a consequence the range of affordances is likely to be limited, and this in turn would seem to leave limited space for the kinds of cross-cultural variations that are best studied by means of interpretive (post hoc) methods.

Conclusion

The two dimensions that we described in the first two sections define four quadrants, (i) system-oriented and relativist (ii) system-oriented and universalist, (iii) convention-oriented and relativist and (iv) convention-oriented and universalist. We proposed that system-oriented approaches are in danger of stereotype-like interpretations of cross-cultural differences. We further suggested that a distinction between constraints and affordances offers a rationale to demarcate realms where culturalist, hermeneutic or action-oriented methods, and realms where universalist psychonomic methods are more appropriate.

In questioning broad generalizations our position may be reminiscent of that of Cole (1996, this volume), but it differs in one essential aspect. There is no need to assume, as Cole does, that culture is a third factor, next to organism and natural environment. He creates in this way a niche for culture as a medium for behavioural development. However, the ontological status of such a conception of culture is unclear (Poortinga, 1997). A similar comment applies to Eckensberger's (1979, 1996, this volume) conception of the person as self-reflexive and capable of acting consciously and intentionally.

A basic difference between our outlook and that of most authors contributing to this volume is that we question the validity of explanations of cross-cultural differences at high levels of generality, including stages in infancy that lead to later cross-cultural differentiation in autonomy and interdependence (e.g. Keller, this volume), and in personality concepts (e.g. Miller, this volume; Kornadt, this volume) that allegedly appear as a consequence of socialization.

It will not be easy to demonstrate that developmental outcomes across cultures are organized in terms of conventions or cultural patterns of limited reach, against the prevalent belief that culture–behaviour relationships are systematic and organized in broad internalized patterns. However, relevant criteria can be formulated. For example, in so far as cultural affordances account for cross-cultural variation, differentiation should take place quite rapidly and early, relative to developmental change within groups. In so far as biological constraints are important, there will be cross-cultural similarity in longitudinal developmental patterns. Moreover, with increasing differences in behaviour repertoires constraints should be more in evidence than affordances, although it is not immediately evident how this condition could be tested.

If we look at cultural variance relative to variance between individuals within cultures, the former tends to be much smaller as soon as measures pertain to broader domains of generalization (such as personality traits and cognitive abilities; cf. Poortinga and van Hemert, 2001). Only at the level of specific beliefs, skills and practices does one find larger variances within than between cultural populations. Finally, non-linear changes should show in discontinuities, but if these discontinuities should be proven to be organizable into more encompassing entities this would go against the notion that affordances can have only a limited reach.

REFERENCES

Aptekar, L. and Stöcklin, D. (1997). Children in particularly difficult circumstances. In J. W. Berry, P. R. Dasen and T. S. Saraswathi (eds.), *Handbook of cross-cultural psychology*, vol. 2. Boston: Allyn and Bacon, pp. 377–412.
Baillargeon, R. (1995). Physical reasoning in infancy. In M. S. Gazzaniga (ed.), *The cognitive neurosciences*. Cambridge, MA: MIT Press, pp. 181–204.
   (1998). Infants' understanding of the physical world. In M. Sabourin and F. Craik (eds.), *Advances in psychological science*, vol. 2. Hove: Psychology Press, pp. 503–29.
Barker, R. G. and Wright, H. F. (1951). *One boy's day: a specimen record of behavior.* New York, Harper.
Barton, S. (1994). Chaos, self-organization, and psychology. *American Psychologist*, 49, 5–14.
Belsky, J., Steinberg, L. and Draper, P. (1991). Childhood experience, interpersonal development, and reproductive strategy: an evolutionary theory of socialization. *Child Development*, 62, 647–70.
Berry, J. W., Poortinga, Y. H., Segall, M. H. and Dasen, P. R. (1992). *Cross-cultural psychology: research and applications.* Cambridge: Cambridge University Press.
Boorstin, D. J. (1985). *The discoverers.* New York: Vintage Books.
Bril, B. and Lehalle, H. (1988). *Le développement psychologique est-il universel?* (Is psychological development universal?). Paris: Presses Universitaires de France.
Buss, D. M. (1989). Sex differences in human mate preferences: evolutionary hypotheses tested in 37 cultures. *Behavioral and Brain Sciences*, 12, 1–49.
Campbell, D. T. and Fiske D. W. (1959). Convergent and discriminant validation by the multitrait-multimethod matrix. *Psychological Bulletin*, 56, 81–105.
Child, I. L. (1954). Socialization. In G. Lindzey (ed.), *Handbook of social psychology*, vol. 2. Cambridge, MA: Addison-Wesley, pp. 655–92.
Cole, M. (1996). *Cultural psychology: a once and future discipline.* Cambridge, MA: Belknap Press.

Dasen, P. R. (1972). Cross-cultural Piagetian research: a summary. *Journal of Cross-Cultural Psychology*, 3, 75–85.

(1975). Concrete operational development in three cultures. *Journal of Cross-Cultural Psychology*, 6, 156–72.

Demetriou, A. and Efklides, A. (eds.) (1994). *Intelligence, mind, and reasoning*. Amsterdam: Elsevier.

Doi, T. (1973). *The anatomy of dependence*. Tokyo: Kodansha International.

Eckensberger, L. H. (1979). A metamethodological evaluation of psychological theories from a cross-cultural perspective. In L. Eckensberger, W. Lonner and Y. H. Poortinga (eds.), *Cross-cultural contributions to psychology*. Lisse: Swets and Zeitlinger, pp. 255–75.

(1996). Agency, action, and culture: three basic concepts for cross-cultural psychology. In J. Pandey, D. Sinha and D. P. S. Bhawuk (eds.), *Asian contributions to cross-cultural psychology*. New Delhi: Sage, pp. 72–102.

Fijneman, Y. A., Willemsen, M. E., Poortinga, Y. H., in cooperation with Erelcin, F. G., Georgas, J., Hui, H. C., Leung, K. and Malpass, R. S. (1996). Individualism-collectivism: An empirical study of a conceptual issue. *Journal of Cross-Cultural Psychology*, 27, 381–402.

Fontaine, J. R. J., Poortinga, Y. H., Setiadi, B. and Markam, S. S. (in press). 'Shame' and 'guilt' in Indonesian and Dutch cognitive emotion structure. *Cognition and Emotion*.

Freeman, D. (1983). *Margaret Mead and Samoa: the making and unmaking of an anthropological myth*. Cambridge, MA: Harvard University Press.

Geertz, C. (1973). *The interpretation of cultures*. New York: Basic Books.

Georgas, J., Christakopoulou, S., Poortinga, Y. H., Angleitner, A., Goodwin, R. and Charalambous, N. (1997). The relationships of family bonds to family structure and function across cultures. *Journal of Cross-Cultural Psychology*, 28, 284–320.

Girndt, T. (2000). Cultural diversity and work-group performance: detecting the rules. Ph.D. thesis, Tilburg University.

Gottlieb, G. (1998). Normally occurring environmental and behavioral influences on gene activity: from central dogma to probabilistic epigenesis. *Psychological Review*, 105, 792–802.

Gould, S. J. (1991). Exaptation: a crucial tool for evolutionary psychology. *Journal of Social Issues*, 47, 43–65.

Greenfield, P. M. (1994). Independence and interdependence as developmental scripts. In P. M. Greenfield and R. Cocking (eds.), *Cross-cultural roots of minority child development*. Hillsdale: Lawrence Erlbaum, pp. 1–37.

(1997). Culture as process: empirical methods for cultural psychology. In J. W. Berry, Y. H. Poortinga and J. Pandey (eds.), *Handbook of cross-cultural psychology*, vol. 1, 2nd edn. Boston: Allyn and Bacon, pp. 301–46.

Gudykunst, W. B. (1983). *Intercultural communication theory*. Beverly Hills: Sage.

Hagen, M. A. and Jones, R. K. (1978). Cultural effects and pictorial perception: how many words is one picture really worth? In R. D. Walk and H. L. Pick (eds.), *Perception and experience*. New York: Plenum Press, pp. 171–209.

Harley, T. R. (1995). *The psychology of language: from data to theory*. Hove: Psychology Press.

Harris, P. and Heelas, P. (1979). Cognitive processes and collective representations. *Archives Européennes de Sociologie*, 20, 211–41.

Heron, A. and Kroeger, E. (1981). Introduction to developmental psychology. In H. C. Triandis, A. Heron and E. Kroeger (eds.), *Handbook of cross-cultural psychology*, vol. 4. Boston: Allyn and Bacon, pp. 1–15.

Hofstede, G. (1980). *Culture's consequences: international differences in work-related values*. London: Sage.

Kagitcibasi, C. (1990). Family and socialization in cross-cultural perspective: A model of change. In J. J. Berman (ed.), *Cross-cultural perspectives: Nebraska symposium on motivation 1989*. Lincoln: University of Nebraska Press, pp. 135–200.

(1996). *Family and human development across countries: a view from the other side*. Hillsdale, NJ: Lawrence Erlbaum.

Keller, H. (1997). Evolutionary approaches. In J. W. Berry Y. H. Poortinga and J. Pandey (eds.), *Handbook of cross-cultural psychology*, vol. 1, 2nd edn. Boston: Allyn and Bacon, pp. 215–55.

Keller, H. and Greenfield, P. M. (2000). History and future of development in cross-cultural psychology. *Journal of Cross-Cultural Psychology*, 31, 52–62.

Kloos, P. (1988). *Door het oog van de antropoloog* (Through the eye of the anthropologist). Muiderberg: Coutinho.

Leung, K. (1988). Some determinants of conflict avoidance. *Journal of Cross-Cultural Psychology*, 19, 125–36.

Lévy-Bruhl, L. (1926). *Primitive mentality*. London: Allen and Unwin.

Lewontin, R. C. (1978). Adaptation. *Scientific American*, 239 (3), 156–69.

Lonner. W. J. and Adamopoulos, J. (1997). Culture as antecedent to behavior. In J. W. Berry, Y. H. Poortinga and J. Pandey (eds.), *Handbook of cross-cultural psychology*, vol. 1, 2nd edn., Boston: Allyn and Bacon, pp. 43–83.

Lumsden, C. J. and Wilson, E. O. (1981). *Genes, mind and culture: the coevolutionary process*. Cambridge, MA: Harvard University Press.

Luria, A. R. (1971). Towards the problem of the historical nature of psychological processes. *International Journal of Psychology*, 6, 259–72.

(1976). *Cognitive development: its cultural and social foundations*. Cambridge, MA: Harvard University Press.

Lutz, C. (1988). *Unnatural emotions: everyday sentiments on a Micronesian atoll and their challenge to Western theory*. Chicago: University of Chicago Press.

Malpass, R. S. and Poortinga, Y. H. (1986). Designs for equivalence. In W. J. Lonner and J. W. Berry (eds.), *Field methods in cross-cultural psychology*. Beverly Hills: Sage, pp. 47–83.

Markus, H. R. and Kitayama, S. (1991). Culture and the self: implications for cognition, emotion and motivation. *Psychological Review*, 98, 244–53.

Masterpasqua, F. and Perna, P. A. (eds.) (1997). *The psychological meaning of chaos: translating theory into practice*. Washington, DC: American Psychological Association.

Mesquita, B. and Frijda, N. H. (1992). Cultural variations in emotions: a review. *Psychological Bulletin*, 112, 179–204.

Miller, J. G. (1984). Culture and the development of everyday social explanation. *Journal of Personality and Social Psychology*, 46, 961–78.

(1997). Theoretical issues in cultural psychology. In J. W. Berry, Y. H. Poortinga and J. Pandey (eds.), *Handbook of cross-cultural psychology*, vol. 1, 2nd edn. Boston: Allyn and Bacon, pp. 85–128.

Piaget, J. (1972). *The principles of genetic epistemology*. London: Routledge.

Poortinga, Y. H. (1992). Towards a conceptualization of culture for psychology. In S. Iwawaki, Y. Kashima and K. Leung (eds.), *Innovations in cross-cultural psychology*. Lisse: Swets and Zeitlinger, pp. 3–17.

 (1997). Towards convergence? In J. W. Berry, Y. H. Poortinga and J. Pandey (eds.), *Handbook of cross-cultural psychology*, vol. 1, 2nd edn. Boston: Allyn and Bacon, pp. 301–46.

 (1998). Cultural diversity and psychological invariance: methodological and theoretical dilemmas of (cross-)cultural psychology. In J. G. Adair, D. Bélanger and K. L. Dion (eds.), *Advances in psychological science*, vol. 1. Hove: Psychology Press, pp. 229–45.

Poortinga, Y. H., Kop, P. F. M. and van de Vijver, F. J. R. (1990). Differences between psychological domains in the range of cross-cultural variation. In P. J. D. Drenth, J. A. Sergeant and R. J. Takens (eds.), *European perspectives in psychology*, vol. 3. Chichester: Wiley, pp. 355–76.

Poortinga, Y. H., van de Vijver, F. J. R., Joe, R. C. and van de Koppel, J. M. H. (1987). Peeling the onion called culture. In C. Kagitcibasi (ed.), *Growth and progress in cross-cultural psychology*. Lisse: Swets and Zeitlinger, pp. 22–34.

Poortinga, Y. H. and van Hemert, D. A. (2001). Personality and culture: demarcating between the common and the unique. *Journal of Personality*, 69, 1033–60.

Rakic, P. (1995). Corticogenesis in human and non-human primates. In M. S. Gazzaniga (ed.), *The cognitive neurosciences*. Cambridge, MA: MIT Press, pp. 127–46.

Rohner, R. (1984). Toward a conception of culture for cross-cultural psychology. *Journal of Cross-Cultural Psychology*, 15, 111–38.

Scribner, S. (1979). Modes of thinking and ways of speaking: culture and logic reconsidered. In R. O. Freddie (ed.), *New directions in discourse processing*. Norway, NJ: Able, pp. 223–43.

Scribner, S. and Cole, M. (1981). *The psychology of literacy*. Cambridge, MA: Harvard University Press.

Segall, M. H., Dasen, P. R., Berry, J. W. and Poortinga, Y. H. (1999). *Human behavior in global perspective*, 2nd edn. Boston: Allyn and Bacon.

Smith, P. B. and Bond, M. R. (1998). *Social psychology across cultures*, 2nd edn. London: Prentice-Hall.

Thelen, E. (1995). Motor development: a new synthesis. *American Psychologist*, 50, 79–95.

Thom, R. (1975). *Structural stability and morphogenesis*. Reading, MA: Benjamin.

Tooby, J. and Cosmides, L. (1992). The psychological foundations of culture. In J. Barkow, L. Cosmides and J. Tooby (eds.), *The adapted mind: evolutionary psychology and the generation of culture*. New York: Oxford University Press, pp. 19–136.

Triandis, H. C. (1989). The self and social behavior in differing cultural contexts. *Psychological Review*, 96, 506–20.

 (1996). The psychological measurement of cultural syndromes. *American Psychologist*, 51, 407–15.

van de Koppel, J. M. H. (1983). *A developmental study of the Biaka pygmies and the Bangandu*. Lisse: Swets and Zeitlinger.

van de Vijver, F. J. R. and Leung, K. (1997a). Methods and data analysis of comparative research. In J. W. Berry, Y. H. Poortinga and J. Pandey (eds.), *Handbook of cross-cultural psychology*, vol. 1, 2nd edn. Boston: Allyn and Bacon, pp. 257–300.

(1997b). *Methods and data analysis for cross-cultural research.* Thousand Oaks, CA: Sage.

van den Heuvel, K. and Poortinga, Y. H. (1999). Material and non-material support modes in Greece and The Netherlands: a test of three models. *International Journal of Psychology*, 34, 1–13.

van Geert, P. (1994). *Dynamic systems of development: change between complexity and chaos.* New York: Harvester Wheatsheaf.

Wierzbicka, A. (1999). *Emotions across languages and cultures: diversity and universals.* Cambridge: Cambridge University Press.

Wimmers, R. H., Savelsbergh, G. J. P., Beek, P. J. and Hopkins B. (1998). Evidence for a phase transition in the early development of prehension. *Developmental Psychobiology*, 32, 235–48.

Wimmers R. H., Savelsbergh, G. J. P., van der Kamp, J. and Hartelman, P. (1998). A developmental transition modeled as a cusp catastrophe. *Developmental Psychobiology*, 32, 23–35.

Zeeman, E. C. (1976). Catastrophe theory. *Scientific American*, 234, 65–83.

15   Paradigms revisited: from incommensurability to respected complementarity

Lutz H. Eckensberger

More than twenty years ago I applied Kuhn's (1970a) concept of paradigms to cross-cultural psychology (Eckensberger, 1979). This early paper was elaborated and extended at several later occasions (Eckensberger, 1995; Eckensberger and Burgard, 1983; Eckensberger and Keller, 1998; Eckensberger, Krewer and Kasper, 1984). In these contributions different paradigms in cross-cultural psychology were not just distinguished; rather cross-cultural psychology was explicitly used as a framework for the evaluation of existing paradigms in psychology in general. This earlier work addressed not only cross-cultural psychologists, but all psychologists – as does the present chapter.

After introducing some distinctions in philosophy of science to provide a basis for my position, discussion of the usefulness of paradigms and recent trends in psychology leads to the specification of four perspectives (paradigms). The elucidation of their interrelationships leads to my conclusion that cultural psychology appears to be a 'metatheory', and not just a sub-branch of psychology, and that the ethic of respected complementarity in psychology is essential for a more complete and differentiated understanding of human beings.

Introductory remarks on philosophy of science

Kuhn's approach: some comments

In psychology the term 'paradigm' has become a part of everyday language, since T. S. Kuhn (1970a) published his short but influential *Structure of scientific revolutions*. Five aspects of this work can help to set the stage for the following discussion:

(1) For Kuhn, 'science of science' was not exclusively *analytical*, but neither was it *normative* in the sense that there is (or should be) one and only one 'royal path' to truth, as is implied, for instance, in Popper's (1959) programme of

I thank Joachim Wutke for critical comments on an earlier version of this chapter. Ype Poortinga and Ingrid Plath helped me to shorten an earlier version by almost half. Ingrid Plath had a tremendous impact beyond this surgery: she not only called relevant literature to my attention, but she also discussed crucial issues of the text, and last but not least she made it readable.

'critical rationalism'. Instead, Kuhn analysed *empirically* how scientific work is realized in the course of history. Hence his argument necessarily implies empirical as well as philosophical aspects, although these have to be kept apart carefully (Michell, 2000).

(2) On the basis of historical cases (primarily from physics), Kuhn claimed that real progress in science is not due to cumulative falsification and/or acceptance of hypotheses, but to radical changes in the (ontological) *pre-assumptions about the nature of a phenomenon* to be explained by a theory. This 'new way of looking' at reality is what he called a *paradigm shift*. Hence the developmental process of science is not 'evolutionary' but 'revolutionary'. Although he used the term 'paradigm' in a variety of ways (Mastermann, 1970), the set of *ontological pre-assumptions* is an essential aspect of a paradigm. The ontological preconditions are assumed to be qualitatively different and mutually exclusive. For this reason paradigms are 'incommensurable'. Kuhn argued that scientists only (or primarily) reflect critically upon their science and theories in times of paradigm shift: a scientific revolution, which is then replaced by the phase of 'normal science', which – more or less – lacks such critical reflections.

(3) These reflective processes themselves and the ensuing 'paradigm shift' (and particularly the acceptance of a new paradigm) are not as exclusively 'objective' or 'rational' as one might expect in science. They are also *social* in the sense that science is *done* by humans, by *groups of scientists* who follow a particular paradigm. This *social basis* of science led to a considerable differentiation of the sociology-of-science concept 'scientific community' in terms of a *disciplinary matrix*, which is *a structured set of guiding beliefs taken for granted by all scientists working within some discipline* (Michell, 2000). This opens the door for the inclusion of *regulatory rule systems* as essential parts of the 'science game', aspects that are usually not assumed to be part of theory construction in science: *conventions* and/or *morality*.

(4) Paradigms are not only based on ontological pre-assumptions, applied and/or accepted within a disciplinary matrix, but also entail the use of *specific methods*, regarded as more adequate, suitable or successful for working under a specific paradigm. These methical ideals or models are called *exemplars*.

(5) Kuhn's conception is based on a *mono-paradigmatic structure* of science. In an established science paradigms follow each other consecutively, they do not exist or compete with each other at the same time. If several paradigms exists simultaneously, then the science is considered *pre-paradigmatic*, which also means *immature*.

Critical reception of Kuhn's approach

Kuhn's analysis was not really discussed critically and in depth in the psychology of the time. But in philosophy of science it was. There his work did not meet with universal approval. Bickhard (1992) regards the view that Kuhn's *Structure of scientific revolution* 'represents the state of the art in philosophy of science' as one of the 'ten myths of science' or 'misconceptions of science in modern psychology' (p. 332). He justifies this assessment by indicating that Kuhn's perspective – despite its historical importance – is outdated, primarily for two reasons: objections to the assumptions that paradigms are incommensurable and that the process of science is irrational to a certain extent. A closer look at these arguments may help to clarify the main points.

In fact it was Popper (1970) who criticized Kuhn's arguments for similar reasons: (1) He charged Kuhn with undermining his own primary goal, namely to distinguish between psychological and logical processes in theory construction. But Kuhn had no reason for retracting the core of his position – there are many factors at work in science that usually are considered 'external' to it, such as convincing others, formation of groups who share the same convictions and use their influence to defend a paradigm etc. (2) Popper accused Kuhn of having introduced *irrationality* into the process of science. This, however, is not Kuhn's intention. He does not assume that paradigms shift in arbitrary ways. Rather he refers to 'good reasons' (which are like basic values of science) that may lead to the choice of a new paradigm. The most important are probably: *accuracy*, *the range of the theory*, *parsimony*, *fruitfulness* and *prognoses* – some of them are, in fact, old friends. (3) Finally, Popper criticized both the concept of paradigm itself (as a 'myth of the framework'), which depicts scientists as 'prisoners caught in the framework of (their)... theories' (p. 56), and the assumption of the *incommensurability* of paradigms, a point important for the present discussion too. Interestingly, this claim is not as clear as one would wish in Kuhn's own writings (cf. Ritsert, 1994). There are numerous statements in which Kuhn seems to argue against the commensurability and possibility of integrating paradigms that follow each other in the wake of scientific revolution. However, he also explicitly claims that paradigms *are comparable* (Kuhn, 1970b, pp. 257ff.). Particularly Bernstein (1983) argued that Popper misinterpreted Kuhn in this respect, because 'Kuhn was not drawing attention to the incommensurability of paradigms to make them incomparable... [but]... to *make them comparable*. Kuhn's expressed intention was to compare paradigms, to compare their profound (and incommensurable) differences' (Slife, 2000, p. 267).

The distinction between commensurability and comparability will be dealt with in more detail later. For the moment it is important to note that Kuhn, to the best of my knowledge, never proposed a neutral 'metalanguage' or scientific language as an integrative framework for different paradigms.

According to Lakatos (1970, 1982), both Popper and Kuhn are disproved by history. He accepts or elaborates concepts of both authors, but leaves numerous questions open. He first argues and demonstrates that Popper's strong falsificationism does not really occur or work. A theory is not given up just because one of its hypotheses is falsified. Hence he accepts Kuhn's argument of *processes* in theory construction, which try to save theories despite falsified hypotheses. He accepts 'theory adjustments' which save theories, and speaks of a 'protective belt', which is built up to avoid rejecting a theory for (maybe) the wrong reasons. Consequently, Lakatos proposes a *sophisticated falsificationism*, which implies that a theory is (and should) only be given up if a new one provides a *better* explanation *of the phenomena* than an earlier one, and *leads to the discovery of new facts* (Lakatos, 1970, p. 113). He does not accept the notion that paradigms shift suddenly, but considers the process of science as being more or less continuous. As far as I can see, Lakatos also implies the simultaneous existence of different (competing) theories. Thus Lakatos does not speak of paradigms but of 'research programmes' or chains of theories. He argues that 'It is not that we propose a theory and nature answers "no!", but we propose a net of theories and nature may possibly answer *"inconsistent"'* (p. 127).

It is not really clear to what extent Lakatos dismisses the idea of a tacit metaphysical foundation in theories, which is the basis of the idea of a paradigm. He particularly seems to reject the notion of *incommensurability* in Kuhn's sense of a paradigm. Yet he develops concepts which come rather close to this notion when he uses the term 'central reference' or explains what he means by a 'positive heuristic' in research, and refers to the 'Cartesian metaphysic' as an example of a research programme.

Feyerabend (1975) underlines Popper's argument that experiences of reality always depend on a theory, and hence doubts that different theories can be tested by the same methods (this is so, because methods themselves produce different realities). Though he is most often cited for his famous credo 'anything goes', he does not call for methodical anarchy (as the translated title of his book 'Against method' suggests), rather he proposes *remaining as open methodologically as possible*, rejecting the *compulsory dictate* of applying just one kind of method (which is much more evident in its German title *Wider den Methodenzwang*). Feyerabend assumes theoretical pluralism, and in his view competing theories can be (or are) 'incommensurable'. Thus, he considers classical falsificationism as too restrictive. Though, historically, major upheavals occur in science, he argues that they are prepared for by unclear (contradictory) bits of data and alternative interpretations. Thus, in Feyerabend's eyes, the strategies of immunization which Lakatos referred to can be productive because they may help to save theories that have not yet broken through. Consequently he proposes that the history of a science should be part of the science itself, including the subjective, long-forgotten, mystic conceptions (Feyerabend, 1975), thus supporting both theoretical pluralism and metaphysical aspects in scientific theories.

Kuhn in retrospect: consensual arguments   Despite differences and controversies, the following arguments still justify the application of Kuhn's basic argument to psychology (see also Machado, Lourenco and Silva, 2000).

(1) There is no doubt that theories (epistemology) determine (to a large extent) what a 'datum', a relevant aspect of reality (ontology), is. Hence the reality that is the object of the theory depends on the theoretical perspective taken (which means that epistemology leads ontology).

(2) Theories do not develop exclusively on a *strictly rational* basis. (a) Generally they are not rejected just because they show anomalies, nor accepted simply because they are empirically supported. (b) The specific principles of scientific rationality that are utilized by science in evaluating theories are not permanently fixed, but change with the development of science. This means *extra-rational* (psychological, sociological) processes are also relevant. (c) The importance and existence of *metaphysical assumptions* in theories seems to be generally accepted. But despite agreement that theory transitions are usually non-cumulative (neither the logical nor the empirical content of earlier theories is wholly preserved when replaced by new ones), the common interest of philosophy of science is in the *historical continuity and change of the metaphysical assumptions in scientific theorizing* (Bickhard, 1992). These extra-rational processes (strategies of immunization) can be disadvantageous, but they can also be rather fruitful. Theories and methods are always carried/defended by social groups. Therefore, the course of science is *not irrational* but rather *culturally rational* (Bickhard, 1992).

(3) There is not just one theory in a science, but many – 'theoretical pluralism' is more or less accepted. Nevertheless, the kinds of relationships existing between the different theories (whether they can be synthesized or translated, or whether they are mutually exclusive) are open to debate. But some basic values of scientific work seem to be accepted (e.g. accuracy, parsimony, range of the theory, prognostic potential). It is plausible, for instance, to argue that if a theory is preferred over another (for 'rational' or social reasons), it should at least explain more than the other one did and it should also lead to new questions/results.

(4) Unfortunately the term 'paradigm' is not as clear as one would wish, but the same is true for other terms (such as 'research programme' or 'positive heuristics').

The usefulness of paradigms: perspectives guide theorizing and research

Because of the fuzziness of the term (Masterman, 1970), we originally decided to use 'paradigm' in psychology to designate an internally coherent pattern based on a model of man, an attached or derived theory and a set of methods, which are also determined by the features of the underlying model of man (Eckensberger, 1979; Eckensberger and Burgard, 1983; Eckensberger et al., 1984). On the basis of different world views ('models of man') underlying theories in developmental psychology I postulated a multi-paradigmatic view of (cross-cultural) psychology in 1979, extending earlier distinctions, particularly those by Reese and Overton (1970; Overton and Reese, 1973; see also Looft, 1973). The proposed paradigms were the paradigm of 'multitude and extent', the mechanistic and organismic paradigms, the eco-behavioural paradigm and the paradigm of potential self-reflective human being. From the perspective of paradigmatic reconstruction of theories (or families of theories), these theories are mutually incommensurable, because the underlying models of man are. As a decision for or against a specific theory (and the implied paradigm) is not possible on the basis of empirical evidence, a theory (and paradigm) can be evaluated only with reference to its usefulness, defined in terms of the issue of one's concern. The main criterion of usefulness specified for theories in cross-cultural psychology, and psychology in general, was the possibility of *dealing with the culture concept in the sense of integrating culture and cultural change into psychology.*

I still consider most of the early distinctions and evaluations valid. Of the five paradigms described only the self-reflective paradigm fulfilled the chosen criterion. It allowed the *integration of culture and behaviour* in the sense of *explaining both culture and the person*, underlined the *significance of development* in terms of interrelating individual and cultural *change* in principle, and encompassed both the *general* and the *unique*. Being based on Kuhn's assumption that paradigms are incommensurable, the whole enterprise focused on a paradigm split (called demarcation by Poortinga, 1997).

But why should one be concerned about paradigms at all; why not just do good empirical work? There are several good reasons to do so, particularly in the multi-paradigmatic situation of psychology.

What does 'good research' mean? From the current viewpoint, there is no such thing as *absolutely* good research: it is 'good' only in terms of a specific perspective. However, paradigms are not just alternative ways of seeing the world, they also *imply evaluation*, and this easily leads to devaluing other approaches, although one approximation of *truth* is not necessarily better than another, as noted. Evidently 'mainstream' psychology is just the 'leading paradigm' of psychology at a particular historical point in time. The social processes in science, as made explicit by Kuhn, imply that the disciplinary matrix (following one paradigm but not another) not only determines what 'good research' is, but largely also structures careers, publication possibilities, acceptance and rejection of papers and chapters in books and journals. In addition, the more funding institutions use economic benefits of research as one (or even the most important) criterion for the evaluation of paradigms, the more psychology is also in danger of being formed or deformed by these extra-scientific criteria (Laucken, 2001). Thus, the explication (limitations and possibilities) of 'hidden assumptions' as well as the justification of the chosen paradigm should undoubtedly be an explicit part of the academic discourse.

The 'self-construals' of psychologists in and outside of cross-cultural psychology were fairly similar in the 1970s. This is one reason, why 'hidden assumptions hunting' in psychology, and particularly in cross-cultural psychology, was probably considered strange or even unnecessary by most colleagues in cross-cultural psychology at that time. Nowadays the fragmentation of the discipline is increasingly recognized. In fact, it has almost become threatening to many colleagues. This is particularly evident in a series of papers recently published in 2000 in the *Journal of Mind and Behaviour*. Here Yanchar and Slife (2000) argue that psychology is fragmented, not only as a discipline, but also in its attempts to address its fragmentation. Some psychologists even call for establishing a strong disciplinary coherence as well as clear demarcations from other disciplines in terms of *concepts* (e.g. Staats, 1998), *methods* (e.g. Fishman, 1990) and *practical implementation* (e.g. Cahill, 1994). Others – like me – call for *theoretical* and *methodical pluralism* (e.g. Rychlak, 1993). Still others propose splitting psychology into more or less independent branches such as *humanistic psychology* and *behaviouristic science* (e.g. Fraley and Vargas, 1986), which is mirrored by the threatening separation of *cross*-cultural and *cultural* psychology, a debate which dominated practically all meetings of the International Association for Cross-Cultural Psychology (IACCP) in the 1990s. There are even proposals to abandon psychology altogether in favour of a *cognitive science*, which is a growing field in the West and comprises many aspects of a unifying perspective (e.g. Gardner, 1992). According to Yanchar and Slife (2000) the complexity of psychology has increased too, because the diversity of psychology has become 'multileveled' in terms of its *ontology* (substance), *epistemology* (means of knowledge) and *axiology* (evaluation). However, the growing discourse on fragmentation allows one to pinpoint the key issues in this debate. These trends and debates make it all the more plausible today than in the 1970s, even essential, to reflect upon psychology and cross-cultural psychology by searching for basic assumptions (paradigms), which may at least allow some order to be brought to the fragmentation psychology is suffering from.

As may be recalled, Kuhn (1970) interpreted paradigm shifts as progress, and fragmentation as 'immaturity'. So, what progress means, or what it can mean in a fragmented psychology, is a serious question (Machado et al., 2000). These discussions show clearly that *unity* (and therefore progress) *can hardly be reached by a common canon of methods*. Yanchar (2000) rightly claims that this can only be done by *subject matter*, by *unique and unifying questions*: 'To merely orient psychology around a method, however, rather than ... (psychological) questions or a clearly defined subject matter begs the question of whether or why psychology should exist in the first place' (p. 250).

Moreover, it has become apparent that 'like any other set of fundamental values, the axioms of the scientific method function as an *implicit morality*.

Because scientists assume that reality is material, atomistic, and universally lawful, they are *obliged* to use a method that is capable of investigating these kinds of phenomena'. And 'there is no guarantee that these values advanced as part of the Enlightenment worldview are true . . . there can be no independent test of their veracity' (Kristensen, Slife and Yanchar, 2000, p. 276, italics added). Some colleagues, who still follow Popper and maintain a distinction between a 'logic of discovery' and a 'logic of explanation', will probably find this insight difficult to swallow. In their view reducing the number of incorrect positions is possible in principle, and is ultimately the path towards at least partial truth.

The fundamental position taken in this chapter is that perspectives lead theorizing and research, 'that they are not "out there" in the data, but "in here" as assumptive frameworks' (Rychlak, 1993, p. 936). In a way my discussion will thus stay within a Kuhnian framework, although it is not followed as rigidly as in 1979 – specifically, the focus will no longer be the mutual exclusiveness and incommensurability of paradigms, but rather their interrelationships. However, the term 'paradigm' will be avoided in the remainder of the chapter, given its inflationary use and criticized aspects. There are various alternatives. One is 'narrative', used by Overton (1998) in his more recent writings. Another term is 'grounding', used by Rychlak (1993), though this term seems to be even stronger than paradigm and thus subject to many of the criticisms summarized above. The broad and unspectacular Wittgensteinian term 'perspective' will be adopted instead. This is intended to trigger the association that the perspectives distinguished are *someone*'s (the theorist's or researcher's) perspectives *about* something (the human being). The term also implies the notion that considering several perspectives may lead to a more complete picture of what is being looked at; in other words, it prepares for the *complementarity* and *coordination of perspectives.*

Recent trends in (cross-cultural) psychology: identifying perspectives in psychology

If one takes a metaperspective to psychology (not just to cross-cultural psychology), then three trends have become visible over the last decades. One represents an increasing preference for *biological theories*. For instance, Bischof (1980) based a major address on a classical and influential paper by Kurt Lewin (1930–1) entitled 'The transition from an Aristotelian to the Galileian worldview in biology and psychology', which aimed at defining psychology as a *natural science*, choosing physics (Galilei) as a model. Bischof agreed that psychology is and should be a natural science, but he accused Lewin of having chosen the wrong way out of Aristotelian thinking. Instead of physics he proposed *biology* as a model for science and Charles Darwin as the key thinker.

It is interesting that Bischof distinguished the same basic orientations, namely a mechanistic and an organismic model, as Reese and Overton (1970) had ten years earlier. There are, however, two significant differences between these positions. One is that, contrary to Reese and Overton, Bischof called for a *paradigm shift*. He explicitly *devalued* the physical model as being insufficient for psychology. The second difference can be clarified best by referring to Piaget's theory as the prime example for organismic theories. While Piaget uses biological concepts such as assimilation and accommodation (adaptation) as a *metaphor*, Bischof (1980) proposed a *literal* (non-metaphorical) *biological interpretation* of psychological concepts. This difference is crucial and will be taken up later. Undoubtedly the salience and frequency of this literal interpretation is increasing in psychology. Sociobiological interpretations in particular are applied to all kinds of human attributes, including human behaviour (Dawkins, 1976; Trivers, 1985; Voland, 2000; Wilson, 1975), but neurophysiological brain research (Roth, 1997; Singer, 2000) has also increased in importance, as have efforts in psychology to define *modules* in the brain, which can explain psychological processes such as cognitive achievements and emotions.

The second trend is that the *culture concept* (the sociocultural per se) has become a perspective in its own right. On the one hand, the 'movement' of *social constructivism* (Gergen, 1985) emerged, and on the other the distinction between *individual* and *collective representations* became influential (cf. the whole issue of *Culture and Psychology*, 4(3), 1998). Moreover, the development of the entire discipline of *cultural psychology* took place (Boesch, 1991; Cole, 1996; Eckensberger, 1990; Price-Williams, 1980; Shweder, 1990). Thus it seems justified and useful, even necessary today, to distinguish a 'cultural perspective' in psychology as a perspective in its own right.

The third recognizable trend is the increasing salience of the perspective of the 'potentially self-reflective' human being (Eckensberger, 1979), and the action theories attached to it, partially paralleling and overlapping the development of cultural psychology. Although the choice of action as the basic unit of analysis for psychology has varied in visibility during the history of psychology, its roots go back to the very beginnings of this 'new science'. This was true for Europe (here names like Pierre Janet, Wilhelm Wundt as well as Münsterberg should be mentioned) as well as for North America (where William James developed a remarkable action theory, see Barbalet, 1997). These roots are discussed in more detail elsewhere (Eckensberger, in press). What needs to be noted here is that these early traditions were overruled by the *neo-positivistic logic of explanation* expounded by the Vienna circle in philosophy, and by behaviourism in psychology.

In recent times, *human action* (or aspects of it) have been taken as a framework for analysis and/or research in many branches of psychology. In addition to the variety of action-based theories in psychology, human action is also focused upon in other human sciences. It is particularly reflected on in philosophy and also has a long tradition in sociology and in cultural and philosophical anthropology (see Eckensberger, in press). Much of Piaget's theory can be affiliated to this perspective, particularly because of his later work (Piaget, 1971, 1974) on the development of consciousness and the increasing importance of 'reflecting abstraction' (see Kesselring, 1981). Moreover, Russian *activity theory*, basically equivalent to action theories with similar roots in Janet's work (Eckensberger, 1995), also has clearly increased in importance through the work of Cole (1996), Rogoff (1990), Valsiner (1987), and Wertsch (1985), to mention but a few authors.

Summarizing these trends one may argue that there are four basic perspectives in psychology. In addition to the most traditional perspective based on the principles of *physics*, there is a second one that relates to *biology*, a third is based on the *potentially self-reflective human being* and a fourth focuses on *culture*. These correspond to the four 'groundings' of *Physikos, Bios, Socius* and *Logos* distinguished by Rychlak (1993).

Characterizing four perspectives in current (cross-cultural) psychology

Distinguishing features

For reasons that are plausible under a Kuhnian perspective, it is not only difficult, but also artificial or even impossible, to describe the ontology implied in the four perspectives as though they were 'pure'. This is so for historical reasons and because the perspectives represent entire sciences (physics, biology, anthropology and psychology), and within these sciences they influence one another, or are shared as working metaphors. Yet it may be helpful to delineate, as more or less independent, the content of the 'world views' (ideologies) from which the perspectives derive. The descriptions will be more like 'caricatures' to simplify matters and accentuate differences, as existing theories are more sophisticated in detail, less clear-cut and to some extent opaque in their assumptions.

Popper's distinction of three worlds appears productive for this purpose (Popper, 1977). *World 1* comprises the 'natural material world' (physical and biological), *World 2* contains 'mental states' (including emotions, dreams etc.) and *World 3* is made up of products of the human mind, be they material (like tools) or immaterial (like scientific theories, myths, rules, social institutions and the like). Clearly this is culture. How these worlds are interpreted and used for interpretation will be discussed in the following.

Figure 15.1 provides a simple depiction of the perspectives, characterized by basic features, and their relation to Popper's three worlds. Their relation

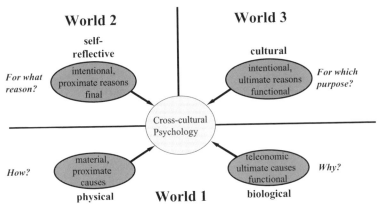

Figure 15.1   Popper's three worlds and their relations to the perspectives.

to psychology and their interrelationship will be discussed later. Three aspects serve as main distinguishing features:

(1) All four perspectives use different *types of interpretation* as basic assumptions in their analyses of *phenomena and processes*. These forms of interpretation in fact define and differentiate the perspectives (Rychlak, 1993) and are largely congruent with the different types of causes already distinguished by Aristotle: The *physical perspective* requires causal explanations, while the *biological perspective* primarily argues in terms of functionality or teleonomy, often also referred to as 'ultimate causes'. The *self-reflective human being* is understood in teleologic or final terms, that is, as exhibiting intentional actions and not just behaviour (see Eckensberger, 1979, 1990, 1996a for details), implying that actions are interpreted in terms of reasons (von Wright, 1971). The *cultural perspective* is also based on an 'intentional world' (Shweder, 1990), but it additionally includes functional aspects. 'Intentions' may become functional over time, as can human actions, e.g. as routines, habits, etc. Therefore, I proposed using the term 'ultimate reasons' as the basis of interpretation (Eckensberger, 1996b).

(2) The *leading questions* of these perspectives also differ (cf. Eckensberger, 1996b; Eckensberger and Keller, 1998; Wuketits, 1981). While the *physical perspective* asks 'how' something works, the *biological perspective* asks 'why' (which does not make sense in physics; Wuketits, 1981), and answers by specifying the adaptive *function* a certain form of behaviour has for survival or for reproductive fitness. The *self-reflective perspective* also asks a 'why' question, but aims at reasons for actions. The *cultural perspective* asks a 'why' question too, but here the purpose (associated with intentionality) is sought (see ultimate reasons, above).

(3) The *developmental processes*, serving as primary focus of the respective perspectives, differ as well. Micro-processes (actual genesis) are more prominent in the *physical* perspective, the *biological perspective* emphasizes phylogenesis, whereas the *cultural* highlights history. The perspective of the *self-reflective human being* primarily tries to integrate microgenesis (actual genesis) and ontogenesis and history (Eckensberger, 1979).

In the following the four perspectives will be explained in some detail, then their 'demarcation' – under the aspect of the 'classical' (conceptual) splits – will be elaborated upon and, finally, these apparent splits will be defined more precisely by introducing different types of relationships between the perspectives. It is important to emphasize that the four perspectives – in so far as they represent whole scientific domains – are all internally fragmented. Hence they are deliberately described only in terms of their influence on psychology – but even so additional choices of which theories to present have to be made.

The physical perspective (mechanistic view of human beings)

Physics as a science has undergone considerable changes during the last century. When classical physics was shaken by quantum mechanics – one of the 'paradigm shifts' in that science – this process made incommensurable and complementary[1] viewpoints of the same phenomenon (light) possible (the wave and particle interpretations). Classical physics was also rocked by Einstein's relativity theory, which itself did not 'fit' quantum theory. Thus, the unity of classical physics was fragmented and the elementarism implied came under attack (Primas, 1984).[2] So, when the physical (mechanistic) world view is adopted as *a perspective* and as *an ideal of research and theorizing* in psychology, then in fact classical Newtonian physics is meant. This is one of the reasons for the saying[3] that 'psychology of the twentieth century is a footnote to physics of the nineteenth century'. This perspective is based on *materialism* and *elementarism* (phenomena can be investigated by means of controlling single variables or a combination of single variables, a procedure which usually also implies decontextualization), on *measurement* (in early physics operationalization and application of mathematics), on *causal explanation* and on *prediction* as a hard test of causality (once more mathematics/statistics are used to test whether predictions hold or not). These are precisely the assumptions on which

---

[1] According to Kugel (1993) it seems that the term 'complementarity' was originally taken by Niels Bohr from his readings of William James' *Principles of psychology* (1890). Interestingly, it seems that it was the physician Wolfgang Pauli who proposed using this term to C. G. Jung to characterize the relationship between the unconscious and conscious as 'complementary'.

[2] It is interesting that these changes were cross-referenced in gestalt psychology (Wertheimer, 1924).

[3] Often this saying is attributed to S. Koch. In fact, I have never read a text where Koch made this remark, but it was attributed to him in various discussions in which I participated.

Table 15.1 *Types of universals in cross-cultural theorizing and research*

Types of universals	Existence of measurement in each culture under study	(plus) **identical metric** of scales in each culture under study	(plus) **identical origin** of the scale (zero) and **same form of distribution** in each culture under study	Types of equivalence
conceptual	−	−	−	assumed
weak	+	−	−	dimensional/functional
strong	+	+	−	metric
strict	+	+	+	full score

Note: Types of universals in cross-cultural theorizing and research from the physical perspective based on the increasing dignity of the scaling level (van de Vijver and Poortinga, 1982), and corresponding types of comparability/equivalence of measures (van de Vijver and Leung, 1997).

almost every method textbook in psychology and cross-cultural psychology are based (Berry et al., 1992; Malpass and Poortinga, 1986; Poortinga and Malpass, 1986; van de Vijver and Leung, 1997). Hence it is not necessary to elaborate on this perspective in detail.

To understand the logic of this approach, particularly in cross-cultural psychology, two aspects require mentioning. The first is that the original 'paradigm of multitude and extent' was integrated into this perspective. This is reasonable, because the physical perspective, as used in psychology and cross-cultural psychology, is largely dominated by methods (quantitative and experimental). The content of the different theories tested under this approach may vary tremendously (it is no longer just learning theory, which constituted the mechanistic model in 1979). The second aspect concerns the meaning of basic concepts in cross-cultural psychology: *comparability* and *universals*. Every paradigm I distinguished in 1979 implies a *logic of comparison* and *assumptions about the universals*, which constitute the '*tertium comparationis*'. Both basic features of the cross-cultural approach (comparability and universals) are exclusively defined by the 'dignity' or power of the methods' level of scaling (reflecting the dictate of methods Feyerabend, 1975, cautioned against). This is exemplified in table 15.1, which is the result of integrating ideas presented in two different papers (cf. Eckensberger and Plath, in press).

The biological perspective (organismic, evolutionary view of human beings)

During the last twenty years sociobiology (Wilson, 1975) really set out to conquer the scientific world. So I will focus on that approach, which is much easier to characterize than other biological models. The theory itself is considered to represent a 'paradigm shift' (Wuketits, 1997), because it took a totally new look at the adaptive processes of organisms in their environment. Although selection always works via the organism (Mayr, 1994) its effects are now primarily defined at the level of genes. Hence social behaviour is understood as mainly serving the function of increasing the inclusive fitness of genes.

The theory of sociobiology is based on the following premises (Keller, 1999): (1) Humans *do not* have a special position in nature, rather they follow the same biological laws and principles that govern all species, that is, they strive for *optimal reproductive success*. (2) Reproductive success is the result of (a) the reproduction of the single organism (Darwinian fitness), and (b) the reproduction of relatives who share some genes (indirect fitness). Both types of fitness together are called the inclusive fitness of an organism (Hamilton, 1964). (3) The analytical unit under an evolutionary perspective is *not* the organism but the gene, although the selection of the genes happens via the phenotype. The individual organism is only the 'carrier of the genes'. Yet the organism plays an important role. First, selection can only work through the phenotype (organism) and hence through ontogeny. Second, the *expression* of the genotype in the phenotype represents the *proximate cause* of body/body attributes. The maximization of the inclusive fitness, i.e. reproductive success, represents the *ultimate cause*. (4) But reproduction also depends on available environmental resources and/or constraints. That is, the gene pool changes owing to *environmental pressures* (resources). These resources also entail social complexity or niches, which are the result of the reproduction of former generations. (5) The reproductive processes shape not only somatic features of the organisms via phylogeny, but also the complex attributes of human beings. (6) Not (just) the adult organism is the product of biological evolution, but also the developmental 'stages' or phases of ontogeny. The individual lifespan is the result of implicit (unconscious, unintended) cost–benefit evaluations: conflicts between parents and offspring, between siblings, as well as partner selection and parental investment strategies, to mention but a few.

This perspective is applied in cross-cultural (Chasiotis and Keller, 1994; Keller, 1997) and developmental psychology (Belsky, Steinberg and Draper, 1991; Chasiotis and Voland, 1998), and in anthropology and social sciences in general (Maxwell, 1991). The interesting point here is that predictions in this model are also made about *ontogenetic* stages. But it is important to understand that although ontogeny is the *object of explanation*, the *explanatory principles* are still phylogenetic ones. Cross-cultural comparisons under this perspective are based upon 'natural universals', i.e. reproductive success and particular resource conditions. Instead of mathematical methods focusing on taxonomies (numerical frequencies) and experimentation, however, a search for homologies, single case studies and observational methods was cultivated (Mayr, 1991).

Recent developments in neurophysiology also represent a 'biological perspective'. Neurophysiological processes, which are assumed to be shaped through phylogeny, can be regarded as mechanisms, which represent *proximate causes*. The impact of this domain of research has been tremendous in recent years. One reason for the explosion of work in this area was the availability of new research methods (Roth, 1997; Singer, 2000), which allow one to measure brain activities while the living brain is working (perceiving, thinking, feeling).

The perspective of the self-reflective human being

Under this perspective humans can be called *Homo interpretans* (Eckensberger, 1993), they are *meaning creating* creatures (an *animal symbolicum*, Cassirer, 1944), hence they struggle with concepts such as truth, morality and beauty.

This perspective is not meant to represent the one-sided cognitive monster Bischof (1993) talks about. It encompasses all classical psychological functions (cognitions, affects, motives), specifically from an action-theory point of view. Action theory is not a unitary theory, agreed upon by the scientific community, but rather a unique perspective. However, those features relevant in the present context will be mentioned (for a recent summary see Eckensberger, in press; Brandtstädter, 1998, gives a comprehensive summary of its use in developmental psychology).

Actions are largely *conscious activities* of an *agency*. The agency has the *potential* to *reflect* upon (a) *his/her actions* as well as (b) upon *him/herself as an agency*. This is why I proposed interpreting action theories as a 'theory family' based on the *potentially self-reflective subject or agency* in 1979. As this perspective is not (part of) mainstream psychology (yet), it requires some elaboration.

To *act* does not mean to *behave*. To speak of an *action* rather than behaviour implies the following features:

Intentionality means that sentences, symbols as well as mental states *refer to* something in the world (Searle, 1980). The intentional state of an action is the *intent of the action*. Its content is the *intended consequence* or *goal*. This implies the so-called 'futurity' (Barbalet, 1997) or future orientation of an action.

Actions are not necessarily observable. If they are, one uses the term *doing* (Groeben, 1986). It is assumed that action involves the *free choice* to do something (A or B), to let something happen or to refrain from doing something (von Wright, 1971). This is strongly related to the (subjective perception) of *free will* (this does not imply that unconscious processes have no influence on human activities; however, they remain the *reasons* for actions).

There are *different types of actions*. If they are directed at the physical/material world and aim at bringing about some effect or suppressing some effect, they are called *instrumental actions* ('letting things happen' also belongs to this type of action; von Wright, 1971). If actions are directed at the social world, i.e. at another agency B, they cannot (causally) 'bring something about' in B, but have to be coordinated with B's intentions. Therefore, agency B's intentions have to be understood (interpreted by agency A). This presupposes a communicative attitude (Habermas, 1984). This type of action is called *communicative action*. If this orientation not only implies *understanding* B, but also *respecting* B's intentions, this is clearly a *moral action*. If B's intentions are simply used for A's benefit it is a *strategic action* (Habermas, 1984). Interestingly, Sinha (1996) points to the fact that in non-Western philosophies/religions (Hinduism, Buddhism, Confucianism) this 'adaptive attitude' and respect for the 'non-A' is extended to the plant and animal worlds. So one may distinguish between two action types that aim at A's *control* of the environment (instrumental and strategic) and two action types that aim at *harmonizing* A with the environment (see Eckensberger, 1996a, for a detailed elaboration of these distinctions).

There is considerable agreement among researchers that actions have more than one goal. They can be seen as a chain or a hierarchy.

The fact that actions are meaningful to an agency implies that *this meaning is precisely* what has to be identified empirically. This calls for *hermeneutic* methods, because actions have to be interpreted. Harré (1977) calls for an ethogenic approach (ethogenics literally means 'meaning-giving'). This does not just refer to the dichotomy between qualitative and quantitative methods in psychology, rather it is a basic methodical feature derived from the theoretical model of an action (it should be noted, however, that no science can do without interpretation). Cross-cultural comparisons under this perspective are therefore based upon the assumption of 'interpretative universals'.

Affects determine the 'valence' of a goal (and therefore of the environment in general). As actions have more than one goal, goals are also 'polyvalent' (Boesch, 1991). Additionally, affects evaluate the course of an action (dealing with barriers, impediments during the action) and the outcome of an action (whether the action was successful or not). Impediments generally *increase consciousness*. Moreover, *regulatory processes* are of special interest in theory and research. They are coping strategies for dealing with occurring affects (*external* or primary control, *action* or secondary control). They are basic for the development and occurrence of conscious processes (Piaget, 1971, 1974). Regarding these regulatory processes as *secondary actions* (as Janet proposed) is attractive from a systematic point of view, because they are in fact 'action-oriented actions' (Eckensberger, 1995).

In empirical work on *agency*, the assumption of *conscious actions* is discussed in different ways. While some authors claim that consciousness is a necessary aspect of an action (which also implies the methodical possibility of asking actors about their actions), others claim that only the potential self-reflectivity of an agency (and a specific action) is crucial (Eckensberger, 1979). This not only implies that self-reflective actions may be rare events, but also *that actions can become automatisms*, etc., and as such still remain actions. This calls for the analysis of the *development of actions*. Development therefore is a genuine and crucial dimension in many action theories (as micro-process or actual genesis, as ontogenesis, and as social/cultural change, see below). In research focusing on the *development of agency*, self-development is central. In this context the agency's experience of *being able to act* (called action potential or communicative competency) as a triggering or incitement condition for agency development is of particular interest. Piaget claims that the development of consciousness begins with the goal to act and agency only develops after this. He even claims that the agency can never be 'self-conscious' in the strict philosophical sense (Kesselring, 1981, p. 132). The development of agency can itself be considered an action – a project of identity development – which has a goal and may fail (Brandtstädter, 1998). I thus proposed calling these identity projects, which have agency-related action structures, 'tertiary actions' (Eckensberger, 1995).

Since the action links an agency to the (social and non-social) environment, the action is the *bridge* between what is called the *internal* and *external action fields*. The *internal action field* is formed during ontogenetic experiences in the sense that actions are internalized as operations (in terms of Piaget's theory) and normative rules (Turiel, 1998) or categories, which, for instance, develop from (action bound) taskonomies to (generalized) taxonomies. These developments as well as control theories, individual rule systems (logic, understanding of morality, law, conventions) and ideas of the self as agency constitute the *internal action* field. Obviously *language* is crucial for and in interaction with other agencies.

This short description should have made evident that the features which characterize human actions and agencies are assumed to be universal. All humans are assumed to develop goals, to coordinate their interests, goals and actions with themselves and others (Eckensberger and Zimba, 1997). They use emotions as regulatory processes, they develop a sense of agency and they communicate. But there is considerable variation in the quality and content of these aspects, which, of course, also leads to the question of cultural comparisons (see Eckensberger, 2000).

The cultural perspective (the historically situated human being)

As mentioned, it is difficult to describe the various perspectives 'in pure terms'. This is particularly evident in the case of the 'cultural perspective'. The reason is that the culture concept itself is usually defined *in relation* to other perspectives, and in particular it is discussed in terms of the tension between the 'double destiny of man as a natural and cultural being' (Jahoda and Krewer, 1997, p. 9).

In addition to this tension two dimensions need to be considered when the culture concept is discussed: (a) Whether it is a *descriptive* or a *prescriptive* term, and (b) whether it is an intentional (individually bound) or a supra-individual phenomenon. This is already evident in the concept of *Volksgeist* that Lazarus and Steinthal (1860) spoke about. In a way this continues in the classical paper on the concept of culture by White (1959), in which he argues for an understanding of culture as *extra-somatic symbols*, called *symbolates*, which are 'ossified' forms of human behaviour. Nowadays, culture is defined as being constituted by *rules* (normative claims), which coordinate human activities in terms of *habits* and *customs*, by *material products* of actions and by *symbolic meanings* (Renner, 1983). No wonder that it was difficult at times to distinguish between psychology and anthropology from a bird's-eye view, and even more so when later, during the 'cognitive shift' in anthropology (cf. D'Andrade, 1984), culture was no longer just considered 'extra-somatic', but also 'intra-somatic', and the relationship between internal and external rule systems became a key issue (Shweder, 1980). Moreover, since Herder's (1784–91) conception of culture (see below), *language* is regarded as a central feature, which at times even led to the identification of culture (mentality of a cultural group) with language. Under this perspective the universals are 'cultural' and refer to material aspects of culture, social regularities (rites, conventions) and symbolic structures which are found in every culture but vary in content.

Demarcation of the four perspectives: classical dichotomies in psychology

The arrangement of the perspectives in figure 15.1 provides a plausible way to localize the 'classical splits' in psychological theorizing at a conceptual level (see figure 15.2).

Going back to the old distinction of Descartes, there are the two worlds: *res extensa* (the material world) and *res cogitans* (the spiritual or mental world). This distinction is not only outdated, but also semantically weak, because the realm of *cogitans* is precisely not *res*. Yet this fundamental distinction is still the basis of the division between natural sciences and humanities, which C. P. Snow (1963) called 'the two cultures' in his famous Cambridge lecture, thereby also pointing to genuine differences in interpreting both the world and humans.

Particularly from the perspective of the self-reflective human being, three specific dichotomies can be identified, representing the *demarcation lines* between the perspectives: the mind/matter dichotomy between the *self-reflective perspective* and the *physical perspective*, which is related to the split between finality and causality as well as that between reasons and causes (Eckensberger, 1996a; von Wright, 1971); and the 'human/animal' split between *biological theories* (like sociobiology and neuroscience) and the *potentially self-reflective*

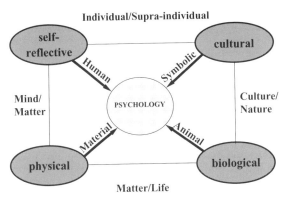

Figure 15.2 Classical (conceptual) dichotomies in psychology as seen from the four perspectives.

human being. Moreover, a dichotomy between the *self-reflective* and the *cultural perspective* can be specified. Whereas culture is a 'super-organic' entity, self-reflectivity relates to the individual (this is an old debate in the culture and personality school; Eckensberger and Römhild, 2000). The question of whether culture is external or internal to the individual (D'Andrade, 1984; Geertz, 1973) is relevant here too, and whether cognitive representations are individual or social (Jahoda, 1988), to mention just some examples.

But there are also classical dichotomies dividing the other perspectives. There is the *nature/culture* dichotomy between the cultural and the biological perspective as well as a *symbolic/material* split between the cultural and the physical perspective, and the *matter/life* dichotomy separating biological and physical theories. This split is related to the one between *causality* and *functionality.* This may not be as salient, but is, however, clearly represented in philosophy of science literature. There it is evident that one is not justified in concluding that, if some *x* serves a distinct function *y*, that this function *y* is therefore also the cause of *x*. This relates to the fact that phenomena in biology usually have multiple functions, which might not all be causes (cf. Hempel, 1959).

Moreover, the perspectives also differ in their *epistemological positions,* pointing to the incommensurability of at least some of them. If we follow Madill, Jordan and Shirley (2000) roughly three epistemological orientations can be distinguished in science of science: (a) the *realist orientation* (with naive, scientific and critical realist sub-orientations), (b) *contextual constructionism,* and (c) *radical constructionism.*

The *realist orientation* is mostly found in natural sciences (physical and biological perspective). Though 'naive realism' is outdated or rare today, scientific and critical realism are not. While naive realists follow a correspondence theory of truth, scientific realists claim that the scientific method can tap true representations of the world. Critical realists state that the way we perceive facts depends partly upon our beliefs and expectations. Although they all assume that knowledge about the world is *discovered*, 'critical realism... has much in common with constructionist positions' (Madill et al., 2000, p. 3). *Contextual constructionists* aim at an analysis of intersubjective meaning, hence this position was primarily developed in social science, where the 'researcher and the subject of research are both conscious beings interpreting and acting on the world around them within networks of cultural meanings' (p. 9). This is one reason why Habermas (1984) proposes 'bifocality' as the stance of social scientists, a simultaneously objectivizing and performatory attitude towards the subjects. Finally, *radical constructionism* challenges the realist foundations of (absolute) knowledge altogether. In this view, the phenomena under study are understood to be more or less constituted by the methodologies used to examine them. 'Hence knowledge is considered a discursive construction, questions of absolute truth or falsity are put to one side, and the spotlight turned toward the ways in which knowledge claims function and are legitimated within overarching "regimes of truth", such as discourses of science' (Madill et al., 2000, p. 13).

These orientations have a clear historical dimension (the increasing 'primacy of the abstract', of theories over facts, a domination of epistemology over ontology; Eckensberger, 2000). Simultaneously these positions also correspond to the 'perspectives' distinguished. *Realism* has much in common with the physical and biological perspectives, whereas the *constructionist positions* are more prevalent in the other two perspectives (the self-reflective human and the cultural).

The perspectives also differ in terms of *methodical standards*, particularly as far as *operationalization and prediction* are concerned. For many psychologists, particularly those advocating the 'physical perspective', operationalization is the method of choice. In this regard the status quo of the concept of operationalization is especially relevant. Even today most textbooks on methods in psychology advocate operationalization as *the* standard procedure. Green (1992) analysed twenty textbooks and only one (!) presented an historical and critical treatment of this concept. This is astonishing, because there is a long and extensive tradition critical of operationalism,[4] the main tenets of which 'have long been rejected by virtually every serious philosopher' (such as Carnap, Frank, Hempel; see Green, 1992, p. 297), including Bridgman himself, who counts as the father of that approach. He wrote in 1954, 'I feel as if I have created a Frankenstein, which has certainly gotten away from me. I abhor the word *operationalism* or *operationism*' (Bridgman, 1954/1961, p. 76).

---

[4] For recent overviews see *Theory and Psychology*, 11(1), 2001.

While in the original operationism (proposed by Bridgman for physics) operations were to *replace* metaphysical concepts, in psychology they are used as *indicators* or *expressions*, or even *to create underlying variables.* So 'they suffer from precisely the problem that Bridgman had attempted to address: what *ontological* sense are you to make of an entity which, in principle, defies observation?' (Green, 1992, p. 300). As Bickhard (1992) puts it, 'Operational definitionalism produced absurdities ... It proved incapable of defining dispositional concepts, such as malleable, ductile, mass, charge, magnetic and other scientifically fundamental concepts ... It is theories as a whole, not just individual words, that have *meaning* about the world. Procedures for measuring or detecting or classifying instances of various concepts can ... *in no case ... change or provide meaning that was not there in the first place*' (p. 323, italics added). Consequently, Bickhard calls it a myth that operationalizations provide and specify meaning.

The limitations outweigh the possibilities of operationalism even within the *physical perspective* (which still generally advocates it). In addition the process of multiple operationalizations (triangulation, convergence) contributed considerably to the fragmentation that psychology is lamenting about. What does this mean for the other perspectives? Is there a common canon of methods, which is independent of the perspective taken?

Rychlak (1993) is quite clear on this issue: Though 'proposals for alternative methods are mushrooming', he argues 'in favour of retaining the rigors of validation even as we liberalize theorizing in psychology ... as a science we must advance to the additional "control and prediction" testing of validation. Anything less is anathema to a scientific profession' (p. 935). If this means that we should follow an experimental 'paradigm' that ultimately defines causality, then I cannot disagree with this statement strongly enough. There are a considerable number of other modes of explanation (Bickhard, 1992, pp. 321f.) that are not causal, yet accepted and useful in science. Apart from this the experiment by its very nature is an *intentionally* controlled situation. *So intentionality (that of the researcher) is a precondition for the definition of causality* (von Wright, 1971). Both the assumption that scientific concepts have to be operationalized and that theories, which contain concepts that cannot be measured, are unscientific, are unmasked as 'myths' still adhered to in psychology by Bickhard (1992). He rightly concludes: 'The genuine empirical constraint is that theories must ultimately be empirically testable, not that their individual concepts are measurable' (p. 325).

The *role of prediction* primarily continues to serve as an essential criterion in realist (physical) approaches. However, even in biological perspectives it is losing its power. Much more often biological research work proceeds on the basis of carefully selected behaviour observations instead of 'controlled predictions' (Mayr, 1994). In constructionism the research aim is to *reconstruct,* not to explain – although cultural agreements like rules and conventions may also allow predictions (Smedslund, 1988). They are, however, not based on assumptions of causality. If predictions are made under these orientations, they have to be made under specific conditions, which may vary (in an uncontrolled manner). Hence, predictions have rather to be made for different *scenarios*.

A closer look at the relationships between perspectives: beyond incommensurability

Obviously, as a whole these 'dichotomies' also imply that the perspectives are meant to be mutually exclusive or incommensurable. This is, for instance, the position taken by Rychlak (1993), who argues that 'the groundings [perspectives in my terms] are no more reconcilable than the wave-particle grounding (which both are competing and incommensurable interpretations of light) in physics' (1993, p. 936).

The issue of what incommensurability means has been differentiated much more post Kuhn. Slife (2000), on the basis of Bernstein's (1983) work, distinguishes between *incompatibility and incommensurability*. *Incompatibility* is the *logical* contradiction between terms or assumptions of two theories. For example, modern neurophysiological theories deny the existence of free will (Singer, 2000), which means that humans cannot act 'otherwise'. However, action theories make free will a basic assumption (see Eckensberger, in press), because they assume that humans can act 'otherwise'. Making both assumptions at the same time is not logically possible. Yet, '*incompatibilities* still imply a common *logical* ground for knowing that they are incompatible or contradictory' (Slife, 2000, p. 266, italics added). *Incommensurability* goes beyond this, and also includes language, background framework, philosophical world view and hence issues of evidence and truth (e.g. the distinctions between modernism and postmodernism).

Two further clarifications are important. First, there is no reason for incommensurable theories not to coexist, or not to be used in a complementary way. Second, '*incommensurability* does not imply *incomparability* and thus absolute relativity and nihilism. Indeed, incommensurability implies, by its very nature, that we know about and can bring into relationships what we consider incommensurable...Discourse communities, in this sense, can have incommensurable languages and methods, but the very fact that we...can know these alternative languages and differing standards means that there is a fundamental basis for comparison' (Slife, 2000, pp. 268f.). So incommensurable theories can be compared. This view forms the basis for possible ways of interrelating perspectives, paradigms or theories.

It prepares the way for interpreting the perspectives distinguished as complementary, namely no longer focusing so much on the demarcations but rather searching for types of interrelationships between the perspectives, which in the long run may lead to integration. Obviously *integration* is a highly valued form of interrelationship. Many attempt to integrate existing theoretical perspectives, e.g. sometimes the nature/nurture dichotomy is called an illusion (Chasiotis and Keller, 1994) or the 'rough distinction' between causality and intentionality (Bischof, 1993). And of course, in most disciplines, including psychology, a 'unified' theory would be preferred. Given the distinctions I proposed, I doubt that this is easily possible though, and some 'integrations' may even turn out to be 'illusions'.

Theoretically there seem to be three (divergent) ways of tackling this problem. One is to attempt a 'meta-analysis', as I do, and by doing so, to find similarities or identities in the underlying 'model of man'. This clearly allows for integration, although the original theories may have quite different histories or origins, and even languages. The second is to get to the 'bottom of reality', to analyse smaller and smaller particles of 'reality' as is done in the 'nano-world' of modern natural science (this is not necessarily identical to a radical realist position, even atoms were constructions at first). As I am not competent in this domain, I will not discuss the possibilities or limitations of these new trends. The third is to refrain from positing different forms of 'reality' altogether, that is to develop a *formal* language that covers all (or some) perspectives. Leibniz wanted to use mathematics for this purpose, and since then efforts to work on developing a 'formal science' are continuing (Küppers, 1994). For instance, principles of German *gestalt psychology* were in a certain sense contained in early quantum mechanics (Primas, 1984), and also used by Benedict (1934) to analyse entire cultures. Systems theory is another candidate that claimed to cover all 'levels' of reality (Haber, 1980), from subatomic particles to the universe. More recently chaos theory (Küppers, 1994) is discussed in this respect. The main problem here is that either the perspectives I distinguished are not really integrated (on the contrary, they are 'lost' because the language chosen is formal), or the different levels distinguished in chaos theory or systems theory are interpreted in terms of the content of one particular level and not understood at the same formal level as defined by the formal language.[5]

This leads to the second most prominent type of integration, *reducing* one theory to another. Different system levels interpreted by the same ontology are an example. Two problems exist with regards to reduction. First, and unfortunately, this term is often used pejoratively, though it is just one effort to unify science. The devaluation often implied is not intended here. Reduction

---

[5] Boulding (1978), for instance, interprets the reconstruction of Warsaw, after 97 per cent of it was destroyed by the Germans in the Second World War, as a 'recovery' of a non-natural ecosystem. This conclusion clearly is a categorical mistake, this 'recovery' is not comparable to the causal and functional processes in the recovery of an ecosystem. It was intended, and was based on the cultural identity of the Poles.

is an acceptable theoretical procedure. However, and this is crucial, it *has* to be justified. The second problem is that the term is extremely opaque in detail, and has a complex history in the science of science (Carrier, 1995). Only a few distinctions will be referred to here. First, reductionism is only justifiable if the terms of two theories are neither incommensurable nor incompatible. Second, in some 'stronger forms' of reductionism it must be possible to translate all terms of a theory into another theory, and all derivations of a theory also have to be possible in the theory to which it is reduced. In a weak form of reductionism (explanatory reductionism) the new (or alternative) theory need only be able to explain (and often to predict) the same 'facts' as the old one. This actually just means replacing one theory by another without really 'reducing' it.

Particularly in the 'rhetoric' understanding of science the term *metaphor* is central. However problematic the relation between epistemology and ontology is on the one hand, and between 'objective truth' and discourse about truth on the other, metaphors have a long tradition and are extremely important in psychology (Soyland, 1994). Reductionism and the use of metaphors have something in common, because using a metaphor is 'giving the thing a name that belongs to something else' (Aristotle cited in Soyland, 1994, p. 106). As every use of a metaphor involves a complicated system of implications, this system obtains an explanatory function, and comes close to at least a weak form of reductionism. Above, Bischof's application of biological models was identified as 'literal' and Piaget's usage of biological terms as 'metaphoric'. This distinction has to be explained. One can argue, like Soyland (1994, p. 121), that the metaphoric use of a term (or concept) is metaphoric only when it is introduced into the scientific discourse, and that it becomes literal when it is no longer new. I agree, but I would like to add two important aspects. First, one can use a comparison literally from the very beginning, and second, in using a metaphor habitually, it obtains a surplus meaning, one it did not necessarily possess initially. Thus, to remember that a term was introduced as a metaphor, and what the metaphor was about, is essential. Metaphoric thinking is '*as if*' 'thinking', and this should be kept in mind.

There is a third category of relationships between theories I consider particularly important in the present context. This is what Harré (1977) calls *enabling conditions*. They are not causal conditions that produce some effects, but rather – in the case of psychology – refer to conditions that enable a psychological phenomenon to occur. So this concept can specify the relationship within and between perspectives too.

The last type of relationship we have to consider is *complementarity*. As long as detailed distinctions and forms of complementarity are avoided (cf. Reich, 1994) this proposal is simple. All perspectives remain separate, as they are, accepting 'that there are different ways to skin a cat'. Most importantly, however, all perspectives have their own truth claims, which are difficult to evaluate objectively. This position was my own in 1979 and it is also implied in the analysis of Reese and Overton (1970). It is Rychlak's (1993) too (although he takes a different position on the relationship between methods and groundings), who, after summarizing divergent 'groundings' of research on emotions, claims that they 'lend different meanings to the target in question, meanings that cannot be welded together' and, later, 'As I noted earlier, according to complementarity it does not matter what the real nature of an emotion *is*' (p. 939, italics in the original). A prominent example (which is also Rychlak's starting point) is the *wave* and *particle theories* of light in physics, both of which are accepted. We simply have to learn that the same thing can be something different if looked at from a different point of view.

Relationships as seen from the physical perspective

It is worth mentioning that historically the *physical* (material, mechanistic, objectivizing) perspective had to be developed by first intentionally separating it from the self-reflective perspective. This is exemplified in terms such as 'energy', 'force' or 'power' (Szabó, 1976), which were taken from human characteristics, but then 'objectivized' by the intentional exclusion of subjectivity from natural sciences (Laucken, 2001, gives excellent references in this connection). Consequently it is no surprise that subjective terms are difficult to grasp under this perspective. Subjectivity is considered *incompatible* with this perspective (because something cannot be objective and subjective at the same time). Moreover, complementarity is not accepted, because it is not part of its methodical and methodological demands. It is interesting, however, that self-reflectivity as such is considered to exist as a phenomenon.[6] Figure 15.3 provides a summary of these and subsequent arguments.

The cultural and biological perspectives are reduced (in the weak form of the term) to methodical standards. The status of the culture concept differs somewhat in different psychological studies: In *differentiation studies*, which investigate the influence of cultural conditions upon psychological concepts, it is reduced to individual variables or a set of variables – it is operationalized (Segall, 1984). Recently, culture has been handled in a more sophisticated way at an aggregate level by using multilevel analyses, which apply the same mathematics at the individual and cultural level and interrelate them by the very same logic of linear equation systems (Leung, 1989; van de Vijver and Leung, 1997). In *generalization studies*, which basically aim at establishing a universal psychology, the goal is 'peeling the onion called culture' (Poortinga, van de Vijver and van de Koppel, 1987). A similar attitude is expressed by

---

[6] For example, Poortinga and Malpass 'do not deny the *reality* of the phenomena which Eckensberger wants to encapsulate. We only see the realm of scientific research in psychology as more restricted than he does' (1986, p. 46, footnote, italics added).

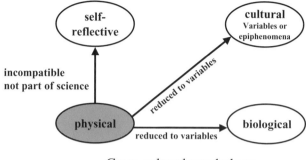

Cross-cultural psychology

Figure 15.3   Relations as seen from the viewpoint of the physical ideal (perspective) in cross-cultural psychology.

Baltes, Nesselroade and Reese (1977), when they elaborate 'As the precision of a theory increases, the general usefulness of comparative developmental work probably decreases' (p. 193). So, in this case culture is considered an epiphenomenon.

In the long tradition of the nature/nurture discussion, the relative 'amount' of cultural and biological influence on behavioural variations is an important question within this perspective. They are assumed to affect different psychological domains or variables directly, but to a different degree (quantitatively). While physiologically based behaviours (including perception) are influenced primarily by biological (genetic) transmissions, personality and social behaviour are shaped largely by cultural transmissions (Poortinga, Kop and van de Vijver, 1989).

Relationships as seen from the biological perspective

It is interesting to note that biology as a science also at first had to explicitly abandon the self-reflective terminology of intentionality (teleology or creation as underlying phylogeny) and to develop such terms as teleonomy and functionality (Wuketits, 1997). It also took an amazingly long time to emancipate itself from causal interpretations, which characterize the (classical) physical perspective, to explain life. It is important to note from a methodical viewpoint that a discussion about methods unique to biology began specifically to achieve a demarcation from (classical) physics (Mayr, 1991). Particularly with regard to the concept of inclusive fitness, it is noteworthy that the gene was considered 'selfish'. Although this is clearly and explicitly understood as a *metaphor* (*'as if'* thinking), it still represents a metaphorical use of self-reflectivity. One can justifiably ask why this is necessary or useful. Figure 15.4 summarizes the main relationships between the biological and the other perspectives distinguished.

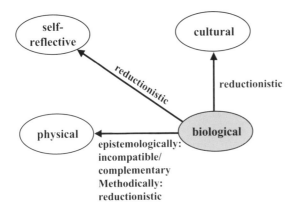

Cross-cultural psychology

Figure 15.4   Relations as seen from the biological perspective in cross-cultural psychology.

The relation between the biological and the physical perspective can justifiably be considered incompatible, if the perspective is taken seriously in psychology. But concrete empirical work done from and within the former perspective still follows the physical model rather consistently. It applies the methodical standards that psychology developed under a physical perspective without any (visible) changes. So, in a way, those psychologists who work under a biological perspective actually use the physical perspective as far as methods are concerned.

The two other perspectives are explicitly treated reductionistically. On the one hand, it is evident that the model of man implied in sociobiology seems to negate the model of man implied in action theories and in the cultural approaches. Neither intentionality nor self-reflectivity is an explicit *category of explanation*. If intentionality and self-reflectivity were accepted as basic features of humans, one would insist that they are results of phylogeny, and as such serve the adaptive function of increasing inclusive fitness – otherwise they would not have developed (Voland, personal communication[7]). In general, human attributes are no more 'unique' than attributes of other species. So intentionality and reflectivity would be as unique to humans as flying is to birds and living under water is to fish.

The same is true for culture. It is interpreted in biological terms and hence reduced to this perspective, as the following citations illustrate. Chasiotis and Keller (1994), for instance, explain that culture 'is a product of selfish individuals, who are forced to live in groups' (p. 77, translation by the author),

---

[7] Statement made in a debate between Voland and Eckensberger in *Spektrum der Wissenschaften*, April 2001.

and they consider it an epiphenomenon. Count (1958) states that 'Culture is man's peculiar elaborate way of expressing the vertebrate biogram' (p. 1049). Or 'in human culture the slow biological evolution is superimposed by a meta-evolution, by the cultural evolution. This offers a huge advantage in fitness to the biogenetically evolved carriers of the culture (human beings). They can adapt to changing environmental conditions much more quickly than would be possible within the frame of (bio)genetic evolution' (Verbeek, 1994, translation by the author).

A similar situation exists in neurobiology. Singer (2000) denies the existence of free will altogether and relegates decisions (which we only become aware of much later) to the brain, which therefore determines what humans do. According to him, intentionality is the result of a cultural attribution, and thus an 'illusion'. Roth et al. (1998) on the other hand, seem to be more cautious. They discuss the problem of reductionism, but avoid it by a 'double operationalization' of psychological variables and brain activities, which can be correlated and are two sides of the same coin. I would call this an example of *complementarity*.

Relationships as seen from the self-reflective perspective

From the self-reflective perspective the relationship to the physical perspective is one of incompatibility. Although some authors try to explain actions by interpreting these intentions as causes of actions, there is agreement at present that actions cannot be *explained* by (efficient material) *causes*, rather they have to be *understood* in terms of their *reasons* (cf. Habermas, 1984; von Wright, 1971).

Several efforts to overcome the interpretive dichotomy implied between explanation in natural science and understanding of actions have been attempted (a comprehensive overview is given in the collection of papers edited by Schurz, 1988). In these efforts the causal interpretation is often extended to actions (with reference to motives, for instance), and the understanding interpretation is extended to natural-science explanations, though actions are still interpreted as based on intentionality even by von Wright (1994, pp. 177f.), which is something other than material causality. Actions are interpreted by referring to a reason (instead of a cause) and I think von Wright's distinction, which implies incompatibility at a very basic level, is still essential for psychologists.

The relation to the biological perspective is different. Clearly the biological preconditions for actions are overwhelming. Janet, for instance, explicitly systematized the transition from animal to human (Schwartz, 1951). He refers to the historical transformation of forms of action, the main concept being that of *adaptation to environmental conditions*, although this was not intended to be strictly biological in all respects. Janet wrote: 'Evolution has not come to an end yet. The action of humans was a source of miracles in the past and it will be so in future' (cited in Schwartz, 1951). Additionally, in order to demonstrate that simpler mechanisms of action tendencies are still present in humans, Janet

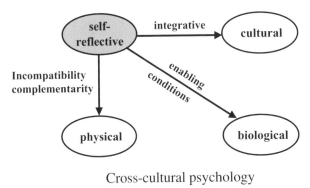

Cross-cultural psychology

Figure 15.5   Relations as seen from the self-reflective perspective in cross-cultural psychology.

repeatedly formulated his arguments within the context of habits and/or pathological states (such as when acting under the influence of drugs). But he also refers to phylogeny. Janet distinguished a total of nine levels of action tendencies, which he combined into three groups: (a) lower action tendencies (simple reflex chains; perceptual and suspended actions; sociopersonal actions and elemental intellectual behaviours); (b) action tendencies of a medium complexity (immediate actions and belief functions; deliberate actions); and (c) highest action tendencies (rational actions, experimental actions, progressive actions).

The first three tendencies were reserved for animals, the fourth tendency is also present in higher-order animals, and in principle human actions begin here. There are, however, already characteristics in perceptual and suspended actions (like an animal hunting other animals), which are precursors of human actions. So in a way there is continuity, but also a clear 'ontological' difference between the activity of animals and the highest tendencies of humans. Tomasello (2001) recently pointed out these differences. He underlines the fact that humans and animals have much in common, but that humans have *specific* cognitive attributes which animals do not have (use of symbols, joint attention, reproduction of intentional acts, collaboration with mental states of others and intentional affordances in object manipulations). The main point here is that this 'uniqueness' of *Homo sapiens* is not to be understood at the same adaptive level as the uniqueness of other species (that fish can swim and birds can fly), but rather that it allows *Homo sapiens* to 'step out of biological constraints'.[8] Humans 'can do otherwise', they can act in a way that is biologically not

---

[8] This fact is impressively described in the metaphor of the 'tree of knowledge' in the Bible and in the Koran: by eating the apple humans become self-reflecting (they 'recognize' themselves) and they are not in Paradise (in nature) any more. (For a more detailed discussion see Eckensberger, 1993.)

adaptive. Even Dawkins (1976), who can be considered as one of the fathers of sociobiology, realized that the application of biological interpretations to humans has limitations, when he elaborated in *The selfish gene*: 'Be warned that if you wish, as I do, to build a society in which individuals cooperate generously and unselfishly towards a common good, *you can expect little help from biological nature.* Let us try to teach generosity and altruism, because we are born selfish' (p. 3). Later he adds, 'We, alone on earth, can rebel against the tyranny of the selfish replicators' (which are the genes of course; Dawkins, 1989, p. 201). No matter how strongly this distinction is made, clearly an epistemological continuity does not necessarily follow from the phylogenetic continuity between man and animal. As Wright (1994) cautions, it is the 'mental organ' (or module) which is 'designed' by natural selection, not the behaviour itself.

Whether or not human actions and their consequences are biologically adaptive and increase inclusive fitness is largely an empirical question.[9] But if this general perspective is justified and plausible, then it follows that humans cannot be interpreted on the basis of biological processes and functions alone. *Biological processes and structures are enabling conditions for human actions, but actions cannot be reduced to them.* Piaget's concept of 'reflective abstraction' points in the same direction, although it is more specific. Piaget (1974) uses the auto-regulatory processes as a 'bridge' between the 'laws of matter and of mind' (Kesselring, 1981, p. 117). He assumes that the biological 'mechanisms of necessity' are akin to logico-mathematical structures, and that the latter emerge by reflecting on the former. Without going into details of Piaget's theory on this difficult matter, it should be clear that he accepts an ontological difference between matter and mind, but interrelates both via developmental processes.

The relationship to the *cultural perspective* is quite different again. Both the self-reflective and the cultural perspective converge in the emerging 'cultural psychology' (see below). Action theory was preferred in the early paper (Eckensberger, 1979) precisely because it allows one to *integrate culture into psychology.*

The action field is not only internal (see above) but also external. Within this theoretical frame an action links the actor (agency) and his/her environment (already mentioned by James, 1897), and cultures are understood as *external action field* (Boesch, 1991; Eckensberger, 1979, 1995). The *external action field* offers opportunities for and constraints to actions, but also assigns values to actions. *Rituals* (as a cultural proffer of organized action clusters) and *myths* (as complements of phantasms at the cultural level) are just as important as

---

[9] Although this problem is difficult to solve empirically. This is so because sociobiological theory is basically built upon an *economic* model (the 'behaviour' of the genes). 'Economic' rationality, however, is also possible in the context of an action theory. So even biologically adaptive behaviour cannot necessarily be interpreted by the sociobiological theory (cf. Casimir and Rao, 1992; Vining, 1986).

personal processes of construction (active production of order in the Piagetian sense). Both the internal and external action fields acquire their *affective meaning* (valence) via actions. Tool construction (not just use of tools) and language mark the beginning (transition) to human actions in Janet's classification of actions (he calls tools 'intellectual objects'). Similarly in Cole's (1996) theory artefacts (cultures) are the mediators between the object and the subject.

The external action field not only prepares for the conceptualization of culture, but also encompasses other agencies. In this context it is important that development is not only a construction or reconstruction on the part of the agency (as is so forcefully underlined by Piaget), but also a co-construction and the intended transmission (education) from one generation to the next is especially relevant (Bruner, 1996).

Although an agency is considered autonomous, actions are not arbitrary, but *follow rules* (see Eckensberger, 1996a, for a detailed description of the different rule systems – prudentiality, conventions, law, ethics and religiosity and their institutionalization as well as their interrelationship). This tension between autonomy and heteronomy is basic to all action theories, which thus also focus on the social/cultural context of actions (cf. Parsons, 1937/1968), an aspect that entails one possible relation to the cultural perspective: cultural rules and their alteration are also *man made*, although the implied intentionality of cultural rules/norms may 'be lost' in time.

There is one aspect of culture which is rarely discussed in psychology, but which is especially plausible from an action-theory perspective. Usually the development of culture is reconstructed in terms of brain evolution and social interactions. Under the perspective of self-reflectivity this view is complemented by the significance of death as the cradle of culture (Morin, 1973), the idea that knowledge and fear of the end of life is a counterpart of self-reflectivity. The body's demise is comprehensible, but death (the end) of subjective existence is not. This led to the development (creation) of religious structures, which have the function of denying the end of subjective existence or 'soul' in all religions (Beltz, 1993). In this context not only rituals and art emerged (Zimmermann, 1998),[10] but all religions also developed ideas about ontology (the development and relation between nature and humans) as well as prescriptions and prohibitions. So the social (ritual) as well as the symbolic structure of culture (rules and meaning systems) are originally bound to death and self-reflectivity. Only much later some of these domains were taken up by science[11] and philosophy.

---

[10] I thank Karl Otto Jung (Department of Fine Arts and Art Education, University of Saarbrücken) for pointing this out.

[11] It is interesting to note that sociobiology – under this perspective – has a religious structure. This is so because the genes survive although the body dies. This is not to say, of course, that sociobiology is a religion, yet one can speculate whether this structure is not one aspect of its success.

Relationships as seen from the cultural perspective

The explications just given lead one to anticipate that the relation to the perspective of the self-reflective subject allows integration. Already Kant gives *human action* a central place, and develops *human autonomy* as a possibility of freeing oneself from one's (natural) inclinations. In this tradition it is understandable that the notion of culture is deeply *normative*. It is the 'goal' of cultivation (and culture) to bring about the *ideal of a general morality* (Kant, 1784). Kant claims that a *constituted society* is the precondition for morality. Later Gehlen (1978) interpreted culture explicitly as an *achievement of humans* that transcends their 'mere nature' (therefore he called culture the 'second nature' of humans). Gehlen distinguished humans from animals by their ability to *act*: Culture, in this view, is something which is *created* (cultivated) by humans via action. This interpretation not only allows an integration with the self-reflective perspective, but also implies that 'nature' is seen as an enabling condition, which at the same time has to be 'cultivated'.

This idea is similar to Shweder's (1990) interpretation of culture as an *intentional world*. This form of integration in fact represents what is called 'cultural psychology', which is pursued by psychologists (Boesch, 1991; Cole, 1996; Eckensberger, 1990; Valsiner, 1987) as well as by anthropologists (Shweder, 1990).

Herder (1784–91) played down the role of rational actions in the development of culture, and instead described this process by *metaphors of biological growth*. Culture is still something special to humans and a 'higher' concept, but it *emerges* from history and also leads to higher forms of morality. These roots (*normativity* and *supra-individualism*) have had a long-lasting effect on later discussions of the culture concept. The question of whether it is a descriptive or a prescriptive term, and whether it is an intentional (individual) or a supra-individual phenomenon remains part of the long and controversial discussion of this concept.

The relationship to the biological perspective was sometimes meant literally, sometimes metaphorically. After the Enlightenment, for instance, the biological basis of humans, and thus universals, were focused upon. This was supplemented by the race concept in the nineteenth century (Jahoda and Krewer, 1997), and implied a 'literal' biological interpretation of culture. On the other hand in general or specific biological models 'nature' was used more or less *metaphorically* by Herder in early German philosophical anthropology, and later by Parsons (1968) as well as by some cross-cultural psychologists (Berry, 1976) and some cultural anthropologists (Rappaport, 1971; for details see Eckensberger et al., 1984). Recently sociobiological interpretations of culture have been proposed. But from a cultural perspective this is seen rather critically.

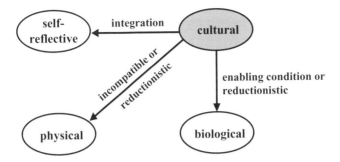

Cross-cultural psychology

Figure 15.6   Relations as seen from the cultural perspective in cross-cultural psychology.

Hallpike, for instance, ends a detailed analysis of sociobiology and its application to human kinship under an anthropological perspective as follows: 'In so far as inclusive fitness theory is a restatement of a naive individualistic reductionism with which social scientists and system theorists have long been familiar it is simply an attempt to reinvent the wheel – and a square wheel at that' (Hallpike, 1984, p. 143).

Frequently, 'bio-cultural *co-evolution*' is claimed to exist (Wuketits, 1997). But this is a misleading notion, if culture itself is not interpreted in biological terms. This is so because biological and cultural processes of change differ greatly in speed and quality. Whereas cultural change is fairly quick, biological change is extremely slow (this is exactly why biological psychologists can assume that even in modern life some regulative processes, rooted in the Pleistocene, are still in force). So one can justifiably claim that nearly all developments (changes) in human life over the last 10 million years can be interpreted as not biological, but primarily cultural changes.

These distinctions do not imply that culture is interpreted as a phenomenon which is independent of biological preconditions. Rather the biological is seen as an enabling condition. It would be quite foolish not to accept that humans emerged through phylogeny, and hence are in many respects a species like any other. But this only means that nothing in humans' development exceeded their biological *capacity* (Fiske, 2000).

The relation to the physical perspective is not as salient, although culture was also sometimes 'measured' and 'clustered' in this tradition (Naroll, 1964; Textor, 1967), as in the case of the ecological correlations that Hofstede (1980) used at the cultural level, triggering most of the research on individualism and collectivism. This is methodically clearly reductionistic.

Cultural psychology: more than a sub-branch of psychology

After all these reflections there are still good reasons to distinguish the four perspectives. However, it should also have become clear that these perspectives are not just incommensurable or incompatible (as I assumed in 1979), but rather that the interrelationships are more complicated. First, the possibility of integrating the self-reflective and cultural perspectives exists without reducing culture to the individual. Second, both the self-reflective and the cultural perspectives tend to interpret the biological heritage of humans as *enabling conditions* and not as conditions humans can be 'reduced' to. The physical perspective, which is mainly defined by methodical standards, primarily implies reductionism, if applied to the cultural as well as to the biological perspective, and it is incompatible with the perspective of the self-reflecting subject.

It turns out that by integrating the self-reflective and the cultural perspective, a cultural psychology should emerge similar to the one which actually has been developed. Concerning the epistemological positions affiliated with these perspectives, a first conclusion is possible, though it appears either over-inclusive or trivial: If culture can be understood in terms of the results of actions, and acts of meaning are creations by the potentially self-reflective *Homo sapiens, then sciences in general (including all four perspectives) are part of culture* in the first place. Science is one aspect of giving meaning to 'reality', and it is embedded in culture and cultural change processes. The development of epistemological orientations (realist, constructionist) turns out to be a cultural interpretation schema which may change over time. Sciences and reflections upon what science is about (relation to reality, truth criteria, rationality etc.) turn out to be part of cultural development (also see Bickhard, 1992). Although Cole (1996) deals with the history of science and the culture concept to some extent, the 'metaperspective' taken in the present context has not been discussed in depth by cultural psychologists as yet. If they did they would in fact follow the 'sociology of science' (Merton, 1959) as well as the 'social psychology of science' (Shadish and Fuller, 1994), which also attempt to analyse the psychological assumptions and aspects of scientific processes in the tradition of Kuhn (1970a). Cultural psychology appears to represent a *metatheory* which tries to include other sciences in its efforts to understand and explain the world.

In taking this 'metaperspective' different rule systems (prudentiality, logical thinking, conventional, legal and ethical thinking, and religiosity) can be distinguished, which are used by the person to interpret different aspects of 'reality' (Much and Shweder, 1978; see Turiel, 1998, for an overview). The same rule systems are also 'materialized' or 'ossified' in cultural institutions (technical knowledge, physics, logic, conventions, law, ethics and religion). And action-theoretical terms can be used not only to distinguish these rule systems and institutions, but also to clarify their interrelationships (Eckensberger, 1996a).

If the development of science is understood as a process of cultural change, then social coordination and cultural constructions are by definition part of this process. At the same time, this implies that the four perspectives distinguished are not 'given' by reality but are themselves cultural constructions, as are constructions of their interrelationship. It is this link in the chain of arguments that leads to the conclusion that science also implies a moral dimension. The groups or 'subcultures' that adopt the different perspectives should first clarify their basic positions and the fruitfulness of these perspectives in different content domains. That is, a cultural discourse should be 'cultivated' which continuously takes different (complementing) perspectives to the same or similar issues. The minimum condition for this discourse to take place is mutual respect – a basic ethical demand for any type of human interaction, including the scientific one. I hope that this chapter constitutes one step in the direction of such a discourse.

REFERENCES

Baltes, P. B., Nesselroade, J. R. and Reese, H. W. (1977). *Life-span development psychology: introduction in research methods.* Belmont: Wadsworth.
Barbalet, J. W. (1997). The Jamesian theory of action. *Sociobiological Review*, 45(1), 102–21.
Belsky, J., Steinberg, L. and Draper, P. (1991). Childhood experience, interpersonal development and reproductive strategy: an evolutionary theory of socialization. *Child Development*, 62, 647–70.
Beltz, W. (ed.), (1993). *Lexikon der letzten Dinge* (Lexicon of last things). Augsburg: Pattloch.
Benedict, R. (1934). *Pattern of culture.* New York: Mentor.
Bernstein, R. J. (1983). *Beyond objectivism and relativism: science, hermeneutics, and praxis.* Philadelphia: University of Pennsylvania Press.
Berry, J. W. (1976). *Human ecology and cognitive style: comparative studies in cultural and psychological adaptation.* London: Sage.
Berry, J. W., Poortinga, Y. H., Segall, M. H. and Dasen, P. R. (1992). *Cross-cultural psychology: research and applications.* Cambridge, MA: Cambridge University Press.
Bickhard, M. H. (1992). Myths of science: misconceptions of science in contemporary psychology. *Theory and Psychology*, 2(3), 321–37.
Bischof, N. (1980). Aristoteles, Galilei, Kurt Lewin – und die Folgen (Aristotle, Galilei, Kurt Lewin – and the consequences). In W. Michaelis (ed.), *Bericht über den 32. Kongress der Deutschen Gesellschaft für Psychologie, Zürich 1980* (Proceedings of the 32nd congress of the German Society of Psychology, Zurich 1980). Göttingen: Verlag für Psychologie, pp. 17–39.
(1993). Untersuchungen zur Systemanalyse der sozialen Motivierung I. Die Regulation der sozialen Distanz – Von der Feldtheorie zur Systemtheorie (Studies on the system analysis of social motivation I. The regulation of social distance – from field theory to systemic theory). *Zeitschrift für Psychologie*, 201(1) 5–43.
Boesch, E. E. (1991). *Symbolic action theory and cultural psychology.* Berlin: Springer.

Boulding, K. E. (1978) *Ecodynamics: a new theory of social evolution.* Beverly Hills: Sage.

Brandtstädter, J. (1998). Action perspectives on human development. In W. Damon and R. M. Lerner (eds.), *Handbook of child psychology*, vol. 1: *Theoretical models of human development*, 5th edn. New York: Wiley, pp. 807–63.

Bridgman, P. W. (1954/1961). The present state of operationalism. In P. Frank (ed.), *The validation of scientific theories*. New York: Collier, pp. 75–80. (Original work published in *Scientific Monthly*, 1954.)

Bruner, J. (1996). *The culture of education.* Cambridge, MA: Harvard University Press.

Cahill, S. P. (1994). A unified training model in a disunified science? Implications of 'psychology's crisis of disunity' for graduate clinical training. *International Newsletter of Uninomic Psychology*, 14, 13–16.

Carrier, M. (1995). Reduktion (Reduction). In J. Mittelstra (ed.), *Enzyklopädie Philosophie und Wissenschaftstheorie* (Encyclopaedia of philosophy and theory of science), vol. 3. Stuttgart/Weimar: J. B. Metzler, pp. 516–20.

Casimir, M. J. and Rao, A. (1992). Kulturziele und Fortpflanzungsunterschiede. Aspekte der Beziehung zwischen Macht, Besitz und Reproduktion bei den nomadischen Bakkarnal im westlichen Himalaya (Cultural goals and reproductive differences. Aspects of the relationship between power, possessions and reproduction among the Bakkarnal in Western Himalaya). In E. Voland (ed.), *Fortpflanzung: Natur und Kultur im Wechselspiel. Versuch eines Dialogs zwischen Biologen und Sozialwissenschaften* (Reproduction: the interplay between nature and culture. Trying out a dialogue between biologists and social scientists). Frankfurt am Main: Suhrkamp, pp. 270–89.

Cassirer, E. (1944). *An essay on man: an introduction to a philosophy of human culture.* New Haven, CT: Yale University Press.

Chasiotis, A. and Keller, H. (1994). Evolutionary psychology and developmental cross-cultural psychology. In A.-M. Bouvy, F. J. R. Van de Vijver, P. Boski and P. Schmitz (eds.), *Journeys into cross-cultural psychology*. Lisse: Swets and Zeitlinger, pp. 68–82.

Chasiotis, A. and Voland, E. (1998). Geschlechtliche Selektion und Individualentwicklung (Sexual selection and individual development). In H. Keller (ed.), *Lehrbuch Entwicklungspsychologie* (Textbook of developmental psychology). Göttingen: Huber, pp. 563–95.

Cole, M. (1996). *Cultural psychology: a once and future discipline.* Cambridge, MA: Belknap Press.

Count, E. W. (1958). The biological basis of human society. *American Anthropology*, 60, 1049–89.

D'Andrade, R. G. (1984). Cultural meaning systems. In R. A. Shweder and R. A. LeVine (eds.), *Cultural theory: essays on mind, self, and emotion*. New York: Cambridge University Press, pp. 88–119.

Dawkins, R. (1976). *The selfish gene.* New York: Oxford University Press.
   (1989). *The selfish gene*, 2nd edn. Oxford: Oxford University Press.

Eckensberger, L. H. (1979). A metamethodological evaluation of psychological theories from a cross-cultural perspective. In L. H. Eckensberger, W. J. Lonner and Y. H. Poortinga (eds.), *Cross-cultural contributions to psychology*. Amsterdam: Swets and Zeitlinger, pp. 255–75.

(1990). From cross-cultural psychology to cultural psychology. *Quarterly Newsletter of the Laboratory of Comparative Human Cognition*, 12(1), 37–52.

(1993). Zur Beziehung zwischen den Kategorien des Glaubens und der Religion in der Psychologie (Concerning the relationship between the categories of belief and religion in psychology). In T. V. Gamkrelidze (ed.), *Brücken. Festgabe für Gert Hummel zum 60. Geburtstag* (Bridges. Dedication to Gert Hummel's 60th birthday). Tbilisi/Konstanz: Verlag der Djawachischwili Staatsuniversität/Universitätsverlag Konstanz, pp. 5–104.

(1995). Activity or action: two different roads towards an integration of culture into psychology? *Psychology and Culture*, 1, 67–80.

(1996a) Agency, action and culture: three basic concepts for cross-cultural psychology. In J. Pandey, D. Sinha and D. P. S. Bhawuk (eds.), *Asian contributions to cross-cultural psychology*. New Delhi: Sage, pp. 72–102.

(1996b). *Nature, culture and the question 'why?'*. Paper presented at a symposium at the 'XIV Biennial Meetings of the ISSBD', Quebec City, 12–16 August.

(2000). Self reflectivity and intentionality as key characteristics of humans: consequences for a cross-cultural cultural psychology. Keynote address in the 15th International Congress of IACCD, Pultusk, Poland, 16–21 July.

(in press). Psychology of action theory. In N. J. Smelser and P. B. Baltes (eds.), *International encyclopedia of the social and behavioral sciences*. Oxford: Elsevier Science.

Eckensberger, L. H. and Burgard, P. (1983). The cross-cultural assessment of normative concepts: some considerations on the affinity between methodological approaches and preferred theories. In S. H. Irvine and J. W. Berry (eds.), *Human assessment and cultural factors*. New York: Plenum Press, pp. 459–80.

Eckensberger, L. H., Krewer, B. and Kasper, E. (1984). Simulation of cultural change by cross-cultural research: some metamethodological considerations. In K. A. McCluskey and H. W. Reese (eds.), *Life-span developmental psychology: historical and generational effects*. Orlando: Academic Press, pp. 73–108.

Eckensberger, L. H., and Plath, I. (in press). Möglichkeiten und Grenzen des 'variablenorientierten' Kulturvergleichs: Von der Kulturvergleichenden Psychologie zur Kulturpsychologie (Possibilities and limitations of a variable-based comparison of cultures: from cross-cultural psychology to cultural psychology). In H. Kaelble and J. Schriewer (eds.), *Vergleich und Transfer – Komparatistik in den Sozial-, Geschichts- und Kulturwissenschaften* (Comparison and transfer – comparability in the social, historical, and cultural sciences). Frankfurt am Main, New York: Campus.

Eckensberger, L. H. and Römhild, R. (2000). Kulturelle Einflüsse (Cultural influences). In M. Amelang (ed.), *Enzyklopädie der Psychologie* (Encyclopaedia of psychology), vol. 4: *Determinanten individueller Unterschiede* (Determinants of individual differences). Göttingen: Hogrefe, pp. 667–731.

Eckensberger, L. H. and Zimba, R. F. (1997). The development of moral judgement. In J. W. Berry, P. R. Dasen and T. S. Saraswathi (eds.), *Handbook of cross-cultural psychology*, vol. 2: *Basic processes and human development*. Boston: Allyn and Bacon, pp. 299–338.

Feyerabend, P. (1975). *Against method: outline of an anarchistic theory of knowledge*. London: New Left Books.

Fishman, D. (1990). Beyond positivism: the pragmatic paradigm in psychology. *International Newsletter of Uninomic Psychology*, 11, 7–16.

Fiske, A. P. (2000). Complementarity theory: why human social capacities evolved to require cultural complements. *Personality and Social Psychology Review*, 4(1), 76–94.

Fraley, L. E. and Vargas, E. A. (1986). Separate disciplines: the study of behavior and the study of the psyche. *Behavior Analyst*, 9, 47–59.

Gardner, H. (1992). Scientific psychology: should we bury it or praise it? *New Ideas in Psychology*, 10, 179–90.

Geertz, C. (1973). Thick description: toward an interpretive theory of culture. In C. Geertz (ed.), *The interpretation of cultures*. New York: Basic Books, pp. 3–30.

Gehlen, A. (1978). *Der Mensch. Seine Natur und seine Stellung in der Welt (1940)* (Mankind. Their nature and position in the world). Wiesbaden: Athenaion.

Gergen, K. J. (1985). The social constructionist movement in modern psychology. *American Psychologist*, 40, 266–75.

Green, C. D. (1992). Of immortal mythological beasts: operationism in psychology. *Theory and Psychology*, 2, 291–320.

Groeben, N. (1986). *Handeln, Tun, Verhalten als Einheiten einer verstehend-erklärenden Psychologie. Wissenschaftstheoretischer Überblick und Programmentwurf zur Integration von Hermeneutik und Empirismus* (Action, conduct, behaviour as units of an understanding/explanatory psychology. A philosophy of science overview and programmatic statement on the integration of hermeneutics and empiricism) Tübingen: Francke.

Haber, W. (1980). Entwicklung und Probleme der Kulturlandschaft im Spiegel ihrer Ökosysteme (Development and problems of cultural landscapes as reflected in their ecosystems). *Forstarchiv*, 51, 245–50.

Habermas, J. (1984). *The theory of communicative action*, vol. 1: *Reason and the rationalization of society*, trans. T. McCarthy. Cambridge: Polity. (Original work published 1981.)

Hallpike, C. R. (1984). The relevance of the theory of inclusive fitness to human society. *Journal of Social Biological Structure*, 7, 131–44.

Hamilton, W. (1964). The genetical evolution of social behavior (I + II). *Journal of Theoretical Biology*, 7, 152.

Harré, R. (1977). The ethnogenic approach: theory and practice. In L. Berkowitz (ed.), *Advances in experimental social psychology*, vol. 10. New York: Academic Press, pp. 284–314.

Hempel, C. G. (1959). The logic of functional analysis. In L. Gross (ed.), *Symposium on sociological theory*. New York: Harper and Row, pp. 271–311.

Herder, J. G. v. (1784–91). *Ideen zur Philosophie der Geschichte der Menschheit* (Ideas on the philosophy of the history of mankind). Riga/Leipzig: Johann Friedrich Hartknoch.

Hofstede, G. (1980). *Culture's consequences: international differences in work-related values*. Newbury Park, CA: Sage.

Jahoda, G. (1988). Critical notes on social representations. *European Journal of Social Psychology*, 18, 195–211.

Jahoda, G. and Krewer, B. (1997). History of cross-cultural and cultural psychology. In J. W. Berry, Y. H. Poortinga and J. Pandey (eds.), *Handbook of cross-cultural psychology*, vol. 1: *Theory and method*. Boston: Allyn and Bacon, pp. 1–42.

James, W. (1890). *Principles of psychology.* New York: Holt, Rinehart and Winston.

(1897). *The will to believe.* London: Longmans, Green and Co.

Kant, I. (1784). Beantwortung der Frage: Was ist Aufklärung? (What is enlightenment?). *Berlinische Monatsschrift, Dezember-Heft*, 481–494.

Keller, H. (1997). Evolutionary approaches. In J. W. Berry, Y. H. Poortinga and J. Pandey (eds.), *Handbook of cross-cultural psychology*, vol. 1: *Theory and method.* Boston: Allyn and Bacon, pp. 215–56.

(1999). Ontogeny as the interface between biology and culture: evolutionary considerations. Nehru lecture presented at the Department of Human Studies and Family Development, M.S. University of Baroda, Vadodara, India.

Keller, H. and Eckensberger, L. H. (1998). Entwicklung und Kultur (Development and culture). In H. Keller (ed.), *Lehrbuch Entwicklungspsychologie* (Textbook of developmental psychology). Bern: Huber, pp. 57–96.

Kesselring, T. (1981). *Entwicklung und Widerspruch. Ein Vergleich zwischen Piagets genetischer Erkenntnistheorie und Hegels Dialektik* (Development and contradiction: a comparison of Piaget's genetic epistemology and Hegel's dialectics). Frankfurt am Main: Suhrkamp.

Kristensen, K. B., Slife, B. D. and Yanchar, S. C. (2000). On what basis are evaluations possible in a fragmented psychology? An alternative to objectivism and relativism. *Journal of Mind and Behavior*, 21, 273–88.

Küppers, B.-O. (1994). Ist die Biologie eine Geisteswissenschaft? (Can biology be regarded as *Geisteswissenschaft*?) In F. Rötzer (ed.), *Vom Chaos zur Endophysik. Wissenschaftler im Gespräch* (From chaos to endophysics. Scientists in dialogue). Munich: Klaus Boer, pp. 68–82.

Kugel, W. (1993). Psychologie der naturwissenschaftlichen Begriffsbildung (Psychology of natural science concept formation). *Zeitschrift für Parapsychologie und Grenzgebiete der Psychologie*, 35(3/4), 231–83.

Kuhn, T. S. (1970a). *The structure of scientific revolutions.* Chicago: University of Chicago Press.

(1970b). Reflections on my critics. In I. Lakatos and A. Musgrave (eds.), *Criticism and the growth of knowledge.* New York: Cambridge University Press, pp. 231–78.

Lakatos, I. (1970). Falsification and the methodology of scientific research programmes. In I. Lakatos and A. Musgrave (eds.), *Criticism and the growth of knowledge.* New York: Cambridge University Press, pp. 91–195.

(1982). Warum hat das Kopernikanische Forschungsprogramm das Ptolemäische überwunden? (Why did the Copernican research programme supersede the Ptolemaic?). In I. Lakatos (ed.), *Die Methodologie der wissenschaftlichen Forschungsprogramme, Philosophische Schriften* (The methodology of scientific research programes, philosophical writings). Braunschweig/Wiesbaden, Germany, p. 182.

Laucken, U. (2001). Wissenschaftliche Denkformen, Sozialpraxen und der Kampf um Ressourcen – demonstriert am Beispiel der Psychologie. Berichte aus dem Institut zur Erforschung von Mensch-Umwelt-Beziehungen (Scientific ways of thinking, social praxis and the competition for resources – the example of psychology). University of Oldenburg, FB 5 – Psychologie. http://www.uni-oldenburg.de/psychologie/mub/psych&komm.htm, 36 (February).

Lazarus, M. and Steinthal, H. (1860). Einleitende Gedanken über Völkerpsychologie als Einladung zu einer Zeitschrift für Völkerpsychologie und Sprachwissenschaft

(Introductory remarks about *Völkerpsychologie* as an invitation for a journal of *Völkerpsychologie* and linguistics). *Zeitschrift für Völkerpsychologie und Sprachwissenschaft*, 1, 1–73.

Leung, K. (1989). Cross-cultural differences: individual-level vs. culture-level analysis. *International Journal of Psychology*, 24, 703–19.

Lewin, K. (1930–1). Der Übergang von der aristotelischen zur galileischen Denkweise in Biologie und Psychologie (The transition from the Aristotelian to the Galileian way of thinking in biology and psychology). *Erkenntnis*, 1, 421–60 (*Annalen der Philosophie*, vol. 9). (Republished Darmstadt: Wissenschaftliche Buchgesellschaft, 1971).

Looft, W. P. (1973). Socialization and personality throughout the life-span: an examination of contemporary psychological approaches. In P. B. Baltes and K. W. Schaie (eds.), *Life-span developmental psychology: personality and socialization*. New York: Academic Press, pp. 26–52.

Machado, A., Lourenco, O. and Silva, F. J. (2000). Facts, concepts, and theories: the shape of psychology's epistemic triangle. *Behavior and Philosophy*, 28, 1–40.

Madill, A., Jordan, A. and Shirley, C. (2000). Objectivity and reliability in qualitative analysis: realist, contextualist and radical constructionist epistemologies. *British Journal of Psychology*, 91, 1–20.

Malpass, R. S. and Poortinga, Y. H. (1986). Making inferences from cross-cultural data. In W. J. Lonner and J. W. Berry (eds.), *Field methods in cross-cultural research*. Beverly Hills: Sage, pp. 47–83.

Mastermann, M. (1970). The nature of a paradigm. In I. Lakatos and A. Musgrave (eds.), *Critism and the growth of knowledge*. Cambridge: Cambridge University Press, pp. 59–89.

Maxwell, M. (ed.) (1991). *The sociobiological imagination*. New York: State University of New York Press.

Mayr, E. (1991). *Eine Philosophie der Biologie* (A philosophy of biology). Munich: Piper.

(1994). Evolution – Grundfragen und Missverständnisse (Evolution – fundamental questions and misunderstandings). *Ethik und Sozialwissenschaften*, 2, 203–9.

Merton, R. K. (1959). Notes on problem-finding in sociology. In R. K. Merton, L. Bloom and L. S. Cottrell, Jr. (eds.), *Sociology today: problems and prospects*. New York: Basic Books, pp. ix–xxxiv.

Michell, J. (2000). Normal science, pathological science and psychometrics. *Theory and Psychology*, 10(5), 639–67.

Morin, E. (1973). *Das Rätsel des Humanen* (The riddle of the humane). Munich/Zurich: Piper.

Much, N. C. and Shweder, R. A. (1978). Speaking of rules: the analysis of culture in breach. In W. Damon (ed.), *New directions for child development: moral development*. San Francisco: Jossey-Bass, pp. 19–39.

Naroll, R. (1964). On ethnic unit classification. *Current Anthropology*, 5, 282–312.

Overton, W. F. (1998). Developmental psychology: philosophy, concepts, and methodology. In R. M. Lerner (ed.), *Handbook of child psychology*, vol. 1: *Theoretical models of human development*, 5th edn. New York: Wiley, pp. 107–88.

Overton, W. F. and Reese, H. W. (1973). Models of development: methodological implications. In J. R. Nesselroade and H. W. Reese (eds.), *Life-span developmental psychology: methodological issues*. New York: Academic Press, pp. 65–8.

Parsons, T. (1937/1968). *The structure of social action.* New York: The Free Press.

Piaget, J. (1971). Inconscient affectif et inconscient cognitif. *Raison présent,* 19, Paris.

(1974). *La prise de conscience.* Paris: Presses Universitaires de France.

Poortinga, Y. H. (1997). Towards convergence? In J. W. Berry, Y. H. Poortinga and J. Pandey (eds.), *Handbook of cross-cultural psychology,* vol. 1: *Theory and method.* Boston: Allyn and Bacon, pp. 347–87.

Poortinga, Y. H., Kop, P. F. M. and van de Vijver, F. J. R. (1989). Differences between psychological domains in the range of cross-cultural variation. In P. J. D. Drenth, J. A. Sergeant and R. J. Takens (eds.), *European perspectives in psychology,* vol. 3. Chichester: Wiley, pp. 355–76.

Poortinga, Y. H. and Malpass, R. S. (1986). Making inferences from cross-cultural data. *Field methods in cross-cultural research,* vol. 8: Cross-cultural research and methodology series, pp. 17–46.

Poortinga, Y. H., van de Vijver, F. J. R. and Van de Koppel, J. M. H. (1987). Peeling the onion called culture: a synopsis. In C. Kagitcibasi (ed.), *Growth and progress in cross-cultural psychology.* Lisse: Swets and Zeitlinger, pp. 22–34.

Popper, K. (1959). *The logic of scientific discovery.* New York: Basic Books.

(1970). Normal science and its dangers. In I. Lakatos and A. Musgrave (eds.), *Criticism and the growth of knowledge.* Cambridge: Cambridge University Press, pp. 51–8.

(1977). Part I. In K. R. Popper and J. C. Eccles (eds.), *The self and its brain.* Berlin: Springer-Verlag, pp. 3–223.

Price-Williams, D. R. (1980). Towards the idea of a cultural psychology: a superordinate theme for study. *Journal of Cross-Cultural Psychology,* 11, 77–88.

Primas, H. (1984). *Elementare Quantenchemie* (Elementary quantum chemistry). Stuttgart: Teubner.

Rappaport, R. A. (1971). Nature, culture, and ecological anthropology. In H. C. Shapiro (ed.), *Man, culture, and society.* London: Oxford University Press, pp. 237–67.

Reese, H. W. and Overton, W. F. (1970). Models of development and theories of development. In L. R. Goulet and P. B. Baltes (eds.), *Life-span developmental psychology: research and theory.* New York: Academic Press, pp. 115–45.

Reich, K. H. (1994). *Der Begriff der Komplementarität in Wissenschaft und Alltag* (The concept of complementarity in science and everyday life). Berichte zur Erziehungswissenschaft, Nr. 105. Freiburg: Pädagogisches Institut der Universität Freiburg.

Renner, E. (1983). Ethnologie und Kultur. Der Kulturbegriff als entwicklungsprägender Faktor der ethnologischen Forschung (Ethnology and culture. The concept of culture as a factor shaping the development of ethnological research). *Zeitschrift für Ethnologie,* 108, 177–217.

Ritsert, J. (1994). *Die Kuhnsche Wende in der Wissenschaftstheorie und ihre Folgen* (The Kuhnian shift in philosophy of science and its consequences). Studienkripte zur Logik der Sozialwissenschaften. Skript 3. Frankfurt am Main: J. W. Goethe-Universität.

Rogoff, B. (1990). *Apprenticeship in thinking.* New York: Oxford University Press.

Roth, G. (1997). *Das Gehirn und seine Wirklichkeit: Kognitive Neurobiologie und ihre Philosophischen Konsequenzen* (The brain and its reality. Cognitive neurobiology and its philosophical consequences), 5th edn. Frankfurt am Main: Suhrkamp.

Roth, G., Schwegler, H., Stadtler, M. and Haynes, J.-D. (1998). Die funktionale Rolle des bewusst Erlebten (The functional role of conscious experiences). *Mathematical Models and Methods in Applied Sciences*, 8, 521–41.

Rychlak, J. F. (1993). A suggested principle of complementarity for psychology. In theory, not method. *American Psychologist Association*, 48(9), 933–42.

Schurz, G. (1988). Was ist wissenschaftliches Verstehen? (Eine Theorie verstehensbewirkender Erklärungsepisoden) (What is scientific understanding? (A theory of explanatory episodes effecting understanding)). In G. Schurz (ed.), *Erklären und Verstehen in der Wissenschaft* (Explaining and understanding in science). Munich: Oldenbourg, pp. 233–88.

Schwartz, L. (1951). *Die Neurosen und die dynamische Psychologie von Pierre Janet* (Neuroses and the dynamic psychology of Pierre Janet). Basel: Schwabe.

Searle, J. R. (1980). The intentionality of intention and action. *Cognition Sciences*, 4, 47–70.

Segall, M. H. (1984). More than we need to know about culture, but are afraid not to ask. *Journal of Cross-Cultural Psychology*, 15, 153–62.

Shadish, W. R. and Fuller, S. (1994) (eds.). *The social psychology of science*. New York, London: Guilford Press.

Shweder, R. A. (1980). Rethinking culture and personality theory. Part III: From genesis and typology to hermeneutics and dynamics. *Ethos*, 8, 60–94.

  (1990). Cultural psychology – what is it? In J. W. Stigler, R. A. Shweder and G. Herdt (eds.), *Cultural psychology: essays on comparative human development*. Cambridge: Cambridge University Press, pp. 1–43.

Singer, W. (2000). Vom Gehirn zum Bewusstsein (From brain to consciousness). In N. Elsner and G. Lüer (eds.), *Das Gehirn und sein Geist* (The brain and its mind). Göttingen: Wallsteinverlag, pp. 189–204.

Sinha, D. (1996). Cross-cultural psychology: the Asian scenario. In J. Pandey, D. Sinha and D. P. S. Bhawuk (eds.), *Asian contributions to cross-cultural psychology*. New Delhi: Sage, pp. 20–41.

Slife, B. D. (2000). Are discourse communities incommensurable in a fragmented psychology? The possibility of disciplinary coherence. *Journal of Mind and Behavior*, 21(3), 261–72.

Smedslund, J. (1988). *Psycho-Logic*. Berlin: Springer.

Snow, C. P. (1963). *The two cultures and the scientific revolution*. New York: Cambridge University Press.

Soyland, A. J. (1994). *Psychology as metaphor*. London: Sage.

Staats, A. W. (1998). Unifying psychology: a scientific or non-scientific theory task? *Journal of Theoretical and Philosophical Psychology*, 18, 70–9.

Szabó, I. (1976). *Geschichte der mechanischen Prinzipien und ihrer wichtigsten Anwendungen* (History of mechanical principles and their most important applications). Basel/Stuttgart: Birkhäuser Verlag.

Textor, R. B. (1967). *A cross-cultural summary*. New Haven, CT: HRAF Press.

Tomasello, M. (2001). Cultural transmission: a view from chimpanzees and human infants. *Journal of Cross-Cultural Psychology*, 32(2), 135–46.

Trivers, R. (1985). *Social evolution*. Menlo Park, CA: Benjamin Cummings.

Turiel, E. (1998). The development of morality. In W. Damon and N. Eisenberg (eds.), *Handbook of child psychology*, vol. 3: *Social, emotional and personality development*, 5th edn. New York: Wiley, pp. 863–932.

Valsiner, J. (1987). *Culture and the development of children's action.* New York: Wiley.

van de Vijver, F. and Leung, K. (1997). *Methods and data analysis for cross-cultural research.* Thousands Oaks, CA: Sage.

van deVijver, F. and Poortinga, Y. H. (1982). Cross-cultural generalizations and universality. *Journal of Cross-Cultural Psychology,* 13, 387–408.

Verbeek, B. (1994). *Die Anthropologie der Umweltzerstörung. Die Evolution und der Schatten der Zukunft* (The anthropology of environmental destruction. Evolution and shadows of the future), 2nd edn. Darmstadt: Wissenschaftliche Buchgesellschaft.

Vining, D. R., Jr. (1986). Social versus reproductive success: the central theoretical problem of human sociobiology. *Behavioral and Brain Science,* 9, 167–216.

Voland, E. (2000). *Grundriss der Soziobiologie* (An outline of sociobiology), 2nd edn. Heidelberg/Berlin: Spektrum, Gustav Fischer.

von Wright, G. H. (1971). *Explanation and understanding.* Ithaca, NY: Cornell University Press.

(1994). *Normen, Werte und Handlungen* (Norms, values and actions). Frankfurt am Main: Suhrkamp.

Wertheimer, M. (1924). Über Gestalttheorie (On Gestalt psychology). *Gestalt Theory,* 7(2), 99–120. Opladen: Westdeutscher Verlag.

Wertsch, J. V. (1985). *Vygotsky and the social formation of mind.* Cambridge, MA: Harvard University Press.

White, L. A. (1959). The concept of culture. *American Anthropologist,* 61, 227–51.

Wilson, E. O. (1975). *Sociobiology: the new synthesis.* Cambridge, MA: Belknap Press.

Wright, R. (1994). *The moral animal: evolutionary psychology and everyday life.* New York: Pantheon.

Wuketits, F. M. (1981). *Biologie und Kausalität* (Biology and causality). Berlin: Paul Paray.

(1997). *Soziobiologie. Die Macht der Gene und die Evolution sozialen Verhaltens* (Sociobiology. The power of genes and the evolution of social behaviour). Heidelberg/Berlin: Spektrum Akademischer Verlag.

Yanchar, S. C. (2000). Progress, unity, and three questions about incommensurability. *Journal of Mind and Behavior,* 21, 243–60.

Yanchar, S. C. and Slife, B. D. (2000). Putting it all together: toward a hermeneutic. *Journal of Mind and Behavior,* 21(3), 315–26.

Zimmermann, R. (1998). *Die Überlistung des Todes. Wozu der Mensch die Kunst erfand* (Outwitting death. Why humans invented art). Munich/Berlin: Deutscher Kunstverlag GmbH.

16 Epilogue: conceptions of ontogenetic development; integrating and demarcating perspectives

Heidi Keller, Ype H. Poortinga, and Axel Schölmerich

The chapters of this book are based on the idea that the relation between biology and culture is essential for understanding ontogenetic development. Moreover, it is agreed that this relation is an essential part of one's orientation and needs to be grounded theoretically, rather than being postulated as some unspecified interaction. Still, the conceptualizations of the authors assembled in this volume vary widely; the volume hosts an array of different, often complementary and sometimes mutually exclusive approaches.

Developmental psychology, like no other area in psychology, has long maintained links to both biology and cultural sciences. For example, early theories of maturation in the foetal phase of the human life cycle drew heavily on evolutionary knowledge of that time (Haeckel, 1866). Likewise, Hall's (1883) conception of development recapitulated not biological but cultural evolution. As informative and stimulating as these links into neighbouring fields were, little progress has been made to specify our conception of the relationship between biology and culture when considering development. Until today, most developmental psychologists can be counted as belonging to one of two camps, one focusing on mind in culture and the other on development of brain structure and evolutionary pressures.

Our overall focus is on ontogenetic development as pivotal in the description of the interplay between culture and biology. The various chapters demonstrate how the understanding of development is central in conceptualizing different perspectives on the interaction between humans and the context in which they live. Development is a broad concept. It serves as a label to indicate the many directional and typically, though not necessarily, irreversible changes in behaviour across the lifespan. It also refers to biological structures and processes that drive and/or enable such changes. Moreover, it refers to the continuous interactional processes between organism and the social and natural environment. Obviously, development cannot be seen as a single process; it encompasses a kaleidoscopic range of events and antecedents within which various theories and research traditions each represent a certain perspective and emphasis.

384

Throughout this chapter we will be guided by the cross-cultural similarities and differences that have been derived from the kind of research conducted by the various contributors. In the first and most extensive section we briefly characterize the main perspectives on development as they are presented in this volume. In the second section we take a closer look at development in terms of the various views on change and continuity. In the third and final section we put forward some suggestions for future theory and research.

Perspectives on development

Cultural context shapes not only development but also developmental theories. As expressions of scientific traditions, theories are bound by ideas prevalent in historical times and locations; additionally, theories represent the individual idiosyncrasies of their authors. Reflections on historical views, as presented in the chapter by Jahoda, allow us to understand the influence of the zeitgeist on conceptions about relationships between biology and culture. The interpretation of empirical evidence tends to be coloured by different views on the nature of the human species. Different scientific paradigms specify different theoretical orientations, even families of theories (Eckensberger, this volume) together with their associated methodologies.

Yet, processes of ontogenetic development are rooted in the biological make-up of the human species, including the psychological processes and the facility for culture that are part of our 'nature'. In addition, culture provides a context for development that in part can fruitfully be conceptualized as a complex of antecedent conditions to individual behaviour as well as concomitant behavioural regulation. All this points to a 'reality out there' that can be explored and should allow us to gain knowledge that goes beyond notions merely held at a particular time and place. Somehow developmental theories should reflect this biological, psychological and eco-cultural reality, specifying the functional relationships between the various aspects during all the phases of the lifespan.

No single theory simultaneously addresses and interrelates all major concerns, and one question that needs to be answered is whether an integrated theory is a feasible goal. In practice there are numerous signs of increasing dispersion, with theorists emphasizing one of the issues implied in these principles while de-emphasizing others. Some approaches with a postmodern or constructivist orientation depict individual development as a person-specific life trajectory that can only be understood retrospectively in its sociocultural and historical context. Others also focus on social context, but at a societal rather than at an individual level. Quite in opposition to these cultural approaches is thinking inspired by psychobiological and sociobiological theories, where development is seen as the expression of genetic propensities under contextual demands.

These demands may not only influence developmental outcomes directly, but also determine types of person–environment interaction processes.

(Mainly) phylogenetic orientations

A phylogenetic perspective on ontogenetic development aims at understanding the interplay between culture and biology from the function that a behaviour pattern or its neurological substrate has for solving a specific problem which has its origins in the evolutionary past of humankind. Approaches informed explicitly by evolutionary theorizing (Casimir and Schnegg, Greenfield, Hewlett and Lamb, Keller, Russon, all in this volume) conceptualize the emergence of culture as an outcome-driven process of adaptation, typically with a focus on regulation of social behaviour in groups of increasing size. Apart from reproduction strategies, such functions include competition and cooperation, defence against predators and exploitation of resources. This kind of thinking allows a functional analysis of various phases of the life cycle with respect to adaptation processes. While global statements garnished with spectacular examples based on such theorizing ensure public attention and strong agreement (or disagreement), more precise and elaborate versions of this approach include consideration of the context-sensitive selection from a range of possible behavioural or developmental pathways, leading, we believe, to more valuable insights.

Cross-cultural surveys have already shown some interesting patterns of similarities in complex behaviours (cf. Voland, 1999). Perhaps the best known is the study by Buss (1989) on preferred characteristics in marriage partners. Men and women students in the thirty-seven societies investigated showed remarkable similarities in what traits they find important in prospective partners, like mutual attraction, love and a dependable character. Moreover, smaller but consistent differences were found between the preferences of men and women, along lines that fit functional differences between the two sexes in reproduction and caretaking. Thus, the young women in this study gave somewhat higher ratings on partner characteristics such as financial prospects and good earning capacity, while the young men placed higher emphasis on good looks and physical attractiveness (presumably signs of health and the capacity to bear children). A related line of thinking has investigated differences between men and women in the preferred age of a partner and the changes in this preference over the lifespan (Kenrick and Keefe, 1992). A large number of sources (such as advertisements for partners and archives with records of marriages) in a range of societies show a similar pattern. With increasing age, the age difference progressively increases to favour older males. In so far as men continue to be able to sire children longer than women are fertile, and resources accumulate over the lifespan, a phylogenetically evolved strategy for females to prefer older partners and for men to prefer younger partners makes sense.

In these and other studies in the tradition of evolutionary psychology it is a basic assumption that all human psychological functions have to be examined in the light of reproductive fitness. Scholars such as Tooby and Cosmides (1992) quite explicitly restrict functions to design features of the human mind that have been shaped by evolutionary processes. On the other hand, those criticizing evolutionary approaches ignore the phylogenetic heritage and continue to explain such differences in terms of social variables that have dominated psychology for the last half century, like the unequal power of men and women (Eagly and Wood, 1999).

What do the present authors contribute to such debates? Greenfield provides an imaginative range of alternative pathways each explaining how culture and biology mutually may define each other. For example, she argues that norms reinforce the biological pattern of newborn motor behaviour in Zinacanteco Indians, or that culture selects from biology with the biological substrate providing the foundation for diverse capacities and the cultural environment reinforcing one particular capacity, as in the case of culturally shared conceptions of parenting. This chapter functions as a warning against a too ready invocation of specific biological pathways by showing the many alternative explanations, which should not be ruled out without closer scrutiny. The tentative nature of evolutionary models on how behaviour is linked to distal precursors is also elucidated by Hewlett and Lamb, who demonstrate diversity within evolutionary thought. They identify three approaches and address these in the light of data on parental care and parent–child interaction in an urban, an agricultural and a hunter-gatherer society. The approaches are complementary in the sense that they focus on somewhat different aspects in explaining caregiver–infant relations.

Russon presents data showing that there is a facility for learning from the sociocultural environment, also in nonhuman species. A phylogenetic perspective allows for a comparative approach between different species. Russon's chapter also deals with the difficult question how culture in great apes is different from human culture. Whereas the creation and maintenance of social practices in nonhuman primates is now widely accepted in the literature, it remains a matter of discussion whether or not processes of social cognition and social learning that are involved in cultural traditions of human beings are equivalent to those of other species (Boesch and Tomasello, 1998; McGrew, 1992, 1998; Tomasello, 2001; Whiten et al., 1999).

Among the present authors, Keller is perhaps the most precise in the formulation of mechanisms underlying different pathways of individual development. She specifies phylogenetic preparedness and epigenetic rules for acquiring specific contextual and cultural information during separate ontogenetic stages. The interactions of phylogenetic heritage and individual social context result in differentiation of life histories.

In all these chapters individuals are the main focus of analysis, rather than developmental processes per se; that is to say, psychological processes are seen as taking place in individuals. A somewhat different perspective is that of Cole. He discusses how phylogenetic preparedness can be integrated with the 'idea of cultural mediation in culturally organized scripted activities' (p. 315). In consonance with his cultural constructivistic perspective, he centres on activity rather than on the individual as the unit of analysis. He emphasizes that it is not single behaviours as such that have evolutionary advantages, but their placement in certain phases of the life cycle. Here psychological lifespan approaches can be linked up with evolutionary life history views (cf. the chapters by Russon and by Hewlett and Lamb).

In sum, a phylogenetic perspective aims at explaining why certain behavioural tendencies exist, and why culture happens to be organized the way it is. Apart from the general problem that phylogenetic precursors can only be specified post hoc, and can only be tested indirectly, we see two sources of confusion in the phylogenetic perspective. One unresolved problem is the time scale of presumed phylogenetic processes, differing so vastly from ontogenetic ones. Second, culturally shaped environments can exert new pressures on reproductive success, or eliminate previously functional selection criteria (Laland, Odling-Smee and Feldman, 1999).

(Mainly) cultural origins

Other authors initiate their discussion with cultural conceptions of life stages as prevalent in various ethnotheoretical traditions. In a general sense, only time can tell to what extent culturally based preconceptions underlying contemporary research have influenced the contents of the various chapters. However, there are two accounts that specify their cultural origins and explicitly do not claim universal validity. The chapter by Zimba acknowledges more specific customs and socioeconomic context and the chapter by Saraswathi and Ganapathy refers more to a religion-based world view, namely the Hindu way of life as it has evolved from the interpretation of time-honoured scriptures.

Zimba draws attention to external circumstances in which children grow up that in many respects can be qualified as dismally poor. He describes contexts for individual development that differ from traditional patterns of socialization in Africa. It cannot be emphasized strongly enough that war and/or poverty is not a valued standard in any culture. At the same time, it is the contextual reality of a large proportion of children in the world. Many consequences of such extreme conditions have not been systematically examined. We know some of the outcomes of poor nutrition for physical and cognitive development (Griesel, Richter and Belciug, 1990; Pollitt, 1994; Zeskind and Ramey, 1981), but the social consequences of growing up in difficult circumstances have hardly been investigated in systematic longitudinal studies (cf. Aptekar and Stöcklin, 1997). In the light of the literature on culture and behaviour, it is perhaps most surprising that so many of the children who survive become responsible citizens of their societies. The notion of 'resilience' that often is used in this context (Werner, 1979) mainly rests on the post hoc observation that there are children who 'make it' in life far beyond expectation, but it leads one to wonder how many human resources remain untapped in children who happen not to show high resilience later in life, but might have done so under even slightly different conditions.

The account by Saraswathi and Ganapathy perhaps refers more to prevailing cultural norms than to the everyday reality of the poor sections of the Indian population. Nevertheless, these norms tend to act as standards for the entire population of India, in many respects even across religious boundaries. Parental ethnotheories reflected in child rearing lead to differential treatment of boys and girls and to cultural rules governing marriage-partner selection. At the level of specific practices the impact of living in one culture or in another can be quite dramatic. Hence the question of broader psychological consequences is a valid one.

These two chapters explicitly refer to the characteristics of certain non-Western societies as a context for development. On the other hand, in an interpretive analysis, Boesch refers to various cultures but does not emphasize distinctions between them. Taking the belief that without suitable measures the world is in danger of falling into disorder (the idea of lurking chaos), Boesch illustrates with respect to a single theme how a range of actions to deal with an existential question is found across various cultures.

Together the three chapters highlight a perspective on development aimed at understanding the developing individual in context. Is it possible to adopt this perspective and at the same time address the interplay between biology and culture? Such an attempt is made by Miller. Her point of departure is that culture serves as a symbolic medium for human development and that participation in culture is necessary for the emergence of all higher-order psychological processes. This position is unassailable in so far as a human environment is an absolute condition for human development; incidental cases of extreme deprivation demonstrate the point. At the same time there are arguments favouring a biological readiness for development of quite specific functions and traits. This can be illustrated by, for example, recognizable facial expressions of emotions among blind children and the development of grammarlike structures in sign languages among the deaf (Goldin-Meadow and Mylander, 1998; Lenneberg, 1967).

In sum, the validity and meaning of descriptive approaches in understanding the emergence of behaviour patterns cannot be denied. However, it appears to be a long leap to explain culture-specifics from a phylogenetic perspective. This shows how using various points of departure helps to paint a fuller picture of development. We can describe the particulars of a given cultural setting looking for understanding, or we can start from an explanatory principle and look for manifestations. So far we have not been very successful in defining the interface between these two approaches.

(Mainly) psychological concerns

The conceptualization of development for understanding the interplay between culture and biology becomes more complex and, consequently, more difficult to understand, when we consider life stages beyond infancy. It is for good reason that infancy traditionally has been the scenario for commonalities whereas adulthood was the arena of cultural and individual peculiarities. Yet a differentiated discussion of the relation between universality and cultural specifics over the whole lifespan has hardly been elaborated until now (cf. Baltes, 1997). Also, the (possibly differential) impact of the ecological and social contexts on human development over the lifespan is not yet well understood. At the same time, clear-cut relations cannot be expected, since interactional processes can lead to similar behavioural outcomes in different contexts and to different behavioural manifestations in similar contexts. Thus, in addition to the effect of the developmental phase and the contextual specificity in moulding universally prepared developmental processes, there are human capacities to develop similar behavioural strategies across diverse contexts.

Killen, McGlothlin, and Kim argue for the universality of individual evaluations of exclusion from social groups and for structural similarities across independent and interdependent societies. Casimir and Schnegg discuss the ontogeny of emotions as illuminating human functions with epigenetic modulation of culture-specific behavioural prescriptions. Both these chapters can be seen as reflecting characteristics of current culture-comparative research. In such studies some form of psychological universalism (see the introductory chapter) is assumed either implicitly or explicitly. The research of Killen, McGlothlin and Kim implies that similar assessment procedures are equivalent in different cultures, an assumption that appears to be supported by their results. Casimir and Schnegg identify similarities and differences at different levels in their analysis of shame, including considerations of the social function of emotional expression.

Although the whole lifespan and life history as the patterning of consecutive life stages are often implied in developmental cross-cultural research, only a few studies actually document developmental processes across different stages. Kornadt presents empirical data demonstrating associations between developmental outcomes in adolescence and earlier socialization as reflected in parental norms and behaviour, attuned to culturally defined developmental goals. This chapter reports various theoretical links to processes beyond the immediate reach of the measurements.

In a sense the chapters reporting empirical culture-comparative research are the core of this volume, since this research tradition continues to form the mainstream in cross-cultural psychology (Berry et al., 1992). In the ideal study there is input from both the life sciences and the social sciences. Moreover, it is recognized that cross-cultural psychology needs a developmental dimension (Heron and Kroeger, 1981; Keller and Greenfield, 2000), while at the same time the analysis of ontogenetic development requires a cross-cultural dimension to broaden its horizon beyond the limitations of time- and place-bound conceptions (e.g. Kessen, 1979). The three chapters mentioned contain all these ingredients in various mixtures.

Three themes

All in all, this volume covers numerous developmental perspectives. Although some of the chapters try to integrate and synthesize across perspectives, the overall picture confirms that integration in an encompassing perspective is still an ideal, and perhaps an ideal that we should not even try to pursue (see below). Nevertheless, during the symposium in Wittenberg (see Acknowledgements) and afterwards some themes emerged that bear upon, and sometimes also transcend, the various perspectives outlined in this section.

A first theme most explicitly discussed by Cole but present in all three chapters of the last part of the book is *level of explanation*, ranging from distal to proximal. In addition to the levels referred to already, both Cole and Eckensberger tend to distinguish a microgenetic level, i.e. the development of patterns of concrete action. These authors emphasize interaction, sometimes even integration of different levels. Poortinga and Soudijn advocate a less integrative view, mentioning demarcation rather than integration as the goal to be pursued and referring to the specific situation as an ('objective') trigger for action, rather than to microgenetic construction of action.

A second theme concerns the *kinds of categories* authors use to make sense of the behaviour patterns found in different societies. First, there is a dimension from more inclusive to less inclusive explanations. Interactions of the person with the context in the conceptions of authors like Greenfield or Keller refer to phylogenetically acquired mechanisms that are selected by style of parental care in (early) childhood. On the other hand, Casimir and Schnegg see culture-specific differences in emotions more as the outcome of conventions. Also Poortinga and Soudijn and Killen et al., while not questioning the attribution of culture-specific meaning at the level of conventions, see little evidence for the validity of broad and inclusive conceptions of cross-cultural differences in terms of social dimensions. A middle position is taken by most authors, who refer to more permanent psychological factors, but limited to historical time at the societal level and the lifetime of the person at the individual level (e.g. the chapters by Zimba and by Saraswathi and Ganapathy).

Variations in perspective are also apparent regarding the antecedents of observed cross-cultural differences. Some authors postulate phylogenetically grounded mechanisms that are supposed to be differentially functional depending on the circumstances in which the child finds itself (e.g. the chapters by Greenfield, Hewlett and Lamb, Keller and Casimir and Schnegg). Others refer to antecedent-consequent relationships between conditions in the context and the individual (e.g. Kornadt and Saraswathi and Ganapathy's contributions). Still others see behaviour primarily as the outcome of intentional actions (Eckensberger, Boesch) or the mediation between context and individual (Miller, Cole). In fact, most of these perspectives are not mutually exclusive, but the orientation of authors has consequences in terms of theory (and paradigm), for methods, for the topics that are selected for study and, ultimately, for the interpretation of data (Eckensberger).

A final difference within the second theme is the dichotomy between relativistic and universalistic orientations that has dominated much of the theoretical and methodological discussion on the relationship between culture and behaviour in the 1990s. Many chapters in this volume could be classified as belonging to one or to the other tradition, but most of our contributors emphasize that this distinction should be seen as complementary rather than controversial. Chapters like those by Miller and by Poortinga and Soudijn describe explicit attempts to bridge the gap but still reflect the individual perspective of the respective authors.

A third general theme centres on the *mechanisms* through which behaviour is transmitted from cultural parents (including teachers, family and friends as well as biological parents) as members of a cultural context to children who are supposed to grow into that cultural context. Here the main differences are in the explicitness with which certain mechanisms, especially those beyond genetic transmission, are put forward, such as cultural transmission (socialization and enculturation), which are shared among individuals within a group, and learning, which is focused more on the individual.

Conceptions of change and continuity

Above all, development is about change: change over the evolutionary past, historical change, ontogenetic change and microgenetic change. In psychology the emphasis is on ontogenetic change, i.e. the lifespan or the life history of the individual person. The nature of various kinds of change raises an array of questions. Is change planned or random; is it a deliberate activity of the self-reflexive individual or is it rather an intuitive strategy serving adaptative purposes; is it predictable or is it chaotic; is it causal or goal directed, or is it the product of self-organizing systems? The answers to these questions in this volume are diverse, reflecting different metaperspectives of development as outlined in the chapters of the last section.

During the course of ontogenetic development the nervous system changes. At the behavioural level such changes can be said to result in qualitatively new processes. For cognitive functions this idea has led to the notion of stages, particularly in the work of Piaget (1970). Also social behaviour may change substantially in association with internal processes like hormonal changes under the influence of regulatory genes, notably during puberty. As already mentioned in the Introduction, the interaction between various processes is not exclusively genetically determined. There is evidence that environmental events can influence regulatory processes (cf. Gottlieb, 1998; Gottlieb, Wahlsten and Lickliter, 1998).

Development is also about continuity. There is evidence in different domains of social-emotional as well as cognitive functioning that earlier developments have systematic effects on later performance. This is evidenced in cognition by the growth of abilities, crystallized in a notion like 'IQ'; similarly the concept of personality is rooted in consistencies of reactions across time and situations. Notably there is continuity in terms of the perception of oneself, and of personal identity. Complementary to this, there tends to be stability in the position that individuals occupy within their reference group.

In this volume the distinction of levels, mentioned before, is central to the understanding of continuities and changes. Three such levels should be mentioned. First, there is the level of phylogenetic development. Russon argues that analysis of the behaviour of species like the orang-utan should lead to insight into human culture. Genetic continuity and the uniqueness of the human species are likely to attract increasing attention as awareness grows of the genetic similarity of humans and related species (International Human Genome Mapping Consortium, 2001). Two more or less complementary lines of thought seem to emerge. The first emphasizes the development of human culture as a lifting of constraints (Tomasello, 2001), the creation of a space for human activities in the form of enabling or facilitating conditions (Eckensberger, this volume) or shifts from constraints to opportunities (Poortinga and Soudijn, this volume). The other focuses more on eco-cultural and sociocultural factors triggering specific patterns of development from the array of biological capabilities (e.g. Greenfield, Keller, both this volume).

The discussion of this issue is obscured by the fact that the expression of many genes is age-dependent as well as situation-dependent, constraining the acceleration of developmental patterns. Thus the identification of continuity or discontinuity of the developmental context is a prerequisite for understanding life histories and the development of adaptation strategies. However, a systematic consideration of contextual change over the life course is not very common in developmental theorizing (Shanahan, Sulloway and Hofer, 2000).

The second level of analysis of continuity and change describes culture as a sociohistorical, and sometimes ecological, context for development of the individual. Effects of the context as antecedent to the development of culture-characteristic behaviour patterns are emphasized by Russon for orangutans grown up in captivity, and by Saraswathi and Ganapathy and Zimba for human societies. Zimba especially shows how practices, including those pertaining to something as culturally central as initiation, can change fairly rapidly under the influence of external pressures (changes in religion, or a need for sexual hygiene). The description of cultural context and associated patterns of behaviour continues to be one of the two main bodies of information for cross-cultural psychology, next to individual-level psychological data.

Continuity of the social and ecological environment is part of and contributes to continuity in behaviour over the course of the lifespan. In biology one finds the notion of the 'ecological niche', specifying aspects of the environment relevant to a species. In cross-cultural psychology Super and Harkness (1986, 1997) have introduced the notion of 'developmental niche', describing the child in interaction with local customs, settings and parental ethnotheories. The notion of development as an interactional process is present also in this description. Individual and context are seen as inextricably interrelated, and continuity and change of the context are part of the developmental process (see also Cole, this volume).

The previous comments are in line with a strong interactional emphasis present in chapters which focus on the third level of analysis, namely the individual, analysing individual-level data. In contrast to the larger part of the developmental literature even today, there is little in this volume on psychological development as an autonomous and universal human process. Interactions between infants and their social environment with consideration of long-term developmental consequences are addressed in particular by Hewlett and Lamb and Keller. Chapters such as those by Killen, McGlothlin and Kim, Casimir and Schnegg, and Kornadt are based on data collected at later stages of development. But these chapters also specifically mention interactions between individual and environment.

Despite all efforts our understanding of the dynamics of change and continuity remains rather unclear. Even the usual modelling of development in terms of linear changes has been challenged theoretically, and lately also empirically, by those who argue that changes tend to be sudden or 'chaotic' (e.g. Thelen, 1995; van Geert, 1994; cf. Poortinga and Soudijn, this volume). Although the notion of chaos is now widely used, it is most often inferred from observed changes, but without any explanatory theory as to how and why the changes occurred. We know, for example, little about the effects of family relationships and the changes in these relationships over time, widely regarded as important in various theoretical approaches. More and more the need for a dynamic view on development instead of static snapshots is emphasized (Georgas, 1997). Consider father absence during early childhood, which in numerous studies has been linked to problem behaviour in adolescence (e.g. Segall et al., 1999). Roopnarine and colleagues (e.g. Roopnarine et al., 2000) have described socialization patterns in the Caribbean, where family life differs greatly from the Euro-American middle-class model. These other family forms have existed for over a century, but it remains largely unclear how children fare in these family configurations. Another example that shows the extent of our ignorance is the difficulty in predicting the changes that result from a large-scale shift towards non-parental day care of infants in Western countries, a consequence triggered in part by sociocultural factors but now sustained in many societies for economic reasons. Mothers have always worked and continue to do so in traditional societies, but their young children are present, or at least near by. Attachment theory as developed by Bowlby (1969) and Ainsworth et al. (1978) emphasizes the importance of constant primary caretakers. What will be the long-term consequences of care systems with frequently changing staff? Longitudinal complexities in the structure of families, such as the availability of resources or the composition of the family in Western (e.g. single, nuclear, patchwork) and non-Western (extended, nuclear) surroundings tend to be neglected in theorizing and in the conceptualization of research designs. Needless to say, such comments pertain equally to other developmental contexts.

Future research and theorizing

Earlier we argued for a position in which ontogenetic development is not merely a sociocultural construction. Even if 'objective reality' in an absolute sense is outside our reach, we do accept that some discourses on development and cross-cultural diversity in development are evidently further removed from this reality than other forms of discourse. We further believe that psychological theorizing and methodology provide tools to gradually remove views inconsistent with carefully collected empirical evidence. The evolutionary epistemology of Campbell (see Overman, 1988) provides a rationale for such a viewpoint. Campbell has argued for analogies of genetic selection at various levels, one of which includes scientific research. This reference to scientific research as an evolutionary process also makes clear why prediction of future trends is at best approximate. For example, adaptations represent changes that escape causality, in the sense of a one-to-one correspondence between some initial state and a later state. However, given an initial state, not all imaginable later states are theoretically equally feasible. And given a certain consistency in outcomes, not all initial states are equally plausible. In an approach like that of Campbell limited certainty about relationships between contextual inputs and behavioural outcomes can be accommodated. They do not make sound research impossible, although they tend to make it complex. To cope with this complexity the design of more comprehensive research projects is needed in which a broader range of alternative explanations is taken into consideration. Increasing technical and methodological sophistication is a recent hallmark of the life sciences, including psychology.

A feature of the present state of affairs in cross-cultural developmental psychology, and in the present book, is the wide variety of perspectives. A major question, already mentioned, is whether these can be integrated in the future. Cole in his chapter refers to interactions between different levels, and so does Eckensberger. However, we do not expect that such integration will readily happen. First, perspectives are rooted in discrepant paradigms and as such are difficult to reconcile (Eckensberger). Second, the range of phenomena and issues they address is only partly overlapping. For example, the phylogenetic time scale of evolutionary approaches is of a different order of magnitude compared with culture-descriptive studies. Third, authors who specify various levels (Cole; Poortinga and Soudijn) are not very clear in specifying relationships between them, and certainly do not indicate how postulated relationships can be critically examined regarding their validity.

If theoretical integration is not feasible, the next question is what the future will be of the perspectives represented in the various chapters. In our view none has reached closure, and this makes it likely that each will continue and presumably be elaborated. This is most evident for evolutionary perspectives, despite the fact that the theoretical postulates, which refer to a presumed state of affairs in the prehistorical past, are not easily accessible to empirical control. The clearest case in point is the status of evolved dispositions. Gould and Lewontin (1979; Gould, 1991), pointing to the pleiotropic functions of genes, have argued that adaptive changes may have resulted in additional functions beyond those that led to these changes initially. In addition there can be features that now enhance fitness, but originally have come about serving another function. For Gould the complex brain is a feature of the human organism that has opened up a large scope for what we commonly call culture (including religion, art and technology), but for which it hardly can have been developed originally. Thus, behaviour patterns characterizing contemporary humans may also be accidental by-products of selection-driven evolutionary processes. These views have been contested by more orthodox evolutionists (Buss et al., 1998; Tooby and Cosmides, 1992), but plausibility of assumptions rather than controllable evidence forms the core of many arguments.

Modes or levels of transmission of information from one generation to the next are typically hardly specified within any of the approaches discussed so far (e.g. Durham, 1982; Plotkin and Odling-Smee, 1981). The role of culture as environmental context has been further elaborated by Laland, Odling-Smee and Feldman (1999). In line with traditional evolutionary theory they recognize that a species through interactions with the environment modifies its environment, called *niche construction*. However, in human populations niche construction is not only a genotypic characteristic of the species. Two other kinds of processes are involved, namely ontogenetic processes of information acquisition (e.g. learning to read and write) and sociohistorical processes. From this perspective constructions can be at the basis of long-term cultural change, and in the long run even of genetic change. This creates the possibility that selective pressures change with the emergence of cultures.

We expect that a certain integration will continue as started already for evolutionary thinking and modern neurosciences. This can redirect the focus of attention from the current emphasis on cognitive neuroscience to affective neuroscience in order to explore the neurobiological basis of interpersonal relationships and their role for the developing mind (Schore, 2000, 2001; Siegel, 1999). Today the bulk of neurobiological research is on the adult rather than on the developing brain. Contemporary neuroscience is not only extending its focus towards early stages of development but also to pathology, seen as developmental failures of the brain (Schore, 2001). The evolutionary functional approach combined with insights from neuroscience can advance our knowledge about the interplay between biology and culture during different developmental stages. Examples like this do not suggest that an integration of all the perspectives presented in this book is feasible.

We have emphasized the complexities of evolutionary models in order to make the point that they are not necessarily more straightforward or less ambiguous than models of cultural transmission. The main difference is that cultural transmission cannot as easily refer to a material substance. A dual transmission model with a cultural inheritance system next to the genetic inheritance system (Boyd and Richerson, 1985), despite its elegance, has to postulate the less tangible notion of learning as a psychological equivalent of the material genes. At the same time, the history of psychology has shown that principles of learning lend themselves to experimental analysis, which has provided quite consistent knowledge. For example, Pavlov's and Skinner's principles of learning seem to be well anchored in empirical evidence.

There is an arena for experimental and functional analysis in so far as a theory states the more or less precise relationships to be expected between aspects of context and behavioural outcomes. Such analysis is more limited in cultural approaches in which historicity and intentionality of psychological processes are key characteristics. Validity of interpretations is an Achilles heel of such qualitative research that is characteristic of culturalist methods, including indigenous psychology (Poortinga, 1997). It is important to note that this comment does not pertain to ethnographic descriptions as presented in the second section of this book, which are largely open to empirical scrutiny. However, it does pertain as soon as non-observable psychological processes and concepts are postulated. For example, in cultural psychology the position that psychological processes are not the same cross-culturally goes beyond description; it is a theoretical axiom, not a testable statement. Of course, the same holds for the universalistic viewpoint that basic processes are identical. Again, we do not emphasize these difficulties to rule out examination of behaviour through other methods as the experiment. A broad range of perspectives in this book may testify to our acceptance of the legitimacy of the concerns expressed in them.

One feature of this book that we especially value is that the contributions are rather unpolemical. By and large, authors seem to respect other viewpoints. Particularly the three chapters in the last section go well beyond the debates on the presumed contrast between culture-comparative and culturalist views of the last decade. We expect that this mutual respect will result in a greater consciousness about the (limited) scope of one's own particular research. It is the need for greater clarity on the reach of various viewpoints that has led us to include the word 'demarcating' in the title of this chapter.

We believe that many of the questions raised can be seriously addressed by the joint efforts of scholars from different disciplinary origins and backgrounds, even if information from different disciplines cannot be fully integrated. Our vision of the future of the field is not that of a unitary or even a uniform science. Development as a unitary process, requiring recognition from many levels, encompassing evolution, embryology, comparative psychology, neurophysiology and anthropology was Arnold Gesell's (futuristic?) view on development at the beginning of the last century (Gesell, 1928; Gesell and Thompson, 1934). Contingent upon their theoretical propositions, some authors may assign priority to one level of analysis, e.g. unidirectional influences between context and individual and vice versa, whereas others rather highlight continuing multidirectional influences among different levels and create configurations of persons and their settings, that again have to be regarded in an ongoing stream of processes of change and continuity. It is probably significant that Gesell's vision still remains a programme rather than an accomplishment; maybe it was a utopian vision to begin with.

In summary, we have argued that the perspectives represented in the various sections of this volume have merits in their own right. Since they apparently cannot be readily integrated we expect that they will continue to exist in parallel. This certainly does not restrict the scope for cooperative research, but points to the need for caution in the interpretation of data from research covering a limited range of developmental phenomena.

Conclusion

What are the main points emphasized in this volume?

First, there is a range of perspectives or paradigms at the interface of biology, culture and ontogenetic development that together address the three concepts and their relationships. This has led to metaperspectives that try to accommodate the entire range of levels from phylogenetic to situational or microgenetic, but there is no cohesive theory that addresses concerns arising from all levels.

A second point following from the first is that researchers invariably argue from their own approach. However, they should be at least aware of the range of alternative perspectives and consider critically how far the explanatory (or interpretive) power of their data and methods is reaching.

A third point refers to the validity of generalizations derived from research on separate developmental phases or levels, limited domains of behaviour and a limited range of cultural variation. Can we conclude that developmental processes are universal, if we consider the restricted and incomplete empirical evidence available so far?

We are convinced that the future will offer serious attempts to refocus the research questions beyond disciplinary boundaries. Many thought-provoking ideas that have been articulated during the last century had their origins in attempts to integrate information and views from different disciplines, such as Darwin's (1872) endeavour to integrate the biology and psychology of emotions, or Piaget's (1967) integration of biology, psychology and philosophy to develop his epistemology, or Bowlby's (1969) idea of attachment grounded in psychoanalysis, ethology and psychiatry.

The main thrust of the argument is that the three concepts of ontogenetic development, culture and biology are all related to one another. Even though the culture–development relationship and the biology–development relationship have received more attention in the literature than the biology–culture relationship, no single relationship is a priori more important than any other.

REFERENCES

Ainsworth, M. D. S., Blehar, M. C., Waters, E. and Wall, S. (1978). *Patterns of attachment: a psychological study of the strange situation.* Hillsdale, NJ: Lawrence Erlbaum.

Aptekar, L. and Stöcklin, D. (1997). Children in particularly difficult circumstances. In J. W. Berry, P. R. Dasen and T. S. Saraswathi (eds.), *Handbook of cross-cultural psychology,* vol. 2: *Basic processes and human development.* Boston: Allyn and Bacon, pp. 377–412.

Baltes. P. (1997). On the incomplete architecture of human ontogeny. *American Psychologis*t, 52, 366–80.

Berry, J. W., Poortinga, Y. H., Segall, M. H. and Dasen, P. R. (1992). *Cross-cultural psychology: research and applications.* Cambridge: Cambridge University Press.

Boesch, C. and Tomasello, M. (1998). Chimpanzee and human cultures. *Current Anthropology,* 39(5), 591–614.

Bowlby, J. (1969). *Attachment and loss,* vol. 1: *Attachment.* New York: Basic Books.

Boyd, R. and Richerson, P. J. (1985). *Culture and the evolutionary process.* Chicago: University of Chicago Press.

Buss, D. M. (1989). Sex differences in human mate preferences: evolutionary hypotheses tested in 37 cultures. *Behavioral and Brain Sciences,* 12, 1–49.

Buss, D. M., Haselton, M. G., Shackelford, T. K., Bleske, A. L. and Wakefield, J. C. (1998). Adaptations, exaptations and spandrels. *American Psychologist*, 53, 533–48.

Darwin, C. (1872). *The expression of emotions in man and animals*. London: John Murray.

Durham, W. H. (1982). Interactions of genetic and cultural evolution: models and examples. *Human Ecology*, 10, 289–323.

Eagly, A. H. and Wood, W. (1999). The origins of sex differences in human behavior: evolved dispositions versus social roles. *American Psychologist*, 54, 408–23.

Georgas, J. (1997). Die griechische Familie (The family in Greece). In B. Nauck and U. Schönpflug (eds.), *Familien in verschiedenen Kulturen* (Families in different cultures), vol. 13. Stuttgart: Enke, pp. 200–13.

Gesell, A. (1928). *Infancy and human growth*. New York: Macmillan.

Gesell, A. and Thompson, H. (1934). *Infant behavior: its genesis and growth*. New York: McGraw-Hill.

Goldin-Meadow, S. and Mylander, C. (1998). Spontaneous sign systems created by deaf children in two cultures. *Nature*, 391, 279–81.

Gottlieb, G. (1998). Normally occurring environmental and behavioral influences on gene activity: from central dogma to probabilistic epigenesis. *Psychological Review*, 105, 792–802.

Gottlieb, G., Wahlsten, D. and Lickliter, R. (1998). The significance of biology for human development: a developmental psychobiological system view. In W. Damon (series ed.) and R. M. Lerner (vol. ed.), *Handbook of child psychology*, vol. 1: *Theoretical models of human development*, 5th edn. New York: Wiley, pp. 233–73.

Gould, S. J. (1991). Exaptation: a crucial tool for evolutionary psychology. *Journal of Social Issues*, 47, 43–65.

Gould, S. J. and Lewontin, R. C. (1979). The spandrels of San Marco and the Panglossian paradigm: a critique of the adaptationist programme. *Proceedings of the Royal Society of London* (Series B), 205, 581–98.

Griesel, R. D., Richter, L. M. and Belciug, M. (1990). Electro-encephalography and performance in a poorly nourished South African population. *South African Medical Journal*, 78, 539–43.

Haeckel, E. (1866). *Generelle Morphologie der Organismen* (General morphology of organisms). Berlin: Reimer.

Hall, G. S. (1883). The contents of children's minds. *Princeton Review*, 11, 249–72.

Heron, A. and Kroeger, E. (1981). Introduction to developmental psychology. In H. C. Triandis and A. Heron (eds.), *Handbook of cross-cultural psychology*, vol. 4: *Developmental psychology*. Boston: Allyn and Bacon, pp. 1–15.

International Human Genome Mapping Consortium (2001). The physical map of the human genome. *Nature*, 409, 934–41.

Keller, H. and Greenfield, P. M. (2000). History and future of development in cross-cultural psychology. *Journal of Cross-Cultural Psychology*, 31, 52–62.

Kenrick, D. T. and Keefe, R. C. (1992). Age preferences reflect sex differences in human reproductive strategies. *Behavioral and Brain Sciences*, 15, 75–133.

Kessen, W. (1979). The American child and other cultural inventions. *American Psychologist*, 34, 815–20.

Laland, K. N., Odling-Smee, F. J. and Feldman, M. W. (1999). Niche construction, biological evolution, and cultural change. *Behavioral and Brain Sciences*, 23, 131–75.

Lenneberg, E. H. (1967). *Biological foundations of language.* New York: Wiley.

McGrew, W. C. (1992). *Chimpanzee material culture.* Cambridge: Cambridge University Press.

(1998). Culture in nonhuman primates? *Annual Review of Anthropology,* 27, 301–28.

Overman, E. S. (ed.) (1988). *Methodology and epistomology for social science: selected papers of Donald T. Campbell.* Chicago: University of Chicago Press.

Piaget, J. (1967). *Biologie et connaissance. Essai sur les relations entre les régulations organiques et les processus cognitifs* (Biology and knowledge. Essay on the relationship between organic regulations and cognitive processes). Paris: P.U.F.

(1970). *The principles of genetic epistemology.* London: Routledge.

Plotkin, H. C. and Odling-Smee, F. J. (1981). A multiple-level model of evolution and its implications for sociobiology. *Behavioral and Brain Sciences,* 4, 225–68.

Pollitt, E. (1994). Poverty and child development: relevance of research in developing countries to the United States. Special issue: 'Children and poverty', *Child Development,* 65, 283–95.

Poortinga, Y. H. (1997). Towards convergence? In J. W. Berry, Y. H. Poortinga and J. Pandey (eds.), *Handbook of cross-cultural psychology,* vol. 1: *Theory and Method.* Boston: Allyn and Bacon, pp. 347–87.

Roopnarine, J. L., Clawson, M. A., Benetti, S. and Lewis, T. Y. (2000). Family structure, parent–child socialization, and involvement among Caribbean families. In A. L. Communian and U. Gielen (eds.), *International perspectives on human development.* Lengerich: Pabst, pp. 309–30.

Schore, A. N. (2000). Attachment and the regulation of the right brain. *Attachment and Human Development,* 2, 23–47.

(2001). The effects of a secure attachment relationship on right brain development, affect regulation, and infant mental health. *Infant Mental Health Journal,* 22, 7–66.

Segall, M. H., Dasen, P. R., Berry, J. W. and Poortinga, Y. H. (1999). *Human behavior in global perspective,* 2nd edn. Boston: Allyn and Bacon.

Shanahan, M. J., Sulloway, F. J. and Hofer, S. M. (2000). Change and constancy in developmental contexts. *International Journal of Behavioral Development,* 24(4), 421–7.

Siegel, D. J. (1999). *The developing mind: toward a neurobiology of interpersonal experience.* New York. Guilford Press.

Super, C. M. and Harkness, S. (1986). The developmental niche: a conceptualization at the interface of child and culture. *International Journal of Behavioral Development,* 9, 545–69.

(1997). The cultural structuring of child development. In J. W. Berry, P. R. Dasen and T. S. Saraswathi (eds.), *Handbook of cross-cultural psychology,* vol. 2: *Basic processes and human development.* Boston: Allyn and Bacon, pp. 1–39.

Thelen, E. (1995). Motor development: a new synthesis. *American Psychologist,* 50, 79–95.

Tomasello, M. (2001). Cultural transmission: a view from chimpanzees and human infants. *Journal of Cross-Cultural Psychology,* 32(1), 151–62.

Tooby, J. and Cosmides, L. (1992). The psychological foundations of culture. In J. Barkow, L. Cosmides and J. Tooby (eds.), *The adapted mind: evolutionary psychology and the generation of culture.* New York: Oxford University Press, pp. 19–136.

van Geert, P. (1994). *Dynamic systems of development: change between complexity and chaos.* New York: Harvester Wheatsheaf.

Voland, E. (1999). On the nature of solidarity. In K. Bayertz (ed.), *Solidarity.* Lancaster: Kluwer, pp. 157–72.

Werner, E. E. (1979). *Cross-cultural child development: a view from the planet Earth.* Monterey, CA: Brooks/Cole.

Whiten, A., Goodall, J., McGrew, W. C., Nishida, T., Reynolds, V., Sugiyama, Y., Tutin, C. E. G., Wrangham, R. W. and Boesch, C. (1999). Cultures in chimpanzees. *Nature,* 399, 682–5.

Zeskind, P. S. and Ramey, C. T. (1981). Preventing intellectual and interactional sequelae of fetal malnutrition: a longitudinal, transactional and synergistic approach to development. *Child Development,* 52, 213–18.

Author index

404   Author index

Subject index

Imitation in Infancy
Jacqueline Nadel and George Butterworth

This is the first book to bring together the extensive modern evidence for innate imitation in babies. Modern research has shown imitation to be a natural mechanism of learning and communication which deserves to be at centre stage in developmental psychology. Yet the very possibility of imitation in newborn humans has had a controversial history. Defining imitation has proved to be far from straightforward and scientific evidence for its existence in neonates is only now becoming accepted, despite more than a century of enquiry. In this book, some of the world's foremost researchers on imitation and intellectual development review evidence for imitation in newborn babies. They discuss the development of imitation in infancy, in both normal and atypical populations and in comparison with other primate species, stressing the fundamental importance of imitation in human development, as a foundation of communication and a precursor to symbolic processes.

Learning to Read and Write: A Cross-Linguistic Perspective

Margaret Harris and Giyoo Hatano

For many years, the development of theories about the way children learn to read and write was dominated by studies of English-speaking populations. As we have learned more about the way that children learn to read and write other scripts – whether they have less regularity in their grapheme–phoneme correspondences or do not make use of alphabetic symbols in all – it has become clear that many of the difficulties that confront children learning to read and write English specifically are less evident, or even non-existent, in other populations. At the same time, some aspects of learning to read and write are very similar across scripts. The unique cross-linguistic perspective offered in this book, including chapters on Japanese, Greek and the Scandinavian languages as well as English, shows how the processes of learning to read and spell are affected by the characteristics of the writing system that children are learning to master.

Children's Understanding of Biology and Health
Michael Siegal and Candida Peterson

This book uses new research and theory to present the first state-of-the-art account of children's understanding of biology and health. The international team of distinguished contributors views children's understanding in these areas to be to some extent adaptive to their well-being and survival and uses evidence collected through a variety of different techniques to consider whether young children are capable of basic theorising and understanding of health and illness. Topics ranging from babies to the elderly including birth, death, contamination and contagion, food and pain are examined and close links between research and practice are made with obvious attendant benefits in terms of education and communication.

Social Processes in Children's Learning
Paul Light and Karen Littleton

This book is about children's learning and problem-solving behaviour. It reflects the increasingly close integration seen in recent years between social and cognitive approaches to researching the learning process. In particular, Paul Light and Karen Littleton examine the ways in which interactions between children influence learning outcomes. They begin by placing this topic in a broad theoretical and empirical context and go on to present a substantial series of their own experimental studies, which focus on children of late primary and early secondary school age. These investigations address peer facilitation of problem solving, social comparison effects on learning and social context effects upon the interpretation of tasks. Many of the studies involve computer-based learning but the findings have implications both for classroom practice and the understanding of the learning process.

This book will be a valuable tool for researchers, teachers and practitioners interested in the social processes of children's learning.

Half a Brain is Enough: The Story of Nico
Antonio M. Battro

Half A Brain Is Enough is the moving and extraordinary story of Nico, a little boy who at the age of three was given a right hemispherectomy to control intractable epilepsy. Antonio Battro, a distinguished neuroscientist and educationalist, charts what he calls Nico's 'neuroeducation' with humour and compassion in an intriguing book which is part case history, part meditation on the nature of consciousness and the brain, and part manifesto. Throughout the book Battro combines the highest standards of scientific scholarship with a warmth and humanity that guide the reader through the intricacies of brain surgery, neuronal architecture and the application of the latest information technology in education, in a way that is accessible and engaging as well as making a significant contribution to the current scientific literature.

Half A Brain Is Enough will be compulsory reading for anyone who is interested in the ways we think and learn.

The Imitative Mind: Development, Evolution and Brain Bases
Andrew N. Meltzoff and Wolfgang Prinz

Imitation guides the behaviour of a range of species. Recent scientific advances in the study of imitation at multiple levels from neurons to behaviour have far-reaching implications for cognitive science, neuroscience, and evolutionary and developmental psychology. This volume provides a state-of-the-art summary of the research on imitation in both Europe and America, including work on infants, adults, and nonhuman primates, with speculations about robotics. A special feature of the book is that it provides a concrete instance of the links between developmental psychology, neuroscience, and cognitive science. It showcases how an interdisciplinary approach to imitation can illuminate long-standing problems in the brain sciences, including consciousness, self, perception-action coding, theory of mind, and intersubjectivity. The book addresses what it means to be human and how we get that way.

Microdevelopment: Transition Processes in Development and Learning

Nira Granott and Jim Parziale

Microdevelopment is the process of change in abilities, knowledge and understanding during short time-spans. This book presents a new process-orientated view of development and learning based on recent innovations in psychology research. Instead of characterizing abilities at different ages, researchers investigate processes of development and learning that evolve through time and explain what enables progress in them. Four themes are highlighted: variability, mechanisms that create transitions to higher levels of knowledge, interrelations between changes in the short time scale of microdevelopment and the life-long scale of macrodevelopment, and the crucial effect of context. Learning and development are analysed in and out of school, in the individual's activities and through social interaction, in relation to simple and complex problems, and in everyday behaviour and novel tasks. With contributions from the foremost researchers in the field, *Microdevelopment* will be essential reading for all interested in cognitive and developmental science.